COMMITTIES AND COMMISSIONS IN INDIA 1947-73

Details of Published Volumes

COMMITTEES AND COMMISSIONS IN INDIA 1947-80

(In 18 Vols.)

Vol. 1	1947-54	Rs. 1500
Vol. 2	1955-57	Rs. 1500
Vol. 3	1958-59	Rs. 1500
Vol. 4	1960-61	Rs. 1500
Vol. 5	1962-63	Rs. 1500
Vol. 6	1964-65	Rs. 1500
Vol. 7	1966	Rs. 1500
Vol. 8	1967	Rs. 1500
Vol. 9	1968-69	Rs. 1500
Vol. 10	1970	Rs. 1500
Vol. 11	1971-73	Rs. 1500
Vol. 12	1974	Rs. 450
Vol. 13	1975	Rs. 450
Vol. 14	1976	Rs. 450
Vol. 15A	1977	Rs. 450
Vol. 15B	1977	Rs. 450
Vol. 15C	1977	Rs. 450
Vol. 15D	1977	Rs. 450
Vol. 16A	1978	Rs. 450
Vol. 16B	1978	Rs. 450
Vol. 17A	1979	Rs. 450
Vol. 17B	1979	Rs. 450
Vol. 18A	1980	Rs. 450
Vol. 18B	1980	Rs. 450

COMMITTIES AND COMMISSIONS IN INDIA 1947-73

Volume VI
1964-65

Virendra Kumar

CONCEPT PUBLISHING COMPANY, NEW DELHI-110059

ISBN 81-7022-215-10 (Vol VI)

First Published 1977
Reprinted 2004

Published and Printed by
Ashok Kumar Mittal
Concept Publishing Company
A/15-16, Commercial Block, Mohan Garden
NEW DELHI-110059 (India)

Phones : 25351460, 25351794
Fax : 091-11-25357103
Email : publishing@conceptpub.com

DEDICATED
TO
MY UNCLE
LATE VIDYA BALLABH KULSRESHTHA

INTRODUCTION

The Sixth Volume attempts to understand and analyse the activities of the various "Committees and Commissions" during the period 1964-1965 which have received as far as the previous volumes are concerned scant attention from even bibliophiles and documentation experts. It is known that the Government all over the world largely rely on the Committees and Commissions for their decisions on particular subjects. Governments make an extensive use of the Instrument of the Public Inquiries which ultimately help in lessening managerial tensions as well as quietening the allegations of misrule. According to John Stuart Mill, "A man seldom judges right, even in his own concerns, still less in those of the public, when he makes habitual use of knowledge but his own or that of some single adviser". Thus the "Committee System" greatly helps the proper functioning of a democratic set-up.

A Commission is a "Governmental Agency created to perform a particular function such as a special investigations or on Governmental regulations of business". It is appointed mainly when it is thought that a matter involves some financial question. There are other reasons for which a Commission is appointed, e.g., in matters pertaining to the Welfare of the State and its Citizens and for improving the efficiency in an administration. The status of a Committee is also the same as that of a Commission, but it does not possess as wide powers as are enjoyed by a Commission and has to limit itself in relation to a specific work assigned to it under its terms of reference. While arriving at decisions in the form of recommendations, a Committee or Commission ensures that such decisions are representatives of interest of various types of people and also a safeguard against abuse of power.

The Committees and Commissions always advise a Government, offering valuable suggestions and recommendations for smooth operation and efficiency in administration for the welfare of the people.

A Committee or a Commission comprises a Chairman, the Members and the Member-Secretary (sometimes there is also a Vice-Chairman and an Assistant Secretary). In some cases there are even One-Man Commissions and enquiries conducted by such Commissions are entrusted to an Official-on-Special Duty or a Judge of the High Court.

The Chairman of a Commission is a person well versed in legal affairs and is often a retired Judge of a High Court or Supreme Court of India. Occasionally, a Member of Parliament is also appointed to the post of Chairman of a Commission. Regarding Committees, the Chairman is usually a specialist in the subject of the Committee. He can be a Leader or a Convener also if he heads a Panel, Study Group, Working Group or a Delegation, etc.

The Members of a Commission, Committee, Panel, Study Group, Working Group, etc., are specialists in their respective fields and provide valuable guidance to the Commission in making recommendations.

The Member-Secretary or Secretary is nominated from among the experienced officials who have the requisite competent knowledge of the subject on which the Commission or the Committee is appointed.

The Study of the "Committees and Commissions" is divided into two main parts :

(I) **Pre-Independence** : From 1772 to August 1947 ; and

(II) **Post-Independence** : From August 1947 to 1973.

The First Volume covers the period from August 1947 to 1954. The Second Volume covers the period from 1955 to 1957. The Third Volume covers the period from 1958 to 1959. The Fourth Volume covers the period from 1960 to 1961. The Fifth Volume covers the period from 1962 to 1963. The present volume, Volume VI in series covers the period from 1964 to 1965.

The Work provides information on subjects like Bibliographical Data of the Committees and Commissions, Chairman, Leader, Convener, etc. Appointments; Terms of Reference ; Contents and Recommendations.

Arrangements : The arrangements in the "Committees and Commissions" are Chronological and items have been arranged according to their dates of appointments and not according to their dates of publication.

I am sure that this reference work will continue into a number of Volumes, for it is unique in nature. I have spared no efforts to make it a comprehensive reference work and it will be of great use to the research scholars, sociologists, historians, economists, students of political science, as well as to all those connected with the study of administration and legal affairs. I have tried my level best to rectify all errors and omissions that I noticed in the previous Volumes. It will be my effort to go on improving these Volumes. The introductory part in Volume I deals with the *why*, *what* and *how* of the "Committees and Commissions".

In the end I must express my gratitude to the Press that reviewed and appreciated the work. I am also indebted to my wife and children who have sacrificed their personal comforts by providing me every facility to make this volume ready for publication within a reasonable short time.

New Delhi
Basant Panchami
February 12, 1978

VIRENDRA KUMAR

CONTENTS

Introduction vii

1964

1. Committee on Integration of Health Services, 1964 1
2. Committee of Secretaries on Government Journals, 1964 3
3. Panel for Literacy among Industrial Workers, 1964 9
4. Study Group on the Study of English in India, 1964 12
5. University Grants Commission, Building Advisory Committee on Teachers' Hostels, 1964 20
6. Study Team on General Insurance Cooperatives, 1964 23
7. Committee on Transport Policy and Coordination, 1964 26
8. Committee on the Methods of Elections to Panchayati Raj Bodies, 1964 48
9. Central Wage Board for Non-Journalist Employees of Newspaper Industry, 1964 53
10. Tariff Revision Committee (Interim), 1964 66
11. Tariff Revision Committee on the Central Excise Tariff, 1964 75
12. Committee to Suggest Ways and Means of Improving Financial Returns from Irrigation Projects, 1964 78
13. Study Group on Wild Life and Wild Life Products, 1964 80
14. Monopolies Inquiry Commission, 1964 82
15. Review Committee on Arabic and Persian Studies in Indian Universities, 1964 107
16. Finance Commission, 1964 109
17. Enquiry Committee on Small Newspapers, 1964 112
18. Liquid Cargo Committee, 1964 128
19. Working Group on Libraries, 1964 130
20. Working Group on Co-operatives in I.A.D.P. Districts, 1964 140
21. Study Team on the Audit of Accounts of Panchayati Raj Bodies, 1964 150
22. Education Commission, 1964 153
23. Air Port Security Committee, 1964 202
24. Sugar Enquiry Commission, 1964 203
25. Committee on Some Problems of University Administration, 1964 217
26. Committee on Cooperative Marketing, 1964 223
27. Study Team on Import and Export Trade Control Organisation, 1964 247
28. Study Team on Directorate General of Technical Development, 1964 256
29. Committee on Cooperation, 1964 264

30. Study Team on the Central Public Works Department, 1964 268
31. One-Man Independent Body to enquire into the Question of Dearness Allowance payable to Central Government Employees, 1964 275
32. Narmada Water Resources Development Committee, 1964 278
33. Committee on Scarce Raw Materials, 1964 284
34. Commission of Railway Safety, Railway Accident, Investigation on Accident to 12 NB Bandel-Naihati Local at Naihati Junction Station of Eastern Railway on 14th September, 1964 290
35. Reviewing Committee of the Telecommunication Research Centre of the Posts and Telegraphs Department, 1964 291
36. Committee to Study the Question of Legalisation of Abortion, 1964 299
37. Mathematics Reforms Committee, 1964 300
38. Ad-hoc Committee on Export of Minor Forest Products, 1964 309
39. Inquiry into the Wash-Away of No. 653 Down Pamban-Dhanushkodi Passenger Train between KMS. 681 and 682 near Dhanushkodi Station (Southern Railway) on 23rd December, 1964 313

1965

40. Group of Experts on Land Acquisition, 1965 315
41. Archaeological Review Committee, 1965 318
42. Committee of Officers on the Reorganization of the Structure and Work Procedures of the Ministry of Works and Housing, 1965 320
43. Commission on the Hill Areas of Assam, 1965-66 322
44. Cancer Committee, 1965 327
45. Committee on Untouchability Economic and Educational Development of the Scheduled Castes and Connected Documents, 1965 333
46. Study Team on Textile Commissioner's Organisation, 1965 340
47. Film Advisory Committee of Members of Parliament, 1965 348
48. Advisory Committee on the Revision of the Lists of Scheduled Castes and Scheduled Tribes, 1965 352
49. Committee on the Indian Foreign Service, 1965 354
50. Tasar Silk Committee, 1965 358
51. The Committee on Cost of Production of Steel, 1965 362
52. Road Transport Taxation Enquiry Committee on Inter-State Transport, 1965 368
53. Committee on Social Science Research, 1965 379
54. Inquiry into the Collision of Down Empty Rake with Rear of No. K-3 Down Local Train at Thana Station (Central Railway), on 14th September, 1965 384
55. Parliamentary Committee on the Demand for Punjabi Suba, 1965 385
56. Panel on Economics in Construction Costs, 1965 388
57. Committee on Customary Rights to Scavenging, 1965 394
Chairman Index 402
Index 403

1964

COMMITTEE ON INTEGRATION OF HEALTH SERVICES, 1964—REPORT

New Delhi, Directorate General of Health Services, 1968, 46p.

Chairman : Dr. N. Jungalwalla.
Members : Dr. D. Bhatia ; Dr. D.N. Sharma ; Dr. (Mrs.) H.M. Sharma ; Dr. C.L. Mukerjee; Dr. T.B. Patel; Dr. Ved Prakash.
Secretary : Dr. P.R. Dutt.

APPOINTMENT

Integration of health services was first mooted in 1937 in India by the Central Advisory Board of health. The principles were recommended by the Health Survey and the Development Committee, 1946 as preliminary step for the delivery of comprehensive health services. This was accepted the Central and State Governments. Implementation was, however, slow and inconsistant. While the Central Government implemented the principle, many of the States lagged behind. This was commented on by the Health Survey and Planning Committee, 1961. In one of its resolutions, the Central Council of Health recommended in 1964 that a Committee of the Directors of Health Services of Gujarat, Punjab, Uttar Pradesh and West Bengal, the Director of Public Health Madras, and a representative of the Indian Medical Association may be constituted. So the Committee on Integration of Health Services was appointed in 1964.

TERMS OF REFERENCE

(i) To examine the various problems including those of service conditions ;

(ii) elimination of private practice ; and

(iii) submit the report to the Government of India.

CONTENTS

Preamble ; Definition ; Integration in Public Health ; Historical Review of Development of 'medical and Health Services' ; Certain Changing Concepts in Health administration ; The present position ; Discussion and Comments ; Recommendations ; Summary ; Appendix 1 and 2.

RECOMMENDATIONS

The Committee noted the tendency to retain organisational structure we had inherited. A fixed organisation has its inherent weakness in that it defeats its own purpose in the presence of a dynamic situation. Some States have reorganised their administrative organisations. Additional steps are necessary to built up a dynamic, fluid and flexible organisation, capable of absorbing present and future responsibilities in an efficient manner. In the reorganisation recent trends should be taken into consideration.

The Committee discussed the various aspects of integration and is firmly of the opinion that services should be integrated right from the highest to the lowest level in service, organisation and personnel. Responsibilities for health of different sections of the Community should be unified in one authority at Central and State levels and medical education be integrated with service. The committee also felt that in developing countries like India, entire health services have to be re-organised. The administration should be more scientifically guided.

The Committee noted that there is greater realisation of inter-independence between Central, State and local governments in health matters including the programmes.

The Committee recommended that the district level should be strengthened sufficiently to undertake comprehensive health work on regionalised basis. The heads of district health organisation may be from curative, preventive or teaching specially, but they must have sufficient re-orientation or training in complicated technical and administrative science of planning and management of integrated medical and health care services so as to provide intelligent educative supervision and guidance in both fields. They should also have experience in Community organization.

A primary health centre is a paramount institution, and medical officer must be in complete administrative control of the staff.

Services are as good as the personnel giving service. It is therefore, necessary that medical officers who are the leaders of the health teams, should have high morale. Morale is, however, influenced by various factors, important being security, chances of progress, technically and financially, provision of adequate safeguards to ensure recognition of good and loyal service, fair and just deal, and provision of pension and gratuity to provide and personnel. Responsibilities for health of different section of minimum living income in old age. The Committee discussed the various aspects including the pay, service conditions and the process by which unification of cadre can be effected. The Committee drew the attention to the example provided by the Army and by the State Governments of West Bengal, Punjab and Mysore. The details may vary but the greatest common measure of agreement should be in terms of :

(a) Single portal of entry,

(b) Common seniority,

(c) Recognition of extra qualification by provision of ante-date or financial advancement,

(d) Equal pay for equal work,

(e) Special pay for specialised work, special programme, research, teaching, public health and extra hazard.

On private practice the Committee felt that no Government medical officer should normally be allowed private practice. Elimination of private service is, however, beset with many problems, financial and administrative. Judicious and more reasonable procedures would be to eliminate private practice on a phased basis ; beginning with teaching or research post health officer, health centre doctor and supervisory posts at the state headquarters and district levels, compensation for the loss of private practice should however be reasonable.

COMMITTEE OF SECRETARIES ON GOVERNMENT JOURNALS, 1964—REPORT

New Delhi, 15p. (Memographed)

Members: Secretary, Ministry of I & B Secretary to the Prime Minister ; Secretary, Finance Ministry.

APPOINTMENT

The Committee of Secretaries on Government Journals was constituted under the Government of India with the approval of the Prime Minister in 1964.

TERMS OF REFERENCE

To examine, in consultation with the sponsoring authorities, the journals brought out by them, to assess their usefulness and recommend their continuance or otherwise.

CONTENTS

Report ; Annexures.

RECOMMENDATIONS

A preliminary survey carried out by the Committee revealed that there were 209 Journals published by the Government and Government-Financed autonomous bodies. Of these there were 17 annuals, 9 half-yearlies, 57 quarterlies, 5 bimonthlies, 78 monthlies, 26 fortnightlies, 14 weeklies and 3 dailies.

The journal can be grouped into four broad categories. There are general purpose journals like BALBHARATI and AJKAL (Hindu and Urdu) which seek to influence the reader's attitude. They aim at making the people conscious of their heritage and inculcate in them such ideals as national unity, social justice and progress. Then these are magazines like India and Foreign Review, Travellers in India, Yojna, Intensive Cultivation, Sainik Samachar which carry information to the reader about policies, programmes and achievements in specific spheres of Governments activity. Thirdly, there are house journals published mainly by the Railways and the Defence Ministry's for promoting a feeling of cohesion between the workers and the employers. To the fourth category belong scientific and technical journals which carry results of research in science and technology and discuss the problems in these fields.

Earlier, an Expert Committee appointed by the Ministry of I & B to survey the journals had reported the existence of 173 journals in 1960. It was thus evident that there was a subsistencial increase in the number of journals between 1960 and 1964.

In every category the Committee observed a tendency for the journals to multiply. The CSIR which used to carry the results of research in a single journal now had a large number of journals, each devoted a specialised field of science. Similarly, the number of ICAR journals has increased manifold in recent years. Many of the Central Ministries and the autonomous bodies under them have started new journals.

Many of the journals were found to have similar or allied themes, contents and roadship. In many other cases although the avowed purpose of the journals was different, their contents were hardly distinguishable. Such journals, the Committee felt, could be merged and overlapping of effort avoided.

Many of the journals examined were found lacking in the requisite standards of taxtual contents, get-up and production. Their sales-although they had been in existence for many years were far from encouraging. Moreover, since to many government journals competed for advertisement from general pool, Government journals generally carried few advertisements and a large number of these were consequently running at loss. Losses compelled the sponsoring authorities to be content with only modest standards of production which, in turn, reduced their appeal to and impact on the readers. Such journals were, therefore, neither effective instruments of publicity nor good business.

While the Committee agreed that a certain measure of subsidy was reasonable and even necessary in the case of publicity journals—which had to be subsidized even in private sector—it felt that journals that had largely failed to establish themselves after several years of existence had no justification for separate existence.

The existing situation, the Committee felt, was undesireable from another angle also. Too many journals, each devoted to a small sector of the Government's activity, tended to blur the image of the country, since few readers could afford to subscribe to an assortment of journals. Fewer well-written and well-produced magazines, it was felt, would make a deeper impression on the reader and better present an integrated picture of progress than many substandard ones.

The Committee noticed that the production values of the journals varied greatly and often had little relationship to what they sought to achieve. Some of these were neither art journals nor designed for foreign readership. In fact, this scarce material was not even put to an effective use. Many of the journals used Indian art paper even though they carried few half-tone illustrations.

Considering the facts enumerated before the Committee came to the conclusion that there was need for rationalisation in production values, reduction in the number of journals to eliminate overlapping. The Committee felt that at the present stage of the country's development when the Government's resources were limited, it would be desirable to concentrate them on bringing out fewer and better journals.

The main reason for the existing unsatisfactory position of Government journals, the Committee thought, was the absence of a well-defined policy and principles in the field of journals and an agency to ensure their observance. As a remedial measure the Committee recommended the following crieteria for: (i) reducing the number of the existing journals, (ii) rationalisation of production standards, (iii) for regulating future development:

1. General purpose and publicity journals which have been in existence for five years and have failed to achieve a paid circulation of 1,000 should be discontinued. In the case of scientific research and teachnical journals the corresponding figures should be 500.

2. Journals with similar and allied contents and more or less common readership should be merged so that fewer journals can be brought out more effectively.

3. Research, science, and technical journals with a print order of less than 500 should be memeographed and only the cover should be printed.

4. Imported art paper should be used only in foreign publicity or prestige journals.

5. Journals of which fewer than a fourth of the pages carry half-tone reproduction should eschew use of Indian art paper.

6. No new journal will be started without the sponsoners seeking the clearance of the Minister for Information and Broadcasting or the Committee of Secretaries.

7. Exemption from the application of the above crieteria will be granted by the Minister for Information and Broadcasting or the Committee of Secretaries.

The crieteria mentioned above were discussed by the Committee with the representatives of the Ministeries and with the Working Group appointed by the Scientific Advisory Committee to the Cabinet and generally accepted.

The Specific recommendations of the Committee in respect of each journal were communicated to the respective Ministries. The final recommendations of the Committee were made in consultations with the representatives of the Ministries concerned.

The Scientific and Technical journals were scrutinised and discussed by the Chairman of the Committee with a Working Group appointed by the Scientific Advisory Committee to the Cabinet. The recommendations of the Working Group have been finalised and circulated for implementation.

To-date the recommendations of the Committee have been finalised in the case of 155 journals. Of these the Committee has recommended discontinuance of 23 journals listed at Appendix 'A' Recommendations that involve reduction in print order, periodicity or bulk have been indicated at Annexure 'B'.

The savings which will accrue as a result of the implementation of recommendations indicated at Annexure 'A' and 'B' are tabulated at Annexure 'F'.

In case of 115 journals the Committee has not recommended any change. These journals are listed at Annexure 'G'.

In respect of some of the recommendations of the Committee, representations have been made by authorities publishing the journals. There are eight such journals listed at Annexure 'C'. The representations will be considered at the next meeting of the Committee. In case of 29 Journals tentative recommendations have been made by the Committee but these have to be discussed with the Ministries publishing these journals at the next meeting of the Committee before final recommendations are made.

Some of the journals have still to be examined by the Committee. These Journals are mentioned at Annexure 'E'.

To sum up, the Committee has finalised recommendations in respect of 155 journals. Of these, it has recommended discontinuance in the case of 23 Journals and suggested reduction in print order, bulk or periodicity in the case of 17. In the case of 115 Journals the Committee has not suggested any change. At a subsequent meeting the Committee will examine representations in respect of 8 Journals. It will also discuss with the representatives of the Ministries concerned tentative recommendations in respect of 29 Journals and scrutinise another 17 Journals.

ANNEXURE 'A'

List Of The Journal Which Are To Be Discontinued
Education (Ministry of)

1. INSDOC—A current Science Literature
2. Bibliography of Scientific Publications of South and South East Asia
3. Bulletin of Regional Research Laboratory
4. Food Science

Food And Agriculture (Ministry of)

5. Indian Livestock
6. Pashu Palan (Hindi)
7. Agricultural Research
8. Rice News Teller
9. Indian Potato Journal
10. Statistical Newsletter and Abstract
11. Indian Coconut Journal
12. Indian Tobacco
13. Arecanut Journal
14. Indian Oil Seeds Journal
15. Indian Sugarcane Journal
16. Sugar Cane Herald—Ishu Sandesh (Hindi & English)
17. Indian Cotton Journal
18. Compost and Sewage Bulletin

Commerce (Ministry of)

19. Metric Measures
20. Metric Maptol (Hindi)
21. Abstracting Service

Information & Broadcasting (Ministry of)

22. Indian Information
23. Bhartiya Samachar (Hindi)

ANNEXURE 'B'

Other Recommendations Including Reduction In Print Order, Bulk Etc.

Education (Ministry Of)

1. C.S.I.R. News	Print order to be reduced from 1,500 to 1,000.
2. Technical Man Power Bulletin	Print order to be reduced from 4,000 to 3,000.
3. Environmental Health	To be reduced half of its present size.
4. Khadya Vijyan (Hindi)	To be converted into a quarterly from Monthly.
5. Khadya Vijyan (Kannada)	To be converted into a quarterly from Monthly.
6. Research and Industry	To be converted into a quarterly from Monthly.
7. Vigyan Pragati (Hindi)	To be brought out once in two months.
8. Leather Science	Director, Central Leather Institute, Madras to examine the possibility of reducing the frequency to once in two months.
9. Indian Journal of Technology 10. Journal of Scientific and Industrial Research	Proposal for the merger of (9) and (10) will be placed before the Executive Council of the Publications Directorate C.S.I.R.

Food And Agriculture (Ministry Of)

11. Indian Journal of Agricultural Science	To incorporate Agricultural Research and to be published once in two months instead of quarterly.

Works And Housing Ministry of)

12. Journal of the National Building Organisation	Number of copies to be printed 1,750 instead of 2,200 and pages to be reduced from 100 to 60.

Commerce (Ministry Of)

13. Coir	The question of discontinuance would be re-examined after a year.

Irrigation And Power (Ministry Of)

14. Irrigation & Power	The Journal should be priced.

Health (Ministry Of)

15. Swasth Hindi 16. Family Planning	The Journal should be re-examined after a year.

Industry And Supply (Ministry Of)

17. Bulletin of Small Scale Industries	The Journal should be priced and the position reviewed after 6 months.

ANNEXURE 'C'

Journals about which recommendations were made by The Committee of Secretaries, but sponsoring authorities have represented against the Recommendations:

Food & Agriculture (Ministry Of)

1. Intensive Agriculture
2. Unnat Krishi (Hindi)
3. Indian Journal of Fisheries
4. Indian Fisheries Bulletin

Commerce (Ministry Of)

5. Indian Journal of Sericulture 6. Indian Silk	On the representation of Ministry of Commerce, the Committee of Secretaries decided not to make any change in these two journals.

7. Indian Trade Journal
8. Journal of Industry and Trade

ANNEXURE 'D'

Journals about which tentative Recommendations were made by the Committee of Secretaries on 11.5.1965 These tentative recommendations are to be discussed with the representatives of the Ministries sponsoring the Journals

Education (Ministry Of)

		Tentative Recommendations	
1.	Cultural Forum	Education Ministry	To continue.
2.	Indo-Asian Culture	Indian Council of for Cultural Relations, New Delhi	Merger with 'Cultural Forum' suggested.
3.	Cultural News Forum India	—do—	In view of the poor scale reduction in print order by 50% suggested .
4.	Sanskriti (Hindi)	Education Ministry	In view of the poor sales discontinuance suggested.
5.	Thaqafat-Ul-Hindi	Indian Council for Cultural Relations New Delhi	Since only 5 out of 2,500 printed are sold, it is presumed that the remaining copies are effectively distributed.
6.	Indian Archives	National Archives New Delhi.	No change.
7.	Indian Literature	Sahitya Akademi, New Delhi	—do—
8.	Lalit Kala	Lalit Kala Akademi New Delhi	—do—
9. 10.	The Education Quarterly Teachers Quarterly (Bengali & English)	Education Ministry Directorate of Extension Project, Calcutta.	To be merged

Central Social Welfare Board

11.	Social Welfare	C.S.W.B., New Delhi	In accordance with the recommendations of the Vidyalankar Study merger of these with 'Yojana' suggested.
12.	Samaj Kalyan (Hindi)	—do—	

Khadi and Village Industries Commission

13.	Khadi Gram Udyog (English)	Khadi & Village Industries Commission	Discontinuance of free distribution.
14.	Khadi Gram Udyog (Hindi)		
15.	Gram Udyog (Marathi)		

16: Jagrati (Hindi)
17. Jagrati (English)

Civil Aviation (Ministry Of)

Rashtriya Panchang	Director General of Observations	To be discontinued
18. English	—	—
19. Hindi	—	—
20. Urdu	—	—
21. Bengali	—	—
22. Gujarati	—	—
23. Kannada	—	—
24. Malayalam	—	—
25. Marathi	—	—
26. Oriya	—	—
27. Sanskrit	—	—
28. Tamil	—	—
29. Telugu	—	—

ANNEXURE 'E'

List Of The Journals Which Have Still To Be Examined By The Committee Of Secretaries :

1. School Science.
2. Journal of Education for Teaching
3. The Young Child
4. Buniyadi Talim
5. Guidance Review
6. Audio-Visual Education
7. Teacher Education
8. Secondary Education
9. Record of the Botanical Survey of India
10. Record of the Indian Museum
11. Nuclear India
12. Indian Minerals
13. The Journal of Parliamentary Information
14. Digest of Central Acts of Constitutional Cases
15. Privileges Digest
16. Memoirs of the Indian Museum
17. Abstract and Index of Reports and Articles.

ANNEXURE 'F'

Savings likely to be accrued to Government on the Implementation of the Recommendations of the Secretaries Committee :

1. Indian Information — Rs. 42,131
2. Bhartiya Samachar — Rs. 24,140
3. Metrick Measures — Rs. 14,685
4. Metric Maptol — Rs. 4,729
5. CSIR Journals — An economy of about 20% of the total in paper and printing cost.
6. Eastern Railway Magazine was using imported art paper. Since changed over to the Indian Art paper. The saving thus accrued on this account is Rs. 15,600.
7. I.C.A.R. Journals—Figures are not received yet.
8. Journal of the National Buildings Organisation Rs. 6,265.

ANNEXURE 'G'

No Change

Education (Ministry of)

1. Annals of Library Science
2. Indian Journal of Chemistry
3. Indian Journal of Pure and applied physics.
4. NML Technical Journal
5. FRI News
6. Indian Journal of Experimental Biology
7. Indian Journal of Biochemistry
8. Central Glass and Ceramic Research Institute, Bulletin
9. Science Reporter
10. Bulletin of the National Geophysical Research Institute.

Food and Agriculture (Ministry of)

11. Indian Farming
12. Kheti (Hindi)
13. Indian Journal of Veterniary Science and Animal Husbandry
14. Indian Horticulture

15. Cocount Bulletin
16. Thengins (Kannada)
17. Nalikera Bulletin (Malayalam)
18. Tobacco Bulletin
19. Tambacu (Hindu)
20. Pogsku (Telugu)
21. Rubber Board Bulletin
22. Bhartiya Tilham Patrika (Hindi)
23. Agricultural Situation in India
24. Agricultural Marketing
25. Gosamvardhan (English)
26. Gosamvardhan (Hindi)

Civil Aviation (Ministry of)

27. Indian Journal of Meteorology and Geophysics
28. Weekly Weather Report
29. Indian Ephemeries and Nautical Almanac
30. Seismological Bulletin
31. Indian Daily Weather Report

Works and Housing (Ministry of)

32. N.B.C. Digest
33. N.B.C. Abstract

Communications (Ministry of)

34. Telecommunications
35. Teleworks Patrika
36. Dak Tar (English)
37. Dak Tar (Hindi)

Petroleum and Chemical (Ministry of)

38. O.N.G.C. Reporter

Industry and Supply (Ministry of)

39. I.S.I. Bulletin
40. Machine Tool Engineer
41. Trade Mark Journal

Cabinet Affairs (Ministry of)

42. Monthly Abstract of Statistics

Commerce (Ministry of)

43. Udhyog Byopar Patrika (Hindi)
44. Forward Market Bulletin
44A. Indian Journal of Sericulture
44B. Indian Silk

Community Development and Cooperation (Ministry of)

45. Kurukshetra
46. Kurukshetra (Hindi)
47. Panchayati Raj

Defence (Ministery of)

48. Sainik Samachar
49. Sainik Samachar (Hindi)
50. Sainik Samachar (Marathi)
51. Sainik Samachar (Punjabi)
52. Sainik Samachar (Tamil)
53. Sainik Samachar (Telugu)
54. Sainik Samachar (Malayalam)
55. Sainik Samachar (Urdu)
56. Sainik Samachar (Gorkhali)
57. Ordnance
58. Indian Air Force
59. Naval Despatch

External Affairs (Ministry Of)

60. Indian and Foreign Review
61. Foreign Affairs Record

Finance (Ministry Of)

62. Quarterly Bulletin of Bombay Gustoms
63. Daily List of Imports
64. Daily List of Exports
65. Reserve Bank of India Bulletin
66. Company News and Notes

Home Affairs (Ministry Of)

67. Indian Police Journal
68. Work Improvement

Information & Broadcasting (Ministry of)

69. Akashvani (English)
70. Akashvani (Hindi)
71. Awaz (Urdu)
72. Betar Jagat (Bengali)
73. Vanoli (Tamil)
74. Vani (Telugu)
75. Akashi (Assamese)
76. Adhaat-ul-Hindi (Arabic)
77. Vinindze Change (Chinese)
78. Saura Henghubung (Indonesian)
79. Sadai Hindi (Persian)
80. Hindi Awaz (Pushtu)
81. Goa Gargi Dratan (Tibetan)
82. I'inde Vouc Parle (French)
83. Indian Calling (Western)
84. Indian Calling (Western)
85. Bal Bharti (Hindi)
86. Ajkal (Hindi)
87. Ajkal (Urdu)

Steel And Mines (Ministry Of)

88. Iron and Steel Control Monthly Bulletin

Irrigation & Power (Ministry Of)

89. Bhagirath

Labour And Employment (Ministry Of)

90. Indian Labour Journal

Planning Commission

91. Yojana
92. Yojana (Hindi)

Railways (Ministry Of)

93. Welfare
94. Kalyan (Hindi)
95. Sankshyaman (Telugu)
96. Kalyan (Bengali)
97. Kalyan (Oriya)
98. Lifeline (English)
99. South Eastern Railway Newsletter
100. Jiwan Marg (Hindi)
101. Jajjog (Bengali)
102. Western Railway Newsletter
103. North Eastern Railway Newsletter
104. Sanjaki
105. Northern Railway Newsletter
106. Northern Railway Magazine
107. Central Railway Magazine
108. South Eastern Railway
109. Eastern Railway Magazine
110. Indian Railways
111. Bhartiya Rail
112. Rail Coach

Transport (Ministry Of)

113. Traveller in India
114. Basic Road Statistics of India
115. Bhartiya Mool Sarak Aankray (Hindi)

PANEL FOR LITERACY AMONG INDUSTRIAL WORKERS, 1964—REPORT

New Delhi, Committee on Plan Projects, 1964. 56p.

Chairman : Dr. M. S. Mehta

Members : Shri R. L. Mehta; Shri B. N. Datar; Shri A. R. Deshpande; Shri C. Balasubramaniam; Shri A. R. Sankaranarayanan; Shri R. Sinha; Dr. S. N. Saraf; Shri I. V. Chunkath; Shri R. C. Saksena; Shri P. Chentsal Rao; Dr. (Mrs.) Maitreyee Bose; Shri K. G. Sriwastwa; Shri Sohan Singh; Shri S. C. Dutta.

Secretary : Shri Jagdish Singh

APPOINTMENT

The Study Team for selected Education Schemes set up by the Committee on Plan Projects (Planning Commission) under the leadership of the late Shri B. N. Jha, who was then Vice-Chancellor Jodhpur University, went closely into the question of adults) (social) education and came to the conclusion "that illiteracy cannot be eradicated by making it purely optional for all age groups and for various categories of illiterate adults. It may be desirable to enforce compulsion in the age groups 15-25 and 26-40 in suitable stages." The Study Team made various recommendations for the eradication of illiteracy among adults. It was suggested that the problem should be broken up into different sectors, the responsibilities for which might be entrusted to the organisations and departments concerned. In this connection it stressed the importance of tackling the problem of illiteracy among industrial workers. One of the recommendations made by the Study Team was that "if the number of illiterate employees in an industrial establishment in the public/private sector is fairly large, it should be its responsibility to run adult literacy classes for such workers before or after working hours as a part of their welfare programme, expenditure on which should be considered as ligitimate."

With a view to studying the problem closely and for formulating concrete proposals for wiping out illiteracy in this important sector, the Committee on Plan Projects of the Planning Commission set up in January 1964, a Panel for Literacy among Industrial Workers under the Chairmanship of the late Shri B. N. Jha (Vice-Chancellor, Jodhpur University). On the sad demise of Shri B. N. Jha on 13th April, 1964, Dr. M. S. Mehta, Vice-Chancellor, University of Rajasthan was asked to be the Chairman of the Panel.

TERMS OF REFERENCE

(i) To enquire into and report on the present position

of literacy among industrial workers both in the public and private sectors.

(ii) To formulate concrete proposals for the eradication of illiteracy among industrial workers.

CONTENTS

Introduction; The problem; Suggested Measures; Summary of Recommendations; Appendices from I to VI.

RECOMMENDATIONS

I-Proposals

1. The programme for the eradication of illiteracy among industrial workers should cover illiterates mainly in the age group 16-45.

2. In the Coal mining Sector, the responsibility for the eradication of illiteracy should be placed on the Coal Mines Labour Welfare Organisation, which should formulate a phased programme for wiping out illiteracy among the mine workers during the next ten years for which a separate budget provision should be made definite targets should be laid down for the purpose. The following suggestions are offered in this respect :

(a) The proposed Central Board for Adult Literacy among Industrial Workers should direct and supervise the adult education programme of the organisation;

(b) The Coal Mines Labour Welfare Commissioner should set up local and regional Advisory Committees for the implementation of these plans;

(c) Arrangements may be made for the training of Adult Education Inspectors and Supervisors at the National Fundamental Education Centre or by some other suitable agency. These Inspectors and Supervisors may, in their turn, organise training courses for adult education instructors employed by the organisation;

(d) A periodical inspection of the adult education centres may be regularly conducted by the appropriate officers of the Organisation and their observations recorded in order to bring about steady improvement in the quality and the extent of the Service;

(e) On completion of the first and second stages of literacy, examinations should be conducted with the help of some recognised and competent educational Board or Institution;

(f) The Ministry of Education and the State of Education Departments should advise in the production of suitable literature for the first and second stages of literacy as well as for the "follow up" programme.

(g) A net-work of libraries should be established at different centres of Coal Mines area. These libraries should be in the charge of trained personnel and should be kept growing in the supply of books and periodical.

3. With regard to tea plantation workers, the eradiction of illiteracy of about 5 lakhs workers (between the age of (16—45) should be entrusted to the following organisations :

(a) The Tea Board;

(b) Tea Planners' Associations located in different States.

4. A similar organisation on the lines suggested for Coal Mines Welfare Organisation may be set up by and within the Tea Board. Definite targets of time and achievement should be laid down for adult literacy work in this sector and funds should be alloted for the same in the Annual Budget of the organisation.

5. The Port Trust authorities and the Dock Labour Board, should pay special attention to undertake literacy programme for dock workers.

6. For the Iron & Steel industry workers in public sector, the Ministry of Steel and Mines should assume the responsibility of eradicating illiteracy from their own resources. For iron and steel workers in private sector, the employers should include a well organised literacy drive in their labour welfare programme.

7. The Indian Jute Mills Association should undertake literacy work for their illiterate employees. A representative Committee of employers, trade unions, voluntary workers and State officers should be set up to keep the literacy drive alive and effective.

8. An appropriate organisation, representative of various interests, may be set up in collaboration with the mill owners' associations to pursue the objective of removing illiteracy among cotton textile workers. One such body at regional level would be ideal for planning as well as for implementation of the programme.

9. The Central and State Governments should assume the responsibility for eradication of illiteracy among workers for companies, Corporations and departmental undertakings run by them. The Labour Welfare Officers of the Central Pool may be made responsible for supervision and control of the working of the scheme. They may be initiated in the techniques of adult education. The scope of their functions should accordingly be enlarged.

10. A separate provision in the budgets of various industrial establishments should be made for literacy of Industrial workers. Periodical targets of achievements may also be laid down.

II Processing Of The Literacy Schemes

11. According to the present practice of processing all schemes of Industrial Welfare through State Labour Advisory Boards and Indian Labour Conference, the

scheme for promoting literacy among Industrial Workers should be placed these bodies.

12. The Planning Commission may convene, at an early date, a representative conference to co-ordinate the various proposals and envolve a suitable scheme for implementation.

III-The Appropriate Agency

13. For the purposes of co-ordination, laying down a general policy, and working out proposals with regard to administration, financial resources, the syllabi, appropriate literature for different stages of literacy, supervision and implementation of policies and programmes, there is a need for an independent semi autonomous body to be called the Central Board for literacy among Industrial Workers, representing the Government, employers, the workers and voluntary Social and Educational Organisation.

14. This Board should have an independent non-official chairman and a whole-time salaried Secretary, assisted by a small technical staff. The Ministries concerned, the organisations of employers and workers and statutory as well as voluntary associations should be represented on the Board. The work of the Board should be carried on through an Executive Commtttee.

15. **Functions**: The Central Board should be responsible for :

(i) A continuing survey of the extent of illiteracy among industrial workers. The nature and magnitude of the problem;

(ii) Stimulattng existing agencies and promoting new agencies for undertaking literacy work among industrial labour;

(iii) Supporting other agencies established with objectives similar to those of the Board ;

(iv) Securing and classifying information on the progress of literacy work among industrial workers and issuing periodical reports ;

(v) Experimental projects in collaboration with official and non-official agencies ;

(vi) Training of personal in collaboration with the Ministry of Education, State Education Departments, University Training Colleges and voluntary organisations ;

(vii) Laying down standards for the first and second stages of functional literacy ;

(viii) Production of suitable books, charts, pamphlets, maps etc ;

(ix) Organising supervision and inspection of literacy and post-literacy centres ;

(x) Arranging, where possible, and securing financial assistance to appropriate organisations.

IV Financial Resources

16. The programme for the eradication of illiteracy amongest industrial workers should be spread over a period of 10 years, to coincide with the 4th and 5th Plans. Thus on an average, 2 lakhs of such workers would be covered every year at an estimated cost of Rs. 50 lakhs per annum, involving a provision of Rs. 2.5 crores in each of the 4th & 5th Plans.

17. Financial resoures for a project of this nature should be drawn from several sources viz. Public exchequer, existing statutory organisations and from employers.

18. The Planning Commission may make a provision of Rs. 2.5 crores in the Fourth Plan period to cover 10 lakhs of industrial workers.

19. The Ministry of Education may also allocate a definite amount, out of its budget for social education, for the literacy programme of industrial workers.

20. The employers may be persuaded to make contributions, on same basis, as may be generally acceptable to them. In the same way, statutory organisations could make provisions in their budgets for the cradicate of illiteracy among their employees during the next ten years.

V-Incentives

21. Industrial establishments may offer such incentive as may be mutually agreed to by the employers' and workers' organisations.

VI-Pilot Projects

22. (a) A few Pilot Projects for the removal of illiteracy among workers be launched in selected industrial towns.

(b) Each such project should be under the guidance of a local organisation representing employers, trade unions, the State Labour and Education Departments, local bodies and adult education associations with a non-official President.

23. Finances for these projects should be drawn from the following sources :

(a) Voluntary contributions by employers ;

(b) Donations from philanthropists ;

(c) Grants from the State Govts ; Local bodies etc.

(d) Subscriptions from workers themselves, when available.

24. These projects should be organised under central direction with some co-ordinating arrangement at the Centre on which the proposed Central Board, the Ministries concerned and the Planning Commission should be represented: The objectives of the pilot projects should be clearly stated and understood.

25. Programmes at the pilot projects should be varied and comprehensive so that they cover as many items of general interest as possible, for examble (i)

cultural and recreational activities; (ii) exhibition of suitable films; (iii) literacy 'and post-literacy classes; (iv) Landicrafts classes for adult men and women and adolescents; (v) music recitals; (vi) dramatic performances.

26. A uniform blue-print for all states, industries or cities is not desirable. Each project should be conceived for a particular centre in keeping with local needs.

27. During the remaining part of the Third Plan itself, such model programme may be taken up in some places like Ahmedabad, Bombay, Bangalore, Culcutta, Coimbatore.

28. The State Labour Commissions should be asked to set up an independent organisation for this purpose.

29. It is necessary to create a proper atmospherr and a climate of public opinion before organising an adult literacy programme.

VIII Organising A Literacy Compaign

30. **Personnel**: The teachers of literacy classes for industrial workers would have to adopt different methods and techniques.

31. Utilising the services of educated workers of the same establishment would be more fruitful. The services of voluntary workers may also be availed of wholetime workers, with specialised training in adult education, will be preferable.

32. Such teachers should be given a thorough training which should be organised under the auspices of the National Fundamental Education Centre or by an accredited organisation. Besides refresher courses should also be conducted periodically for trained workers.

33. **Supervision**: The supervision and inspection of adult literacy centres for workers should ordinarily be carried out by persons conversant with the techniques and methods of adult education. These people should receive a short training at the National Fundamental Education Centre of the Ministry of Education or at another similar institution.

34. **Syllabus**: The Syllabus for industrial workers should be different from that prescribed for illiterate rural adults and be related to their daily lives and surroundings.

35. The Syllabus by the Ministry of Education for first and second States of literacy should be considerably simplified. A suggested syllabus is given in Appendix-V.

36. The Central Broad should conduct investigations to determine the minimum period required for making a worker functionally literate.

37. Some of the industrial units have taken up research in various stors of industry. Their research staff should also conduct investigations in respect of literacy.

38. The universities and other organisations like the National Fundamental Education Centre should assist in the research programmes on these subjects & other related matters.

39. **Libraries**: The role of small libraries in industrial establishments in providing the necessary motivation and facility for maintaining the interest of the workers in their newly-acquired literacy should be emphasized.

40. A systematic "follow-up" programme for improving the reading and writing skills of adults, after completion of their first and second stages of literacy, is most essential.

41. It would not be enough to make worker literate. He must be given opportunities to become an "educated" worker capable of appreciating the nature of his job and to develop a sense of "belonging" to the establishment.

STUDY GROUP ON THE STUDY OF ENGLISH IN INDIA 1964—REPORT

New Delhi, Ministry of Education, 1967. 271p.

Chairman: Prof. V. K. Gokak.
Members: Shri A.E.T. Borrow; Prof. C. S. Bhandari; Smt. M. Choksi; Shri A. R. Dawood; Mr. J. M. Ure.

APPOINTMENT

The Study Group on the Teaching of English at the School Stage was appointed by the Government of India,, Ministry of Education in 1964.

TERMS OF REFERENCE

1. The Position of English in School education as it would be when English would cease to be the medium of instruction at the University stage and would be

replaced by Hindi or other modern Indian languages.

2. The extent of the knowledge of English which a student should have at the end of the secondary stage and at the University stage with a view to maintenance of standards.

3. The re-orientation of course in the teaching of English at the school stage in view of the findings under (1) and (2) above;

4. The problems involved in the teaching of English at the School stage, such as (a) the class in which the teaching of English should begin, (b) the methods of teaching to be employed, (c) the preparation of text-books and handbooks for teachers, and (d) the preparation of teachers of English for schools in adequate numbers;

5. Improvement of standards of English in Secondary schools to meet the present situation of English being the medium of instruction in Universities and the regional languages in the secondary schools; and

6. Any other matters which may be relevant to study.

It was agreed, after an explanatory discussion and consideration of the working papers produced by some of the members of the Group that the proper interpretation of the first and fifth terms of reference would be as follows :

1. Apart from the details of a time scheduled regarding the replacement of English as medium of instruction at the University stage, which is beyond the purview of this Group, what needs to be considered is the quantum of English required by those students who will receive their education through the regional medium, once the change comes about. The Group should also set forth the alterations in the methods of teaching English to pupils and of testing their attainment in it, consequent on the change of medium of instruction and examination.

2. At present students continue to be instructed and examined through English. It is possible that, even when the medium has been regionalised. Some students will continue to use English as their medium in some schools. The Study Group should, therefore, define the quantum of English which has to be mastered by students who use English as their medium of instruction and examination, now or later and either wholly or partially. Further the Group should set forth the measures to be adopted for ensuring this achievement on the part of Student.

CONTENTS

Part I: Recommendations

The Study Group : Terms of Reference, Meetings Acknowledgements; English as Medium of Instruction and as Second Language—A Historical Review; English as Medium of Instruction; English as Compulsory Second Language; A Programme for Teaching English in Schools; A Programme for Teaching English in Colleges; A Training Programme for Teachers of English; Measures to improve the present Situation; A Programme of Priorities; Summary of Findings and Recommendations.

II Part : Appendices from 1 to 13.

Summary Of Findings And Recommendations

For convenience of reference, we give below a summary of our main findings and recommendations, arranged according to chapters.

Chapter Two : English As Medium Of Instruction And As Second Language

A Historical Review

Owing to the pressure of historical circumstances, English became the unchallenged medium of instruction at the higher level during the second quarter of the 19th century in India. In spite of Wood's Despatch (1854) which held the hope that English and the modern Indian languages would be media at the secondary stage, English became the sole medium. The study of English dominated the entire school curriculum. Though the system of education could hardly be regarded as sound, it maintained consistently the same medium of instruction at both the secondary and university level-English.

With the advent of Diarchy on the provincial level in the twenties, modern Indian languages were adopted as media of education at the secondary school level. This change came gradually and unobstructively all over the country.

We are faced with a similar transition at the university level today. The continuance of English as university medium with the regional medium current in school, is fraught with ruinous consequences to education itself. It is a pity that this was not foreseen when the medium in secondary schools was regionalised. We have lost nearly fourty years during which the universities could have been prepared for the new medium by a phased programme of translations.

One may legitimately demand that the unity of academic life in the country should be ensured through due safeguards like an intensive study of English and Hindi as link languages. But we are not justified in condemning the regional medium itself as a fissiparous and disintegrated force.

A vicious circle has established itself in the teaching of English—the yonger lecturers being often incorrect in their use of English. It is possible to promote in students the comprehension of reading materials in English for purposes of supplementary study. But correct expression in English and the continuation of English as medium of higher education is now beyond the reach of our students. The only hope for higher education now lies in regionalising the medium without any further delay.

The transition from English to the regional medium should be a carefully planned and phased programme. The following may be envisaged as some of the possible steps in this process: (a) Permission given to candidates to answer the examination papers on some of their subjects in the regional languages; (b) Permission given to colleges to continue to teach either through or the regional medium, depending upon the preparedness of their teachers and the willingness of the parents and guardians: (c) The decision to regionalise the university medium should be taken simultaneously all over the country and not spreadically by a university here and a university there : (d) A planned programme for the production of textbooks on all academic subjects in the regional language is essential. This should not be left to the vagaries of the book-trade as it was when the school medium was regionalised.

Modern Indian languages should be firmly established as media in most of our universities by 1975, the last year of the Fifth Five-Year Plan. All the steps necessary in the field of book-production should be taken according to this time-schedule. We suggest this in view of the vicious circle that has established itself in the teaching of English in schools and colleges. We do not believe that correct expression in English can be salvaged as part of the equipment of an average student in the present state of the learning and teaching of English. The state of affairs cannot be improved sufficiently to such an extent as to ensure correctness of expression in English as the general and habitual acquisition of average students.

The ideal of national education as one that preserves the mobility of the student and the teacher should be carefully provided for, while regionalising the medium. This can be done by teaching English and Hindi to students so intensively that B.A. special and M.A. students are able to follow lectures in English or Hindi with ease and are responsive to them as media of instruction though not of examination. All instruction will normally take place through the regional medium. But the possibility that a few lectures may come from other parts of India should always be envisaged and arranged for.

Once the university medium is regionalised, the need for each student to study a modern Indian language other than his own will be more apparent than ever. Experts in different subjects are employed today as external examiners by each university. Unless experts are available for each subject who know the regional language which is the medium of a university, the valuaion of examination scripts will have to depend only on internal examiners. It is, therefore, necessary to encourage each student to study a regional language other than his own both at school and in college.

The Constitution laid down in 1950, after considerable controversy in the Constituent Assembly and outside, that Hindi in Devanagari script would be the official language of India. This meant that special provision had to be made for the teaching of Hindi in schools in the non-Hindi speaking areas.

The Central Advisory Board of Education evolved the three-language formula in 1956 to remove this inequality in the language load on children. Its outstanding geature was that it recommended Hindi as a compulsory language in the non-Hindi areas and a modern Indian language in the Hindi areas.

The formula was simplified at the Chief Ministers' Conference in 1961 so as to permit 'any other Indian language' even a classical language like Sanskrit or Persian—to be studied as a compulsory language in the Hindi areas.

The Three-language formula has been accepted in principle but not implemented satisfactorily. There are certain difficulties inherent in the national situation itself which come in the way of its implementation.

Hindi will be the official language by 1965. But English may, to quote from Clause 3 of the Official Languages Act, as from the appointed day, continue to be used in addition to Hindi for all the official purposes of the Union. This may be for an indefinite period.

The educational significance of the study of English as a second language is now being increasingly realised.

Chapter Three : A Programme For Teaching English in Schools

The three-language formula should be modified. Only two languages and not three, should be studied compulsorily in Classes V, VI and VII and the study of the third languages should be taken up in Classes VIII, IX and X. Assuming that the duration of the school course is 12 years, three languages may continue to be studied in Classes XI and XII, but in a modified form.

The modified form of the three-language formula is given below :

A-Primary

Classes I-IV

The only compulsory language at this stage will be the mother tongue or the regional language which will be the medium of instruction.

Classes V-VII

For Non-Hindi speaking Areas

(i) The mother tongue or the regional language

(ii) One of the two official languages—English or Hindi

For Hindi Speaking Areas

(i) The mother tongue or the regional language

(ii) English or Hindi, if English is already taken as the mother tongue under (i)

B. Secondary

Classes VIII-X

For Non-Hindi Speaking Areas

(i) The mother tongue or the regional language
(ii) English
(iii) Hindi

For Hindi-Speaking Areas

(i) The mother tongue or the regional language

(ii) English or Hindi, if English is already taken as the mother tongue under (i)

(iii) A modern Indian language other than Hindi

C. Higher Secondary or Pre-University

(i) University Preparatory Group

For Non-Hindi Speaking Areas

(i) The mother tongue or the regional language
(ii) English
(iii) Hindi

For Hindi Speaking Areas

(i) The mother tongue or the regional language

(ii) English or Hindi, where English is already taken as the mother tongue under (i)

(iii) A modern Indian language other than Hindi

2. Vocational or Semi-Vocational Oroups

The mother tongue or the regional language will be the medium of instruction for these groups as for the others. But it may not be a subject of study. There will be compulsory study of English or Hindi or any other modern European or Indian language, depending on the type of occupation to be followed.

The level of attainment desirable in English can be reached after studying English for eight years at school at the rate of six periods a week in Classes V to X, both inclusive, and six periods a week for the lower level in Classes XI and XII (and eight periods a week for the higher level).

A pupil who has studied English or Hindi for three years only upto Class X, will have to undergo a special course in English or Hindi for a year before he can be admitted to Class XI.

English will continue to occupy an important place in the language curriculum from the point of view of the time devoted to a study of it. This is so because English will for a long time continue to be the chief source of all scientific or technological knowledge. The fact that English will be the additional official language lends further support to this position.

In a 12-year school course, it is assumed that there will be a bifurcation at the end of the tenth year, separating pupils for whom the school course will be a terminal stage from those who wish to pursue their studies further at the university. The language requirements are bound to vary from one vocational course to another. They will have to be examined in detail by the committees of courses for the various vocations.

A twelve-year school course followed by a three-year course at the university is the pattern that has been accepted by the Conference of Education Ministers in 1964. This should be implemented immediately and the pattern $4 \times 3 \times 3 \times 2$ should be accepted for the school course.

The introduction of English as a second language earlier than Class V should be discouraged.

Pupils who seek admission to Class VIII without studying English for the three preceding years should be required to study English for a whole year and pass a test in English.

In Classes XI and XII, English should be taught at least six periods a week. Four of these should be utilised to meet class sections of 20 each and help pupils to cultivate language skills directly. The other two periods should be used for class-work on text materials and some points of usage. If the higher secondary or pre-university year is only one, as it is today, English should be taught for eight periods during the year, five of these periods being devoted to class-section meetings.

English will have to be studied at two levels at the higher secondary stage. When the medium of instruction at the university stage is regionalised, comprehension will be a more important language skill than expression for the large majority of students. Comprehension will decidedly be a more important language skill than expression at the lower level course which has been designed to meet the needs of the average university student.

The higher level course in English is designed for that class of students from among whom teachers of English will have to be recruited in the future. Those who complete the higher level courses in English at the higher secondary stage is given below :

(a) **Objectives (Lower Level)**

At the end of the course a pupil should be able to—

(i) Understand a talk on a subject within his experience, provided the pace of the talk is not too fast and that unusual words or expressions are avoided,

(ii) Reply intelligibly in speach in English, to straight

forward questions, within his experience,

(iii) Read with fluency and understand a simple passage of prose in English, and

(iv) Express himself with a reasonable degree of accuracy in speech and in writing in English on subjects within his linguistic experience.

(b) **(Objective Higher Level)**

At the end of this course a pupil should be able to—

(I) Understand a talk (including a radio or tape-recorded talk) on a subject of general interest within his experience.

(ii) (a) Carry on a natural conversation with clarity of expression on a topic within his experience, (b) arrange, present and explain his ideas intelligently, on a topic selected by him,

(iii) understand the main statements or ideas in a written passage and be able to reproduce them, in the order in which they are given, in a simple workmanlike manner, and

(iv) express himself in writing with relevance and accuracy on :

(a) a subject of general interest within his experience, (b) a topic chosen from a subject within the curriculum which entails a vocabulary relating specially to that branch of knowledge.

A student should study English for eight years in order to acquire the quantum of the language necessary to qualify him for admission to the lower level examination at the end of the twelth year. A student who has studied English for three years only upto Class X should undergo a special course in English for a year before he can be admitted to Class XI of the pre-university course. This is true also with regard to admissions to Class XI for certain vocational courses.

Syllabuses for both the lower and higher level courses based on the structural approach, are given in Appendices Two and Three. The lower level course aims at the acquisition of an active vocabulary of 2,000 and a passive vocabulary of 1,500 words as well as the mastery of 337 teaching points. The higher level course aims at the mastery of an additional 38 teaching points and an active as well as a passive vocabulary of another 500 words each. Certain additional material (elements in word formation, formulas, phrasal verbs, etc.) should be distributed appropriately over the entire course,

The two syllabuses (higher and lower) presuppose the prescription of two papers or course units—one on language skills with text and the other on language skills without texts. Simplified reading material is prescribed for the lower level, and unsimplified reading for the higher level. The snpplementary reader prescribed for the higher level should have a greater range of vocabulary.

Appendices Four and Five contain some specimen test techniques, and questions meant for the lower and higher level examinations in English at the end of the higher secondary stage (Classes XI and XII) are given in Appendices Four and Five. A comparison of the two appendices will bring out the following distinctions; (a) The lower level stresses comrehension rather than expression, both written and spoken; (b) The difficulty level of the questions on comprehension and on spoken English is greater at the higher level; (c) Pupils have to answer the question on a passage given for comprehension through the regional language at the lower level; at the higher level, only some of the questions may be so answered; (d) There are two questions on free composition at the higher level, but only one at the lower. The pupil examined at the higher level is tested more in continuous composition and in a wider areas of usage.

Aural-oral tests are necessary at both the lower and higher levels. These will have to be arranged as internal tests in view of the large number of peoples involved. Since these tests have to be internal, two safeguards are recommended; (a) No pass or class should be awarded on the basis of the marks given internally. If the candidate has passed in the internal test, this should be shown in the certificate, (b) Roving officers should supervise the internal examination in different centres. (c) A correction should also be attempted between marks given internally and externally and the results circulated to affiliated institutions.

Chapter Four : The Teaching of English in Colleges

Compulsory English should be taught throughout the three-year degree course, for six periods a week during the first two years and for three periods a week during the third year. Of the six periods, there should be used as preceptorial or practical exercise periods for class-section meetings. All the three periods, there should be used as preceptorial or practical exercise periods for class-section meetings. All three periods should be so used during the third year. The course should consist of a paper on skills through texts and another on skills without texts. A subject classic should be prescribed under the text paper to facilitate reading on the student's own special subject. Simple, original writing can now be prescribed for study in the form of a book of prose and poetry selections, novels, collections of short stories of one-act plays, biographies, travelogues, etc. A certain level of continuity should be maintained between the pre-university and the compulsory English course while prescribing books.

What is stated above regarding the course in compulsory English applies to the measure of reform recomended for the transition period. In addition to the two papers, there should be a half paper of the duration of one and a half hours in summary and translations.

The regionalisation of the medium of instruction at university level necessitates another innovation. Each department in a college should have, in its own subject, an additional lecturer whose duty it will be to introduce to students the literature in English on the subject. Provision should be made for this work for two periods a week during the first year of the three-year degree course. This kind of guidance should keep pace with the topics taught each week.

A specimen syllabus of the higher level course in compulsory English is given in Appendix Seven. It is meant for students who have studied English at the higher level at the higher secondary stage. There is a greater emphasis on expression in this course since teachers of English for the higher secondary and compulsory English classes are expected to emerge from this category of students.

Those who specialise in subsidiary English in the three-year degree course should take up the higher level course in compulsory English and not the lower level. The syllabus for subsidiary English should be revised so as to include a course unit on a linguistic description of the language.

A good part of the teaching under both the subsidiary and principal courses in English should be conducted through preceptorials and through tutorials at the M. A. stage.

Apart from a common core of literature, the M. A. course should contain an optional section consisting of the history of the English language, a statement of the problems involved in the teaching of English as a second language and a discussion of more advanced topics in the phonetics of English and in structural linguistics with special reference to Engligh. A viva-voce should be a part of the M. A. examination.

A reorientation of courses as mentioned above will result in bringing about a sharp distinction between lecturers in the English language and lecturers in English literature. This is not only a valid distinction but one which has a great significance for the future. Most of the departments of English may be expected to be language-oriented departments during the next twenty years. Specialisation in Engligh literature as such may be confined to some of the older postgraduate centres.

There is considerable need for research on the problems arising from the teaching of English in India. A degree like M. Ed. should really be conferred on those who do outstanding work in the field of textbooks, anthologies, simplified books, teachers' handbooks, workbooks, test papers, etc. A research degree should need not be insisted on for university teachers of English in the same manner in which it is insisted on for other subjects.

Chapter Five : A Training Programme For Teachers Of English

A programme should be worked out for each State, on the basis of the qualifications prescribed, the number of teachers required for each stage and the number of training schools and training colleges and teacher-educators required. The programme should be so scheduled as to begin in April 1965 and end by March 1971. The number of additional teachers of English that will have to be trained for the whole country during the next ten years is approximately as follows :

Stage	No. of additional teachers to be trained per year	
	Fourth Plan	Fifth Plan
Middle School	16,000	15,000
High School	7,000	7,000
Higher Secondary or Intermediate	2,800	3,000
Three-year Degree Course	2,300	2,400

The following qualifications are recommended for teachers of English at each of these stages :

(a) **Middle School :** A graduate with a year's training in a training college; or, a person who has completed the higher secondary course, with a year's training in a content and methods course in English.

(b) **High School :** A graduate with subsidiary or principal English and a year's training in a training college; or, a person who has graduated after passing the Indian School Certificate Examination and who has been trained in the teaching of English in a special programme for a year; or, a graduate who has, in addition to being trained for a year in the methods of teaching English in a training college, also undergone a special content course in English for a year.

(c) **The Higher Secondary and Three-year Degree Stage :** A postgraduate degree in English with a diploma in the teaching of English as a second language; or, a second class graduate with principal English and with a diploma as above (as a transitory measures).

The training of teachers of English should be organised on the following lines :

Middle School Teachers : Most of the teachers at this level will have passed the S. S. C. examination. Many more training schools should be established to provide an intensive content and methods programme for a year as outlined in Appendix Nine.

High School Teachers ; Only graduates with subsidiary or principal English should be admitted to a year's training programme in training colleges. Others should be admitted to the course only after being trained for a year in the content course only, after being trained for a year in the content course the higher level compulsory English course along with a course unit in a linguistic description of English and the other papers. Arrangement should be made to teach this content course in colleges or in training colleges. The number of training colleges should be increased considerably. The admissions to the four-month course in the Capital Institute of English should also be increased.

Higher Secondary and Compulsory English Course Teachers: The Central Institute of English should be expanded considerably so as to double the number of key personnel that it trains every year. In addition; a number of teachers will also have to be trained in training colleges. Admissions to the B. A. special English and M. A. English courses in colleges and university departments should also be increased.

The following steps should be taken for training teacher-educators for the training institutions of English at various levels, The teacher-trainers in training schools, who should be graduates with subsidiary or principal English, should be trained for a year in training colleges or at a four-month course in the Central Institute of English. The teacher-educators in training colleges, who should be M. A.'s in English should be trained on a diploma course in the teaching of English at Hyderabad or a course equivalent to it.

The following measures should be taken as soon as possible without waiting for a change of medium at the university level : (a) the appointment of subject-inspectors for English; (b) the organisation of orientation courses in the teaching of English for other inspecting officers and of refresher courses once in five years for teachers of English in service; (c) and the sanction of a suitable allowance or of two advance increments to those teachers of English who undergo the training required for their level of teaching.

The B. Ed. course in English should be revised as indicated in Appendix Ten.

Chapter Six : Measures To Improve The Present Situation

A State Institute of English should be established in each State by September 1965.

The Central Institute of English should be expanded in the following manner :

(a) Trainees should be admitted exclusively from colleges and polytechnics and from training colleges to the sixty places that are now available at the Institute. Sixty more places should be created for a four-month course for training a number of additional persons per year.

(b) An examination wing should be organised and a bank of test papers created to test students on the curricula current in State departments of education, secondary education boards, training schools and colleges and university departments of English. Fees may be charged for these test papers.

(c) A close liaison should be established between the Central, Institute of English, Hyderabad and the State Institute of English.

(d) Arrangements should be made to increase the number of admission to the B.A. subsidiary and principal courses in English and the M A. course in English in colleges and university departments of English in each State depending on the number of teachers of English required for teaching at high school and higher secondary levels.

Graduates who have studied English only in the compulsory English course and are desirous of getting trained in the methods of teaching English, should be required to undergo a special content course for a year-a course which amalgamates higher compulsory English and subsidiary English. Teachers trained in this way can teach in high schools. The University Grants Commission should assist universities to set up these courses in selected colleges. The arrangements should start in 1966.

Reform in the preparation and prescription of text-books in English at the secondary stage is necessary. A body of experts in this field should be appointed to prepare a few series of course books, work books and teacher's handbooks, not for one department but for several departments of education together, on the basis of a common syllabus. This will mean a great saving of time and effort. Regional variations of pattern are desirable and should be observed in the preparation of such books.

The mass media of communication should be used increasingly for English-teaching programmes. The A.I.R., the State departmets of education and the State institutes of English can co-operate in such a programme.

A radical change in the structure of our examination at all levels is necessary. The cultivation of language skills, which is the prime aim in language learning, is relegated to the background and obscured by the study of course books for their own sake. Paper-setters should be trained in new techniques and given more time and better remuneration for their work. A bank of test papers should be welcome to the board and university authorities, if one can be organised.

In view of the abrupt change of medium which a student experiences in his transfer from school to college, it is necessary to organise 'bridge' or special preparatory courses during the long vacation. The necessary materials and methods of teaching such a course have been evolved by the Central Institute of English. University authorities should organise and run such courses,

Full details of a lower and a higher level course in English are given in Appendices Two and Three. Teachers of English should make sure that the school-leaving student has the minimum equipment represented by the lower level of English given in Appendix Two.

Chapter Seven : A Programme Of Priorities

The recommendations contained in this Report should be examined immediately by the Ministry of Education and circulated to State Governments for their consideration and for the inclusion of concrete schemes to improve the teaching of English on the lines recommended by us, in their Fourth Five Year Plans.

The two crucial measures for improving the teaching of English on the national level are :

(i) The expansion of the Central Institute of English, Hyderabad ; and

(ii) The establishment of an institute of English in each State.

Both these problems should be examined by the Ministry of Education. A suitable programme of expansion for the Central Institute of English, Hyderabad, till the end of the Fourth Five Year Plan should be drawn up and financial provision for it should be made by the Ministry of Education in its budget for this year and for the next. Similarly, a programme for establishing an institute of English in each State and for assisting the State institutes that are already established should be provided for in the Centrally-sponsored sector.

The following arrangements should be regarded as the minimum necessary for a State institute of English :

(i) An independent building in which all the classes and the offices of the institute can be housed.

(ii) An independent building in which the institute hostel can be housed, with satisfactory accommodation for the teacher-trainees that will be admitted to the institute.

(iii) The institute should have independent status. It should not be attached to any other institution under the State Department of Education.

(iv) Specially trained teaching personnel should be recruited to posts at the institute and they should be given the U.G.C. Grades meant for readers and professors. The Director of the Institute should at least have a professor's status. The minimum qualifications for a member of the teaching staff at a State Institute, including the Director, should be a good M.A. degree in English and a diploma from the Central Institute of English, Hyderabad, or a qualification equivalent to it.

(v) The grants for the expansion of a State Institute should be made available through the Central Institute of English, which will co-ordinate training programmes so as to help the institutes to function effectively in their areas. Further, in order that the State institutes may get adequate technical assistance for their proper functioning, there should be an effective contact between them and the Central Institute of English, Hyderabad.

Immediate steps should be taken to :

(i) Determine the number of training institutions required for training teachers of English for middle and secondary schools ;

(ii) Prepare the teacher-educators for staffing these institutions ; and

(iii) Establish such institutions forthwith all over the country.

Steps will also have to be taken during the remaining eighteen months of the Third Plan as advance action towards impelementing these three measures and the funds required for this purpose should be made available in the Centrally sponsored sector.

The main body of recommendations made in this report is concerned with the place of English in our schools and colleges after the medium of higher education has been regionalised. Effective action on them would be possible only if an executive machinery is devised at the national level. This executive body should be representative of all the authorities concerned with this problem. It should function at a sufficiently high level and command adequate financial resources required for this programme of action.

The broad programme for the development of English in the Fourth Five Year Plan should include the following :

(i) The expansion of the Central Institute of English on the lines suggested in our recommendations.

(ii) The establishment of an Institute of English in each State.

(iii) The revision of curricula at all stages of education and the use of mass media for the teaching of English.

(iv) The establishment of special institution for the training of teachers for middle, secondary and higher secondary schools in adequate numbers.

(v) The upgrading of the qualifications of teachers of English at different levels in the manner discussed in the Report.

(vi) The organisation of one-year current courses for teachers of English in secondary schools on an adequate scale.

(vii) The expansion of facilities for teaching the course in special English at the undergraduate and postgraduate stages so that an adequate number of teachers of English is forthcoming for higher secondary schools and colleges.

(viii) Provision for posts of subject-inspectors of English.

(ix) Organisation of orientation courses for the inspecting officers of middle and secondary schools.

(x) The establishment of an Educational Testing Service and orientation courses for teachers of English in evaluation techniques.

The change of medium at the university level will be fully impelemented during the period of the Fifth Five Year Plan.

In this Plan, it will also be necessary to organise refresher courses for teachers of English so that every teacher of English can undergo a refresher course extending from one to three months once in every five years of his service.

UNIVERSITY GRANTS COMMISSION, BUILDING ADVISORY COMMITTEE, ON TEACHERS' HOSTELS, 1964—REPORT

New Delhi, University Grants Commission, 1964. 8p.

Chairman : Shri K.L. Joshi.
Members : Prof. F. C. Auluck ; Shri H. Rahman ; Shri B.P. Mathur.
Member-Secretary : Shri R.K. Chhabra.

APPOINTMENT

There is an acute shortage of properly qualified and experienced teachers in the Universities and Colleges. To attract and retain the best available talent to the teaching profession it is felt that besides attractive scales of pay some more facilities have to be provided. Environments and living conditions play a predominant part in moulding the personality of a teacher and the quality of education imparted by him. Provision of residential accommodation for the teachers near the University Campus will not only be a potent factor in checking the drift of talent to avenues other than teaching but also prove advantageous to the students. It will help in building a corporate community life within the campus.

During recent years there has been a rapid increase in the number of students resulting in additional number of teachers in the Universities. The provision of residential accommodation for teachers, however, has not kept pace with the increase in teaching staff. In most cases the teachers have to seek rented accommodation which is expensive, inconvenient and difficult to secure.

The University Grants Commission has been aware of this difficulty and a Committee of the Commission is separately looking into the problem of provision of residential accommodation for students and teachers. The provision of housing in a regular scale to all the teachers in the Universities would be a prohibitive programme in the context of the present limited resources. As an interim measure the University Grants Commission has decided to appoint a Committee for the construction of Teachers, Hostels in 1964.

TERMS OF REFERENCE

(i) That in addition to assistance for the construction of Staff Quarters, the Universities may be assisted for the construction of 'Teachers' Hostels'.

(ii) To lay down the norms in general for the provision of various facilities in the Teachers' Hostel for the guidance of the Universities.

CONTENTS

Introduction ; Purpose ; Siting, Location and Expansion ; Space Utilization ; Living Room or Multi-purpose Room ; Bed Room ; Kitchenette ; Bath Room ; Entrance Hall ; Sleeping Terrace ; Choice of Material ; Services; Combination of Hostels; Appendices I and II.

RECOMMENDATIONS

Purpose

The teachers' flats are intended for single, newly-married or senior teachers who do not have large families and can manage with a suite of two rooms with other facilities provided. While recommending the norms, the Committee feels that the following facilities and areas should be provided in each of the flats :—

(1)	Living room or multi-purpose room living, study and dining)	165 sq. ft.
(2)	Bed room (including wardrobe)	125 sq. ft.
(3)	Kitchenette	55 sq. ft.
(4)	Toilet	40 sq. ft.
(5)	Sleeping balcony	60 sq. ft.

(6) Circulation entrance lobby — 7-1/2% of the carpet area.

(7) For thickness of walls, staircases and circulation space. — 50% of the carpet area

(8) Total carpet area per flat — 480 sq. ft.

(9) Total built-up area per flat — 720 sq. ft.

Due to special climatic conditions in certain parts of the country it may not be necessary to provide balconies in the flats everywhere. In such cases the area so surrendered could be usefully utilised for providing increased carpet area in flats, provided that the total built-up area per flat as recommended does not exceed the limit indicated.

Siting, Location And Expansion

In the proposal for the construction of teachers' hostels, apart from the living and other accommodation made available, a small kitchenette may be provided in each flat. Some Universities may desire to provide in addition to these arrangements, a common dining hall and lounge for the residents. Most of the Universities already have provision for guest houses-cum-staff clubs. These blocks of teachers' hostels may be so located that the facilities already available for dining hall etc. could be made available to residents of these flats.

Space Utilisation

The Commission has been examining plans submitted by some Universities. The building team is of the opinion that flats for teachers should be planned around an entrance lobby from where all the rooms including bath and kitchen could be entered directly. The shape of the room should be determined by the particular furniture necessary in the room, and the unit of flat should determine the overall shape of the building. In case, where corridor access is used, it will be seen that the circulation space is disproportionately high. The building Committee is of the view that flats around a central staircase may be found to be most economical.

Living Room Or Multi-Purpose Room

This room is intended to serve as a dining room as well as for entertainment, eating and study. For utility and convenience it has been found that an oblong shaped room offers a better arrangement. The design of this room should be such that there is sufficient light and ventilation and enough of space.

The multi-purpose room should be able to accommodate the following furniture :

1. A Divan, which could be used for sitting during the day and may function as a bed for a guest at night, if need be.
2. Two sofa chairs.
3. Central or Coffee table.
4. A standard lamp.
5. A study table.
6. Built in bookshelf for about 150 books.
7. A dining table for four (3′′-9′′ × 3′-9′′)
8. Four dining chairs.

Note :—One of the dining chairs could be utilised for the study table.

Bed Room

The bed room is the most important component of the flat. Care should be taken to study its proportions and the arrangements of furniture. The Committee has observed that many a times the bed rooms are large enough but the beds can not be arranged conveniently. Moreover there is hardly enough space round the beds to move conveniently either to reach the bath room or to leave the bed room or even to reach the electric light controls. These defects could be overcome by proper arrangement of doors and windows and study of the furniture layout. The bed room should contain the following furniture:

1. Two beds.
2. Two built-in Wardrobes.
3. Built-in type dressing table.
4. A book niche.

Kitchenette

This is intended for the cooking of food for the small family. As already recommended that for large entertainments or parties the use of the University club dining hall and lounge may be made by locating the flats near the club building.

The kitchen should be well designed and the use of fire wood and coal may be replaced with gas or oil-fed ovens, whichever proves economical both in the installation and running cost. Whatever be the system of cooking a hood above the cooking range is necessary to take away the fumes. It is also necessary to fit up the kitchen with a large pantry sink with an elbow control tap. Further a provision for a garbage chute is considered very desirable. Sufficient thought should be given to the planning of garbage chutes and the collection and disposal of the garbage.

Following is the list of furniture and fittings for the Kichenette :

1. A sitting stool.
2. Cooking range with two plates (Electric, gas or oil-fed).
3. Pantry sink with drainboard and elbow control tap.
4. Storage cupboard.
5. Plate rack above the sink.
6. Garbage chute with a shutter.
7. An extra power plug to operate other electric gadgets like an electric kettle etc.

Bath Room

The bath room should be attached to the bed room. At the same time it should be possible to enter it direct from the enterance hall so that one may not have to enter the bed room to reach the bath room.

The bath room should have a W.C., wash basin, a shower, towel rail, mirror and medicine chest.

In our country it is absolutely necessary to provide effective ventilation and light in the bath rooms. Most of the Municipal Committees insist that the bath room should have an external wall. This is laid down with a view to achieving good ventilation in the bath-rooms.

Entrance Hall

An entrance hall is necessary to provide entry to the various components of the flats and could also be utilised for ventilation of the flats. The entrance hall should have provision for a telephone, where a socket may be provided, while laying the wiring in the flat. It should also have a cupboard for raincoat, shoes, old newspaper etc., which may be found very useful to the occupants of the flat.

Sleeping Terrace

In most parts of our country a sleeping terrace is very essential and should be large enough to take two beds conveniently. As far as possible the terrace should be approachable both from the living room and the bed room. An ideal terrace should have winter sun and be free from afternoon summer sun.

As far as possible solid masonery rails to the terrace should be avoided as they radiate heat and add to the discomfort of summer nights, but at the same time the other type of rails should as well not be of very open type and should provide sufficient safety.

In structures of more than 2 storeys the sleeping terrace should be so arranged that it may provide sufficient privacy and at the same time be open from sides for undisturbed flow of breeze and at least radiation from the walls. Generally the sleeping terrace should be 1/2" lower than the level of the living or bed room so that the rain water may not enter the room.

As already stated where sleeping terraces are not required the area for the sleeping terrace as recommended could be utilised for increasing the size of the rooms in the flat. It is entirely at the discretion of the universities to utilise this area in the manner they consider most desirable.

Choice Of Material

It has been found that a structure consisting of ground, first and second floors can easily be built upon 1 inch thick load bearing brick wall. In case it is desired to make the flats more than four storeys high a R.C.C. frame structure with panels may be more economical than a brick structure.

Detailed discussion regarding the number of storeys that may be provided has already been made in the report on Residential buildings. It has been pointed out that a single storey structure is certainly not economical to build, even if there is plenty of cheap land available. High structures may have their own disadvantages but are very economical as regards circulation space.

Local materials normally are the cheapest to use. Since the prices of Steel and Cement are uniform in the country it is possible to lay terrazzo floors in the flats specially in bath rooms and kichens, and use R.C.C. roofs and R. C. C. staircases.

Services

It is a general practice to fix the waste pipes on the external face of the building. This, is very objectionable from the aesthetic point of view, and it is recommended that all pipes from toilet & kichen should be planned in a duct. In order to achieve economy in the piping it has already been recommended that wherever possible single pipe system should be adopted. It is further recommended at that horizontal pipes embedded in floors should be of the shortest possible length, and effective provision should be made for roding them conveniently.

The kitchen waste pipe is normally 2" in diameter. The size of this pipe should be increased to at least 3" and 4" dia pipe will be prefe rred.

The electric wiring should be in conduit. The position of the electric main should be such that the meter reader should be able to come at any time without disturbing the inmates of the flat or without even entering the flat.

Combination Of Hostels

On the basis of the recommendations a few lines drawing have been prepared and are enclosed as appendices. These are meant only to give an idea of the basis on which the above recommendations have been made by the Committee and could be modified to suit requirements of the universities. It may be that in certain cases the universities may like to provide, instead of two-room (flats) a single-room flat (with a small kitchenette and an attached bath) or a single room with attached bath room for the teachers. These three types could be grouped, if so desired, together in a block, according to requirements of each university.

STUDY TEAM ON GENERAL INSURANCE COOPERATIVES, 1964 —REPORT

New Delhi, Ministry of Community Development and Cooperation (Department of Cooperation), 1964. 63p.

Chairman : Shri L. N. Bongirwar.
Members : Shri C. L. Jain; Shri Madhav Rao Anwari.
Member-Secretary : Shri R. Vengu.

APPOINTMENT

The question of drawing up specific programmes for the development of general insurance cooperative societies on sound lines has been under the consideration of the Government. The Government of India appointed a Study Team to examine the working of the general insurance cooperative societies, to suggest measures for their development and to recommend the future line of development vide their Resolution No. F.9-26/63 Coord., dated January 14, 1964.

TERMS OF REFERENCE

(i) To review the present functioning of Cooperative societies in the field of general insurance;

(ii) To recommend specific measures for their development on sound lines; and

(iii) To indicate the promotional steps and future programmes for the organisation and working of cooperatives in the general insurance sector, particularly in the Third and Fourth Plan Periods.

CONTENTS

Introduction; Present position of General Insurance Cooperative in the Country; Basic approach to the problems of Insurance in the Cooperative Sector; Role of the State in Cooperative General Insurance; Pattern of Organisation; Insurance of deposits in Cooperatives; Cattle and Crop Insurance; Programme in the Third and Fourth Plan Periods; Conclusions and Recommendations; Appendices from I to V.

RECOMMENDATIONS

There are four cooperative general insurance societies in India with headquarters at Madras, Hyderabad, Bombay and Cuttack. The total gross premium increased from Rs. 27.8 lakhs in 1958 to Rs. 120.03 lakhs in 1963. Of this the premium from the business of cooperative institutions was Rs. 43 lakhs during 1962.

In addition there is a cooperative insurance society in Orissa writing the business of third party insurance under the Indian Motor Vehicles Act.

Similarly a Cooperative Insurance Society is functioning nominally in Bihar. A Cooperative General Insurance Society has recently been registered in Maharashtra State and will commence business as soon as it secures the necessary registration under the Insurance Act, 1938.

By and large the standard of their working including financial management and services rendered by the institutions is such as should justify the confidence of policy holders. Though all the societies have their area of operation throughout the country. Their representation is mainly from the Co-operative institutions in their State. None of the institutions could thus be said to be of all India Character.

About a third of the investment of the societies is in the Cooperative Sector and if certain local priorities with regard to investment are changed they could invest considerably more funds in the cooperative sector.

Uniformly in all these institutions individual policy holders are not given participation in the management. This is not in accordance with cooperative principles.

Mutuality and collective cooperation are the basic principles of insurance and the State should accept the cooperative form of organisation in the insurance sector as the desirable approach, and as an integrated part of national policy. Organisation of insurance by cooperative institutions for servicing their insurance needs is the logical process in the development of the fuller development of the sector. Nationalisation can never be a substitute for cooperativisation. The State should consequently promote the cooperative organisation in the insurance sector.

Property and business of cooperatives is public property with insurable interests. There is, however, no built-in mechanism to ensure that all cooperatives insure their insurable interests. Registrars of Cooperative Societies should draw up a schedule of insurable interests for different types of cooperatives and provide in the rules for compulsory insurance of such insurable interests by each cooperative society. There should thus be no discretion left to any society in the matter of insuring its insurable interests

Cooperative institutions should insure compulsorily with approved cooperative insurance organisations. State Governments and Registrars should frame appropriate rules for the purpose.

Some State Governments have made it obligatory on the part of some cooperative organisations to insure with the Insurance Fund or Insurance Pool and State aid has been made a lever of this policy. This should be removed and there should be no compulsion direct or indirect to make a society insure with any organisation other than an approved cooperative insurance society.

Similarly the Life Insurance Corporatio -should not insist on cooperatives, to whom it has given assistance, insuring with a particular insurance society.

Insurance of business which may be called incidental to cooperative business, e.g., loans by cooperative societies to members for purchase of milch cattle, pumping sets etc. should be exclusively with approved cooperative insurance organisations. The cooperative societies issuing such loans should make this a condition of their loan.

Cooperative business essentially a of rural character like the property of panchayats stocks, in warehouses should be reserved exclusively for approved cooperative insurance societies.

Cooperative insurance societies will not have to incur expenditure on agency commission for getting the business of cooperative organisations, business incidental thereto and buisness of rural character. The benefit of such consequential reduction in agency commission should be passed on to the policy-holder. If necessary, the Insurance Act and Rules should be amended for the purpose.

It should be possible for approved co-operative insurance societies to take advantage of the expertise available in the Life Insurance Corporation and work out arrangements for reinsurance and other business relationship to their mutual benefit.

Co-operative societies are of considerable assistance in procuring life business for L.I.C. They could similarly be of considerable assistance in arranging the business of cooperative insurance organisations.

Co-operative insurance societies should function efficiently and in a manner calculated to sustain the confidence of the State and policy-holder. The national federation of the insurance societies should actively supervise and guide their work.

There should be a strong cell headed by a senior officer in the State Cooperative Departments to guide, supervise and assist the societies. The cost of this cell be shared equally by the Central and State Governments as the case of all departmental staff.

A co-operative insurance society with proper representation of all cooperative institutions in the State is more conducive for developing the business of cooperative institutions than a society from outside. Besides cooperation is a State subject and the State Governments are responsible for promoting the sound growth of the movement. As a general policy organisation of State level Cooperative General Insurance Societies should be promoted wherever there is adequate business potential.

A minimum annual business of Rs. 5 lakhs gross premium is necessary for the organisation of a cooperative general insurance society. Business of this order would be available immediately for State level societies in Gujarat, Mysore, Uttar Pradesh and Madhya Pradesh. State Governments should consequently promote societies in these States immediately. It should be possible to organise State level societies in most of the other States in the early years of the Fourth plan.

For development of insurance as a proper service and real cooperative endeavour individual policy holders should be associated in the management if necessary through an electoral college.

(a) The State level societies should federate into a national federation. In addition to coordinating the activities of State level societies, laying down policies and supervising their functioning should arrange the reinsurance of all the State level societies.

(b) The existing insurance societies will have to fit in themselves into the broad structure, i.e., fit State level societies and national federation.

(c) In the arrangement suggested under Para (b) due note should be taken to safeguard the interests of the present employees.

(d) Under the pattern suggested there will be an authorised Cooperative In urance Organisation in each State. The business of all cooperative institutions in the State will be compulsorily placed with this organisation.

In areas where State units are yet to come up, suitable arrangement may be made by the federation or through some sort of insure pool of the State units or by permitting individual state units to undertake business in adjoining areas as may be convenient.

(e) It would be useful to provide a specific number of seats to different distinct sectors like Cooperative Sugar Factories, Marketing Societies, Consumer Stores, etc. on the Board of management of a State Unit.

(f) Membership of the national federation should consist of approved State level societies.

L.I.C. should also become a member of this federation.

(g) National federation must engage competent technical personnel in consultation with and through the good offices of L.I.C.

The national federation will require a strong capital base. Government may contribute an initial capital of Rs. 20 lakhs and further capital as business expands upto a maximum of Rs. 50 lakhs on matching basis. Similarly in the case of State level Societies Government may contribute Rs. 2 lakhs initially and increase it to a maximum of Rs. 10 lakhs as business expands.

When Government becomes a shareholder it may nominate 3 directors on the Board of management or 1/3 of the total number of directors whichever is less.

An important item of insurance may be insurance of Government property like fertiliser stock, stocks of foodgrains etc., which are stored by Cooperatives as agents of Government or in pursuance of certain contracted arrangements made for implementation of the State policy. Wherever any question of insurance of such property arises cooperative insurance organisations should have a prior responsibility for undertaking such insurance, in preference to any other alternative arrangement like a State insurance pool or a State sponsored insurance organisation.

Even in the field of insurance of deposits of cooperatives, Cooperative insurance organisations should be allowed to play their role. It should not be difficult for the cooperative insurance organisation to handle the business and make adequate reinsurance arrangements. The arrangements contemplated and the organisation proposed to be set up for insurance of deposits in Cooperatives should be reviewed in the light of these considerations.

It is necessary to evolve schemes for protecting farmers against risks to crop and cattle. Government should take an active part in promoting this.

Cattle insurance has to be a promotional programme in the initial stages in which Government will be fully involved. The pilot scheme formulated by the Central Government should be undertaken in areas where a high degree of technical assistance could be provided. It is, however, essential that such work is organised in association with the Cooperative General Insurance Societies as any large scale programme of cattle insurance has to be undertaken by these societies and they should be enabled to acquire the necessary experience. Wherever general insurance cooperatives come forward to run the scheme they should be enabled to do so. Assistance from Government should be available to them when the claims exceed a predetermined percentage of the insured amount.

Under the model scheme for crop insurance formulated by the Central Government insurance of crops is compulsory. The technical feasibility of undertaking an alternative seheme in which insurance will be voluntary but spread over a larger area and limited to a single money value crop may be examined. However, in whatever form the experiments on crop insurance are undertaken Government should be fully involved. As in the case of cattle insurance the experiments should be undertaken in association with or through the cooperative general insurance societies.

The establishment and operation of an effective crop and cattle insurance scheme will involve the Government fully in many ways ; general direction, guidance and supervision, providing adequate technical know how.

Conditions are appropriate for organising State level general insurance cooperative immediately in Gujarat, Mysore, Uttar Pradesh and Madhya Pradesh. This programme should be completed in the Third Plan. The national federation will also come up simultaneously. It should be possible to organise societies in most of the other States in the early years of the Fourth Plan.

Provision of Rs. 24 lakhs in the State plans and Rs. 20 lakhs in the Central Plan will be required for giving share capital to the societies in the Third Plan. Provision required in the Fourth Plan for this purpose will be Rs. 36 lakhs in the Central Plan.

The entire amount required by State Government for contribution to the share capital of State level societies may be given as a long term loan by the Central Government.

A few pilot projects on cattle insurance should be undertaken in the Third Plan. Provision should be made for undertaking this work in 2 or 3 compact areas in each State.

Experiments on crop insurance may be undertaken in the Fourth Plan in the IADP Districts and appropriate provision included for this purpose.

COMMITTEE ON TRANSPORT POLICY AND COORDINATION, 1964—FINAL REPORT

New Delhi, Planning Commission, 1966. 340p,

Chairman : Shri Tarlok Singh.
Members : Shri R.L. Gupta ; Shri S. Ranganathan ; Shri Kirpal Singh ; Shri S. Bhootalingam ; Dr. Nagendra Singh ; Dr. I.G. Patel ; Shri G.V. Ayyar.
Secretary : Shri K.L. Luthra,

APPOINTMENT

The Planning Commission and the Ministries of Railways and Transport and Communications have had under consideration for some time past suggestions relating to the coordination of different means of transportation, especially rail and road transport, and their future development having regard to the needs of the growing economy of the country. It has been felt that a comprehensive examination of these problems at this stage will be of material assistance in the formulation of plans of future development in the field of transportation. It has accordingly been agreed in consultation with the Ministries of Railways and Transport and Communications to constitute a committee to study the problems involved, and to make recommendations on the measures required to secure the necessary coordination between different means of transport and on long-term policies and coordinations which should guide their future development. So the Committee on Transport Policy and Coordination was constituted vide Planning Commission Resolution No. PC (TPT) 3/6/59 dated July, 22, 1959. The committee was reconstituted in February, 1964

TERMS OF REFERENCE

(a) What broadly should be long-term transport policy of the country, so that the development of the transport machinery growing needs with economy and efficiency avoiding duplication to the maximum extent practicable ;

(b) in keeping with the policy defined under item (a) what should be the role of the various means of transport in the country during the next 5 to 10 years ; and

(c) What is the best mechanism for the regulation and coordination of the various means of transport, so that the transport needs of the country are met in an efficient and economic manner consistent with the larger interests of the country ?

CONTENTS

Introduction ; Trends in the Development of Transport—A Broad View (Transport in the National Economy ; Trends in Goods and Passenger Traffic ; Imbalances in Transport ; Changes in composition of Traffic) ; Approach to Problems of Coordination (Objective of Coordination ; Rail and Road Costs ; Methods of Achieving Coordination) ; Railways (Public Service Obligations of the Railways ; Financial Trends ; Railway Rating Policy : Operational Efficiency) : Road Development and Road Policy (Review of Progress ; Emerging Problems and Need for Systematic Road Planning ; Finance of Road Development ; Road Research and Construction Techniques ; Administrative Organisation Road Transport (Road Transport Industry ; Legislative Provisions ; Present System of Regulation ; Comments and Recommendations ; Fares and Freight Rates ; Reorganisation of the Road Transport Industry in the Private Sector ; Scope of the Public Sector in Road Transport ; Management of State Transport Services) ; Annexure : Taxation of Commercial Motor Transport (Main features of existing Taxation ; Consolidation of Taxes and other Reforms; Motor Taxation and Inter-State Movements) ; Coastal Shipping and Rail-Sea Coordination (Growth of Coastal Traffic ; Prospects of Coastal Traffic ; Coal ; Salt ; Cement ; Oil Traffic ; General Cargo ; Future of Coastal Shipping ; The Coastal Shipping Industry) : Ports and Harbours ; Inland Water Transport (Development under the First Three Plans ; Problems of Development ; Waterways in the North East Region ; The Ganga River System; Waterways in Kerala ; Waterways in other regions) ; Pipelines and Roadways ; Air Transport ; Machinery for Coordinating Transport Programmes and Policies (Policy Assumptions ; Scope of Coordination ; some General considerations ; Recommendations concerning Machinery for Coordination ; Research and Training in Transport) ; Organisation and Collection of Data on Traffic Flows and Transport Costs (Traffic Flows ; Appraisal of Transport Costs) ; Concluding Observations ; Main conclusions and Recommendation ; Appendices.

RECOMMENDATIONS

The capacity of each mode of transport has to be

developed to meet the specific demands for it as well as in relation to the rest of the transport system. The system as a whole has to be viewed at each step both as an integrated structure as well as in terms of relationships between different transport services.

Trends In The Development of Transport—A Broad View

As part of a planned national economy, looking to continuous and cumulative growth, with deep-rooted structural problems being resolved step by step, the transport system has now to subserve a much wider range of purposes than before and has a crucial role in economic, social and technical development at the national and regional levels as well as in the expansion of international trade.

Since transportation requirements are always of a specific nature, much depends on the accuracy with which they are assessed in advance. The requirements may also change at short notice on account of changes in the industrial and economic situation. Thus, even within a few weeks or months, in particular section of the transport system, bottlenecks may develop or spare capacities may be shown up.

Assessment of transport needs calls for close and continuous appreciation of the progress of plans for industrial development and the functioning of the entire industrial and agricultural economy as well as for systematic and consistent projections for the future. In determining ahead and planning for capacities to meet the requirements for transport, a coordinated view has to be taken of various media and, in particular, of rail and road transport.

A national transport policy must seek to build a transport structure of the right size and pattern, consistent with the scheme of economic development envisaged under the Plans and capable of meeting the demands of the future.

In seeking the objective of coordination, it will be necessary not only to establish appropriate criteria for the distribution, of traffic between different modes of transport, but also to consider in the given conditions of India, the economic policies and the organisation and structure through which these criteria can be given practical effect in the day to day working of the transport system.

Approach To Problems Of Coordination

If the transport system is viewed as an integrated network, disregarding the fact that each service may be operated by a different agency, frequently under diverse ownership, the objective of coordination may be stated to be to develop the various modes of transport as complementary services in such proportion and combinations as will meet the total need of the community at each given stage at minimum cost to the economy.

The problem of coordination in transport has to be co nsidere in the dyramic context of growth, the essential elements to be reckoned being changes in the volume and composition from period to period of the services needed by the economy and the costs at which these services can be established and operated.

As between different transport services, the more important aspect is complementar'ty through within a gange determined by users' preferences and the prices at which individual services become available, there is also a significant element of substitutability.

In considering the problem of coordination in transport, the social costs are decisive. While reckoning social costs, the social benefits derived from the services must also be considered. These are not always easy to measure. They may reflect the social values and judgement of the community functioning through its various organs and may in factive of great importance in reaching conclusions on public policy for transport.

Planning for transport involves decisions, which often remain only implicit, concerning the distribution of traffic between different modes of transport. These determine the quantum of resources—CAPITAL, For Capital—foreign exchange, scarce meterials and personnel—which should be devoted to the development of different services during any given period, the prices at which the services are made available and the return on investment in the development of transport.

The central purpose of transport policy is to create such technical, economic and other conditions for the distribution of traffic between different modes of transport as will help ensure to the greatest extent feasible that facilities in each mode are developed in such proportions and operated in such manner as would meet the total needs of the economy at minimum cost to the community. It is important that every effort be made to achieve progressively as close an approximation to the objective as may be possible and, to this and, to develop systematically the necessary economic and statistical information for different modes of transport and changes in the demand for various services and in the composition of traffic.

Both for rail and road transport, it is necessary to conduct over a period a series of investigations into costs, both total and marginal, for specific sections and specific streams of traffic so as to build up a body of data on which dependable policy judgements may be based.

In comparing rail and road costs, it is somewhat risky to generalise on the basis of average costs. Therefore, it is necessary to obtain comparative data on costs pertaining to specific flows of traffic.

Basic to any scheme of cost determination on the existence of a suitable accounting system at each level of the industry which will permit ready ascertainment and analysis of costs for specific flows of traffic.

For accurate comparisons to be made between rail and road transport costs, it is essential that on key issues of definition, criteria and methods of analysis, a common approach should be developed between the authorities concerned.

Account will need to be taken, through appropriate money values being set, where possible, on the social aspects of costs and benefits of alternative modes of transport, such as in the case of road transport, door to door service or saving in time, employment possibilities or developmental role in relation to rural areas or hilly tracts.

In interpreting cost data due attention has to be given to the different economic and technological characteristics of rail and road transport since these necessarily influence their suitability for different types of traffic.

In allocating traffic in terms of the economy as a whole or for different regions, or in relation to different classes of goods, it is necessary to take a forward looking view regarding the technical and economic possibilities presented by alternative modes of transport. While being checked in terms of performance from time to time, this view should be, at each stage, for a period of years and should not be restricted too closely to the effects of the current transport situation or to trends over very short periods.

In the less developed economies, the role of transport is even more fundamental and dynamic than in the more advanced countries. The growth of basis capacities in transport, increase in mobility, diffusion of industry and economic activity and changes in the structure of production and consumption will call for adjustments in the prespectives and instruments of policy for the future.

Recently there has been greater recognition that the various transport services should be considered, both in theory and for policy and practical action, as a composite network in which each element should be complementary to the rest to the greatest extent possible. This objective will be facilitated by systematic application of investment and cost benefit criteria the transport sector. With this approach in mind in the Ministries of Railways and Transport and the Planning Commission, through the Joint Technical Group for Transport Planning, have initiated a series of technical and economic studies.

These studies will, it is hoped, make it possible to and economic more accurately than in the past the transport capacities needed in relation to principal commodities moving or expected in the future to move between important centres of activity for the country as a whole as well as for different regions. It should be possible on the basis of the results of these studies to draw up programmes for the development of different transport media on an integrated basis and to relate them sufficiently closely to development in other sectors of the economy.

In a country like India where major developments in the transportation system are expected to take place in future as part of plans for the growth of the economy as a whole, it should be possible to take care of the problem of coordination of different transport services largely through investment policies under the Plans. These should be directed towards with the needs of growing traffic.

Most of the new investment on the railways will have to be devoted to building up an increasingly efficient rail transport system rather than to the expansion of the network itself. Road transport facilities will be needed on a much larger scale than even before to open up new and less developed areas, to carry economic development and social services to the farthest village, to promote the growth of agriculture and the rural economy and to provide for INTRA—CITY TRANSPORT SERVICES. Wherever possible, inland water transport and costal shipping should provide useful supplementary services to cater particularly for movement of bulk traffic over long distances. Further investments in these services will have to be directed to modernisation of the services and technological improvements for reducing their costs etc. Other means of transport such as ropeways and pipelines, have still to be developed on a significant scale and it should be possible to integrate their development into the transportation system as a whole.

The pricing or rate policies adopted by different modes of transport will influence not onty the distribution of traffic between different transport services, but also their relative profitability and, therefore, future growth potential.

Pricing policy for major undertakings should be such as to yield a net return which corresponds to the scarcity value of capital in the economy in general. Taken as a whole, the operations of each system of transport, therefore, should earn at least that rate if return which cannot be considered low in relation to the return obtained in alternative forms of investment. Equally, it can be said that the price charged for a particular transport service should cover at least the marginal cost of providing that service.

The profitability of each mode of transport, given fully cost-based pricing, will serve as an indicator for future investment decisions. While there is some theoretical justification for fully cost-based pricing systems, it is based on a number of assumptions which are not always fulfilled in real life. Costs may not always measure social costs and consumer preference as expressed in the market do not always reflect social benefits and the consequences envisaged in theory can ensure in practice only under more or less perfect competitive conditions.

Granted the fact that at any given time, competition between different modes of transport can at best be imperfect, departures from a fully cost-based pricing system would become inevitable—in the absence of regulation-in response to the desire to take advantage of specific demand situations.

In the case of railways, investment takes the form of large generally indivisible and associated with similar complementary investments. The railways are a Government undertaking and are charged with important public service obligations. This implies non-discrimination and stability in rates and liability to provide services in accordance with published schedules. The Indian Railways have already taken steps to develop their accounting system along commercial lines ; yet to bring about approximation of rates to the costs of services is process which will inevitably be spread over several years. Because of the very wide variation in costs in different conditions of operation, it is difficult for the railways to adjust rates on the basis of costs in all cases.

The road transport industry consists of large number of single truck operators and there are yet no organised associations in the industry which can assist public interest and assisting small operators in obtaining steady business.

An essential condition for the operation of competition in a basic public utility like transport is that short-term imbalances between supply and demand should lead to appropriate remedial action rather than to large fluctuations in prices. The availability of vehicles and the capacity of the automobile industry are an inevitable constraint on the supply of road transport in the short period.

For any period, both for the economy as a whole and for regions, the essential ingredients in the plan of development for transport are the scheme of allocation of traffic and the investment plan. But, by themselves, they are not likely to be sufficient for putting the plan into effect.

Three types of supporting measures have to be considered and incorporated into the development plan before an effective scheme of coordination between rail and road transport or for that matter any alternative mode of transport can be formulated. These are : (a) fiscal measures and pricing policies, (b) regulation, and (c) integration in organisation and operations.

Despite their limitations, taxes and subsidies can be expected to assist by way of incentives or disincentives in the use of given forms of transport for specific traffics within the overall scheme of allocation of traffic. They have considerable value in securing a degree of self-regulation in the allocation of traffic between alternative modes of transport and in translating the overall economic judgement of the community as a whole not specific measures.

Regulation of road transport has to be thought of as a positive means for fulfilling the role assigned to the road transport industry in the total transport plan and not, as was stressed in the past, for the purpose transport of affording a measure of protection to a long established and mature transport service such as railways.

Regulation of road transport has to be exercised largely through control over licensing. We make a broad distinction between inter-State and intra-State road transport and propose that the former should be the special responsibility of the Central Government and the latter of State Governments. We recognise that there are a few sizeable regions which can be identified as being markedly backward and in which transport facilities have considerably lagged behind. In these particular regions, we see the need for integrated transport plans with special emphasis on the development of the road network and to an extent licensing of vehicles on a regional basis, accompanied by concessional tax rates and other incentives to operators to provide transport services in these regions.

The approach of integration can be extended worth advantage in three principal directions. Firstly, wherever possible, joint rail-road transport for passengers and goods should be facilitated through arrangements arrived at mutually between the Indian Railways and State Road Transport operations as well as Corporations which the Central Government might set up for operating on specified inter-State routes. Secondly, efforts should be made to develop the operations of the Central and State Corporations, with the participation of the Indian Railways, on a scale sufficient to give them a significant share of the traffic. Thirdly, wherever at present public transport enterprises are organised as departmental undertakings, they should become Corporations or companies so that they can operate on wholly commercial lines.

More and more, road transport should take on the character of a well-organised industry, working on the basis of responsibility to the community as a whole, functioning, wherever necessary, in a complementary relationship to the railways and taking generally a leading role in opening up the countryside and stimulating the growth of the less developed regions.

Railways

On the whole, there is national advantage in continuing the obligations of the railways as a public carrier and in enabling the Central Government to give such directions to the railways from time to time in the public interest, for according preference to the transport of such goods or class of goods as may be specified.

Having regard to the developments in the transport system, it is essential to review from time to time the extent which each branch line is subserving the needs of an area and the combination of transport services which should be made available in its economic development. Suitable tests or criteria need to be evolved for considering a line uneconomic depending of the purposes it serves and the cost of providing alternative means of transport.

If alternative facilities have been or are capable of being developed to a point that the requirements for transport can be met substantially by means other than the railways at no higher cost to the economy, there should be no hesitation in giving up an existing branch line which is proving unremunerative and will not serve any object which cannot be met otherwise and at lesser cost.

Where road transport has to be expanded considerably to facilitate the discontinuance of unremunerative lines, the railways may consider, in consultation with State Governments, whether and in what form they could participate or assist in the growth of road transport services.

In the light of these considerations, in the wider economic interests of the country, as much as of the railways as an enterprise, the financial working of branch lines and the transport needs and plans of areas served by them should be reviewed periodically.

Suggestions concerning unremunerative branch lines would also apply generally to the light railways. As in the past, in future also, the general approach adopted has to be consider each case on merits and to take over such lines as would justify convert to broad gauge or metre gauge on the basis of the traffic handled by them and the prospects of traffic growth. In other cases, the lines might be dismantled and the services provided by them might be allowed to be replaced by road transport.

The problem of suburban railway transport has to be dealt with in any long-term solution as part of the problem of metropolitan transport, involving a coordinated approach to rail and road transport, development of roads and urban and regional development around major cities such as Callcutta, Bombay, Madras and Delhi.

The value of freight concessions on export goods should be carefully assessed so that the costs and the benefits may be appraised and from time to time special efforts may be made to raise the level of efficiency in the industries concerned.

In the past, almost everywhere, the railways were the basic form of transport, and construction of new railway lines was virtually synonymous with the provision of new transport facilities in an area. This is still a eidly prevalent view and leads to demands for construction of new railway lines. The merits of each such proposal have to be studied carefully and schemes to be undertaken within the resources allocated by the Plan.

In the strategy of economic and industrial development, the more completely road communications and rail and road transport services are thought of together, as complementary services forming part of a single, integrated plan, the more rapid is the progress likely to be achieved. The railways are inherently better suited for long distance and bulk traffic and the extension of the railway system in future has to be directed principally towards meeting the needs of basic and heavy industries and of traffic in minerals like coal and iron ore. The programme for construction of new railway lines has to be conceived mainly in this context and the new lines which are built in future should ordinarily be expected to yield, over a period of time, a reasonable return on the investment.

In the planning of transport in future, the need for ensuring the financial solvency of the railways has to be kept in view, the railways should be expected to earn a a reasonable return on capital.

It is in the overall economic interest as also in the interest of railway finances that once the capacities for additional traffic have been built on the railways, they should be as fully utilised as possible, due advantage being taken of the economies inhent in large scale operations on the railways.

In the foreseeable future the railways should be called upon to continue to bear obligation imposed on them because of larger public service consideration. The financial implications of such obligations should be identified and given due consideration in adopting policies for the future. Having regard to the present stage of development of different modes of transport and in view of the requirements of a planned economy, the obligations of common carrier will have to maintained. However, it is necessary to reconsider the approach to be followed in the construction of new railway lines in future. Lines which are expected to be unremunerative even after a few years of their opening should be taken up only in exceptional circumstances. In all such cases provision should be made to compensate the railways for the losses involved.

The concessions given by the railways in fares and freight rates have to be considered on merits. To the extent that these concessions are granted in the larger public interest and involve losses to the railways, account should be taken of them in determining the railways' commitments to the general finances. When obligations for uneconomic services arise from executive decision should be critically scrutinised.

During the past two or three years, the railways have introduced significant changes in the direction of adjusting the existing rates from ad valorem to cost basis, but the process will necessarily be spread over several years. Further changes and adjustments may be proposed in the future. However, there are limits to the railways' ability to adjust rates on the basis of costs fully in all cases. These limits stem (a) from the wide variations in costs on the railways, and (b) their obligation, as a national undertaking, to have uniform rates all over the railway system.

The present scheme of presentation of efficency data as described in the Railway Board's annual "Review of the Performance of the Indian Government Railways" should be reviewed so as to facilitate objective interpretation not only for the railway system as whole, but also for specific zones and areas, under comparable conditions and in relation to past trend.

The fullest cooperation of trade and industry should be secured by the railways in introducing technical and operational improvements which can help them to reduce their carrying costs.

The beginnings, which have been already made in the use of devices like containers and piggy-backs should be followed up and other forms of joint rail-road services should be encouraged.

In the past, the railways were able to rely wholly on traffic coming to them without special effort on their part. However, with many new varieties of goods being produced and likely to be produced in the future in many new centres, railway administrations at the zonal and local levels should study the needs of potential customers much more closely.

Through market research and other ways, they should study the needs of potential customers much more closely and find ways of meeting them more readily and in a more flexible manner than was necessary in the earlier phases.

The Indian Railways are well placed for extending to their operations modern economic accounting and statistical concepts such as are coming increasingly into use in large-scale enterprise for measuring efficiency, improving reporting systems, reducing captial and operational costs, securing more scientific programming and scheduling of projects and creating a greater sense of personal incentive and achievement. This would help to bring the accounting and statistical systems more into line with one another.

Road Development and Road Policy

The dimensions of the road problem in India are such that adequate progress is possible only if at each level—from the local rural community and the town and the city to the region, the State and the nation—there is readiness to pay for the construction and maintenance of roads, to discover ways both, direct and indirect, and of shouldering this enormous and continuing responsibilty. At the same time, the possibilities of science technological research must be exploited to the full so as to reduce the costs of construction and maintenance of roads and promote the use of local materials and other resources to the greatest extent possible.

Roads are so crucial to national and regional development and the resources involved are of such substantial magnitude that careful planning and constant search for economy must be regarded as the keystones of road programmes in the future, whether these are undertaken by the Centre or the States or by local authorities.

In view of the large investments now involved, it is important to adopt economic criteria to the utmost extent possible, to undertake careful traffic surveys and forecasts and, in the choice of major road projects, to proceed on the basis of cost-benefit studies before committing substantial resources.

Road plans should take full account of the industrial and other development needs as these are likely to arise over a period of years. They should be informed by the same long-term perspective of development as are the programmes for agriculture, industry, power and other aspects of the economy, both for the country as a whole and within each State and region.

In each State phased programmes for the development of rural roads should be drawn up on a district and area basis. Priority should be given to areas in which intensive agricultural development plans are being undertaken or where new resources, such as irrigation and power, have come into use and their fullest utilisation, along with complementary development, is likely to promote rapid economic growth.

In such cases, the development of communications and of marketing facilities constitutes an integrated activity and should be undertaken as a matter of considerable urgency. In other areas, depending upon the study of conditions and assessment of needs, the development of local communication networks may be accomplished in stages over a longer period.

State Governments should definitely earmark a proportion of the allocation for roads in their plans for rural market roads and for assisting villages in the construction of approach roads connecting villages with one another and with market roads. Each State has to consider the proportion of funds to be so earmarked, but about a fifth of the State Plan allocation for roads should be regarded as the minimum. As part of the scheme of Central assistance for the plans of States, assistance given specifically for rural roads should take the form of a grant to the extent of one-third of the actual expenditure incurred by each State under the annual plan.

In lifting the economy of the more backward areas, such as scheduled areas, hill areas, coastal areas and others, improved road communications can make a contribution for exceeding the investments needed. Such investments should, therefore, have high priority in plans for the development of markedly backward region which should be specified in advance in the plan of each State. As in the case of rural roads, Central assistance should be given for road development in the specified regions by way of grant to the extent one-third of the outlay incurred by the State Government.

In metropolitan and other large cities, it is necessary to take an overall long-term view of transport needs both for passengers and for goods, and to plan road development, development of road transport services and, where necessary, suburban rail transport as parts of a comprehensive and integrated scheme. In these cities, the planning of transport has to be closely related to the scheme of long-term urban planning and location of industrial and economic activities. In evolving transport plans there has to be the possible closest collaboration between the various agencies of the State Government, the local municipal administration and planning authorities and those responsible for operating road and rail transport services. The Committee on Plan Projects has recently appointed an expert study team on Metropolitan Transport to investigate these problems in relation to Calcutta, Madras, Bombay and Delhi. It is hoped that as part of the process of drawing up the road plans State Governments will give similar attention to the transport problems of other large cities.

The Transport Development Council has recommended the setting up of Road Planning Boards by the Central Government and the States. These Boards are intended to be high-level technical advisory bodies, which will consider plans to road development in the wider economic perspective and in relation to the economic and other criteria. Working in close cooperation with one another, the Central and State Road Planning Boards are expected to evolve an integrated national road network and to give attention to various important aspects of planning such as traffic surveys, cost benefit studies, economic in construction costs, maintenance norms, maximisation of the benefits of road development through greater coordination with development in other sectors, road development is backward regions, rural roads and road development in metropolitan and other cities. Their task is to ensure that roads can make the maximum contribution to economic development. Road development now demands a degree of continuity, accuracy, planning in detail and freedom from arbitrary cuts in allocations, once the initial allocations have been determined for a five-year period. It is hoped that through their working the Central and State Road Planning Boards will help create these essential conditions.

It is important that National Highway network should expand steadily. This will strengthen the trunk communications from the point of view of the country as a whole and enable States to devote greater attention to the improvements of roads in the interior, to rural roads and to roads designed to achieve rapid development in the more backward regions.

Road plans at the Centre should contain adequate provision for selected roads which provide inter-state links or have special economic importance. These roads are a convenient and flexible means of removing important gaps in communications between States, ensuring coordination in planning and assisting States in expediting the construction of costly road projects which are important both from the national and regional considerations. In inter-State road schemes, the Centre could assist for instance, in the construction of bridges, the road lengths being provided by the States concerned in an integrated programme forming part of their respective road plans.

Provisions for maintenance have in recent years been less than adequate both for National and for State Highways. It is important that suitable forms should be set for this purpose and arrangements for ensuring effective maintenance strengthened further.

It is essential that the construction of village approach roads undertaken through local effort, supported by a measure of assistance for masonry works, should itself be part of a larger area plan, which provides both for continuous maintenance and gradual change-over to higher specifications. Local authorities, such as Panchayat Samitis and Village Panchayats should be made responsible for village approach roads and should be placed in a position to support local voluntary effort, specially in respect of masonary works.

The scope and financing of the Central Road Fund calls for a fresh review. In principle, there is considerable advantage in maintaining a non-lapsing Central Road Fund which may be utilised for financing selected schemes, such as are apt to be lost sight of in the ordinary course. These may include specially research and experimental work on a much larger scale than is being currently undertaken, regional transport surveys, traffic studies and construction of bye-passes and over and under-bridges at rail-road crossings on trunk roads in large cities.

In the interest of systematic long-term road development, the resources available from the Central Road Fund at the Centre need to be enlarged. How best this may be done should be considered by the Ministry of Transport in consultation with the Ministry of Finance. A flexible non-lapsing source of this nature, from which certain types of specific schemes can be initiated by the Centre has advantages which are not to be measured only by the actual amounts allotted.

A general levy of tolls is not desirable. However, tolls should be applied relatively to major projects involving heavy costs such as major and costly bridges, large tunnels and express highways.

On many routes the existing road pavements are proving inadequate in width as well as in strength. Long Lengths of completely new roads of high standards have also to be built in some cases and the old methods of stage construction are not always applicable because traffic develops very fast soon after the road is built. Under these circumstances, there is need to adopt modern and advanced construction techniques. Techniques in evolving efficient use of available materials have to be introduced so as to achieve overall economy. This requires detailed testing of materials and control of quality for highway works. In addition to facilities for research, it is necessary to provide for a chain of testing and control laboratories, so that full advantage may be taken of the new techniques evolved in India as well as in other countries.

Testing and control laboratories should be set up in all States. Progressively, they should develop research activities on their own and in association with the Central Road Research Institute. Each State should also have a number of mobile field laboratories for on-the-spot testing and quality control of road and bridge construction. It is also necessary to carry out an extensive survey of road building materials and to arrange for their systematic testing. The results of the surveys and tests should be suitably compiled and published.

A Highway Research Board should be set-up at the national level for bringing together the results of research work done in various laboratories and disseminating them.

Both to gain speed in operations and to ensure control over quality, special steps have to be taken to promote the manufacture of all essential road construction equipment within the country.

The tasks to be fulfilled through continuous research should be carefully specified from time to time in relation to the road development programme of each region and, besides provisions of funds, the necessary organizations for follow-up should be established.

To encourage the adoption of the results of research and to promote the use of new techniques of road construction, local materials etc., the Government of India set up in 1961 a Central Assessment Committee, which underwrites any loss or excess costs incurred by a State on account of the failure of a new technique adopted by it. In the light of the experience gained the work of the Committee should be reviewed and its programme and organisation strengthened.

In the past enough attention has not been given to planning for the entire road system of a State in an integrated manner, including in it both National Highways and roads for which the State Governments are responsible. There has also been need for greater work on district road plans, so that, within the framework provided by the State road plan, roads connecting market centres, small towns and villages could be planned and executed in a systematic manner.

There is need for a road construction agency with the Central Government which can supplement the State agencies to the extent necessary and, on the basis of agreed programmes, can also take up some of the difficult works. The construction organisation at the Centre should maintain a pool of road construction machinery which could be made available as and when required by State agencies engaged in completing works of an emergency nature or works requiring superior technical standards.

In several States the volume of road construction work is now large enough to justify the setting up of separate Highways Departments with specialised highway and bridge engineering personnel who are able to provide the technical planning and supervision needed in highway road and bridge construction and to ensure the standards required on high specification roads.

Special Traffic Engineering Cells devoted to and equipped for the task of carrying out traffic studies and giving attention to the problems of traffic engineering and road safety should become a normal feature of organisation in public works and Highway Departments.

In respect of major road projects, before decisions to commit large funds are made, cost benefit studies should be undertaken. This will assist in the application of sound economic criteria and help obtain the maximum results from investment on road development.

Each Road Planning Board should make its final recommendations regarding plans of road development after taking into consideration the requirements of the State and its different regions as well as the results of economic and technical studies.

CHAPTER IV—Road Transport

The practices now in vogue for the regulation of road transport suggest that far from being a common approach for the country as a whole or an adequate rationale, in several respects policies and, even more, the manner of their implementation differ greatly from State to State. There is, therefore, imperative need to simplify and introduce greater uniformity in the existing approach to procedures for regulation of road transport and bring these into confirmity with the changing and growing transport requirements of an economy developing in a planner manner.

The requirements of the future differ greatly in scale and composition from those in the past. The existing scheme of regulation of road transport suffers from many drawbacks and calls for large changes. SOME MEASURE OF REGULATION of operations, appears necessary for the following reasons :

(i) The need to evolve and put into effect a common scheme of allocation of traffic or a development plan for transport, which provides for various modes of transport as a composite network serving the needs of the economy;

(ii) Safeguards against mis-allocation of scarce resources, including materials, foreign exchange and long-term credit ; and

(iii) Ensuring priorities in the development of road transport.

A vast increase in road transport services is called for, for instance, for integrating the large rural sector of the economy with the country's urban and industrial economy, for opening up isolated and underdeveloped regions and for providing cheap and efficient mass transport in the towns. But, for several years to come, there will be limitations on the supply of vehicles. Special steps will be needed to ensure that the transport requirements of underdeveloped and backward regions in the country and of rural areas are adequately met.

The conclusion which emerges, therefore, is that regulation of road transport, conceived as a tool of planned and coordinated development, rather than as a restrictive device, has a functional role in the development of road transport in keeping with the growing needs of the economy and as an integral part of the total transport system of the country.

In the future development of passenger services, although passenger services have to be licensed for specified routes, a regional approach has value in as much as it stresses the requirements of the local economy, helps adapt the forms of investment to the needs as established, ensures closer coordination with railway services and provides a continuing best of progress in reaching into the interior. Secondly, special steps should be taken to encourage the rapid growth of passenger road transport in the more backward districts and regions. This object has to be achieved by accelerating road development in these regions and eliminating the large deficiencies in the road system which now exist. There would be need also for concessional terms such as charging lower rates of taxes for road transport services in these regions.

Passenger services between connecting points situated in different States should be in future be licensed under the authority of the Inter-State Transport Commission, which must no doubt act in consultation with the States concerned. In the scheme of regulation, the system of reciprocal agreements between different States for determining the number of permits to be issued will be given up.

The present practice under which licensing authorities invite and hear objections from operators, including the Railways, before they grant permits for the operation of passenger services, serves a useful purpose and provides an assurance of a fair deal to operators and should, therefore, be continued.

In the regulation of goods transport, the concept of 'region' as defined in the Motor Vehicles Act and as operated in practice in many States is not suited to present needs. Regions should be determined, not only on considerations of administrative convenience, as at present, but even more on economic considerations which take into account the natural flows of traffic. While the present system of inviting and hearing objections before granting fresh permits should be continued, the precedure by which the Regional Transport Authorities are required to function, involving frequently a system of counter signature of permits is cumbrous, leads to vezatious delays and needs to be changed. Moreover, in the States, the focus in the regulation of road transport should shift from the region and the Regional Transport Authority to the State and its economic needs, and to the State Transport Authority which should function as an organ assisting in formulating and implementing the State's economic development plan.

In any system of regulation of road transport modified to meet present needs, inter-state movement of goods by road, which must be in the main long-distance movement, will call for special attention and study in the scheme of allocation of traffic. It will also require adequate machinery for implementation.

Within the scheme of road transport regulation, it would be necessary to treat the problems of rapid development of transport in large underdeveloped regions and in metropolitan cities as special problems calling for somewhat wider planning and for provision of adequate resources for development.

In making specific proposals, the details of regulations should be in line with the objective of providing cheap, efficient and expanding transport facilities and of obtaining the utmost value from all available modes of transport.

A system under which States have to negotiate and bargain with one another to determine the number of permits which each may issue to its own operators is bad in principle and proves even worse in practice. The place of reciprocal agreements should be taken by a system of inter-State permits issued under the authority of the Inter-State Transport Commission which, in the interest of precision, could be redesignated as the Inter-State Road Transport Commission. This body, working in close collaboration with State Transport Authorities and the Railways, should assess at intervals of two to three years the requirements of inter-State road transport and should determine the volume of transport and the number of vehicles which should be made available and the broad terms on which the services should be provided. The requirements should be arrived at on the basis of careful technical and economic studies, with progressively greater knowledge of relative costs, keeping in view the needs of coordination between different services and the relative contribution due from each. The proposals should be always conceived with reference to a total plan of development.

Having decided upon the quantum of road transport to be provided over a given period on any long distance or inter-State route the permits could be issued by the State Transport Authorities on behalf of the Inter-State Transport Commission.

To what extent each State should be able to issue permits to applicants from among its own operators could be determined on some agreed principle of equity such as route mileage, volume of traffic originating etc. If the requisite number of operators are not forthcoming in a State at one stage, either the permits could be issued when suitable applicants are available or, for the time being, applicants from outside the State could be attracted.

For all inter-State permits, there would be uniform rules for motor taxation. There would be no question of seeking special authority to pass through the territory of any State lying on route or of obtaining countersignatures. To distinguish vehicle operating on inter-State routes under permits issued on the authority of the Inter-State Transport Commission, it would be useful to prescribe a common clour to be adopted throughout the country. Action on this aspect has already been initiated by the Inter-State Transport Commission.

It is essential that the Inter-State Transport Commission should be considerably strengthened. It should have a full-time Chairman of high status preferably drawn from public life. The complete range of powers contemplated for the commission under Section 63A(2) of the Motor Vehicles Act, including the power to grant, revoke or suspend permits for the operation of transport vehicles on inter-State routes, should be given by the commission and its existing powers should be utilised effectively.

In its present mode of functioning the Inter-State Transport commission is unable to fulfil the role assigned to it under the Motor Vehicles Act. In future the commission should be equipped with machinery to elicit information concerning traffic requirements on inter-State routes and should be placed in a position to coordinate plans of road transport development with the States as well as with the Railways.

In view of the fast growing and changing needs of the economp, in licensing goods road transport vehicles for intra-State operations, the traditional forms of distance limits are no longer appropriate. Having due regard to the various means of transport which can be harnessed—rail network, road system and inland water transport—and the assessment of present and future traffic, the State Transport Authority should propose the extent to which road transport facilities are to be expanded in any given period, the distribution in different parts of the State, the kind of vehicles required etc. Such assessment should form an integral part of the scheme of transport planning for the future and would have the advantage of furnishing a sound basis for the allocation of traffic and development of transport. State Transport Authorities should be equipped with appropriate personnel.

As a general rule, it is visualised that permits for intra-State operations will be valid for the State as a whole. However, there are a few large regions in the country which are markedly underdeveloped in terms of transport facilities. In these, it would be desirable to formulate integrated regional transport plans within the framework of the transport plan of the State as a whole. The regions in question are the Telangana districts in Andhra Pradesh, North Bihar, Chhatisgarh Division and the eastern districts in Madhya Pradesh, Vidarbha and Marathwada in Maharashtra; the coastal and hill districts of Mysore, Uttarakhand and the eastern districts in Uttar Pradesh. In these regions, particular stress should be laid on accelerated development of the road network. State Governments should also consider whether facilities for procuring vehicles and some measure of concessions in taxes levied on motor vehicles could not also be usefully given in respect of permits for operation within the region as distinguished from operation over the State as a whole. If such concessions were available for a period of, say, up to five year, levels of development in transport in these regions should come up to the general level in the State more speedily than might otherwise be possible.

Under the proposed scheme of regulation, the scope for temporary permits will diminish considerably. Basically, temporary permits should be issued only for special temporary purposes to meet unexpected requirements. The same authority which issues regular permits should also be the one which issues temporary permits as and when needed. Thus, temporary permits should become an exception to be resorted to only for meeting special and short terms needs.

In putting forward proposals for two sets of permits —inter-State permits and intra-State permits—the approach is that of planned and coordinated development of all modes of transport. The principal consideration is how every part of the country may be helped to obtain as fully and as speedily as possible the communications and the transport services needed for its overall economic development. The area of conflict between different modes of transport is by no means considerable. Even such conflict as there may be, can be practically eliminated by a system of planning based on careful assessment of needs and costs and recognition of common interest and on active cooperation at each stage between those responsible for different media at the regional, State and national level.

While the existing powers for regulating fares and freights in the public interest are generally adequate, in certain situations the objective of road-rail coordination could be served more effectively if minimum rates were also laid down. Therefore, legislation shou'd clearly empower the State Transport Authority to fix both maximum and minimum as well as specified fares and freights as might be necessary. The main problem in respect of fares and freights, specially the latter, concerns the means by which the prescribed rates can be enforced. It is necessary to ensure that in each State a sufficient number of goods vehicles are licensed to prevent scarcity. A satisfactory solution to the problem of enforcement of freight rates in particular cannot be found without establishing, on a State and regional basis, of Road Transport Associations which are capable of performing a responsible role in advising on freight rates and in giving effect to rates fixed by State Transport Authorities.

To secure the required measure of expansion as well as to obtain higher standards of efficiency in the services rendered, it is essential that a steadily increasing proportion of the private industry engaged in road transport should take the form of viable and well-organised units.

Reorganisation of the road transport industry has to be considered in three main directions. Firstly, small operators should be helped to join together to form viable units. For practical purposes, a fleet of 10 or more vehicles may be held to constitute a viable unit. To encourage operators to merge into viable units capable of rendering efficient service, certain concessions and facilities could be offered. Secondly, cooperative transport undertakings should be actively promoted as a matter of public policy. Thirdly, it is essential to provide in the legislation for the formation at the State and regional level of associations of transport operators with specific functions and responsibilities.

Unless banks and other financial institutions come forward to provide financing and refinancing facilities in a big way, it will not be possible to secure the development of the road transport industry along sound and efficient lines, or to realise the measure of development envisaged for the Fourth Five Year Plan. This is a problem of such critical importance and dimensions as to demand the special attention of the Ministries of Finance and Transport and of the Reserve Bank of India and the State Bank of India.

With the growth of towns and cities and more rapid development in the countryside, passenger transport service constitute a business completely free from risk, highly profitable as an investment and essentially a public utility suitable for operation on a public and semi-public basis. Therefore, there are valid economic grounds in favour of State Governments proceeding towards enlargement of their own share and the share of municipal and cooperative undertakings in passenger transport. State Governments should give a due place in their Five Year Plans to the development of passenger transport in the State, municipal and cooperative sectors, each State determining the extent of advance in any given period according to its assessment of development needs in different regions, specially those still inadequately developed, and the resources it can make available. To a large extent, such development can and should be self-financing, the profits and reserves of existing undertakings being ploughed back into the industry. From this aspect, the question of forms of management of road transport undertakings owned and operated by State Governments is of very great importance. The quality of management is the crucial factor in the rapid development of road transport as a public enterprise. The expansion of Government's role and the form of organisation should not be considered to be separate and unrelated issues.

In the field of goods transport, so far, the problems presented by road transport has not received sufficient consideration of the terms of the scale of development called for, the requirements of the more backward regions, coordination in relation to rail transport and other services and the question of finance of operators. These are some of the basic issues in transport policy at the national level. The existing legislation has failed to secure the development of the industry along sound and efficient lines, or to achieve proper coordination between rail and road transport. Instead, it has provided the basis for a restrictive and unintegrated approach to the development of road transport.

The question whether Government should participate in goods services has to be considered with reference to certain objective facts :

(i) During the Fourth Plan, goods traffic is likely to increase by about 70 per cent. It is hoped that the private sector will be able to undertake a large part of this development, but it may well be necessary to supplement this effort.

(ii) In several States, there are substantial regions in which development has lagged behind and in whose future growth road transport can make an important contribution, private industry does not always move readily into such areas. Even after allowing for suitable encouragement and concessions to existing and potential private operators there may be need in certain situations for promoting State and cooperative enterprises.

(iii) In the Assam region and in Jammu and Kashmir, the economy is affected adversely by high costs of transport as well as by inadequacy of transport. Experience suggests that private services in these regions are more likely to be developed and maintained on a reasonable scale if, at the same time, there is a significant area of public activity, such as will continue uninterrupted even under different circumstances.

(iv) Reorganisation of the road transport industry along sound and economic lines in public undertakings could fill important gaps in the network of the services in a complex and growing economy, which is yet lacking in balance in many ways, and could help speed the reorganisation of the road transport industry along sound and economic lines. They could set standards of performance which could be applied progressively to the industry as a whole, besides providing fair opportunity to small operators, encouraging them to come into viable units and helping to link up their operations more closely with the larger undertakings.

(v) Public undertakings can facilitate the active participation of the railways in long distance goods transport by road and thus promote overall transport development.

For these reasons, as the resources permit, State Governments should make a beginning in the operation of goods transport services, associating the railways as partners in this activity. As a first step, they may extend the scope of existing State Road Transport Undertakings and, where necessary, new corporate undertakings could be set up. Such public participation in goods transport is visualised, not as a scheme of nationalisation to be put through now or in the future, but as an attempt to forge a necessary instrument for strengthening the road transport industry as a whole and achieving coordination between different forms of transport in the interest of the national economy. How far this effort may proceed will depend upon the economic results achieved and the efficiency with which the services are operated. However, considering all the facts and the claims on their resources, in most States, the advance in the direction of public participation in goods transport during the Fourth Plan is not likely to be on any significant scale.

In relation to long-distance inter-state routes, it is considered necessary to promote some measures of public participation so as to bring together the Central and State Governments and the Railways as partners in an effort to achieve such coordination between rail and road transport as will help expand road transport, reduce the existing restrictions, bring about cheaper and more efficient transport, induce suitable adjustments in railway rating policies and promote a coordinated and planned approach to the development of transport services. Therefore, it is proposed that a corporation to operate long-distance goods transport services on selected inter-State routes may be formed. In this the Central Government, through the Ministry of Transport, the Railway Board and the States concerned, may provide capital in suitable proportions, for instance, in the ratio of 30, 30 and 40 respectively. The corporation should work in close cooperation with undertakings sponsored by States and with associations of road transport operators and should, in particular, give special support to small operators.

It is already Governments' policy to encourage the formation of cooperative transport organisations. These could be of value in several fields, notably, in the transport of agricultural produce, in hilly regions and other areas where existing road transport services are inadequate, and for carrying fruits and vegetables, milk, fish and perishable goods. It is of course important that cooperative organisations should be both genuine and well managed and every care must be taken to see that the support and concessions which it is necessary to give to cooperatives are not misused.

In addition to bringing about greater coordination in services, Corporations are essential for mobilising the internal resources needed for the continuous expansion of road transport undertakings and for measuring and enforcing standards of efficient management. Corporations would have much greater autonomy in the management and operation of commercial services, in the use of internal resources and in mobilising resources for future development than obtain in the case of departmental undertakings.

It is hoped that states which have not so far set up corporations will agree to re-examine their earlier views specially in the context of future development and expansion of goods transport services. This would facilitate planned and coordinated development of road transport in which both public and private operators and the Railways have a valuable part to play.

The work of the Association of State Transport Undertakings should help in bringing about uniformity of practices and better tests of efficiency among State and municipal transport undertakings and promote schemes for strengthening the economy of small operators and achieving greater coordination with the services offered by the Zonal Railways.

Chapter VII—Taxation of Commercial Motor Transport

Question concerning the level and quantum of taxation falling on the road transport industry and its incidence are being enquired into by another Committee constituted by the Ministry of Transport. The issues for consideration in this Report are (a) whether the various taxes which motor transport bears cannot be consolidated and their diversity reduced, (b) whether means can be found to bring about greater uniformity in taxation prevailing in different parts of the country, and (c) whether the system of motor taxation can be brought into closer harmony with the scheme of regulation recommended in the Report.

The broad approach to the taxation of commercial motor transport should be in line with the principles which determine the regulation and development of road transport. The tax system should be so devised as to contribute to the maximum extent to the development of an efficient, well organised and technologically progressive road transport industry.

Both in respect of taxes on passengers and taxes on goods, satisfactory principles have still to be evolved. In a number of ways these taxes are a source of inconvenience. In particular, in the case of goods taxes, where a route passes through more than one State, taxes have to be paid separately within each State and for each trip, even though the operator may not be authorised to pick up or deliver goods in the intermediate territories. This difficulty has recently diminished in the case of regulor permits through arrangements for compounding the tax on an annual or quarterly basis.

Octroi duties should be abolished. There has been general agreement on the vaxatious and inhibitary nature of octroi duties and the abuses to which they are prone, but action leading to their abolition has proceeded very slowly.

Tolls slow down traffic, but can be justified under certain circumstances, as in the case of costly works which might not be otherwise undertaken.

Since the State Government levies a motor vehicles tax to enable a vehicle to operate on various specified routes, the imposition of a further wheel tax is hardly justified.

Where passenger and goods taxes exist, they should be levied on a simplified basis as a lumpsum paid along with the motor vehicles tax for periods, such as a year, or a quarter or even on monthly basis. In fact, passenger and goods taxes should not be levied separately and should be consolidated with motor vehicles tax as has been done in Andhra Pradesh. Further, the same agency should be responsible for the collection of the motor vehicles tax and of passenger and goods taxes.

In respect of vehicles operating on inter-State routes, all State Governments have agreed to single point taxation, but this applies only to vehicles operating on regular permits. The greater part of the inter-State traffic is being undertaken on the basis of temporary permits, which tend to be renewed for future periods. Besides the financial burden, the system leads to a great deal of harassment.

Unless the system of taxation of commercial motor transport is modified to meet the requirements of inter-State traffic, it may not be possible to implement the recommendations made in the Report for regulation and development of road transport. Therefore, certain minimum changes in the tax system are a necessary ingredient in the scheme of road transport development.

There would be greater uniformity in levels if taxation of motor vehicles throughout the country were regulated under Union legislation and this would assist the development of road transport. For reasons explained earlier, it is felt that the minimum change needed is to bring taxation, now under the exclusive jurisdiction of State Legislatures, under Entries 56 and 57 of the State List within the concurrent jurisdiction of the States and the Centre under the Seventh Schedule of the Constitution.

Where taxes are levied and collected under the authority of Parliament, the proceeds should be assigned to the States, for which the necessary provision already exists in Article 269 of the Constitution as amended a few years ago.

It is envisaged that Parliamentary authority will be used to determine taxation pertaining to inter-State movement and to support, thus, the scheme of regulation of inter-State road transport and road-rail coordination which we have rcommended.

In accordance with the general principles of motor vehicles taxation laid down by Parliament, individual States should be free to determine tax rates as applicable to operations on inter-State routes.

An amendment of the Constitution on the lines proposed above (item 9) will be in the best national interest. It is hoped that the Central Government will find it possible to take the necessary initiative in the near future.

This proposal retains the existing legislative power of the States, without making it exclusive and, at the same time, it safeguards their financial interest in as much as the proceeds of any taxation which is imposed by virtue of Palriament's authority will be distributed wholly to the States.

The advantages of the proposals outlined above would be that the scheme of road transport regulation which is recommended here will become capable of practical implementation. On inter-State routes there will be a single motor vehicles tax, the rates being adjusted according to capacity and distance of operation, but applicable uniformly throughout the country. The tax will be paid at the place of registration, although the proceeds will be distributed among various States according to appropriate criteria.

On inter-State routes, there should be no need to levy separate passenger and goods taxes. Vehicles operating on these routes, being distinctive also in colour, can be exempted from octroi and local taxes other than special tolls on bridges, tunnels etc. Moreover, since, uniform principles of motor vehicles taxation will be adopted, and tax rates proposed by the Centre for inter-State routes will provide a broad guide and some kind of upper limit for taxes levied directly by State Governments on vehicles operating on permits issued under their own authority.

With greater uniformity in motor taxation and more common norms being established, it should be possible also to devise suitable concessions and incentives to stimulate the growth of road transport in the more backward regions, in hilly areas and in tracts in which, in the past, transport facilities have tended to lag behind.

Chapter VIII—Coastal Shipping And Rail Sea Coordination

The future role of coastal shipping has to be considered in relation to its over all national and strategic importance.

The future expansion of coastal shipping has to be planned with reference to a few selected commodities which constitute important components of coastal cargo, namely, coal, salt and cement.

As regards the future of coastal shipment of coal, in principle, there is a good case for continuing shipments from the Bengal-Bihar coalfields to southern and western India at the level of about 1.5 million tonnes per annum, subject to minor variations. In the existing conditions, casts of coastal shipping compare unfavourably with railway casts except in the case of Tuticorin, Goa and Kandla. However, with the development of Haldia port and with suitable improvements in the design of ships, significant economies in costs of coastal shipping should be possible. The policy for building up a coastal tonnage and programmes for giving effect to it have to be based on long-term national considerations.

As regards traffic in salt and cement, in so far as this could be carried by collieries in the direction of empty movement, it should considerably help the economics of coastal shipping. The quantities to be moved by the sea route should be assessed after considering the comparative costs of production and movement in different regions of the country and changes in the patterns of production and consumption anticipated over the next decade or so.

The advantage of coastal shipping for the movement of general cargo will increase if steps are taken to arrange for through booking facilities with the railways and the necessary facilities are developed at a number of ports in the country.

It would be desirable to provide for specially designed vessels suited for carrying general cargo from port to port.

Having regard to low incomes and standards of living in the coastal areas, it is essential to evolve programmes for promoting economic and industrial development in these areas. General cargo services touching on a large number of minor ports could be encouraged and, to begin with, such services might be organised for selected ports.

It will be desirable for the Government to ensure that a certain minimum of tonnage is retained on the coast so that the requirements of coastal traffic are not starved. At the same time, the composition of the coastal fleet should be such that a proportion of the ships can be shifted to overseas trade if there is not sufficient demand for them on the coast. This will help ensure efficient utilisation of the ships.

It is essential to consider whether important economies in capital cost and operational expenses will not be secured if, in place of as many as 27 companies of varying size, many of them operating their small fleets in an indifferent manner round the coast, a scheme for unified control and operation cannot be evolved with the cooperation of the industry. This could take the form of a Corporation promoted by the Central Government to which the Central Government and the existing shipping companies might subscribe. A single Corporation operating the coastal fleet will be in a position to secure fuller utilisation of the existing ships, provide regular services, improve operational efficiency, both directly and, through improvement of facilities at the ports and take steps to replace overaged ships. The Corporation could also operate shipping services to neighbouring countries. The Corporation should endeavour to carry a large share of the imported crude oil. Since a part of the movement of coal by sea is sustained by the railways, if they so desired, the railways could also subscribe towards the capital of the Corporation. Steps along these lines will help improve the comparative costs of coastal shipping and facilitate coordination in rates and traffic with the railways.

In the last analysis it will be by creating conditions in which coastal sea transport can be operated more efficiently and at lower cost that it can become a viable national industry. When the basic facts of the situation are so clearly established, it would be an error to let the coastal shipping industry continue with its present unorganised and ill-equipped structure.

Chapter IX-Ports And Harbours

The Central Government should insist on Port Trusts, specially in the larger ports, finding all the internal resources they can for development. They should be encouraged to seek loans directly from the market and to this end they should receive the necessary support from the Reserve Bank of India and the Government of India. As a matter of policy, Port Trusts should be expected to manage their operations as to be able to draw a least part of their capital from the market.

The industrial and engineering capacities available in the country can be harnessed to much greater advantage than at present. If this is done, most of the equipment required by ports can be provided within the country in a comparatively short period. For this purpose, it is essential to strengthen the existing technical arrangements available within the Central Government. It is suggested that a special unit should be established within the Department of Technical Development to assist the Ministry of Transport, Port Administrations and the industry in mobilising indigenous manufacturing capacity for meeting the requirements of ports. Port Administrations should be enabled to prepare forward plans continuously for three or four years and place firm orders on indigenous manufacturers. It would be worthwhile to explore the possibility of establishing groups of manfacturers of different categories of port equipment and other related equipment and assist them with the balancing plants needed as well as the minimum supply of components and spares.

Engineering organisations in the Ports should be sterngthened and each Port Administration should be asked to lay down a phased programme for this purpose.

It is essential to take steps to establish a Central Organisation which can assist the major ports in preparing designs and specifications and in working out detailed project reports and where necessary in supervising construction operations in selected intermediate and minor ports. The office of the Development Adviser under the Transport Ministry provides nucleus for such a technical organisation but, as at present organised, it is clearly inadequate.

The building up of an adequate technical organisation for port construction and development is a basic national and a matter calling for urgent action on the part of the Central Government.

It would be an advantage if the period of rapid and accelerated port construction now coming to a close could be followed by a period of consolidation and efforts to improve operational efficiency. At the same time as new construction projects have to be taken up, it is suggested that port development plans should embody schemes for increasing capacities as well as programmes for efficient utilisation of the capacities created.

Each port should have a long-term programme of development, extending at least to a period of ten to fifteen years. The plan should be supported by more adequate economic studies and projections than have been available in the past. Ports like Calcutta, Bombay, Madras, Visakhapatnam and Cochin should be equipped with economic intelligence units of adequate quality.

The Ministry of Transport, in consultation with the Planning Commission and the Ministries concerned, should initiate a concerted effort in which all the major ports would cooperate in formulating a long-term plan of port development for the country as a whole. Within this broad framework, which will need to be revised at appropriate intervals, it should be possible for each port to determine its own plan in fuller detail.

For the higher levels of technical and administrative personnel there should be some kind of common 'pool' jointly maintained by the major ports. Such a 'pool' will provide all ports with trained and experienced personnel to fill positions involving higher responsibilities. Common system for recruitment of officer cadres should also be evolved. From the aspect of efficiency of management, it is essential that considerable proportion of the top positions in the ports should be filled by individuals who have spent the greater part of their careers working in the ports. It is hoped that the Ministry of Transport will take early steps to evolve a suitable scheme in consultation with Port Authorities.

It is necessary to develop institutional facilities for training in harbour engineering. A beginning in this direction has been made at the Institute of Technology in Bombay, but there is need to plan facilities on a larger scale and to utilise them more adequately than at present. There is scope also for close cooperation between the major ports in providing in-service training programmes for various categories of personnel.

It is important that costs of various services rendered by port authorities should be known precisely and that port charges should be related to known costs. It is also essential that each port should have a cell for pursuing programmes for reducing the time taken and the costs incurred in different operations. Such a programme must necessarily be undertaken with the support of labour and should be based on efforts to raise the level of labour productivity through incentive schemes and other means.

Development of port capacities and efforts to increase operational efficiency should be regarded as continuous processes. Essential port development schemes should be approved at the earliest possible stage feasible and their execution expedited, so that the capacity of the ports to handle traffic should be developed in advance of actual need. At the larger ports, and specially in Bombay and Calcutta (of which Haldia will be a subsidiary port), there should be a fair amount of reserve capacity which can be drawn upon readily.

There has been already a measure of delay in initiating advance action on several port development schemes in anticipation of the Fourth Five Year Plan. It is suggested that an early review should be made by the Ministry of Transport of the position in all the ports and specially at Bombay, Calcutta and Visakhapatnam, so that appropriate action may be taken at an early data.

Chapter X—Inland Water Transport

Problems of development of inland water transport have to be considered in different regions separately according to the nature of the water-ways and conditions of traffic available in each region.

In the interest of overall economic development and utilisation of available communication facilities, it is important that the waterways potential of different regions should be put to productive use. Advantage should be taken of recent techological advances to achieve possible economies offered by this natural mode of transport, for instance, of better mechanically operated craft with greater power and capacity to move traffic in bulk.

Development of inland water transport has to be viewed in each region in the context of integrated regional transport plans within the framework of the transport plan of the country as a whole. It is of the utmost importance that in each region, to the extent necessary, water transport services should be fully coorndinated with services provided by the railways and by road transport.

To ensure development of waterways potential, where natural conditions are favourable, it is necessary to work out long-term plans, keeping in view a perspective of at least ten to fifteen years.

A beginning with the setting up of an organisation for inland water transport has been recently made by the Ministry of Transport. If this organisation is adequately developed, it should be possible for the Centre to assist the States in evolving suitable plans for future development.

Having regard to initial costs of development, some of the waterways may not be financially viable at least for a period. Efforts, therefore, should be made to work into the plans of regional development of waterways, principles and methods of direct or indirect financial support to be given to waterways services, say, for a period of five years or so. The necessary resources for devevlopment should be provided under the Five Year Plans.

In the north-eastern region, while railway services on the metre gauge line could be made self-contained, the broad gauge services have necessarily to be integrated, with waterways and road services. Traffic terminating on the broad gauge line at Jogigopa has to be carried further inside the region by waterways and road services. Similarly, certain types of traffic originating in the region such as are intended for destinations in India on the broad gauge railway system could best be carried up to Jogigopa by road and river. The traffic in respect of which integrated transport services have specially to be organised will consist largely of jute, tea and wax in the outgoing direction and cement, foodgrains, fertilisers and salt in the incoming direction. In order that rail, road and water transport services function as parts of a composite network in the region, it will be necessary to work out arrangements for pooling their operations and also to have facilities like common booking and transhipment and through freights and fares.

Having regard to the location of Assam and other adjoining States in the north-east region, it is of the utmost importance that costs of transport of essential goods moving from or to the region are kept to the minimum. It is from this point of view that it will be desirable to work progressively towards a scheme of pooling of rates and fares, and to consider possibilities of cross-subsidisation of different transport services so that, over a period, as the economy of the Assam region develops, the system can pay for itself. Plans for the development of waterways have to be thought of in this wider perspective.

Having regard to the nature of conservancy work involved in the Brahmaputra and its tributaries, and, for that matter in other major river systems in the country, overall responsibility for conservancy should be accepted by the Central Government. It will be necessary to ensure systematic study of the methods of river training and conservancy, the improvements needed, the capital required for conservancy works, and the organisational arrangements which may be required. The costs of conservancy have to be carefully worked out. It will also be essential to have an adequate organisation at the State level, and to assign to it effective responsibility for developing and maintaining the waterways in the region.

Having regard particularly to the needs of relatively undeveloped areas such as Eastern Uttar Pradesh and North Bihar served by the rivers will be drawn up and integrated with the general economic development plans of comparatively less developed areas in wh.ch every resource offered by nature needs to be stretched to the maximum advantage.

The success of plans for development of inland services in the Ganga river system will depend, in a large measure, on the feasibility of maintaining navigable channels in the rivers, a serious problem in this connection being bank erosion. River training works and adequate conservancy arrangements are, therefore, of great importance.

In view of the construction of the Farakka Barrage and the connected development of the river Bhagirathi, it is necessary to make a fresh appraisal of potential of the All-India waterways between Calcutta through Patna and Uttar Pradesh. Technical and economic problems connected with this development should be considered as part of this appraisal.

An essential step is to build up a suitable organisation which can undertake responsibility for developing and maintaining the waterways in Kerala, including introduction of better craft and for organising and assisting boatmen with a view to enabling them to provide services on a commercial basis. This organisation should work out detailed plans for the development and operation of waterways as an integral part of the transport system in the State covering a period of ten to fifteen years.

A detailed project for the development of Mormugao port is now under preparation. Along with this project, it is necessary to prepare a plan for the development of waterways with a view to realising their economies in the transport of iron ore to the maxim m extent possible.

Paradeep has been developed as an all-weather port with alongside facilities and an express highway which will provide a direct road link from the mines to the port is about to be completed. The future of waterways, particularly from the point of view of export of iron ore through Paradeep, has to be assessed afresh in the context of these developments.

In Andhra Pradesh, the Krishna and the Godavari delta canals provide vital lines of communication connecting the Kakinada and Masulipatnam ports and suggestions have been made for development of these waterways. In other States also, particularly Maharashtra and Gujarat, there are waterways whose potential could be developed further.

Measures have to be considered for utilising the potential offered by the Damodar Valley Corporation Canal.

Chapter XI—Pipelines And Ropeways

In India pipelines have come into increasing use in recent years and may be expected to play a larger role in the future due to developments like movement of crude oil, oil exploration, oil refining and petro-chemical industries.

Pipelines entail heavy fixed costs, but their operating costs are low, average costs per tonne-kilometre depending largely on the throughput.

However, since pipelines must be used for specific products, it is important that projections of future traffic requirements should be made with special care.

(i) In view of the capital intensive character of investment in pipelines, it is suggested that the Ministry of Petroleum and Chemical Industries should make an early appraisal so as to establish operational cost data which may provide guidance in future projects ;

(ii) Though the experience gained so far is limited, it should still be possible to verify the assumption and estimates made at the time of taking the initial investment decisions and to set appropriate norms for future development and operation of pipelines;

(iii) In respect of product pipelines, distribution costs in relation to various consuming centres should be assessed and an attempt be made to ascertain the cost to the economy as a whole ;

(iv) While comparing the economics of pipelines and rail or road transport it will be important to assess the extent of capacity already available and the desirability of putting existing investments to full use, taking into account the foreign exchange costs of pipelines.

Pipelines have also a significant role to play in respect of petrol-chemical industries and fertiliser production. Scope or use of pipelines to supply coal from washeries to nearby steel plants and power houses deserves closer investigation.

(i) Ropeways are used mainly for carrying bulk materials like sand, coal, stone, ore etc. They are suitable for comparatively short hauls over terrain where construction of roads or provision of other transport is either not feasible or is too expensive, provided also that there is a steady flow of material to be moved;

(ii) In view of the high capital cost and the large foreign exchange component, the economic feasibility of costlier ropeway projects should be examined closely before approval is given.

Chapter XII—Air Transport

The present is an appropriate time to undertake a

fresh review of the existing fare and freight structure, the pricing followed as well as the system of cost and budgetary control employed by Indian Airlines Corporation. having regard specially to the programme of development envisaged for the Fourth Plan Period. While there might be marginal adjustments from year to year, as a matter of policy, these various aspects should receive fresh and systematic scrutiny on the part of the Corporation and the Government at regular intervals.

The existing network of services is relatively adequate in relation to trunk routes. These are operated with comparatively greater efficiency and provide a higher level of services than the regional routes. While steps are being taken by the Ministry of Civil Aviation to bring about improvements on many of the regional routes, civil aviation and communication facilities are admittedly deficient.

Several new and growing centres of economic and industrial importance need to be better served, for instance, the industrial complexes of the coal-steel belt. Economic development in a number of regions in the country could be accelerated and their administration greatly facilitated if more adequate air services could be provided. Of these, the most important instance is that of the Assam region, where a regional network of services based on the area itself is a priority requirement equally from the economic, administrative and political aspects. Large tracts in the country, specially in Madhya Pradesh, Orissa and parts of Andhra Pradesh need to be served more effectively than at present. In the Southern region also, there is scope for developing new sources of traffic. It is, therefore, suggested that a reappraisal of the existing structure of air services should be undertaken by the Indian Airlines Corporation in consultation with the Government.

The objectives of development and profitability would have to be carefully reconciled in the context of the present economic and industrial requirements and likely development over the next few years.

By its very nature, air transport offers somewhat limited scope for coordination with other modes of transport. Nevertheless, specially in the regions referred to above, air transport requirements need to be studied along with the requirements of other transport services so that, to the extent possible, plans of development could take such assessment into account. It would be desirable to evolve a carefully worked out overall plan for the future development of domestic air services. Along with these, complementary civil aviation and aeronautical facilities will also need to be planned for.

For a period, it would be necessary to take special steps to diminish possible losses. Fares and freights might vary in different regions. As a matter of policy various measures may be necessary to assure the volume of traffic needed to facilitate economic operation. Composite cargo passenger services may be found feasible. Decisions of this nature have to be taken by the Government as part of coordinated regional transport plans.

The Civil Aviation Department Fund recently set up by the Government of India should assist in developing services along the lines proposed above.

The introduction or discontinuance of a particular air service should in each case be considered in relation to the total transport requirements of a region and the requisite traffic and the possibilities of economic operation should be explored as far as possible through a coordinated scheme of development which encompasses all the principal modes of transport. As resources permit and favourable technological developments occur over a period, the effort should be to introduce aircraft which can operate at low cost even over short distance.

It is suggested that there should be a re-examination by the Indian Airlines Corporation and the Government of existing arrangements for the operation and control of domestic air services at the regional level. It is realised that trunk air services account for about 70 per cent of the total revenue and there are limits to the regionalisation of services. However, if regional organisations were more adequately equipped and could serve as semi-autonomous and self-contained units for costs, profits, etc. there might be gains in performance both operationally and in economic terms. Taking Delhi, Bombay, Calcutta and Madras as the principal centres for regional operation, it would be appropriate also to separate headquarters costs from those of the Delhi, Bombay and Calcutta regions. Also, specially in the case of Calcutta, in view of the difficulties of operation and other problems which have come into prominence more recently, there would be advantage in establishing a subordinate unit for operations within the Assam region. If need be, within the Assam region, the resources of private operators could also be pooled and utilised as part of a wider system under the control and direction of the Indian Airlines Corporation.

With the economic and industrial development now under way and that projected for the future, air transport will have a larger and more significant role. Questions bearing on coordinated operations of air services along with other services will now call for closer study, More specially, in relation to the requirements of large parts of the country, such as the Assam region, the coal-steel belt and the southern region, the possible contribution of air transport to future development will have to be identified and provided for in future plans.

Air services have a vital role in the promotion of tourism. From this aspect it is necessary to stress the quality of service available, both on regional and on trunk routes, and the need to improve the existing travel facilities, transport, accommodation, catering and other conveniences, specially outside the metropolitan centres.

Chapter XIII—Machinery For Coordinating Transport Programmes And Policies

For achieving coordination between transport programmes and policies, it is essential to develop adequate machinery, organisation and instruments for giving effect to approved programmes and policies and reviewing them from time to time as part of a functioning system, in which all the agencies concerned, both at the Centre and in the States, act as partners working within a framework of common policies and assumptions. Any machinery that may be devised must change and grow over a period until it becomes more adequate to the task entrusted to it and can operate with the necessary knowledge of facts and problems and a degree of flexibility in dealing with changing situations.

It is essential to devise suitable machinery within the Central Government as well as at the State level for carrying out the policies outlined in the Report and, more specially, for assessing the volume and composition of traffic, coordinating investments, obtaining data or relative costs, fares and freights, proposing from time to time appropriate fiscal measures and pricing policies and changes in the scheme of regulation, and promoting greater integration between different services.

Action by way of 'coordination' lies between 'planning' at one end and 'operations' at the other. The principal tasks to be undertaken by way of coordination are:

(a) To study from time to time the relative costs of providing different transport services and Government's fiscal and pricing policies and related fare and freight structures, having regard to the scheme of allocation of traffic under the approved plan of development;

(b) To propose measures for correcting imbalances between availability of transport and the requirements of the economy in respect of different modes of transport both in the agreegate and in different parts of the country; and

(c) To suggest specific measures for the regulation of transport in pursuance of principles and policies approved by Government, including traffic envisaged for different services.

'Coordination' has to be achieved in the following principal contexts :

(a) Between the network of transport services taken together and the requirements of transport for the economy as a whole;

(b) Between different transport services interse and, more specially between ;

(i) Rail and road transport

(ii) Rail, road and inland water transport; and

(iii) Rail and coastal sea transport;

(c) Within the Central Government, between the Ministries concerned with transport and problems of policy affecting transport;

(d) Between the Central Government and each of the State Governments; and

(e) Within each State or region, between different transport services, specially rail, road, inland water transport and ports.

In a sense, these are different facets of a common problem which arise inevitably as between various modes of transport and at different levels within the national economy.

In the field of transport, the overall responsibility of the Central Government is a necessary condition of planned and coordinated development. The Central Government is in a position to see the picture as a whole in relation to the present and future needs of the economy and to integrate with these the requirements of national defence. It can provide an appropriate framework of policy—economic, social and legal—within which State Governments may undertake development in the spheres assigned to them and ensure the necessary coordination between different transport services.

Within the Central Government, three main agencies are at present responsible for providing transport services—the Ministry of Railways, the Ministry of Transport and the Ministry of Civil Aviation. In principle, it is possible that functions entrusted to these Ministries could be assigned to a single Ministry incharge of transport. This would be in itself an extremely heavy burden to carry. While such a course may make it easier to view the various media of transport as a composite network and as a total service to be provided in adequate quantity and at the appropriate level of efficiency, problems and coordination of transport go far beyond this limited issue. In either case, there will be need for special arrangements for achieving coordination on a continuing basis. The problem of creating a suitable machinery for the coordination of transport and equipping it adequately with resources and personnel for studying relative costs of providing different transport services and Government's fiscal and pricing policies and related fare and freight structures, framing policies for the regulation of transport and participating and correcting short term imbalances should be regarded as distinctive one.

For any coordination machinery to function effectively, the first condition is the building of an organisation capable of undertaking independent studies and economic appraisals, providing data on relative costs and following up decisions with authorities responsible for implementation. The nucleus of such an organisation is now available in the Joint Technical Group for Transport Planning. This unit should be strengthened and equipped adequately for undertaking studies and collection of data required for coordinating between development programmes and rating policies in respect of different modes of transport.

The existing Planning Committee on Transport which guides the work of the Joint Technical Group for Transport Planning should be reconstituted and should function as the Transport Planning and Coordination Committee. The Joint Technical Group for Transport Planning should serve as the Technical Secretariat of the Transport Planning and Coordination Committee The Committee should meet at regular intervals and consider reports and studies prepared by the Joint Technical Group and research organisations in the Ministries of Railways, Transport and Civil Aviation as well as in the States.

To facilitate consideration of important questions of policy and to provide guidance from time to time to the Transport Planning and Coordination Committee and to the Ministries, we suggest that the Prime Minister may constitute a Committee of Ministers, consisting of the Ministers incharge of Railways, Transport and Civil Aviation, Minister of Industry, Minister of Planning, Minister of State in the Ministry of Finance, and the Member of Planning Commission incharge of Transport. The Prime Minister may appoint a member of the Committee to serve as a Chairman.

The existing agencies for development and coordination at the national level include the National Harbour Board and the Transport Development Council, the latter being supported by an Advisory Committee for Roads and Inland Water Transport. The Transport Development Council has served as a useful forum for the consideration of common problems affecting the development specially of those sectors of transport which fall within the plans of States. In relation to these, it has done much to help evolve a consensus from the point of view of the country as a whole.

To secure an adequate measure of coordinated action by way of implementation, the necessary machinery should exist and should be in a position to function continuously and with the support of the Centre and the States. These considerations have led to the recommendation for the setting up of the Council for Transport Coordination. This body would be concerned with the general and overall problems of coordination, and besides reviewing implementation of measures and policies pertaining to the coordination of transport, it would provide direction and guidance to the road transport industry and other interests as well as advise on programmes of studies to be undertaken by the Joint Technical Group for Transport Planning, by research organisations in the Ministries and technical units established in the State. The Council would be composed of members of the Committee of Ministers on Transport at the Centre and State Ministers incharge of Transport and Roads. The Council for Transport Coordination would supplement and carry further the work of the Transport Development Council, specially in fields where larger considerations of policy demand unified action between the Centre and the States and problems of the transport sector as a whole have to be considered in their wider setting. The Chairman of the Committee of Ministers would serve as Chairman of the Council for Transport Coordination. The three organisations proposed above, namely, the Transport Planning and Coordination Committee, the Central Committee of Ministers on Transport and the Council for Transport Coordination may be set up under a Resolution of the Government of India in the Cabinet Secretariat.

In the Scheme of coordination for road transport proposed in the Report, the broad line of distinction is between inter-State Road Traffic and intra-State road traffic. Corresponding to this, responsibility for coordinating road transport within a State would devolve on the State Transport Authority. Since an overall view has to be taken of the requirements of road transport in terms of the integrated development of transport facilities, State Transport Authorities should function increasingly on the basis of systematic assessment of requirements for road transport made by them and, for the country as a whole, by the Inter-State Road Transport Commission. On wider questions bearing on policy and coordination, the Transport Planning and Coordination Committee at the Centre could provide a measure of support to the State Transport Authorities.

To facilitate formulation of integrated transport plans for individual States or regions, it is recommended that each State Government should constitute a State Advisory Tansport Board. Besides the principal agencies of the State Government, such as the Road Planning Board, the State Transport Authority, the Transport Commissioner or Secretary of the Transport Department and the Development Commissioner, others to be represented on the Board might be the General Managers of the main Zonal Railways, the Chairman of the Port Authority of the major port (if one exists in the State) and persons drawn from the road transport industry, both public and private. State Advisory Transport Boards are expected to give material help in the formulation and review of composite transport plans for the Fourth and Fifth Plan Periods which it is hoped, will emerge as a consequence of the regional transport surveys which are now under way in different parts of the country.

To stimulate transport research and studies, both within the Government and the universities, it is recommended that a Centre for Transport Research and Training should be developed. The Centre should undertake Research into the basic problems of long term transport development, including studies of comparative costs, and should assist the Central Ministries and the States in undertaking special investigations and surveys. It should provide facilities for work and training to persons, drawn from Central and State Organisations concerned with different transport services, from the road transport and other transport industries and from universities. After it has made some headway, the Centre could provide not only intensive training courses for specialised personnel engaged in or required for research in transport problems, but also shorter orientation courses for senior personnel drawn from the railways, from road transport organisations, port administrations, shipping and major industrial projects. In due course, the work of the Centre should come to exert increasing influence on the quality of data available for planning and coordination and on methods of planning in the transport sector.

Such a Centre could be set up as a non-government institution fully supported by the Planning Commission and the Ministries of Railways, Transport and Civil Aviation and Finance and also the States. A detailed project should be drawn up and provided for as a specific scheme in the Fourth Five Year Plan.

Chapter XIV—Organisation And Collection Of Data On Traffic Flows And Transport Costs

In the discussion in this Report of problems of planning and coordination of different transport services, the need for two sets of key data has emerged repeatedly. These relate to traffic flows and transport costs.

For achieving a rational allocation of traffic and, therefore, a plan of investment in the interest of the economy as a whole, it is of the greatest importance to obain accurate information regarding the demand for the movement of commodities by different modes of transport and the relative costs of carrying them. Without these, it is not possible to work out pricing policies which may be justified on economic criteria or to know fully the implications of pricing policies which may in practice be followed.

Unless it becomes possible to establish and compare costs for given flows of traffic for different modes of transport, the essential objective of transport policy, namely, to develop the various modes as complementary services in such proportion and combinations as will meet the total need of the community, at a minimum cost to the economy, cannot be secured. It is also essential to view this central objective in the context of growth, more specially of changes in volume and composition in the services needed by the economy from period to period, and, having regard to technological and other changes, the costs at which these services can be provided.

At present, information on rail movements by commodities along specific routes or sections is not readily available and has to be processed afresh from primary data. With the mechanisation of traffic accounts and statistics on the Indian Railways and simplification of procedures now in progress, it should become relatively easier in the future to obtain such data both more speedily and at regular intervals.

In the work of the Joint Technical Group for Transport Planning, it has been envisaged that with the preparation of each Five Year Plan, opportunity should be taken to review progress, collect afresh the basic data needed and project the long term transportation plan for a further period of ten or fifteen years. It is expected that the studies now in progress will enable the Central Ministries concerned, in cooperation with the Planning Commission and the States, to implement with fuller knowledge of detail and to elaborate further plans formulated for the development of transport for the Fourth Five Year Plan Period. They should also assist the Planning Commission and other agencies in working out a broad plan for the period 1971-76, sufficient at least to facilitate some of the basic decisions, and perhaps also suggest certain guidelines for the period 1976-1981.

On the basis of the work initiated, it is proposed that the Government of India should organise an all-India transportation survey at five yearly intervals. The survey should also collect data for the last year of each plan period. It should take advantage of all available data and should be undertaken as for as possible through existing research organisations in the Central Ministries and in the States. The help of research organisations outside the Government should also be taken. The detailed scope and methodology of the survey will need be considered carefully in the light of the experience gained in commodity studies and the regional transport surveys. We believe that such a survey of transportation, covering all modes of transport and undertaken at regular intervals, will be of great value in the planning and development of transport as well as in projecting the long term transportation requirements of the country and of different regions.

It has now become incumbent on every transtport enterprise, specially those operated by State undertakings and indeed in the transport sector as a whole, to develop adequate costing sytems and to pursue the objective of cost reduction continuously and as a matter of general policy. This is a necessary condition if investments in the development of transport capacities are to make the contribution due from them to the rapid growth of the national economy.

Comparisons between costs of different modes of transport of their aggregation in a meaningful way call for a degree of uniformity in the basic accounting and statistical concepts which are adopted as well as in the methods of analysis. It is in this sense that the introduction of the practices of management accounting has become a matter of high priority in several fields, notably in the management of ports. Also for similar enterprises, such as road transport undertakings there is need for uniform accounting systems.

For undertaking the tasks in the area of transport cost studies, special steps should now be taken to strengthen the necessary administrative and technical arrangements. The cell within the Directorate of Statistics in the Railway Board for the study of costs could be readily strengthened. The Directorate of Transport Research in the Ministry of Transport should be equipped with a unit which could study specially costs of services provided in different ports and by different road transport undertakings and also undertake cost-benefit studies. Port authorities, road transport undertakings and other public enterprises in the field of transport should also organise cost studies so that continuous efforts may be made to reduce costs and enlarge surpluses for development. Within the Joint Technical Group for Transport Planning also, there is need to set up a cell for cost studies which could interpret the results of studies concerning costs of different modes of transport. In cooperation with the Ministries of Railways and Transport and the Management Group of the Committee on Plan Projects, this cell could help evolve a common approach to questions of definition, criteria and methods of analysis in the presentation of basic cost and accounting data in the field of transport.

The Transport Planning and Coordination Committee should initiate a series of case studies on transport costs. These should relate to specific movements of commodities in which transport costs constitute a significant element, as in exports of iron ore, or where greater knowledge of costs will assist in evolving policies for coordination between different modes of transport.

Chapter XV—Concluding Observations

Transport is a highly capital intensive field of development. Therefore, application of appropriate cost-benefit criteria for selecting projects, careful attention to their preparation and execution according to schedule, the building up of adequate technical organisations, collection on a continuing basis of economic and statistical data and projections of future growth, determination of costs, adoption of programming techniques and sound management practices, correct pricing policies and studied efforts to reduce costs of transport and foreign exchange expenditure are essential to the successful operation of transport services and the generation of internal resources for future development to the greatest extent possible.

There is an important common area of planning between transport, industry and energy to which the Planning Commission and the Ministries should give much greater attention in the future. Its two main aspects are the promotion of indigenous manufacture of various types of equipment required in transport operations and fuel policies in relation to transport development. Similarly, while manufacturing developments bearing on rail transport and road transport are receiving considerable attention, much remains to be done in respect of road construction equipment, cargo handling equipment, harbour craft and different types of marine engines. Though these subjects are beyond the scope of this Report, attention is drawn to them, as they have an important bearing, both on the growth of industries within the country, on which depends the uninterrupted development, of transport services, and on reduction in the foreign exchange costs of transport projects, which is at present an urgent aspect of transport planning.

COMMITTEE ON THE METHODS OF ELECTIONS TO PANCHAYATI RAJ BODIES, 1964—REPORT

New Delhi, Ministry of Community Development and Cooperation, 1965. 132p.

Chairman : Shri K. Santhanam ;
Members : Shri P. Govinda Menon ; Shri T.H. Sonavane ; Shri Rajishwar Patel ; Shri V.B. Raju ; Miss Maya Banerjee ; Dr. J. N. Khosla ;
Secretary : Shri Shiromani Sharma.

APPOINTMENT

Panchayati Raj introduced first in Rajasthan and Andhra Pradesh in 1959, is now under implementation in 10 States. In Bihar, Madhya Pradesh and West Bengal, necessary legislation has been enacted and arrangements are under way for the establishment of the higher-tier institutions. The experience so far has underlined the significance of the relationship between the method of elections to the Panchayati Raj bodies and their democratic functioning. Different methods are now being followed in the States ranging from direct to indirect elections ; there are also variations in the procedures for cooption and the reservation of seats for Scheduled Castes and Tribes, women etc. The pattern of association of Members of Parliament and State legislatures with the Panchayati Raj Bodies is also not uniform.

These and other allied matters have been exercising the mind of the Government for some time. The Government of India, Ministry of Community Development and Cooperation has accordingly decided to set up a Committee to Study the methods of election being followed in various States and other related matters and to make detailed recommendations Vide their Resolution No. 16/5/64-PR dated February 22, 1964.

TERMS OF REFERENCE

(i) The strength and composition of and the method of elections to the Panchayati Raj bodies at village, block and district levels as can ensure the democratic and efficient functioning of these bodies and the evolution of harmonious and coordinated pattern of representative institutions ;

(ii) The need for cooption, the categories to which cooption should be appplied, the manner of its application and other related matters ;

(iii) The measures for ensuring adequate and effective representation to the weaker sections on these bodies ;

(iv) The method of election of office-bearer of these bodies ;

(v) The association of the Members of Parliament and State Legislatures with the Panchayati Raj bodies ;

(vi) The term of membership and the periodicity of elections to Panchayti Raj bodies ;

(vii) How far unanimity in elections is practicable consistent with the growth of democratic processes ;

(viii) Whether and to what extent political parties should participate in Panchayati Raj elections ; and

(ix) The measures required to ensure free and fair elections to the Panchayati Raj bodies and the desirability of setting up a State level Commission for the purpose.

CONTENTS

Introductory ; Historical ; Some General Principles ; The Village Panchayat ; Panchayat Samiti ; Zila Parishad ; Association of Members of Parliament and State Legislatures with Panchayati Raj Institutions ; Representation for special Groups ; Qualifications and Disqualifications ; Conduct of Elections ; Role of Political Parties ; The scope for unanimity in Panchayati Elections ; Supervision and Control ; Miscellaneous ; Conclusion; Summary of Recommendations and Suggestions ; Table showing the proposed composition of Panchayati Raj Bodies ; Appendices from I to XIX.

RECOMMENDATIONS

The Village Panchayats

A panchayat should consist of not less than 9 and not more than 19 members. The actual number of members should be fixed on the following scale ;

(a) Panchayats with population less than 2000;	9 members.
(b) Panchayats with population 2000—7000	1 additional member for every increase of 1000 or part thereof.
(c) Panchayats with population 7000—17000	1 additional member for every increase of 2000 or part thereof.
(d) Panchayats with population above 1700	19 members.

All the members of the panchayats, including representatives of women, scheduled castes/tribes should be elected and there should be no coopted, nominated or ex-officio members.

The panchayat election should be held by secret ballot and in single member wards into which each panchayat would be divided.

Any person who is a voter of the village and whose name appears in the electoral roll of the panchayat should be entitled to contest as a condidate in any ward.

It should be made compulsory for all voters to cast their ballot in panchayat elections. The voter who fails to do so should be fined Rupee one.

In every panchayat, there should be two seats reserved for women. The reserved wards for women should be rotated at every election to the panchayat.

There should be one seat reserved for scheduled castes where their population is less than 10 percent and where their population is more than 10 per cent, two seats should be reserved for them. In all panchayats where the population of scheduled tribes is more than 5 per cent, there should be one reserved seat for them. The reserved wards for scheduled castes/tribes may also be rotated but only among the wards where they have some people belonging to them.

Women, scheduled castes and tribes should also be free to contest for unreserved seats.

The sarpanch should be elected directly by the voters of the panchayats.

A person may be permitted to be a candidate for the office of the sarpanch as well as for membership of the panchayat.

In case a person who is not a member, is elected as a Sarpanch he should be deemed to be an additional member of the Panchayat, the strength of the panchayat being thereby increased automatically by one.

If the sarpanch dies, resigns or is removed, his successor will be elected indirectly for the remaining period of the term by the members of the panchayat from among themselves.

The up-sarpanch should be elected indirectly by members of the panchayat from among themselves.

The term of office of the members of the panchayats, the sarpanch and the up-sarpanch should be five years.

All the panchayats in a state should have the same term, beginning and ending on the same dates. All mid-term elections should be for the remaining term only.

There is no need of standing committees for the village panchayats but ad-hoc committees may be set up for supervising particular works.

Panchayat Samiti

A panchayat samiti should have between 20-40 members.

Where a Panchayat Samiti consists of not less than 20 and more than 40 village panchayats, the sarpanch of every panchayat should be an ex-officio member of the samiti.

Where the number of panchayats in samiti is more than 40 :—

(a) Panchayats with population of about, say 3000 or more should have their sarpanch as ex-officio member of the samiti ;

(b) Panchayats of population less than 3000 should be suitably grouped, each group consisting of two or three panchayats and there should be one representative for each group. Each sarpanch of the group will be a member of the samiti for half the period if it is a group of two and for two years in turn if it is a group of three.

If the number of panchayats in the samiti is less than 20, panchayats with a population of 3000 in Orissa and 7000 in Kerala should each have one representative. Panchayats with population 3000-5000 in Orissa and 7000-10,000 in Kerala will have two representatives. Panchayats with higher population will have three representatives. The sarpanch will be an ex-officio representative in all cases and the other representatives will be elected by members of the panchayats. Where there are two additional representatives, the election will be by single transferable vote.

Four women members should be coopted by every samiti out of the elected women members of the panchayats comprised in the samiti.

If the population of scheduled castes in a Samiti area is less than 10 percent, the Samiti shall co-opt two members of the scheduled castes out of the elected scheduled castes members of its constituent panchayats. If the population is more than 10 percent, four such representatives will be coopted.

If the population of scheduled tribes in a Panchayat Samiti area is more than 5 percent, two representatives of the scheduled tribes will be coopted.

The cooption of the representatives mentioned above will be by single transferable vote subject to the further condition that no two representatives of women, scheduled castes or Tribes should be from the same village panchayat. These coopted representatives will be in addition to those coming in as sarpanches or elected additional members.

The Chairman of the Samiti shall be elected by an electoral college consisting of the members of all the village panchayat comprised in the Samiti area. This election should be conducted not later than fourteen days after the panchayat elections.

A candidate for the chairmanship need not be a sarpanch or a panchayat member but should be a voter in a village of the Panchayat Samiti.

If a sarpanch is elected as Samiti Chairman, his position as sarpanch will be in abeyance and the up-sarpanch will act as sarpanch. If, for any reason, he relinquishes his office as chairman, he should be entitled to resume his office as sarpanch.

In case of a vacancy in the office of the Samiti Chairman by reason of resignation, death or any other cause, the successor will be elected for the remaining period by the members of the Panchayat Samiti.

The Vice-Chairman of the Samiti will be elected by its members from among themselves.

The term of office of the Samiti, the Chairman and the Vice-Chairman shall be five years.

Every member of the Samiti should be on some Standing Committee or the other and no person should be on more than two Committees.

The Chairman or the Vice-Chairman of the Samiti should not preside over more than one Committee. The Chairman of these Committees need not be elected but should be nominated by Samiti Chairman.

For coordinating the work of the various committees there should be an executive committee consisting of the Chairmen of all Standing Committees.

In Maharashtra, the election of some common members to the Samiti and the Parishad may continue, but instead of electing two sarpanches from each electoral division, the grouping of villages and the method of representation recommended above may be followed and the strength of the Samiti increased as suggested before.

Zila Parishads

The Zila Parishad should have 40-60 members.

The Chairman of the Panchayat Samitis comprised in the Parishad should be ex-officio member of Zila Parishad. In addition, each Panchayat Samiti should elect another member for the Parishad. In districts having less than fifteen samitis, a second additional member may also be elected by every Samiti and in those districts, the two additional members may be elected by single transferable vote.

There should be 8 women members in the Parishad coopted by its members, out of the women members of the constituent Samitis.

If the scheduled caste population in a district is less than 10 per cent, there should be four representatives of scheduled castes coopted from such representatives in the Panchayat Samitis. If their population should exceed 10 per cent, there should be 8 representatives.

For Scheduled Tribes, four reprsentatives should be coopted in like manner if their population is not less than 5 per cent of the total population.

The cooption of the representatives listed above will be by single transferable vote, subject to the further condition that no two representatives of women, Scheduled Castes or Tribes shall be from the same Samiti. These coopted representatives will be in addition to those coming in as Samiti Chairman or additional elected members.

The President of the Zila Parishad should be elected by an electoral college consisting of members of panchayats comprised within the Jurisdiction of the Parishad and this election should be held simultaneously with that of the Chairman of the Panchayat Samiti.

A candidate for the Presidentship of the Parishad need not be a member of a Panchayat or a Panchayat Samiti and it would be sufficient if he is a primary voter in any panchayat of the district.

A candidate who is standing for the chairmanship of a Panchayat Samiti should not, in the same election, stand also for the Presidentship of the Zila Parishad.

If there is an interim vacancy in the office of the Presidentship of a Parishad, his successor should be elected for the remaining period by the members of the Parishad.

The Vice-President of the Zila Parishad should be elected by the members of the Parishad.

The term of office of the Zila Parishad, the President and the Vice-President should be five years.

Every member of the Parishad should be a member of at least one standing Committee but no one should be a member in more than two Committees.

The President or the Vice-President of the Parishad should not preside over more than one Committee. The Chairman of these Committees need not be elected but may be nominated by the Parishad President.

For coordinating the work of the various committees, there should be an Executive Committee consisting of the Chairmen of all the standing Commiitees.

Where the Zila Parishad is purely an advisory and coordinating body without any executive functions or finances of its own, its composition may be as recommended for other States; but its President need not be elected by a wide electoral college. It would be sufficient if he is indirectly elected by the members of the Parishad.

The District Collector should not be the ex-officio President of the Zila Parishad or its Standing Committees.

In Maharashtra, direct election to membership of the Zila Parishad is not necessary. The electoral college consisting of members of village Panchayats in the Parishad may elect, besides the Chairman of the Samiti, two or three members to the Parishad. The Parishad President may also be elected by the same electoral college at the same time.

Association of Members of Parliament and State Legislatures with Panchayati Raj Institutions.

Menbers of Parliament and State Legislatures should be prohibited from becoming elected members or heads of the Village Panchayats, Panchayat Samitis or Zila Parishads.

Members of the Rajya Sabha and the State Legislative Councils who are indirectly elected and who are not direct representatives of voters in any Samiti or Parishad, should not be given any ex-officio status in either.

A member of the State Legislative Assembly should be an ex-officio associate member without the right to vote or to hold office of all the Panchayat Samitis which are wholly in his constituency.

A member of Parliament should be an associate member in only one Samiti where he normally resides.

In the Zila Parishad, all members of Parliament and State Legislative Assembly, elected by constituencies within the district (except those elected from city constituencies) should be associate members without right to vote or to hold office. If the Zila Parishad is purely an advisory body without any functions or finances of its own, the right to vote has not much political significances and may be given to them.

Representation For Special Groups

No representation to any sections other than women and Scheduled Castes/Tribes need be provided in Panchayati Raj institutions.

There is no need to provide institutional representation to the Cooperative organisations in Panchayati Raj Bodies. If at all their representation is considered desirable, they should be only associate members without any right to vote or hold office.

There should be no nomination or cooption of outsiders on the score of eminence or experience.

Functional Committees may be permitted to coopt outsiders with special experience; but they will be only associate members without any right to vote or hold office.

No official should be a member—full associate.

Official of the appropriate category should attend as adviser wherever requested to do so.

The chief executive officers should function only as official Secretaries and not as members.

Qualifications & Disqualifications

The disqulifications for voters at present embodied in some Panchayat Acts should be removed and instead it should be provided that every voter whose name is included in the rolls of the State Assembly relating to a Panchayat should be deemed to be a qualified voter without any further question.

Disqualifications for membership in a village Panchayat at present embodied in the Panchayat Acts of the various States other than those mentioned below are either superfluous or purposeless and may, therefore, be removed.

A person should be disqualified for membership only if he—(a) Is not registered on the Assembly electoral rolls; (relating to the Panchayat).

(b) Is an undischarged insolvent.

(c) Is interested in a subsisting contract, etc. with the Panchayat.

(d) Is in the service of Government or other local bodies including the Panchayat, Samiti or the Parishad.

(e) Has been dismissed by any such body for wrongful conduct.

(f) Has been convicted for an offence and sentenced to a term of imprisonment for not less than two years.

(g) Has been bound down for good behaviour under section 110 of the G.P.C.

The disqualifications listed from (e) to (g) should operate only for a period of three years after the dismissal, expiry of the sentence or the expiry of the period for which he is bound down.

The failure to pay panchayat dues should not be a disqualification for standing for election to the Panchayat.

No educational qualification need be prescribed for membership of the village panchayat. However, the candidate should not be allowed to affix his thumb impression in the nomination paper but should sign his name.

Ability to read and write the local language should be laid down as the minimum qualification for becoming a Sarpanch. No special age qualifications are necessary.

Ability to read and write the local language should be laid down as the minimum qualification for membership or office in the Panchayat Samiti and the Zila Parishad.

Conduct of Elections

Elections to Panchayati Raj institutions should not be held simultaneously with the elections of Parliament and the State Assembly.

The Chief Electoral Officer of the State, who is responsible for the conduct of elections to Parliament and the State Assembly must be statutory Election Authority, supervising the elections to Panchayati Raj institutions also.

The electoral rolls maintained for elections to the State Assembly and Parliament should be used in panchayat elections also. For the purpose of facility, these rolls should be maintained panchayat-wise. Each panchayat may be given a serial number and a separate part of the roll prepared for it.

The electoral rolls as they exist at the time of issuing the notification announcing the Panchayat elections should be deemed to be final. No additions or alterations should be permitted after such notification.

There is no need for a proposer or seconder for nomination of candidates in panchayat elections. A simple nomination paper requiring the candidate to express his intention of contesting the elections should be enough.

No security deposit should be prescribed at the time of filing nominations ; but in order to discourage frivolous nominations, a non-refundable nomination fee at the following rates may be prescribed.

(a) Rs. 5/- for membership of village Panchayats.
(b) Rs. 10/- for Sarpanch.
(c) Rs. 20/- for Samiti Chairman.
(d) Rs. 50/- for Parishad President.

An appeal against scrutiny of nomination should be provided only where the nomination paper is rejected.

For Panchayat elections, standard ballot paper consisting only of symbols should be printed in advance and kept in stock. The symbols should be different from the party symbols allotted in the elections to Parliament and State Assemblies and should be such that they do not suggest any association with religious or communal sentiments.

The candidates should not be given choice for symbols. They should either be allotted by lot or in alphabetical order. For the convenience of the voters, notice Boards indicating the names and symbols of candidates should be prominently displaced of the polling booths.

As the Sarpanch has to be directly elected simultaneously with the members, there should be two ballot boxes in every polling booth and every voter would have to be supplied with two ballot papers—one for the ward membership and the other for Sarpanch. It may be desirable to have the ballot papers for the members and the Sarpanch in different colours.

Elections to offices of Chairman and President will be held simultaneously and two ballot boxes—one for the Chairman and another for the President—will have to be provided at each polling station set up for the purpose. There should be one polling station in each panchayat or in a group of 3-5 panchayats. Voting should be by marking system on ballot papers with symbols only.

There symbols should be different from those used in panchayat elections.

Elections to Panchayati Raj Bodies should be completed within a period of two months after the notification.

The list of corrupt practices given in the Representation of the People Act, 1951, with the omission of the one relating to election expenses, may be adopted for Panchayat elections also.

The following administrative steps may be desirable specially during the elections to Samiti Chaiman and Parishad President :

(a) Organising of camps for voters where food and drinks are served, should be banned.

(b) Appropriate restrictions should be placed on the number of motor vehicles used and the manner of their use by candidates and by those who are working for them.

(c) In non-prohibition areas, liquor shops should be closed for one week preceding the panchayat elections and for 3 days preceding the elections of the Samiti Chairman and the Parishad President.

With a view to prevent undue interference by courts in the conduct of panchayat elections, Article 329 of the constitution should be made applicable to matters relating to such elections also. Besides, provisions similar to Section 30 of the Representation of the People Act, 1950 and Section 170 of the Representation of the People Act, 1951, should also be made in respect of elections to Panchayati Raj institutions.

There is no need for a separate Election Commission for every State for panchayat elections. The overall supervision of the Chief Electoral Officer should be sufficient to ensure free and fair elections.

The Role of Political Parties

There should be no legal provision prohibiting political parties from influencing Panchayati Raj Elections.

No political party symbols should be issued in any election to Panchayati Raj institutions.

No representations from political parties should be entertained in relation to Panchayati Raj institutions.

Official recognition should not be accorded to political party groupings among members of Panchayat Raj bodies.

The Score for Unanimity in Panchayati Raj Elections

No cash Prizes or material inducements or incentives should be offered for unanimity in panchayat elections.

No official organisations, like the State Panchayat Parishads should be encouraged to do propaganda for unanimity and consensus and half help to reduce bitterness and conflict based on caste, communal or religious prejudices.

Supervision and Control

At the District level a District Panchayat Commissoner be appointed for six years in whom all the powers of guidance, inspection, supervision and control over the Panchayati Raj institutions will be concentrated.

He will do this work in a semi-judicial capacity and will be assisted by the District Panchayat Officers and Panchayat Supervisors who will be placed under him.

In the alternative, the District Collector may be entrusted with this work, provided he is kept at this post for not less than 4 years, does this work in a semi-judicial capacity and is designated as District Panchayat Commissioner functioning through District Panchayat Officers and Panchayat Supervisors.

At the State level a Panchayati Raj Board on the lines of the Board of Revenue may be set up. The Board would prepare an annual report on the working of Panchayati Raj institutions in the State and submit it to the State Government. The State Government should place the report before the State Legislature.

Miscellaneous

The area of a village panchayat, a panchayat samiti or a zila parishad should be fixed except where it has to be changed for unavoidable reasons. Where a change becomes necessary, the initiative should come from the District Panchayat Commissioner and this should be supported by the State Panchayati Raj Board. Alternatively, the State Panchayat Parishad should be consulted in the matter. There should also be provision for consultation with the Panchayati Raj institutions affected and their views should be taken into consideration before any change is made.

A rigid adherence to the normal terms of Panchayati Raj institutions should become a building convention. This should be departed from, only when the law and order situation or the occurrence of natural calamities makes it physically impossible to hold elections.

The existing Sarpanch, Chairman or President should continue in office till their successor are duly elected; even though their five year term might have expired.

A quorum of 50 per cent for the village panchayats, 40 per cent with a minimum of 10 members for the Panchayat Samiti and one-third with a minimum of 10 members for Zila Parishad may be prescribed.

A panchayat member should be liable to forfeit his membership if he absents himself continuously for 3 meetings. There should be a review at the end of each year and members who have not been present at not less than one-third of the meetings should be called upon to offer their explanations. If their explanations are not considered satisfactory, the prescribed authority may terminate their membership.

In the case of ex-officio members of the Panchayat Samiti and the Zila Parishad, the Executive Officers of the respective bodies should write to the Panchayat or Samiti concerned about the continuous absence of the ex-officio member and such communications should be placed before the meeting of the Panchayat and the Samiti so that the Sarpanch or the Chairman has to justify his absence. In the case of other members, the ordinary rules providing for loss of membership may hold good.

A two-third majority should be required to pass a no confidence motion. No such motion should be permitted in the first year of assumption of office and there should be a minimum interval of one year between any two no confidence motions.

No one should be permitted to hold the office of Sarpanch, Samiti Chairman or Parishad President for more than two consecutive terms.

CENTRAL WAGE BOARD FOR NON-JOURNALIST EMPLOYEES OF NEWSPAPER INDUSTRY, 1964—REPORT

New Delhi, Ministry of Labour, Employment and Rehabilitation, 1967. 101p.

Chairman : Shri G.K. Shinde.

Members : Shri Sidheshwar Prasad; Shri P. Brahmayya; Shri Narendra Tiwari; Shri P.K. Roy (resigned. Replaced by Shri Upendra Acharya—Shri Upendra Acharya also resigned and replaced by Shri K. M. Mathew); Shri Amarnath Vidyalankar; Shri S. Y. Kolhatkar (replaced by Shri H.L. Parvana—resigned. replaced by Shri T. M. Nagarajan).

Secretary : Shri V. R. Kulkarni.

APPOINTMENT

The Government of India constituted a separate Wage Board for fixing the rates of wages of the non-Journalist employees of the newspaper establishments vide its Resolution No. WB-17 (2)/63, dated the 25th February, 1964. The Resolution runs as follows :

A wage Board for the Working Journalists has been set up by the Government of India by their notification, S.O. 3202, dated the 1th November, 1963. It has been decided to set up a separate Wage Board for fixing the rates of wages of the non-Journalist employees of the Newspaper establishments i.e., those who are not covered by the definition of the term 'Working Journalist in section 2(f) of the Working Journalists (conditions of service) and Miscellaneous Provisions Act, 1955 (No. 45 of 1955). While making its recommendations, the Wage Board for non-Journalists shall have regard to the cost of living, the prevalent rates of wages for comparable employments, the circumstances relating to the newspaper industry in different regions of the country and to any other circumstances which to the Board may seem relevant.

TERMS OF REFERENCE

While making its recommendations, the Wage Board for non-Journalists shall have regard to the cost of living, the prevalent rates of wages for comparable employments, the circumstances relating to the newspaper industry in different regions of the country and to any other circumstances which to the Board may seem relevant.

The Board shall also consider the demand for grant of gratuity to non-Journalist employees of the newspaper establishments.

CONTENTS

Constitution of the Wage Board and the Procedure adopted by it ; General Principles governing the Wage Structure ; Grounds Underlying the Recommendations ; Recommendations of the Wage Board for Non-Journalist Employees of Newspaper Establishments; Miscellaneous; Schedule ; Minutes of dissent ; Annexures I to V.

RECOMMENDATIONS

Preliminary

Definitions : In the following paragraphs the following expression shall have the meanings assigned to them.

"Non-Journalist employee" means all full-time employees including out-station staff of a newspaper establishment excluding Working Journalists and those who are employed mainly in a managerial or administrative capacity.

Note—Persons who can take initiative and pass independent orders will be the only persons who will be treated as those who are in a managerial or administrative capacity.

"Working Journalists" this term will have the same definition as defined in Working Journalists (conditions of service) and Miscellaneous Provisions Act, 1955.

"Newspaper Establishment" means an establishment including a printing press, under the control of any person or body of persons, whether incorporated or not, for the production or publication of one or more newspapers or for conducting any news-agency or syndicate.

"Accounting Year" used with reference to a particular year shall, in the case of a newspaper establishment whose accounting year is a calendar year, mean that calendar year and shall in the case of newspaper establishment whose accounting year is different from the calendar year, mean that accounting year of the establishment of which more than half falls in the particular calendar year. In the case of a newspaper where accounting year starts from Ist of July, the accounting year would be the year in which the first six months fall.

Example : If the accounting year of a newspaper establishment starts from April Ist reference to the accounting year 1962 in the succeeding paragraph shall be construed as reference to the accounting year 1962-63 of such establishment. On the other hand, if the accounting year of a newspaper establishment starts from 1st October, reference to the accounting year 1962 in these paragraphs will be construed as reference to the accounting year 1961-62 of that establishment.

"Category" means any of the kind of employees mentioned under the groups set out in paragraph 23.

"Gross revenue" (a)—In the case of a newspaper means the entire revenue earned by the establishment from one centre. Revenue in respect of circulation and advertisement shall be taken to be the amount arrived at after deducting the commission actually allowed to the extent to which the amount of commission allowed by the income-tax authorities. In the case of a group the entire revenue of a unit is to be calculated as follows :

The circulation and advertisement revenue of each unit be separated. The remaining revenue is to be apportioned to each unit in proportion to its circulation and advertisement revenue.

Provided that in a newspaper establishment in regard to the activity of other departments, which have nothing to do with the income and expenditure of the newspaper, including the depreciation on the machinery employed by the newspaper establishment, the net income of those of other departments is to be excluded from the income of the newspaper.

In the case of a news-agency, means the entire revenue of the establishment by whatever sources earned by the establishment.

"Group" means two or more newspapers published by a newspaper establishment from the same centre.

"Multiple Unit" means the same newspaper published from more than one centre by a newspaper establishment.

"Chain" means more than one newspaper published by a newspaper establishment from more than one centre.

"Metropolitan Centre" or "Metropolitan City" means the city of Bombay, Calcutta, Delhi and Madras.

Classification of Newspaper Establishments: For the purpose of fixation of wages of Non-Journalists, Newspapers and News-agencies should be classified in the manner hereinafter provided.

Classification of newspaper establishment should be based on the average revenues of the three accounting years 1963, 1964 and 1965.

In the case of a newspaper establishment completing two out of the aforesaid three accounting years, its classification should be determined on the basis of its average revenues for those two years.

In the case of newspaper establishment which has completed only one year of the said accounting years, its classification should be determined on the basis of its revenues for that year.

The classification determined in accordance with the provisions of paragraphs 3, 4 and 5 should continue until the newspaper establishment is reclassified in accordance with the provisions of paragraph 21.

A newspaper establishment or news-agency started after the year 1965 should be deemed to fall within the lowest class of newspaper establishment and should continue to remain in that class until it is reclassified according to the provisions of paragraph 21.

Dailies: Newspaper establishment should, subject to the provisions of the succeeding paragraphs, be classified under the following seven classes on the basis of its gross revenue—

Class	Gross Revenue
I	Rs. 200 lakhs and above.
II	Rs. 100 lakhs and above and less than Rs. 200 lakhs.
III	Rs. 50 lakhs and above and less than Rs. 100 lakhs.
IV	Rs. 30 lakhs and above and less than Rs. 50 lakhs.
V	Rs. 15 lakhs and above and less than Rs. 30 lakhs.
VI	Rs. 5 lakhs and above and less than Rs. 15 lakhs
VII	Less than Rs. 5 lakhs.

If the ownership of a newspaper establishment is transferred by one person to another at any time after the accountting year 1961, the provisions of paragraphs 3 to 7 should apply to such news paper establishment as if the revenues of the newspaper establishment for the relevant accounting years under the previous owner were its revenues for those years under the new owner.

If the advertisement revenue of any such newspaper not being a newspaper falling in Class VII, is less than 40 per cent of its gross revenue reduced by advertisement revenue, it should be placed in the Class next below that in which it would fall on the basis of its gross revenue.

Groups, Multiple Units and Chains: In the case of a multiple unit, all constituent units should be placed in the highest of the classes in which they are taken separately, would fall, under the foregoing provisions, provided that no such unit should as a result of the provisions of this paragraph be placed more than two classes above the class in which it would fall on the basis of its own revenues in accordance with the provisions of paragraph 9.

In the case of a group, English daily newspapers including the 7th day edition by whatever name it is called published from one centre by a newspaper establishment will form one unit and all Indian language daily newspapers published from one centre including the 7th day edition by whatever name it is called will also form one unit.

Provided that common staff on non-Journlist employees for the purpose of scales of pay and allowances shall be placed in highest class of the unit.

In the case of a newspaper establishment having more than one unit at one centre of publication as defined in paragraph 12 the weaker unit at that centre will be given a weightage of two classes, if the stronger unit falls in class I, II or III and one class if the stronger unit falls in class IV, V or VI.

Provided that where the weaker unit is only one class below the other unit of that centre then it will be placed in the class of the other unit.

Where a newspaper establishment publishes one newspaper from one centre and another newspaper from another centre they will be classified according to their own individual revenue. Where a newspaper forms part of a multiple or group the papers falling in these categories will be governed by the principles laid down in paras 11 and 12.

Weeklies and other Periodicals: Newspaper establishment owning weeklies and other periodicals should be classified on the basis of their gross revenue as follows :—

Class	Gross Revenue
I	Rs. 50 lakhs and above
II	Rs. 30 lakhs and above and less than Rs. 50 lakhs.
III	Rs. 15 lakhs and above and less than Rs. 30 lakhs.
IV	Rs. 5 lakhs and above and less than Rs. 15 lakhs.
V	Rs. 2 and half lakhs and above and less than Rs. 5 lakhs.
VI	Less than Rs. 2 and half lakhs.

A weekly which is substantially the 7th day edition of a daily or a special edition of a daily by whatever name it may be called should be deemed to be part of the daily and should be dealt with in accordance with the provisions of paragraphs 11, 12, 13 and 14.

All bi-weeklies, tri-weeklies and other periodicals should be classified on the basis of their gross revenue in accordance with the provisions of paragraph 14.

The weaker units of weeklies, fortnightlies, bi-weeklies, tri-weeklies, monthlies and other periodicals forming part of a group shall be placed one class above the class to which they belong on the basis of gross revenue as per paragraph 15. In the case of a multiple, principles laid down in para 11 should be followed.

News-Agencies : News-agency should be classified on the basis of their gross revenue as follows :

Class	Gross Revenue
I	Rs. 200 lakhs and above.
II	Rs. 100 lakhs and above and less than Rs. 200 lakhs.
III	Rs. 50 lakhs and above and less than Rs. 10 lakhs.
IV	Rs. 30 lakhs and above and less than Rs. 50 lakhs
V	Rs. 15 lakhs and above and less than Rs. 30 lakhs.
VI	Rs. 5 lakhs and above and less than Rs. 15 lakhs.
VII	Less than Rs. 5 lakhs.

A foreign news-agency, that is to say, news-agency which operates in India but whose principle office is situated outside India would be treated as par with the Press Trust of India in respect of classification.

Reclassification : It should be open either to the employer or to the employees to seek reclassification of a newspaper establishment at any time after the accounting year 1968 on the basis of the average revenues of the three immediately preceding accounting years provided that such reclassification should not be sought more than once in any period of three consecutive accounting years.

Classification of Areas : For the payment of dearness allowance to full time employees, areas should be classified as follows :

Area No. I : Metropolitan Cities.

Area No. II : Towns with the population of 5 lakhs and above but excluding metropolitan cities.

Area No. III : Other places.

The population figures as published in the last available all India Census Report should be taken to be the figures for the purpose of the above publication.

Grouping of Non-Journalists

I. Administrative Staff : (a) In daily newspapers Class I, Class II and Class III and weeklies and periodicals class I :

Group I : General Manager, Manager and Secretary.

Group II : Departmental Managers (those who are Incharge of Circulation, Advertisement Departments, Personnel etc.), Chief Accountant (Accountant) P.R.Os. (Class I and II daily newspapers).

Group III : Liaison Officers, Accounts Officers, Chief Internal Auditor, Assistant Advertisement Managers and Assistant Circulation Managers, Personnel Officers.

Group IV : Sectional Heads (supervising work of 5 clerks), Business Convassers, Sales Representatives, Head Clerks, Personal Assistants (Steno-Secretaries), Assistant Accountant, Advertisement Representative.

Group V : Stenographers, Assistants, Ledger Clerks, Cashiers, Clerks working on Balance sheets or Costing, Watch and Ward Inspectors, Assistant Cashiers, Circulation Inspectors, Advertisement Translators, Clerks doing independent correspondance, Scheduling work for advertisements or making advertisement dummy, Computists, Clerks doing work relating to tax matters like Sales Tax, Income Tax, Excise Duty, Persons dealing with the preparation of abstracts under the Payment of Wages Act, Minimum Wages Act, Circulating E.S.I. and Provident Fund, those working on Accounting Machines, Teleprinter Operators, Field Organisers and those doing ABC.

Group VI : Factory Clerks, Works Clerks, Record keepers, Clerks doing simple copying work, Filing work, those preparing bills, Challans for bills, circulation receipts, Time keepers (Time office, Advt. Box sorters), Typists, Telephone Operators, Addressographers, Receptionists, Railway Despatch Clerks, Parcel Clerks, Despatchers, Franking Machine Operators, Sanitary Inspectors, . Persons dealing with the acceptance of advertisements, sale of publications.

Group VII : Bill Collectors, Daftry or those doing semi-clinical work.

Group VIII: Peon, Sweeper, Chowkidar, Bearer, Cleaner, Call boy, Canteen boy, Water boy and Mali.

(b) In daily newspapers Class IV, Class V, Class VI and Class VII—

Group I: General Manager, Manager and Secretary.

Group II: Departmental Managers (those who are Incharge of Circulation, Advertisement Departments, Personnel etc.), Chief Accountant (Accountant), P.R.Os. (Class I and II papers), Chief Internal Auditor.

Group III: Sectional Heads (supervising work of 5 clerks). Business Canvassers, Sales Representatives, Head Clerks, Personal Assistants (Steno-Secretaries).

Group IV: Stenographers, Assistants, Ledger Clerks, Clerks working on Balance Sheets or Costing, Cashiers, Watch and Ward Inspectors,. Assistant Cashiers, Circulation Inspectors, Advertisement Translators, Clerks doing independent correspondence, scheduling work for advertisements or making advertisement dummy, Computist, Clerks doing work relating to Tax matters like Sales Tax, Income Tax, Excise Duty. Persons dealing with the preparation of abstracts under the Payment of Wages Act, Minimum Wages Act, Calculating E.S.I. and Provident Fund, those working on Accounting Machines, Teleprinter Operators, Field Organiser and those doing ABC,

Group V: Factory Clerks, Work clerks, Record Keepers, Clerks doing simple copying work, Filing work, those preparing bills, challans for bills, Circulation Receipts, Timekeepers (Time Office, Advertisement Box Sorters), Typists, Telephone Operators, Addressographers, Receptionists, Railway Despatch Clerks, Parcel Clerks, Despatchers, Franking Machine Operators, Sanitary Inspectors, Persons dealing with the acceptance of advertisements, sale of publications.

Group VI: Bill Collectors, Daftry or those doing semi-clerical work.

Group VII: Peons, Sweeper, Chowkidar, Bearer, Cleaner, Call boy, Canteen boy, Water boy and Mali.

(c) In Weeklies and Pariodicals—(other than Class I).

Group I: General Manager, Manager and Secretary.

Group II: Departmental Managers (those who are incharge of Circulations, Advertisement Departments Personnel etc.), Chief Accountant (Accountant), P.R.Os. (Class I & II papers), Chief Internal Auditor.

Group III: Sectional Heads (supervising work of 5 clerks), Business Canvassers, Sales Representatives, Head Clerks, Personal Assistants (Steno-Secretaries).

Group IV: Stenographers, Assistants, Ledger Clerks, working on Balance Sheets or Costing, Cashiers, Watch and Ward Inspectors, Assistant Cashier, Circulation Inspectors, Advertisement Translators, Clerks doing independent correspondence, scheduling work for advertisements or making advertisement dummy, Computist, Clerks doing work relating to Tax matters, like Sales Tax, Income Tax, Excise Duty. Persons dealing with the preparation of abtsracts under the Payment of Wages Act, Minimum Wages Act, calculating ESI and Provident Fund, those working on Accounting Machines, Teleprinter Operators, Field Organisers and those doing ABC.

Group V: Factory Clerks, Works Clerks. Record Keepers, Clerks doing simple copying work, filing work, those preparing Bills, Challans for bills, Circulation Receipts, Timekeepers (Time Office, Advertisement Box sorters), Typists, Telephone Operators, Addressographers, Receptionists, Railway Despatch Clerks, Parcel Clerks, Despatchers, Franking Machine Operators, Sanitary Inspectors. Persons dealing with the acceptance of advertisements, sale of publications.

Group VI: Bill Collectors, Daftry or those doing semi-clerical work.

Group VII: Peon, Sweeper, Chowkidar, Bearer, Cleaner, Call boy, Canteen boy, Water boy and Mali.

II. Factory Staff—(d) Factory Workers of Daily newspapers—

Group I: Lino-Mechanics, Mono-Mechanics, Motor-Mechanics, Rotary Mechanics, Armature Winder, Lino Operator; Mono Operator, Colour-Etcher, Printer (Forman, Composing, Supervisor), Rotary Machine Shift Incharge (Minder).

Group II: Sarang, Stereo-Caster, Corrector, Make-up Man, Hand Compositor (for classes I, II, III, & IV), Imposer, Driver (for Classes I, II, III, & IV), Ludlow Operator, APL Operator, Half-tone Etcher, Camera Operator, Rotary Machineman (General),

Group III: Caster, Monocaster, Electrician, Cutter, Carpenter, Copyholder, Dark Room Assistant. Mistry, Fitter, Machineman (Except Rotary Machineman), Roller Maker, Moulder, Mangleman, Mason, Plate Maker (Black & White), Stereoman, Turner, Wireman, Welder, Hand Compositor (for Classes V, VI, & VII) Driver (for Classes V, VI, & VII).

Group IV: Tradleman, Lino-Etcher, Blacksmith Cook, Distributor.

Group V: Semi-skilled Baller, Binder, Flyboy. Knife-Sharpner, Monnter, Plate-Grinder, Rollerman, Router. Reel Winder, Stitcher, Colour work Examiner, Barman Counter, Daftry, Dhobi, Galley Pressman, Inkman, Interlay Cutter, Liftman, Lock up Man, Lead Melter, Numberer, Proof Puller, Feeder, Paperman, Head Peon, Havildar, Jamadar.

Group VI: Mazdoor, Reel Loader and Unloader, Trolleyman, Baller.

(e) Factory Workers of Weeklies and Periodicals—

Group I: Lino-Mechanics, Mono-Mechanics, Motor-Mechanics, Rotary Mechanics, Armature Winder, Lino

Operators, Mono-Operator, Colour Etcher, Printer (Foreman, Composing Supervisor), Rotary Machine Shift Incharge (Minder).

Group II : Sarang, Stereo Caster, Corrector, Make-up Man, Hand Compositor (for Classes I and II). Imposer, Driver (for Classes I & II), Ludlow Operator, APL Operator Half-tone Etcher, Camera Operator Rotary Machineman (General).

Group III : Caster, Monocaster, Electrician, Cutter, Carpenter, Copy holder, Dark Room Assistant, Mistry, Fitter, Machineman (Except Rotary Machineman), Roller Maker, Moulder, Mangleman, Mason, Plate-maker (Black and While), Stereoman, Turner, Wireman, Welder, Hand Compositor (for Classes III, IV, V and VI), Driver (for Classes III, IV. V and VI).

Group IV : Tradleman, Line-etcher, Blacksmith, Cook, Distributor.

Group V : Semi-Skilled Baller, Binder, Fly-boy, Knife-sharpner, Mounter, Plate-grinder, Rollerman. Router, Reel Winder, Stitcher, Colour Work Examiner, Barman, Counter, Daftry, Dhobi, Galley Pressman, Inkman, Interlay Cutter, Liftman, Lockup Man, Lead Melter, Numberer, Proof Puller, Feeder, Paperman Head Peon, Havildar, Jamadar.

Group VI : Mazdoor, Reel loader and unloader, Trollyman, Baller.

(f) Grouping of Non-Journalist Employees News Agencies—

Administrative Staff

Group I : General Manager, Chief Accountant;
Group II : Accountant;
Group III : Office-Secretary, Store Officer;
Group IV : Cashier, Assistant Accountant, Commercial Assistant, Stores Assistants;
Group V : Senior Clerks;
Group VI : Junoir Clerks, Car Driver;
Group VII : Havildars;
Group VIII : Peons, Hammals, Sweepers, etc.

Engineering Dept., Transmission Dept. and Production Dept.]

Group I : Chief Engineer;
Group II : Engineer, Superintendent;
Group III ; Assistant Engineer, Transmission Incharge;
Group IV : Selection Grade and Die-maker;
Group V : Senior Technician/Senior Operator;
Group VI : Technician/Operator;
Group VII : Machine Attender/Transmission Boys;

Remarks

1. It is not obligatory for a newspaper establishment to comply any or all catagories of employees grouped above. Some of the functions may be combined. The non-Journalist employees shall continue to discharge the functions which they had been performing before the coming into force of these recommendations.

2. If any employee or any category of employees, is not included in the above grouping, they should be placed in such groups as would be determined by mutual negotiations between the management and the representatives of employees.

3. Due to paucity of data, scale of wages of non-Journalist employees in Enginieening, Transmission and Production Departments of news-agencies other than P.T.I. have not been prescribed.

Remuneration—Wages, Scales and Grades:

Administrative Staff and Daily Newspapers

Class	Group of Employees	Scale	Years
1	2	3	4
I. (Rs. 200 lakhs and above)	I	No Scale	
	II	50-30-650-40-850-75-1225	(15 years)
	III	400-20-500-40-700-50-950	(15 years)
	IV	275-13-340-24-460-45-685	(15 years)
	V	250-12-310-24-430-50-680	(15 years)
	VI	190-10-240-16-320-30-380	(12 years)
	VII	125-3-140-5-175	(12 years)
	VIII	110-5-160	(10 years)
II. (Rs. 100 lakhs and above and less than Rs. 200 lakhs)	I	No Scale	
	II	350-14-420-34-590-55-865	(15 years)
	III	300-14-370-26-500-50-750	(15 years)
	IV	240-12-300-24-400-40-620	(15 years)

1	2	3	4
	V	225-10-275-21-380-42-590	(15 years)
	VI	175-11-230-14-300-25-350	(12 years)
	VII	115-3-130-5-165	(12 years)
	VIII	100-5-150	(10 years)
III. (Rs. 50 lakhs and above and less than Rs. 100 lakhs)	I	No Scale	
	II	300-14-370-26-500-50-750	(15 years)
	III	275-13-340-24-460-45-685	(15 years)
	IV	225-10-275-20-375-40-575	(15 years)
	V	200-10-250-18-340-30-490	(15 years)
	VI	160-8-200-16-280-20-300	(12 years)
	VII	105-3-120-5-155	(12 years)
	VIII	90-5-140	(10 years)
IV. (Rs. 30 lakhs and above and less than Rs. 50 lakhs)	I	No Scale	
	II	250-12-310-20-410-45-500	(12 years)
	III	200-10-250-20-350-25-400	(12 years)
	IV	165-9-210-12-270-25-320	(12 years)
	V	130-8-170-13-235-20-275	(12 years)
	VI	95-3-110-5-145	(12 years)
	VII	80-2-100	(10 years)
V. (Rs. 15 lakhs and above and less than Rs. 30 lakhs)	I	No Scale	
	II	220-12-280-18-370-35-440	(12 years)
	III	190-10-240-16-320-20-360	(12 years)
	IV	150-8-190-16-270-20-310	(12 years)
	V	115-6-145-12-205-15-235	(12 years)
	VI	85-2-95-5-130	(12 years)
	VII	70-1-1/2-85	(10 years)
VI. (Rs. 5 lakhs and above and less than Rs. 15 lakhs)	I	No Scale	
	II	200-10-250-20-350-25-400	(12 years)
	III	175-9-220-12-280-24-330	(12 years)
	IV	140-8-180-10-230-25-280	(12 years)
	V	105-5-130-11-185-15-215	(12 years)
	VI	75-2-85-5-120	(12 years)
	VII	60-1-70	(10 years)
VII. (Less than Rs. 5 lakhs)	I	No Scale	
	II	175-9-220-12-280-25-330	(12 years)
	III	150-8-190-10-240-25-290	(12 years)
	IV	125-8-165-12-225-15-255	(12 years)
	V	95-5-120-10-170-12-1/2-195	(12 years)
	VI	65-2-75-5-110	(12 years)
	VII	50-1-60	(10 years)

Weeklies And Periodicals

1	2	3	4
I. (Rs. 50 lakhs and above)	I	No Scale	
	II	300-14-370-26-500-50-750	(15 years)
	III	275-13-340-24-460-45-685	(15 years)
	IV	225-10-275-20-375-40-575	(15 years)

1	2	3	4
	V	200-10-250-18-340-30-490	(15 years)
	VI	160-8-200-16-280-20-320	(12 years)
	VII	105-3-120-5-155	(12 years)
	VIII	90-5-140	(10 years)
II. (Rs. 30 lakhs and above and less than Rs. 50 lakhs)	I	No Scale	
	II	250-12-310-20-410-45-500	(12 years)
	III	200-10-250-20-350-25-400	(12 years)
	IV	165-9-210-12-270-25-320	(12 years)
	V	130-8-170-13-235-20-275	(12 years)
	VI	95-3-110-5-145	(12 years)
	VII	80-2-100	(10 years)
III. (Rs. 15 lakhs and above and less than Rs. 30 lakhs)	I	No Scale	
	II	220-12-280-18-370-35-440	(12 years)
	III	190-10-240-16-320-20-360	(12 years)
	IV	150-8-190-16-270-20-310	(12 years)
	V	115-6-145-12-205-15-235	(12 years)
	VI	85-2-95-5-130	(12 years)
	VII	70-1-1/2-85	(10 years)
IV. (Rs. 5 lakhs and above and less than Rs. 15 lakhs)	I	No Scale	
	II	200-10-250-20-350-25-400	(12 years)
	III	175-9-220-12-280-25-330	(12 years)
	IV	140-8-180-10-230-25-280	(12 years)
	V	105-5-130-11-185-15-215	(12 years)
	VI	75-2-85-5-120	(12 years)
	VII	60-1-70	(10 years)
V. (Rs. 2-1/2 lakhs and above and less than Rs. 5 lakhs)	I	Ne Scale	
	II	175-9-220-12-280-25-330	(12 years)
	III	150-8-190-10-240-25-290	(12 years)
	IV	125-8-165-12-225-15-255	(12 years)
	V	95-5-120-10-170-12-1/2-195	(12 years)
	VI	65-2-75-5-110	(12 years)
	VII	50-1-60	(10 years)
VI. (Less than Rs. 2 1/2 lakhs)	I	No Scale	
	II	150-8-190-10-240-25-290	(12 years)
	III	130-7-165-11-220-20-260	(12 years)
	IV	105-5-130-11-185-15-215	(12 years)
	V	95-5-155	(12 years)
	VI	65-1-70-2-83-5-90	(12 years)
	VII	50-50 paise-55	(10 years)

Factory Employees—Daily Newspapers

1	2	3	4
I. (Rs. 200 lakhs and above)	I	250-12-310-24-430-50-680	(15 years)
	II	210-10-260-20-360-30-420	(12 years)
	III	190-10-240-20-340-30-400	(12 years)
	IV	175-9-220-16-300-25-350	(12 years)
	V	150-7-185-15-260-20-300	(12 years)
	VI	110-5-160	(10 years)

1	2	3	4
II. (Rs. 100 lakhs aad above and less than Rs. 200 lakhs)	I	225-10-275-21-380-42-590	(15 years)
	II	200-10-250-18-340-30-400	(12 years)
	III	175-9-220-16-300-25-350	(12 years)
	IV	160-8-200-14-270-25-320	(12 years)
	V	140-8-180-12-240-20-280	(12 years)
	VI	100-5-150	(10 years)
III. (Rs. 50 lakhs and above and less than Rs. 100 lakhs)	I	200-10-250-18-340-30-490	(15 rears)
	II	175-9-220-16-300-25-350	(12 years)
	III	160-8-200-20-300-25-350	(12 years)
	IV	145-7-180-12-240-25-290	(12 years)
	V	125-7-160-12-220-15-250	(12 years)
	VI	90-5-140	(10 years)
IV. (Rs. 30 lakhs and above and less than Rs. 50 lakhs)	I	175-9-220-16-300-25-425	(15 years)
	II	140-8-180-12-240-20-280	(12 years)
	III	110-6-140-10-190-20-230	(12 years)
	IV	105-5-130-10-180-20-220	(12 years)
	V	95-5-120-10-170-12-1/2-195	(12 years)
	VI	80-2-100	(10 years)
V. (Rs. 15 lakhs and above and less than Rs. 30 lakhs)	I	150-8-190-14-260-20-360	(15 years)
	II	120-6-150-10-200-20-240	(12 years)
	III	100-5-125-10-175-12-1/2-200	(12 years)
	IV	90-5-115-8-155-12-1/2-180	(12 years)
	V	85-5-110-8-150-10-170	(12 years)
	VI	70-1-1/2-85	(10 years)
VI. (Rs. 5 lakhs and above and less than Rs. 15 lakhs)	I	135-7-170-12-230-20-330	(15 years)
	II	110-5-135-11-190-15-220	(12 years)
	III	95-5-120-10-170-12-1/2-195	(12 years)
	IV	80-5-105-7-140-15-170	(12 years)
	V	75-5-100-8-140-12 1/2-165	(12 years)
	VI	60-1-70	(10 years)
VII. (Less than Rs. 5 lakhs)	I	125-8-165-12-225-15-300	(15 years)
	II	100-5-125-10-175-12 1/2-200	(12 years)
	III	85-5-110-8-150-12-1/2-175	(12 years)
	IV	70-5-95-8-135-10-155	(12 years)
	V	65-5-90-7-125-10-145	(12 years)
	VI	50-1-60	(10 years)

Factory Employees Of The Weeklies And Periodicals

1	2	3	4
I. (Rs. 50 lakhs and above)	I	200-10-250-18-340-30-490	(15 years)
	II	175-9-220-16-300-25-350	(12 years)
	III	160-8-200-20-300-25-350	(12 pears)
	IV	145-7-180-12-240-25-290	(12 pears)
	V	125-7-160-12-220-15-250	(12 years)
	VI	90-5-140	(10 years)

1	2	3	4
II. (Rs. 30 lakhs and above and less than Rs. 50 lakhs)	I	175-9-220-16-300-25-425	(15 years)
	II	140-8-180-12-240-20-280	(12 years)
	III	110-6-140-10-190-20-230	(12 years)
	IV	105-5-130-10-180-20-220	(12 years)
	V	95-5-120-10-170-12 1/2-195	(12 years)
	VI	80-2-100	(10 years)
III. (Rs. 15 lakhs and above and less than Rs. 30 lakhs)	I	150-8-190-14-260-20-360	(15 years)
	II	120-6-150-10-200-20-240	(12 years)
	III	100-5-125-10-175-12-1/2-200	(12 years)
	IV	90-5-115-8-155-12 1/2-180	(12 years)
	V	85-5-110-8-150-10-170	(12 years)
	VI	70-1-1-2-85	(10 years)
IV. (Rs. 5 lakhs and above and less than Rs. 15 lakhs)	I	135-7-170-12-230-30-380	(15 years)
	II	110-5-135-11-190-15-220	(12 years)
	III	95-5-120-10-170-12-1/2-195	(12 years)
	IV	80-5-105-7-140-15-170	(12 years)
	V	75-5-100-8-140-12-1/2-165	(12 years)
	VI	60-1-70	(10 years)
V. (Rs. 2-1/2 lakhs and above and less than Rs. 5 lakhs)	I	125-8-165-12-225-15-300	(15 years)
	II	100-5-125-10-175-12-1/2-200	(12 years)
	III	85-5-110-8-150-12-1/2-175	(12 years)
	IV	70-5-95-8-135-10-155	(12 years)
	V	65-5-90-7-125-10-145	(12 years)
	VI	50-1-60	(10 years)
VI. Less than Rs. 2-1/2 lakhs)	I	120-5-145-7-180-12-240	(15 years)
	II	100-5-160	(12 years)
	III	80-5-140	(12 years)
	IV	75-5-135	(12 years)
	V	60-5-120	(12 years)
	VI	50-50 paise-55	(10 years)

Pay Scale For News Agencies—Administrative Staff

1	2	3	4
I. (Rs. 200 lakhs and above)	I	No Scale	
	II	500-30-650-40-850-75-1225	(15 years)
	III	400-20-500-40-700-50-950	(15 years)
	IV	275-13-340-24-460-45-685	(15 years)
	V	250-12-310-24-430-50-680	(15 years)
	VI	190-10-240-16-320-30-380	(12 years)
	VII	125-3-140-5-175	(12 years)
	VIII	110-5-160	(10 years)
II. (Rs. 100 lakhs and above and less than Rs. 200 lakhs)	I	No Scale	
	II	400-20-500-35-675-55-900	(15 years)
	III	300-14-370-26-500-50-750	(15 years)
	IV	250-12-310-28-450-40-650	(15 years)
	V	225-10-275-21-380-42-590	(15 years)
	VI	175-11-230-14-300-25-350	(12 years)
	VII	115-3-130-5-165	(12 years)
	VIII	100-5-150	(10 years)

1	2	3	4
III. Rs. 50 lakhs	I	No Scale	
and above and less	II	300-14-370-26-500-50-750	(15 years)
than Rs. 100 lakhs)	III	275-13-340-24-460-45-685	(15 years)
	IV	225-10-275-20-375-40-575	(15 years)
	V	200-10-250-18-340-30-490	(15 years)
	VI	160-8-200-16-280-20-320	(12 years)
	VII	105-3-120-5-155	(12 years)
	VIII	90-5-140	(10 years)
IV. (Rs. 30 lakhs	I	No Scale	
and above and less	II	250-12-310-20-410-45-500	(12 years)
than Rs. 50 lakhs)	III	200-10-250-20-350-25-400	(12 years)
	IV	190-10-240-16-320-20-360	(12 years)
	V	165-9-210-12-270-25-320	(12 years)
	VI	130-8-170-13-235-20-275	(12 years)
	VII	95-3-110-5-145	(12 years)
	VIII	80-2-100	(10 years)
V. (Rs. 15 lakhs	I	No Scale	
and above and less	II	220-12-280-18-370-35-440	(12 years)
than Rs. 30 lakhs)	III	190-10-240-16-320-20-360	(12 years)
	IV	175-9-220-12-280-25-330	(12 years)
	V	150-8-190-16-270-20-310	(12 years)
	VI	115-6-145-12-205-15-235	(12 years)
	VII	85-2-95-5-130	(12 years)
	VIII	70-1-1/2-85	(10 years)
VI. (Rs. 5 lakhs	I	No Scale	
and above and less	II	200-10-250-20-350-25-400	(12 years)
than Rs. 15 lakhs)	III	175-9-220-12-280-25-330	(12 years)
	IV	160-8-200-16-280-20-320	(12 years)
	V	140-8-180-10-230-25-280	(12 years)
	VI	105-5-130-11-185-15-215	(12 years)
	VII	75-2-85-5-120	(12 years)
	VIII	60-1-70	(10 years)
VII. (Less than	I	No Scale	
Rs. 5 lakhs)	II	175-9-220-12-280-25-330	(12 years)
	III	150-8-190-10-240-25-290	(12 years)
	IV	140-7-175-11-230-25-280	(12 years)
	V	125-8-165-12-225-15-255	(12 years)
	VI	95-5-120-10-170-12-1/2-195	(12 years)
	VII	65-2-75-5-110	(12 years)
	VIII	50-1-60	(10 years)

Pay Scales Of Press Trust Of India Engineering, Transmission And Production Branch

1	2	3
I	No Scale	
II	500-30-650-40-850-75-1000	(12 years)
III	450-20-550-40-750-75-900	(12 years)
IV	375-15-450-30-600-50-700	(12 years)

1	2	3
V	300-15-375-35-550-50-650	(12 years)
VI	175-10-225-15-300-25-350	(12 years)
VII	115-3-130-5-165	(12 years)

Dearness Allowance—Dearness allowance should be paid to non-Journalists at the following rates :—

Range of Basic Pay	Area		
	III	II	
	Rs.	Rs.	Rs.
1	2	3	4
Below Rs. 100	30	40	50
Rs. 100 to Rs. 200	40	55	70
Above Rs. 200 and upto Rs. 300	50	65	80
Above Rs. 300 and upto Rs. 400	60	75	90
Above Rs. 400 and upto Rs. 500	70	85	100
Above Rs. 500 and upto Rs. 800	85	100	110
Above Rs. 800 and upto Rs. 1,200	100	115	130
Above Rs. 1,200	120	140	150

The proposed scales of pay and dearness allowance are to be linked up with the average consumer price index number for the year 1965 of the All India Average Consumer Price Index numbers for working class (with 1949 equal to 100) as base, i.e., 166, The dearness allowance should be revised every year either upwards or downwards on the basis of the average of the previous 12 months. The first revision is to take place in January 1968 as soon as average consumer price index number for the year 1967 is available. If the average of the year 1967 differs from the average of the year 1965 by 10 points or more upwards or downwards the dearness allowance is to be revised at the rate of 50 paise per point upwards or downwards as the case may be. After 1968 revision is to be made every year in January on the basis of the average of the previous year as soon as the figures are available, provided the average of the 12 months differs by 10 points or more from the average of the year immediately preceding the previous year. The rate of revision is to be 50 paise per point

Other Allowances : The Board recommends that the fixation of conveyance, entertainment, travelling, night shift allowances etc., should be left to collective bargaining between the non-Journalists and the newspaper establishments concerned.

The gratuity scheme as applicable to Working Journalists as per the provisions contained in the Working Journalists (Conditions of Service) and Miscellaneous Provisions Act, 1955 subject to the decisions of the Supreme Court shall be applicable to all the non-Journalist employees. If there be any gratuity scheme applicable to non-Journalists immediately before coming of these recommendations into force in that case at his option he can continue to be governed by that scheme instead of the one recommended above.

Fitment : For the purpose of fitment :—

(i) Relevant dates means—

In the case of Classes I, II & III of newspapers and News Agencies and Class I Periodicals-Ist January, 1967.

In the case of all others—Ist July, 1967.

(ii) The present emolument of a non-Journalist shall mean his basic pay plus the D.A. and the amount of interim relief payable to him immediately before the relevant date.

(iii) The revised scale shall mean the scale of pay applicable as per para 24 of these recommendations.

(iv) The assumed basic pay for a non-Journalist shall mean the amount arrived at after reducing the present emolument by the amount of D.A. for the minimum of revised scale applicable in his case as per paras 24 and 25 respectively.

If the assumed basic pay of a non-Journalist is less than the revised scale, his initial pay will be brought to the level of the minimum of the revised scale.

In case the assumed basic pay is higher than the minimum of the revised scale and equal to any stage in the revised scale it will be fixed at that stage.

In case the assumed basic pay is higher than the minimum of the revised scale but not at level with any stage in the revised scale then it will be brought upward to thel evel of the time nearest stage of the scale.

After the initial fixation of basic pay of a non-Journalist as set forth in paragraphs 2, 3, 4 above each non-Journalist, shall be given one increment on the basis of each five years completed service in the group he was immediately before coming into operation of these recommendations.

Provided that in no case more than three increments shall be given; and provided further that by fixation of his pay in the manner suggested above no one will get more than the maximum of the revised scale.

After the initial fixation of the basic pay of a non-Journalist as set forth in the foregoing sub-paragraphs the D.A. as per para 25 shall be payable from the relevant dates on the basic wage so arrived.

A non-Journalist at his option can retain the present scale. This option he has to exercise within a period of two months from the date of publication of Government decision on this recommendation. Option once exercised shall be final.

When a non-Journalist is fitted into a scale in accordance with the provisions of sub-paragraphs 1 to 7 as on the relevant date, he should be entitled to count increments in the appropriate scales as from that date.

In no case, should the total of the existing basic pay and dearness allowance, if any, be reduced as a result of the operation of the provisions contained in these recommendations.

When a newspaper establishment is reclassified in accordance with paragraph 21, the employee should be fitted into the new scale, applicable to him as his existing basic pay. When the basic pay does not coincide with a stage in the new scale, the employee should be fitted at the next higher stage when the classification goes up and at the next lower stage when the classfication goes down. In the latter case, the higher existing basic pay should be protected and the difference between the existing basic pay and the pay to which he is so fitted may be absorbed in a future increment.

Miscellaneous : The interim rates of wages fixed by the Government vide Notification No. WB. 17 (13)/64, dated 9th April, 1965 shall cease to be in operation from the relevant date.

The age of retirement of a non-Journalist shall be 58 years. However, a non-Journalist shall be continued in service upto the age of 60 years, on production of a fitness certificate from any registered medical practitioner.

Re-employment shall be on the basis of the last pay drawn by the employee at the time of retirement.

An apprentice is a person who is only a learner and not an employee in a newspaper. The period of apprenticeship shall not exceed two years.

Subject to the provisions of the standing orders applicable to a newspaper establishment a non-Journalist may be employed as a probationer for a period not exceeding one year during which he shall be paid basic pay not less than the minimum of the scale applicable to the class of establishment and the group in which he is a probationer alongwith allowances attached to the post. In case a non-Journalist acting as a probationer on a higher post is drawing more than the minimum pay of the higher post then he should get 10 per cent of the minimum pay of the higher post in addition to his salary of the lowe post during the probationary period.

Date of Operation : These recommendations should be operative in respect of each newspaper, news-agency, and periodical as from the relevant date applicable to it in accordance with paragraph 29 sub-para (1).

Total arrears payable by the newspapers or news-agencies to its non-Journalists as a result of retrospective operation provided in paragraph 35 should be paid in one instalment, not later than six months from the date of the publication of the order of the Central Government :

Provided that if services of non-Journalists are terminated by the employer before the arrears are paid they will become payable immediately on such termination.

It is recommended that contractual labour should not be allowed in Printing Presses by establishments. However, this restriction would not apply in the case of work of a casual nature.

TARIFF REVISION COMMITTEE, (INTERIM), 1964—REPORT

New Delhi, Directorate of Commercial Publicity, Ministry of Commerce, 1965. iii, 45 p.

Chairman : Shri S. Subramanian.

Members : Shri P. Chentsal Rao; Shri R. V. Leyden; Shri Y. A. Fazalbhoy; Shri Gulabchand G. Siraj; Shri R. C. Shah; Shri M. Panchappa; Dr. B. D. Kalelkar; Shri C. Balasubramaniam; Shri S. C. Mukherjee; Shri S. P. Gugnani; Shri S. D. Bhambri; Shri J. Banerjee; Shri V. A. Padmanabhan; Dr. P. K. Mukherjee; Dr. P. V. Gunishastri; Shri K. L. Saxena; Shri S. P. Jain; Shri E. S. Krishnamoorthy.

Secretary : Shri S. Venkatesan.

APPOINTMENT

The Tariff Revision Committee was constituted by the Government of India in the late Ministry of International Trade by their Resolution No. 10(8)/63-GATT, dated the 17th March, 1964, to conduct a comprehensive enquiry into the structure of the Indian Customs Tariff and recommend the lines on which it might be revised and improved.

TERMS OF REFERENCE

1. To examine the present structure of the Indian Customs Tariff (Import and Export) Schedule with reference to the composition of products and pattern of India's import and export trade.

2. In the light of the examination made under item (1) and having regard to the international developments and changed pattern of trade, to recommend whether the Import Tariff Schedule should be based on the Brussels Tariff Nomenclature or other international nomenclature or whether India may continue to have its separate Import Tariff Schedule after necessary improvement.

3. To advise the Government of India regarding the lines on which the Customs Tariff Schedule should be revised, with particular reference to the need for—

(a) The creation of additional tariff items for articles of recent development and of commercial importance;

(b) Revision of the classification of machinery, iron and steel and textiles in the context of the changed pattern of trade; and

(c) Provision for assessment of parts of articles;

4 To recommend suitable amendments to the classifications and nomenclature of the Export Tariff Schedule;

(5) To review the substantive provisions of the Indian Tariff Act, 1934, Tariff (Amendment) Act, 1949 as well as other relevant legislations and to recommend modifications or amendments required in respect of them. ;

6. To make such other recommendations as may seem germane to the objective of the enquiry.

CONTENTS

Genesis and progress of work; Examination of the terminology, classification and structure of the existing Indian Customs Tariff; Basis of the new tariff; The classification of articles of machinery; Correspondence between the Tariff, I.T.C. and Statistical Classifications; Method to be followed in constructing the new tariff; Conclusion; Appendices I to IV.

RECOMMENDATIONS

Examination Of The Terminology, Classification And Structure Of The Existing Indian Customs Tariff

Before deciding how a tariff classification should be revised, it would be profitable to identify some of the drawbacks which have been noticed in the existing classification. The export tariff is not considered here, as it presents a much more limited problem. What is considered is the import customs tariff, forming the First Schedule to Indian Tariff Act, 1934, and referred to in brief as the "Tariff Schedule". This Schedule broadly follows the draft customs nomenclature of the League of Nations evolved in 1931. Though the Schedule has been amended a number of times since its enactment for purposes of granting protection to indigenous industries, for raising additional revenue, for honouring international commitments, and so on, its basic framework is the same as that adopted in 1934.

There have been complaints that the nomenclature of the Tariff Schedule contains some anomalies, complexities and uncertainties which result in illogical classifications and delays and difficulties in the clearance of goods. It is evident that so long as a tariff contains differing rates of duty, there is always some scope for disputes; and no country has succeeded in totally eliminating such disputes. Nevertheless, it cannot be gainsaid that the Tariff Schedule suffers from a number of shortcomings, some of which no doubt have originated from, or been accentuated by, differences in the circumstances which prevailed in 1934 and those which prevail 30 years later. We are giving below details of some of these shortcomings with a view to providing a possible basis in preparing a revised tariff:—

(1) Lack Of Adaptation To Changes In The Pattern Of Trade

It may be necessary for trade agreement or protective purposes to have separate tariff headings for articles, imports of which are small. It is, however, generally not desirable that there should be too many items of negligible revenue in the long term. Nor is it desirable that a very large volume of trade should come under a single tariff heading, as that would make it difficult to distinguish between different articles which may be able to bear different rates of duty, or may require different degrees of incentive or disincentive to their importation, through the fixing of appropriate rates of duty. The following table shows the order of the duty realizations in 1963-64 under different tariff headings :

Order of Duty Realizations	No. of Items (including protective items shown in brackets)
Upto Rs. 5 lakhs	392 (13)
Between 5 and 10 lakhs	29 (2)
Between 10 and 25 lakhs	37 (6)
Between 25 and 50 lakhs	40 (8)
Between 50 lakhs and 1 crore	21 (3)
Between 1 crore and 5 crores	31 (4)
Between 5 crores and 10 crores	7 (1)
Over 10 crores	6 (—)
Total	563 (37)

It will be seen that, against an overall average revenue collection of about Rs. 60 lakhs for each tariff item, over two-thirds of the tariff items accounted for less than Rs. 5 lakhs each. In many cases the figure was far less than Rs. 5 lakhs, and the revenue collected was either a few hundred rupees or nil. Some examples of headings which are practically inoperative are No. 17 (3) 'Sugar-candy', 22(7) 'Vinegar in casks', 28(10) 'Saecharine tablets', 32(4) 'Candles', 42 'Furniture of wickerwork or bamboo'. 49(5) 'Ghoonsis and muktakesis', 50(4) 'Ropes cotton', 63(29) 'Enamelled iron-ware', 70(9) 'Type metal', 71(7) 'Hurricane Lanterns', 72(17) 'Metal working machinery other than machine tools' and 75(13) 'Parts of mechanically propelled vehicles and accessories N.O.S'. The total revenue collection in 1963-64 under all these 12 headings together was only Rs. 4,902,00, or less than two-millionths of the total revenue. This imbalance in the structure of the tariff, which is no doubt due in a large measure to the change in the pattern of our imports, will have to be remedied when evolving a new tariff. We are, however, conscious at the same time that in any tariff such an imbalance is likely to exist to some extent.

(2) Unnecessary Sub-Division Of Tariff Headings

This is connected to some extent with (1) above. The reasons which necessitated the introduction of several rates of duty in respect of certain groups of articles no longer obtain, though such differing rates, and the separate tariff headings introduced to provide for the different rates, continue to exist. This is seen especially in Section XV "Base metals and articles made therefrom". In pursuance of the policy of discriminating protection to the iron and steel industry, as recommended by the late Tariff Board, various distinctions were made in the tariff—between galvanised and non-galvanised, fabricated and non-fabricated and British and non-British goods; goods made of cast iron or iron or steel; tramway rails and other rails; rails of less than 30 lbs. per yard and over, and rails of a lesser weight; and so on. Each of these categorisations provided for the levy of different rates of duty. The iron and steel industry is no longer under tariff protection and imports are resorted to only to bridge the gap between demand and indigenous supply. The elaborate tariff headings and sub-headings which were considered necessary in the past may not now be necessary in the same degree of detail, whereas there may be a need to provide for new sub-divisions in certain other cases.

(3) Failure To Take Account Of New Products

This is also connected with (1) above. While the range and variety of imported goods has been continuously expanding in the post-war period and many new products have come into existence, there has been no corresponding elaboration of the Customs Tariff Schedule Consequently, even some quite important products of industry have to be classified under one or other of the "N.O.S." provisions. For example, plastics (except phenol formaidehyde moulding powder and P.V.C. sheets, unsupported) are assessed under the general residuary item 87; earth moving machinery and material, handling equipment like mobile cranes, and fork-lift trucks are assessable as "conveyances N.O.S." under item 75 I.C.T.

The Tariff Schedule also contains some odd gaps even in respect of articles which are not very new. An example is the case of domestic sewing machines. There is no single heading for a complete domestic sewing machine; the head and hand attachment are specified in item 72(11)(a) which carries one rate of duty, while, "other parts" fall under item 72(11) (b) with another rate. We understand that there are historical reasons for the headings being worded in this manner, but we nevertheless think it anomalous that such a common and comparatively simple article should have had to be constructively dismantled prior to assessment, and assessed at two different rates, as we understand was the case until recently. [The Central Board of Excise and Customs have since ruled that a complete sewing machine should be assessed under item 72 (11)(a)]. Similarly, there is no specific heading for a complete vehicular diesel engine, which has been ruled to be assessable under item 75(10)(i), covering certain specified engine components.

In drafting a new tariff, these and other less obvious shortcomings would have to be rectified.

(4) Excessive Scope Of "N.O.S," Provisions

The present Tariff Schedule contains a number of "N.O.S." items (that is, residual items with a "not otherwise specified" clause) such as item 63(28) "All sorts of Iron and Steel and manufacturers thereof not otherwise specified", items 73 and 77 relating to electrical and non-electrical instruments, apparatus and appliances and item 87, the general residuary item. Such residual items are no doubt necessary, since individual tariff items cannot conveniently specify all conceivable articles. Nevertheless, the scope of some of these "N.O.S." or miscellaneous items is far too wide. It has been pointed out, for instance, that about 12 per cent of the customs revenue realised in 1963-64 came from the general miscellaneous item No. 87 "All other articles not otherwise specified". Classification under such residual items results from a process of elimination or exclusion, and sometimes results in unforeseen classifications. For example, semi-finished hosiery needles are classifiable as iron and steel manufacturers N.O.S. under item 63(28) on which the rate of duty is 60 per cent ad valorem, unfinished clinical thermometers are classifiable as glass and glassware N.O.S. under item 60 on which the rate of duty is 60 per cent ad valorem, and fork-lift trucks and mobile cranes are assessable as conveyances N.O.S. under item 75 I.C.T. at the rate of 50 per cent ad valorem. Similarly, raw materials like silicon, raw asbestos, oil extended synthetic rubber etc. are classifiable under the residuary item 87 on which the rate of duty is 60 per cent ad valorem.

In all the above cases the hardship resulting from the application of a higher rate of duty, which was not appropriate or not intended to apply, had to be alleviated by the issue of notifications under the Customs law, making them free of duty or subject to appropriate reduced rates of duty.

We consider it necessary that the tariff headings in general should be made as specific as possible, so that the volume of articles assessed under the residual heads may be kept to the minimum. This will ensure that the rates of duty levied are fixed with close reference to the nature of the articles, and anomalous cases like those referred to are avoided.

(5) Tariff Loopholes Due To Lack Of Precision

As indicated under sub-paragraph (1), quite a number of the 563 headings in the Tariff Schedule are ineffective in practice. The effective tariff headings which remain have been found inadequate both in number and in their precision and degree of detail, and both Importers and the Customs Authorities frequently find themselves in doubt regarding the scope of various headings. For instance, art silk yarn and thread have been specified in item 47(2) I.C.T., while twine is assessable under item 53. Since there are no definite criteria to distinguish between yarn, thread and twine, considerable difficulty has been experienced in determining which of the two headings would apply in particular cases.

Again, "Scientific instruments" [item 77(2)] have not been further specified, nor "Optical instruments" [item 77(4)] with the result that quite elaborate, and complicated measuring instruments are sometimes excluded from the lower rates of duty applicable to these items, whereas a simple magnifying glass gets the benefit. We do not propose to multiply instances, but we have to observe that many more such examples could be given.

Apart from causing difficulty to the ordinary importer, lack of precision in wording also provides loopholes which less scrupulous importers have been only too prone to exploit. It is an accepted principle that fiscal statutes should be construed strictly in favour of the assessee and that the latter is entitled to base his stand on the wording of the tariff, irrespective of what the intention of its framers might have been. However, in the larger public interest it is undesirable that such intentions should be made ineffective by faulty wording, particularly because the I.T.C. Schedule, is also connected with the Tariff Schedule, and loopholes in wording can result in the evasion of I.T.C. regulations. We, therefore, consider that expressions commonly used in Customs terminology, such as machinery, instruments, appliances and equipment should be amplified or defined as precisely as possible.

We agree that no system of nomenclature is likely to eliminate doubts and disputes completely; but it is clearly necessary and possible to make the tariff headings sufficiently precise and detailed so as to reduce the scope for disputes to the minimum. We also agree with the demand for a general simplification of the Tariff Schedule. However, we would point out at the same time that simplicity in application does not necessarily go with simplicity of wording. For the present we would only say that, in order to facilitate classification and avoid disputes, more detailed and more-numerous headings are required for important articles of import rather than apparently simple headings with a wide and undefined scope.

(6) Provision For Assessment Of Parts Of Articles

By the Indian Tariff (Amendment) Act, 1963, the Tariff Schedule was amended to provide for component parts of various articles being assessed under the same items as the articles themselves. However, there are still some items in the tariff which refer to the whole article and not to its parts, e.g., items 63(18), 70(11), 77(6), 77(7) etc. In cases where the items refer to the complete article and not to its parts, doubts arise regarding the appropriate item or items under which the parts should be assessed. It would make the tariff more precise, if provisions were made for assessment of the parts of such articles, either in the specific items or through a general provision.

(7) Assessment Of Articles Of Machinery

The assessment of machinery and component parts has in particular given rise to a number of problems, and it was because of this fact, apart from the importance of machinery to the economy, that one of the two Sub-committees which the Committee set up at its very first meeting was concerned with the classification of articles of machinery.

In the Resolution setting up the Committee, it was stated that the Committee is not required to go into the question of the rates of duty applicable in respect of individual products or the different classses of products and it will not be concerned with the level of duty applicable under the Customs Tariff. We think therefore that it would not be appropriate for us, in this report, to make any recommendations for adjustments in the rates of duty on specific articles. At the same time it is not possible in practice to keep our study of tariff classification entirely free of any reference to rates of duty as such, particularly as the representatives of the trade and industry who cooperated in the Committee's work raised numerous valid points turning on anomalies in tariff rates. We have accordingly considered that it would be useful to refer in somewhat general terms to such types of anomalies or inconsistencies which would have to be avoided in framing the new Tariff.

(i) Too Many Rates Of Duty

The Customs Re-organisation Committee, which submitted its report in 1958, referred to the existence in the Tariff Schedule of too wide a range of ad valorem rates of duty, which must inevitably add to the difficulties in the day-to-day application of the tariff, particularly when tariff descriptions carrying different duties could apply to the same article. They had said -

"Almost all multiples of 5 upto 100 are to be found in these rates. We appreciate that a Customs Tariff should normally make a distinction between various categories of goods, as for example : (1) essential and non-essential consumer articles, (2) raw materials for essential and non-essential industries, (3) protected and non-protected items, but the reasons for prescribing different ad valorem rates of duty for articles falling within the same category is not clear."

We appreciate that this multiplicity of rates is in many cases due to the rates on individual items having been altered separately, at different times, for revenue purposes. It is, however, obviously necessary, when a comprehensive review of the tariff is being undertaken to harmonise the rates of duty on different articles and avoid unnecessary distributions.

(ii) Iron And Steel

The specific rates of duty on certain articles of iron and steel were fixed several years ago. Because of a steady rise in prices, the relationship between the specific and ad valorem rates of duty has been upset, with the result that where there are alternative specific and ad valorem rates of duty. the specific rates have lost all significance, having become wholly ineffective, as the duty at the ad valorem rate is invariably higher than the specific duty. Owing to the use of alternative ad valorem and specific rates of duty, it has also been found necessary to issue exemption notifications, to prevent the 'favourable' rate of duty on British goods becoming higher than the rate on non-British goods. In the process of rationalisation of the tariff, such redundant specific rates of duty should be eliminated. The ineffective distinctions between British and non-British goods can also be given up.

Basis Of The New Tariff

The first and most important point which the Committee bad to decide was whether the existing framework of the Tariff Schedule should be preserved, with amendments and improvements, wherever necessary, or whether the revised tariff should be based on a Standard Classification like the Brussels Tariff Nomenclature (B.T.N.) or the Standard International Trade Classification (S.I.T.C.) (Revised), or the Revised Indian Trade Classification (R.I.T.C.), which is based on the S.I.T.C. (Revised) but considerably amplified and amended to take account of India's pattern of Trade.

The features of the various classifications were considered by the Sub-committee on the principles of classification, of which Mr. R. V. Leyden was the Convener. This Sub-committee recommended that the B.T.N., should form the basis for the new Indian Customs Tariff, and that this tariff should maintain the basic structure of the B.T.N., subject to the contraction of the main headings wherever necessary, and also expansion of the main headings by the introduction of sub-headings to suit the pattern of our trade as it exists and as it may be expected to develop in the forseeable future. In determining these sub-headings, the R.I.T.C. should be of great value. The detailed reasons for the Sub-committee's conclusion were as below :—

(i) The B.T.N. has been designed inter alia with a view to the international comparability of tariffs and has been adopted by a large number of countries as the basis of their tariffs.

(ii) While it is quite comprehensive, the number of headings (1097) is manageable, in contrast to the R.I.T.C. with its 5000 headings.

(iii) It is correlated to the Statistical Classifications of trade data such as the S.I.T.C. (Revised) and the R.I.T.C.

(iv) It has the same origin as, and is broadly similar to, the present Indian Customs Tariff, and, therefore, a transition from the present tariff to a new one based on the B.T.N. would not be too difficult.

(v) It is backed by readily available technical guidance in the form of exhaustive Explanatory Notes, Classification Opinions etc., which are under constant review by expert bodies to ensure that they are always abreast of technological progress. There are also Alphabetical Indexes to facilitate easy location of any goods in the Nomenclature as well as in the Explanatory Notes.

(vi) Being a scientific system of four-digit classification, capable of being expanded to a further number of digits on the same pattern ; it would also facilitate the application of modern data processing devices when they are adopted in India.

(vii) It has already been agreed between the U.N.O., and the Customs Cooperation Council that it is the B.T.N. which should be recommended for adoption as a basis for Customs tariffs.

The Committee, at its second meeting, tentatively accepted the conclusions of the Sub-committee. It did not take a final decision at that stage, as the replies to the questionnaire were still due and it was not possible to take fully into account the opinion of the public and Government departments.

The Committee has since seen an analysis of the replies received to the part of the questionnaire dealing with the basis of the revised tariff. It will be seen from this statement that practically all those who have expressed any views on this point are in favour of basing the new tariff on one of the two standard nomenclatures, namely, the B.T.N., or the S.I.T.C. (Revised), (or the R.I.T.C., which is the S.I.T.C., Revised, adapted for India's needs). While the majority opinion is in favour of a tariff based on the B.T.N., the formula proposed by the Sub-committee, namely, a tariff based on the B.T.N. with modifications and making use of the R.I.T.C. for its sub-headings, would to some extent meet the views even of those bodies and persons who have suggested a tariff based on the S.I.T.C., Revised or the R.I.T.C.

After considering all aspects, our conclusion is broadly what it was before. We would, however, make it clear that the broad structure of the B.T.N. should be accepted in principle although it may not be practicable to adopt the B.T.N. as it is and in all its details. The general structure of the B.T.N., and the sequence and broad scope of its sections and chapters, will serve to provide a convenient frame of reference, which in fact would in many cases approximate to the provisions of the existing staff. In several cases, the wording of the B.T.N. headings could also be adopted. The device of having section and chapter notes, to impart precision without making the individual headings too lengthy, can also be usefully adopted. Subject to these considerations, the freedom should be retained to evolve headings in accordance with the requirements of our economy, making free use of the headings in the R.I.T.C.

We would like to explain some of the reasons which have led us to prefer the B.T.N. as a base and not the S.I.T.C. Revised. We observe that each of these classifications has been evolved as a result of the sustained efforts of experts of several countries. Though each has been evolved for a different purpose, steps have been taken to correlate them It has also been agreed between the United Nations and the Customs Cooperation Council, the bodies administering the two Classifications, that it is the B.T.N. which should be recommended for tariff purposes.

So far as the public in India are concerned, the S.I.T.C., Revised, is likely to be of greater appeal, since it is more or less familiar to them. But this is only a transient advantage. If proper steps are taken, as should be done, to enable the public to familiarise themselves in advance with a B.T.N.-based tariff, it will become equally familiar to all concerned, particularly because under the scheme which we have proposed, the individual headings would be fully correlated with the statistical headings of the R.I.T.C.

We further consider that as a base for tariff purposes, the B.T.N. has the following impo tant advantages over the S.I.T.C., Revised :

1. **Precision**: The B.T.N. has been evolved as a basis for Customs Tariffs, where the interpretation of the various headings can involve substantial differences in the duty leviable. Therefore, it has been so worded as to be as exact and precise as possible, even though this involves the use of comparatively long headings in places, and detailed Section and Chapter Notes. We would observe here that simplicity in a Customs Tariff can only be relative. Particularly in an economy like that of India, whose industries are in the process of development, the goods that are imported range from the simplest to the most sophisticated product. Many of them are balancing or semi-finished components, to complement indigenous production. Our Customs duties have therefore to provide the necessary gradation to allow for the present needs of the economy while providing a sufficient incentive for local manufacturers to supply such needs in time. The Customs tariff must, therefore, have the necessary flexibility to allow for differentiation in duties between articles, or different stages of manufacture of the same article, to achieve these twin objects. To provide this flexibility, it is necessary that the tariff should be fairly detailed. (Even otherwise, for I.T.C. and statistical purposes, a fairly detailed classification is necessary). With a detailed classification and different rates of duty, the need for precision in definition is very great. Otherwise, there is room for doubts, disputes and delays. A detailed classification which leaves as little scope for doubt as possible, would help not merely to resolve disputes but also to avoid them, by enabling the importer to know in advance what the tariff classification would be. To achieve this object, it will be necessary to be detailed to the point, at times, of appearing complicated. It is the experience of Customs administrations that this degree of detail and "complication" is preferable to a surface simplicity which leaves wide scope for differences of interpretation and opinion. In this respect, the B.T.N. differs markedly from the S.I.T.C., Revised, whose headings, having no fiscal implications, have been worded in brief and comparatively less precise terms. The examples given below of how the same commodities are defined in the B.T.N. and in the S.I.T.C., Revised, respectively will bring out the force of this point :

B.T.N.	Heading and Description	Corresponding S.I.T.C, (R) Heading and Description
15.12	Animal or vegetable fats and oils, hydrogenated, whether or not refined but not further prepared.	431.2 Hydrogenated oils and fats.
29.38	Provitamins, and vitamins, natural or reproduced by synthesis, including concentrates and intermixtures, whether or not in any solvent.	541.1 Vitamins and provitamins.
70.15	Clock and watch glasses and similar glasses (including glass of a kind used for sunglasses but excluding glass suitable for corrective lenses), curved, bent, hollowed, and the like ; glass spheres and segments of spheres, of a kind used for the manufacture of clock and watch glasses and the like.	664.9(3) Clock and watch glasses etc.

2. **Aids to Interpretation**: Even after making the headings as detailed and precise as possible, it would be too optimistic to believe that disputes can be avoided altogether. To provide for resolving such disputes, an elaborate system has been set up by the Customs Co-operation Council. This includes publications like the Explanatory Notes and Classification Opinions and arrangements whereby doubts regarding classification are referred to the Nomenclature Committee and the Council itself. Even if these arrangements are not made legally binding with reference to the revised Indian Tariff, they would be of great help is coming to a decision on matters of interpretation.

3. **International Comparability**: We learn that

nearly a hundred countries have based, or are proposing to base, their tariff on the B.T.N. Naturally, the B.T.N. has become the "language" for international customs discussions. In tariff negotiations, almost all countries (including India) have come to express their offers and request lists in terms of the B.T.N. In a matter like the Customs Tariff whose significance so obviously extends beyond national frontiers, we consider that there are clear advantages in falling in line with the great majority of countries.

It would also appear that at least one country which had based its tariff on the S.I.T.C. Revised has been forced to think of going over to the B.T.N. A communication from the Newzealand Ministry of External Affairs, received by our Mission in Wellington, states that "Operation of the S.I.T.C., Revised as a Customs Tariff has revealed numerous shortcomings not foreseen when the decision to adopt this form of Tariff was made. There is a proposal to adopt a B.T.N. Tariff, but preliminary steps have still to be taken . . ."

It seems to us that a basis which has been found acceptable to nearly a hundred countries, in all stages of development, should be capable of adoption by India, which had already based its tariff on the League of Nations' Draft Nomenclature, the forerunner of the B.T.N. There is a feeling that the B.T.N. as it stands would not be suitable for Indian conditions, being too detailed in certain parts and not sufficiently so in others, but this particular objection is, we consider, fully taken care of by the freedom allowed to contract or expand the Nomenclature according to national needs. The relative unfamiliarity of the B.T.N. has been responsible for the lurking hesitation to accept it; but as we have explained earlier, this unfamiliarity would be a passing phase. One other difficulty which has been pointed out is that the acceptance of the B.T.N. as a basis might lay an obligation on the customs administration and the Government to accept tariff rulings and opinions with which they may not always agree To this we would say that the use of the B.T.N. carries no obligation whatever as regards the rate of duty to be levied on any article. The Nomenclature is concerned exclusively with the question as to which heading is considered more appropriate to cover a particular article. It seems to us that the prospect of having such technical problems discussed by technical experts of a number of countries, who would not be affected by the duty implications in any particular country, should be welcome to the public, and even to the Government. We feel that, if the Government does not wish to formally bind itself, through a provision in law, to the rulings and opinions of the Customs Cooperation Council and its Nomenclature Committee, it can benefit by making use of them to the greatest possible extent while reserving to itself or the Customs Authorities, as the case may be, the power to take a decision. We have no doubt that a suitable formula can be devised for this purpose.

Our conclusion, therefore, is that the revised Indian Customs Tariff should adopt the broad structure of the B.T.N. with suitable contractions and expansions as may be necessary in the light of the country's trade pattern, development needs and other factors, and that in the matter of expansion, i.e., opening of sub-headings, reference should be freely made to the R.I.T.C. This would provide a happy compromise as well as the best solution.

We might add at this point that the transformation of the existing Indian Customs Tariff into the general form of the B.T.N. would not be a routine operation, but one requiring an intelligent appreciation of the rationale of classification and its applications. Although the broad rate structure of the Tariff Schedule has to be maintained, a certain degree of rationalisation is essential; if an attempt were made to maintain exactly the same rate of duty as exists at present on every individual article, this would result in need less complication of the Schedule.

The Classification of Articles of Machinery

One of the most important sections of the tariff is that dealing with articles of machinery. Its revenue importance is considerable ; the two main machinery items in the Tariff Schedule, namely, Nos. 72 and 72(3), by themselves accounted for 17.2 per cent of the total customs in 1963-64. Apart from its revenue significance, one has to take into account the intrinsic importance of machinery in a fast developing economy, and the need to ensure that its importation is not hindered by inadequate classification. It may be added that a large proportion of the difficulties in assessment occur in connection with the items of machinery.

The wording of items 72 and 72(3) of the existing tariff, which account for the bulk of the imports of machinery and plant is based on the report of the Lloyd Committee of 1922. This report has been reproduced in Chapter V in the last few editions of the Indian Customs Tariff Guide. The Committee's report is a model of compression and lucidity but its recommendations, although relevant to the period when there was practically no manufacture of machinery in the country, are inapplicable to the conditions in present-day India, with its greatly transformed economy.

We do not propose, in this interim report, to comment at length on the conclusions of the Lloyd Committee. We do, however, feel that it would be useful to set out its main conclusions, which were as follows :—

1. The Committee tried broadly to bring within the favourable machinery rate of duty as much as possible of the equipment of industrial plants, while keeping out as far as was practicable, such portions as were suitable for other uses. The Committee was not in favour of extending the machinery rate to importations by industrial concerns as against importations by stock-holders, that is, of a system of assessment based on the end-use to which an individual importer would put the goods. [This is, however, qualified by (6) below].

2. Equipment essential to the erection of a factory, but not to the actual operation of the system installed—for example, electric lamps, wiring, fire bricks and building material—was excluded from the definition of machinery.

3. It was decided to exclude "non-industrial machines of low horse power", viz., those requiring less than 1/4 horse power for their operation, and also machines to be worked by manual or animal labour. No reason has been given for the 1/4 horse-power rule, except that it was necessary in order to give proper effect to the intentions of the framers of the tariff of 1894 (hardly a valid argument in 1965).

4. Control and transmission gear used for transmission of power from the power-house to the machine, lighting system, tram-car, etc. was also to be covered by the definition.

5. As regards component parts, two main provisions were made. The first of these was that component parts in general should: (i) be essential for the working of the machine or apparatus, and (ii) have been given for that purpose some special shape or quality which would not be essential for their use for any other purpose. The latter clause does not mean, as is sometimes thought, that the article is incapable of use for any other purpose, but only that it has been manufactured as a component part of a particular machine or type of machine. The somewhat involved wording adopted by the Committee to deal with a situation which was fairly difficult has however resulted in undeserved criticism from those who do not fully appreciate the difficulty involved in framing a satisfactory definition.

The second and equally important provision regarding 'component parts', which is embodied in the proviso to item 72(3) of the I.C.T., is that even interchangeable articles (which do not have the required "special shape or quality") can be assessed at the favourable machinery rate, provided they are imported as parts of a complete machine in an unassembled condition. No provision was made for a portion of a machine being imported, and complemented by local manufacture; this is an instance of an approach which was wholly adequate in 1922 being found woefully inadequate to meet present requirements, as it serves to discourage actively the manufacture of machinery in the country. The proviso, however, permits articles like transformer oil and lubricants, which are more in the nature of consumable stores to get the benefit of the machinery rate of duty when imported for the first installation of the machine.

7. In coming to its conclusions, the Machinery Sub-Committee noted that the B.T.N. provided for the solution of the main difficulties referred to in paragraph 4 above. Under the B.T.N., an incomplete machine is to be assessed under the same heading as the complete machine, provided it has the essential character of such complete machine. Machinery parts which are not finished ready for use (but not rough forging of iron or steel) are to be classified under the headings for the finished parts. The B.T.N. therefore, helps immediately to overcome two of the major difficulties experienced with the existing tariff. The desirable points in the Lloyd Committee's conclusions referred to in sub-paras (1) and (2) of paragraph 3 above are preserved under the B.T.N. In certain respects the scope of the machinery items as recommended by the Lloyd Committee is wider than those of the relevant B.T N. headings. For instance, according to the Lloyd Committee's report the favourable rate is applicable even to articles in the nature of consumable stores, when imported for first installation, and also to fire-bricks with special qualities and tools specially designed for the working of a machine. We would not venture to express any firm opinion on the claims of such individual articles for a favourable rate of duty. They do not necessarily fall within the definition of machinery, but if it is desired on policy grounds that they should get the benefit of a low rate of duty, this could no doubt be provided for. On the whole, we consider that for machinery as for other commodities, a tariff having a broad structure of the B.T.N. with modifications here and there would provide the best solution.

In considering the suitability of the B.T.N. as the basis of the tariff, our Machinery Sub-Committee had the benefit of the first hand impressions of its convener, Shri Chentsal Rao, who had the opportunity of a discussion with officials of the Customs Cooperation Council during his recent visit to Brussels in another connection, Shri Chentsal Rao gathered, inter alia that if the Government of India considered that certain headings in the Nomenclature were not precise, and could suggest improvements, the Council Secretariat would be quite prepared to give the most careful consideration to the suggestions, and if necessary, to initiate action to carry out the necessary amendments. They also offered their general cooperation in regard to the finalisation of the new tariff. At is second meeting the Committee felt that, as a test case, the Government of India might suggest to the Council Secretariat some amendments to the B.T.N., for example, in heading No. 84.17, which is somewhat ambiguous. A reference on these lines has since been made to the Council Secretariat through our Mission in Brussels.

Correspondence Between The Tariff, I T.C. And Statistical Classifications

Although our terms of reference do not mention the I.T.C. classification, we refer to it because of the view widely expressed by representatives of trade as well as Government, that it would be quite useful to correlate the Customs tariff with the I.T.C. Schedule, and if possible, with the Statistical Classification as well. This aspect has been considered by Shri P.M. Mukerji in his report as Officer on Special Duty, and by the Mudaliar Committee. Among the salient points made by Shri Mukerji in his Report were :

1. The Import Trade Control Schedule is based on considerations of foreign exchange and of allowing the entry of only such imports as are vitally necessary for the economy of the country as well as the availabillity of goods of indigenous manufacture. The Customs Tariff, on the other hand, has essentially revenue considerations in view and the protective features pertaining to certain categories of goods manufactured in the country.

2. Infusion of the two systems may cause difficulties, since, in the absence of a timely rulling from the Customs as to the classification of the items, licencing work may be held up and vice-versa. In the case of Import Trade Control, it would be necessary to take a decision as to the classification of an item prior to importation on the basis of such literature and samples as may be available. While, on the other hand, Customs are rather concerned with goods after importation when a more systematic scrutiny would be possible. In several cases, where there have been differences in the matter of classification of items from the point of view of tariff and import trade control, executive instructions have been issued by the Import Trade Control Authorities for the purpose of clearance of goods, and this indicates that unification is not the remedy for existing difficulties.

In conclusion, Shri Mukerji considered that a complete merger of the Import Trade Control Schedule and the Indian Customs Tariff, though seemingly attractive, should not be the goal. It should, however, be ensured that the two systems worked in close liaison with each other. Where details are not mentioned in the Import Trade Control Schedule, obviously reliance will be placed on customs practice and usage. The fundamental need, according to Shri Mukreji, was to establish adequate understanding between the I.T.C. and the Customs authorities and to establish machinery for a quicker resolution of difficulties of interpretation and classification of items, both prior and subsequent to importation. This point has been pursued in somewhat greater detail by the Mudaliar Committee and we would not like to burden our Interim Report with detailed comments on these matters, and in particular, on the best form of machinery for the resolution of difficulties. We propose to devote a whole Chapter in our Final Report to the subject of best machinery for the resolution of disputes.

Upon the whole, it seems to us, from the different views expressed, that while correspondence of the headings in the Tariff and the I.T.C. Schedules is certainly desirable, it involves at the same time certain difficulties, due mainly to the facts that; (a) the two Schedules are administered by different Ministries for different purposes, and (b) the Tariff Schedule, being part of a statutory Act, is less flexible and more difficult to amend than the I.T.C. Schedule. While reserving our considered views for our final report, we would point out here that, if our recommendation regarding the basis of the revised tariff is accepted, correspondence can be achieved to a reasonable extent. It may be noted that there can be different degrees of correspondence, which we call for convenience "correlation" and "aligument". By "correlation" of two classifications we mean that each heading in one classification corresponds, and is cross referenced, to one or more headings in the order. By "alignment" we mean a closer degree of agreement, where both classifications have the same sequence and the same numbering system, but one being in general more detailed than the other. In other words, one or the other classification would have more digits and more sub-divisions, but the main headings in both classifications would have the same serial numbers and the same scope.

We have been informed that the Revised Indian Trade Classification has been put into effect from 1st April 1965. We also understand that it is proposed to recast the I.T.C. Schedule and base it on the R.I.T.C., since the I.T.C. policy relies largely on import statistics. If the R.I.T.C. could be modified so as to align it with the B.T.N., it would be possible to align all the three classifications. If, however, in view of the agreement between the United Nations and the Customs Cooperation Council to which we have referred in Chapter "Basis of the New Tariff", it is considered that the S.I T.C., Revised, should be preferred to the B.T.N. For statistical purposes, it would still be possible to have a proper correlation of the R.I.T.C. and the new tariff, with a few changes in the R.I.T.C. The question would then arise whether the I.T.C. Schedule should be aligned with the Tariff Schedule and correlated to the R.I.T.C., or whether it should be aligned with the R.I.T.C. and correlated to the Tariff Schedule. We think that the former would be the better course. Alignment of the Tariff and the I.T.C. Schedules would greatly simplify matters in the Custom House, where a large number of consignments have to be classified every day for tariff and I.T.C. purposes. The occasions when it is necessary to refer to the statistics of imports of goods falling under particular Serial Numbers of the I.T.C. Schedule are much less frequent, arising more from the requirements of policy formulation than in the course of every day transactions. It would not cause any appreciable inconvenience to the I.T.C. authorities on those few occasions to have to refer to the import statistics through a correlation code rather than through direct alignment of the I.T.C. Schedule and the Statistical Classification.

It would be advisable to hold over the introduction of the R.I.T.C. for I.T.C. purposes till a final decision can be taken regarding the possibility of aligning the I.T.C. Schedule with the Tariff Schedule. The introduction of a new I.T.C. Schedule is a complex matter, which would affect the public to a great extent. There is also a possibility of the R.I.T.C. having to undergo some amendment in the light of actual working and of new factors which may come to light while drafting the new Tariff Schedule. Whichever view prevails, however, there would be no bar to the acceptance of a tariff structurally based broadly on the B.T.N. but with sub-headings based on the R.I.T.C. wherever necessary.

Method To Be Followed In Constructing The New Tariff

In the light of the conclusions of the Committee, the Sub-Committees are proceeding to construct the revised draft tariff in the following manner :

(a) The basic structure of the B.T.N., with its 21 Sections, 99 Chapters and 1095 main headings, will be maintained, except that some of the main headings, which are unimportant in our trade, would be merged together. In this process, advantage should be taken of the assistance available from the Customs Cooperation Council. Except for the changes necessitated by such contractions, the main headings will broadly maintain the sequence and wording in the B.T.N.;

(b) The main headings will be split up wherever necessary into sub-headings covering specific commodities which are important in India's trade. The headings and sub-headings in the R.I.T.C. will be freely referred to for this purpose;

(c) Sub-headings will also be created wherever necessary for preserving the levels of duty applicable under the present tariff. Separate sub-headings will be provided for important articles which are assessed at concessional rates of duty under exemption notifications (where the notifications are of a durable nature). In the interests of rationalisation, where a particular sub-heading has to be split up purely for the purpose of showing the existing differences in the rates of duty, and there appears to be no special justification (such as protective duties or trade agreements) for such splitting up, it will be recommended that sub-headings may be merged to the extent possible with such rates of duty as Government may decide;

(d) In the above process the considerations laid down by the Committee, any difficulties known to have been experienced in the past and also suggestions received by the Committee will be taken into account.

The Sub-committees have been advised that in respect of any changes in the rates of duty, which in the opinion of the sub-committee are necessary in order to remove tariff amomalies or for similar reasons [i.e., those not covered by para 1(c) above], they may bring the matter separately to the notice of the Secretariat of the Committee.

TARIFF REVISION COMMITTEE ON THE CENTRAL EXCISE TARIFF, 1964—REPORT

New Delhi, Ministry of Commerce (Directorate of Commercial Publicity), 1968. 111p.+vp.

Chairman : Shri S. Subramanian.

Members : Shri R. V. Leyden; Shri D. S. Mulla; Shri Gulabchand G. Siraj; Shri R. C. Shah; Dr. R. G. Agrawal; Shri E. S. Krishnamoorthy; Shri K. Narasimhan; Shri P. L. Sahgal; Shri C. Balasubramaniam; Shri S. C. Mukherjee; Shri S. P. Gugnani; Shri A. P. Verma (replaced by Shri K. G.

Paranjpe); Shri Ram Saran; Dr. P. V. Gunishastri; Shri P. V. Raghavan; Dr. S. G. Rao; Shri P. M. Mukerji.

Secretary : Shri S. Venkatesan.

APPOINTMENT

The present structure of Indian Customs Tariff follows, in its broad aspects, the League of Nations Draft Customs Nomenclature, prepared by the Sub-Committee of Experts of the Economic Committee of the League of Nations, set up in 1927. In the post-war period, new classifications and nomenclature of products have been evolved to suit the changed pattern of international trade. One of them is the "Brussels Tariff Nomenclature" prepared by the European Customs Union Study Group, 1955, which claims to have taken into account the common features of the tariff nomenclatures of the seventeen European countries which constituted the Group and also the latest technological and commercial developments. Another is the "Standard International Trade Classification" prepared by the United Nations Organisation for compilation of national trade statistics on a uniform basis.

With the implementation of the successive Five Year Plans, considerable progress has been made in industrial and economic development leading to a substantial change in the composition and pattern of India's external trade. Both, the Government of India and the business community have, therefore, felt the need for a detailed study of the present tariff with a view to revising it on modern lines, and in a manner which, having regard to the pattern and composition of India's external trade, will be more appropriate. The need for a complete reforms of the Indian Customs Tariff has also been stressed in the reports submitted by the various Committees and Commissions set up by the Government of India from time to time, most recent among them being the Shri A. Ramaswami Mudaliar Committee. The Government of India have accordingly decided to appoint a Committee to conduct a comprehensive enquiry into the Indian Customs Tariff structure and to recommend the lines on which it may be revised and improved. This committee was constituted under the Ministry of International Trade vide their Resolution No. 10(8)/63-GATT, dated 17th March, 1964.

TERMS OF REFERENCE

1. To examine the present structure of the Indian Customs Tariff (Import and Export) Schedule with reference to the composition of products and pattern of India's import and export trade.

2. In the light of the examination made under item (1) and having regard to the international developments changed pattern of trade, to recommend whether the Import Tariff Schedule should be based on the Brussels Tariff Nomenclature or other international nomenclature or whether India may continue to have its separate Import Tariff Schedule after necessary improvement.

3. To advise Government of India regarding the lines on which the Customs Tariff Schedule should be revised, with particular reference to the need for :

(a) The creation of additional tariff items for articles of recent development and of commercial importance;

(b) Revision of the classification of machinery, iron and steel and textiles in the context of the changed pattern of trade; and

(c) Provision for assessment of parts of articles.

4. To recommend suitable amendments to the classifications and nomenclature of the Export Tariff Schedule.

5. To review the substantive provisions of the Indian Tariff Act, 1934, Tariff (Amendment) Act, 1949 as well as other relevent legislations and to recommend modifications or amendments required in respect of them.

6. To make such other recommendations as may seem germane to the objective of the enquiry.

In modification of the Resolution of the late Ministry of International Trade No. 10(8)/63-GATT, dated the 17th March, 1964, the Government of India have decided to entrust the Tariff Revision Committee with the revision of the Import Trade Control Schedule and the Central Excise Tariff Schedule vide their Resolution No. 1(54)TRC/66, dated 1st February, 1966.

Accordingly, the aforesaid Resolution shall be further amended as indicated below :

1. For the words "Customs Tariff" appearing as the subject of Resolution, the following words shall be substituted :

"Customs Tariff, Import Trade Control and Central Excise Tariff Nomenclure".

2. In paragraph 4, after sub-paragraph (5), the following sub-paragraphs shall be inserted :

"(5A) to examine the classification of commodities in the Import Trade Control Schedule and make recommendations for its revision, taking into account in particular :

(a) The proposed Import Tariff Schedule and the need for consistency between the interpretation of the Tariff and the Import Trade Control Schedules;

(b) The need for correlation of the Import Trade Control Schedule with the statistical classification of commodities in the import and export trade, so as to facilitate the framing of Import Trade Control policy in greater detail.

(5B) To scrutinize the nomenclature adopted in the Central Excises Tariff Schedule (viz., the First Schedule to the Central Excises and Salt Act, 1944), and to suggest suitable amendments thereto; in doing so the

Committee will :

(a) Examine the desirability of achieving a closer alignment between the Customs Import Tariff Schedule and the Central Excise Tariff Schedule with a view to—

(i) Ensuring as far as practicable, uniformity in the interpretation and administration of the two Schedules; and

(ii) facilitating the removal of doubts and difficulties in the levy of countervailing duties :

(b) Examine also the question whether, and to what extent, the Central Excise Tariff Schedule can be aligned, for statistical purposes, with the system adopted for the maintenance of statistics of "import and export trade."

The following sentence shall be added at the end of paragraph 5 :—

"Similarly, the Committee will be concerned with the Nomenclature and not with the rate structure as such of the Central Excise Tariff Schedule."

The following words shall be added at the end of paragraph 7 :

"Or such extended period as Government may decide."

CONTENTS

Part I: Introduction ; Framework of Revised Central Excise Tariff ; Format of the Schedule ; Other Recommendations ; Summary of Conclusions and Recommendations ; Acknowledgements ; Appendices, 1 to 9 ; Part II; Draft Schedule and Covering Note.

RECOMMENDATIONS

Framework Of The Revised Central Excise Tariff Schedule

It is necessary that the revision of the Central Excise Tariff Schedule should be on a scientific basis so as to put it in a form capable of logical and orderly expansion. The alignment of the Central Excise Tariff Schedule with the Customs Tariff Schedule would go a long way to ensure uniformity in the administration and interpretation of the two Schedules, particularly because at many levels the authorities administering them are the same.

The Central Excise Schedule should continue to be selective, as at present, and should by and large cover only articles on which duty is actually being levied.

The need to levy countervailing duty on imported articles has placed a burden on customs assessing staff which is out of proportion to the revenue involved in such a levy, and the alignment of the Central Excise Tariff Schedule with the Customs Tariff Schedule would simplify the levy of countervailing duty.

The Customs Tariff Schedule and the Central Excise Tarifl Schedule should be aligned and should have a common nomenclature to the extent possible.

A complete alignment of the two Schedules is not feasible where it would seriously affect the compactness of the existing Central Excise headings, or in a few instances where the accepted terminology in India differs considerably from that for imported goods, as in the case of textile fabrics.

While the specifications laid down by the I.S.I. could usefully be referred to in many cases, it would not be practicable to adopt those specifications for taxation purposes.

Rule 56-A of the Central Excise Rules, 1944, may be suitably amended or exemption secured otherwise, so that credit of daty paid on raw materials and component parts, which is now admissible, is not denied to manufacturers merely as a result of the existing Central Excise headings having been split up.

There would be no particular advantge in attempting an alignment of the Central Excise Tariff Schedule with the R.I.T.C. Any such attempt is likely to make the Schecule unduly complicated.

The revised Schedule does not incorporate exemption notifications based on the scale of output of the manufacturing unit, the end-use of the article, and similar factors, but general exemptions which appear to be permanent have been incorporated.

The omission of headings for salt and silver has been suggested.

The levy of countervailing duty should be selective, and should be confined to a list of specified articles. It would be convenient to achieve this object through a general exemption notification.

It is desirable to have a grouping of the Central Excise headings into sections. These should however be based on the Sections of the R.C.T. and not on the Sections of the S.I.T.C. as at present.

It is desirable, on balance to give the same number to the headings in the Central Excise Schedule as the numbers of the corresponding R.C.T. headings.

Format Of The Schedule

The format of the Statutory Schedule is simple and does not need amendment, except for a slight modification of the column headings.

The lay-out of the Working Schedule has to be such as to show in the most convenient manner the effect of the several exemption notifications in force.

A revised lay-out, which will show at a glance the statutory rates of duty on any commodity (whether under the Central Excises and Salt Act, 1944 or under any other Central Act), as well as the effective rates of duty, has been suggested.

The adoption of the revised lay-out will involve the interpretation of exemption notification. The task of compiling the Working Schedule on these lines may therefore be carried out by the Statistics and Intelligence Branch of the Central Board of Excise and Customs under the supervision of the Director of Inspection.

The Working Schedule should contain an indication that the effective rates have been shown for convenience and that this publication should not be regarded as an overriding authority.

Exemption notifications may if possible be grouped separately according as they affect or do not affect the levy of countervailing duty.

The Working Schedule may be brought out as a supplement to the Indian Trade Journal. If this arrangement does not come up to expectations, the Committee has suggested alternative methods to reduce delays in publication. There should be atleast two issues in a year, of which the first should be published immediately after the enactment of the Finance Bill.

Other Recommendations

The Committee has accepted the principle that some kind of encouragement should be given to cottage and small-scale industries. The degree of encouragement should however be in a form and quantity that would stimulate efficiency.

It would not be practicable at present to replace rate concessions to cottage and small scale industries by subsidies.

The system of giving effect to rate concessions to cottage and small scale industries through exemption notifications will have to be retained for the present.

The duty differentials in the above-mentioned cases may be fixed in consultation with the Tariff-Commission.

There is a widespread demand for the setting up of an independent appellate tribunal for deciding Central Excise disputes.

The appointment of Appellate Collectors of Central Excise will not satisfy the demand for an independent tribunal.

The Tariff Commission would not be able to function as an appellate tribunal, in the near future. Nor would it be feasible for it to issue general tariff rulings.

There should be an independent tribunal to deal with Central Excise disputes at the revision stage, with a revision for reference to the High Courts on points of law. The same tribunal could deal with both Customs and Central Excise disputes for the same area.

Tariff rulings issued by the Government of India and the Central Board of Excise and Customs should ordinarily apply to both the Customs and the Central Excise Schedules.

Any order by the Government or the Board in Revision or appeal which implicity incorporates a tariff ruling should be followed by a regular tariff ruling.

There is no need for an elaborate programme of training to field officers prior to the introduction of the revised Schedule, nor for a "trial run". However, the Revised Tariff should be made available in advance to the public and to the administration.

The adoption of the Revised Shedule is not likely to impose any extra strain on the departmental laboratories. However, this factor may be taken into account while making an assessment of the requirements of the departmental laboratories in connection with the adoption of the revised Customs Tariff Schedule.

COMMITTEE TO SUGGEST WAYS AND MEANS OF IMPROVING FINANCIAL RETURNS FROM IRRIGATION PROJECTS, 1964—REPORT

New Delhi, Ministry of Irrigation and Power, 1964. v. 81p, (Memographed)

Convener : Shri S. Nijalingappa.
Members : Shri Balwant Rai Mehta; Shri S. B. Chavan; Shri Girdhari lal; Shri A. C. Subba Reddy; Choudhary Ranbir Singh (replaced by Shri Rizk Ram); Shri M. P. Sinha; Shri S. Bhattacharjee; Shri V. V. Chari; Shri B.S. Nag.
Secretary : Shri S.S. Lamba.

APPOINTMENT

The working of the irrigation projects in relation to their financial returns has received considerable attention during recent years and proposals suggesting ways and means of improving the financial returns from the projects have been made from time to time. The subject was also discussed at the Conference of Irrigation and Power Ministers held at New Delhi on the 3rd and 4th January, 1964. Since irrigation projects are not giving adequate returns and the response in respect of betterment levy is not encouraging. So the Government of India, Ministry of Irrigation and Power Constituted a Committee to examine the whole question and suggest ways and means for improving the financial returns from the Projects Vide their Resolution No. DW. II-31 (2)/64 dated April 3, 1964.

TERMS OF REFERENCE

(i) To suggest ways and means of improving financ'al returns from the projects.

(ii) To review and suggest criteria for sanctioning new projects.

(iii) To consider the feasibility of future beneficiaries contributing towards the cost of schemes beginning from the construction stage itself.

CONTENTS

Part I : Letter of Transmittal ; Introduction ; Report ; Recommendations ; Statements from 1 to 6.

Part II : Appendices from 1 to 7.

RECOMMENDATIONS

Projects Under Construction

Projects already under execution should be completed at the optimum pace technologically feasible, and within the limitation of available resources, adequate provision of funds should be made for these in the State Plans.

New Projects

New projects should be sponsored only after these have been fully investigated, their feasibility established beyond doubt, and a complete project report with carefully worked out estimates of cost, benefits etc. prepared.

The various components of works in a project should be so planned and coordinated that benefits to the extent feasible are obtained at various stages of construction. It is of utmost importance to plan well in advance for controlled and scarce materials, heavy machinery, their spare parts and personnel Requirements of foreign exchange and finance should be realistically worked out and phased well in advance so that availability of foreign exchange is assured when a project is sanctioned. For the assessment of foreign exchange and its expeditions availability for such projects, necessary steps should be taken to set up a cell at the centre, consisting of the representatives of the concerned Ministries, and the Planning Commission. For speedy execution of large irrigation projects, additional financial assistance from the Centre may become necessary. This additional assistance could be taken into consideration while fixing the ceilling of the State Plan.

It should also be ensured that new schemes are not sponsored to the detriment of continuing schemes.

Priority For Major And Medium Projects

Irrigation should be treated as one coordinated problem. While due importance may be given to minor irrigation, no secondary place should be allotted to major and medium irrigation schemes, which yield in the long run more stable resources for increasing food production. This will also bring food financial returns.

Funds allotted to Irrigation Sector, should not be diverted on any account.

Rivision Of Water Rates

Water rates should be on the basis of a suitable percentage of the additional net benefit to the farmer from an irrigated crop where with the available data, this can be worked out. These rates may be fixed at 25 percent to 40 percent of the additional net benefit keeping in view factors like rainfall, water requirement, yield and value of crop etc. Where it is not feasible to work out the additional net benefit, water rates may be fixed, to start with, as a suitable percentage of gross income to the farmer from the irrigated crop. Rates in this case may be 5 to 12 percent of the gross income, and should be worked upto.

Water rates should be reviwed every 5 years. Required data regarding additional net benefit should be continuously collected for this purpose.

Introduction Of Irrigation Facility Charge

In States where irrigation charge are optional, in consideration of the irrigation facilities, having been made available for an area, there should be a 'charge' to cover at least the maintenance and operation charges, whether the facility is actually made use of or not. This should be levied on the entire C.C.A., that is, "the gross area commanded less the area of unculturable land included in the gross area", as defined in the "Glossary of Irrigation and Hydro-electric Terms and Standard Notations used in India", published by the Central Board of Irrigation & Power. On carrying out actual irrigation, this facility charge paid in respect of the area should be deducted from the total irrigation dues for the year will form part of the water rate.

Recovery Of Betterment Or Capital Levy

A betterment or capital levy should be charged on irrigation projects, the quantum and mode of recovery being determined by the State Governments.

Optimum Utilisation Of Irrigation Potential Created Area Programmes

"After Frogrammes" for development of irrigation in the commanded area should proceed space with the project, so that, optimum utilisation of irrigation potential is achieved, with maximum speed, through coordination of efforts of all concerned Departments.

Coordination Between Agriculture Department And Irrigation Department

A senior and experienced officer of the Agriculture Department, with adequate supporting staff, should be attached to the State Irrigation Department, to advise an agricultural aspects of major and medium irrigation projects, such as cropping pattern, water requirements of various crops, suitability of areas for irrigation, both for new and existing projects.

Criteria For Sanctioning A Project

Economic benefit criterion should be adopted for sanctioning irrigation projects instead of the present financial criterion. For this purpose, it will be necessary to lay down detailed instructions for working out the "benefit cost Ratio". As a general rule, a project should be considered worthwhile only if the benefit cost ratio as already explained is not less than 1.5. Exceptional cases such as those for scarcity and backward areas, may however, continue to receive special consideration.

Advance Contribution Towards Cost Of Schemes

In deciding inter-se priorities of irrigation projects accepted for inclusion in a Plan, schemes in respect of which beneficiaries are ready to pay betterment or capital levy in advance, should receive special consideration.

STUDY GROUP ON WILD LIFE & WILD LIFE PRODUCTS, 1964—REPORT

New Delhi, Department of Agriculture, 1967, 42p. (Memographed)

Chairman : Shri Hari Singh

Members : Shri K.S. Dharmakumar Singh Ji ;
Dr. Salim Ali (he expressed his inability to serve a member), and his place was taken by Shri Humayun Abdulali) ;
Shri M.A. Rahman (Shri Rahman retired from the Government service and his place was taken by Shri T.N. Srivastava);
Dr. M. L. Roonwal (Since succeeded by Dr. A.P. Kapur);
Shri F.C. Gera (Left the Department on March, 1966 succeeded by Shri J. S. Sarma) ;
Shri V. D. Gangal (Succeeded by Shri S.K. Sarkar) ;
Shri H.K. Singh (Replaced by Smt. S.L. Singla);

Secretary : Shri R.R. Gupta.

APPOINTMENT

This Study Group was set up by Government of India in the Ministry of Food, Agriculture, Community Development and Cooperation to examine the possibility of increasing exports of those species of Wild Life and Wild Life Products for which there is a demand in Foreign markets, so as to increase foreign exchange earnings. On the other hand, there is a strong opinion in the country that due to its indiscriminate exploitation of commercial and other purposes. Our Wild life has been reduced to the status where many species are now rare and some even on the verge of extinction. They feel that the amount of foreign exchange earned from the export of Wild life and its products did not warrant an incentive in the form of increased exports to the killing of Wild life. The Study Group was appointed by No. F. 14-9/64-E.P. Government of India, Ministry of Food and Agriculture (Department of Agriculture), (Export Promotion Division) New Delhi, dated the 4th April, 1964.

TERMS OF REFERENCE

The Terms of reference of the Study Group will be as under :

(i) To estimate on the basis of available material the availability of these species of the Wild life and Wild life Products;

(ii) To consider and suggest long term policies to be adopted for the export to Wild life and Products of Wild life;

(iii) To recommend steps to be taken for increasing the availability of Wild life and Products there from for export purposes, and

(iv) To suggest specific schemes with estimates of expenditure involved for developing various species of wild life for export purposes.

CONTENTS

Preface, Chapter; Introduction, Peacock feathers, Crocodiles and Crocodile skins, Pythons; and python skin, Water lizard and other monitor lizards and their Skins, Jungle Fowl feathers and necks, Deer Musk, Deer Horns, Lesser Panda, Slow Loris and Slender Loris, Leopard or Panther Skins, Langurs, Jha Committee Exports of India goods a Souvenirs.

RECOMMENDATIONS

Peacock feathers

The quota for export of peacock feathers may be reduced from the existing quota of 3000 kgs. to 2500 kgs. per annum. Only complete feathers should be allowed for export. The export of articles manufactured out of Peacock feathers should be freely allowed for a period of six months and it, at the end of this period, such exports are found to fall short of 500 kgs., the difference could be made up by the export of Peacock feathers.

The Ministry of Commerce may be requested to collect data on the type, quantity and value of articles made out of Peacock feathers that are being exported by the trade.

The Zoological Survey of India and the State Governments may be requested to take up the question of conducting Census/ecological survey of this species.

Crocodile And Crocodile Skins

The Zoological Survey of India and the State Government may be requested to take up the question of conducting Census/ecological survey for all the three species of Crocodile. The extent of Crocodile skins should be completely banned.

The State Government should be asked to declare the Crocodile as protected species where this has not yet been done.

Python & Python Skins

The Zoological Survey of India and the State Governments may be requested to take up the question of conducting Census/ecological survey in connection with the Indian Rock Python.

The existing policy of an export quota of 250 (in numbers) python skins of not less than 12″ width per annum may continue for the present.

The State Governments may be requested to declare the python a protected species where this has not been done, and this subject be placed before the I.B.W.L.

The Ministry of Commerce should be requested to maintain separate data for the export of pythons and python skins by numbers and not by weight.

Water Lizards And Other Monitor Lizards & Their Skins

The Zoological Survey of India and the State Governments may be requested to take up the question of conducting census/ecological survey in connection with Water Monitors.

Since Monitor Lizards other than Water Lizards are useful for controlling rates and mice it is necessary that some control is imposed on the export of lizard skins with a view to checking the large scale killing of those raptiles. This question should therefore be pursued in consultation with the Director, Zoological Survey of India.

The existing policy of limiting the export of Water Lizard skins to quota of 500 skins of a width not less than 10" per annum, may continue to the present.

Jungle Fowl Feathers And Necks

The export of (1) Skins of Grey Jungle Fowl, and (ii) Grey Jungle-cock necks and neck feathers should be brought under Part 'A' of Schedule I to the Export (Control) Order, 1962.

Deer Musk

The existing export quota of 300 kgs. of musk per annum may continue till the proposed investigations regarding purity of the exported musk is completed. After this investigation is completed, the question of banning completely the export of deer musk may be re-examined.

The Ministry of Food and Agriculture may get in touch with the National Chemical Laboratory, Poona with a view to encouraging the use of synthetic musk in the perfumery trade.

Deer Horns

The existing policy of allowing freely the export of deer horns on the production of a certificate from a Divisional Forest Officer (that the horns were dropped or naturally shed) be continued.

The State Chief Conservators of Forests should be asked to furnish information on the quantity of horns for which such certificates had been issued during the period from 1st October, 1965 to 30th September, 1966.

Lesser Panda

As the Lesser Panda is a rare animal in the country, it is necessary to recommend that the export of the Lesser Panda should be completely banned.

Slow Loris And Slender Loris

The export of these lamurs should be completely banned and they should be brought under Part 'A' of Schedule I to the Export (Control) order.

Leopard and Panther Skins

It is recommended that the export of Panther and Leopard skins should be allowed freely till a decision in this regard is taken by the Indian Board for Wild Life.

Langurs

The export of the Lakhimpur, Nilgiri, Malabar and Travancore langurs should not be allowed. These species should, therefore, be included under Part 'A' of the Schedule I to the Export (Control) Order, 1962.

The existing policy of allowing the export of 100 common langurs per annum should from States other than Maharashtra, Gujarat and Himachal Pradesh. Where the quota celling does not apply subject to the production of the specified certificates be continued.

Jha Committee Report: Exports Of Indian Goods As Souvenirs

It is recommended that there should be no restrictions on the export of articles made of peacock feathers and crocodile skins which are exported as accompanied baggage of the travellers.

MONOPOLIES INQUIRY COMMISSION, 1964—REPORT

Delhi, Manager of Publications, 1965. 438p.

Chairman : Shri K.C. Das Gupta.
Members : Shri G. R. Rajagopaul ; Shri K. R. P. Aiyangar ; Shri R.C. Dutt ; Shri I.G. Patel.

APPOINTMENT

The Government of India, in Ministry of Finance appointed the Monopolies Inquiry Commission under the Commission of Inquiry Act, 1952 Vide their Notification of April 16, 1964.

TERMS OF REFERENCE

(a) To inquire into the extent and effect of concentration of economic power in private hands and the prevalence of monopolistic and restrictive practices in important sectors of economic activity other than agriculture with special reference to :

(i) The factors responsible for such concentration and monopolistic and restrictive practice ;

(ii) Their social and economic consequences, and the extent to which they might work to the common detriment ; and

(b) To suggest such legislative and other measures that might be considered necessary in the light of such enquiry, including, in particular, any new legislation to protect essential public interests and the procedure and agency for the enforcement of such legislation.

The Notification further authorises to report on any other matter bearing on any aspect of national economy or functioning of the private sector and financial institutions that may deem necessary to look into in connection with the terms of reference.

CONTENTS

Introduction

Vol. I., Part 1. Concentration of Economic Power defined ; Causes of concentration ; Product-wise concentration. Country-wise concentration. Part II. Monopolistic and Restrictive Practices ; Consequences of concentration ; Recommendations (Non-Legislative) ; Foreign Legislation ; Recommendations (Legislative) ; Other Matters ; Conclusion ; Note of Dissent by Shri R. C. Dutt.

Vol. II. Appendices from A to E.

RECOMMENDATION

The foregoing study has convinced us that the dangers from concentrated economic power and monopolistic and restrictive practices are not imaginary but do exist in a large measure either at present or potentially. It is therefore necessary to proceed to the consideration of the proper measures we can recommend to Government and Parliament to avert or at least to minimize these dangers. In making our recommendations we are assuming that the planned economy and development as envisaged in the Industrial Policy resolutions will continue in this country for many years to come and that the operation of the industry will be shared between the public sector, with the necessary allocation of capital resources, foreign exchange and import of raw materials or necessary components between the two sectors that planning entails.

We are clearly of opinion that a permanent body should be set up with the duty and responsibility for exercising and for taking action to protect the country against the dangers that we think do exist. We are fortified in this view by the general support of many of the Chambers of Commerce representing big business in the country who appeared before us.

The suggestion for constituting such a body was made by the very first witness examined by us (Dr. Lokanathan). In our opinion, this step is absolutely necessary if anything is to be done to fight restrictive and monopolistic practices. That same body would be in a position to take whatever action is proper to fight other evils arising from concentration of economic power.

The Bengal Chamber of Commerce which represented a large section of European business houses in eastern India recognised in its own memorandum the need of having some kind of authority to investigate complaints about antisocial practices in particular trades and industries. The Associated Chamber of Commerce also expressed itself in favour of the constitution of such an authority. Some of the other Chambers of Commerce and other associations of industrialists present in their written memorandum the view that the powers placed in the hands of Government by various provisions of the Companies Act, Industries (Developmemt & Regulation) Act, Control of Capital Issues Act, Essential Commodities Act, the Tarrif Commission Act and certain other statutes provide sufficient safeguard against the growth of concentration of economic power, rise of monopolistic conditions and the danger from monopolistic and restrictive practices. They were not able to show how far these various laws were directly effective in practice in checking monopolistic and restrictive practices or others aspects of concentration of economic power. The representatives of some of these fairly agreed as a result of their discussions with us about the need of a permanent body to deal with these matters. The Indian Chamber of Commerce's delegation finally put the matter thus :

"If after examining all the facts, you come to the conclusion that there has been really a kind of exploitation on a large scale of the consumer by monopolistic tendencies in some industries and there is no other remedy, that the present machinery of Government is such that even with this legislation, the Essential Commodities Act and other Acts, the Government is not in a position to curb these tendencies, on the basis of that finding, we will have no case before you to say that you should not have such a body."

The delegation from the Engineering Association of India which at the commencement of the discussion was very emphatic in its opposition to any more legislation and the setting up of any authority, also approved ultimately of the suggestion to set up a permanent body.

The Bharat Chamber of Commerce's delegation after saying in the course of discussion that it had no objection to vigilance being kept against dominant concerns doing anything against national interests and that it was not opposed to any permanent body being set up to deal with restrictive practices in industries ended by saying that the setting up of a body to examine judicialy all complaints against concentration of economic power or monopolistic and restrictive practices would be a boon to industrialists.

Speaking on behalf of the Gujarat Chamber of Commerce, Mr. Amin made the following observations :

"I agree that some sort of machinery is necessary with power to make enquiries ; when complaints are made, this body after hearing all the parties concerned, will pass an order whether a particular monopolistic practice or restrictive practice exists or not and take action. This permanent body should only be more by way of corrective action without creating further restrictions and further complications."

Mr. J.R.D. Tata expressed himself wholly in favour of such a body, but was anxious that this should be really independent of Government. Expressing a similar view another leading industrialist Mr. Mafatlal, said, : "In principle I think that the creation of a body of that nature is absolutely a very good thing. The only thing I wanted to tell you is proper constitution and proper approach."

We are convinced that the existing powers of Government have not been able to check the growth of concentration of economic power in private hands or to eliminate the evils of monopolistic and restrictive practices. The experience of other countries, when faced with similar situations show that a body specially entrusted with the duty of looking after these matters can be of great use in preventing excessive concentration of economic power or the evils resulting therefrom and also evils that frequently result from monopolistic and restrictive practices.

The question as to how this body should be constituted and what powers and functions should be entrusted to it will require careful consideration. But we are conscious that, however, much such a body may be expected to accomplish, resolute action in other spheres will also be necessary to attain the objective. Before examining the question of the powers and functions of the permanent body, we shall indicate what action in other spheres we consider essential,

Most important of these is the political sphere. It has long been thought in America that too much concentration of economic power is dangerous to political democracy. The same feeling has been voiced before us by many. Our own apprehension as regards this danger has already been mentioned by us in a previous portion of this report. The best protection from the danger can be provided by the practice of discipline by the political parties themselves. A first step towards that may well be the refusal by politicians to accept financial or other assistance from business houses in their election campaigns. A strict observations of a rule towards this end is likely to go a long way to remove the danger of big business corroding the democratic machinery. While it is not our purpose to tell the political parties, what to do and what not to do, we shall be failing in our duty if we do not add that politicians whether belonging to the party in power or to the opposition parties must also discipline themselves against accepting anything from big business for themselves or for their children or friends or relatives—directly or indirectly—if they are to free their thought and action from the incumbrance of favours received.

Hand in hand with this should go measures to remove corruption from the administrative machinery. For many years in the past, the permanent services—with the exception of only a few sections—enjoyed a great reputation for integrity which was the envy of many. That bright picture seems to have faded now. With the increase in the power of officialdom in the matter of helping or hindering traders and industrialists, there has been, it is often alleged, a rapid deterioration in the standards of honsety of government officials. Even responsible members of Government have sometimes voiced their fears about the corrupting influence of some business interest on public officials. Not unnaturally critics of Government have been more out-spoken and much more serve in their allegations of corruption among Government officials. Without expressing any opinion on the degree of corruption that is rampant, we think it only proper to say that complacency that all is well and nothing needs to be done will be no less dangerous than serving corruption at every corner. We are here concerned only with that aspect of corruption which influences and is in turn influenced by concentration of economic power. We are convinced that officials totally freed from the vice of corruption may exert great influence against unnecessary concentration of economic power.

It is hardly necessary to add that once politicians free themselves from the corrupting influence, if any, of big business, it will be easier for them to deal with any corruption of government officials.

We have anxiously considered whether we can usefully make any recommendation on the question of industrial licensing. Some think that to diminish the concentration of economic power, one of the most effective ways would be to do away with such licensing. Such a step, it has been claimed, would remove the main obstacle to the free entry of entrepreneurs into different industries and would bring in competitors in many of the fields where concentration now exists.

The total abolution of the licensing system is not however, at the present stage, a practical proposition. The law requiring such licensing was enacted after a careful considaration of all aspects of the national economy and is now an integral part of the country's economic policy. We do not think it possible to recommend the wholesale repeal of these provisions merely on the ground that might reduce concentration of economic power.

But, what we can do and recommend is that licensing policy should be liberalised. Much has been written in recent months about 'streamining the procedure' for grant of licences and some steps have apparently been taken, specially after the reports of the Swaminathan Committee, the Lokanathan Committee and the Mathur Committee. Much more, we think, can be done, to make it easy for the comparatively smaller entrepreneurs to get industrial and import licences without undue expenses and wasteful delay. Many of the leading industrialists, we understand, have found it necessary to maintain expensive establishments in the capital, for facilitating the obtaining of licences. Those who cannot afford the expenses of running such establishments-which include sometimes, it seems, large amounts required to employ highly paid "contactmen", and to give lavish parties—are at a disadvantage. One small entrepreneur complained some time ago to our Member Mr. R.C. Dutt that he could not afford to fly to Delhi again and again in the attempt to obtain a licence. There are, we convinced, many others who have been in similar predicament and have given up the idea to enter an industry in sheer disgust and despair.

We believe that responsible officers of the Government are aware of all that and doing what they can to remove the causes of such complaints. Even so, we have thought it our duty to mention this matter and to recommend that more positive action should be taken to liberalise the issue of licences. For, we are convinced that making it easier to obtain licences without having to spend unnecessarily and to wait indefinitely would be a potent factor in removing concentration.

So long as the system of industrial licensing does

remain, and it is not easy to see that it can be brought to an end soon, it can be used to good purpose by Government in fighting concentration wherever necessary in the interests of the country. Thus, where a choice lies between a big industrialists and many other entreprenuer Government may very well adopt the policy of leaning in favour of the latter provided this can be done without much risk to the paramount needs of efficient production. Such a policy will be justified by the directive principle in article 39 of the Constitution, which calls upon the State to see that the operation of the economic system does not result in the concentration of wealth and means of production to the common detriment.

It has been suggested to us that the provision in Section 372 of the Companies Act as regards inter-corporate investments-specially the power of Government to grant or withhold approval to inter-corporate investments exceeding the limits specified in the section—are available as a means of controlling concentration of economic power. We are doubtful how far this will be effective in actual practice. If also seems to us that the question of concentration of economic power is wholly outside the scheme and purpose of the above provision. We do not think therefore that it would be right or proper to use the powers of Government under the section for the purpose of controlling concentration as suggested. On the question whether such use of the power would be legal or not we express no opinion.

Our direction in which administrative action can be fruitfully taken with regard to monopolies is in the matter of the issue of import licences and in preventing abuses of licences granted whether to actual users or established importers. Complaints have been made to us by more than one trade organisation that the issue of import licences to a select few has had the effect of concentrating economic power as regards the supply of these goods to industrial and other consumers. In view of the stringent foreign exchange situation, it is not possible for us to recommend the liberal issue of import licences, to remedy the evil. It should be possible, however, we think, for the authorities to insist upon proper distribution, on reasonable terms, by those who get the licences among all those who use the imported commodity—whether for industrial purposes or for direct consumption.

We also recommend that in shaping the import policy of the Government should, as far as possible, pay due regard to the need of protecting the consumers against exploitation by enterprises enjoying monopolistic or near monopolistic position largely because of their shelter of restricted or prohibited imports or a high tariff wall. There are certain industries, specially some producing consumer goods, in which we are convinced, cost of production has remained high due to the fact that the top enterprises have not exerted themselves sufficiently, to improve technology or bring down costs, secure in their belief that in the absence of competition from abroad there was little risk of these enterprises a healthy stimulus to decrease costs by increasing production or by other means. This would be specially important and indeed effective in industries where the elasticity of demand is high so that with a little reduction in price, demand would register an appreciable increase.

Dr. P. S. Lokanathan, Director-General of the National Council of Applied Economic Research, was emphatic in his opinion that the only effective way to bring down costs and thereby price was to promote imports. "If you really want to bring down costs", the learned professor told us, "you must be a little merciless, you must use the mechanism of prices. You must allow some imports to come and see that over a period of years, our prices come to international standards. That should be our goal." Returning to this point later in the discussion, he said: "what we should do is to bring more and imports and force the Indian businessman to reduce prices as in other countries. The whole mechanics has got to be revised". When it was put to him that if we are not able to export, it would not be possible to increase imports, Dr. Lokanathan replied: "You must have a phased programme by which you say that over a period of certain years if you cannot produce so much you will have to go out."

We are bound to say that there is some force in this view. We are also aware of a somewhat similar provision in the Canadian legislation to fight monopolistic practices. At the same time, faced as the Government of India is with a difficult position about the foreign exchange, it may not be possible to give practical effect to the theory that the best way of inducing Indian businessman to reduce prices is to confront them with the likelihood imports being allowed. Even so, we think that the Government may in future years, specially if the balance of payment position improves, be able to take some action in this direction.

Countervailing action by the public sector may sometimes prove useful to prevent concentration of economic power and its evil effects. It is rightly said that in many industries a very large amount of capital, exceeding sometimes several crores of rupees, is required to set up an economic unit of production; only big business can bring in such amounts. No small enterprise will ordinarily apply for licence for such production, and if it does apply, it is not likely to receive favourable consideration. So, big business steps in and necessarily there is growth of concentration. A rival unit, if at all can only come from another big businessman. Government may usefully consider in such cases the setting up of the new unit of production in the public sector. This may be considered not only when an altogether new industry is proposed to be started, but also where an existing industry requires expansion. Assuming, for example, that a particular capital intensive industry is in need of expansion it would be worthwhile—as a countervailing measure—to start one or two units of production in the public sector. That would not only prevent the growth of concentration that would otherwise occur in private hands, if a private industry was allowed to start the unit but might also be helpful to counteract the monopolistic practices by combinations between the few companies already in the field.

In making this recommendation, we are not unaware of the risk that a 'competitive' unit in the public sector may not have the efficiency to enable it to compete. "If a public enterprise is put into counteract private sector then the efficiency will further go down", was the opinion expressed by the Indian Chamber of Commerce delegation. There is certainly the risk that an inefficient public sector unit will have a harmful effect on the private sector units and will prove expensive to the consumer or to the general tax payer.

We are permitting ourselves, however, to hope that in course of time the efficiency of the public sector will increase considerably ; besides, where a public sector enterprise is set up to counteract unfair practices of one or more private sector enterprises, it will be spurred to great efforts to be efficient. Where such an enterprise is started, special action might be called for to maintain its efficiency both as regards cost and quality.

The production of small scale industries has been of some importance in combating the effect of concentration in certain industries. In matches, for example, though Western India Match Co. is by far the largest producer, and has immense resources, a restraining influence on its power and its conduct is undoubtedly exercised by the numerous small producers of matches, operating mostly in cottages without even the assistance of any mechanised factory. In soaps, though Hindustan Lever and Tatas are the big producers and are probably the price leaders, they cannot ignore the reality, that if the price was fixed too high, many of their present customers, would transfer their patronage to the sopas made by the small scale producers, whose outturn is substantial. In sewing machines, bicycles and radios also, the small scale manufacturers are known to play an important part in checking the power in the hands of big business.

It appears to us that the Government is fully conscious of the importance of helping the growth of small scale industries. Various steps have already been taken for that purpose and others are being contemplated as a result of the recommendations of the Lokanathan Committee and other Committees. It is therefore unnecessary for us to make any special recommendation in this respect.

Consumer co-operative societies can play an important part in the distribution channel as a means of keeping unscrupulous traders within control. It has to be recognised that there has to be a considerable increase in the number of consumer cooperative societies and substantial improvement in their working before one can expect them to play a really important part. The Mirdha Committee which has recently examined the working of co-operative societies has made a number of suggestions which we believe will prove useful.

A more difficult question is what part co-operative societies can play in checking concentration of economic power in the production of goods. One instance of success in this direction in the Kaira-Cooperative Society (the makers of Amul Milk products) which was able to break the virtual monopoly of Glaxo in Baby Food some years ago. Cooperative sugar factories have also been working successfully in Maharashtra but it has to be noticed that even before that there was no concentration in the production of sugar. On the materials we could collect, we have not been able to reach any firm conclusion as to the usefulness of co-operative enterprises in fighting concentration of economic power generally.

Purchasing departments of Government may sometimes be able to take action that will curb the power of dominant concerns in some industries. Some of the smaller industrialists complained to us that far from helping them, Government policy in purchase tended to strengthen the hold of monopolistic concerns. Special favour, we are told, was shown to such dominating concerns as Dunlops in tyres, and the members of ELMI in electric lamps. We can see no reason why authorities like the D.G.S.D. who is in charge of purchases of various articles for the Government of India, and purchasing autborities of the State Governments, should not give more of their patronage to the smaller and weaker concerns, provided this can be done without harming the tax payer's interests. Such assistance will go some way—if not always a long way—in breaking the domination of the big concerns, by bringing up stronger competition.

One other direction in which action can be profitably taken to reduce the evil effect of concentrated economic power and monopolistic and restrictive practices is the establishment of consumer societies. This suggestion came from an experienced industrialist,

Mr. Lindsay, who led the delegation from the Bengal Chamber of Commerce. "It is a matter of the consumers organising themselves. He has got to do something" said he. We consider this a very helpful and important suggestion.

The history of how labour trade unions have helped workmen in the industries in their bargaining with employers is too well known to require any detailed description. There is no reason why consumer societies should not with proper encouragement gather sufficient strength in course of time to be able to fight back against practices of industrialists—whether manufacturer, or trader—which tend to injure consumer's interests.

In Calcutta, which has been notorious in recent years for hoarding and profiteering practices, consumers have from time to time taken action by way of boycotting certain traders and by collective refusal to buy, with good results. Unfortunately, because of lack of proper organisation, the more vigorous section of consumers have on such occasions often come into conflict with the guardians of law and order, so that the police arm of the State promptly and heavily came down on the side of the traders and the movement failed.

Delhi also saw last year a price of resistance movement which achieved some degree of success. Ad hoc consumers' bodies took up the purchase and sale of milk and vegetables, and were able to curve to some extent the extensive profiteering that was going on. As was to be expected, however, these activities did not continue for long.

What we have in our mind are consumers' societies, which will not carry on trade themselves; but will operate as the watch dogs of consumers' interest. With proper guidance such consumers' societies may be expected to try to achieve their objective by peaceful means which will in the long run prove more effective than violent outbursts. Some financial resources will be necessary; but that should not prove difficult. Their success will, however, depend principally on the support of the members—consumers themselves and the ability of those at the head of the organisation to evoke a sufficient degree of self-denial—by refusal to purchase at an unreasonable price—if so directed by the society.

These should be purely unofficial bodies—preferably registered. If they are to be useful, they must eschew politics. Organisation of some such societies in the principal cities of every State? By persons of known integrity and organisational ability who have kept away from politics—and there should be no dearth of such men and women in our country—should not prove difficult. Once the principal cities lead the way small centres of population will not be slow to follow their example.

Well established consumer societies are likely to be of great assistance in bringing the grievances of consumers to the permanent body contemplated by us. One of the several ways in which such a body should be able to initiate action to remedy the consequences of restrictive practices, including hoarding, cornering, and profiteering will necessarily be the investigation of complaints from the persons most affected by them—whether they are producers, traders or consumers. Producers and traders are frequently organised in associations and it will be possible for them to take appropriate action through the association. Unless and until consumers have also their associations they can only make individual complaints. There is, however, the obvious risk in such individual complaints, of many being made frivolously; and it will be difficult to discriminate between the numerous complaints that may be made, If there is a well established society with a fair number of consumers in a local market as its members so that it can be considered to be representative of the local consumers taken as a whole, the permanent body will be in a much better position to take cognisance of such complaints, and to pass proper orders.

RECOMMENDATIONS Legislative

In trying to profit from the experience of other countries we cannot afford to lose sight of the many vital differences between them and our land as regards political history and economic conditions. A bird's eye view of the special circumstances that are relevant in this connection will therefore be useful.

Ours is an under-developed country, hopefully claiming to have a developing economy. Centuries of foreign dominition have sapped the people's energy and enterprise. A large part of the population is on the verge of starvation. Of the remainder the vast majority is a long way from affluence. The pressure of population is high and still it continues to increase at a tremendous pace. The incidence of unemployment and underemployment is very great. Foreign debt incurred mostly to assist the necessary process of industrialisation has been steadily accumulating.

Sustained improvements in exports is urgently required in order that an excess of exports over imports can be achieved to ensure repayment of part at least of the foreign debt, lightening the burden of debt service. For this purpose, and for reducing unemployment and alleviating the plight of the common man, vastly increased production is essential, both in industries and agriculture. Rapid industrialisation, on which Parliament and Government have rightly set their hears is bound, however, to bring with it even greater concentration of economic power than before, as time goes on and is likely to give rise to monopolistic conditions, often bringing in their train various monopolistic practices. Persistent shortage of commodities has generally proved too strong a temptation for many businessmen to maintain fair trade practices, and hoarding and cornering and profiteering have been common. Other restrictive practices have also been widely practised. The attempts of Government by price control and other means to ease the situation have met with only partial success and general discontent due in a large measure to the frustration of the hopes and aspirations that the advent of independence has awakened in all with its potential threat to the stability of the political and economic structure of the country has been growing.

The above background highlights two important principles of securing the highest production possible and of ensuring that it is achieved with the least damage to the people at large and secures to them the maximum benefit. These two principles indicate important considerations for the formulation of the legislative policy:

(1) We need not strike at concentration of economic power as such, but should do so only when it becomes a menace to the best production (in quality and quantity) or to fair distribution.

(2) To accomplish this a consant watch must be kept by a body independent of Government—in addition to what is being done by Government and Parliament—that big business does not misuse its power.

(3) Monopolistic conditions in any industrial sphere are to be discouraged, if this can be done without injury to the interests of the general public.

(4) Monopolistic and restrictive practices must be curbed except when they conduce to the common good.

We trust that in formulating the principles as above we have been able to give full effect to the directive principles in article 39 of the Constitution. That article which has already been set out in a previous portion of the Report requires the State to direct its policy towards securing . . . that the operation of the economic system does not result in concentration of wealth and means of production to the common detriment. Clearly, what is directived to be guarded against is not concentration of economic power per set but such concentration as may be to the common detriment.

Applying these principles, we are of opinion that the primary function of the permanent body—we may conveniently refer to it as the "Commission"—should be directed against restrictive practices and monopolistic practices. To accomplish this task a beginning should be made with the compulsory registration of all restrictive practices. Such registration as we have already notices is an usual feature of the anti-trust legislation in European countries. There is considerable difference, however, between these countries as regards the consequence of such registration. We think that in the peculiar circumstances of this country, it would be wise to provide that registration of a practice should not mean either its approval or condemnation. The register should be open to public inspection so that wide publicity is given to restrictive practices that prevail in different trades and industries. The light of publicity may itself be of some use in inducing many to stop such practices as are likely to attract general public criticism and so to damage the reputation of the concerns. At the same time, the registration would facilitate the work of investigation of complaints from consumers and other members of the public, against restrictive practices.

The success of the Commission in curbing restrictive practices would largely depend upon fair and quick investigation of all such complaints. We consider it essential that the question whether a restrictive practice is to the common detriment or not should be decided judicially by those at the head of the permanent body; but for proper and systematic working it will be desirable that the judicial examination will take place ordinarily only if the Investigation Branch has reported that there is a prima facie reason to believe that any practice is to the common detriment.

This work of investigation should be the charge a Director of Investigation, to be attached to the permanent body. His task (as we apprehend it) would be something analoguous to that of the committing magistrate who holds a preliminary enquiry, whether certain cases should be committed for trial to the Court of Sessions or not.

The Director of Investigation should have power to institute an enquiry not only on receipt of complaint from the public but also on his own motion, if on information from any source whatsoever, he thinks fit so to do. The Central Government or State Government may also, report that restrictive practices believed to be injurious to the public interest are being pursued by any enterprise or a number of enterprises. The Commission should proceed to examine such charge, without any preliminary investigation by the Director.

Where the judicial examination results in a finding that no restrictive practice is being pursued or that though such a practice is being pursued, it is in the interest of the general public, or that it does not work to the common detriment, no further action need be taken, except that the decision should be given proper publicity in a suitable way. Where the decision is otherwise—in other words—where the finding is that one or more enterprises are guilty of pursuing a restrictive practice which is to the common detriment, something in addition to giving publicity to the finding is called for. We think the most fruitful line of action would be the issue by the Commission itself of an order to discontinue the practice. We are also of opinion that this should be final, subject only to an appeal to the Supreme Court and that it should have mandatory force.

We are happy to find that not one of the many industrialists who appeared before us raised any objection to these orders being mandatory. On the contrary, several of them spoke strongly and clearly in support of the view that if the permanent body is to be really useful, and not remain a mere 'paper tiger', it is essential that its decisions arrived at, after hearing all parties to the controversy, Special mention ought to be made in this connection of the views expressed by Mr. J.R.D. Tata and Mr. Choksi who appeared before us on behalf of the Tata Group of Industries and by Mr. Tandon, the head of the Lever Group of Industries in India. When it was put to Mr. Tata that to give the order of the proposed permanent body mandatory force, might embarrass Government, Mr. Tata made no secret of his apprehension that unless these orders were clearly made mandatory by law the status of the permanent body would become emasculated purely on political grounds or without any ground at all. Mr. Choksi was equally emphasitic in support of the suggestion that the permanent body's orders should have binding force subject to an appeal to the Supreme Court, and that it would not be open to a Department of Government to sit in judgement over its decisions. Mr. Tandon, who had in the course of discussions with us emphasized the importance of having such a body to create confidence in the public about the doings of the corporate sector, also agreed without hesitation that the decision of the proposed body should prevail. 'Government will have to make up its mind', he added, if it is going to appoint a Commission 'that it will have to be independent'.

We do not see any reasonable basis for the apprehension that by giving this body's decision mandatory force, the Government will be abdicating its role. After all, in a democracy, Government as the chosen instrument of the people, has and should have the right to decide policies. That body would be concerned not with laying down any policy but with the implementation of policies laid down by Government and Parliament. Thus, it is only if the Government decide on a policy that monopolistic and restrictive practices should be curbed and Parliament approves of it, that the permanent body could take action as regards such practices. Once the policy has been decided the Government should, we venture to say, have confidence in a body of the nature proposed by us that it would give effect to the Government policies truly and faithfully.

It will be, in our opinion worse than useless to create such a body and make its opinion only recommendatory. Far from allaying public apprehension, the removal of which is one of the major justifications for setting up such a body, the creation of a body with only a power to recommend and unable to take action itself would add fuel to the fire of public discontent.

It is, therefore, clearly necessary, in our opinion, that the orders of this body should be given a mandatory force and should be final, subject only to an appeal to the Supreme Court. In order that the mandate may be effective it would be necessary to provide for a daily fine for every day of disobedience of the order.

We have considered the question whether the Commission of an objectionable restrictive practice should be made punishable with imprisonment, where it is not already so, under the ordinary criminal law. In our opinion, such a course would be unwise in the circumstances of our country ; we think that the effect of a fine for disobedience of a "discontinuance" order should be watched for some years ; and the step of making the Commission of a restrictive practice punishable with imprisonment should be seriously considered only if experience shows that these remedies are ineffective in practice. We think it desirable, however, that where the guilty party is a corporation, the Directors themselves should be personally liable to pay the fine.

While this should be the general pattern of dealing with restrictive practices, some of these practices will require special treatment. One such is resale price maintenance. We have already noticed in our examination of foreign legislation that several countries consider resale price maintenance harmful and objectionable, per se. In that view, Canada, Sweden, Denmark and recently England has prohibited resale price maintenance. The main argument in support of resale price maintenance is that it enable small traders and shopkeepers to survive the competition of big merchants and powerful chain stores. Against this is to be weighed the injury to the public in general as a result of reduction competition in efficient salesmanship. It seems to be generally true to say that the consumers have to pay higher prices than would be the case if the maintenance of a fixed or minimum price was not insisted upon.

Mention must be made in this connection of the valuable opinion of the eminent industrialist, Mr. Arvind Mafatlal, "any competition between distributors will be partly neutralised", he said, "if there is a term that below this price, you must not sell." ". . . competition between distributors", he went to say, "should not be disturbed".

On an anxious consideration of the problem, we have come to the conclusion that the harmful effect of resale price maintenance for out-weight its advantages. In our opinion, the interests of the general public demand that resale price maintenance should be prohibited subject to exceptions being made as regards loss leader sales.

The other species of restrictive practices, apart from resale price maintenance for which special provision requires to be made is the practice of hoarding, cornering and profiteering. There is hardly anybody in India who has not been a victim of this practice from time to time. Whenever there is a slight shortage-even temporarily-in any consumer goods for which the demand is urgent and inelastic, almost every trader—it is perhaps unnecessary to use the qualification "almost"—conceals his stock and blandly tells the customers that he has not got the commodity in stock, often putting the blame on producers for keeping him in short supply. After some time when the customer can no longer do without the goods, he proceeds to dispose of his stock "underground stock" at exorbitant prices to such customers who are prepared to pay the high price and—this is important—who would not insist upon a cash memo showing the price that is charged and is not likely to be difficult. Wheat, rice, sugar, edible oils, drugs, baby food—each of these commodities and many others have had their share of hoarding and cornering practice. There is hardly anybody—except perhaps the traders themselves—who has not condemned these practices. They have been called wicked, anti-social, criminal, but still these make their appearance every time there is any apprehension of even a slight shortage of such commodities.

While most of the industrialists appeared to condemn these practices many of them seem to think that these practices could arise only in situations of shortages and that the only way of curing this malady in the body economic is to increase production so that shortages would disappear. We are inclined to agree that if the quantity available is well above the demand at the market price, cornering will not be ordinarily a profitable venture. We think however, that even where the supply is only slightly below the demand a creation of artificial scarsity by cornering goods is possible and has actually happened. We are convinced that these practices of cornering and profiteering are so dangerous to the body politics, apart from their serious effect on the poorer sections of the people that no stone should be left unturned to remove or at least reduce them. That is why we think that over and above all the other efforts being made by Government through the agency of the criminal courts and otherwise, the permanent body proposed by us should also play its part in this important task.

For this purpose, the body should be vested with the power to take action against any enterprise—which refuses to sell at the usual rate—except on reasonable grounds. The French Code contains a provision on these lies and we understand that it has proved useful. The most effective action for the body to take would be to suspend or cancel the licence to carry on the trade or industry, in addition to the imposition of a fine. Mr. Lindsay, leading the Bengal Chamber of Commerce, said that it would be worth trying such a step to fight hoarding.

To give relief against monopolistic practices, the Commission will have to proceed on several different lines of action. First and foremost, it will have to give its verdict about the reasonable price to be charged by the enterprises holding monopolistic position, where it is satisfied that unreasonable prices are being charged ; when such a verdict has been given, after of course, hearing all parties, that would be binding. The Commission may pass such other orders as it may think fit to remedy or prevent any mischief resulting from the monopolistic practice. These may include regulation of production or supply, prohibiting any practice likely to lessen competition or fixing standards for the goods. The Commission may also declare particular agreements as unlawful and require any party to determine the agreement.

As monopolistic positions tend to create complacency and to destroy the urge to improved methods of production, the Commission will have to examine, from time to time, the structure in the monopoly industry, so that it can suggest suitable ways for effecting improvement and avoiding obsolescence.

Mergers and amalgamations which often pave the way to monopoly, have been comparatively few in this country. But, there is every prospect of their becoming more frequent in future. In deciding what action to take about these to prevent the emergence of monopolistic conditions, we have to remember, however, that mergers and amalgamations may sometimes be called for in the best interests of the country. Horizontal mergers and amalgamations may often be an essential mode to improve efficiency and to achieve economies of scale, while vertical mergers and amalgamations may also help to cut costs. It will, in our opinion, be wrong to look upon mergers or amalgamations to be per se harmful to public interest. A cautious approach to the problem is therefore desirable.

Bearing that in mind we think it desirable that where a big enterprise which already holds a dominant position as regards any particular commodity wants to go in for merger or amalgamation with any other concern it should apply directly to the Commission. It will be proper, in our opinion, to take the production, supply or distribution of 1/3rd of a particular commodity or service produced, supplied or distributed in the country as the index of "dominance" for this purpose. In deciding whether an enterprise is dominant or not in the above sense, it is necessary to take into account not only what is produced, supplied or distributed by one particular undertaking but also what is produced by other units of inter-connected undertakings. We think that the possession of one crore or more of assets would be the proper measure of bigness that should attract this recommendation. The Commission should not give its approved to the proposal unless it is satisfied that its harmful effect in aggravating the monopolistic position is clearly less than its beneficial-effects on the economy in the shape of higher production, lesser costs and improvement in quality. Refusal of sanction by the Commission should totally bar the merger or amalgamation. In our opinion, attempts of 'take-over' should be dealt with in the same manner as merger or amalgamation.

We have considered the question whether the Commission should have the power to prevent such expansion of similar dominant enterprises as might be harmful to public interests. The majority is of the view that it is necessary to vest the Commission with such power. Exercise of such power is not likely to run counter ordinarily to Governmental policy in these matters. For this purpose, it will be convenient to provide that whenever such an enterprise applies to the Government for substantial expansion, (i.e. not less than 25 per cent) of its present line of production it shall give notice to the Commission of the proposed application. The Commission should decide as early as possible whether such expansion is or is not likely to be detrimental to public interests. If within a period of 30 days no action is taken in the matter by the Commission, the prayer of expansion will be dealt with by the relevant authority on its merits. If however the Commission decides to inquire into the matter by issue of notice to all interested parties, including the Government, expansion should not be allowed until and unless the Commission has approved of it on finding that it is not detrimental to public interests. Mr. R.C. Dutt (who has recorded his views in a separate note) and Dr. I.G. Patel do not share the above views. In their opinion, all matters of expansion should be left entirely to the Government.

We also think it desirable that no person who is a director of a big dominant undertaking shall be appointed director of another undertaking engaged in the same line of business without obtaining the prior approval of the Commission. This will not apply to inter-connected undertakings. The Commission should not refuse approval unless satisfied that the effect of such interlocking directorate would be to reduce competition unreasonably.

Apart from all this, the Commission will have to keep a watch generally over dominant concerns—particularly the big ones. For this purpose, it may be made obligatory for all such concerns to submit annual returns to the Commission, containing details about their organisation, business, conduct, practices, management, costs of production and connections with other undertakings as may be prescribed by the Commission by Rules.

We see no reason why monopolies arising from parents should not be subject to the Commission's jurisdiction in the same manner (as regards monopolistic and restrictive practices and other matters) just as other monopolies are. In order to avoid any conflict with the operation of the parent law, we however think it desirable that a definite provision should be made to this effect that no order made by the Commission with respect of monopolistic or restrictive trade practice shall operate so as to restrict, (a) the right of any person to restrain any infringement of a patent granted in India or (b) to restrict any person as to the conditions which he attaches to a licence to do anything the doing of which but for the licence would be an infringement of patent granted in India.

The next important question is: what powers the Commission should be given as regards country-wise concentration of economic power. Stated briefly, such power, as we have already seen, arises from some successful entrepreneurs launching into diversified lines of production, or a number of entrepreneurs engaged in different lines of production forming one single group for the purpose of improved efficiency or better financial resources or other benefits. In the ultimate analysis, every such case is an instance of diversified production. Thus, country-wise concentration of economic power is inextricably bound up with diversification in industry. It is difficult, if not impossible, to prevent country-wise concentration, without distroying the process of diversification. It was pressed before us by all the industrialists that diversification is very necessary for the rapid industrialisation of the country on the right lines. Similar opinion was also expressed by the economists. "diversification of business", said Dr. Lokanathan, "is a very important and legitimate form of expansion for industry." "There is some advantage", said Dr. Muranjan, "in diversification of production". There is, in our opinion, considerable force in this view. In all the developed countries of the world, diversification into many products by one concern or by a group of concerns, held together by the relationship of holding company and subsidiary company, or otherwise, has been found to be a useful step in the process of industrialisation. It is rightly claimed that such diversification provides on the one hand a cushion for the group as a whole against the risks that are inherent in any particular line of production by changes of fashion, variance in the world position of supply and demand, introduction of new products and various other causes; and on the other, by making available to the several lines of production in the group larger financial resources, wider technical know-how and expertise, the ability to cultivate foreign markets, greater bargaining power with Government and others, than would otherwise have been possible.

We are aware of the strong feeling of aversion and antipathy for these industrial empires. We are also not unmindful of the unhealthy effect these industrial colossues m y have on the political and social fields, even where they do not indulge in conduct which are clearly shown to be harmful in the economic sphere. In a previous portion of the report we have mentioned the risk of the power big business has to corrupt political democracy. We have discussed also at some length the evil social effects that the concentration of wealth produces by concentration of economic power. The temptation to solve this even by dismembering the existing industrial empires and to curb the formation of future empires of this nature is great indeed. It may indeed not even be difficult to evolve measures for this purpose.

We are however of opinion, in the light of experience of other countries and having regard to the urgent need of the country's Industrial development that diversification with its necessary concomitant countrywise concentration of economic power, even though an evil in some respects, is a necessary evil in the economic interests of the country. It would not be right at the present stage of our industrial development to attempt to place any curb on diversification (which in turn gives rise to country-wise concentration) that may result in a slowing down of the pace of such development.

We are fully conscious that the constitution makers, in speaking of concentration of wealth and means of production in Art. 39, had in mind not only productwise concentration but also country-wise concentration. As we have pointed out above, the directive principle in Art. 39 does not condemn concentration as such, but only such concentration of economic power as may be to the common detriment.

In Chapter VII we have already recommended the use by Government of the powers conferred on them by the law as respects licensing to prevent the growth of concentration wherever it is to the common detriment. The legislative measures we have already recommended, if adopted, will enable the Commission, which would also be required under the proposed law to keep a watchful eye on all dominant enterprises, to take suitable action where industrialists who have achieved concentration, whether country-wise or product-wise, are guilty of monopolistic or restrictive practices. Where there is a risk of such concentration corroding the political machinery, the remedy lies in proper action being taken by the political parties themselves. As regards its evil effects in the social field, the emergence of a strong public opinion against corruption, helped by the right emphasis on values is the ultimate remedy. We believe that by proper use of licensing and other powers vested in Government under the existing laws Government can effectively prevent the growth of of country-wise concentration wherever it is to the common detriment. We do not think it necessary to vest the Commission with any power in this behalf.

Coming now to the constitution of the commission, we recommend that while the minimum number of members should be three, the maximum may for the present be fixed at nine. The work of the commission would be to a great extent judicial in nature. Most of the industrialists strongly expressed the view that the commission should be strong and independent. We recommend that the chairman of the commission should be appointed from among persons who are or have been judges of the Supreme Court or Chief Justices of a High Court. Membership should, in our opinion, be limited to persons who are not less than 50 years of age. Only men of ability integrity and standing who have adequate knowledge or experience, or have shown capacity, in dealing with problems relating to economics, law, commerce, industry, public affairs or administration should be appointed as members.

We do not wish to make any specific recommendation as regards salaries and allowances for the Chairman and Members. We have no doubt that the Central Government will take care to fix these so as to attract the best talent in the country.

It will be necessary to have a Registrar for registration of restrictive practices. This officer may be appointed by the central Government, but should work in accordance with the directions of the Commission. The Director of Investigation should be an officer of the Commission and should be appointed by it.

We give below the draft of a Bill that has been prepared by us to give effect to the recommendations that we have made above. In this draft we have included a definition of monopolistic and restrictive practices in amplification of what has been already stated in Chapter V. This has been done in order to facilitate the administration of the law by the commission. Other consequential details and procedural matters have also been included in the draft. These, we believe, will explain themselves and do not require any discusssion here. Provision has been made also in the Draft Bill as regards penalties for infringement of the law.

DRAFT BILL

The Monopolies And Restrictive Trade Practices Bill, 1965

A Bill to provide that the operation of the economic system does not result in the concentration of economic power to the common detriment for the control of monopolies and the prohibition of monopolistic and restric tive trade practices when found contrary to the public interest and for matters connected therewith or incidental thereto.

Be it enacted by Parliament in the Sixteen Year of the Republic of India as follow :

Chapter I

Parliamentary

Short title extent and commencement: This Act may be called the Monopolies and Restrictive Trade Practices Act, 1965.

It extends to the whole of India except the State of Jammu and Kashmir.

It shall come into force on such date as the Central Government by notification in the Official Gazette may appoint.

Definition : In this Act, unless the context otherwise requires,—

'Agreement' includes any agreement, arrangement or understanding whether or not it is intended to be enforceable (apart from any provision of this Act) by legal proceedings;

'Commission' means the Monopolies and Restrictive Trade Practices Commission established under section 5;

'Director' means the Director of Investigations appointed under section 9;

'Dominant undertaking' means an undertaking which, either by itself or along with inter-connected undertakings :—

(a) Produces, supplies or distributes at least one-third or the goods (including imported goods) or any description that are produced, supplied or distributed in India; or

(b) Provides at least one-third of any service in India; and where the production, supply or distribution of any goods or the provision of any service within the meaning if this clause is shared by inter-connected undertakings, each such undertaking shall be deemed to be a dominant undertaking for the purposes of this Act.

'India' means the territories to which this Act extends;

"Inter-connected undertaking" an undertaking is said to be inter-connected with another—

In the case of firms, if they have one or more common partners; and

In the case of bodies corporate, if—

One owns or manages the other; or

One is a subsidiary of the other; or

The two undertakings have a common management, or a common holding company; or

A majority of shareholders of the one holds a majority of shares in the other; or

In any other manner, one exercises control over the other;

'Member' means a member of the Commission;

'Prescribed' means prescribed by rules or regulations made under this Act;

'Price', in relation to the sale of any goods or to the performance of any service, includes every valuable consideration whatsoever, whether direct or indirect; and includes any consideration which in effect relates to the sale of any goods or to the performance of any service, although ostensibly relating to any other matter or thing;

'Register' means the register kept by the Registrar under Section 24;

'Registrar' means the Registrar of Restrictive Trade Agreements appointed under Section 22;

'Retailer', in relation to the sale of any goods, includes every person, other than a wholesaler, who sells the goods to any other person, and in respect of the sale of goods by a wholesaler to any person for any purpose other than re-sale, includes that wholesaler ;

'Service' means service of any description which is made available to potential users, and includes the provision of facilities in connection with banking, insurance, transport, the supply of electrical or other energy, boarding and lodging, entertainment, amusement or the purveying of news or other information, but does not include the rendering of service free of charge or under a contract of service;

'Trade' means any trade, business, industry, profession, occupation or undertaking relating to the production, supply or distribution of goods;

'Trade association' means a body of persons (whether incorporated or not) which is formed for the purpose of furthering the trade interests of its members, or of persons represented by its members;

'Trade practice' means any practice relating to the carrying on of any trade; and includes anything done by any person which controls or affects the price charged by, or the method of trading of, any trader or any class of traders; and includes also a single or isolated action of any person in relation to any trade;

'Undertaking' means an industrial or a commercial undertaking engaged in the production, supply of distribution of goods (including imported goods) of any description or the provision of any service, whether the undertaking is owned by an individual or is a firm or a body corporate;

'Wholesaler', in relation to the sale of any goods, means a person who sells the goods to any person for the purpose of resale.

Expressions used but n t defined in th's Act, and defined in Ccmpanies Act, 1956 (1 of 1956), have the meanings assigned to them in that Act.

Act not to apply in certain casss : Unless the Government, by notification in the Official Gazette, otherwise directs, this Act shall not apply to—

(a) Any undertaking owned or controlled by the Government, including a Government Company;

(b) Any trade union or other association of workmen or employees formed for their own reasonable protection as such workmen or employees;

(c) Any corporation established under a special law, whether a Central, Provincial or State Act;

(d) Any undertaking engaged in an industry, the control of which has been taken over by the Union under a Central Act as being expedient in the public interest, to the extent to which the provisions of that Act or any rules there-under relating to the production, supply or distribution or any goods by the undertaking are inconsistent with the provisions of this Act.

Application of other laws not barred : Save as otherwise expressly provided herein, the provisions of this Act shall be in addition to, and not in derogation of, any other law for the time being in force.

Chapter II

The Monopolies And Restrictive Trade Practices Commission

Establishment and Constitution of Commission : (1) For the purposes of this Act, the Central Government shall establish a commission to be known as the Monopolies and Restrictive Trade Practices Commission which shall consist of not less than three and not more than nine members to be appointed by the Central Government.

One of the members, who shall be appointed the Chairman thereof, shall be a person who is or has been a judge of the Supreme Court or the Chief Justice of a High Court, and the other members to be appointed shall be men of ability, integrity and standing who have adequate knowledge or experience, or have shown capacity, in dealing with problems relating to economics, law, commerce, industry, public affairs or administration.

Before appointing a person to be a member, the Central Government satisfy itself that the person will have no such financial or other interest as is likely to affect prejudicially his functions as such member.

No person shall be appointed as a member unless he has attained the age of fifty years.

Condition of service of members : (1) Every member shall hold office for such period not exceeding five years as may be specified in the instrument of his appointment, but shall be eligible for re-appointment.

Notwithstanding anything contained in sub-section (1) a member may—

(a) By writing under his hand addressed to the Central Government resign his office at any time;

(b) Be removed from office in accordance with the provisions contained in Section 7.

There shall be paid to a member such salaries and allowances at the Central Government may determine :

Provided that such salaries and allowances shall not be varied to the disadvantage of the member after his appointment.

A member ceasing to hold office as such shall not hold any appointment in, or be connected with the management or administration of, any private industry or undertaking for a period of five years from so ceasing to hold office.

Removal of members from office in certain circumstances : (1) The Central Government may remove from office any member who:

(a) Has been adjudged an insolvent; or

(b) Has been convicted of an offence which, in the opinion of the Central Government, involves moral turpitude; or

(c) Has become physically or mentally incapable of acting as such member; or

(d) Has acquired such financial or other interest as is likely to affect prejudicially his functions as a member; or

(e) Has so abused his position as to render his continuance in office detrimental to the public interest.

Notwithstanding anything contained in Sub-section (1), no member shall be removed from his office on the ground specified in clause (d) or clause (e) of that subsection unless the Supreme Court, on a reference being made to it in this behalf, has, on inquiry held in accordance with such procedure as it may prescribe in this behalf, reported that the member ought on such ground to be removed.

The removal of any member under Sub-section (a) shall be reported as soon as may be to both Houses of Parliament.

Oath of office by members : Every person appointed to be a member shall, before he enters upon in office, make and subscribe before the person specified by the Central Government in this behalf an oath according to the form set out hereunder:—

"I, A.B., having been appointed a member of the Monopolies and Restrictive Trade Practices Commission do swear/affirm that I will bear true faith and allegiance to the constitution of India as by law established and I will duly and faithfully and to the best of my ability, knowledge and judgement perform the duties of my office without fear or favour, affection or ill-will".

Staff of the Commission : Subject to such rules as may be made in this behalf, the Commission may appoint an officer to be known as the Director of Investigations for making any investigation for the purposes of this Act, and in addition, may appoint such member of other officers and employees as it may think fit for the purpose of enabling it to efficiently exercise its powers or discharge its functions.

The conditions of service of all persons appointed by the Commission shall be such as it may, by regulations made in this behalf, determine.

Salaries etc. of staff to be charged on this Consolidated Fund : The salaries and allowances payable to members and the administrative expenses of the Commission, including all salaries, allowances and pensions payable to or in respect of officers and others employees appointed by the Commission shall be charged on the Consolidated Fund of India.

Chapter III

Concentration Of Economic Powers

Application of Chapter : This Chapter shall apply to a dominant undertaking only if its assets are not less than one crore of rupees in value.

Expansion of dominant undertakings : Subject to the provisions contained in Section 13, where a dominant undertaking to which this Chapter applies, for the purpose of increasing its share in the production, supply or distribution of goods (including imported goods) of any description or in any service provided by it in India, proposes to substantially expand its activities by the issue of fresh capital or by the installation of new machinery or other equipment or in any other manner, it shall, before taking any action to give effect to the expansion, give to the Commission, notice of the expansion in writing in the prescribed form, and, it within a period of thirty days from the date of receipt of the notice by the Commission no action is taken by the Commission thereon, the expansion may be given effect to, subject to the provisions of any other law for the time being in force.

The Commission may, within the period of thirty days aforesaid, call upon the undertaking to satisfy it that the expansion is not likely to be detrimental to the public interest and, where it does so, an order in writing of the Commission approving the expansion shall be necessary before the expansion is given effect to under this or any other law for the time being in force.

Explanation : For the purposes of this action, an undertaking is said to substantially expand its activities if after such expansion the production, supply or distribution of any goods or the provision of any service by the undertaking is likely to result in an increase by not less than twenty-five per cent, of its production, supply or distribution or the service provided by it, as the case may be, before the expansion.

Mergers and amalgamations : Where a merger or amalgamation is proposed between—

(a) Two or more bodies corporate and one of them is a dominant undertaking to which this Chapter applies; or

(b) A body corporate having assets not less than one crore of rupees in value and another body corporate as a result of which the share of the undertaking resulting from the merger or amalgamation in the production, supply or distribution of goods (including imported goods) of any description in India or in the provision of any service in India is likely to be one half or more ;

The merger of amalgamation shall not be sanctioned by any court under the Companis Act, 1956 (1 of 1956), or under any other law for the time being in force or be recognised for any purpose unless the Commission in the first instance has approved of the merger or amalgamation, by order in writing, after being satisfied, on application made to it in this behalf, that the merger or amalgamation is not likely to be detrimental to the public interest.

The provisions of sub-section (1) shall apply in relation to the take over of one undertaking by another, both being bodies corporate, as they apply in relation to mergers for amalgamation.

Nothing contained in sub-section (1) shall apply in the case of any amalgamation for which provision is made by order of the Central Government under Section 396 of the Companies Act, 1956 (1 of 1956).

Duty of undertakings to furnish information : (1) Every undertaking to which this section applies shall furnish to the Commission at such intervals and in such form as may be prescribed full information as to the nature and extent of the activities carried on by it, the connection between it and any other undertaking over which it may have control, as well as such other information relating to its organisation, business, cost of production, conduct, practices, management and connection with other undertakings as may be prescribed, to enable the Commission to effectively discharge its functions under this Act.

This section applies to—

(a) Every dominant undertaking to which this Chapter applies,

(b) Every undertaking not falling within clause

(a) whose assets, whether individually or in conjunction with the assets of any other undertaking over which it may have control, are five crores of rupees or more in value;

(c) Any undertaking which may be called upon by the Commission, by general or special order, to furnish any such information as may be required by this section.

Directors of dominant undertakings not to be appointed directors of competing undertakings—(1) After the commencement of this Act, no person who is a director of a dominant undertaking to which this Chapter applies shall be appointed as a director of another undertaking engaged in the same line of business, not being an inter-connected undertaking, except with the prior approval of the Commission, and any appointment contrary to the provisions of this section shall be void.

(2) The approval of the Commission to any such appointment as is referred to in sub-section (1) shall not be refused unless the Commission is satisfied that the effect of such appointment is, or would be, to unreasonably reduce or limit competition in that line of business.

Explanation—For the purposes of this section, the expression 'undertaking engaged in the same line of business' means an undertaking—

(a) Engaged in the production of any raw material intended for use of which may be used in the production of the goods by either of the undertakings ;

(b) Engaged in the production of the same goods as those produced by the other undertaking or any other goods which are or may be used as substitutes therefor.

Powers under Chapter how to be exercised (1) In exercising its powers under this Chapter, the Commission shall take into account all matters which appear in the particular circumstances to be relevant and, among other things, regard shall be had to the need, consistently with the general economic position of the country:—

(a) To achieve the production, supply and distribution by the most efficient and economical means of goods of such types and qualities, in such volume and at such prices as will best meet the requirements of the home and overseas markets ;

(b) To have the industry organised in such a way that its efficiency is progressively increased ;

(c) To ensure the best use and distribution of men, materials and industrial capacity in India ;

(d) To effect technical and technological improvements in the industry and the expansion of existing markets and the opening up of new markets ;

(e) To encourage new enterprises for stimulating competition and to prevent excessive concentration of economic power.

Before making any order under this Chapter the Commission shall give an opportunity to the Central Government and to any other person who in its opinion may be interested in the matter to be heard.

Chapter IV

Monopolistic Practices

Monopolistic undertaking defined : For the purposes of this Chapter, 'monopolistic undertaking' means—

(a) A dominant undertaking ; or

(b) An undertaking which, together with not more than two other independent undertakings, produces, supplies or distributes not less than one-half of the goods (including imported goods) of any description that are produced, supplies or distributed in India, or provides not less than one-half of any service in India.

Monopolistic trade practices : A monopolistic undertaking is said to indulge in a monopolistic trade practice if—

(a) By limiting, reducing or otherwise controlling the production, supply or distribution of goods of any specified description or the supply of any service or in any other manner it seeks to maintain prices at an unreasonable level;

(b) It adopts any practices or pursues any commercial policy which has or is likely to have the effect of unreasonably preventing or lessening competition in the production, supply or distribution of any goods or in the supply of any service;

(c) Due to lack of competition, it limits technical development or capital investment to the detriment of national economy, or allows the quality of its goods to deteriorate.

Investigation by Commission of monopolistic trade practices : (1) Subject to the other provisions contained in this Act and the rules made thereunder, it shall be the duty of the Commission to inquire into every case which may come before it under this Act in which a monopolistic undertaking is said to be indulging in a monopolistic trade practice and, if as a result of such inquiry, the Commission is of opinion that, having regard to the economic conditions prevailing in the country and to all other matters which appear in the particular circumstances to be relevant, the practice operates or may be expected to operate against the public interest, it may pass such orders as it may think fit to remedy or prevent any mischiefs which result or may result form such practice.

2. Any order made under this section may include an order :

(a) Regulating the production, supply or distribution of any goods by the undertaking or the supply of any service by it and fixing the prices or terms of sale thereof ;

(b) Prohibiting the undertaking from resorting to any act or practice which might lessen competition in such production, distribution or supply;

(c) Fixing standards for the goo s produced by the undertaking;

(d) Declaring to be unlawful, except to such extent and in such circumstances as may be provided by or under the order, the making or carrying out of any such agreement as may be specified or described in the order;

(e) Requiring any party to any such agreement as may be so specified or described to determine the agreement within such time as may be so specified, either wholly or to such extent as may be specified.

3. Where in respect of an undertaking—

(a) An inquiry under this Act is pending before the Commission, then, notwithstanding anything contained in the Industris (Development and Regulation) Act, 1951 (65 of 1951), the Central Government shall not make or cause to be made an investigation in respect of that undertaking under section 15 of that Act; or

(b) An investigation under section 15 aforesaid is pending or any directions issued under that section are in force, nothing contained in this Chapter shall be deemed to authorise the Commission to undertake an inquiry in respect of that undertaking.

Chapter V

Restrictive Trade Practices

Restrictive trade practice defined: A trade practice is said to be a restrictive trade practice if it has, or may have, the effect of preventing, distorting or restricting competition in any manner; and, in particular, if it tends to obstruct the flow of capital or resources into the stream of production or to the manipulation of prices, conditions of delivery or the flow of supplies in the market relating to specified goods or services in such a manner as to impose on consumers unjustified costs or restrictions.

Registrable agreements relating to restrictive trade practice: (1) Any agreement relating to a restrictive trade practice falling within one or more of the following categories shall be subject to registration in accordance with the provisions of this Chapter:

(a) Any agreement between producers or, as the case may be, wholesalers to restrict by any method the persons or classes of persons to whom they sell;

(b) Any agreement between wholesalers or, as the case may be, retailers to restrict by any method the persons or classes of persons from whom they buy;

(c) Any agreement between producers, wholesalers or retailers, as the case may be, to sell goods only at prices agreed upon between themselves;

(d) Any agreement requiring a purchaser of goods as a condition of such purchase to purchase some other goods of the seller;

(e) Any agreement restricting in any manner the purchaser in the course of his trade from acquiring or otherwise dealing in any goods other than those of the seller;

(f) Any agreement between producers, wholesalers or contractors, as the case may be, to purchase goods or tender for the sale or purchase of goods only at prices or on terms agreed upon between themselves;

(g) Any agreement between producers and wholesalers or between wholesalers and retailers or any combination of them to grant or allow concessions or benefits, including allowances, discounts, rebates or credit, in connection with, or by reason of dealings;

(h) Any agreement to sell goods on condition that the prices to be charged on resale by the purchaser shall be the prices stipulated by the seller, unless it is clearly stated that prices lower than those prices may be charged;

(i) Any agreement between producers or wholesalers or between a producer any and other person to limit, restrict or withhold the output or supply of any goods or allocate any area or market for the disposal of any goods;

(j) Any agreement between producers not to employ or restrict the employment of any method, machinery or process in the manufacture of goods;

(k) Any agreement for the unjustifiable exclusion from any trade association of any person carrying on, or intending to carry on, in good faith the trade in relation to which the trade association is formed;

(l) Any agreement not hereinbefore referred to in this section which the Central Government may, by notification in the Official Gazette, specify as being one relating to a restrictive trade practice within the meaning of this sub-section, pursuant to any recommendation made by the Commission in this behalf;

(m) Any agreement to enforce the carrying out of any such agreement as is referred to in this sub-section.

(2) The provisions of this section shall apply, so far as may be, in relation to agreements making provision for services as they apply in relation to agreements connected with the production, supply or distribution of goods.

Registration of restrictive trade agreement Registrar of Restricrive Trade Agreements: For maintaining a register of agreements subject io registration and for performing the other functions imposed on him under this Act there shall be appointed by the Central Government an Officer to be known as the Registrar of Restrictive Trade Agreements who shall be subject to the control of the Commission in the performance of his functions.

Registration of agreements : (1) The Central Government shall, by notification in the Official Gazette, specify a day (hereinafter referred to as the appointed day) as the day on and from which every agreement falling within section 21 shall become registerable under this Act.

Within three months after the appointed day in the case of any agreement existing on that day, and in the case of any agreement made after the appointed day, within three months after the making thereof, there shall be furnished to the Registrar in respect of every agreement which is subject to registration, the following particulars, namely :

(a) The names of the persons who are parties to the agreement ; and

(b) The whole of the terms of the agreement.

If at any time after the agreement has been registered under this section of the agreement is varied (whether in respect of the parties or in respect of the terms) or determined otherwise than by effuxion of time, particulars of the variation or determination shall be furnished to the Registrar within one month after the date of the variation or determination.

The particulars to be furnished under this section in respect of an agreement shall be furnished—

(a) In so for as the agreement or any variation or determination of the agreement is made by an instrument in writing, by the production of the original or a true copy of that instrument ; and

(b) In so far as the agreement or any variation or determination of the agreement is not so made, by the production of a memorandum in writing signed by the person by whom the particulars are furnished.

The particulars to be furnished under this section shall be furnished by or on behalf of any person who is a party to the agreement or, as the case may be, was a party thereto immediately before its determination, and where the particulars are duly furnished by or on behalf of any such person, the provisions of this section shall be deemed to be complied with on the part of all such persons.

Notwithstanding anything contained in this section, no agreement falling within section 21 shall be subject to registration under this section if it is expressly authorised by or under any law for the time being in force.

Explanation 1—Where any agreement subject to registration under this section relates to the production, supply or distribution of goods or the performance of any service in India and any party to the agreement carries on business in India, the agreement shall be deemed to be an agreement within the meaning of this section, notwithstanding that any other party to the agreement does not carry on business in India.

Explanation 2—Where an agreement is made by a trade association, the agreement for the purposes of this section shall be deemed to be made by all persons who are members of the association or represented thereon as if each such person were a party to the agreement.

Explanation 3—Where specific recommendations, whether express or implied, are made by or on behalf of a trade association to its members or to any class of its members as to the action to be taken or not to be taken by them in relation to any matter affecting the trading conditions of those members, this section shall apply in relation to the agreement for the constitution of the association notwithstanding any provision to the contrary therein as if it contained a term by which each such member and any person represented on the association by any such member agreed with the association to comply with those recommendations and any subsequent recommendations affecting those recommendations.

Keeping the Register—(1) For the purposes of this Act, the Registrar shall keep a register in the prescribed form, and shall enter therein the prescribed particulars as regards agreements subject to registration.

(2) The Registrar shall provide for the maintenance of a special section of the register for the entry or filling in that section of such particulars as the Commission may direct, being—

(a) Particulars containing information the publication of which would, in the opinion of the Comission, be contrary to the public interest ;

(b) Particulars containing information as to any matter, being information the publication of which, in the opinion of the Commission, would substantially damage the legitimate business interests of any person.

Any party to an agreement required to be registered under section 23 may apply to the Registrar for the agreement or any part of the agreement to be excluded from the provisions of this Chapter relating to registration on the ground that the agreement or the part thereof has no substantial economic significance or may apply to the Registrar for the inclusion of any provision of the agreement in the special section, and the Registrar shall dispose of the matter in conformity with any general or special directions issued by the Commission in this behalf.

Power of Registrar to obtain information : If the Registrar has reasonable cause to believe that any person is a party to an agreement subject to registration under section 23, he may give notice to that person requiring him within such time as may be specified in the notice to notify the Registrar whether he is a party to any such agreement and, if so, to furnish to the Registrar such particulars as may be so specified of the agreement.

The Registrar may give notice to any person by whom particulars are furnished under section 23 in respect of an agreement or to any other person being party to the agreement requiring him to furnish to the Registrar such further documents or information in his possession or control as the Registrar considers expedient for the purpose of, or in connection with, the registration of the agreement.

Where a notice under this section is given to a trade association, the notice may be given to the Secretary, Manager or other similar officer of the association ; and for the purposes of this section any such association shall be treated as a party to any agreement to which members of the association, or persons represented on the association by those members, are parties as such.

Control of certein restrictive trade practices—Investigation, into restrictive trade practices by Commission : The Commission may inquire into any restrictive trade practice, whether the agreement, if any, relating thereto has been registered under section 23 or not, which may come before it for inquiry, and if, after such inquiry, it is of opinion that the practice is contrary to the public interest, the Commission may, by order, direct that—

(a) The practice shall be discontinued or shall not be repeated ; or

(b) The agreement relating thereto, if any, shall be void in respect of such restrictive trade practice or shall stand modified in respect thereof in such manner as may be specified in the order.

The Commission may, instead of making any order under this section, permit the party to any restrictive trade practice, if he so applies, to take such steps within the time specified in this behalf by the Commission, as may be necessary to ensure that the trade practice is no longer contrary to the public interest, and, in any such case, if the Commission is satisfied that the necessary steps have been taken within the time specified, it may decide not to make any order under this section in respect of that trade practice.

No order shall be made under sub-section (1) in respect of :

(a) Any agreement between buyers relating to goods which are bought by the buyers for consumption and not for resale ; or

(b) A trade practice expressly authorised by any law for the time being in force.

Trade practices when deemed to be contrary to public interest : A restrictive trade practice shall be deemed to be contrary to the public interest if, in the opinion of the Commission, the effect of the practice, having regard to the economic conditions prevailing in the country and to all other matters which appear to the Commission to be relevant in the particular circumstances, is, or would be—

(a) To increase unreasonably the cost relating to the production, supply or distribution of goods or the performance of any service ;

(b) To increase unreasonably the prices at which goods are sold or the profits derived from the production, supply or distribution of the goods or from the performance of any service ;

(c) To reduce or limit unreasonably competition in the production, supply or distribution of any goods (including their sale or purchase), or in the provision of any service ;

(d) To limit or prevent the supply of goods to consumers.

Special provision for avoidance of condition for maintaining resale prices : 1. Withuut prejudice to the provisions of this Act with respect to registration and to any of the powers of the Commission under this Act, any term or condition of a contract for the sale of goods by a person to a wholesaler or retailer or any agreement between a person and a wholesaler or retailer relating to such a sale shall be void in so far as it purports to establish or provide for the establishment of minimum prices to be charged on the resale of the goods in India.

2. After the commencement of this Act no supplier of goods whether directly or through any person acting on his behalf, shall notify to dealers, or otherwise publish on, or in relation to any goods, a price stated or calculated to be understood as the minimum price which may be charged on the resale of the goods in India.

3. Nothing contained in sub-section (a) shall be as precluding a supplier or any person acting on his behalf from notifying to dealers or otherwise publishing prices recommended as appropriate for the resale of goods supplied or to be supplied by the supplier.

Prohibition of other measures for maintaining resale prices : (1) Without prejudice to the provisions of this Act with respect to registration and to any of the powers of the Commission under this Act, no supplier shall withhold supplies of any goods from a wholesaler or retailer seeking to obtain them for resale in India on the ground that the wholesaler or retailer—

(a) Has sold in India at a price below the resale price goods obtained, either directly or indirectly, from that supplier, or has supplied such goods, either directly or indirectly, to a third party who had done so ; or

(b) Is likely, if the goods are supplied to him, to sell them in India at a price below that price or supply them, either directly or indirectly, to a third party who would be likely to do so.

Nothing contained in sub-section (1) shall render it unlawful for a supplier to withhold supplies of goods from any wholesaler or retailer, or to cause or procure another supplier to do so, if he has reasonable cause to believe that the wholesaler or retailer has been using as loss leaders any goods of the same or a similar description, whether obtained from that supplier or not.

Explanation 1. "Resale price", in relation to a sale of any description, means any price notified to the wholesaler or dealer or otherwise published by or on behalf of the supplier of the goods in question (whether lawfully or not) as the price or minimum price which is to be charged on, or is recommended as appropriate for, a sale of that description, or any price prescribed or purporting to be prescribed for that purpose by any contract or agreement between the wholesaler or retailer and any such supplier.

Explanation 2. A wholesaler or retailer is said to use goods as loss leaders when he re-sells them otherwise than in a genuine seasonal or clearance sale, not for the purpose of making a profit on the re-sale, but for the purpose of attracting to the establishment at which the goods are sold customers likely to purchase other goods or otherwise for the purpose of advertising his business.

Power of Commission to exempt particular classes of goods from sections 28 and 29 : (1) The Commission may, on a reference made to it by the Registrar or by any other person interested, by order, direct that goods of any class specified in the order shall be exempt from the operation of sections 28 and 29 if the Commission is satisfied that in default of a system of maintained resale prices applicable to those goods—

(a) The quality of the goods available for sale, or the varieties of the goods so available, would be substantially reduced to the detriments of the public as consumers or users of those goods ; or

(b) The prices at which the goods are sold by retail would in general and in the long run be increased to the detriment of the public as such consumers of users ; or

(c) Any necessary services actually provided in con nection with or after the resale of the goods by retail would cease to be so provided or would be substan tially reduced to the deteriment of the public as such consumers or users.

2. On a reference under this section in respect of- goods of any class which have been the subject of proceedings before the Commission under Section 26, the Commission may treat as conclusive any finding of fact made in those proceedings.

Refusal to sell goods—If any wholesaler or retailer refuses to satisfy to the best of his ability and upon the customary trade terms any request for the purchase of goods which is made in good faith and which has no abnormal character and is not forbidden by law, the Commission may, having regard to the previous conduct of the wholesaler or retailer in the trade and to all other matters which appear in the particular cirumstances to be relevant, pass such orders as it may think fit to prevent the recurrence thereof.

Any order made under this section may include an order—

(a) For the imposition of a fine upon the wholesaler or retailer;

(b) For the temporary or permanent closure of the whole or any part of the business carried on by him;

(c) For the suspension or cancellation of any licence granted to him under any law for the time being in force, authorising him to carry on any business as such wholesaler or retailer;

(d) For the modification or determination of any agreement entered into by him entitling him to the supply of goods for the purpose of resale.

Chapter VI

Jurisdiction, Powers And Procedure Of The Commission

Cognizance of monopolistic or restrictive trade practices by Commission—The Commission may inquire into any monopolistic or restrictive trade practice :

(a) Upon receiving a complaint of facts which constitute such practice from any trade or consumers' Association or from any seven or more individual consumers; or

(b) Upon a reference made to it by the Central or a State Government; or

(c) Upon application made to it by the Registrar or the Director.

Investigation by Director before issue of process in certain cases—In respect of any monopolistic or restrictive trade practice of which complaint is made under clause (a) of section 32, the Commission shall, before issuing any process for requing the attendance of the person complained against, cause a preliminary investigation to be made by the Director in such magner as it may direct for the purpose nf satisfying itself that the complaint requires to be inquired into.

Powers of the Commission (1) For the purposes of this Act, the Commission shall have all the powers of a civil court while trying a suit under the Code of Civil Procedure, 1908 (5 of 1908), in respect of the following matters :

(a) Summoning and enforcing the attendance of any person and examining him on oath;

(b) Discovery and production of documents;

(c) Receiving evidence on affidavits;

(d) Requisitioning any public record or copy thereof from any court or office;

(e) Issuing commissions for the examination of witnesses or documents;

(f) Any other matter which may be prescribed.

In particular, the Commission shall have power to require any person—

(a) To produce before, and allow to be examined by, an officer of the Commission specified in this behalf such books, accounts or other documents in the custody or under the control of the person so required as may be specified or described in the requisition, being documents relating to the transaction or business the examination of which may be required for the purposes of this Act; and

(b) To furnish to an officer so specified such information as respects the transaction or business as may be required for the purposes of this Act or such other information as may be in his possession in relation to the business carried on by any other person.

The Commission shall be deemed to be a civil court for the purposes of sections 480 and 482 of the Code of Criminal Procedure, 1898 (5 of 1898), and any proceeding before the Commission shall be deemed to be a judicial proceeding within the meaning of sections 193 and 228 of the Indian Penal Code (46 of 1860).

For the purpose of enforcing the attendance of witnesses, the local limits of the Commission's jurisdiction shall be the limits of the territory of India.

Order of Commission may be subject to conditions etc.—(1) In making any order under this Act, the Comimission may make such provisions not inconsistent with this Act, as it may think necessary or desirable for the proper administration of the order to ensure compliance with the terms thereof, and any person who commits a breach of, or fails to comply with, any obligation imposed on him by any such provision shall be deemed to be guilty of an offence under this Act.

Any order made by the Commission may be amended or revoked at any time in the manner in which it was made.

An order made by the Commission may be general in its application or may he limited to any particular class of traders or to an individual trader or to a particular class of trade practices or to a particular trade practice or to a particular locality.

Orders where party concerned does not carry on business in India—Where a monopolistic or restrictive trade practice relating to the production, supply or distribution of goods (including imported goods) of any description or the provision of any service is substantially within one or more of the practices falling within this Act and any party to the practice does not carry on business in India, an order may be made under this Act with respect to that part of the practice which is carried on in India.

Restriction on application of Orders in certain cases—No order made under this Act with respect to a monopolistic or restrictive trade practice shall operate so as to restrict—

(a) The right of any person to restrain any infringement of a patent granted in India; or

(b) Any person as to the conditions which he attaches to a licence to do anything the doing of which but for the licence would be an infringement of a patent granted in India; or

(c) The right of any person to export goods from India, to the extent to which the monopolistic or restrictive trade practice relates exclusively to the production, supply or distribution of goods for such export.

Place of sittings of the Commission—The Central Office of the Commission shall be in Delhi, but the Commission may sit at such places in India and at such times as may be most convenient for the exercise of its powers or functions under this Act.

Benches of the Commission—The powers or functions of the Commission may be exercised or discharged by benches convened by the Chairman from among the members.

Hearing to be in public except in special circumstances (1) Subject to the provisions of sub-section (2), the hearing of proceeding before the Commission shall be in public.

Where the Commission is satisfied that it is desirable to do so by reason of the confidential nature of any evidence or matter or for any other reason, the Commission may—

(a) Hear the proceeding or any part thereof in private;

(b) Give directions as to the persons who may be present thereat;

(c) Prohibit or restrict the publication of evidence given before the Commission (whether in public or in private) or of matters contained in documents filed before the Commission.

Procedure of the Commission—(1) Subject to the provisions of this Act and the rules made thereunder, if any, the Commission shall have powers to regulate:

(a) The procedure and conduct of its business;

(b) The formation, places of sitting and the procedure of benches of the Commission;

(c) The delegation to one or more members of the Commission of such powers or fuction as the Commission may specify.

In particular and without prejudice to the generality of the foregoing provisions, the powers of the Commission shall include the power to determine the extent to which persons interested or claiming to be interested in the subject-matter of any proceeding before it are allowed to be present or to be heard either by themselves or by their representatives or to cross examine witnesses or otherwise to take part in the proceedings.

Proceedings of Commission to be conducted with

expedition. The Commission shall have its proceedings conducted with as little formality and technicality, and with such expedition, as the requirements of this Act and a proper consideration of the matters before the Commission permit.

Orders of the Commission to be noted in the register The Commission shall cause a copy of every order made by it in respect of a monapolistic or restrictive trade practice to be forwarded to the Registrar, who shall have it recorded in such a manner as may be prescribed.

Chapter VII

Offences And Penalties

Penalty for contravention of Section 12 or Section 13: If any person contravenes the provisions contained in section 12 or section 13, he shall be punishable with fine which may extend to ten thousaad rupees.

Penalty for failure to register certain agreements— If any person fails without reasonable cause to register an agreement which is subject to registration under this Act, he shall be punishable with fine which may extend to five thousand rupees.

Penalty for offences in relation to furnishing of information—If any person fails without reasonable cause to furnish any information required under section 14 or to comply with any notice duly given to him under section 25, he shall be punishable with fine which may extend to two thousand rupees or with imprisonment which may extend to three months or with both.

If any person who furnishes or is required to furnish any particulars, documents or information under this Act—

(a) Makes any statement or furnishes any document which he knows or has reason to believe to be false in any material particular; or

(b) Wilfully alters, suppresses or destroys any document which is required to be furnished as aforesaid; he shall be punishable with fine which may extend to five thousand rupees or with imprisonment which may extend to six months or with both.

Penalty for offences in relation to Orders of Commission—If any person contravenes any order made under section 19 or under section 26 or section 35, he shall be punishable with fine which may extend to five thousand rupees; and, in the case of a continuing offence, with an additional fine which may extend to five hundered rupees for every day during which the offence continues after conviction for the first such offence.

Penalty for offences in relation to re-sale price maintenance—If any person contravenes the provisions contained in section 28 or section 29, he shall be punishable with fine which may extend to five thousand rupees.

Penalty for wrongful disclosure of information— If any person discloses any information in contravention of section 57, he shall be punishable with imprisonment for a term which may extend to six months or with fine which may extend to five thousand rupees or with both.

Offences by companies—(1) Where an offence under this Act has been committed by a company, every person who at the time the offence was committed was incharge of, and was responsible to, the company for the conduct of the business of the company, as well as the company, shall be deemed to be guilty of the offence and shall be liable to be proceeded against and punished accordingly:

Provided that nothing contained in this sub-section shall render any such person liable to any punishment if he proves that the offence was committed without his knowledge or that he exercised all due diligence to prevent the commission of such offence.

Notwithstanding anything contained in sub-section (1), where an offence under this Act has been committed by a company and it is proved that the offence has been committed with the consent or connivance of, or is attributable to any negligence on the part of any Director, Manager, Secretary or other officer of the company, such Director, Manager, Secretary or other officer shall also be deemed to be guilty of that offence and shall be liable to be proceeded against and punished accordingly.

Explanation—For the purposes of this section :

(a) "company" means a body corporate and includes a firm or other association of individuals; and

(b) "Directors", in relation to a firm, means a partner in the firm.

Chapter VIII

Miscellaneous

Appeals—A person aggrieved by an order of the Commission under section 19 or section 26 may, within sixty days of the date of the order, prefer an appeal to the Supreme Court.

Jurisdiction of Courts in respect of Offences—No court inferior to that of a presidency magisterate or a magistrate of the first class shall try any offence under this Act.

Cognizance of Offences—No court shall take cognizance of any offence punishable under this Act except on a report in writing of the facts constituting such offence made by a person who is a public servant as defined in section 21 of the Indian Panel Code (45 of 1860).

Special Provision regarding Fines—Notwithstanding anything contained in section 32 of the Code of Criminal

Procedure,. 1898 (5 of 1898), it shall be lawful for any presidency magistrate or magistrate of the first class to pass a sentence of fine exceeding two thousand rupees on any person convicted of an offence under this Act.

Statements made by persons to the Commission—No statement made by a person in the course of giving statement before the Commission shall subject him to, or be used against him in, any civil or criminal proceedings except a prosecution for giving false evidence by such statement:

Provided that the statement—

(a) is made in respect to a question which he is required to answer by the Commission; and

(b) is relevant to the subject matter of the inquiry.

Inspection of any extracts from register—The register, other than the special section, shall be open to public inspection during such hours and subject to the payment of such fees as may be prescribed.

Any person may, upon payment of such fee as may be prescribed, require the Registrar to supply to him a copy of, or extract from, any particulars entered or filed in the register, other than the special section, certified by the Registrar to be a true copy or extract.

A copy of, or extract from any document entered or filed in the register certified under the hand of the Registrar or any officer authorised to act on his behalf, shall in all legal proceedings, be admissible in evidence as of equal validity with the original.

Restriction on disclosure of information—No information relating to any undertaking has been obtained by or on behalf of the Commission for the purposes of this Act shall, without the previous consent in writing of the owner for the time being of the undertaking, be disclosed otherwise than in compliance with or for the purposes of this Act.

Nothing contained in sub-section (1) Shall apply to the disclosure of any information made for the purpose of any legal proceeding pursuant to this Act or of any criminal proceeding which may be taken, whether pursuant to this Act or otherwise, or for the purposes of any report relating to any such procceding.

Reports of Commission to be placed before Parliament—The Central Government shall cause to be laid before both Houses of Parliament every report pertaining to the execution of this Act which may be submitted to it by the Commission from time to time.

Members to the public servants—All members to the Commission, the Director and the Registrar shall be deemed, while acting or purporting to act in pursuance of any of the provisions of this Act, to be public servants within the meaning of section 21 of the Indian Penal Code (45 of 1860).

Protection of action taken in good faith—No suit, prosecution or other legal proceeding shall lie against the Commission or any member, officer or servant of the Commission, or the Registrar in respect of anything which is in good faith done or intended to be done under this Act.

Power to make Regulations—The Commission may make regulations for the efficient performance of its functions under this Act, and, in particular, such regulation may provide for :

(a) The conditions of service of persons appointed by it ;

(b) The form and manner in which notices may be given or applications may be made to it under this Act and the fee payable therefor;

(c) The particulars to be furnished under this Act and the form and manner in which and the intervals within which they may be furnished;

(d) The issue of processes to Government and to other persons and the manner in which they may be served;

(e) The manner in which the special section of the register shall be maintained and the particulars to be entered or filed therein;

(f) The duties and functions of the Registrar and the Directors;

(g) The payment of cost of any proceeding before it by the parties concerned and the procedure and conduct of its business generally.

Power to make Rules— (1) The Central Government may, by notification in the Official Gazette, make rules to carry out the purposes of the Act.

In particular, and without prejudice to the generality of the foregoing power, such rules may provide for—

(a) The conditions of service of members of the Commission and the Registrar;

(b) The places and the manner in which the register shall be maintained by the Registrar and the particulars to be entered therein;

(c) she fees payable for inspection of the register, and for obtaining certified copies of particulars from the register;

(d) the travelling and other expenses payable to persons summoned by the Commission to appear before it;

(e) the criterion to be adopted for determining the circumstances in which an undertaking may be said to control another or for determining any of the tests for measuring concentration (whether based on value, quantity, capacity, number or otherwise).

Every rule made by the Central Government under this Act shall be laid as soon as may be after it is made before each House of Parliament while it is in session for a total period of thirty days which may be comprised in one session or in two successive sessions; and if, before the expiry of the session in which it is so laid or the session immediately following, both Houses agree in making any modification in the rule or both Houses agree that the rule should not be made, the rule shall thereafter have effect only in such modified form or be of no effect, as the case may be; so however, that any such modification or annulment shall be without prejudice to the validity of anything previously done under that rule.

Chapter X

Other Matters

The economic activities of the public sector and of agriculture are not directly within the terms of our reference. Obviously, there was not much necessity of including agriculture in a study of this nature. For in India, as everywhere else in the world, agricultural activities are widely dispersed over thousands of farms of different sizes. This process has been accentuated by the land reform legislation in the States, which has among other things placed ceilings for land holdings. There is, therefore, little scope for concentration of economic power or emergence of monopoly in agricultural production. For restrictive practices also there is hardly any scope in agricultural operations. These presumedly are the principal reasons why agriculture has been omitted from our terms of reference.

In marked contrast with agricultural activities concentration of economic power, attended with monopolistic positions is conspicuously present in some of the public sector activities. Thus, in the Steel Industry the public sector concern, Hindustan Steel Ltd. with units at Rourkela, Bhilai and Durgapur, account for the lion's share of the steel production in the country. A still greater share is likely to be attained when Bokaro Steel Ltd. goes into production. In the Fertilizer Industry, Fertilizer Corporation of India Ltd. and F.A.C.T. produce the major share of the total production of fertilisers in the country. The Posts and Telegraphs Department has always been a monopoly. So, also is the case with the Railways (which were formerly in the private sector), and the Defence Industries. The All-India Radio also enjoys a monopoly in broadcasting services. In road transport, the bus services run by the various State Transport Corporations wield monopolistic power in many of the States. In air transport, the Indian Airlines Corporation enjoys a monopolistic position as regards carriage of passengers. The National Newsprint and Paper Mills Ltd., Madhya Pradesh, while producing 20% of the annual consumption in India is the only concern engaged in making newsprint. The State Trading Corporation and the Mineral and Metal Trading Corporation have also been given exclusive rights of import and export in certain commodities. We shall not be far from the truth, if we state, that speaking generally, many of the public sector concerns whether statutory corporations, or corporations under the Companies Act or run by Government departments-it appears, enjoy a high degree of concentration of economic power which in most cases, gives them a monopolistic position.

Many industrialists as also some Members of Parliament who gave us the benefit of their opinions, have gone to the length of saying that high concentration of economic power can be found only in the public sector. They went on to say that in case, we were satisfied, as a result of our investigation that high concentration of economic power and monopolistic or restrictive practices did exist in the private sector also and we thought fit to make recommendations to fight the evils resulting from them it was only just and proper that as far as possible these recommendations should be made applicable to public sector activities also. Monopolies may be bad, they say, whether they are owned by the State or whether by private persons; and there is no reason they say, why the Commission we are contemplating for vigilance and action against private monopolists when they act or appear likely to act against the interest of public, should not have power to act against monopolies in the public sector also.

The possibility cannot be ruled out that monopolies in the public sector no less capable of charging unreasonable prices and supplying inferior qualities of goods and services than private monopolists. The danger of monopolistic enterprises in the public sector clinging to obsolescent processes and inefficient management are likely to be at least no less than in the case of similar enterprises in the private sector. It cannot therefore, be gainsaid that the public are entitled to proper safeguards against the evil effects of monopolies in the public sector.

We are not in a position to make any definite recommendations, as regards public sector concerns, since they are not directly within the terms of our reference. It is fair to mention, however, that public sector concerns are subject to some amount of supervision by Parliament, which does not apply to the private sector. Some Committees have also recently been set up for examining the performances of the public sector concerns. An annual report and balance sheet of each industry and commercial concern of the Central Government is presented to Parliament every year. With effect from 1960-61 an annual report on their combined working is also being presented to Parliament

Though doubts have been expressed about the effectiveness of the supervision by Parliament, we are not in a position to express any opinion in the matter. We think it legitimate, however, to say that if Government and Parliament think it right that something more than the kind of supervision that has hitherto been exercised over the public sector concerns enjoying monopolistic power is desirable, the Permanent Commission proposed by us for vigilant supervision over private sector enterprises would be eminently suitable for the purpose.

Several industrialists made the point that public sector concerns get special and favourable treatment from Government in many matters for which there was no justification. In this connection, they urged that where the public sector concern was in a competitive field, competing with private sector enterprise, it would be wholly unfair that while the latter should be subjected to the jurisdiction of the Permanent Commission proposed by us, the competing public sector enterprises should remain outside. It was rightly pointed out that such public sector enterprises are no less capable of indulging in restrictive practices that may be harmful to the general public than their private sector competitors ; and if the latter require, in the public interest, the controlling supervision of the Commission, such controlling supervision is equally needed for the public sector enterprises. We are bound to say that there is considerable force in these contentions ; and that the Government and Parliament should seriously consider whether these public sector enterprises should be allowed to enjoy special immunity or whether they should be made subject to the Commission's jurisdiction in the same manner as the private sector concerns, in respect of any restrictive practices.

The next aspect of national economy that we have thought necessary to look into, in connection with the terms of reference, is the alleged control of big business over the daily press It has been said that such connection of big business with the press has an unhealthy influence on society, inasmuch as it obstructs the free formation of public opinion and mould people's minds in a manner unduly favourable to the selfish interests of businessmen.

We find it to be true that an appreciable section of the press is either owned or controlled by persons or corporations who are themselves big businessmen or closely connected with big business. Instances of these are: "Times of India Journals and Newspapers", including three English dailies, the "Times of India", Bombay, The Times of India, Delhi and the "Evening News of India", Bombay, a Hindi Daily, the "Navbharat Times", Delhi and a daily financial paper. "The Economic Times", Bombay, apart from several monthlies and weeklies. Bennet Coleman and Company Ltd. publishes these journals and papers and is controlled by Mr. Shanti Prasad Jain and others closely connected with him. The Birlas appear to control the "Hindustan Times" and allied publications including among others, the English daily, the "Hindustan Times", Delhi, and a Hindi daily, the "Hindustan", Delhi, and an English daily, "Leader" and a Hindi daily, "Bharat", published in Allahabad, and an English daily, "Searchlight" and a Hindi daily "Pradeep" published in Patna, They also control a financial weekly the "Eastern Economist". The leading English daily newspaper "Statesman" appears to be under the control of a consortium of business houses.

We have read many of the issues of the daily and weekly press which is within the control of these businessmen and we are inclined to think that in spite of the so called "editorial independence", these newspapers or financial journals do tend to prejudice the reader in favour of businessmen in general, and big business in particular. It would be unfair to ignore, however, the fact that some of these papers have frequently brought to the public notice, the malpractices and misdemeanours discovered from time to time to prevail in certain branches of business activity.

Even so, there seems to be some force in the contention that the section of the press that is under the control of big business tends to obstruct the free formation of public opinion, by presenting too rosy a picture of the performances and practices of big business in general by slurring over many of their malpractices. But, we do not think that much can be done to remedy this state of things, so long as independent persons—independent in the sense of not being under the control of big businessmen—do not come forward in sufficient numbers to start newspapers and journals, with a more objective presentation of news and views. It is proper to mention, that there is even now an appreciable section of the press that appears to be independent in the above sense. Among the papers which appear to us to be independent of big business may be mentioned the "Hindu" of Madras, the "Amrita Bazar Patrika", the "Ananda Bazar Patrika", the "Hindustan Standard" and the "Jugantar" of Bengal and the "Vir Arjun", "Milap", "Pratap" and "Patriot" of Delhi and the "Free Press Journal" of Bombay. The chain of Express Newspapers, with a circulation of more than a million is under the control of Ramnath Goenka, but his own industrial interests (outside the press) do not appear to be large.

Divergent opinions were expressed before us on the question of big business controlling newspapers. "Industrialists", said Dr. Lokanathan, "should not exercise control over newspapers". I would like the "financial institutions and newspapers to be independent of big business, if it can be done", said another eminent economist. Some others were, however, of opinion that while newspapers can be used or abused for ndustrial purpose to create an opinion and to over emphasise a certain point as against other points of view, it would be unwise to interfere.

As was to be expected, the industrialists saw no harm in big business having connection or control over newspapers. Their point of view was most clearly and elaborately put by the leader of the Bharat Chamber of Commerce delegation thus :

"In our democracy everybody has a right to express freely. If a newspaper given its opinion, I do not think it is doing anything wrong, if it does not do anything socially bad, in my opinion, there is nothing wrong.

I think to maintain democracy and the life of the private sector it is highly essential that the private sector must pay some more attention to the publicity of their activities to create public opinion that we are doing something good for the country and for the public. Now we find that economics cannot be divorced from politics. If we want to maintain democracy, if we want to maintain free enterprise and the private sector, we will have to create public opinion--the press and the platform. Of course, proper or improper utilisation of of the press is a different issue. But I say it is for the common good and ¡is in the interests of the country to allow or permit industrialists or business community to have newspapers.

Political parties are dominating the newspapers and we are not getting free and unbiased news for proper education of public opinion. If the views of politician big guns are dominating the field, I for one feel that the business community should also have the right to run newspapers so that there will be control on both sides."

The essence of the matter is that the Constitution has guaranteed to all citizens of India, the fundamental right of free expression of their opinion, subject only to reasonable restrictions in the interests of security of State, friendly relations with foreign States, public order, decency or morality, contempt of court or defamation. Any attempt to curtail big businessmen's control over newspapers which impedes the exercise of this fundamental right in so far as it is guaranteed by the Constitution must therefore be ruled out.

At the same time we have no hesitation in saying that it is necessary and desirable that more and more independent newspapers and journals free from sectional affiliations should come into existence and prosper. We are not trying to suggest ways and means to achieve this object as that would really be beyond our province.

What we have said above does not touch the question of any monopoly that may exist in any section of the press by ownership or control. We have not found it possible to investigate whether in fact any such monopoly exists. If any monopoly does exist, in any section of the press, the Commission proposed by us will be competent to give relief against any monopolistic practice, by those who control the newspaper or journal concerned. The Commission will be able also to take steps against any restrictive practice which such people indulge in.

Some may enquire why we have made no recommendations as regards the abolition or control of managing agency system, even though we mentioned in an earlier Chapter the important part played by this system in the growth of concentration of economic power. The reasons are more than one. The most important of these is that we are doubtful whether even the total abolition of the managing agency system at the present stage would have any marked effect in curbing the growth of concentration of economic power. We are inclined to believe that even if the managing agency system goes, its place would quickly be taken by some other system of group management, or some other method which it will not be practicable to prevent. Secondly, the question of what action, if any, should be taken as regards managing agency system has to be decided—what action, if any, in addition to what is provided in the Companies Act—not only on a consideration of its effect on concentration of economic power but on full and careful assessment of the effects of any proposed action on the process of Industrial advancement in the country, which is hardly possible for this Commission to undertake. Another consideration which weighed with us was the fact that as recently as 1960 Parliament has carefully considered the question of appropriate action to be taken to control the operation of managing agencies and it seems too early to reopen the question now. Further. it has to be mentioned that the question of the abolition of the managing agency system as regards selected industries is already under the consideration of a Committee appointed by Government.

REVIEW COMMITTEE ON ARABIC AND PERSIAN STUDIES IN INDIAN UNIVERSITIES, 1964—REPORT

University Grants Commission, New Delhi, 1968. 16p.

Chairman : Dr. M.Z. Siddiqi ;
Members : Prof. Nazir Ahmed ; Prof. Khwaja Ahmed Faruqi ; Prof. M. A. Muid Khan ; Prof. N. A. Nadvi ; Dr. M. S. Agwani ; Dr. P. M. Joshi ; Shri Badr-ud-din Tyabji ; Shri A. A. A. Fyzee ; Dr. Abdul Sattar Siddiqui ;
Secretary : Dr. G. S. Mansukhani.

APPOINTMENT

The Review Committee on Arabic and Persian Studies in Indian Universities was appointed in May, 1964.

TERMS OF REFERENCE

Following are the terms of reference of the Committee :

(i) To suggest ways and means for improving the standards of teaching and research in Arabic and Persian ; and

(ii) To make recommendations to the Commission with regard to the modernisation and improvement of the courses of study provided in Arabic and Persian in our Universities.

CONTENTS

Foreword ; Introduction ; Existing position ; Recommendations ; Appendices I and II.

RECOMMENDATIONS

The Committee after careful consideration of the cultural as well as political and international importance of Arabic and Persian Studies, the existing facilities and future requirements, came to the conclusion that there is a real need for developing such studies at centres where suitable conditions and demand exist. The Committee suggests that the study of Arabic and Persian on modern scientific lines should be encouraged.

The problem of attracting bright and promising students to the study of Arabic and Persian needs to be tackled seriously. For this purpose it is essential that employment opportunities, particularly in the fields of business, teaching, interpreting, area studies, newspapers and translation work, might be brought to the notice of students. It is expected that in the coming years the number of students taking up these languages will increase in view of the new avenues of employment.

The Committee considered the syllabi in Arabic and Persian in Indian Universities and felt that there was need for modification. There has been in recent years a shift of emphasis from the study of classical Arabic and Persian to their modern forms. Persian has not changed very much through the ages, but on the other hand, modern Arabic is very much different from its Classical form.

The Committee suggests that the syllabi for B.A. Honours Course in Arabic and Persian might be reviewed in the light of the courses prescribed by the Delhi University. The B. A. Honours Course in Arabic in Delhi University consists of 8 papers as under :

Paper I Classical Prose
Paper II Classical Poetry ;
Paper III Modern Prose ;
Paper IV Modern Poetry ;
Paper V Grammar, Prosody and Rhetoric ;
Paper VI History of Literature ;
Paper VII Any one of the following options ;
(a) Islamic History ;
(b) Islamic Studies ;
(c) Persian Classical Prose & Poetry ;
Paper VIII Essay and Translation.

The B. A. Honours Course in Persian consists of the following papers :

Paper I Classical Prose ;
Paper II Classical Poetry ;
Paper III Modern Prose ;
Paper IV Modern Poetry ;
Paper V Indo-Persian Literature ;
Paper VI History of Literature (from Firdausi to Saadi) ;
Paper VII Any one of the following options ;
(a) Sufistic Literature ;
(b) Early Period of Islamic History ;
(c) Arabic ;
(d) Pahalvi;
Paper VIII Essay and Translation.

The Committee thinks that the problem of the study of language, as distinct from literature, has to be considered at the M.A. level. In order to make the study of language fruitful, some make the study of language of linguistic and philosophy may be provided. There should be some specialisation either in language or literature at the M. A. level. The M.A. syllabi in

Arabic and Persian should consist of two parts. The first part may have four compulsory papers which should acquaint the students with the history, culture, and modern trends of the region in which the languages are current. The second part may include two options : literature produced in India on account of the impact of that language, besides classical prose and poetry ; the paper relating to language may include linguistics and knowledge of allied language.

The following papers for M. A. in Persian are suggested :

Four Compulsory papers :

Paper I : An Outline of the History of Iran from Earliest Times up-to-date including Study of Antiquities of Iran ;

Paper II : Literary History from the Arabic Conquest of Parsia onwards ;

Paper III: Prosody, Elements of Comparative Phonetics of Indo-European Languages and Translation of Unseen Passages ;

Paper IV : Modern Persian Prose and Poetry between 1875-1945.

Group 'A' Literature

Paper I Classical Poetry ;
Paper II Classical Prose ;
Paper III Historical and Philosophical Texts ;
Paper IV Indo-Persian Literature and the influence of Persian on Modern Indian Languages:

Group 'B' Philosophy

Paper I : Principles of Linguistics (History of Persian Scripts);

Paper II : Zend and Old Persian Including Elements of Grammar ;

Paper III : Pahalvi Texts including Elements of Grammar ;

Paper IV : Historical Grammar of Iranian Languages and Elementary Sanskrit.

The following papers for M.A. in Arabic are suggested :

Four Compulsory Papers

Paper I : An Outline of the History of Arabs from the Earliest Tunes upto 1945;

Paper II : Literary History of the Arabs from Pre-Islamic Times upto 1945 ;

Paper III: Prosody. Element of Comparative Philosophy of Semitic Langauges and Translation of unseen passages ;

Paper IV : Modern Arabic Prose and Poetry from 1800 to 1945.

Four optional papers either in Group 'A' or in Group 'B'.

Group 'A' Literature

Paper I Poetry including Pre-Islamic Poetry ;
Paper II Classical Prose ;
Paper III Historical and Philosophical Texts ;
Paper IV Portions of Quran and Hadith with critical commentary.

Group 'B' Language and Philosophy

Paper I Principles of Linguistics;
Paper II Arabic Grammar and Phonetics ;
Paper III Hebrew ;
Paper IV Syriac.

Universities and colleges may provide incentives for the study of Arabic and Persian by providing scholarships, studentships and possibly by giving some weightage in admissions to students offering these subjects. It may be noted that the number of scholars for these languages can be increased if the employment potential is made known to them. Moreover, such studies may also prove useful for students of area studies and allied disciplines.

In order to improve teaching in the two languages, selected teachers in Indian Universities may be deputed to West Asian or African Countries for further Studies, and the possibility of sending some teachers abroad under the cultural exchange programmes with foreign countries may be explored.

Seminars and Conferences may be convened by selected universities for considering problems relating to the development of Studies in Arabic and Persian and the improvement of curricula. It would be useful if selected teachers and research scholars are brought together for discussion regarding the improvement of the standards of research and teaching in these subjects at one of the centres annually.

The value and importance of the studies of Arabic and Persian may brought home to the people through radio talks, extension lectures and small pamphlets. The university departments of Arabic and Persian should take initiative in this field. It is necessary to popularise the study of Arabic and Persian and it is suggested that a popular history of Arabic/Persian language and literature should be produced. Besides this, a popular brochure entitled "Why should we read Arabic/Persian ?" may prove helpful.

The existing curricula in Arabic and Persian, which have a classical bias, may be reviewed in the light of recent developments. Apart from the knowledge of modern prose and poetry, the study of allied languages such as Hebrew, Syriac, Turkish, Modern French and German may be useful. Moreover, a student of Persian should know some Arabic and vice-versa.

In order to improve the standard of teaching, it is

suggested that the staff of the university departments may deliver lectures in Arabic and Persian in the local colleges. This will require close co-operation between the University and the affiliated colleges.

The possibility of providing a short-term Correspondence Course in Modern Arabic and Persian, supplemented, if possible by a co-ordinated series of radio lessons, may be explored for the benefit of those living in places where provision for the teaching of the language does not exist. The idea behind such a course is that the candidate may acquire a working knowledge of the language so that he may be able to speak the language, read the newspapers and carry on ordinary correspondence. This may be treated as an experiment or pilot project at one University centre.

Some universities (and at least one university in each State) may develop an intensive short-term diploma course in Modern Arabic and Persian. Such a course would be useful to students of allied disciplines particularly the scholars and teachers of medieval Indian History. Language laboratories, tape-recorders and other modern audio-visual aids will be useful.

In some universities vacancies in the staff for Persian and Arabic have not been filled up. It is urged that suitable steps be taken to fill up these vacancies in the interests of teaching and research. The possibility of obtaining the services of rented teachers from abroad for specfic period could also be explored.

Library facilities for research scholars are inadequate. Most of the books in Persian and Arabic are published in foreign countries and there is a great difficulty in obtaining these books. Foreign exchange is necessary for obtaining such books.

Numerous manuscripts are lying in a precarious condition in private libraries and museums. Attempts should be made to obtain these manuscripts and preserve them in university libraries. These manuscripts should be sorted out and important ones microfilmed to provide valuable research material for research scholars. Besides this, many manuscripts are lying in university libraries. These should be catalogued and brought to notice of teachers and scholars.

Universities providing post-graduate teaching in the two languages might publish catalogues of manuscripts including those in the local libraries and museums. For the benefit of research scholars books on the cultural and socio-economic aspects of West Asian countries and research methodology may also be made available in the libraries. With regard to the research in the two languages it is necessary that duplication be avoided through coordination and mutual consultation. It is necessary to indicate the fields in which useful research may be undertaken. It is also suggested that the teacher must first satisfy himself whether the candidate has the necessary background and aptitude for research on the topic selected. It may be necessary to hold a suitable test for the selection of research scholars. A course in research methodology and technique will be of great benefit to candidates in dealing with their source materials.

FINANCE COMMISSION, 1964—REPORT

Manager of Publications, Delhi, 1965. 234p.

Chairman : Dr. P.V. Rajamannar
Members : Shri Mohan Lal Gautam ; Shri D.G. Karve ; Prof. Bhabatosh Datta
Secretary : Shri P.C. Mathew

APPOINTMENT

The Finance Commission was constituted under Govt. of India by the President, vide his order, dated 5-5-1964.

TERMS OF REFERENCE

In addition to the matters on which, under the provisions of sub-clauses (a) and (b) of clause (3) of article 280 of the Constitution, the Commission is required to make recommendations, the Commission should also make recommendations in regard to :

(a) The States which are in need of assistance by way of grants-in-aid of their revenues under Article 275, and the sums to be paid to those States other than the sums specified in the provisions to clause (1) of that article, having regard, among other considerations to :

(i) The revenue resources of those States for the five years ending with the financial year 1970-71 on the basis of the levels of taxation likely to be reached in the financial year 1965-66;

(ii) The requirements of those States to meet the

committed expenditure on maintenance and upkeep of Plan Schemes completed during the Third Plan ;

(iii) Any further expenditure likely to devolve upon those States for the servicing of their debt ;

(iv) Creation of a fund out of the excess, if any, over a limit to be specified by the Commission of the net proceeds of estate duty on property other than agricultural land accruing to a State in any financial year, for the repayment of the State's debt to the Central Government ; and

(v) The scope for economy consistent with efficiency, which may be effected by the States in their administrative expenditure ;

(b) The changes, if any, to be made in the principles governing the distribution amongst the States under article 269 of the net proceeds in any financial year of estate duty in respect of property other than agricultural land ;

(c) The changes, if any, to be made in the principles governing the distribution amongst the States of the grant to be made available to the States in lieu of taxes on Railway fares ;

(d) The changes, if any, to be made in the principles governing the distribution of the net proceeds in any financial year of the additional excise duties levied on each of the following commodities, namely :—

(i) Cotton fabrics,
(ii) Silk fabrics,
(iii) Rayon or artificial silk fabrics,
(iv) Woollen fabrics,
(v) Sugar; and
(vi) Tobacco (including manufactured tobacco).

In replacement of the State's sales taxes formerly levied by the State Governments:

Provided that the share according to each State shall not be less than the revenue realised from the levy of the sales tax for the financial year 1956-57 in that State ;

(e) The effect of the combined incidence of a State's sales tax and Union duties of excise on the production, consumption or export of commodities or products, the duties on which are shareable with the States, and the adjustments, if any, to be made in the State's share of Union excise duties if there is any increase in the States' sales tax on such commodities or products over a limit to be specified by the Commission.

The recommendations of the Commission shall, in each of the above cases, cover the period of five years commencing from the Ist day of April, 1966.

CONTENTS

Introduction ; Union-State Financial relations—Our basic approach ; Estate Duty ; Grant in lieu of Taxes on Railway Fares ; Income-tax ; Union Excise Duties ; Additional Duties of Excise in lieu of Sales Taxes ; Coordination between Sales Taxes and Union Excise Duties ; Principles governing grants-in-aid of revenues ; Forecast of Revenue and Expenditure. Grants-in-aid under Article 275 of the Constitutions; General observations and suggestions ; Summary of Recommendations ; Acknowledgements ; Minute of Dissent by Shri Mohan Lal Gautam ; Observations on the Minute of Dissent ; Minute by Dr. P.V. Rajamannar ; Minute by Prof. Bhabatosh Datta ; Annexures 1 and 2, Appendices I to VII.

RECOMMENDATIONS

Under article 269 of the Constitution :

I. Estate Duty : In each of the five years commencing from 1st April, 1966 :

(i) Out of the net proceeds of the duty in each financial year, a sum equal to two per cent be retained by the Union as proceeds attributable to Union Territories ;

(ii) The balance be apportioned between immovable property and other property in the ratio of the gross value of all such properties brought into assessment in that year ;

(iii) The sum thus apportioned to immovable property be distributed among the States in proportion to the gross value of the immovable property located in each State ; and

(iv) The sum apportioned to property other than immovable property be distributed among the States as follows :

States	Percentage
Andhra Pradesh	8.34
Assam	2.75
Bihar	10.76
Gujarat	4.78
Jammu & Kashmir	0.83
Kerala	3.92
Madhya Pradesh	7.50
Madras	7.80
Maharashtra	9.16
Mysore	5.46
Nagaland	0.09
Orissa	4.07
Punjab	4.70
Rajasthan	4.67
Uttar Pradesh	17.03
West Bengal	8.09
Total	100.00

II. Grant In lieu of Taxes on Railway Fares: In each of the five years commencing from 1st April, 1966, the amount of grant made available on the basis of the recommendations of the Railway Convention Committee be distributed among the States as follows :—

States	Percen age
Andhra Pradesh	9 05
Assam	2.79
Bihar	9.99
Gujarat	7.11
Jammu & Kashmir	—
Kerala	1.85
Madhya Pradesh	9.85
Madras	5.81
Maharashtra	8.98
Mysore	3.98
Nagaland	0.01
Orissa	2.12
Punjab	7.43
Rajasthan	6.40
Uttar Pradesh	18.23
West Bengal	6.40
Total	100.00

Under Article 270 of the Constitution

III. Income Tax: In each of the five years commencing from 1st April, 1966 :

(i) The percentage of the net proceeds in any financial year of taxes on income other than agricultural income, except in so far as these proceeds represent proceeds attributable to Union territories or to taxes payable in respect of Union emoluments to be assigned to the States be 75 (Seventy five) per cent ;

(ii) The percentage of the net proceeds of taxes on income which shall be deemed to represent proceeds attributable to Union Territories be 2-1/2 per cent ; and

(iii) The percentage of the net proceeds assigned to the States be distributed among them as follows :

States	Percentage
Andhra Pradesh	7.37
Assam	2.44
Bihar	9.04
Gujarat	5.29
Jammu & Kashmir	0.73
Kerala	3.59
Madhya Pradesh	6.47
Madras	8.34
Maharashtra	14.28
Mysore	5.14
Nagaland	0.07
Orissa	3.40
Punjab	4.36
Rajasthan	3.97
Uttar Pradesh	14.60
West Bengal	10.91
Total	100.00

Under Article 272 of the Constitution

IV. Union Excise: In each of the five years commencing from 1st April, 1966, a sum equal to 20 (twenty) per cent of the net proceeds of the Union duties of excises on all articles levied and collected in that particular year, excepting regulatory duties, special excises and duties and cesses earmarked for specific purposes be paid out of the Consolidated Fund of India to the States and distributed among them as follows :

States	Percentage
Andhra Pradesh	7.77
Assam	3.32
Bihar	10.03
Gujarat	4.80
Jammu and Kashmir	2.26
Kerala	4.16
Madhya Pradesh	7.40
Madras	7.18
Maharashtra	8.23
Mysore	5.41
Nagaland	2.21
Orissa	4.82
Punjab	4.86
Rajasthan	5.06
Uttar Pradesh	14.98
West Bengal	7.51
Total	100.00

V. Additional Duties of Excise: In each of the five years commencing from 1st April, 1966, out of the total net proceeds of additional duties of excise on cotton fabrics, silk fabrics, rayon or artificial silk fabrics, woolen fabrics, sugar and tobacco including manufactured tobacco :

(i) A sum equal to 1.00 (one) per cent of the net proceeds be retained by the Union as proceeds attributable to Union Territories ;

(ii) A sum equal to 1.50 (one and a half) per cent of the net proceeds be paid to the State of Jammu and Kashmir ;

(iii) A sum equal to 0.05 (one twentieth) per cent of

the net proceeds be paid to the State of Nagaland ; and

(iv) Out of the balance (i.e., 97.45 per cent) of the net proceeds of the duties, i.e., after the deduction of the amounts mentioned in sub-paragraphs (i) to (iii) above, the following sums representing the revenue realised in 1956-57 by each State on account of Sales Taxes on the six commodities, be first paid to the following States :

States	(Rupees in lakhs)
Andhra Pradesh	235.24
Assam	85.08
Bihar	130.16
Gujarat	323.45
Kerala	95.08
Madhya Pradesh	155.17
Madras	285.34
Maharashtra	637.77
Mysore	100.10
Orissa	85.10
Punjab	175.19
Rajasthan	90.10
Uttar Pradesh	575.81
West Bengal	280.41
Total	3254.00

(v) The remaining sum, if any, be distributed among the 14 (fourteen) States, as specified below :

States	Percentage
Andhra Pradesh	7.42
Assam	1.98
Bihar	6.17
Gujarat	7.43
Kerala	5.65
Madhya Pradesh	4 62
Madras	11.13
Maharashtra	19.87
Mysore	5.21
Orissa	2.58
Punjab	5.01
Rajasthan	3.17
Uttar Pradesh	7.83
West Bengal	11.93
Total	100.00

Under Article 275(1) of the Constitution

VI. **Grants-in-Aid :** Under the substantive portion of article 275(1) of the Constitution, in each of the five financial years commencing from 1st April 1966, the sums specified below be charged on the Consolidated Fund of India as grants-in-aid of the revenues of the States mentioned against them :

States	(Rs. in crores)
Andhra Pradesh	7.22
Assam	16.52
Jammu & Kashmir	6.57
Kerala	20.82
Madhya Pradesh	2.70
Madras	6.84
Mysore	18.24
Nagaland	7.07
Orissa	29.18
Rajasthan	6.73
Total	121.89

ENQUIRY COMMITTEE ON SMALL NEWSPAPERS, 1964—REPORT

Ministry of Information and Broadcasting, New Delhi, 1966. 308p.

Chairman : Shri R. R. Diwakar

Vice-Chairman : Shri A. D. Mani.

Members : Shri A. R. Bhat; Shri Joachim Alva; Prof. Hiren Mukerjee; Shri Banarsi Das Chaturved (resigned and replaced by Shri M. Yunus Dehlvi); Shri Premnarayan Indernarayan; Shri Durga Das; Shri Hayat Ullah Ansari.

Secretary : Shri D. R. Khanna.

APPOINTMENT

The question of making an enquiry into the difficulties and problems facing small newspapers, especially those published in the languages mentioned in the VIII Schedule to the Constitution of India with a view to ameliorating their position, has been engaging the attention of the Government of India for some time.

The Government of India have now decided to set up an Enquiry Committee on Small Newspapers, consisting of non-officials to make an investigation into the matter and to advise Government on the measures to be taken for assisting the small newspapers published in various languages. In pursuance of the above decision the Government of India in the Ministry of Information and Broadcasting appointed the Enquiry Committee on Small Newspapers vide their Resolution No. 28/2/64-IP dated May 12, 1964.

TERMS OF REFERENCE

(i) To make an investigation into the matter ;

(ii) To advise government on the measures to be taken for assisting the small newspapers published in various languages; and

(iii) The Committee shall enquire into the present conditions of small newspapers and periodicals in the country and make recommendations on the steps to be taken by the Government for the development of such newspapers.

CONTENTS

Course of Enquiry; The perspective; The Small Newspaper/periodical and its Definition; Difficulties and Problems of Small Newspapers in different States; Circulation; Performance of Small Newspapers; Printing Machinery of Small Newspapers; Communication and Transport; News Services; Information Services; Training facilities for Staff; Association of Newspapers; Credit Facilities and Consultancy Service; Newsprint; Advertisements; Price-Page Schedule; Summary of Conclusions and Recommendations; Minute of Dissent; Supplementary Notes; Appendices from I to XVI.

Summary Of Conclusions And Recommendations

Our recommendations in the various chapters are based on two assumptions : (i) that in view of the tendencies towards concentrations of power in a few big newspapers, Government are now eager to formulate a long-term plan for a balanced development of the Press, and (ii) that the measures we are proposing would help not only towards stabilising the economy of the small papers now in existence but would also encourage the birth of new opinion forming newspapers.

A long-term plan must take into account three considerations : (1) the growth of the Press must keep pace with the growth of population and the spread of literacy; (2) the Government must play a positive role by treating small newspaper as not merely an industry like any other but as an industry essential for the growth of democracy; and (3) steps must be taken to ensure that the growth of the Press is along healthy lines.

We should urge Government to keep a strict watch on unbalanced developments in the matter of growth of chains of newspapers and concentration of readership and devise suitable measures to curb them. We note in this connection that the provisions of the Press Council Bill empower the Council to deal with such matters.

The following criteria are recommended for classification of newspapers/periodicals as small newspapers-/periodicals.

Dailies : Circulation not exceeding 20,000 copies and annual gross revenue not exceeding Rs. 12 1/2 lakhs.

Other publications, including tri-weeklies, bi-weeklies, weeklies, fortnightlies and monthlies—Circulation not exceeding 15,000 copies and annual gross revenue not exceeding Rs. 5 lakhs.

Gross revenue in the case of a newspaper/periodical means the total of its circulation revenue (including subscription revenue) and advertisement revenue.

The foregoing definition of a small newspaper and periodical should not apply to newspapers and periodicals which belong to chains/groups of newspapers.

In the case of multiple-unit newspapers, all Constituent units will be eligible for classification as a small newspaper on the basis of the criteria applicable to each individual unit.

All dailies including the seven-day edition of a daily, by whatever name called, published by a newspaper establishment in the same language from the same centre, should be taken together and treated as if they form one unit and the revenues of all such papers put together should be deemed to be the revenue of such a unit.

No minimum circulation need be prescribed for eligibility as small newspaper/periodical, but it would be open to the authorities concerned for the grant of a concession to satisfy themselves about the regularity or standard of production of the newspaper concerned.

The Press Registrar should be declared as the authority for certifying whether a newspaper/periodical answers the criteria prescribed above for classification as a small newspaper/periodical.

The above definition may be reviewed after five years in the light of circumstances then existing.

Circulations

The practice so far followed in the scrutinies of circulation of newspapers undertaken by the Press Registrar has been to compare the current circulations (say, for 1963-64) on verification with the 1961-62 circulations, which is the basic year for allotment of newsprint, according to the present policy. Where the verified circulation was less than that of the basic year, the publisher has been allowed to get away on the plea that his circulalion had fallen since 1961-62 (basic-year) and his present circulation was so much. But the point to note is that the publisher has submitted in respect of that year (1963-64) a certificate, duly verified by Chartered accountant placing the circulation in 1963-64 at a particular figure. If this circulation is not sustained on verification, it is evident that a certain excess amount of newsprint was issued to the publisher. The Committee is of the opinion that in such cases the newspaper's current year's quota of newsprint should be reduced to that extent, besides any other effective action being taken. The practice, among other things, will serve to deter the publishers from submitting exaggerated claims.

Since all circulation claims (exceeding 2,000 copies) submitted by a publisher to the Press Registrar have to be certified as correct by a chartered accountant or a qualified auditor, the latter can be deemed to be a party to any exaggerated claims that might be made, in violation of his professional code of conduct. Such cases should invariably be brought to the notice of the professional body, namely the Institutes of Chartered Accountants for suitable action.

The Press Registrar informed us that he was experiencing considerable difficulties in examining the circulation claims of a Calcutta daily whose publishers have failed to submit for scrutiny the necessary account books. In such cases, the advice of the Ministry of Law should be sought for putting the legal process in motion.

The present proforma for ascertaining figures of news papers and periodicals is not comprehensive and it needs no strain on anyone's thinking to concede that the proforma can lend itself to easy manipulation at the hands of unscrupulous people. This proforma as well as the certificate from the chartered accountant or a qualified auditor, should be reviewed not with a view to causing undue hardship to publishers of newspapers and periodicals, but to enable the auditors to examine the relevant books to arrive at reliable circulation figures. The Press Registrar should specify the books and accounts which should be maintained by the publisher andscrutinised by an auditor. The forms and specimens of these documents, which should not be elaborate, should be prescribed. Along with the statement of information, the publisher must also submit a statement of the books and accounts maintained and submitted by him to the auditor, who should certify the documents examined by him before authenticating the publisher's claimed circulation. Each statement so received should be checked in the office of the Press Registrar before it is admitted for entry in the Press Register. The assistance of commercial auditors. who have had the experience of circulation audits, may be sought by Government in evolving revised proforma to be completed by publishers and auditors.

In our view, the Press Registrar, before effecting a reduction in the accepted circulation of a newspaper, should issue to it a show cause notice giving reasons for the proposed reduction, and give an opportunity to the newspaper concerned to state its case. Where a newspaper challenges the conclusions of the Press Registrar, the Press Registrar should arrange a re-check of newspaper's circulation by an independent commercial auditor nominated by him. The cost of such re-check should be met by Government.

It is recommended that uncertified figures should not be accepted by the Press Registrar and in such cases the letters "N. S." (not submitted) should be recorded in the Report against the name of newspaper concerned.

The Committee has noticed that some newspapers do not file their returns in time so that their circulations are not recorded in the annual report though they do supply the circulation figures to the Press Registrar at a subsequent date. In some cases, this is cover against falling circulations. The practice needs to be plugged by suitable legal action.

Under the existing rules, it is not necessary for publishers claiming circulations up to 2,000 copies submit an auditor's certificate. Representations have been made that this limit should be raised to 5,000 copies or even to 10,000 copies. We cannot support this suggestion.

Three successive issues of a Hindi fortnightly of Delhi were placed before the Committee with identical material. This seems to be a device to keep the declaration alive; obviously it is an abuse of the law and deserves to be firmly discouraged. The entitlement of newsprint in such cases can rightly be questioned.

The Committee saw three publications with different titles, bearing different dates but having the same contents. At present, there is not provision under the law to deal with such cases or to prevent the issue of newsprint to them. The lacuna in the law should be removed.

The Committee hope that the Press Registrar will take suitable steps to ensure that all current newspapers are entered in the Register of Newspapers and included in the Annual Report.

Evidently, there is need for greater collaboration between the Central and State authorities to ensure that both the births and deaths of newspapers are promptly reported to the Press Registrar, so that the national Press Register is always up to date and authentic.

Under the law, publishers of newspapers are required to supply copies of their newspapers and periodicals, within the prescribed time limit, to the Press Registrar. Copies of newspapers published in Engiish, Hindi and Urdu are supplied to the Press Registrar's branch office at Simla whereas copies of others are to be supplied to the branch/regional offices of the Press Information Bureau located in different centres. We have been told by several branch officers of the PIB that this duty is extraneous to their normal work and cannot be expected to be discharged properly owing, inter alia, to lack of adequate staff. This must be telling adversely on the maintenance of records regarding regularity of the publications as well as their commencement and closure, in the Office of the Press Registrar. The Press Registrar should go into this matter and evolve suitable machinery for maintenance of up to date statistics of newspapers for the Press Register.

Representations have been made about the delay in the acceptance of declarations of newspapers. The following steps are proposed to cut short the time lag in the disposal of such references by the Press Registrar:

(a) On submitting an application to the Magistrate of his intention to file a declaration, the publisher should simultaneously forward a copy direct to the Press Registrar, who should convey clearance or otherwise of the title to the District Magistrate concerned without waiting for a formal reference from the District Magistrate. The Press Registrar should, at the same time, inform the applicant that he should contact the Magistrate. A copy of the report of the Press Registrar should be available with each District Officer or the authority dealing with declarations of newspapers, for reference, among other things, about the availability of the title applied for ;

(b) The State Governments should instruct their information Departments or the concerned authorities to keep a watch on the publications for which declarations have been authenticated and report to the Press Registrar immediately, a paper starts publication. Moreover, they should also instruct the District Magistrate to intimate to Press Registrar immediately where the newspaper has not commenced publication within the time prescribed under Rule 5 of Section 5 of the Press and Registration of Books Act ;

(c) The Publishers may, on their own, suggest more than one title in order to preference so that if one title is not available or there is an element of doubt about its availability, the second or third alternative may be found acceptable ;

(d) The Press Registrar should also enquire from the District Magistrate and the publishers concerned as to whether or not a newspaper with a particular litte for which clearance had been given had come out within the prescribed period. This procedure will also help in the maintenance of up to date records in the office of the Press Registrar ;

(e) The period between the date of submission of application for a declaration and its acceptance should not normally exceed one month ;

(f) In case where a title has been recommended to a Magistrate for a particular newspaper and the publisher had not fled any declaration, the said magistrate should inform the Press Registrar about it so that the title may not remain blocked.

We recommended that the Press and Registration of Books Act, 1867, should be amended suitably to fix responsibility for the publication of a journal on the publisher and the editor alone and to eliminate the responsibility of the printer.

We would recommend that A.B.C. should not insist in the case of small newspapers and periodicals on the banking of cash every day, as many of them have slender financial resources and do not have adequate staff facilities.

The following suggestions made by the Indian languages Newspapers Association deserve adoption by the Audit Bureau of circulation :

(i) The A.B.C. may fix a minimum standard which the auditors should primarily consider ;

(ii) Appointments of auditors should be made after giving due consideration to distance and time likely to be taken up in audit ;

(iii) A maximum period be fixed within which the auditors should be advised to furnish their final report ;

(iv) Personal representation should be allowed to the publisher so that the Bureau may have the other side also ;

(v) Difficulties about loans, despatch notes, local purchases should be given due allowance.

We recommend that in cases where the A.B.C. is satisfied that the dues are genuine, circulations passed on such claims should be admitted for the circulation certificate till the suits filed are disposed of by the appropriate Court of Law.

Small newspapers have limited resources and many of them have to depend heavily on sales It is, therefore, necessary that publishers should pay only a reasonable percentage of commission to newspaper agents. We would recommend to the publishers to restrict the percentage of commission for copies sold by agents up to 40 per cent. A higher percentage of commission would be uneconomic for small newspapers.

In view of the complaints made before the Committee that the paper agents do not settle their dues in time, publishers may consider the possibility of maintaining on a regional basis a list of approved agents on the lines of the list of recognised advertisers maintained by the Indian and Eastern Newspapers Society. A condition for the accreditation of a newspaper agent should be that he should settle his dues to the members of the regional body within the prescribed time limit and that if he fails to settle his dues to any member of that body he will be disaccredited by the body with the result that he would not be entitled to receive more than 10 percent as commission for the sale of copies any member of the regional body. Such a sanction will enable publishers to receive their dues in time from defaulting agents.

Performance Of Small Newspapers

Sometime is bound to elapse before the Press Council is established and its influence is felt by the entire body of the Press, there was hardly any obscene publications in the country. It may be that we can not quite have the same kind of sober and serious journalism which has been happily more or less the rule in India, since we live in a period of very quick changes and certain values, formerly cherished, are in the melting pot. While we are prepared to welcome changes in the tone of many of our popular journals, and even a certain amount of verve and colourfulness, there are limits which, in all decency, should not be overstepped. It is in this spirit that we make our criticisms and recommendations.

As regards the question of tightening up of the law of obscenity as applicable to news papers and periodicals, we hope that as the influence of the Perss Council grows, it may not be necessary to resort to legal measures in this regard.

The Committee was informed that many of the weeklies in Gujarat as well as some journals in other states publish astrological predictions. We are aware that astrological predictions have the effect of boosting sales of a newspaper, provided the writer has established a reputation for some measures and alarm in the minds of the Public. Predictions, forecasting illnesses of persons in authority or possibility of external threat or internal disorder can cause alarm among the public and such predictions should find no place in the columns of journals.

In order to improve the production standards of small newspapers and periodicals, it is recommended that separate annual awards should be instituted for small newspapers and periodicals in each language given in Schedule VIII of the Constitution of India. There should be three cash prizes in each of the categories of dailies, weeklies and fortnightlies and monthlies together.

The value of cash prizes should be as follows :

Periodicity	First Prize Rs.	Second Prize Rs.	Third Prize Rs.
(1) Dailies	5,000	2,000	1,000
(2) Weeklies	3,000	1,000	750
(3) Fortnightlies and Monthlies	2,000	1,000	500

State Governments may consider instituting their own State Awards in addition, for the purpose of encouraging small newspapers and periodicals published in the State concerned.

Printing Machinery For Small Newspapers

Small newspapers have been denied facilities for obtaining printing machinery on hire-purchase basis through the National Small Industries Corporation-they give facilities only to newspapers working on cooperative basis. To remedy this basic handicap and in the interest of development of small newspapers and periodicals, Government should make special efforts to help small newspapers in obtaining printing machinery of their requirements. One of the ways is that Government should consider the requirements of small newspapers, on a preferential basis, in granting licences for import of printing machinery. We were informed by Government that there was no specific reservation for small newspapers and periodicals in the allotment of import licences for printing machinery, but that their applications were given sympathetic consideration by the authorities responsible for the issue of import licences.

Since the Government is interested in the development of small newspapers, we recommend that 50 per cent of the current and future allocations of foreign exchange for the import of printing machinery should be set apart for the requirements of small newspapers and periodicals.

The Committee has been informed of the possibility of importing rebuilt machines from foreign countries. These are second hand machines discarded by flourishing newspapers in favour of fresh models in foreign countries. They are in good working order and can be had at comparatively lower prices then bend new machinery. Government should explore the possibility of importing such machines from abroad through the STC. By this arrangement, there will be a saving in foreign exchange besides helping in meeting the shortage of printing machinery at home.

It has been represented to us that the machinery imported from the Rupee Area is not as good and efficient in performance as that available in the General Area, particularly from Japan and West Germany. While our imports have to flow from the area which the needs of foreign exchange warrant, we would recommend to Government to examine whether the machinery received from the Rupee Currency Area is as good as from free foreign exchange sources and whether the same type of machinery could not be had cheaper from other Areas, at less expenditure of foreign exchange.

The Committee has received representations from certain newspapers that State Governments should set up printing presses for the common use of newspapers and periodicals at economical rates. Some of the Governments seem to be inclined to favour this proposition. The proposal has certain merits in that small newsp.pers with little capital would be spread large investments on printing machinery.

It is understood that in some of the Government presses, spare capacity is available for doing such jobs as block-making on behalf of newspaper establishments. This possibility should also be explored by State Governments to assist small newspapers. We were informed that in a State, the spare capacity available with the Government Printing Press could not be fully utilized for block-macking facilities for the benefit of small newspapers, as the hours of working of the printing Press were not convenient to be able to serve the needs of small newspapers in time. An obvious solution is that the working hou s of the staff concerned with the block-making facilities should be so arranged as to enable them to make blocks etc. for newspepers in time.

The Committee was informed of the difficulty experienced in the castin g of types for printing presses owing to the cut in the imports of antimony and metal components. This further hits developmet of type varieties in various languages. As regards the type faces, a certain amount of research is called for, and we recommend that the Development Wing of the Ministry of Industry and supply should examine this matter in consultation with printing interests.

Shortage of spare parts for the printing machinery is another handicap in the way of the development of small newspapers and periodicals. While we would recommend that import licences should be issued to the actual users for the import of spare parts for printing machinery, the STC should in our opinion set up a spare parts depot for the requirements of the Press.

Communications And Transport

The conversion to the decimal coinage system has resulted in a higher financial burden on newspapers, both from the point of view of the weight as well as the postal charge. It is understood that the Indian Language Newspapers Association had drawn attention to this hardship on small newspapers as far back as 1956.

The Committee have examined this question in detail. Most of the small newspapers weigh less than 50 grams. We, therefore, recommend that the postage rate be reduced to one paisa for each single copy weighing up to 50 grams. This concession will be of considerable advantage to small newspapers and periodicals.

We recommend that where a newspaper, on account of some unforeseen circumstances, is obliged to delay the date of publication, the rule of three clear days notice before the due date of posting should not be insisted upon. Further, the power to relax the rule should be delegated by the Post Master General to the local Post Master, so that speedy action can be taken on such applications.

It is recommended that the suitable instructions may be issued by the Post and Telegraph Department to the Post Masters to clarify the provisions of the rules with regard to delays in the date of posting of publications and to take into consideration other delays also.

It was represented to the Committee that in the case of monthly publications, where delays in production resulted in an interval of more than 31 days between the date of last posting and the date when the delayed posting was sought to be made, the postal authorities do not permit such delays on the plea that, as per definition of a registered newspaper under the Post Office Act, they could not accept the publications coming out at longer intervals than 31 days as newspapers. The Committee recommends that the postal authorities should liberally interpret the definition and treat all periodicals which normally come out at intervals of not more than 31 days as newspapers regardless of occasional delays in their production and posting.

Express Delivery service is mainly used by newspapers and their correspondents and the Committee recommends that it should be properly organised by the postal authorities with a view to prompt delivery.

We hope that the P&T. Department would pay special attention to setting right the genuine grievances of the present users of telegraphic and teleprinter facilities. We recommend that applications from newspapers/periodicals and news and feature agencies should be given top priority in allocation. Special concessional rates should be allowed for press connections.

Telephone connections to newspaper representatives, Press Correspondents, journalists, etc. are being provided by the P&T. Department under the 'exempted' category in O.Y.T. (Own Your Telephone) stations and "Priority" category in non-OYT stations. The heads of Circles/Districts are competent to register such requests for provision of telephone connections in these categories. We recommend that high priority should be given for the demands of telephone connections from bonafide Press interests. Normally it should be possible for the Department to sanction a new connection within three months from the date of application, and to instal the telephone within a period not exceeding a month from the date of sanction.

We further recommend that applications for Telex connections from bonafide Press interests should also be accorded high priority in the matter of sanctioning and installing of connections within the periods specified above.

A rebate of 12-1/2% is allowed on Press trunk calls which can be booked from any telephone number or Public Call Office but only to a telephone number which has been registered as a Press telephone. These calls are treated on the same footing as trunk calls from the general public. Such calls should clearly relate to matter intended for publication in a news paper. The Committee recommends that to facilitate press traffic the maximum duration of such calls should be raised to 12 minutes, and they should be accorded priority in bookings.

Newspapers are an essential commodity concerned with purveying news and information. Delay in the circulation of newspapers, particularly in emergencies, may give rise to rumours and unconfined news causing law and order problems. The Committee, therefore, recommends that news paper consignments should, where off-loading is unavoidable, be given preferential treatment in subsequent shipments by the I.A.C.

We recommend that in order to facilitate the development of small newspapers, representatives of small newspapers should also be given suitable concession in air fares by the Airlines Corporation and other carriers.

It will greatly facilitate matters if the Indian Airlines Corporation could undertake home delivery of the parcels to the addresses without any extra charge, especially in the case of consignments of newspapers and periodicals.

We recommend that the Railways should throw open to newspaper hawkers all those stations where no bookstalls exist at present for the sale of newspapers and periodicals. Representatives of the newspapers, etc. should be permitted to enter the railway platforms when the trains arrive, to hawk their copies around the compartments. Where book stalls have already been contracted on long-term basis, Railways should insist that they should also stock local and district newspapers and periodicals. Some of these stalls do not have adequate arrangements for the sall of newspapers etc. around the compartments when the trains are parking. Railways should see to it that such arrangements are made for the convenience of the passengers.

At present there are no arrangements at all for the sale of newspapers in running trains. The reading habits of the public are spreading fast and arrangements for the supply of copies of newspapers would be in keeping with the spirit of the times. Such arrangements appear easy in the case of vestibule trains. However, the Railway Board should apply its mind on the question of providing facilities for the sale of newspapers and periodicals on running trains.

News Services

The Committee is out of the view that an Indian news agency should be entrusted by the Central Govt. with the task of preparing a 1,500 word news bulletin and news feature to be broadcast thrice during the course of the day by A.I.R. This material could be prepared in English, by the Delhi Office or the agency concerned, and handed over to the office of AIR at Delhi. The same bulletin could simultaneously be given to different regional stations of AIR over the creed. The Delhi Station of AIR would translate the bulletins into Hindi and broadcast them over the radio. Similarly, the other AIR stations would translate the bulletins in the respective regional languages and broadcast them over the radio. at dictation speed at stated times. The newspapers can pick up the bulletins through the shorthand writes or by the use of taperecorders. If the agency is prepared to give the bulletins in Indian languages too, that would eliminate delay in translation. The aim of this scheme is that the bulletins should be prepared objectively and that there be no Government interference in their preparation. AIR should only give its free service for translation and announcements for the benefit of the small newspapers.

It was also suggested to the Committee that a small fee should be levied on the small newspapers who would make use of this service. The Committee, however, is of the opinion that the collection of such a fee from small newspapers by Government would present difficulties. The newspapers, for example, can assert that they had not made use of the special bulletins of AIR and that their source of news was different. Similarly, it was suggested should be asked to pay a special licence fee. We are of the view that small newspapers with their limited resources cannot afford to pay for such costs. The Committee, therefore, recommends that no fee should be levied on the small newspapers making use of special news broadcast service of AIR, at least for a period of five years, and that the fee payable by Government to the news and feature agencies be met by the Ministry of Information and Broadcasting.

Information Services

The Committee recommends that the State Governments should include representatives of small newspapers in conducted tours and the Press information Bureau should also plan its tours in such a way that in each tour there is an adequate number of representatives from small newspapers.

It has been brought to the notice of the Committee that in some tours organised by State Governments preference is given to representatives of the metropolitan Press over correspondents stationed in their own State and representatives of small newspapers. We are unable to appriciate this practice and would strongly urge that State newspapers, particularly small ones, should be given their due place in conducted tours sponsored by State Governments. State Governments should also endeavour to provide free transport to accredited representatives of State papers to cover important events in the State.

The Committee is of the opinion that the Central and the State Governments should jointly organise tours in which press parties from one region are taken to the other region. Such tours will provide healthy informational intercourse and serve the purpose of national integration.

It was brought to the notice of the Committee that recently when the Prime Minister went abroad, only a limited number of press correspondents were invited to accompany him, it being impossible to send out a large contingent because of foreign exchange difficulties.

The Principal information officer, however, made arrangements with these Pressmen that, besides filing stories for their own papers, each correspondent should also feed four or five other papers, particularly Indian language papers, with his stories, and that this service should be supplied free of charge, with the consent of the sponsoring paper. In such cases, the representatives of news and feature agencies should be adequately represented, so that a large number of newspapers, particularly small ones can avail of their stories. In this connection, the Committee has noted with some concern the inadequacy of the grant placed at the disposal of the Bureau. We were informed that against the current year's allocation, of Rs. 50,000, the P.I.O. had to spend away as much as Rs. 47,000 on one tour to Kutch alone. The Committee recommends a substantial increase in the Bureau's budgetary allocation to meet the requirements of such tours.

Press information Bureau should check its mailing lists periodically with the recipients, to make sure that those requiring its services are provided with the necessary material, while it may be withdrawn from those who do not need it.

Representatives of several newspapers, particulary of those published from the border areas in Tripura, Manipur and Assam, told the Committee that on certain occasions, e.g. Republic and independence Days, the material sent by the Bureau reaches newspapers late so that proper use of it cannot be made. This is an important matter, and it is to be hoped that the Bureau will remedy the drawback where it exists.

The Committee is aware that both the Rajya Sabha and the Lok Sabha prepare daily synopsis of the discussions in Parliament, highlighting the significant items of the day. We consider that the Press Information Bureau should arrange with the Secretariat of the two Houses to obtain copies of these synopses for supply to small newspapers and periodicals, particularly to dailies and weeklies.

There is a great demand for blocks from newspapers and periodicals, and the Bureau should adopt measures for a larger output of ebonoid blocks to meet the growing needs of small newspapers and periodicals. We recommend that the Bureau should operate a block-making plant under its own auspices. We are given to understand that it is possible to have a block-making plant installed in the premises of an office. In this connection, the Urdu papers printed on a litho press have represented that what they require is charbas instead of ebonoid blocks, Charba is a proof of a block taken on a yellow "treated" paper with a special link. It is much cheaper than an ebonoid block, requires no further processing and can go into the press without involing any effort on the part of the sub-editors and others. We, therefore, recommend that the press information Bureau should make arrangements for the supply of charbas to such Urdu newspapers and periodicals, as may want them.

Feature Services : The Bureau's fealure services need to be further expanded, to cover the regional needs of newspapers/periodicals. For this purpose; it is necessary that the Bureau should set up feature units at different stations to cover regional needs. Some of the newspapers have expressed a keen desire for a feature service on such items as science, agriculture, industry, education, health, opportunities for training and employment, etc. We recommend that the Bureau's feature services should be expanded to meet this demand.

We would recommend that the strength of the Bureau's staff in different regional offices should be reviewed any inadequacy, where it exists, should be remedied.

We would recommend to Government the opening of offices of the Press Information Bureau at such centres as Allahabad, Hubli, Rajkot, Agra, Kanpur and Aurangabad. In addition, we would also recommend the opening by the Bureau of their offices in border areas like Tripura and Manipur.

The Committee recommends that Government should provide motor transport to the Bureau's offices, in the interests of speedy service to newspapers and periodicals.

We are of the opinion that Central and State Governments should supply to the newspapers and periodicals material in the languages in which they are published even though, in some cases, such languages may not be regarded as regional languages in those areas.

The State Governments should review their existing machinery for the issue of information services, to ensure promtness in the issue of material in an acceptable language. The U. P. Government brought to the notice of the committee that the Information Department of the State Government had started a daily 200-250 word telegraphic news service from Lucknow regarding governmental activities, for the benefit of small dailies. This serxice has been welcomed by the recipient newspapers. The expenditure is estimated Rs. 900 a month. We commend this experiment to the notice of the other State Governments. It is necessary to add that such a telegraphic service should be objective and factual and should not contain comments on news and events.

The evidence submitted before the committee makes it clear that foreign Embassies in India are more conscious of the value of publicity in small newspapers than most Government publicity departments are.

Photo And Feature Services: Only a few States have organised photo and feature services. There is a good deal of demand for feature articles, news letters, etc. from small newspapers. Small newspapers are not in a position to pay the writers adequately and, therefore, do not get material of the required standard. If feature articles relating to science, technology, agriculture, etc. are made available to small papers we are of the view that they would be in a position to use the material.

Some states supply photographs to newspapers but only a few states supply ebonoid blocks and that supply, too, is not regular. It was brought to the notice of the committee that in one of the states a deposit of Rs. 5 is asked for from small newspapers as caution money for the return of blocks issued to them, where as no such deposit is insisted upon in the case of other papers. This is an unusual practice and the committee feels that photographs and ebonoid blocks should be supplied free to all newspapers and periodicals.

The committee is of the opinion that all States Governments should make arrangements for the accreditation of press correspondents at district headquarters. District officers should hold press conferences from time to time on matters of importance under their jurisdiction, to which district accredited correspondents should be invited. Facilities should also be provided for the travel of such correspondents within the district to cover important assignments. For this purpose, State Governments may issue to them free passes on State-operated and state licensed buses. We would also recommend that the Railways should allow travel at coucessional rates to correspondents accredited to district headquarters for travel upto 1,000 Kms. in a year for bonafide journeys. These facilities will be useful instruments in enlarging the vision of the press correspondents as well as in providing news and other informational fare to the readers of the district press.

Priority should be accorded to the correspondents accredited to district headquarters in the matter of allotment of accommodation-officers and residential as well as telephones.

It is recommended that the accreditation rules in respect of district head quarters may provide for facilities to those correspondents whose main calling is journalism. It may be noted that the rules provide for the withdrawl of accreditation facilities in the event of their misuse, the committee believes that our home Information services have a good deal to do in the way of competing with the services provided by foreign embassies operating in India.

Training Facilities For Staff

Staff Training: Unfortunately, there are not adequate facilities in the country for imparting training to the staff of small newspapers and periodicals. In the circumstances, it is not possible to expert a good standard of production on the part of small newspapers. The committee, therefore, feels that adequate means should be devised for the training of staff employed in small newspapers and periodicals in the different branches of production.

The committee is firmly convinced that the greatest single factor which will contribute to the improvements of standards and development of responsible journalism in the country is the quality of mind of the new entrants into the profession, and the acquisition of professional technique by them.

The press council which is to be set up shortly, or the press organisations in the country, would be well-advised to constitute a National Council for training of journalists in different departments of newspapers production, with branches at various publications centres. The exnanses of the National Council to Training of Journalists will lay down qualifications for new entrants into journalism and conclude arrangments for practical training with newspapers, periodicals and news and feature agencies.

The National Council for training of Journalists may also organise schools of training in printing for the benefit of newspaper employees and those seeking careers in newspapers establishments.

We would urge that the National Small Industries

organisation should launch special courses to suit the needs of small newspapers and periodicals particularly in the field of maintenance of accounts, sales promotion etc.

Katibs : It is recommended that a school for the training of Katibs should be set up at a suitable centre, under the auspices of the Government of India, to which qualified students from all States may be admitted. An alternative may be to introduce calligraphy as a subject in polytechnic institute in suitable centres. The course may be of four to six months duration. The minimum academic qualification for a candidate should be the Matriculation Examination. In view of the fact that the chances of advancement are limited, the Katibs should be given a reasonable start. We think a minimum of Rs. 150 per month should do.

Association Of Newspapers

The Committee is of opinion that to safeguard their interests, small newspapers should form regional organisations which may eventually develop into a federal form of organisation. If for any reason such organisations can not be formed, the Committee is of opinion that small newspapers and periodicals should join the existing newspaper organisations, and the latter should form special panels with their organisations, to look after the problems of small newspapers. However, this is a matter in which small newspapers have to take an initiative and decide what form of organisational set up would be suitable from their point of view.

Credit Facilities And Consultancy Services

We recommend, the Government should expand the definition of small scale industrial units to include newspapers and periodicals with fixed capital investment not exceeding rupees five lakhs, which have their own printing presses or are intending to have them. The facility of receiving machinery on a hire-purchase basis through the National Small Industries Corporation, would not be available to small newspapers whose fixed capital investment exceeds Rs. 5 lakhs. The State Financial Corporations can meet the needs of such papers if they are brought within their purview of operations. In fact we have learnt that in Ahmedabad the State Financial Corporation has advanced loans to a printing press, which bringing out a daily newspaper. In other words, newspapers not owning printing presses are at a disadvantage. There is a reasonable justification for extending the scope of the definition of the term 'industry' to cover newspapers and periodicals. We believe that the requirements of newspapers and periodicals for credit facilities would be sufficiently met if they are allowed to avail of the facilities of the existing institutions mentioned above.

If for any reasons, it is not possible for small newspapers and periodicals to secure printing machinery under the hire-purchase scheme of the National Small Industries Corporation or long-term loans from the State Financial Corporations, the only other alternative is that a separate finance corporation should be set up by the Government of India to provide credit facilities to small newspapers for buying printing machinery and newsprint and for buildings. etc.

We recommend that the Government should request the National Small Industries Organisation to provide the small newspapers and periodicals advisory services in regard to selection of printing machinery, occasional assistance in the removal of defects etc. therein, maintenance of accounts in a proper manner, sales promotion, organisation of circulations, building up of advertisement revenue and general measures for economies in expenditure. It, for any reasons, this organisation is unable to undertake these assignments, a special organisation to serve exclusively the needs of small newspapers would be necessary. Alternatively, Government may tell some of the existing commercial firms in the line and ask them to undertake the service to small newspapers and periodicals at economical rates, their losses being under-written by Government.

Newsprint

There is no denying the fact that the newsprint distribution policy is highly restrictive. Far from promoting the growth of newspapers, it has been hindering their circulations. Newspapers are a source of information, instruction and entertainment, and their utility in a developing country like India need hardly be stressed. Thus, the Government's present restrictive policy on newsprint distribution comes in the way of the spread of information, education and entertainment among the masses.

We recommend that Government should review its newsprint import policy and increase the annual allocation of foreign exchange in gradual instalments.

We are of the view that small newspapers which, by and large, are powerful instuments for the communication of information and education to the rural areas, should be encouraged to develop in an unrestricted manner. To meet this requirement, an increase in circulation to the tune of 20 per cent over the previous year's circulation should be allowed up to the ceiling in terms of the definition of a small newspaper as given by the Committee, provided, however, that newspapers and periodicals with a circulation of less than, 10,000 copies be permitted to develop upto that level without the said restriction.

The Information and Broadcasting Ministry has

detailed knowledge of the conditions of the newspaper industry, and we recommend that the subject of newsprint—import and distribution—should continue to be dealt with by the Ministry.

The Committee finds that the policy is unduly restrictive in the case of new periodicals. We recommend that new periodicals should be allowed to develop and build up an average circulation upto a maximum of 10,000 copies of the size equivalent to 16 pages of the standard size of a daily newspaper, during the first year after the commencement of the publication. They should be granted their full requirements of newsprint from imported supplies.

Policy Announcement

The annual policy announcement in regard to newsprint imports, which takes effect from 1st April each year, is generally made three or four weeks later. This timelag should be avoided. In the past there have been frequent changes in the newsprint policy, sometime in the middle of the licensing period, with the result that it has not been possible for newspapers to chalk out their future plans accurately. We recommend that the broad outlines of the policy in regard to newsprint imports should be announced on a long-term basis.

Delay In The Issue Of Import Licences

The Committee has received numerous complaints from newspaper proprietors that applications for import licences are not sanctioned quickly. We have ourselves examined about a dozen instances in consultation with the Press Registrar. The minimum time taken for the issue of an import licence is six weeks, and in several cases it has exceeded 15 weeks. The Committee feel that the Press Registrar should draw up a definite drill to ensure that applications for newsprint import licences are vetted in his office within a week. Another week should suffice for the issue of the licence by the office of the Chief Controller of Imports and Exports so that the time taken for the issue of a licence should not exceed two to three weeks in all. Where certain enquiries have to be made, the Press Registrar should issue an advance quota representing 50% of the quota of the previous year on application by the newspaper/periodical, so that the publisher is not put to undue hardship.

Application Forms : A large number of small newspapers have represented before us that application forms for issue of newsprint import licences are very cumbersome. The data asked for is so detailed that small newspapers do not have the means to collect and furnish the required information. Some newspapers representatives told the Committee that they could not apply for newsprint quotas owing to non-availability of forms; this is particularly so in district towns. We recommend that, in addition to the existing arrangements, forms should be made available to the regional offices of the Press Information Bureau, so that copies can be supplied by them to newspapers/periodicals on request.

It is recommended that the State Trading Corporation should make arrangements at the port towns for cutting the reels into sheets without an extra charge on the newspapers before transport to destination.

The Committee have received representations from a large number of weeklies and periodicals originating from the districts that they had not been issued any newsprint quota inspite of the fact that they had been in existence for many years. The stand of the Press Registrar was that since these weeklies and periodicals were not given any newsprint quota in the crucial period, no newsprint quota could be issued to them, for they were treated as new periodicals to whom no newsprint quota was given. The Committee's opinion is that this policy decision was unfortunate. It drove the proprietors of small weeklies and periodicals into buying newsprint in the black market or white printing paper, which is prohibitive in cost. While the policy has since been revised granting some relief to such periodicals, it does not meet the requirements of the situation. To treat such old periodicals as new ones is unjust. The Committee recommends that they should be allotted imported newsprint to cover their full quotas.

Under the present newsprint distribution policy, no certificate from a Chartered Accountant is required in the case of publications claiming circulations up to 2,000 copies, for purposes of receiving newsprint quotas. Representations have been made to the Committee that this ceiling should be raised upwards to 5,000 copies or even 10,000 copies. The Committee have sympathy —exchange for import of newsprint, it is not possible for them to make a recommendation for raising the present ceiling for issue of newsprint quota without an audited circulation certificate beyond the present figures of 2,000 copies, as we are of the view that if a newspaper has a circulation of more than 2,000 copies, it should be presumed to have resources to enable it to have its accounts properly maintained and audited.

The Committee endorses the recommendations of the Lok Sabha Committee on Public Undertaking regarding Nepa Mills which reads as under :

"This Committee hope that every effort will be made to get the tariff rates of power and steam reduced as early as possible as these items constitute about 25 per cent of the cost of production. We further feel that there is enough scope for curtailing expenditure on other items also. In view of the fact that the cost of Nepa newsprint is already very high, it is essential that the management should exercise strict control over costs by following modern methods of cost control. An expert study to bring down costs may be arranged if considered necessary."

It is obvious that the quality of Nepa newsprint is not up to the normal standard and that there is considerable room for its improvement. We may add here that good quality newsprint is essential for proper reproduction of advertisement and reading matter. We expect that the authorities of the Nepa Mills as well as Government will pay serious attention towards raising the production standard of this commodity. In this connection it is interesting to note that the Nepa Mills incurred the following expenditure on laboratory tests and research :

1961-62	Rs. 14,780
1962-63	Rs. 20,355
1963-64	Rs. 26,329

While it is qualifying to note that some attention in this direction has been paid in the last few years, which must have given adequate returns, the quantum of expenditure incurred is obviously inadequate and the research sections need to be strengthened considerably. Experts from abroad may be attached to various sections of the manufactory for quite some time, to examine the defects in the various stages of the manufacture of this commodity and to suggest remedial measures therefore.

The attention of the Committee has been drawn in this connection to the following recommendation made by the Planning Commission in their publication "Programme of Industrial Development" (1961-63) reading :

"The Development Council of the Planning Commission had recommended that an institute for pulp, paper and allied industries should be set up, supported by the industry and the Government to foster research, development and technology of the industry and also to co-ordinate the work done by other research organisations, on lines similar to that of the Textile Industry Research Association and the Indian Jute Mills Research Association."

We consider that this is a sound recommendation and hope that effective steps will be taken to ensure that an institute of the kind recommended comes into being as early as possible to render service to the paper making mills of the country. It may be noted that paper is the most indispensible material for the spread of literacy as well as newspaper circulation in the country.

We have seen above that Nepa newsprint cannot compare with the imported newsprint either in quality or cost. The cost factor results in a heavy burden on small newspapers and periodicals whose financial position is far from strong. We, therefore, recommended that only imported newsprint should be allotted to small newspapers and periodicals, and their requirements should have a prior charge on the total imports of newsprint in the country. It is hoped that the recommendation will be implemented as soon as possible. Pending that arrangement, small newspapers will have to continue to depend on indigenous sources of supply for part of their requirements.

We consider that the Nepa Newsprint Mills, being a public sector undertaking, should regard it as an act of public service to supply quality newsprint to newspapers. Since the financial resources of the small newspapers are limited, any deposit of money against the despatch of newsprint, either in full or part value, is hardship. We would, therefore, recommend to the Nepa Mills that they should follow the usual procedure adopted by private firms in this matter and send documents relating to the despatch of newsprint through banks, so that money which would be otherwise useful to small newspapers is not locked up in the form of deposits.

The Nepa Mills have reported (May 1965) that their monthly capacity is 2,500 m. tons in reels and 100—150 m. tons in sheets. The authorisations in hand with the Mills issued by the Press Registrar were sufficient to cover the manufacturing capacity of the Mills for about 6-1/2 months, so that any fresh authorisations could be complied with only after that period. Cases of the kind mentioned above do not help build-up respect for the authorisations issued by the Press Registrar.

The latter should not go on issuing authorisations, if the supplies are expected to mature after a long time. In fact, there should be close coordination between the Nepa Mills and the Press Registrar, so that the latter is kept informed of the supplies ordered and supplies made, with a view to staggering fresh authorisations as far as possible. It is suggested that the Press Registrar should, in consultation with the Nepa Mills, evolve a procedure to rationalise the issue of authorisations, so as to conform to the rate of production of the Mills and thus reduce the inconvenience caused to newspapers, particularly small newspapers and periodicals to the minimum. We recommended that a certain percentage of the Mill's production (say 25%) should be set apart for meeting indents up to 100 metric tonnes.

It is recommended that the Nepa Mills should re-examine their packing arrangements to ensure that the packing is sufficiently strong to stand rough handling in transit.

We recommend that Nepa Mills should arrange to insure all consignments of newsprint, wherever a newspaper asks for such cover. Nepa Mills will thus be enabled to secure a favourable rate because of bulk placement of business. This insurance cover may be obtained from the General Insurance Department of Life Insurance Corporation of India or from any other General Insurance Company willing to cover the risk.

We recommend that in order to bridge the gap between the demand and the supply of newsprint, Government should consider the starting of one or more newsprint factories in the public sector.

Supplying Mills, in the interests of their own reputation, should make arrangements for secure packing of newsprint reels, and the Press Registrar may, on behalf of Government, address them a suitable circular letter on this subject. We would also urge that the importers should try to take delivery from the Ports as quickly as possible. The Press Registrar should intervene with the Port Commissioners to evolve a satisfactory procedure for the clearance of newsprint consignments.

The Committee strongly recommends that the Railway Board should issue instructions that newsprint should be treated as an essential commodity and be given "A" priority in rail movement.

We are of the opinion that black marketing transactions indulged in by some newspapers whether as buyers or as sellers, are reprehensible and both the Central and the State Governments should take dell deterrent action against such transactions.

We are of the opinion that where newspapers themselves admit the existence of black market in newsprint, there should be an investigation to locate the sources of the black market.

One of the witnesses, who is a responsible district official, stated that he was not aware that detection of the black market in newsprint was among the duties of the district authorities. In view of the uncertainty that seems to exist in some States on the subject, we would recommend that the concerned Ministry of the Government of India should issue instructions to the State Governments to detect sources of the blackmarket in newsprint, where it may exist and take appropriate proceeding under the law.

Another case of alleged misuse of newsprint has come to the notice of the Committee. A certain quota of newsprint was allotted to a new daily from Calcutta.

The quota was drawn, but the publication never saw the light of the day. We questioned the Press Registrar about this when he appeared before us. We understand that the matter is still being enquired into and we, therefore, refrain from further comments, except to say that we are surprised to find that the name of this newspaper appears in the printed report of the Press Registrars as a running paper.

Considering the financial difficulties faced by small newspapers and periodicals, we would recommend that Government should consider giving some relief in import duty on newsprint required by small newspaper either by removing the duty altogether or by reducing it at least.

While we appriciate the steps taken by the Central Government to reduce the financial burden on the newspaper industry, we would recommend that the Central and State Governments should go a step further and exempt the newsprint and white printing paper required by small newspapers and periodicals from sales tax altogether. The loss in revenue would be small, but the relief to small newspapers and periodicals would be quite considerable.

We recommend that the Central and State Governments should issue instructions for the exemption of newsprint from municipal octroi or any other duty of that kind.

Repeated representations have been made to the Committee that the State Trading Corporation should open depots at important publication centres like Hyderabad, Gauhati, Bangalore, Cuttack, Rajkot, Ahmedabad, Imphal, Tripura, Nagpur, etc. In endorsing these suggestions the Committee recommends that the STC should evolve some way by which bulk supplies of newsprint can be made available at the more important publication centres for newspapers to draw upon locally against authorisations issued by the competent authorities.

In view of the high cost of white printing paper as well as of Nepa newsprint, we recommend that small newspapers should be spared the necessity of buying such supplies, and they should be supplied with imported newsprint only.

Advertisements

Display Advertisements Of The Central Government

Mass Campaigns : The Committee recommends that not less than 50% of the advertisement allocation set apart for mass educational campaigns should be released to small newspapers which primarily circulate in the district, towns and rural areas.

Sales Promotion Advertisements : We recommend that not less than 50% of the advertising budget on these campaigns should be allocated to the small newspapers. Further, if the advertising space for some of the releases is reduced, it should be possible to cover a larger number of small newspapers and periodicals within the same budgeted amount.

Announcements and Notifications : We are of the opinion that the scope for advertising in small newspapers for this category of campaigns is comparatively limited, but we do not concede that such releases should be denied to Indian language newspapers. In fact such releases should be given to Indian language and small newspapers as extensively as possible.

Defence Recruitment Advertisements : We agree that the wishes of the client Department should be respected where possible, but the choice of the media should, by and large, be made by the Director of Advertising and Visual Publicity, who has the necessary expert knowledge of the pulling power and readership etc. of the different media. To strengthen his hands, Government should issue a clear-cut directive to all Departments that, as far as possible, the recommendations of the Director of Advertising and Visual Publicity in this regard should be accepted by them.

We, therefore, recommend that in such cases the quantum of space should be reduced, so that a large number of newspapers could be accommodated within the same budget.

Notifications regarding Admission to Educational, Technical and Training Institutes: We consider that it should be possible to buy some space in district newspapers as well for advertisements of this kind in order to be able to draw candidates from the readers among whom the district newspapers circulate.

Statutory Notices and Miscellaneous Announcements : We think that advertisements of this kind can with advantage be placed is small newspapers as well, taking into consideration the area of their circulation and readership.

After careful thought, the Committee has come to the conclusion that taking tnto consideration the pulling power, influence and the readership served by small newspapers, and with a view to assisting them in development, the Central Gevernment should so arrange their advertising that at least 50 per cent of the expenditure on display is apportioned to small newspapers and periodicals. In the case of classified advertisements, the small newspapers may be utilised to the maximum extent possible to suit the needs of a particular advertisement.

Advertisement Tariff : We recommend that the Government should revise its policy. Either the tariff fixed by the Press Commission (which needs to be revised upwards in view of the tremendous rise in prices since 1954) may be introduced in the case of all newspapers and periodicals of small newspapers may, as in the case of big newspapers, be permitted to raise their advertising rates from time to time, so as to conform to the minimum rate accepted by commercial advertisers.

Payment of Advertising Bills by DAVP : We would recommend that the Directorate of Advertising and Visual Publicity and other Governmental Authorities should further tighten up their machinery for the payment of advertisement bills to ensure that the bills are paid within 75 days of the date of their submission. We were imformed in the oral evidence that one of the causes of the delay was that newspapers do not submit voucher copies with the bills or that sometimes voucher copies are lost and have to be sent for again. In order to obviate unnecessary delays in the Government offices, Advertisement Managers should submit their bills complete in all respects so that no back reference is called for.

We would strongly urge upon the Government that the Director of Advertising and Visual Publicity should be authorised to make payments by cheques issued by him to newspapers and periodicals. This would be in conformity with the practice obtaining in commercial offices. There is an arrangement whereby advertising agencies settle the bills of newspapers, which are members of the Indian and Eastern Newspaper Society, within 75 days. On that analogy the Directorate of Advertising and Visual Publicity should also settle advertisement bills of all newspapers within 75 days, In the case of bills held up beyond that period, a monthly statement should be submitted by the Directorate of Advertising and Visual Publicity to the Secretary of the Information and Broadcasting Ministry with reasons for the delay. We further recommend that Government should examine the question of making payments of 90 per cent of the value of the advertisement bill on submission and the remaining 10 per cent within 75 days from the date of submission of the bills.

What is said in the preceding two paragraphs applies mutatis mutandis to State Governments, Railways and Public Undertaking as well, in regard to the settlement of advertisement bills of the newspapers. Complaints of delay on their part have also been numerous, and we would suggest that State Governments and other public authorities would gear up their bill payment machinery so that all bills are paid within 75 days of the date of submission.

The Directorate of Advertising and Visual Publicity, while issuing certain advertisements, fixes the space within which the material should be printed. Some of the representatives of small newspapers stated before the Committee that due to non-availability of variety of types with them, it was not always possible for them to cover the material within the required space. They were obliged to overstep the limit imposed, but the Directorate of Advertising and Visual Publicity insisted on paying them for the prescribed space only. The grievance was that the small newspapers were put to an unnecessary hardship for no fault of their own. The Committee expects that the Directorate of Advertising and Visual Publicity would bear this grievance in mind while fixing space limits for advertisement releases.

Criteria for Selection of Advertisement Media by Central and State Government : We recommend as follows :

(i) Every State Government should frame a set of rules for the issue of their advertisements which should be notified in the Government Gazette, and any amendments thereto should also be similarly notified from time to time.

(ii) The main objective to be kept in view in the release of Government advertisements to newspapers and periodicals should be : (a) to secure the widest possible coverage within the funds available ; (b) to reach as wide a public as possible, particularly where advertisements carry a message to the people. Subject to these two objectives, preference should be given to small newspapers.

(iii) In selecting newspapers and periodicals due regard should be paid to : (a) effective circulation ; (b) regularity of publication ; (c) class of readership ; (d) journalistic code ; (e) production standard ; (f) language ; and (g) area to be covered.

(iv) The political affiliation of a newspaper should not influence the release of Government advertisements.

(v) The budget and the distribution of advertisements of State Governments should be entrusted to a Department other than the States Information and Publicity Department.

(vi) Some of the State Governments advertise extensively in papers published outside the State. We concede that there may be adequate justification for such releases at times. For example, the Rajasthan Government may like to advertise for nurses in newspapers published in Kerala, from which State a number of candidates of the required qualifications may be available. But we have come across cases where a State places a large volume of its advertising in the metropolitan papers published outside the State. The message contained in these advertisements is meant primarily for dissemination inside the State of origin. The number of copies of newspapers published from the metropolitan city circulating in the State concerned is comparatively small, whereas the advertising State has to pay for the advertisement at a high rate in relation to the total circulation figure of the newspaper. In the words of the Press Commission, the rate payable for such advetisements works out to 'fantastic figure'.

Advertising Allocation of Central and State Governments : We recommend that the Central and State Governments should make larger allocations for expenditure on advertisements in newspapers and periodicals. We propose that it should be not less than 1 per cent of the annual budget on revenue account of the Central/State Government expenditure.

The Committee has noticed that small newspapers are not usually supplied with copies of the results of university examinations for publication, whereas copies thereof are supplied to big newspapers. This puts the small newspapers at a disadvantage. We recommend that the Education Ministry should be approached to request universities that copies of their examination results should be supplied by them to small newspapers also in their areas for publication.

A large number of newspapers bring out special supplements on occasions like Diwali, Puja holidays, Id, etc. Government should make efforts to release special advertisements to small newspapers on such occasions.

Since the Central Government itself is the biggest advertiser, it is necessary that they should set up some machinery to study the reader's tastes as well as the effect of the advertising placed by them from time to time.

New Income Tax Rules regarding Advertisement Expenditure : It is our strong recommendation that the expenditure incurred on advertising in small newspapers and periodicals should be exempted from any ceiling on advertisement expenditure that may be placed by Government. Any ceiling on advertising expenditure would lead to the ruination of small newspapers.

Advertisements of Railways and Public Undertakings : Railways are commercial organisations no doubt, and have, in their advertising, which is largely of the character of classified advertisements, to be guided mostly by commercial consideration. At the same time, it must be remembered that they are public utility concerns and have to be popular in addition to being useful. We, therefore, feel that the principles we have enunciated in the case of Government advertising should be applicable mutatis mutandis to the newspaper advertising of the Railways as well. We also feel that the same principles, with suitable changes, should also be applied to the newspaper advertising of all public undertakings which in many cases are monopolistic. It would be desirable that the rules framed in this connection should be gazetted and any amendments thereto should also be notified in the Gazette from time to time for the information of all concerned.

Two suggestions have been placed before the Committee which we recommend for consideration by small newspapers. The first is that most of the advertising agencies operate from metropolitan cities and handle the advertising business of the national advertisers. There are hardly any agencies which handle business of a local character for service to the district newspapers and periodicals. There is, therefore, urgent need for regional advertising agencies, i.e., those equipped to handle advertising business of small advertisers in the districts for placement in the district's publications, Small newspapers and periodicals should, with the cooperation of their associations, explore the possibility of the recognition of such agencies.

Another suggestion was that the district newspapers should combine and evolve a joint advertisement rate, for national advertisements, which can compete favourably with the advertisement rates of the metropolitan dailies. The revenue received could be distributed among participating newspapers on the basis of their circulations. The experiment could be extended further in having joint special correspondents and business representatives.

A newspaper is a saleable commodity. Its customers are its readers. In order that it may gain and retain its popularity, it should aim at becoming attractive in presentation as well as in contents. It fact, it should develop its own distinctive features such as, news coverage, editorial and feature articles, book reviews, cartoons, strips, humour, columns, reportage of local events and social engagements, etc. The factors which contribute to the presentation of the publication inter alia are the quality of the paper, illustrations and general get up.

A newspaper must aim at meeting the requirements of its clients, the readers. It must study their tastes and provide material accordingly. A small newspaper, whose beat is usually the district of origin or the neighbouring areas, should attempt to cater to the needs of the area of its circulation. It should specialise in the news of the district and comments on problems of the area in which it circulates. There is no bar whatsoever to a small newspaper giving national and international news and comments thereon, but it should primarily concentrate on the coverage of the news of the area of its circulation. In other words, it must develop a local character, which implies a larger budget of local news. social engagements and activities, so that its bond with its readers is strengthened. In short, the district paper should aim at becoming an organ of information, instruction and entertainment of the people of the district or the region of its circulation. A district paper need not, therefore, attempt to wear the pattern of a metropolitan paper.

As for its sources of advertisement, a district paper should tap the local sources first such as local merchants, Panchayats and Zila Parishads. Advertising is not popular at present with the traders in the district, towns and rural areas. But as the development programmes percolate into the rural areas, there is bound to be a greater consciousness for advertising among the district traders and merchants. Small newspapers must, therefore, take the initiative of educating the traders and the industrialists in the area about the advantages of advertising. It may at times be desirable to give free space to potential advertisers with a view to promoting good will. Small newspapers should offer to the local retailers a special rate, called the local advertising rate, for a customer may not like to pay for the full circulation of a paper when he aims at reaching his clients in a limited area.

There is growing scope for classified advertisements also in the district areas. Examples of such advertisements are P.W.D. tenders, court notices, employment notices, college and school admissions, matrimonials etc.

Most of the advertising agencies do not negotiate and settle rates with newspapers individually. They accept the trade rates fixed by a newspaper. The Committee has, however, been told that some advertising agencies also negotiate rates with newspapers and the case of Rintas has been mentioned as an illustrations. This practice is unfair and should be discouraged as it weakens small newspapers.

The Committee has been informed that advertising agencies are charging various rates of commission from small newspapers. We have been informed by the advertising agencies that these rates are offered by small newspapers on their own with a view of securing business from the advertising agencies. We feel that this is an exploitation of the weaker limb of the Press. No newspaper should allow more than 15 per cent commission to recognised agencies and more than 10 per cent to provisionally recognised agencies.

After a newspaper has built its prestige as a good medium of local advertising, the time would then be ripe for it to approach the national advertiser to include it in his media list. The usual technique in such matter is for the newspapers to bring out printed rate cards or folders describing their specialities as well as the area of their circulation. Multiple readership of small newspapers circulating in the rural areas is a factor in their favour. If a small newspaper can convince a national advertiser of the potentialities of the market for his goods, this will facilitate its task.

Price-Page Schedule

The majority of the Committee considers the introduction of a price-page schedule of fundamental importance to promote the growth of small newspapers. However, since the Supreme Court of India has struck down the Newspapers (Price and Page) Act, 1956 and the Daily Newspaper (Price and Page) order, 1960 issued under it as ultra vires of clause (2) (a) of Article 19(1) of the Constitution, the Committee recommends that the Government should take steps to amend the Constitution with a view to enlarging restrictions in clause (2) of Article 19 to make possible the enactment of the Newspaper (Price and Page) Act.

To cover the period involved in amending the Constitution, the Committee further recommends that Government should immediately formulate and enforce the schedule under the Essential Commodities Act. The Committee notes that in the existing national emergency, the fundamental rights guaranteed by the Constitution stand suspended and therefore the Supreme Court's judgement is no bar to the introduction of a statutory price-page schedule.

The Committee is of the view that the Act enabling introduction of a price-page schedule may lapse after a period of ten years from the date of the Newspaper (Price and Page) Order issued under it, unless re-enacted by a fresh law by Parliament.

The majority, also recommends that it should be prescribed in the price-page schedule that not more than 40 per cent of the space in the newspaper shall be occupied by advertisements.

LIQUID CARGO COMMITTEE, 1964 –REPORT

Manager of Publications, Delhi, 1965. 43p.

Chairman : Shri B. P. Patel.

Members : Shri P. A. Narielwala ; Shri C. D. Thakkar; Shri C. P. Srivastava; Shri A. Seetharamiah ; Shri S. Rajgopalan (replaced by Shri M. P. Sathaye); Shri K. Ranganathan.

Secretary : Shri F. R. Bijli.

APPOINTMENT

The Government have had under consideration for some time past the question of undertaking a study of the possibilities of arranging for bulk transportation, storage and handling of liquid cargoes exported from and imported into India as a means of increasing the efficiency of operations, reducing costs and maximising foreign exchange earnings. The Committee on liquid Cargo was constituted by the then Ministry of International Trade vide their Office Memorandum No. 7(1)/64—BOT, dated May 15, 1964.

TERMS OF REFERENCE

(a) To assess the annual export from and imports into India of liquid Cargoes other than petroleum products during the next 10 years;

(b) To review the existing port, shipping and ancillary facilities available for the transportation, shortage and handling of liquid cargoes at present;

(c) To determine the extent to which it would be possible to organise the handling of bulk shipments of liquid cargoes exported from and imported into India with a view to improving the efficiency of operations, reducing costs and maximising foreign exchange earnings;

(d) To recommend measures for the installation of the port storage facilities and for acquisition of tankers necessary for achieving the above objective;

(e) To formulate a comprehensive scheme for the bulk transportation, storage and handling of liquid cargoes and to recommend a suitable agency or agencies which should be entrusted with the administration of such a scheme; and

(f) To make recommendations on such ancillary measures as it may consider necessary for improving the efficiency of operations in the transportation, storage and handling of liquid cargoes.

In dealing with the terms of reference the Committee has considered not only the liquid cargo in vegetable oils and chemicals but also Cashew shell liquid oil generally exported from the ports of Cochin and Mangalore.

CONTENTS

Introduction; Import and Export of Liquid Cargoes in bulk; Export/Import Trade of Vegetable Oils; Export/Import of Liquid Chemicals; Central Agency; Conclusion; Summary of Recommendations of the Liquid Cargo Committee; Appendices from I to VIII.

Summary Of Recommendations Of The Liquid Cargo Committee Set Up By The Board Of Trade

Handling of liquid chemicals in bulk for storage and distribution, would result in the saving on packing and freight to the extent of 20 per cent. Excess payment is a charge on the foreign exchange outgo. It is, therefore, recommended that liquid chemicals should be imported in bulk to the extent possible.

The tank farms that would be established at the various ports should consist of standard units as large in number as possible but the smallest unit should not be less than 250 tons' capacity. The tank farm that would be established for storing vegetable oils for export should be utilised for storing imported palm oil/soyabean oil and tallow.

Simultaneously with the construction of tank farms at the various ports, steps should be taken to instal meters and weighbridges with a view to adopting the modern methods of weighment and accounting.

Government should take steps to permit cotton seed being crushed into oil. The exportable surplus of this oil is estimated around 1,00,000 tons annually and this should supplement or even replace exports of groundnut oil. Certain technical difficulties will have to be got over and the rules which do not permit the use of solvent extraction oil for edible purposes may have to be amended in the light of the imports of soyabean oil, which is obtained only by solvent extraction process.

The Ministry of Railways should be requested to buiid the following "Tank Wagons":

	By the end of the 4th Plan BG	MG
Vegetable oils	2,0C0	1,200
*For liquid chemicals other than Molasses and coaltar	750	50

* In the case of distribution of these vehicles for different categories of chemicals, the increase proposed should be more or less in the same proportion as was followed for planning the increase for the Third Plan period over the position at the end of the Second Plan.

In the case of molasses what is necessary for proper utilisation of the availability of molasses is to provide for: (a) expansion of storage facilities at the factory sites to hold molasses for export, and (b) advance planning of the requirements of molasses by the distileries and the supply thereof according to a schedule of deliveries.

A planned allocation of the total availability of ethyl alcohol in the country between the domestic requirements and exports would result in the availability of substantial quantities of surplus alcohol for exports.

The coastal movement of these commodities in bulk should not be neglected as this has a great potential for improved efficiency and net saving of freight compared to movements over land.

The absence of bulk storage facilities for exporting vegetable oils at the important port towns retard speedy shipments of vegetable oils. It is, therefore, recommended that the following storage facilities should be built:

(i) Bombay Port 4,000 tonnes
Comprising :
6 tanks of 250 tonnes capacity
5 tanks of 500 tonnes capacity

(ii) Bhavnagar Port 1,000 tonnes (Addl.)
Comprising :
2 tanks of 250 tonnes capacity
1 tank of 500 tonnes capacity

(iii) Veraval Port 6C0 tonnes
Comprising :
2 tanks of 200 tonnes capacity

(iv) Bedi Bunder There is no need to construct any storage tanks. The existing tank of the private party can be taken over by the port/central agency for providing the facility.

Considering the economies involved in importing bulk liquid chemicals for subsequent distribution and keeping in view the quantum of liquid chemicals that would have to be imported annually, the additional tank installations would have to be imported annually. The following additional tanks installations would have to be built for this purpose:

(i) Bombay Port 2,000 tonnes
Comprising :
2 tanks of 250 tonnes capacity
3 tanks of 500 tonnes capacity

* (ii) Calcutta Port 2,000 tonnes
Comprising :
4 tanks of 250 tonnes capacity
2 tanks of 500 tonnes capacity
4 tanks of 250 tonnes capacity
2 tanks of 500 tonnes capacity

(iii) Madras Port 1,000 tonnes
Comprising :
2 tanks of 250 tonnes capacity
1 tank of 500 tonnes capacitys.

The total number of tanks to be established are:

(i) Bombay Port 6,000 tonnes
Comprising :
8 tanks of 250 tonnes capacity
8 tanks of 500 tonnes capacity

*(ii) Calcutta Port 2,000 tonnes
Comprising :
4 tanks of 250 tonnes capacity
2 tanks of 500 tonnes capacity

(iii) Madras Port 1,000 tonnes
Comprising :
2 tanks of 250 tonnes capacity
1 tank of 500 tonnes capacity

(iv) Bhavnagar Port 1,000 tonnes
Comprising :
2 tanks of 250 tonnes capacity
1 tank of 500 tonnes capacity.

*At Calcutta it is suggested that the possibilities of taking advantage of the tank already constructed by

M/s. R. Sen and Co. at Calcutta on a rental basis, in the initial stages, should, be explored. Construction of additional tanks should be undertaken only after tapping these sources. It is recommended that the Budge-Budge area should be preferred for such additional storage.

(v) Veraval Port 600 tonnes

Comprising :
2 tanks of 300 tonnes capacity
Total capacity of 10,000 tonnes.

The tank farms to be established at Bombay/Calcutta/Madras should preferably be composite ones for the storage of vegetable oils, tallow and chemicals designed to bring about flexibility and occupational ratio. The Committee recommends that it would be sufficient if ordinary mild steel tanks are constructed and that there is no need to go in for stainless tanks for the present.

N.B. : The tanks at Bhavnagar and Veraval should be exclusively for bulk storage of vegetable oils.

The construction of tanks need not be taken in hand all at a time. This could be staggered and a phased programme will have to be evolved based on demand that would be anticipated, but a beginning should be made at all the ports other than Calcutta.

It has been emphasised in the report that currently the world trend has been to sell commodities on c.i.f. basis. In order that a beginning in this direction is made with the bulk storage facilities proposed for vegetable oils/chemicals, an Indian flag tanker of an advanced design with 4,000 tonnes to 5,000 tonnes capacity should be acquired.

Imports of palm oil/soyabean oil/tallow and liquid chemicals are made on the basis of carefully estimated requirements of numerous actual users and established importers. The economies that would accrue from bulk imports and subsequent redistribution according to the needs are lost under the present practice of individual imports in small lots. It would be desirable, therefore, to import the requirements in bulk through one or more limited agencies for storage and subsequent redistribution in smaller quantities as would be needed from time to time.

"Tank farms" should be established and managed by a Central Agency whose approach should be to offer the services to any one without discrimination and favour. In the initial stages, in the Port Trust at Bombay and Madras and the Director of Ports, Gujarat (for Bhavnagar and Veraval). In the case of Bombay and Madras Port Trusts and the Director of Ports, Gujarat are not willing to undertake this work, the Committee suggests that this task should be taken up by the State Trading Corporation of India Ltd., who have the requisite experience in the export of vegetable oils, especially groundnut oils and import of liquid chemicals the State Trading Corporation should put in initially all the funds required for various installations but should associate the local commodity associations in the management of the respective installations so as to avail of their experience. As and when the activities expand and there are prospectus of collecting substantial capital from the trade the question of forming a separate corporate body for this purpose could be examined.

WORKING GROUP ON LIBRARIES, 1964—REPORT

New Delhi, Planning Commission, 1967. 94p.

Chairman : Shri Sohan Singh.
Members : Shri B.L. Bharadwaja ; Shri N.C. Chakravarty.

APPOINTMENT

The Working Group on Libraries was constituted to consider the Library Development Programmes during Fourth Plan by the Planning Commission on a decision of Prof. V.K.R.V. Rao, member, Planning Commission, which was communicated by Shri D. P. Nayar, Chief Education Division, Planning Commission vide D.O. letter No. 15/21/64, dated June 15, 1964.

TERMS OF REFERENCE

The terms of reference of the Working Group was to work out the details of the library development programme with special reference to the administrative setup required, personnel training, library legislation, the public library system and children's libraries.

CONTENTS

Preface ; Introduction ; Findings & Recommendations ; Annexures from I to V ; Appendices I to VIII.

RECOMMENDATIONS

A. Administrative And Advisory Organisations At The Central And State Levels

The Group is firmly of the opinion that the Central and State Governments should share among them the entire responsibility of providing adequate public library services to the citizens. To give effect to this recommendation, creation of certain new Government Departmental agencies and non-official organisations are essential. The Governmental Agencies are :

1. A Division/Branch in the Central Ministry of Education headed by a duly qualified officer competent to deal with all work relating to libraries.

2. A Directorate of Libraries in each State headed by a duly qualified Director to deal with all library matters at the State level.

The officers in the organisations, referred to at 1 and 2 above should be made fully responsible for implementing Government policy and programmes in respect of public library development in their respective jurisdiction. As no operations, like working out details of programmes, keeping watch over progress and assessing results, are possible without such organisations, it is imperative that the Central and State Governments should setup these organisations well before the commencement of the Fourth Plan. As soon as these organisations are brought into being they should apply themselves to the task of taking advance action necessary to implement the public library development programmes under the Fourth Plan in their respective sphere of operation. The non-official organisations are :—

3. An all India Library Advisory Council with the following as members to advise the Central Government on broad policy matters with regard to all library matters at the national level:

Union Minister of Education (Chairman).
Secretary, Union Ministy of Education.
Officer in charge of Libraries in the Union Ministry of Education—Secretary.
One representative each of the Union Ministry of Community Development and Planning Commission.
Chairmen of the State Library Councils.
One representative each of the Indian Library Association and Indian Association of Special Libraries & Information Centres.
Two Vice-Chancellors of Universities.
Two Members of the Parliament.
Two persons co-opted for their expert knowledge of libraries.

(A) A State Library Advisory Council in each State composed of members as follows :

Minister incharge of Education (Chairman).
Secretary, Department of Education.
Secretary, Department of Community Development.
Director of Public Instruction/Director of Education.
The Librarian of the State Central Library.
One in four of the Chairmen of District Library Committees.
One representative of each Univesity in the State.
Chairman/President, State Library Association.
Director of State Library Directorate (Secretary).
Two members of the State Legislature.
Not more than four non-officials having special knowledge of libraries to be nominated by the Chairman of the Council, provided that the Council must have atleast 4 professional librarians as members.

For information of the All India Council the existence of a well organised Libraries Division/Branch in the Union Ministry of Education under the charge of a competent officer, who should serve as its Ex-officio Secretary, is an absolute prerequisite. The same is the case in all respects with regard to the Directorates of Libraries in the State Departments of Education vis-a-vis, the formation of the State Library Advisory Councils. As soon as they are set up the Libraries Division/Branch in the Union Government and the Directorates of Libraries in the State Governments should take steps to form respectively the All-India Council and the Councils at the State level. In those States where Library Legislations have already been passed, formation of the State Library Councils should conform to the provisions made in this behalf in the relevant State Acts.

B. Public Library Development Programmes

After detailed study of the issues involved and in consideration of the resources that may be available the Working Group came to the conclusion that a minimum sum of Rs. 30.99 crores should be spent on Public Library Development during the Fourth Plan. A scheme of phased and co-ordinated programmes, laying in the course of the Fourth Plan, the foundation of an efficient and progressive system of public library service, spread evenly over all parts of the country, is outlined below :

1. State Central Liberaries—Rs. 3,10,00,000

In four states (Madhya Pradesh, Mysore, Nagaland and Orissa) out of the sixteen States, Central Libraries are yet to be established. Orisa, however, is understood to have got a new building for its State Central Library. Only five States, (Andhra Pradesh, Assam, Kerala, Orissa and Punjab) have got newly constructed buildings for their State Central Libraries. The buildings in which the other existing 8 State Central Libraries are housed generally offer very inadequate and unsuitable accommodation for the purpose. In all 11 State Central

Libraries will need new buildings or extensive renovation of their existing buildings.

Each of the existing State Central Libraries spend on a sum of Rs. 1,50,000 only per annum. Such a low financial provision has severely restricted the growth and functions of these libraries, expected to be centres of inspiration and guidance to the entire State-wide library systems. At present most of them are obliged to serve under many handicaps merely as local public libraries in the cities of their locations. The staff of these libraries must be immediately strengthened and offered adequate pay and prospects. Adequate funds should also be made available to them to buildup their book stocks and new services. Keeping all these in a view the following programme of development is recommended :

Year	Building & Equipment	Improving emoluments & strengthening of Staff, Stock & Services	Total
1	2	3	4 (2+3)
1966-67	50,00,000	30,00,000	80,00,000
1967-68	60,00,000	40,00,000	1,00,00,000
1968-69		40,00,000	40,00,000
1969-70		40,00,000	40,00,000
1970-71		50,00,000	50,00,000
Grand Total	1,10,00,000	2,00,00,000	3,10,00,000

The above provision envisages construction of buildings for 11 State Central Libraries (@ Rs. 10,00,000 per unit) by the second year of the Plan. While during the first year only the existing 12 libraries will be aided at the rate of Rs. 2,50,000 per unit over and above their current rates of expenditure, during the following 3 years the aid will be at the same rate to 16 Libraries each of which will receive Rs. 3,12,500 during the last year of the Plan.

One of the conditions of the aid should be the maintenance of a well-equipped children's section as a compulsory feature in a State Central Library. Further, in the interest of the quality and extent of services to be rendered, it is provided that by the last year of the Plan the rate of expenditure on staff should reach a level that it is at least 5o% of the total recurring expenditure in each State Central Library.

2. District Libraries—Rs. 10,00,00,000

In all some 335 District Libraries (providing for two libraries for a few exceptionally big and populous districts) are necessary for organising public library service at the Distriet level. The data collected show the number of District Libraries so far established to be 205. This leaves 130 more District Libraries to be established. All these District Libraries must be established during the first two years of the Fourth Plan, if it is desired to lay the foundation of a well-organised and evenly laid public library system during this period. It is considered that the minimum cost of a building and equipment for a District Library should be taken as Rs. 2,00,000 and its minimum annual recurring cost be fixed at Rs. 75,000 to start with. At present the existing 205 District Libraries spend on an average nearly Rs. 30,000 per annum only. To raise their expenditure to the level of the minimum requirement each of these libraries will have to be provided with additional funds of Rs. 45,000 annually.

Thus the year-wise recurring expenditure on District Libraries may be tabulated as follows :

(In Rupees)

Year	New Libraries (130)	Existing Libraries (205)	Total
1	2	3	4 (2+3)
1966-67	16,25,000	92,25,000	1,08,50,000
1967-68	30,00,000	92,25,000	1,22,25,000
1968-69	97,50,000	92,25,000	1,89,75,000
1969-70	97,50,000	92,25,000	1,89,75,000
1970-71	97,50,000	92,25,000	1,89,75,000
Total	3,38,75,000	4,61,25,000	8,00,00,000

Further, it is essential that at least some of the District Libraries should be provided with new buildings. A sum of Rs. 2,00,00,000 is set apart for the purpose to allow 100 Library buildings to be constructed. The buildings may be evenly spread over the country and given such priority as to complete construction of all the 100 buildings latest by the second year of the Plan.

According to the estimates given above the total expenditure of Rs. 10,00,00,000 on District Labraries which fall under two main heads is shown below ;

	Rs.
Recurring expenditure on books, staff and services	8,00,00,000
Buildings (100)	2,00,00,000
	10,00,00,000

Each District Library must maintain a well-equipped section to render service to children.

3. Block Libraries—Rs. 13,75,00,000

According to available data 1394 out of 5223 Blocks,

spread over the rural areas in the whole country, have got Block Libraries. This means that nearly three-fourths of the Blocks are to be provided with libraries. Further, the services rendered by the existing Block Libraries are very poor. Annual recurring expenditure per unit may not be even Rs. 10,000 in many cases.

The Block Libraries will be the main centres of the State Library System that will directly render service to the rural population and further extend, in due course, such services through village level libraries. As the resources are not enough to establish and maintain self-contained village level libraries during the Fourth Plan great care should be taken to build up a base in the Block Libraries for village level service during this period. It must, therefore, be provided that the foundation of fairly well-equipped Block Libraries is established atleast 75% of the Blocks during this Plan. This will mean establishment of nearly 2,500 new libraries and improving the services of the less efficient among the existing ones. Under the present circumstances the minimum recurring expenditure per annum on a Block Library may be fixed at Rs. 15,000. According to this scale of expenditure a phased programme of establishing 2,500 Block Libraries may be drawn up :

(In Rupees)

Year	No. of new Libraries to be established	Cost of maintenance
1966-67	200	30,00,000
1967-68	400	90,00,000
1968-69	600	1,80,00,000
1969-70	600	2,70,00,000
1970-71	700	3,75,00,000
Total	2,500	9,45,00,000

Further it is provided that half the number of existing Block Libraries be provided with additional funds at the rate of Rs. 5,000 per annum during this Plan to improve their services. Thus 700 Libraries will receive a total sum of Rs. 1,75,000 in 5 years at an uniform rate.

Available resoures do not permit any extensive building projects for Block Libraries during the Fourth Plan. However, to erect models of such buildings suitable to accomodate Block Libraries with extension services in years to come, 1,020, buildings at a total cost of Rs. 2,55,00,000 (@ Rs. 25,000 per unit) may be constructed at selected Block headquarters distributed all over the country.

The expenditure of Block Libraries will thus fall under the following main heads :

	Rs.
Newly established Libraries	9,45,00,000
Additional aids to existing Libraries	1,75,00,000
Buildings	2,55,00,000
	13,75,00,000

The Block Libraries must cater to the needs of all citizens including children.

4. Branch Libraries—Rs. 1,00,00,000

It is a well-known fact that quite a few libraries in both urban and rural areas, mostly supported by donations and subscriptions from philanthropists and members using them, have been rendering for many years valuable services to the people under very trying circumstances with regard to their accomodation, stock and staff.

Provision is being made to earmark a sum of Rs. 1 core to be distributed as grants-in-aid to such libraries during the Fourth Plan. Each library may be sanctioned, according to some carefully prepared rules, any sum between Rs. 1,000 to Rs. 5,000 per annum. Taking Rs. 2,000 as the average annual grants-in-aid per library a programme may be drawn up as follows :

(In Rupees)

Year	No. of Libraries to be assisted	Amount
1966-67	500	10,00,000
1967-68	500	10,00,000
1968-69	1,000	20,00,000
1969-70	1,000	20,00,000
1970-71	2,000	40,00,000
Total	5,000	1,00,00,000

5. Model Public Libraries—Rs. 60,00,000

In the scheme of programmes envisaged it is proposed to set up public libraries on the model of Delhi Public Library with a view to demonstrating atleast to some more areas the various services and the standards thereof to be maintained by public libraries in the country. Owing to paucity of funds it will be possible to set up only three such libraries during the Fourth Plan with allocations as shown below :

	Rs.
Buildings (3) @ Rs. 10,00,000 per unit	30,00,000
Recurring expenses	30,00,000
Total	60,00,000

The sites for location of the libraries should be selected and buildings may be completed by the end of the Plan Period. The provision of Rs. 30,00,000 is on an ad-hcc basis ; but the progress of the project should be such that by the end of the Plan all the three libraries should start functioning fully and the recurring expenditure per unit reaches a level of Rs. 3,00,000 per annum.

6. Public Library Development In Union Territories And Other Areas—Rs. 1,60,00,000

The Delhi Public Library which was established about 15 years ago as a pilot project, co-sponsored by the Unesco and the Government of India has proved to be a success. The library immediately needs suitable buildings. A sum of Rs. 40,00,000 may be provided for the purpose.

The Institute of Library Science, set up by the Ministry of Education in 1958-59, after functioning for a few years, is at present in a state of suspended animation. Revival of this Institute will go a long way to support the elaborate development schemes under consideration by providing suitably trained personnel. A sum of Rs. 10,00,000 may be provided for the Institute to function in all the five years of the Plan. The remaining sum of Rs 1,10,00,000 should be utilised during the Plan period for developing public library services in the Union Territories and other areas for which the Central Government holds special responsibility. The detailed sehemes for these will have to be evolved in consideration of the widely varying social and economic conditions of the areas involved. Thus the broad heads of expenditure under this item will be as under :

	Rs.
Department of Public Library Service in the Union Territories and other	1,10,00,000
Building for Delhi Public Library	40,00,000
Institute of Library Science (Central)	10,00,000
Total	1,60,00,000

7. Training Of Library Personnel—Rs. 40,00,000

The programmes of Public Library Service costing Rs. 30,05,00,000 as detailed under II B-1-6 above, must be supported by supplies of trained staff to tackle the work, at all stages, progressively in keeping with the tempo of development. It has been estimated that atleast 12,000 fresh trained library personnel will be required during the Fourth Plan. Of these 12,000 half should be at the graduate and the other half at the under-graduate levels of general education and professional qualifications. To train the future librarians at these two levels within the crucial period, Institutes of Library Science at the State level after the pattern of the Inststute of Library Science founded by the Government of India, may be established in the States. The Library Associations in the country under the leadership of the Indian Library Association should also undertake the responsibility of training the required number of undergraduate librarians.

Taking on the average the expenditure per trainee as Rs. 300 we may make the following provision :

	Rs.
Initial administrative expenses	4,00,000
Training of 12,000 Librarians	36,00,000
Total	40,00,000

It may be noted in this context that a sum of Rs. 10,00,000 has been shown under II B-7 as expenditure on the Institute of Library Science (Central). This Institute should concentrate on training library personnel for senior executive and professional jobs.

8. Grants-In-Aid To Library Associations—Rs. 10,00,000

For creating public opinion in favour of the massive programme, outlined above, for rendering technical advice to the library authorities and for assisting in training of libraians and production of library literature through seminars, surveys reports, etc. the All-India and State Library Associations should be given financial assistance according to some rules formulated for the purpose. Financial assistance during the Plan may be as follows :

	Rs.
1966-67	1,50,000
1967-68	1,50,000
1968-69	2,00,000
1969-70	2,50,000
1970-71	2,50,000
Total	10,00,000

9. Central Government, Ministry Of Education And State Governments' Directorate of Libraries—Rs. 44,00,000

A sum of Rs. 44,00,000 is provided for setting up Administrative and Advisory Organisations shown under II A-1-4 above. As already explained, action in this behalf should be taken well in advance of the commencement of the Fourth Plan Period in April, 1966. May be that this amount will not be sufficient for the entire period of five years if all the indirect administrative expenses are taken into account. But, it is expected, once the Governments take up implementation of the public library development progammes costing a little over Rs. 30 crores, additional expenditure of a few lakhs in excess of what has been provided for herein for administrative operations, will be made available.

C. Library Legislation

The Working Group attaches great importance to enactment of legislations for providing adequate public library service to the citizens, and, as such, it has carefully examined the existing Library Acts in Madras and Andhra Pradesh as also the Model Library Bill prepared some years ago by the Union Ministry of Education. In view of the varying social, political and cultural conditions obtaining in different States of the Union the Group has prepared a Draft Bill for consideration of all concerned. Further, it has prepared a memorandum explaining the basic issues involved. The Draft Bill, read with the memorandum, it is expected, will present the complete case wilh regard to problems of library legislation in India today.

It is recommended that the Draft Bill together with the memorandum (Annexure IV) may be given due publicity as soon as possible.

D. Production Of Books

The Group felt seriously concerned with the state of book production in this country. Currently 30,000 publications are issued every year in India. Of these 50% are unfit for public libraries. Considering the number of languages, a few of which rank very high in the world list of major languages (in the context of number of people using them), this rate of production is very poor. Further, the quality of production of books, particularly books intended for children, is very unsatisfactory. Again, contents of books in respect of their merit and subjects generally lack standards and variety. The state of affairs is such that concerted action by Central and State Governments and non-official promotional organisations like the Sahitya-Akademi, the National Book Trust, the Southern Language Book Trust, the Children's Book Trust, University Faculties, Research & Cultural Organisations, having production of literature as one of their functions, should immediately take steps to improve matters. The problems of producing quality literature that can be used in public libraries should be tackled simultaneously with the problem of developing public library in the country.

Production of the right kind of paper for book production in adequate quantities should be encouraged in all possible ways. The existing printing presses also need bigger capacities and better tools. There is also need for quite a few more good printing presses all over the country. The authorities concerned with paper, printing, binding and other related industries should be approached to render help in this regard. Publishing should be treated as an industry eligible for loans and other facilities from Govts. under the relevant Central and State Acts governing sueh provisions.

The Group feels that the import control on books should not operate in a manner that may sieve out scholarly and technical books in favour of cheap fiction and other literature of elementary nature.

The Group recommends that at least a sum of Rs. 20 crores should be spent on well-thoughtout schemes [for promotion of book production during the Fourth Plan.

E. Outline Of A Ten-Year Programme In Perspective

The programmes for development, outlined under B 1-9 above, provide sufficient basis for consideration of similar programmes during the Fifth Plan. The ten-year period, 1966-67 to 1975-76 may be treated as a period of construction after which the work of consolidation may start with the commencement of the Sixth Plan in 1976-77.

1. Village Level Libraries—Rs. 30,50,00,000

The Fourth Plan schemes provide for completing establishment of all the 16 State Central Libraries, all the 335 District Libraries, 3 Model Libraries as well as for improving their buildings, stock, staff and services.

These also provide for establishment of as many as 2,500 new Block Libraries bringing their total number to 3,894. Provision has also been made to improve the services and maintain a minimum standard all along the line. Some provisions have also been made to assist the subscription Libraries whith grants-in-aid. Allocations have also been made for training of Librarians, assistance to Library Associations and other related schemes. The schemes together make a well-knit whole and indicate efforts necessary to complete the public library structure during the next Plan.

During the Fifth Plan public library service points in rural areas may be carried further down from the Block to the Village Level. Out of nearly 56,500 villages in the country 4,169 have population of 5,000 or above and nearly 26,000 have population ranging from 2,000 to 5,000. 4,169 villages with 5,000 or more population are expected to be fully covered by the scheme of developing 5,223 Book Libraries. Allowing for changes owing to movement of population and regrouping of villages it may be assumed that if 25,000 of the 26,000 villages with a population ranging from 2,000 to 5,000 are provided with Village Level Libraries during the Fifth Plan the entire rural India will be covered by the system. It is expected that by the end of the Fourth Plan each such village will have its own primary school and/or Village Community Centre. The Village Panchayat controlling primary education and community Centre will surely like to accommodate the public library in the school building/community centre. Location of the Library in the school/community centres premises will be the ideal arrangement from all points of view. No separate provision needs, therefore, be made for construction of building for Village Level Libraries at this stage. Taking Rs. 5,000 as the recurring maintenance cost per unit the following programme of development is suggested :—

(In Rupees)

Year	No. of Libraries	Maintenance
1871-72	2,000	1,00,00,000
1972-73	4,000	3,00,00,000
1973-74	5,000	5,50,00,000
1974-75	6,000	8,50,00,000
1975-76	8,000	12,50,00,000
Total	25,000	30,50,00,000

2. Block Libraries—Rs. 5,00,00,000

1329 Block will be left without Block Libraries at the end of the Fourth Plan. By the end of the second year of the Fifth Plan all these Blocks should be provided with libraries. The total expenditure at the rate of Rs. 15,000 per unit on this account is estimated to be Rs. 5,00,00,000 during the Fifth Plan Period.

3. Schemes Carried Forward From The Fourth Plan—Rs. 46,00,00,000

Detailed examinations of the requirement of maintenance and development of the schemes carried from the Fourth Plan provide data to show that a minimum sum of Rs. 46,00,00,000, registering an increase of nearly 50% over the Fourth Plan, will be needed for the purpose. This will allow maintenance of the services all along the line as well as construction/renovation of some more buildings for State Central Libraries, Districts Libraries and Block Libraries. This will also bring the stock and services of the State, Central District and Block Libraries to a point from which they will be able to guide and feed the units next below reaching the lowest service point at the village level.

Thus the total outlay during the Fifth Plan will amount to Rs. 81,50,00,000 as compared to Rs. 30,99,00,000 during the Fourth Plan. The recurring annual expenditure at the end of the Fourth Plan will reach the level of 7 crores and the same at the end of the Fifth Plan will approximate a sum of a little over Rs. 22 crores. Thereafter the rate of increase in expenditure will slow down. As far as can be seen in ten years more i.e., by the end of the 7th Plan (1985-86) the total recurring expenditure may rise to Rs. 35 crores per annum.

Though the outlay is not much as compared to many other sectors of development, the schemes are so elaborate and cover such extensive areas that after completion of the Fifth Plan the achievements should be fully reviewed and the future programmes framed to achieve the double objectives of consolidation and development.

ANNEXURE IV

Memorandum On The Model Public/Libraries Bill Prepared By The Working Group On Libraries Of The Planning Commission

The Planning Commission's Working Group for Libraries has embodied in the Model Library Bill attached herewith what, in its opinion, is the best way of providing public library service in a State. However, the Group realises that social and political conditions in a State may need a different approach to the problem of providing public library services than the one adopted in the Model Bill and therefore the Group feels that it should assist the State Governments by suggesting a set of alternative choices.

On one point, however, the Group is unanimous and firm, namely, that there is no alternative to library legislation. Social & economic forces in modern society are permitting no choice to the Government except to push ahead in the fields of primary, secondary, university and technical and professional education. Such pressures are not left in the matter of public library services. But these services are an integral part of the educational structure of society and already the discerning among us have felt that for lack of public libraries, our people are being deprived of the full fruits of our educational advance. In the absence of social and political pressures on behalf of public libraries, therefore, the Government on their own must accept a measure of self-discipline in the matter of providing the machinery and the resources to build an adequate public library service. Library legislation provides this self-discipline.

Essentially, the responsibility of providing public library services belongs to the Government. However, the Government can discharge the responsibility either directly or through statutory bodies—generally called Library Authorities, especially created for organising public libraries. The Library Authorities, again, may be of two types : There may be one Library Authority for the whole State, or there may be separate Library Authorities for various districts and sometimes also ities. The latter alternative has been adopted in the Library Legislation enacted so far in India. The Working Group having noted some deficiencies in the library organisations set up under these laws has preferred that the State Governments should discharge their library responsibility directly.

In any course that may be adopted, the people must be associated at all levels of public library organisation. Accordingly even though the Model Bill requires the State Government to provide library services, it has posted a State Library Council at the State level and District Library Committees at the district level with advisory functions.

The administrative set-up for public libraries also could be of different types. The Library Authorities may set up their own administrative machinery or they may utilise governmental machinery for providing public library services. The former alternative exists in U.S. and U.K., the latter has been adopted in India. The Government machinery itself may be of two types, either a new and independent Department (or Directorate) of libraries may be created specifically for organising library services, or an existing Department, almost invariably the Education Department, may organise the services. So far the latter has been the invariable practice in India. Here, again, the Working Group, dissatisfied with the way the Education Departments have discharged their public library functions, has preferred that these functions be discharged by an independent department called the Directorate of Libraries. However. it is for a State Government to choose any of the alternatives.

The public library machinery in any country must provide for the competance and morale of the personnel manning this service. In the existing set-up in India only Government can provide proper terms and conditions of service of the personnel. In fact, that is one main reason why we have accepted the principle of the Government's taking up direct responsibility in this field. Further, it may be observed, that since public library services are essentially educational services, the terms and conditions of the service of library personnel at different levels of responsibility must correspond to those of educational personnel. The two cadres may be separate or unified into a single cadre.

Finally, it is important to consider various ways of financing public libraries. Two methods compete with one another in this field. The necessary funds may be provided by the Government from its general revenues or a special library cess may be levied on taxes already being levied by the Government, such as house tax, property tax, land revenue etc. It has been found that the proceeds from the cess will not itself suffice to provide adequate library services and it has to be supplemented by grants from Government.

However, the Working Group on Libraries has noted the difference of opinion on the question of library cess and has, therefore, considered it advisable to leave it to the State Governments to take decision on this issue. The Group is of the view that a great harm has already resulted to the intellectual and cultural life of the nation by the absence of public library system and if the cess is likely to spoil the chance of its coming up, it is no use insisting on it. It, therefore, suggests an alternative device which will assure an adequate flow of funds into the library system.

Whatever method of financing public libraries is adopted i.e., financing entirely out of general revenues or out of funds collected from a special cess supplemented by grants from general revenues, the Group feels it necessary to emphasise that the Central Government must share in a generous manner, the financial burden of providing adequate public library services in the country, and that the provision for public libraries should be such that the annual expenditure thereon is in no case less than 1.5% of the total annual expenditure on education.

Model Public Libraries Bill

A bill to provide for the establishment, maintenance and development of public libraries in the State of........ Be it enacted by the Legislature of the State of.............. in the..................year of the Republic of India as follows :

1. **Short title, extent and commencement:** 1. This Act may be called the...............Public Libraries Act 196..............

2. It extends to the whole of the State of...........

3. It shall come into force on such date as the State Government may by notification in the Official Gazette, appoint.

2. **Definitions**—In this Act, unless the context otherwise requires, (1) book includes :

(i) Every volume, part or division of a volume and pamphlet in any language;

(ii) Every sheet of music, map, chart or plan separately printed or lithographed;

(iii) Newspapers, periodicals, films and other audio-visual materials.

2. 'Book service' means reference service, lending out books to members of public libraries, helping groups with books, helping people to know the whereabouts of a book or books and helping them to procure the book they need.

3. 'Prescribed' means prescribed by rules made under this Act.

4. 'Public Library' means a library within the public library system of the State maintained from

public funds, which permits borrowing without charging any fees, deposits, subscriptions or asking for any other form of guarantee.

5. 'Reference service' means assistance by the library staff to the reader or user of the library to enable him to know, locate and consult books and other materials, and to secure from such books and materials information relevant to his purpose.

6. 'Regional language' means the regional language or any of the regional languages of the State.

7. 'State' means the State of.............

8. 'Year' means the financial year.

3. **State Government to establish, maintain and develop library services**—1. The State Government shall establish, maintain and develop an integrated and adequate public library service in the State.

2. For carrying out the purposes of sub-section (1) the State Government may:

(a) Appoint a Committee of experts to be constituted in the prescribed manner once in every five years to prescribe the standards of service to be maintained in respect of the public library service at different levels and to recommend the steps that may be necessary to ensure the maintenance of the standards so prescribed.

(b) Acquire for its public library system :

(i) Book published in the State;

(ii) Books published in the regional language;

(iii) Books bearing on the State, its people and the regional language;

(iv) State Government publications;

(v) A representative collection of English books and books in other foreign languages;

(vi) A representative collection of books in Indian languages other than the regional languages for the use of linguistic minorities in the State.

(c) Offer in its public library system an adequate book service and reference service to the people of the State;

(d) Promote the use of books for the benefit of the people;

(e) Establish and sponsor organisations and institutions with a view to promoting public interest and participation in the public library system;

(f) Provide library training facilities to ensure adequately trained personnel for libraries in the State;

(g) Provide or secure suitable conditions of service for the library personnel in the State;

(h) Promote cooperation between the public libraries and cultural and educational institutions in the country;

(i) Promote production and publication of useful literature.

4. **Machinery for Library Service** : The State Government shall discharge its responsibility unde section 3 through the State Library Directorate ir consultation with the State Library Council.

5. **State Library Council**—(1) The State Library Council (hereinafter referred to as the Council) shal consist of :

(i) The following ex-officio members :

(a) The Minister in Charge of Education, who shal be the Chairman;

(b) The Secretary, Education Department;

(c) The Director of Public Instruction/Director o Education;

(d) The State Librarian;

(e) One in four of the Chairmen of District Library Committees;

(f) One representative of each university in the State

(g) The Secretary, State Community Developmen Department;

(h) The Chairman President State Library Asso ciation;

(i) The Director of the State Library Directorat who shall be the Secretary;

(j) The members representing Sahitya Parishads and other cultural organisations;

(k) Two members of the State Legislature interestec in Library development;

1. Not more than four non-officials having specia knowledge of libraries to be nominated by the Chairmar of the Coancil.

Provided that the Council must have on it atleas 4 professional librarians.

2. The Council shall advise the State Governmen on all matters arising under section 3 and also i regard to promotion and development of library servic in the State.

3. The Council shall meet atleast once in year.

4. The term of office of the members of the Counci other than ex-officio members shall be four years an any casual vacancy in the office of any such member shall be filled by nomination and a member nominate to fill a casual vacancy shall hold office only so long a the member in whose place he is nominated would hav been entitled to hold office if the vacancy had no occured.

5. The Council shall frame regulations for trans acting its business and for matters in respect of whicl regulations are to be framed by it under this Act an may appoint sub-committees.

(6) **State Library Directorate**—(1). There shall be State Library Directorate. The functions of the Stat Library Directorate shall be as follows:

(a) To prepare the annual as well as short or long term plans for libraries in the State in cooperation wit the Development and other concerned Departments o he State Government and of the Central Government.

(b) To prepare and publish descriptive and statistical eports on the working of all libraries in the Public Library System in the State;

(c) To arrange or to secure training of various categories of library employees;

(d) To conduct inspection of and render advisory ervices to the District, Block and other libraries in the State;

(e) To administer the system of grants-in-aid to he subscription libraries and to undertake their inspection;

(f) To fix the boundaries of operation of District Libraries and of different libraries in a district.

(2) The Director of Libraries shall be the ex-officio Secretary of the Council.

3. The Director of Libraries shall have adequate cademic and professional qualifications.

4. The State Library Directorate shall have a staff vith adequate qualifications and training.

5. The Director shall perform the following duties:

(a) He shall participate in all meetings of the Council nd the Committees which may be set up by the Council;

(b) He shall be responsible for carrying out such of he recommendations of the Council as have been approved by the State Government;

(c) He shall perform such other duties as may be prescribed in the regulations made by the Council;

(d) Subject to any rules made by the State Government :

(i) The Director shall be responsible for implementing the programme of work for the year as approved by the Council;

(ii) He shall administer the grant-in-aid system to subscription libraries;

(iii) He may absorb a subscription library into the public library system of the State;

(iv) He shall decide where District and other libraries in the public library system of the State are to be et up, and approve the constitution and bye-laws of public library.

7. **Public Library System—The set-up**—The Public Library System in the State shall consist of :

(a) The State Central Library;

(b) The State Regional Libraries (only in bilingual states) ;

(c) The District Library System including Block, Anchal/Panchayat/Rural and Subscription Libraries.

8. **State Central Library**—There shall be a State Central Library located in the State capital.

9. **Book stock of the State Central Library**—The stock of books in the State Central Library shall consist of books acquired through any legislation for the time being in force providing for compulsory acquisition of books published in the State, books acquired otherwise by purchase, exchange, gifts and requests and its own publications.

10. **Functions of the State Central Library**—The functions of the State Central Library should be as follows :

(a) To serve as the depository of books received under the Books Registration Act;

(b) To undertake bibliographical works including subject bibliographies for the use of scholars and research workers and to prepare useful catalogues and bibliographies in the regional language;

(c) To organise library seminars, conferences and book exhibitions;

(d) To provide technical guidance and assistance to libraries in the State maintained or aided by the Government;

(e) To act as the centre for book exchange and inter-library lending within the State, as well as with libraries outside the State;

(f) To publish professional literature, such as library manuals, codes etc :

(g) To prepare and issue reports on the working of libraries, espeeially public libraries in the State;

(h) To function as information and reference centre for the State in general and State Legislature in particular;

(i) Provide library service for children;

(j) Provide library service for the handicapped.

(11) **State Librarians**—1. The officer incharge of the State Central Library shall be known as the State Librarian and he shall be a professionally qualified person.

2. The State Librarian shall be responsible for management of the State Central Library and shall conduct all approved activities of the State Central Library.

12. **The District Library System**—(1) An integrated system, giving book service to the residents of a district shall constitute the Distric Library System.

2. The District Library System shall consist of the following categories of libraries :

1. District Library;
2. Municipal/City/Town Library;
3. Block Library;
4. Anchal/Panchayat Library;
5. Village Library; and
6. Small book deposit centres.

13. **Functions of a District Library**—The functions of a District Library shall be as follows :

(a) To provide reference and bibliographical service in the district;

(b) To give special reference service to the members of the Municipal Committee/Corporation of the town/city in which it is situated;

(c) To give special service to student-groups, study circles and other educational groups;

(d) To extend library service in the urban and rural areas by setting up branch libraries, mobile libraries and deposit-centres and to extend similar services in the district through the various Block Libraries and other Library units;

(e) To feed Block Libraries with supply of suitable books;

(f) To cooperate with and help the subscription libraries in the district in accordance with the instructions of the Director;

(g) To cooperate with other institutions and groups, especially the social education institutions and workers, in promoting library mindedness among the people;

(h) To arrange conferences, camps and seminars of librarians and other library workers in the district;

(i) To provide refresher courses for workers in the district library system.

14. **District Library Committee**—1. There shall be a District Library Committee for each District Library System in the State which shall be constituted in accordance with such regulations as may be framed by the Director in consultation with the Council.

2. The District Library Committee shall, subject to the approval of the Director as advised by the Council, frame its rules of business and proceduce for carrying out the purposes of the District Library System.

15. **Employees of the Public Library System**—1. The State Government on the advice of the Council shall create cadres of the State Library Employees similar to those of the State Education Department and lay down the qualifications and the other terms and conditions of service for those cadres.

2. Within a year of its first constitution, the Director shall frame service rules for the various categorie of library employees.

3. No librarian shall be asked to furnish securit for his being in charge of library books, nor shall librarian be required to pay for loss of damage to book unless negligence or dishonesty is proved against him.

16. **Public Library System—Finance—**The Stat Library Council shall, within a year of its constitution prepare a perspective plan to cover the entire State wit a public library system in a specified period whic shall not exceed 25 years. The State Governments sha frame the annual budgets of the Directorate of Librarie and the Public Library System in the State within th broad framework of this plan.

17. **Power to make Rules**—1. The State Government, in consultation with the Council, may, by noti cation in the Official Gazette, make rules for carryin out the purposes of this Act.

2. In particular and without prejudice to the gener ality of the foregoing power, such rules may provid for all or any of the following matters, namely :

(a) Establishment of a Committee of experts a mentioned in clause 3('), and the procedure to b followed by such Committee;

(b) Establishment of organisations and institution to promote and impart education and training fo librarianship.

(c) Constitution and procedure of work of the Stat Library Council;

(d) Appointment of Director, laying down hi powers, responsibilities and the manner of dischargin his responsibilities;

(e) Appointment of the State Librarian, laying dow his powers, responsibilities and the manner he sha discharge his responsibilities.

WORKING GROUP ON CO-OPERATIVES IN I.A.D.P. DISTRICTS, 1964—REPORT

New Delhi, Ministry of Food, Agriculture, Community Development & Cooperation (Department of Cooperation), 1967, 177p.

Chairman : Shri N.P. Chatterjee.

Members : Shri R.S. Singh ; Director (Cooperation), Planning Commission ; Shri Vishwa Nath Puri ; The Chief Officer, Agricultural Credit Deptt. ; R.B.I. or, his nominee; Shri H. Miles ; Dr. D. Brown ; Dr. M.P. Singh ; Shri M.L. Batra.

Secretary : Shri J.K. Verma.

APPOINTMENT

The Expert Committee on Assessment and Evalua tion of the Intensive Agricultural District Programm appointed by the Ministry of Food and Agriculture in its first report, inter alia brought out that one of the limiting factors in the speedy implementation of the intensive agricultural district programme is to be sought in the weakness of the institutions particularly the cooperatives to handle a large programme like this. The Ministry of C.D. and Cooperation after considering this report, vide their notification No. F. 13-34/64-IADP/Plans, dated the 22nd June, 1964, appointed the above working group.

TERMS OF REFERENCE

The terms of reference of the Working Group were :

(a) To make an intensive study of the cooperatives in the intensive agricultural district programme areas with a view to assessing their shortcomings and deficiencies.

(b) To recommend ways and means of making them vital and effective instruments for the furtherance of the intensive agricultural district programme.

(c) To formulate an "Action Programme" for launching in the cooperative sector, intensive area development projects in regard to agricultural credit, marketing, supplies, processing and storage, animal husbandry, dairy, fisheries and consumer services in rural areas in selected IADP districts viz : (i) Thanjavur, (ii) West Godavari, (iii) Ludhiana, (iv) Raipur, (v) Surat, (vi) Mandya, and (vii) Burdwan ; and

(d) To make a broad assessment of the requirements of agricultural credit, vis-a-vis, the various inputs envisaged in the intensive agricultural district programme and to suggest measures for strengthening the cooperative structure to meet this need.

CONTENTS

Introduction ; Cooperative Credit ; Farm Supplies and Consumer Services in Rural Areas ; Marketing ; Processing and Storage ; Animal Husbandry and Fishery Cooperatives ; Cooperative Administration ; Training and Coordination : Summary of Main Recommendations ; Appendix I ; Annexures from I to XVIII.

RECOMMENDATIONS

A programme of reorganisation and revitalisation of the primary agricultural credit societies should be drawn up without delay for the package districts on the basis of a careful survey of the present position and steps taken to implement this programme according to an agreed time-schedule.

In certain districts primary societies are required to repay as much as 80 to 100 per cent of the dues to the central cooperative banks if they are to be provided with fresh finance conditions of such severity need to be relaxed and as envisaged in the "action programme" this proportion may be fixed at 50 to 75 per cent of the dues.

A phased programme should be drawn up for each block for the enrolment of new members and implemented with the cooperation of the various agencies working together in the package programme.

The average loan per society worked out to less than Rs. 20,000 in all districts excepting Palghat, West Godavari, Thanjavur, Ludhiana, Mandya, Sambalpur, Aligarh, and Surat. This emphasised the need for buildingup primary societies satisfying certain minimum standards of viability based on reasonable area of operation and a fairly sizeable level of lending.

The system of group secretaries or part-time secretaries in vague in some districts is hardly conducive to raising the level of operational efficiency of the cooperatives. Each society should have a full-time paid secretary, There is also need to ensure that as many societies as possible have an office of their own to which the cultivator can look for the services which he requires.

In each State the Registrar of Cooperative Societies, the authorities of the apex and central cooperative bank margin be retained by primary societies of their credit and non-credit business and determine reasonable levels of margins.

State assistance in future should be made available only to those agricultural credit societies, as reconstituted on the basis of a survey, to be viable or potentially viable units and in respect of which a programme for re-organisation and development has been drawn up and is being implemented.

While progress towards viable units will itself help to bring to the fore good leadership, every effort should be made in mobilising local leadership and associating them with the various tasks in the programme so as to give them a sense of responsibility and participation as also to secure for the programme, the full benefit of their local knowledge.

There has been a general trend in the package districts towards liberalisation of individual maximum borrowing power and the present levels compared favourably with what may be taken to represent the requirements of the cultivator with an average holding in these districts, considered with reference to the scale of finance per acre in force for the principal crop in the district. It is, however, important that a general rationalisation should be broughtout keeping in view the following considerations :

(i) The individual maximum borrowing power should be such as to cover requirements of the generality of cultivators.

(ii) Special needs of crops, such as sugarcane and banana, which call for relatively high outlays should be taken into account.

(iii) The need for rationing the available resources with a view to preventing the accrual of the benefit of cooperative credit to a small section of the population.

(iv) Bigger cultivators should be expected to find an increasing proportion of the outlay on production from their own resources.

The individual maximum borrowing power should be raised to Rs. 2,000 if the existing level is less than this and progressively raised, in due course, to Rs. 5,000 in unirrigated areas and to Rs. 10,000 in irrigated areas.

Wherever no general increase in the individual maximum borrowing power is justified, a relaxation of the limits in deserving cases may be made permissible, provided resources are available and a case for a larger loan is established on the basis of the production programme and repaying capacity of the borrower. Circumstances under which such a relaxation should be allowed should be determined by the central financing agency and the procedure for giving effect to any such relaxation should be simple and quick.

The limits upto which loans can be given to a member on the basis of personal sureties have been raised in some of the districts. Even so it is low in most of districts like Burdwan, West Godavari, Mandya and Shahabad. Normally a cooperative should provide short-term loans for production purposes on the basis of two personal sureties, subject of course, to a maximum limit prescribed by it for such loans. In case a cultivator needs a higher quantum of credit than has been prescribed under such a limit, charge on land or on the crop should be obtained as security and mortgage security need be insisted only as a last resort.

Provision for the creation of a charge on land exists only in the Cooperative Societies Acts of Punjab, Maharashtra, Rajasthan, Mysore, Madhya Pradesh, Madras, Gujarat and Andhra Pradesh. This should be incorporated in other States early.

Oral tenants are being denied requisite production credit in the absence of record of tenancy rights. Oral tenants should be eligible to apply for loans, furnishing details of land proposed to be caltivated by them. Such information should be verified by supervisors of the cooperative bank or the extension officer and on the basis of such verification, credit should be provided to them irrespective of whether they have farm plans or not.

Convention should be established on having atleast one member of the Board of Directors of the central cooperative bank from amongst landless tenants.

Discrimination in the provision of credit has been introduced in certain areas against cultivator with small holdings. Credit should not be denied to any cultivator howsoever small, unless his lack of credit worthiness is established.

Cooperative credit institutions have not so far been positively involved in evolving loaning policies and procedures suited to agricultural production programmes. Every effort should be made to carry the cooperative credit agencies with the programme by providing them sufficient autonomy and scope for initiative in framing policies and procedures in the light of needs.

The cooperative credit agencies on their part should begin to play a positive role in the entire programme and bring all their experience, knowledge and leadership to bear on the task of the devising ways and means of providing effective credit support to the I A.D.P.

Farm plan should not be treated as a credit document. Crop loan system should be introduced in all the I.A.D P. districts.

Eligibility for medium-term loans should also be fixed on a per acre/crop basis......

Consultancy service, to begin with may be organised in package districts to provide technical advice to cultivators on adoption of improved practices and on investments like water lifting equipment etc.

Fullest advantage should be taken of the refinance facilities which Agricultural Refinance Corporation can provide for long as well as medium-term credits.

In Maharashtra and in a few other States determination of credit needs of farmers may be started in November, December or even earlier, so that the sanction of drawals from the limit from Kharif crops can be made before the commencement of the sowing season. A similar procedure, suitably adjusted to local conditions be developed in all States.

A system of sanction of credit limits well in advance of the season should be introduced. It will be necessary for a society to be allowed to draw upon the limits, even before it attains eligibility, provided the funds are drawn for meeting the credit needs of non-defaulting participants to the extent atleast of the cost involved in the adoption of improved practices. Managers of central banks should be given authority in this respect.

The Central Bank should seek the advice of field workers conference for determining seasonality in lending and repayments.

Recently a scheme has been envolved on the basis of conclusions reached by the Standing Advisory Committee of Rural and Cooperative Credit of the Reserve Bank in regard to the manner in which and the levels upto which Stabilisation Funds should be built up and circumstances, under which stabilisation facility should be provided with the support of these funds and the National Stabilisation Fund of the Reserve Bank of

India. Steps should be taken on these lines in the I.A.D.P. districts also without delay.

Cooperative credit institutions should not be called upon to finance wilful defaulters. Financing of defaulters of cooperative societies by Government in the form of fertilizers, taccavi etc. would only tend to undermine the discipline of cooperative credit and affect its serviceability in the area on a long-term basis.

Where there are more than two cooperative central banks in the district, care should be taken to see that there is proper coordination between them.

Of the 20 central cooperative banks in the IADP districts only 11 which command a business of Rs. 1 crore and above can be said to be viable according to the standards laid down by the Standing Advisory Committee on Rural and Cooperative Credit.

Individual members in the central cooperative bank should not have more than one representative on the Board of Directors and wherever their representation is larger it should accordingly be reduced.

Apart from instituting and filling the 4 key posts of Executive Officer, Manager, Accountant and an officer for developing cooperative marketing, it is important to see that persons employed have the necessary qualifications and are suitably trained for the jobs.

Though the number of cooperative supervisors appears to be generally satisfactory, there is general need to tone up the quality of supervision.

In many of the districts such as Ludhiana, Mandi, Pali, Delhi, Aligarh and Shahabad, cooperative supervisors are not under the control of central cooperative banks. Early steps should be taken to transfer the work of supervision to the cooperative banks. The central banks which are not willing to take over departmental supervisors should be allowed to appoint additional supervisors up to the required extent over and above their normal strength and provided with subsidy for this purpose.

A programme of opening branches by central banks should be drawn up in each of the districts and implemented so that in the next few years every central cooperative bank has atleast one branch in each taluka, or a block headquarters. A scheme of subsidising uneconomic branches during the initial years of their working should be drawn up and implemented.

Central banks and apex banks should be represented on the district level and State-level Coordination Committees respectively. These Committees should meet frequently.

The ratio of the share capital to borrowing should be 1 : 5 between central bank and societies. The practice of collecting share capital over and above 20 per cent of the borrowing in respect of primary credit societies in Bhandara should be given up.

State Governments and cooperative banks should draw for the next 5 years a programme for increasing State contribution to the share capital of each bank to the required extent.

The central cooperative banks should make active efforts in different directions to mobilise larger deposits by :

(i) Locating their offices in business areas ;

(ii) Improving their services to their clients ;

(iii) Securing deposits of local bodies, educational institutions etc. with the help of the State Government ;

(iv) Offering competitive rates of interest ;

(v) Opening more branches ; and

(vi) Organising campaigns for mobilising deposits in each block with assistance of the block administration.

Each bank should make a periodical review of the progress in deposits with reference to targets which may be laid down from time to time.

In any saving drive which may be undertaken by the State Government's through their officials, the practice of fixing targets for the cooperatives or pressing them to invest their funds in such Government securities should be discontinued.

Excepting for a few districts like Ludhiana, Surat, Palghat and Alleppey the contribution which the primaries are making to the cooperative credit structure from the point of view of resources is negligible and needs to be stepped up appreciably.

Primary societies should collect compulsory thrift deposits at 5 per cent of the borrowings each year after the share capital contribution of members has reached a limit of 20 per cent of their borrowings.

The deposits collected by credit societies should be permitted to be utilised in the business of the societies themselves.

Many of the central banks could not utilise the credit limits sanctioned by Reserve Bank fully in view of their inability to satisfy the condition regarding non-overdue cover. The Reserve Bank may give sympathetic consideration to deserving cooperative banks in the package districts where the banks are unable to satisfy this condition in the short run to ensure that credit support to the programme in these districts is not jeopardised.

The present policy of obtaining Government guarantee for sanction of credit limits by the Reserve Bank of India for all central banks in package districts needs to be reviewed.

The apex cooperative bank should take the land in planning the programme of provision of medium-term credit. It is also the responsibility of the apex bank to initiate, support and foster dezirable changes in operational policies at the central bank level particularly in respect of central banks which are relatively week in organisational and financial terms.

It is recommended that:

(a) No taccavi should be provided to members of cooperatives ;

(b) Taccavi should not be provided on such terms and in such a manner that makes cooperative credit unattractive and undermines the discipline of cooperative credit ; and

(c) There should be a gradual reduction in the quantum of direct taccavi and such funds should increasingly be placed at the disposal of the cooperatives.

By and large the record of cooperatives has been such as to show an increasing degree of responsiveness to the programme and to demonstrate to their suitability for the role assigned to them in this coordinated effort and promising of improving performance in the future. Quantitative strengthening and improvement of cooperative credit on the lines recommended, is, however necessary.

The estimates of credit needs in these districts are complicated and difficult. Based on certain assumptions given the local credit to be advanced by agricultural credit societies for production purposes is likely of the order of Rs. 38 crores in 1966-67.

Farm Supplies And Consumer Services In Rural Areas

There would appear to be considerable scope for opening more retail depots in some of the districts like Mandi, Burdwan, Raipur and Surat. The objective should be that, ordinarily no cultivator is required to travel more than 4 to 5 miles to obtain his requirements of fertilizers.

In the interest of cooperative development and agricultural production, the Government should give active support and positive preference to cooperatives in the matter of distribution of fertilisers, particularly to those allotted from Central Fertiliser Pool. The progress of the programme through a production-oriented system of credit in the cooperative sector will suffer to the extent the cooperatives are not unable to handle this business.

Panchayats and other agencies should withdraw from distribution of fertilisers at the earliest in areas where this work can be performed by the cooperatives satisfactorily.

It would be convenient to farmers and also help cooperatives become viable units if they deal with entire range of fertilisers. Government should provide all possible assistance to cooperatives in this regard.

Instead of the State Government taking a decision to entrust cooperatives with the distribution of fertilisers, from year to year, as in Burdwan, a long-term decision will help cooperatives to make necessary, financial, administrative and other arrangements for effective distribution of fertilisers.

The higher level cooperative organisations like the district marketing societies should not open retail depots excepting in areas where the concerned primary societies are unable to do so for one reason or the other. Once a primary society is able and willing to undertake this activity, the higher level cooperatives should withdraw from retail distribution in that area.

In many districts it was represented that consumption of fertilisers would have been higher if fertilisers had been made available in large quantities. The State/Central Governments should take appropriate steps to ensure that adequate quantities of fertilisers are secured for cooperatives in such areas.

Cooperatives should undertake preparation of manure mixtures which are becoming increasingly popular. Higher level organisations like the district marketing societies, apex marketing societies should undertake this work, employing necessary technical personnel. Block capital required for installation of equipment for this purpose should be provided by the State Governments as long-term loans to co-operatives. The National Cooperative Development Corporation should make available necessary funds to the State Governments for this purpose.

Considering the relatively weak financial positions of primary credit societies, the need for their stocking fertilisers well in advance of the season and long before the cultivators actually demand them and also the obligation of the societies to stock and supply fertilisers to non-members also, there is an obvious advantage in a primary society obtaining fertilisers on consignment basis.

In many districts primary societies are not getting adequate margins for undertaking distribution of fertilisers. Although the work of farm supplies undertaken by a cooperatives is a service function, it should necessarily be viewed as a business activity and the adequate margins should be allowed to cooperatives to cover various items of expenditure like handling charges, godowns charges, interest, shortages and also a reasonable margin of profit to faciliate capital accumulation in societies.

In some of the districts it was observed that the cooperatives were required to insist on the lifting of recommended doses of fertilisers before a member allowed the cash portion of the loan sanctioned to him. Instead of exercising compulsion, the media of publicity, propaganda and demonstration should be employed. Though it is the extension agency which has the major responsibility in the matter of education and administration, cooperatives should not be content with playing a passive role in this regard and they should develop aggressive salesmanship. The scheme suggested by the National Cooperative Development Corporation envisaging that the State Apex Marketing Societies should take the initiative in planning and executing the programme of sales promotion, is endorsed. Tnis scheme, to begin with, be introduced in the IADP districts in collaboration with agricultural specialists at the district level.

Fertiliser's fairs/melas as in Madras should be organised by the primary marketing/district marketing societies with the assistance of Agriculture and Cooperative Departments.

The cooperatives, to begin with, should associate themselves with the distribution of seeds and later, when some experience is gained, they may undertake the work relating to multiplication of seeds also.

Primary marketing societies should obtain supplies of seeds from the Seed Corporation or the registered growers direct and make available the required quantities to the primary societies on a consignment basis.

The State Agricultural Department should provide necessary technical assistance to the cooperatives, in this regard.

The marketing societies should instal suitable equipment for seed cleaning and treatment. Government should provide 50 per cent of the cost of such equipment as subsidy and the balance as loan.

The State Governments may consider the question of providing necessary finance to the cooperatives or make suitable arrangements with financing institutions by giving them the requisite gaurantee to meet the working capital requirements of the marketing societies for procuring seed.

The present position in regard to margins available to cooperatives for distribution of seeds should be examined and fair margins be determined.

The Central Government had suggested to the State Governments the following arrangements for distribution of agricultural implements to cooperatives :

(a) Implements which the State Departments manufacture in their own workshops or obtained from private manufacturers should be distributed through marketing societies. The Department of Agriculture should make payment to the manufacturers for such supplies. The marketing societies should deposit the sale proceeds in the Government treasury from time to time;

(b) Marketing societies should be entitled to commission to meet distribution charges which they could share with the primaries; and

(c) In due course the marketing societies should make their own arrangements for procurement and distribution of implements.

The above approach is endorsed.

As the use of improved implements is an important ingredient of the package of practices, credit facilities should be made by the primary societies to their members for the purchase of improved agricultural implements.

The Government of India has suggested the following arrangements regarding distribution of pesticides by cooperatives :

(i) The Department of Agriculture may procure various pesticides needed from different manufacturers on a rate contract basis. Adequate stocks should however be made available to the marketing societies for distribution to individual growers and primary societies. Department of Agriculture should make payment to the manufacturers for the supply of pesticides. Marketing societies should be required to deposit the sale proceeds in the Government Treasury from time to time. They may also be allowed commission to be shared with primary societies. Subsidies made available to the growers from the Department of Agriculture should be routed through the cooperatives instead o being given directly;

(ii) Cooperatives should not restrict themselves to the distribution of pesticides supplied by the Department of Agriculture. They should also be allowed to procure necessary quantities and types from private manufacturers;

(iii) As marketing cooperatives gain experience in field, the apex marketing societies should undertake to procure the entire supply necessary, including the procurement done by Department of Agriculture. The Department of Agriculture should, however, provide technical guidance; and

(iv) The Department of Agriculture should procure spraying and dusting equipments and hand them over to cooperatives on consignment basis.

The above approach is endorsed.

It was noticed in many districts that pesticides sold by the Agriculture Department carried a subsidy of 25 per cent; but such subsidy was denied in respect of pesticides distributed by cooperatives. State Governments should encourages distribution of pesticides through cooperatives and provide them with such subsidy as is made available for distribution done through the Agriculture Departments.

In most of the districts satisfactory arrangements for regular procurement of consumer articles on behalf of primary societies do not exist. It is possible for the marketing societies or the whole-sale stores to undertake this work. If the whole sale stores are to be entrusted with this work, village societies will have to be given adequate representation on the management of such institutions. It is important that the marketing society or the wholesale stores, which undertake this work, reorient its business practices and policies to meet the consumer needs of the farming community.

Arrangements should be made with the cooperative

banks and other banks for provision of requisite funds to the marketing societies, if necessary, on Government gurantee. With a view to enabling the marketing socities to build-up the requisite share capital base for undertaking the various supply functions in addition to their marketing activities, Government participation in the share capital should be made without insisting upon corresponding matching contribution.

At present, there is no institutional agency for providing loans to cooperatives for affording common services such as tractors etc., to cultivators. Development of an institutional agency for this purpose is recommended and until this is done, Government should provide necessary funds to the cooperatives for this purpose.

Marketing, Processing And Storage

Although the progress of cooperative marketing in the IADP districts as a whole compares favourably with that of other districts in the country, there is still substantial scope for further intensification of cooperative marketing in all the IADP districts. Each IADP district should have a specific programme for development of cooperative marketing of agricultural produce. The apex and the district marketing societies should be fully involved in drawing up and implementing the district programmes.

A few socities should be selected for development of cooperative marketing and processing on the basis of optimum support in all the directions so as to throw light on all the relevant factors in the situation and determine the best means of achieving the optimum degree of progress.

There is scope for organizing more marketing societies in Sambalpur. In Raipur and Burdwan, the number of marketing societies exceeds the number of important markets and need, therefore, to be reorganised.

In some of the districts, like Shahabad, marketing societies are not located at the market centres. In such cases the possibility of shifting the headquarters of the society to the market centre, or, atleast opening a branch of the society at the principal marketing centre should be considered.

In Burdwan, besides the district marketing society, there is also a regional marketing federation with headquarters at Burdwan. The need for two higher level organisations at the intermediate level is not obvious and needs to be examined.

The percentage of village societies affiliated to marketing societies is of the order of 76 in the IADP districts. To bring about an organic link between credit and marketing it should be ensured that all credit societies are affiliated to the marketing societies in the area as early as possible.

In some of the districts, like Mandya, Sambalpur and Alleppey, restrictions are placed on enlarging individual membership in primary marketing societies. Besides removing the existing restrictions, positive steps should be taken to expand individual membership as it would help in augmenting the capital base of marketing societies, facilitate expansion of the business and also make it possible to bring into the management of marketing societies producers who are directly availing of their service.

To promote individual membership in primary societies, representation should be given to individual members on the Board of Management of the marketing society though credit societies may be given a majority of seats.

A suggestion made in the 'Action Programme' formulated by the Ministry of CD&C that credit societies should invest 2 per cent of their loan turnover as share capital in the marketing societies is endorsed. To begin with a credit society may be required to invest a certain percentage of its own share capital in the primary marketing society, the proportion being determined in the light of local conditions.

It was noticed in some districts that while Government were providing additional share capital assistance to primary marketing societies, the cooperatives were simultaneously being required to retire a part of share capital contributed earlier by the Government. This anomally needs to be rectified by a suitable modification of the policy in regard to the retirements of Government contribution.

Initially, individual members should be required to contribute Rs. 5.00 to Rs. 10.00 towards share capital of marketing societies. Once their loyalty is assured, their contribution to share capital should be stepped up to say, to a rate of one per cent of their sales every year subject to a suitable maximum.

When cooperatives undertake procurement of foodgrains for the Food Corporation of Government they should act as agents only. It should also be ensured that cooperatives are not required to hold stocks for longer periods.

The practice of utilising the service of private commission agents for procurement work by cooperatives is highly undesirable. Higher level organisations should operate only through the primary marketing societies and primary credit societies.

In Raipur the provisions of the Agricultural Produce Market Act have created difficulties for cooperative marketing societies in regard to purchase of paddy from the members at the village level. The State Government should examine and remove such difficulties.

As the scheme of Government contribution to Price Fluctuation Fund of marketing societies introduced in

1964-65, cover only 200 societies in the country, most of the marketing societies in the IADP districts could not be covered by the scheme. When the scheme is extended to a large number of societies, more societies in the IADP districts should be selected under the scheme on a priority basis.

Various suggestions made in para 4.24 for bringing about an effective link between credit and marketing need to be implemented.

As pledge loans play a significant part in the scheme of agricultural credit particularly in double-crop areas and as this would eventually facilitate development of marketing functions, cooperatives should develop this business of pledge loans.

The majority of us are of opinion that the Reserve Bank should review its policy regarding provision of working capital loans to marketing societies by co-operative banks with a view to ensuring a smooth flow of finance to meet the requirements of the expanding programme of cooperative marketing.

Considering that the main objective of marketing cooperatives is to benefit the cultivators and also to hold the price line, the State Bank should increasingly undertake to finance cooperative marketing.

While the practice of taking on deputation of developmental officers to work as managers of marketing societies should be desirable in the initial stages and while the State-level institutions could help a great deal by employing a number of trained men to be lent on deputation to affiliated marketing societies, the best course would be for individual marketing societies to recruit their own men and train them up by offering suitable and attractive service conditions.

The Government of India are considering the setting up of a Central Institute of Management for the training of co-operative personnel in the entire country. This will provide satisfactory arrangements for training of managers of marketing societies. Meanwhile, full use may be made of the facilities provided in the various training centres managed by the Committee for Co-operative Training.

Periodical refresher course for short duration of a week or fortnight should also be organised for managers of Marketing Societies on a regional basis.

Intensive programme for development of marketing and its linking with credit should immediately be undertaken in the districts where modern rice mills are being established.

The apex marketing societies, in consultation with the State Cooperative Unions should draw of a programme for training of managers of processing units.

There is a fairly heavy backlog in the construction of godowns for which Government assistance was given, in the districts of Aligarh, Pali, Raipur, West Godavari, Mandya, Cachar and Surat. Steps should be taken to ensure the completion of the programme according to schedule.

State Cooperative Department should undertake a detailed survey in each IADP district to consider the economies of the existing godowns and take effective steps to make them viable units.

The possibility of constructing godowns of 40 to 50 tonnes capacity should be considered instead of uniformally allotting 100 tonnes godowns to all primary credit societies.

The district/apex marketing societies should arrange for a short training of the godownkeepers at the block/district level in consultation with the officers of the Agriculture Department in the District.

Animal Husbandry And Fishery Co-operatives

Significant development of animal husbandry and fishery cooperative is possible only if there is intensive programme representing comprehensive package of services such as extension, credit, marketing, processing etc. In view of the limitations of resources in terms of supplies, personnel, etc., it is necessary that, to begin with such a programme should be restricted to areas selected from the point of view of suitability for the purpose and developed on a phased basis.

Effective stimulus of this kind of development may come from a milk plan to serve the requirements of one or more cities, or, of the demand of large and expanding establishments.

It is as a part of such a plan that arrangements would have to be made for the provision of facilities and services which are necessary.

It is when the development of the activity receives a special impetus from an important market or source of demand and a project is built-up on this basis that there will be a wide scope and an urgent need for the organisation of functional cooperatives, federated suitably into a union of their own, through which the various aids can be provided, requisites such as feed, credit etc., can be supplied and the products collected, processed and marketed.

Every effort should be made to take advantage of the facilities available from the Agricultural Refinance Corporation for such Projects.

As cooperative organisations for certain common purposes develop, the assistance from Government should be utilised for meeting the needs of long-term funds for investment. The working capital requirements in such cases would have to be ordinarily met by the central banks and in areas where such banks are not equal to undertake the responsibility, by the Government itself.

One of the weaknesses of dairy cooperatives in

IADP districts is that the membership is small, and share capital structure extremely is weak. As suggested by the Working Group on Dairy and Animal Husbandry Cooperatives appointed by the Union Ministry of Food & Agriculture, the work relating to milk collection and financing of members should be entrusted to village service societies and that independent milk societies should be organised only when there is no effective village service cooperative in the area or where there is a concentration of rural milk producers, subject to the conditions that such societies will be economically viable. These service cooperatives and primary village societies should federate into the unions which should undertake processing and marketing of milk.

An early decision should be taken on the recommendation of the Working Group on Animal Husbandary and Dairy Cooperatives that the 50 per cent of the cost of milk processing plant with capacity upto 5,000 litres should be subscribed by the Government.

Capital accumulation in the cooperatives is to be brought about by compulsory deductions for milk price payable to members towards their share capital deposit accounts.

Through primary milk societies, according to the existing pattern of assistance, are eligible for a subsidy of Rs. 2,000 for equipment etc., in practice, this assistance is hardly being given to the cooperatives. The subsidy should be made available to societies in IADP districts which are eligible for it.

As recommended by the Working Group on Dairy and Animal Husbandry Cooperatives Government may contribute 12-1/2 per cent of the block cost of milk unions as share capital for meeting the working capital requirements of the unions.

Loans for milch animals should be given at least for a duration of two laciation periods as against for 10 months in Ludhiana and West Godavari.

There is considerable scope for organising creamaries in Mandya and also in the Kalana-Katwa areas in Burdwan.

There was a proposal to establish 18 farm coolers of 2,000 litres each at 18 centres in Ludhiana under the composite scheme which was to be undertaken with UNICEF assistance. The possbilities of organising separate milk supply societies or entrusting milk collection to primary societies at these centres should be explored.

The possibility of including the milk producing centres in West Godavari in the milk shed of the proposed milk project coming up in the public sector in Krishna district should be considered.

A survey should be conducted in each of the districts to locate pockets where milk production is concentrated. On the basis of the survey, a specific programme should be drawn up to link these selected production centres with the urban consuming centres.

In the IADP districts there are a number of towns with population of over 10,000 which are not at present served by any milk supply union. The possibility of organising milk supply unions in these urban centres and also installation of processing plants by the unions should be considered.

The experience of Punjab in poultry farming indicates that independent primary poultry cooperatives should be organised subject to their economic viability. The facilities provided by the poultry cooperatives to their members should also be made available to the existing village service societies in their jurisdiction wherever the societies need such facilities.

A poultry cooperative to begin with may concentrate on supply of feed and collection and marketing of poultry and poultry products.

The recommendations of the Working Group on Dairy and Animal Husbandry Cooperatives that in respect of capital equipment, poultry cooperatives should be given 50 per cent of the cost of such equipment as subsidy, 12-1/2 per cent of the cost as share capital contribution by Government and the remaining 37 and 1/2 per cent as loan from Government may be accepted.

All Government loans to individual members of Cooperatives should be routed through the Cooperatives only.

Intensification of poultry programme is being undertaken in select blocks. The poultry cooperatives could be organised first in these intensive development blocks so that all Government assistance for these areas may be available for cooperatives.

Marketing societies, should, wherever necessary, assist the poultry societies in procuring and arranging for supply of poultry feed at economic rates.

It would substantially faciliate the growth of poultry cooperatives if link between the production centres and the terminal markets like Delhi, Calcutta and Bombay and also big industrial towns like Bhilai, Durgapur, etc. is established.

The extent to which the consumer cooperatives in these industrial areas and towns could assist the cooperatives in marketing poultry and poultry products, also deserve attention.

Admission of a large number of nonfishermen in societies as in Raipur is not conducive to the healthy growth of fishermen cooperatives.

The suggestion made by the Union Ministry of Food & Agriculture that a primary society should consist of about 150 fishermen and that 10 or 15 of such primary societies should be federated into a marketing union which will undertake the sale of fish and fish products and also provide facilities for fish procuring yards, cold storage etc., is endorsed.

The Central Government have recommended certain pattern of financial assistance to be provided by the State Governments to the Fishermen Cooperatives but they are not receiving the assistance on the pattern recommended. Besides making available assistance on the accepted pattern there should also be flexibility in the pattern so that larger assistance, if necessary, could be provided to certain societies depending upon their need.

Organisation of new fishermen societies or reorganisation of existing fishermen societies should be undertaken in the areas where the scheme of intensive development of fisheries is being undertaken so that the Government assistance available for the intensive and general schemes could be routed through the cooperatives.

Adequate Cooperative Supervisory as well as Technical Staff should be provided in each of these districts for development of animal husbandry and fishery cooperatives.

If a technical department is incharge of these cooperatives they should obtain the services of a cooperative officer ar the district level and vise-versa. It should be the responsibility of the concerned disirict officer to draw a specific action programme in consultation with the Assistant/Deputy Registrar of Cooperative Societies for organisation of these various types of societies in these districts.

Cooperative Administration, Training and Coordination

The State Cooperative Departments should take upon themselves the responsibility of supervising the cooperative aspect of the programme irrespective of the fact whether the cost of the additional staff is met by the Agricultural Department or not.

The distinction between package and normal extension officers obtaining in certain districts should be abolished and the work between the two be distributed on a territorial basis.

In Shahabad district the Deputy Registrar may be placed in charge of the district as a whole. Under the present arrangement there is one Assistant Registrar for each block. Instead one Assistant Registrar may be provided for each circle comprising an on average of about 7 blocks.

Every district should be provided with an adequate number of Marketing Inspectors to assist in developing and intensifying the marketing programme and ensuring proper supervision of the supply line and distribution work.

The integration of the supervisory machinery under the unified control of the Central Cooperative Bank is vital to the efficient operation of the credit programme,

Adequate staff of the category of Sub-inspectors will have to be provided in each district to undertake supervision work of distribution of agricultural requisites.

The Assistant Registrar (Package) working in the district should be in the hierarchy of the Cooperative Department so that he may be able to work under the directions of the Deputy Registrar who would be of Class I status and incharge of the entire cooperative programme in the district.

The balance of advantage would lie in having a Class I Officer in each IADP district to be in overall charge of the cooperative aspect of the programme. He should have adequate supporting staff both in office and for specific jobs like marketing, processing, consumers etc.

The question of providing suitable additional staff in each district of promoting cooperative marketing, processing and supplies be given necessary consideration.

The normal cooperative staff, particularly in respect of audit, liquidation, amalgamation, revitalisation, arbitration and execution of awards has to be adequately strengthened in accordance with the recommendations of the Committee on Cooperative Administration (1963).

A Joint Registrar at the State level has to be placed incharge of intensive agricultural areas including the IADP districts. Such a post should be created in every State and a suitable officer of sufficient seniority be appointed thereto. He should be provided with a jeep to facilitate his touring throughout the State.

The Director (Cooperation) incharge of IADP in the Ministry at Centre has to be adequately assisted by a suitable number of officers and other staff. The Ministry may take appropriate action early in the matter.

The Managing Committee of societies should be given full discretion in the matter of appointment and control of their staff. Higher level organisations or cooperative departments should not exercise any direct control over such staff.

One vehicle out of the IADP pool should be execlusively placed incharge of the Deputy Registrar.

The Deputy/Joint Registrars of IADP districts should be given orientation training in the business aspects of all activities which the cooperatives are called upon to undertake.

The present arrangement for training the members/Committee Members of the cooperatives, is inadequate. An instructor should not normally be made to cover an area exceeding 2 development blocks with about

60 to 80 cooperatives. Necessary financial assistance may be provided to the National Cooperative Union to enable it to engage 100 to 150 more Instructors in a period of two years to conduct the training programme more effectively. An officer may be appointed at the district level, on the cadre of the State Cooperative Union, to be attached to the District Cooperative Union who should assist the Deputy Registrar in the direction and coordination of the educational programme throughout the district.

The education officer of the State Cooperative Unions should get themselves closely associated with the IADP in their respective areas. The Chairman of the District Cooperative Union or its Chief Executive Officer should be included in the Cooperation Sub-Committee at the district level.

Besides the initial courses of 4 to 6 weeks to be organised by the National Cooperative Union of India every year, for Instructors of the peripatetic units, a refresher course for 2 or 3 districts should be held by National Cooperative Union of India every year as a normal feature of its activity.

There is need for coodination between the agricultural information unit in IADP districts and the State/District Cooperative Unions, in regard to publicity. Specific measures be taken to bring this about.

The District and State Level Coordination Committees were not meeting regularly. Steps should be taken to ensure that these Committees meet regularly and review the progress of the programme.

STUDY TEAM ON THE AUDIT OF ACCOUNTS OF PANCHATI RAJ BODIES, 1964—REPORT

New Delhi, Ministry of Community Development and Corporation (Department of Community Development), 1965. 54p.

Chairman : Shri R. K. Khanna.
Member : Shri J. C Luther.
Secretary : Shri K. K. Uppal.
Assistant Secretary : Shri P. K. Ramachandran.

APPOINTMENT

Panchayati Raj is now under implementation in ten States. In three more States, necessary legislation has been enacted and arrangements are under way for the establishment of higher tier institutions. By the end of the Third Plan Period the entire country will have been covered by Panchayati Raj Institutions. In this context the need for timely and efficient audit of the accounts of Panchayati Raj Institutions assumes special significance.

The Study Group on Budgeting and Accounting Procedure of Panchayati Raj Institutions set up in July 1962, incidently went into the question of audit and found that the arrangements in vogue in the States were generally satisfactory. They recommended that the States should aim at cent per cent audit of accounts of Panchyati Raj Institutions and that there should be a system test audit of expenditure of grants by the Accountant Generals. These recommendations are under various stages of implementation by the State Governments.

With the progressive devolution of resources and functions to Panchayati Raj Institutions the need for ensuring soundness and propriety in their financial transactions has become urgent. It has, therefore, become necessary to undertake a detailed examination of the actual working of the present system of audit of the accounts of Panchayati Raj Institutions, to locate the deficiencies, to devise measures to strengthen the system and to suggest a basic pattern of audit suitable for all States, allowing for local modifications. The Government of India have accordingly decided to set up a Study Team to go into the question and to make detailed recommendations in the Ministry of Community Development and Cooperation by their Resolution No. 9/1/64, dated June, 27, 1964.

TERMS OF REFERENCE

(i) To study the practical working of the system of audit of accounts of the Panchayati Raj Institutions at various levels and to suggest a basic pattern of audit for adoption with necessary modifications to suit local conditions ;

(ii) To recommend, in particular, measures for

strengthening the system of audit so as to ensure its adequacy` in relation both to quantum and frequancy;

(iii) To suggest, if necessary, a phased programme of the revised system for adoption, with due regard, among other things, to its financial implifications and the availability of trained and experienced personnel; and

(iv) To make such other recommendations of an incidental and consequential nature, bearing on the budgeting and accounting procedures of panchayati Raj Bodies, as the Study Team may consider necessary, to realise the objective in view.

CONTENTS

Part I : Introductory Background; Accounts; Audit; Followup of Audit; Surcharge; Role of Accountant General; Submmission of Reports to Legislature; Epilogue; Summary of the Recommendations; **Part II**; Annexures from I to VI.

RECOMMENDATIONS

Serial No.	Chapter	Paragraph	Summary of the Recommendations
1.	III	3.4	Panchayats with income over Rs. 10,000 should have a full-time Secretary and others grouped so that one Secretary looks after not more than five panchayats. If Panchayats are not able to meet the cost, suitable subsidy to be given by Government which may be progressively withdrawn.
2.		3.6	The capacity of training institutions for Panchayat Secretaries should be enlarged to cover the remaining untrained personnel within a period of two years.
3.		3.8	Panchayati Raj accounting personnel should be constituted into a cadre under the Development or Panchayati Raj Department. Shortage may be met by deputation from the staff of the Accountants General.
4.		3.11	Central Government may consider rationalisation and simplification in the accounting procedure in the flow of funds from the Centre and States to Panchayati Raj Institutions.
5.		3.12	State Government should undertake periodical review of farms and registers for further simplification and reduction in numbers.
6.	IV	4.3	Audit of Panchayats should be taken up by Examiner Local Funds Accounts where it is not so far done.
7.		4.4	A Primary Auditor should be placed at the Panchayati Samiti for audit of 40-50 Village Panchyats. Suitable regrouping may be done for placement of the Primary Auditor when there is more or less number of Village Panchayats in a Samiti.
8.		4.7	Audit should be conducted annually of 3-4 months' accounts including the month of March.
9		4.8	Each State should workout the actual shortage of audit personnel on the basis of norm suggested, and the following other factors: (a) Number of institutions. (b) Average time taken for audit. (c) Quantum of backlog. (d) Need for prompt scrutiny of replies to the audit objections.
10.		4.9	Expenditure on audit should not exceed 2 per cent of the income of the institutions.
11.		4.10	Audit should not be confined to a voucher check but also see that the sanction to expenditure is in order and is related to performance.
12.		4.12	The audit party may preferably consist of 1 Senior Auditor and 2 Junior Auditors and located at each of the district headquarters. Adequate Gazetted Supervision to be provided for groups of districts. One special party can be located at the headquarters of the State for any special audit.
13.		4.13	A cadre under the Examiner should be formed to cover the Audit Personnel of Panchayati Raj. In the initial stages officers may be obtained on deputation from the audit department to meet shortage.
14.		4.16	Audit memoes for Village Panchayats should be issued in the regional language.

15.		4.17	A manual for Panchayati Raj Bodies for imparting guidance in accounting and audit procedure should be prepared.
16.		4.18	Status, power and functions of the Examiner should be inscribed in the Statute, He should be drawn from the I.A.&A.S. atleast in the initial stages and till the cadre comes to fruition.
17.		4.19	Examiner should have powers of waiver upto Rs. 100. Further delegation may be made for appropriate reduced amounts for gazetted staff under him.
18.		4.20	Audit fee should not be recovered from Panchayati Raj Institutions.
19.		5.3	The period between the conclusion of audit and issue of the report should not exceed two months, preliminary replies should be obtained on the spot. Reports need not be printed.
20.		5.7	Old objections pertaining to erstwhile District Boards and other local bodies may be reviewed. procedural and technical objections dropped, irrecoverable amounts written off and a vigorous drive for recovery be launched in other cases.
21.		5.8	Higher tiers should supervise the lower ones. General body meetings at each tier may be held once in three months to review the outstanding objections.
22.		5.9	Government should have power to clamp pre-audit for prescribed period in case of persistent financial defauls.
23.		5.14	Provision of a special machinery like Triangular Committee consisting of the representatives of the Accountant General, Development Commissioner and the Examiner, as in Orissa, recommended at the State and district levels to review the outstanding objections. Stringent action to ensue against officials reponsible for serious delays in compliance.
24.		5.15	The internal audit machinery of the Development Department should assist the accounts staff of the Panchayati Raj Bodies, especially at the lower tiers in the disposal of audit objections and educate them in accounts matters.
25.	VI	6.4	The Examiner should be given the power of the surcharge.
26.		6.7	For the option to the aggrieved party to appeal against surcharge either to State Government or to the Civil/Court may remain. As early as practicable the State Governments should divert themselves of this power and the appeal should lie only to the Civil Court. Alternatively Panchayati Raj Tribunals may be set up for heariag of appeals in surcharge cases and other matters.
27.		6.8	The limitation period for instituting surcharge proceedings should be four years.
28.		6.9	Surcharge should also be made applicable to the lowest tier in States where it is not already so provided.
29.		6.10	Surcharge proceeding should be instituted only against non-officials and direct employees of the Panchayati Raj bodies. In the case of Government Servants on deputation the matter should be reported to the parent department for instituting necessary action.
30.		6.11	Surcharge should not include an element of fine though there may be a provision for recovery of interest.
31.	VII	7.6	Apart from the audit by the Examiner, a supplementary independent test by the Accountant General is recommended.
32.		7.15	A provision may be included in the proposed Bill under Article 149 of the Constitution, defining the powers and duties of the Comptroller and Auditor General, to the effect that audit of Panchayati Bodies may be entrusted to him by the State Government after consultation with him.

33	VIII	8.5	A consolidated finance account with an audit review on the working of Panchayati Raj Bodies may be submitted to the Legislature. It would inter alia mention :— (i) The number of institutions of each type; (ii) Funds placed at the disposal of the institutions; (iii) The number of the units which have not finalised their accounts; (iv) The number of units for which audit could not be taken up; (v) Number and broad category of objections pending settlement; and (vi) The efforts made for their clearance.
34.		8.6	The Secretary, Panchayati Raj Department may continue to appear and answer the queries of the Public Accounts Committee in respect of these bodies and carry out its recommendations.
35.		8.8	The conventional audit report under Article 151(2) of the Constitution may include : (i) A resume of the grants given by various departments to the Panchayati Raj Bodies; (ii) Comments on the adequacy of examination by Government before the release of grants; (iii) Salient points from the Report of the Examiner; (iv) Results of statutory test audit by the Accountant General.

EDUCATION COMMISSION, 1964—REPORT

Delhi, Manager of Publications, 1966. 692p.+xiiip.

Chairman : Prof. D.S. Kothari.
Members : Shri A. R. Dawood ; Mr. H. L. Elvin ; Shri R.A. Gopalaswami ; Prof. Sadatoshi Ihara ; Dr. V. S. Jha ; Shri P.N. Kirpal ; Prof. M. V. Mathur ; Dr. B. P. Pal ; Kumari S. Panandikar ; Prof. Roger Revelle ; Dr. K.G. Saiyidain ; Dr. T. Sen ; Prof. S. A. Shumovsky ; Mon. Jean Thomas.
Associate-Secretary : Mr. J.F. McDougall.
Secretary : Shri J.P. Naik.

APPOINTMENT

The Education Commission was appointed by the Government of India by Resolution, dated 14th July, 1964 to advise Government on the national pattern of education and on the general principles and policies for the development of education at all stages and in all aspects.

TERMS OF REFERENCE

To advise Government on the national pattern of education and on the general principles and policies for the development of education at all stages and in all aspects.

CONTENTS

Foreword ; **Part One** : General Problems—Education and National Objectives ; The Educational System : Structure and Standards ; Teacher Status ; Teacher Education ; Enrolments and Manpower ; Towards Equalization of Education Opportunity ; **Part Two** : Education at Different Stages and In Different Sectors—School Education : Problems of Expansion ; School Curriculum ; Teaching Method, Guidance and Evaluation ; School Education : Administration and Supervision; Higher Education : Objectives and Improvement, Higher Education : Enrolments and Programmes ; The Governance of Universities ; Education for Agriculture; Vocational, Technical and Engineering Education ; Science Education and Research ; Adult Education ; **Part Three** : Implementation—Educational Planning and Administration ; Educational Finance ; Need for Vigorous and Sustained Implementation ; Supplemental Notes ; **Part Four** : Supplementary Papers—Minute of

Supplementation ; Appendices I to IX; Summary of Recommendations ; Index ; List of Tables ; List of Charts ; List of Abbreviations.

RECOMMENDATIONS

Education And National Objectives

The most important and urgent reform needed in education is to transform it, to endeavour, to relate it to the life, needs and aspirations of the people and thereby make it a powerful instrument of social, economic and cultural transformation necessary for the realization of the national goals. For this purpose, education should be developed so as to increase productivity, achieve social and national integration, accelerate the process of modernization and cultivate social, moral and spiritual values.

Education and Productivity : The following programmes are needed to relate education to productivity:

Science Education : Science education should become an integral part of school education and ultimately become a part of all courses at university stage also.

Work Experience : Work-experience should be introduced as an integral part of all education.

Every attempt should be made to orient work experience to technology and industrialization and to the application of science to productive processes, including agriculture.

Vocationalization : Secondary education should be increasingly and largely vocationalized and in higher education, a greater emphasis should be placed on agricultural and technical education.

Social and National Integration : The achievement of social and national integration is an important objective of the educational system and the following steps should: be taken to strengthen national consciousness and unity

The Common School : The common school system of public education should be adopted as a national goal and effectively implemented in a phased programme spread over 20 years.

Social and National Service : Social and national service should be made obligatory for all students at all stages. These programmes should be organized cocurrently with academic studies in schools and colleges.

At the primary stage, programmes of social service should be developed in all schools on the lines of those developed in basic education.

At the secondary stage, social service for a total of 30 days at the lower secondary stage and 20 days at the higher secondary stage (10 days a year) should be obligatory for all students. It may be done in one or more stretches.

At the undergraduate stage, social service for 60 days in total (to be done in one or more stretches) should be obligatory for all students.

Every educational institution should try to develop a programme of social and community service of its own in which all its students would be suitably involved for periods indicated above.

Labour and social service camps should be organized by creating a special machinery for them in each district. Participation in such camps should be obligatory for all students for whom no programmes of social service have been organized in the educational institutions they attend.

N.C.C. should be continued on its present basis till the end of the Fourth Five Year Plan. The authorities concerned should explore the possibility of providing this training, on a whole-time basis, in a continuous programme of about 60 days at the undergraduate stage. In the meanwhile, alternate forms of social service should be developed and as they come into operation, the NCC should be made voluntary.

Language Policy : The development of an appropriate language policy can materially assist in social and national integration.

Mother-tongue has a pre-eminent claim as the medium of education at the school and college stages. Moreover, the medium of education in school and higher education should generally be the same. The regional languages should, therefore, be adopted as the media of education in higher education.

The UGC and the universities should workout a programme for the adoption of these recommendations suitably for each university or a group of universities. The change-over should be completed with in ten years.

Energetic action is needed to produce books and literature, particularly scientific and technical, in regional languages. This should be made a responsibilty of universities assisted by UGC.

All-India institutions should continue to use English as the medium of education for the time being. The eventual adoption of Hindi should, however, be considered in due course, subject to certain safeguards.

The regional languages should also be made the languages of administration for the regions concerned as early as possible so that higher services are not barred to those who study in the regional medium.

The teaching and study of English should continue to be promoted right from the school stage. Encouragement should be given also to the study of other languages of international communication. The study of Russian needs special attention.

It would be desirable to set up a few institutions, both at the school and university levels, with some of the important world languages as media of education.

English will serve as a link-language in higher education for academic work and intellectual inter-communication. It is, however, equally obvious that English cannot serve as the link-language for the majority of the people. It is only Hindi which can and should take this place in due course. As it is the official language of the Union and the link language of the people, all measures should be adopted to spread it in the non-Hindi areas.

In addition to Hindi, it is essential to provide multiple channels of inter-State communication in all modern Indian languages. In every linguistic region, there should be a number of persons who know the other modern Indian languages and some who are familiar with their literature and able to contribute to them. For this purpose, there should be adequate arragements, both in schools and colleges, for teaching different modern Indian languages. In addition, steps should be taken to establish strong departments in some of the modern Indian languages in every university. At the B.A. and M.A. levels, it should be possible to combine two modern Indian languages.

Promotion of National Consciousness : Promoting national consciousness should be an important objective of the school system. This should be attempted through the promotion of understanding and re-evaluation of our cultural heritage and the creation of a strong driving faith in the future towards which we aspire :

(a) The first would be promoted by well-organized teaching of the languages and literatures, philosophy, religions and history of India, and by introducing the students to Indian architecture, sculpture, painting, music, dance and drama. In addition, it would be desirable to promote greater knowledge, understanding and appreciation of the different parts of India by including their study in the curricula, by the exchange of teachers. wherever possible, by the development of fraternal relations between educational institutions in different parts of the country, and the organization of holiday camps and summer schools on an inter-State basis, designed to break down regional or linguistic barriers.

(b) Creation of a faith in the future would involve an attempt, as a part of the courses in citizenship, to bring home to the students the principles of the Constitution, the great human values referred to in its Preamble, the nature of the democratic-socialistic society which we desire to create and the Five Year Plans of national development.

There is no contradiction between the promotion of national consciousness and the development of international understanding which education should simultaneously strive to promote.

The educational programme in schools and colleges should be designed to inculcate democratic values.

Education and Modernization : In a modern society, knowledge increases at a terrific pace and social change is very rapid. This needs a radical transformation in the educational system. Education is no longer taken as concerned primarily with the imparting of knowledge or the preparation of a finished product, but with the awakening of curiosity, the development of proper interests, attitudes and values and the building-up of such essential skills such as independent study and capacity to think and judge for oneself. This also involves a radical alteration in the methods of teaching and in the training of teachers.

To modernise itself, a society has to educate itself. Apart from raising the educational level of the averaage citizen, it must try to create an intelligentsia of adequate size and competence, which comes from all strata of society and whose loyalties and aspirations are rooted to the Indian soil.

Social, Moral and Spiritual Values : The education system should emphasize the development of fundamental, social, moral and spiritual values. From this point of view :

(a) The Central and State Governments should adopt measures to introduce education in moral, social and spiritual values in all institutions under their (or local authority) control on the lines recommended by the University Education Commission and the Committee on Religious and Moral Instruction ;

(b) The privately managed institutions should also be expected to follow suit ;

(c) Apart from education in such values being made an integral part of school programmes generally, some periods, should be set apart in the time-table for this purpose. They should be taken, not by specially recruited teachers but by general teachers, preferably from different communities, considered suitable for the purpose. It should be one of the important objectives of training institutions to prepare them for it ;

(d) The University departments in Comparative Religion should be specially concerned with the ways in which these values can be taught wisely and effectively and should undertake preparation of special literature for use by students and teachers.

Education about Religions : It is necessary for a multi-religions democratic State to promote a tolerant study of all religions so that its citizens can understand each other better and live amicably together. A syllabus giving well chosen information about each of the major religions shou'd be included as a part of the course in citizenship or as part of general education to be introduced in schools and colleges up to the first degree. It should highlight the fundamental similarities in the great religions of the world and the emphasis they place on the cultivation of certain broadly comparable and moral and spiritual values. It would be a great advantage to have a common course on this subject in all parts of the country and common textbooks which should be prepared at the national level by the competent and suitable experts in each religion.

The Educational System : Structure And Standards

Structure and Duration : The standards in any given system of education at a given time depend upon four essential elements : (a) the structure or the division of the educational pyramid into different levels or stages and their inter-relationships ; (b) the duration or total period covered by the different stages ; (c) the quality of teachers, curricula, methods of teachings and evaluation, equipment and buildings ; and (d) the utilization of available facilities. All these elements are inter-related, but they are not of equal significance.

The structure which may be regarded as the skeleton of the educational system, is of the least importance.

The duration or total period of education plays a more significant role ; but it becomes crucial only when the available facilities are utilized to the full and no further improvement can be expected without the addition of time.

The quality of different inputs is even more important, and with an improvement in these, it is possible to raise the standards considerably without affecting the structure or increasing duration.

But probably the most important is utilizatoin of available facilities and obtaining the maximum return at the existing level of inputs.

The immediate efforts on which attention should be concentrated at the school stage are two : increasing the intensity of utilization and improving the quality of inputs, other than time. With these, it is possible to add about a year of content to the school course. In addition, it is also necessary to increase the duration of the higher secondary stage to two years under a phased programme which will begin in the Fifth Plan and be completed by 1985.

The new educational structure should consist of—

One to three years of pre-school education.

A ten-year period of general education which may be subdivided into a primary stage of 7 to 8 years (a lower primary stage of 4 or 5 years and a higher primary stage of 3 or 2 years) and lower secondary stage of 3 or 2 years of general education or one to three years of vocational education (the enrolment in vocational courses being raised to 50 per cent of the total).

A higher secondary stage of two years of general education or one to three years of vocational education (the enrolments in vocational education being raised to 50 per cent of the total).

A higher education stage having a course of three years or more for the first degree and followed by courses of varying durations for the second or research degrees.

The age of admission to Class I should ordinarily be not less than 6+.

The first public external examination should come at the end of the first ten years of schooling.

The system of streaming in schools of general education from Class IX should be abandoned and no attempt at specialization made until beyond Class X.

Secondary schools should be of two types—high schools providing a ten year course and higher secondary schools providing a course of 11 or 12 years.

Attempts to upgrade every secondary school to the higher secondary stage should be abandoned. Only the bigger and more efficient schools—about one-fourth of the total number—should be upgraded. The status of the existing higher secondary schools should be reviewed from this point of view and, if necessary, those that do not deserve the higher secondary status should be downgraded.

A new higher secondary course, beginning in Class XI, should be instituted. Classes XI and XII (and during the transitional period Class XI only) should provide specialised studies in different subjects. Where, however, existing higher secondary schools with integrated course in Classes IX, X and XI are running satisfactorily, the arrangement may continue until Class XII is added.

Transfer of the Pre-University Course : The pre-university course should be transferred from the universities and affiliated colleges to secondary schools by 1975-76 and duration of the course should be lengthened to two years by 1985-86.

The UGC should be responsible for effecting the transfer of all pre-university or intermediate work from university and affiliated colleges to schools.

Simultaneously higher secondary class or classes should be started in selected schools by State Education Departments, as self-contained units, and assisted with adequate recurring grants.

Boards of Secondary Education should be reconstituted to accept the responsibility for the higher secondary stage also.

Lengthening the Duration of the Higher Secondary Stage : In the Fourth Plan, efforts should be concentrated on securing a better utilization of existing facilities, on making the necessary preparation for implementing the programme and on lengthening the duration of the course in a few selected institutions as pilot projects.

The programme of lengthening the duration of the higher secondary stage should begin in the Fifth Plan and be completed by the end of the Seventh Plan.

Reorganization of the University Stage : The duration of the first degree should not be less than three-years. The duration of the second degree may be 2 to 3 years.

Some universities should start graduate schools with a three-year Master's degree course in certain subjects.

Three-year special courses for the first degree which begin at the end of the first year of the present three-year degree courses should be started in selected subjects and in selected institutions.

Suitable bridges should be built between the existing courses and the new (longer) courses.

Incentives in the form of scholarships, etc., should be provided for those who take the longer courses.

In Uttar Pradesh, the lengthening of the first degree course should begin with the establishment of three-year graduate schools in selected subjects and in selected universities. The first degree courses in other colleges should be raised to 3 years in a period of 15-20 years.

Utilization of Facilities : Emphasis should be laid, in plans of educational reconstruction, on programmes of intensive utilization of existing facilities.

The number of instructional days in the year should be increased to about 39 weeks for schools and 36 weeks for colleges and pre-primary schools.

A standard calendar should be worked-out by the Ministry of Education and the UGC in consultation with the State Governments and universities respectively. The number of other holidays should be cut down to ten in the year. Loss of instructional days due to examinations and other reasons should not exceed 21 days in the case of schools and 27 days in the case of colleges.

Vacations should be utilized fully through participation in studies, social service camps, production experience, literacy drives, etc.

The duration of the working days should be increased at the school stage. At the university stage, adequate facilities for self-study should be provided.

Steps should be taken to ensure full utilization of institutional facilities such as libraries, laboratories, workshops, craftsheds, etc., all the year round.

Dynamic and Evolving Standards : An intensive effort should be made to raise standards continually for all stages of education. The first ten years of school education should be qualitatively improved so that the wastage at this stage is reduced to the minimum. Within a period of ten years, the standards reached at the end of Class X should be that now attained at the end of the higher secondary course. Similar efforts should be made to raise the standard of the university degrees by adding one year of content.

A continual improvement of standards and their comparability between different parts of the country should be secured at the school stage through the creation of an adequate and efficient machinery at the State and National levels which will define, revise and evaluate national standards at the end of the primary and the lower and higher secondary stages.

In order to raise standards, it is necessary to secure better coordination between different stages of education and to break the isolation in which educational institutions generally function. From this point of view :

(a) Universities and colleges should assist secondary schools in improving their efficiency through a variety of measures ; and

(b) School complexes should be formed. Each complex should consist of a secondary school and all the lower and higher primary schools within its neighbourhood. All the schools in such a complex should form a cooperative group working for improvement.

Part-time Education : Part-time and own-time education should be developed on a larger scale at every stage and in every sector of education and should be given the same status as full time education.

Nomenclature : A uniform system of nomenclature for the different stages and sub-stages of education should be evolved by the Government of India in consultation with State Governments.

Teacher Status

Intensive and continuous efforts are necessary to raise the economic, social and professional status of teachers and to feed back talented young persons into the profession.

Remuneration : The most urgent need is to upgrade the remuneration of teachers substantially, particularly, at the school stage.

The Government of India should lay down for the school stage, minimum scales of pay for teachers and assist the States and Union Territories to adopt equivalent or higher scales to suit their conditions.

Scales of pay of school teachers belonging to the same category but working under different managements such as Government, Local Bodies or private managements should be the same. This principle of parity should be adopted forthwith. But its full implementation may, if necessary, be phased over a programme of five years.

Please see next page for pay scales as proposed by the Commission)

N.B. (1) One-third of the professors to be in the senior scale of Rs. 1500-1800. Scales comparable to the supertime scales in IAS to be introduced for exceptionally meritorious persons and in selected centres of Advanced Studies.

(2) The proportions of junior (lecturers) staff to senior (readers/professors) staff in the universities which is now about 3 : 1 should be gradually changed to 2 : 1.

The Commission proposes the following scales of pay :

Teachers	Remuneration	Rs.
1. Teachers who have completed the secondary course and have received two years of professional training.	Minimum for trained teachers.	150
	Maximum salary (to be reached in a period of about 20 years).	250
	Selection grade (for about 15 p.c. of the cadre).	250—300

N.B. The minimum salary of a primary teacher who has completed the secondary course should be immediately raised to Rs. 100 ; and in a period of five years, it should be raised to Rs. 125. Similarly, the minimum pay of a teacher, who has received two years of training, should be raised immediately to Rs. 125 ; and it should be raised to Rs. 150 in a period of five years. Untrained persons with the requisite academic qualifications should work on the starting salary until they are trained and become eligible for the scale.

Teachers	Remuneration	Rs.
2. Graduates who have received one year's professional training.	Minimum for trained graduates.	200
	Maximum salary (to be reached in a period of 20 years).	400
	Selection grade (for about 15 p.c. of the cadre).	300—500

N.B. Untrained graduates should remain on their starting salary of Rs. 220 p.m. until they are trained and become eligible for the scale.

Teachers	Remuneration	Rs.
3. Teachers working in secondary schools and having postgraduate qualifications.		300—500

N.B. On being trained, they should get one additional increment.

Teachers	Remuneration	Rs.
4. Heads of secondary schools.	Depending upon the size and quality of the school and also on their qualifications, the headmasters should have one or other of the scales of pay for affiliated colleges recommended below :	
	Lecturer	Rs.
5. Teachers in Affiliated Colleges.	Junior scale	300—25—600
	Junior scale	400—30—640——40—800
	Senior Lecturer/Reader	700—40—1100
	Principal I	700—40—1100
	,, II	800—50—1500
	,, III	1000—50—1500

N.B. The proportion of lecturers in the senior scale to those in the junior scale should be progressively improved. By the end of the Fifth Plan, this proportion should be raised to about 75 per cent on an average.

Teachers	Remuneration	Rs.
6. Teaching in university department.	Lecturer	500—40—800—50—950
	Reader	700—50—1250
	Professor	1000—50—1300—60—1600

Notes. (a) The above scales of pay for school teachers are at the current price level and include the existing dearness allowances. Suitable increases will, however, have to be made due to rise in prices from time to time.

(b) Compensatory cost of living allowance given in cities, house-rent allowance or other allowances are not included. These will be in addition to the salary recommended above and should be given on a basis of parity.

(c) The scales of pay are to be integrally related to the programmes of qualitative improvement of teachers through improved methods of selection and improvement in general and professional education.

(d) The scales are to be given to all teachers—Government, local authority or private – on the basis of parity.

Implementation of Scales at the University Stage : The scales proposed above for teachers in higher education have already been approved by Government. To facilitate their introduction, assistance from the Centre should be provided to meet additional expenditure on a sharing basis of 80 per cent from Central and 20 per cent from State funds. In the case of private colleges, Central assistance may even be provided on a 100 per cent basis.

The introduction of these scales of pay should be linked with improvement in the qualifications of teachers and improvement in the selection procedures for their appointment. This should be done on the lines of recommendations of the Committee on Model Act for Universities. For the recruitment of professors, a slightly different procedure has been suggested.

The qualifications of teachers in affiliated colleges should be the same as those for teachers in the universities. The method of recruitment for them should also be similar. A discriminating approach should be adopted, in regard to these, for privately managed colleges. Good institutions should be allowed greater freedom in the choice of their teachers and stricter control should be exercised where the management is not satisfactory.

Implementation of Scales for School Teachers : Three main scales of pay should be recognised for school teachers.

(a) For teachers who have completed the secondary school stage and are trained ;

(b) For trained graduates ;

(c) For teachers with postgraduate qualifications.

There should be no teacher at the primary stage who has not completed the secondary school course and did not have two years of professional training.

Headmasters of higher primary and lower primary schools with enrolments of more than 200 should be trained graduates. Their salaries should be the same as those of trained graduate teachers in secondary schools.

The practice of creating posts in lower scales of pay and recruiting to these—either teachers with lower qualifications when qualified teachers are available or recruiting qualified teachers to these posts—and paying them at lower scales, should be abandoned.

Scales of pay of secondary school teachers should be related to scales of pay for teachers in affiliated colleges and universities on the one hand and to those of primary teachers on the other.

Scales of pay for headmasters of lower and higher secondary schools should have a definite relationship with those of teachers in affiliated colleges or even universities. That is to say, the scale of pay for headmasters should be the same as that for lecturers, readers, or even professors, depending upon the size, function and quality of the school.

The proportion of teachers with postgraduate qualification in lower secondary schools should vary from 10 to 30 per cent, depending upon the size, function and quality of the school.

Teachers with first and second class B.A./B.Sc. or M.A./M.Sc. or with M.Ed., degree should be given advance increments in the scale.

Professional training should be obligatory for all secondary school teachers.

State Boards of School Education and the State Education Departments should prescribe qualifications of teachers similar to those in Government institutions; every post to be filled should be adequately advertised and interviews held by duly constituted Selection Committees; and no grants-in-aid should be paid for the salary of a teacher appointed outside the rules.

Promotional Prospects : It is necessary to improve promotional prospects in the teaching profession in order to attract and retain men of talent. From this point of view, the following suggestions are made :

(1) **School Stage :** Qualified and trained teachers in primary schools should be considered for promotion as Headmasters or Inspectors of schools.

(2) Trained graduate teachers in secondary schools who have done outstanding work should be eligible for promotion to posts carrying salaries of teachers with postgraduate qualifications;

(3) Secondary school teachers with the necessary aptitude and competence could be enabled to become university and college teachers. The UGC should give ad hoc grants to outstanding teachers to do research into problems to encourage them and incidentally to qualify themselves for work at the universities;

(4) Advance increments for teachers doing outstanding work should be made possible.[1] Normally, a teacher reaches the maximum of his scale in a period of 20

years. It should be possible for about five per cent of the teachers to reach the top of the scale in about ten years and for another five per cent of teachers to reach the same in about fifteen years.

(5) **University Stage** : Ad hoc temporary posts in a higher grade should be created for a lecturer or reader who has done outstanding work and who cannot be given promotion for non-availability of a suitable post.

(6) In Departments doing postgraduate work, the number of posts at professional level should be determined on the basis of requirements.

(7) It should be open to a university in consulation with UGC to offer remuneration, even beyond the special scale of 1600-1800 to outstanding persons.

Relating Salaries to Costs of Living : All teachers' salaries should be reviewed every five years and the dearness allowances paid to teachers should be the same as that paid to Government Servants with the same salary.

Welfare Services : A general programme of welfare services for all school teachers should be organised in each State and Union Territory, the funds being contributed by teachers (at 1-1/2 per cent of the salaries) and an equal amount being given by the State. The fund should be administered by Joint Cemmittees of representatives of teachers and Government. When, such a fund is organized, the existing teacher's welfare fund set up by the Government of India may be advantageously merged in it.

Need for Central Assistance : The proposals for the improvement of salaries of school teachers should be given effect to immediately. Generous Central assistance should be made available to State Governments for this purpose.

Retirement Benefits : The system of retirement benefits to teachers should also be reorganized on the principles of uniformity and parity, That is to say, the retirement benefits given to employees of the Government of India should be extended automatically to teachers in the service of the State Governments in the first instance and then to teachers working under local authorities and private management.

As an interim measure, the triple-benefit scheme should be more widely adopted both for teachers in local authority and private schools as well as for the university and college teachers.

The normal retirement age for teachers in schools, colleges and universities should be made 60 years with provision for extension upto 65 years.

A higher rate of interest should be given to teachers on their provident fund and for this purpose, a better system of investing these funds should be devised.

Conditions of Work and Service : The conditions of work in educational institutions should be such so as to enable teachers to function at their highest level of efficiency.

The minimum facilities required for efficient work should be provided in all educational institutions.

Adequate facilities for professional advancement should be provided to all teachers.

In fixing the hours of work, not only actual classroom teaching, but all other work a teacher has to do, should be taken into consideration.

A scheme should also be drawn up under which every teacher will get a concessional railway pass to any part of India once in five years on payment of a reasonable contribution related to his salary.

New conduct and disciplinary rules suitable for the teaching profession should be framed for teachers in Government services.

The terms and conditions of service of teachers in private schools should be the same as for Government schools.

The provision of residential accommodation for teachers is extremely important. For this purpose, it is suggested that:

(a) Every effort should be made to increase residential accommodation for teachers in rural areas and State subsidies should be made available for the purpose ;

(b) A programme of building construction and grant of adequate house rent allowance should be adopted in all big cities;

(c) Cooperative housing schemes for teachers should be encouraged and loans on favourable terms should be made available for construction of houses ; and

(d) In universities and colleges, the target should be fived to provide residential accommodation to about 50 per cent of the teachers in the universities and 20 per cent of them in affiliated colleges.

Private tuitions should be discouraged and controlled. Special coaching for children, who need it, should be provided on an institutional basis.

At the university stage, part-time consultancy or additional work, such as research by teachers in higher education, should be permitted and no payment should be required to be made to the institution if the earnings do not exceed 50 per cent of the salary.

Teachers should be free to exercise all civic rights and should be eligible for public office at the local, district, State or National levels. No legal restriction should be placed on their participation in elections, but when they do so, they should be expected to proceed on leave.

Women Teachers : The employment of women teachers should be encouraged at all stages and in all sectors of education. Opportunities for part-time employment should be provided for them on a large scale.

Adequate provisions should be made for residential accommodation particularly in rural areas.

The condensed courses for adult women operated by the Central Social Welfare Board should be expanded.

Increasing facilities should be provided for education through correspondence courses.

Wherever necessary, special allowances should be given to women teachers working in rural areas.

Teachers for Tribal Areas : Teachers for tribal areas should be given special allowances, and assistance for the education of their children and residential accommodation.

Provision should be made for giving special training to teachers who are to work in tribal areas.

Teachers' Organizations : Professional organizations of teachers which carryout work for the improvement of the profession and of education should be recognized by the Central and the State Governments and consulted on matters relating to school education, general and professional education of teachers and their salaries and conditions of work.

Joint Teachers, Councils should be constituted in each State and Union Territory to discuss all matters relating to teachers' salaries, conditions of work and service and welfare service. These should consist of representatives of teachers' organizations and officers of the State Education Department. Conventions should be developed to the effect that unanimous recommendations of the Council would de accepted by Government. In certain matters, there should be provision for arbitration when negotiations fail.

National Awards : The Ministry of Education should consider the following suggestions :

The number of national awards should be increased ;

The selection committees should be strengthened : and

Travelling allowance given to the awardees should be similar to that sanctioned for Clase I officers of Government.

Teacher Education

The professional preparation of teachers, being crucial for the qualitative improvement of education, should be treated as a key area in educational development and adequate financial provision should be made for it, both at the State and national levels.

Removing the Isolation of Teacher Training : In order to make the professional preparation of teacher's effective, teachers education must be brought into the mainstream of the academic life of the universities on the one hand and of school life and educational developments on the other.

To remove the existing isolation of teacher education from university life:—

(a) education, as distinguished from pedagogy, should be recognised as an independent academic discipline and introduced as an elective subject in courses for the first and second degree ; and

(b) schools of education should be established in selected universities to develop programmes in teacher education and studies and research in education, in collaboration with other university disciplines.

To remove the existing isolation of teacher education from schools:

(a) Extension work should be regarded as an essential function of a teacher training institution and an Extension Service Department should be established in each institution-pre-primary, primary and secondary—as an integral part of it ;

(b) Effective alumni associations should be established to bring all students and faculty together to discuss and plan programme for curricula ;

(c) Practice-teaching for teachers under training should be organized in active collaboration with selected schools which should receive recognition from the Education Department as cooperating schools and special grants for equipment and supervision ; and

(d) Periodic exchange of the staff of the cooperating schools and the teacher training institutions should be arranged.

An intensive effort should be made to remove the existing separation among the institutions preparing teachers for different stages of education or for special fields such as craft or art or physical education by :

(a) Implementing a phased programme of upgrading all training institutions to the collegiate standard with the ultimate objective of bringing all teacher education under the universities ;

(b) Establishing comprehensive colleges of education in each State on a planned basis ;

(c) Establishing a State Board of Teacher Education in each State to be responsible for all functions related to teacher education at all levels and in all fields.

Improving Professional Education : The essence of a programme of teacher education is 'quality' and in its absence, teacher education becomes, not only a financial waste but a source of overall deterioration in educational standards. A programme of highest importance, therefore, is to improve the quality of teacher education. This can be done through :

(1) Organisation of well-planned subject-orientation or content courses, in collaboration with university departments (or postgraduate colleges), leading to insight into basic concepts, objectives and implications of subjects to be taught ;

(2) Introducing integrated courses of general and professional education in universities ;

(3) Vitalising professional studies and basing them on Indian conditions through the development of educational research ;

(4) Using improved methods of teaching which leave greater scope for self-study and discussion and improved methods of evaluation which include continuous internal assessment of practical and sessional work as well as practice-teachings ;

(5) Improving practice-teaching and making it a comprehensive programme of internship ;

(6) Developing special courses and programmes ; and

(7) Revising the curricula and programmes at all levels of teacher education in the light of the fundamental objectives of preparing teachers for their varied responsibilities in an evolving system of education.

Duration of Training Course : The duration of the professional courses should be two years for primary teachers who have completed the secondary school course. It should be one year for the graduate students ; but the number of working days in a year should be increased to 230.

The State Boards of Teacher Education should conduct a survey of teacher education programmes and curricula and initiate the necessary revision.

New professional courses must be developed to orientate headmasters and teacher educators in their special field of work.

The postgraduate courses of education should be flexible and be planned to promote an academic and scientific study of education and to prepare personnel for specific fields requiring special knowledge of initiation. The duration of the courses should be increased to three terms. Quality is crucial at this stage and only institutions having properly qualified staff and facilities should be allowed to conduct them.

Improving the Quality of Training Institutions : Early steps should be taken to improve training institutions for teachers on the following lines :

(1) **Secondary Teachers** : (a) The staff of secondary training colleges should have a double Master's degree in an academic subject and in education. A fair proportion of them should hold Dectorate degrees. They should all have taken induction or orientation courses in teacher education;

(b) Qualified specialists in subjects like Psychology, Sociology, Science or Mathematics may be appointed on the staff even if they have not had professional training ;

(c) Summer institutes should be organized for the in-service training of staff;

(d) No student should be allowed to specialize in the teaching of a subject unless he has studied it for his first degree or obtained an equivalent qualifications prior to training ;

(e) States and Union Territories should adopt a rule that teachers in secondary schools will ordinarily teach only those subjects which they had studied for a university degree. If they are required to teach subjects other than those they have studied, they should take a special course therein either by correspondance or in the Summer Institutes;

(f) Attempts should be made to recruit first and good second class students to teacher training institutions and adequate scholarships should be provided for them.

(2) **Primary Teachers** : (a) The staff in institutions for training primary teachers should hold a Master's degree either in Education or in an Academic subject as well as in B. Ed., and should have undergone special induction courses in teacher education at the primary level;

(b) New appointments of primary teachers should be restricted to those who have completed atleast ten years of general education ; exceptions may be made for women teachers and teachers in tribal areas ;

(c) Correspondence courses and liberal concessions for study leave should be made available to unqualified teachers in primary schools to improve their qualifications ;

(d) Special courses should be organized for graduates entering primary teaching ;

(e) The duration of the training course for primary teachers should be uniformly two years for those who have completed the secondary school course. Teachers with different educational qualifications should not be put into the same course.

(3) **General**: It is necessary to introduce the following reforms in training institutions for primary as well as secondary teachers :

(a) All tuition fees in training institutions should be abolished and liberal provision made for stipends and loans ;

(b) Every training institution should have an experimental or a demonstration school attached to it ;

(c) Adequate hostel facilities for trainees and residential accommodation for staff should be provided ;

(d) Libraries, laboratories, workshops, etc., are very inadequate at present in most institutions, especially at the primary level. These need to be improved.

(4) **Other Teachers** : Reforms on the above lines should be carried out in the training programmes for other categories of teachers.

Expansion of Training Facilities : The training facilities should be expanded on a priority basis. The objective should be to ensure that every teacher in a primary or a secondary school is either already trained at the time of his appointment or receives such training within three years of his appointment. From this point of view :

(1) Each State should prepare a plan for the expansion of training facilities in its area so that the output of trained teachers meets the demand for teachers as well as the needs for in-service education;

(2) Part-time facilities and correspondence courses should be provided on a large scale and care should be taken to see that standards in full-time institutions are not diluted ;

(3) The backlog of untrained teachers should be cleared at an early date through measures of the type recommended in the Report ;

(4) The size of the institutions should be fairly large and then should be located on a planned basis.

In-Service Education of School Teachers : A large scale and coordinated programme of in-service education for teachers should be organized by universities, training institutions and teachers' organizations for teachers at all levels. The target should be that every teacher will receive atleast two or three month's in-service education in every five years of his service.

The programme of summer institutes for the in-service training of secondary school teachers should be extended, with systematic follow-up and active collaboration among the agencies concerned.

Professional Preparation of Teachers in Higher Education : Some orientation to professional education is necessary for junior lecturers in higher education and suitable arrangements should be made for the purpose.

Newly appointed lecturers should be given some time to acclimatize themselves to the institution and should be encouraged to attend lectures of good teachers.

Regular orientation courses for new staff should be organized in every university and where possible, in every college.

In the bigger universities, or groups of universities, these courses may be placed on a permanent basis by establishing a staff college.

Standards in Teacher Education : At the national level, the UGC should take the responsibility for the maintenance of standards in teacher education. The State Boards of Teacher Education should be responsible for the raising of standards at the State level.

A substantial allocation of funds should be made available to the UGC in the Forth Five Year Plan for improvement in teacher education in the universities.

The UGC should set-up a Joint Standing Committee for teacher education in collaboration with the NCERT. It should consist of competent persons from the profession and should be responsible for the maintenance of standards in teacher education.

The Government of India should make provision of funds in the Centrally-sponsored sector to assist State Governments to develop teacher education which is now outside the universities.

Enrolments And Manpower

A National Enrolment Policy : During the next twenty years, the national enrolment policy should have the following broad objectives :

To provide effective general education of not less than seven years' duration to every child, on a free and compulsory basis ; and to expand lower secondary education on as large a scale as possible ;

(1) To provide higher secondary and university education to those who are willing and qualified to receive such education, consistent with the demands for trained manpower and the need to manitain essential standards ; and to provide adequate financial assistance to those who are economically handicapped ;

(2) To emphasize the development of professional, technical and vocational education and to prepare skilled personnel needed for the development of agriculture and industry ;

(3) To identify talent and to help it grow to its full potential ;

(4) To liquidate mass illiteracy and to provide an adequate progamme of adult and continuing education; and

(5) To strive continuously to equalize educational opportunities, beginning with the elimination of atleast some of the more glazing inequalities.

Raising the Educational Level of the Average Citizen : High priority should be given to programmes of raising the educational level of the average citizen :

(1) By providing five years of effective primary education to all children by 1975-76 and seven years of such education by 1985-86 ;

(2) By making part-time education for one year compulsory for all children in the age-group 11-14 who have not completed the lower primary stage and are not attending schools. The aim will be to make these children functionally literate and stop all further additions to the ranks of adult illiterates ; and

(3) By developing programmes to liquidate adult illiteracy.

Enrolment Policies in Secondary and Higher Education : The enrolment policies in post-primary education should be based on a combination of four criteria : public demand for secondary and higher education ; full development of the pool of natural ability ; capacity of society to provide educational facilities at required levels of quality ; and manpower requirements.

The public demand for secondary and bigher education has increased immensely in the first three plans and will continue to increase in future. It sets up a high target which is beyond the resources of the country in terms of men, money or materials. It is, therefore, necessary to adopt a policy of selective admissions to higher secondary and university education in order to bridge the gap between the public demand and available facilities.

Providing secondary and higher education to all potentially-able students also sets up a high target which even affluent societies find it difficult to achieve. It will be obviously beyond our reach, atleast in the immediate future. While striving towards this goal, therefore, the immediate objective of the national enrolment policy should be to ensure that atleast all the gifted students (5 to 15 per cent of all the students) who complete primary or secondary education are enabled to study further and that their financial handicaps are overcome through the institution of a liberal programme of scholarships.

There are internal constraints in every educational system which limit expansion of facilities, especially in secondary and higher education, viz., the availability of competent teachers, physical plant and finance. These constraints have often been set aside in the past to meet the pressures of public demand and standards have been diluted. This temptation will have to be resisted in the larger interests of the country.

Estimated requirements of manpower needs or available job opportunities form a good basis for planning the expansion of educational facilities. This broad recommendation has to be understood in the light of three reservations :

(a) A continuous effort should be made to improve the collection of necessary data and the techniques of forecasting and the estimates of manpower needs should be continuously revised and kept up-to-date ;

(b) The quality of manpower produced should be equally emphasized ; and

(c) The estimates of manpower needs should not be regarded as the only criterion—it should be suitably combined with other criteria in taking final decisions about expansion of educational facilities.

A Strategy of Development : The capacity of society to expand educational facilities in terms of real resources sets up minimum targets whereas the maximum targets are suggested by the public demand for secondary and higher aducation or the need to develop the available pool of native talent. The gap between these high and low targets can be bridged by considerations which emerge from the necessity to relate the output of the educational system to manpower needs and to equalize educational opportunities. These will indicate the priorities to be adopted, the different courses of study to be developed, the extent to which facilities should be provided in the different courses, and the manner in which enrolments in them could be made to include, after equality of access is provided for all, atleast the best students in the community.

Future Requirements of Educated Manpower : The ISI/ISE Estimates : We broadly accept the estimates of future requirements of educated manpower given in the ISI/LSE Paper. This will, however, have to be continually revised in the light of the best data available and kept up-to-date. The table given on page 95 (Table 5.3) shows the estimates of the required workers, stock and out-turn of educated persons during the next twenty years.

Educational Implications of the Estimates : The following are the main policy implications of these estimates :

To restrict the unplanned and uncontrolled expansion of general secondary and higher education, if massive educated unemployment is to be avoided ;

To make special and intensive efforts to vocationalize secondary education and to develop professional education at the university stage ; and

To devise suitable machinery, both at the national and State levels, which will relate the estimates of manpower needs effectively to the output of the educational system so that, by and large, there is some assurance that a suitably trained person would be available for every job to be done and every educated person would find a job appropriate for his education and professional training.

Enrolments : The enrolments implied in these targets of out-turn, workers and stock have been discussed in the appropriate context in the different sections of this Report.

Machinery for Manpower Planning : The first-two of these have been discussed in their appropriate context in tater chapters. With regard to the third, the following recommendations are made :

At the national level, the Planning Commission, which is responsible for preparing estimates of manpower requirements in all sectors of national development, should set up a Standing Committee for Manpower. Its main responsibility should be to prepare and revise, from time to time, manpower forecasts for the overall output of the educational system as well as for different categories of specialists.

At the State level, it may be desirable to set up State Committees on Manpower on the broad lines of the Standing Committee for Manpower at the Centre and having similar functions and responsibilities.

Relating Manpower Estimates to Output of Educational Institutions : The following measures will have to be taken to relate the output of the education system to manpower needs :

National Level : Planning at the national level should be done by the Centre in consultation with the States and should cover all sectors, crucial for national development, where the mobility of trained personnel is or should be high, where it is very costly to set up institutions for training personnel or where the very high level staff required for such institutions as in short supply. These should include engineering, agricultural and medical education, and the preparation of teachers for higher education.

State Level : The planning of the remaining sectors should be done at the State level by State Governments. The planning of facilities in secondary and higher education (excluding the sectors for which planning would be done at the Central level) should be done at the State level.

The Provision of vocational education—both of school and college standard—will have to be expanded in all areas on a priority basis in keeping with manpower needs.

For enrolments in general education, however, which is underdeveloped in others, a policy of equalization will have to be adopted. Decisions will have to be made by each State in view of its conditions ; but as a general basis, the following may be suggested :

(a) In all areas where the level of expansion reached is below the national average in 1966, steps should be taken to promote expansion ;

(b) In all areas where the level of expansion reached is about equal to the national average expected in 1986, a restrictive policy should be adopted, unless there are special reasons to the contrary ;

(c) It will be for the Government of India to suggest the targets to be reached from time to time, at the State level. State Governments may, in their turn, indicate suitable targets at the district level ;

(d) The planning of higher education should be done on a State-basis. All universities in the State should be involved in this. Each university should be required to prepare a five-year plan of the facilities to be provided in all its teaching departments and affiliated colleges and the output therefrom and these should be approved after bringing them into accord with manpower needs. In granting affiliations or expanding their departments, the universities should be required to follow these plans.

(e) It is also essential to have an authority at the district level which can plan all school education. This authority will plan in the light of general directives given from the Centre and the State. In order to assist in its work, local studies of manpower needs, etc., will have to be carried out.

Education and Employment : We should move in the direction of giving every graduate an offer of employment alongwith his degree or diploma. From this point of view, the system of one year internship now prescribed for medical graduates should be extended to other categories of graduates.

A Wider Perspective : The basic problem of human resource development can be solved only against a wider perspective. From this point of view, it is necessary to formulate and implement integrated plans which will have three objectives. (1) To reduce the birth-rate by about half ; (2) To bring about an expansion of employment ; and (3) To provide such education as will qualify young people for specific jobs. Such integrated plans are needed at the National, State and District levels.

Towards Equilization Of Educational Opportunities

Fees in Education : The country should work towards a stage when all education would be tuition free. From this point of view :

(1) Tuition fees at the primary stage should be abolished in all Government, local authority and aided private schools as early as possible and preferably before the end of the Fourth Plan.

(2) Lower secondary education should be made tuition free in all Government, local authority or aided private institutions as early as possible and preferably before the end of the Fifth Plan. If necessary, a phased programme may be drawn up for the purpose.

(3) For the next ten years, the main effort with regard to fees in higher secondary and university education should be to extend provision of tuition free education to all needing and deserving students. As a first step, the proportion of free studentships should be increased to 30 per cent of the enrolment.

Other Private Costs : Other private costs in education have increased greatly in recent years and not necessarily for educational reasons. Efforts are needed to reduce them to the minimum.

Free textbooks and writing materials should be provided at the primary stage. Children freshly joining schools should be welcomed at a school function and presented with a complete set of books for the next year as soon as the results of the annual examinations are declared and before the long vacation starts so that they can use the vacations for further study.

A programme of book-banks should be developed in secondary schools and institutions of higher education. The State Education Departments should have a fund at their disposal from which they can encourage the establishment of book-banks in secondary schools and a similar fund should be placed at the disposal of the UGC for organizing them in the universities and affiliated colleges.

The libraries of secondary schools and institutions of higher education should contain an adequate number of sets of textbooks so that the students can have easy access to them.

Grants for the purchase of books, which need not necessarily be textbooks, should be made to talented students—the top 10 per cent—in educational institutions. The scheme should begin in the universities and lateron be extended to affiliated colleges and secondary schools.

Scholarships : The programme of scholarships has received considerable emphasis in recent years, but it needs reorganization on the following lines:

The scholarships programme is a continuous process and has to be organised at all stages of education. At present, the programme is weak and needs to be strengthened at the school stage.

It is necessary to evolve a more equitable and egalitarian basis for the award of scholarships.

A scholarships programme will yield better results if it is accompanied by a programme to maintain an adequate number of quality institutions at every stage and in every sector and an attempt is made to place the talented students in these institutions.

A careful watch should be kept at all points of transfer from one stage or sub-stage of education to another to ensure that all the abler students continue their studies further.

An adequate machinery should be created for administering this combined programme of scholarships, placement and maintenance of quality institutions.

The following programme of scholarships is proposed at the different stages of education :

Primary Stage : Steps should be taken to ensure that, at the end of the lower primary stage, no promising child is prevented from continuing his studies further and to this end, a scholarship of an adequate amount will have to be provided to every child that may need it. It has been assumed that the target should be to provide scholarships for 2,5 per cent of the enrolement at the higher primary stage by 1975-76 and to 5 per cent of the same enrolment by 1985-86.

Secondary Stage: Steps should be taken to ensure that the top 15 per cent of the children in the age-group do get scholarships from higher primary to secondary stage. To this end, the necessary financial assistance should be provided to about 10 per cent of the top students in Claas VII or VIII in each higher primary school. Atleast one good secondary school, with adequate residential facilities, should be developed in each Community Development Block and admission to such institutions should be regulated on the basis of merit.

In every school, there should be a programme for the identification of talented students who should be provided with special enrichment programmes to suit their needs and to help in their growth.

University Stage : At the university stage the target for the provision for scholarships should be as follows :

(a) Scholarships should be available to atleast 15 per cent of enrolment at the undergraduate stage by 1976 and to 25 per cent of such enrolement by 1986 ; and

(b) Scholarships should be available to atleast 25 per cent of the enrolment at the postgraduate stage by 1976 and to 50 per cent of such enrolement by 1986.

There should be two kinds of scholarships:

(a) For those who have to stay in hostels these should cover all the direct and indirect costs on education, such as tuition fees, books, supplies etc.; and

(b) For those who can stay at home and attend schools or colleges. These should mainly cover direct and indirect costs.

At the lower stages, the scholarships of the second type would be most needed. As one goes up the educational ladder, the proportion of scholarships of the first type would have to be increased.

Steps should be taken to study the indirect costs of education and living costs and to reduce them to the minimum. In particular, it is necessary to cut down hostel expenses by reducing the number of servants, etc.

The amount of scholarships should be regulated in such a manner as to cover all costs.

National Scholarships : The scheme of National scholarships should be expanded. The target to be reached should be to cover the top 5 per cent of the students who pass out of the examinations by 1975-76 and 10 per cent of such students by 1985-86. The administration of the scheme should be still further simplified and decentralized. In particular, the power to issue entitlement cards should be delegated to the authorities holding the examinations at which these scholarships have been instituted.

With a view to introducing a greater egalitarian element in the award of these scholarships, it is suggested that 50 per cent of these scholarships should be awarded, as at present, on the State basis. The remaining 50 per cent should be awarded on the 'school-cluster' basis in which a group of schools with similar socio-economic background of students are grouped into a cluster and the top students from each cluster are awarded the scholarships.

University Scholarships : To supplement the above, a scheme of university scholarships should be instituted and implemented through the UGC. The target to be reached should be to cover 10 per cent of the enrolment at the undergraduate stage and 20 per cent of the enrolment at the postgraduate stage by 1976.

A Standing Committee on Postgraduate and Research Scholarships shoutd be set up at the national level in the Ministry of Education. It should consist of the representatives of the Ministries which award scholarships at the postgraduate stage and its main function would be to coordinate the different scholarship programmes.

Scholarships in Vocational Education : With regard to

scholarships in vocational education, the following reforms are necessary:

It is necessary to make a more intensive effort to introduce an egalitarian element in admissions.

The admission examinations of IITs should be held in English and also in regional languages and the best students from each linguistic group should be selected, if necessary, on the basis of the quota related to population. If some of these students are not quite up to the standard in English, this deficiency should be overcome by giving an intensive training in English to the selected students in their first year at the institute.

At the school stage, about 30 per cent of the students should be given scholarships; and this proportion should be increased to 50 per cent at the collegiate stage.

Scholarships for Study Abroad : There should be a national programme for the award of scholarships to the best talented students for study abroad About 500 scholarships should be awarded each year.

Loan Scholarships : It is necessary to institute a programme of loan scholarships to supplement the outright grant scholarships described above. It should be organised on the following lines ;

The programme would be a supplement to that of outright scholarships which should be provided on the scale we have suggested.

It would be essentially meant for students in the sciences and the professional courses where the chances of employment and levels of earning are comparatively better and are more likely to make the scheme successful. There should be no upper limit to the number of such loan scholarships in this sector and an attempt should be made to provide financial assistance to every needy student. To a limited extent and in deserving cases, the programme should be extended to cover arts students also.

If a person who holds a loan scholarship joins the teaching profession, one-tenth of the loan should be written off for each year of service. This will encourage good students to join this profession.

For convenient administration of the loan scholarships programme a National Loan Scholarships Board may be set up as recommended in the Report.

Other Forms of Student Aid : Some other forms of student aid need development.

Transport facilities should be provided imaginatively to reduce the cost on hostels and scholarships, e.g., we have seen schools in rural areas which provide bicycles to students who come from a distance.

Day-Study Centres and lodging houses (i.e., places where the students can stay throughout the day and even at night but can go home for food) should be provided on a liberal scale.

Facilities for students to earn and pay a part of their educational expenses should be developed.

General : In all programmes of scholarships, preferential consideration should be given to the needs of girls.

The Government of India should assume the bulk of the responsibility for providing scholarships in higher education. At the school stage, this responsibility should vest in the State Governments. To develop a good programme of scholarships at the school stage, however, the funds needed for it should be provided in the Centrally-sponsered sector in the next two Plans. The State Governments may be able to develop the programme on their own thereafter.

Handicapped Children : The progress in providing educational facilities to handicapped children will be limited by two main considerations: lack of teachers and financial resources. A reasonable target will, however, be to provide, by 1986, education for about 15 per cent of the blind, deaf and orthopaedically handicapped children and to about 5 per cent of the mental retarded ones. This will mean the provision of educational facilities for about 10 per cent of the total number of handicapped children. As a part of this programme, it should be possible to have atleast one good institution for the education of the handicapped children in each district.

In the educationally advanced countries, a great deal of stress is now being laid on the integration of the handicapped children into regular school programmes. We feel that experimentation with integrated programmes is urgently required in our country and that every attempt should be made to bring as many children into the integrated programmes as possible.

In addition, it will be desirable to develop services on a pilot basis for some other categories of children who have peculiar educational needs, viz., the partially-sighted, the speech-handicapped, the aphasic, the brain-injured and the mentally disturbed.

To develop the above programmes for the education of the handicapped children on proper lines, it will be necessary to emphasize the training of teachers, the coordination of the efforts of the different agencies working in the field and to promote adequate research into the problem.

Regional Imbalances : There are wide differences in the educational development in the different States. These become wider still at the district level. A reduction of these differences to the minimum is desirable and the programme for this will have to be pursued side by side with the wider programmes for reducing the imbalances in the socio-economic development of the different States and districts in the country. The solution of this complex problem will, however, be facilitated if action is taken on the following lines :

A total elimination of these differences in educ tional development is neither possible nor desirable. What is needed, however, is a balancing factor, a deliberate and sustained effort to assist the less advanced areas to come up to atleast certain minimum levels so that the gap between them and the advanced areas will be reduced.

The district should be adopted as the basic unit for educational planning and development

At the State level, there should be a deliberate policy of equalization of educational development in the different districts and the necessary administrative and financial measures to this end should be taken.

At the national level, it should be regarded as the responsibility of the Government of India to secure equalization of educational development in the different States. The necessary programmes for this, including special assistance to the less advanced States, should be developed.

Education of Women. We fully endorse the recommendations of the three Committees which have examined the problem of women's education in recent years: (a) The National Committee on the Education of Women under the chairmanship of Shrimati Durgabai Deshmukh; (b) The Committee on Differentiation of Curricula between Boys and Girls under the chairmanship of Shrimati Hansa Mehta; and (c) The Committee under the chairmanship of Shri M. Bhaktavatsalam which studied the problem in the six States where the education of girls in less developed.

We invite special attention to the following recommendations of the National Committee on Women's Education :

(1) The education of women should be regarded as a major programme of education for some years to come and a bold and determined effort should be made to face the difficulties involved and to close the existing gap between the education of men and women in as short a time as possible;

(2) Special schemes should be prepared for this purpose and the funds required for them should be provided on a priority basis; and

(3) Both at the Centre and in the States, there should be a special machinery to look after the education of girls and women. It should bring together officials and non-officials in the planning and implementation of programmes for women's education.

In addition, it will also necessary to give adequate attention to the education of girls at all stages and in all sectors.

The role of women outside the home has become an important feature of the social and economic life of the country and, in the years to come, this will become still more significant. From this point of view, greater attention will have to be paid to the problems of training and employment of women. Opportunities for part-time employment which would enable women to look after their homes and to have a career outside will have to be largely expanded. As the age of marriage continues to rise, full-time employment will have to be provided for almost all young and married women. As the programme of family planning develops, older women whose children have grown up, will also need employment opportunities. Teaching, nursing and social service are well-recognised areas where women can have a useful role to play. In addition, several new avenues will have to be opened out to them.

Education of the Backward Classes: The existing programme for the education of the Scheduled Castes should continue be the expanded.

Greater efforts are needed to provide educational facilities for the nomadic and semi-nomadic groups.

Hostels should be provided for the children of the denotified communities.

Education of the Tribal People: The education of the tribal people deserves great emphasis and attention. We broadly agree with the recommendations made in this respect by the Commission on Scheduled Castes and Scheduled Tribes under the chairmanship of Shri U. N. Dhebar and in the seminars on the Education and Employment of the Tribal People organised by the Planning Commission and the NCERT. We invite special attention to the following programmes in this content:

At the primary stage, the provision of facilities will have to be improved and Ashram/schools will have to be established in sparsely populated areas. The teachers should be invariably conversant with tribal languages. The medium of education for the first two years of the school should be the tribal language; and during this period, the children should be given oral instruction in the regional language. By the third year, the regional language should become the medium of education. The programmes of the schools should be attuned to tribal life and atmosphere.

At the secondary stage, provision of schools, hostel facilities and scholarships has to be greatly expanded.

In higher education, the administration of the scholarships programme will have to be decentralized and made more efficient.

Provision for special tuition will have to be made both at the secondary and university stages.

It is essential to develop cadres of persons who will devote themselves to the service of the tribal people. In the early stages, these cadres will consist mostly of non-tribals but an effort has to be made to develop such cadres among the tribals themselves From this point of view:

(a) Non-official organisations working in the tribal areas should be encouraged;

(b) Special sub-cadres shou'd be formed among the official ranks with the object of selecting persons to work in the tribal areas. The emoluments for these sub-cadres should be good enough to attract the best persons available ;

(c) Promising young persons from the tribals should be selected and specially trained to work in tribal areas. The usual prescriptions regarding recruitment or minimum qualifications will often have to be set aside in this programme.

School Education : Problems Of Expansion

The entire pre-university period of education should be treated as one single and continuous unit. It may be sub-divided into sub-standards such as pre-primary, ower and higher primary, and lower and higher seconlary. But it has to be noted that the similarities between the problems of the different sub-stages are nore significant than the differences.

Pre-Primary Education : Pre-primary education is of reat significance to the physical, emotional and intellctual development of children, especially those with nsatisfactory home backgrounds. An enrolment of ive per cent of the population in the age group 3 to 5 in he pre-primary schools proper and of 50 per cent in he age-group 5-6 in pre-school classes will be a reasonble target to be attained by 1986.

Pre-primary education should be developed on the ollowing lines during the next twenty years :

State-level development centres for pre-primary eduation should be set up in each State Institute of Eduation; in addition, a district level centre should be set p in each district for the development, supervision nd guidance of pre-primary education in the area.

Private enterprise should be made largely responsile for setting up and running pre-primary centres, the tate assisting with grants-in-aid on the basis of equalition.

Experimentation in pre-primary education should e encouraged especially to devise less costly methods of xpanding it. This may be done on the Madras pattern. the alternative children's play centres should be tached to as many primary schools as possible and ould function as pre-school classes.

The State should maintain State and District levels ay centres, train pre-primary teachers, look after rearch and preparation of literature on pre-primary edution, supervise and guide pre-primary schools and aining institutions, assist private agencies with grants--aid and run model pre-primary schools.

The programme of pre-primary schools should be flexible and consist of various types of play, mannual and learning activities accompanied by sensosial education.

Expansion of Primary Education : The objective of primary education should be to prepare individuals to be responsible and useful citizens.

The constitutional directive of providing free and compulsory education for every child upto the age of 14 years is an educational objective of the highest priority and should be fulfilled in all parts of the country through the development of the following programmes :

Five years of good and effective reducation should be provided to all children by 1975-76.

Seven years of such education should be provided by 1985-86.

Emphasis should be laid on the reduction of wastage and stagnation. The objective should be to ensure that not less than 80 per cent of the children that enter Class I reach Class VII in a period of seven years.

Children who are not yet fourteen years old at the end of Class VII and who do not wish to study further should be retained in the educational system till they complete 14 years of age but should be provided with short vocational courses of their choice.

Each State and district should be required to prepare a perspective plan for the development of primary education in its area in the light of the targets stated above and its local conditions. It should be given full assistance to move forward at its best pace; and care should be taken to see that its progress is not held up for want of financial resources.

Universal Provision of Schools . The expansion of primary schools should be so planned that a lower primary school is available within a distance of about a mile from the home of every child. A higher primary school should be available within one to three miles from the home of every child.

Universal Enrolment : A programme of universal enrolment should be organised simultaneously with emphasis on the following :

(1) The present heterogeneity of cohort in Class I should be reduced and the bulk of the students in this class should consist of children in the age-group 5-6 or 6-7;

(2) A system of pre-registration should be introduced;

(3) The transfer rate of students from the end of the lower primary stage to the higher primary (which is now about 80 per cent) should be raised to 100 per cent by the end of the Fifth Plan.

Universality of Retention : The most important programme to be implemented during the next ten years is to improve the quality of primary education and to reduce stagnation and wastage to the minimum. The target should be to reduce stagnation and wastage by about half by 1976 and to almost eliminate them by 1986.

Stagnation and wastage are very high in Class I and their reduction should be a major programme. Of the various measures to be adopted for the purpose, three are very important :

(a) Treating Classes I and II (and wherever possible even Classes I—IV) as one integrated unit;

(b) Introducing a year of pre-school education; and

(c) Adopting play-way techniques in Class I,

Stagnation and wastage in other classes should be reduced by providing various forms of part-time education, by implementing a nation-wide programme of school improvement, and by an intensive programme of parental education.

All children in the age-group 11-14 not attending schools and who have not completed the primary stage of education and become functionally literate, should be required to attend literacy classes for a period of atleast one year. The classes should be organized in primary schools and in a flexible manner to suit the convenience of the pupils. They should begin on a voluntary basis; but compulsion may be tried when the local community has become familiar with the concept.

Similar facilities for part-time education should be provided for children who have completed the lower primary stage and who desire to study further. (Their magnitude may be 10 per cent of the total enrolment in 1975-76 and 20 per cent in 1985-86. The curriculum may follow the general education pattern or contain a large vocational element as required by local needs.

Education of Girls—Primary Stage : The education of girls requires special attention in fulfilling the constitutional directive and should be accelerated on the lines of the measures recommended by the National Committee on Women's Education.

Improvement of Quality : Expansion of facilities at the primary stage and programmes of universal enrolment and retention should be accompanied by qualitative improvement.

Expansion of Secondary Education : Enrolments in secondary education should be regulated during the next 20 years by : (a) proper planning of the location of secondary schools, (b) maintaining adequate standards and to that end, by determining the enrolment in terms of facilities available, and (c) selecting the best students.

A development plan for secondary education should be prepared for each district and implemented in a period of ten years. All new institutions should satisfy essential standards, and existing institutions should be raised to the minimum level.

The best students should be selected for admission into secondary schools, through a process of self-selection at the lower secondary stage, and on the basis of external examination results and school records at the higher secondary stage.

Vocationalizing Secondary Education : Secondary education should be vocationalized in a larger measure and enrolments in vocational courses raised to 20 per cent of total enrolment at the lower secondary stage and 50 per cent of total enrolment at the higher secondary stage by 1986.

A variety of part-time and full-time facilities in vocational education should be available at both these stages to meet the needs of boys and girls, in urban and rural areas. Special sections should be set up in the Education Departments to help young people who drop out after Class VII or VIII to obtain training on a full-time or part-time basis, and to be in overall charge of the organization of these courses.

The Central Government should provide special grants to State Governments in the Centrally-sponsored sector for the vocationalization of secondary education.

Part-time Education: Facilities for part-time education should be provided on a large scale at the lower and higher secondary stages, in general and vocational courses. A desirable target would be 20 per cent of the total enrolment at the lower secondary stage and 25 per cent at the higher secondary stage. Special emphasis will have to be placed on agricultural courses for those who have taken to farming as a vocation and on courses in home science or household industries for girls.

Education of Girls—Secondary Stage : Efforts should be made to accelerate the expansion of girls education so that the proportion of girls to boys reaches 1 : 2 at the lower secondary stage and 1 : 3 at the higher secondary stage in 20 years.

Emphasis should be placed on establishing separate schools for girls, provision of hostels and scholarships, and part-time and vocational courses.

Planning and Location of Schools : A national policy for the location of new institutions of each category should be adopted so as to avoid waste and duplication. The second education survey should be used for the careful planning of the location of educational institutions.

Public opinion should be educated to accept mixed schools at the primary stage and the sharing of bigger and efficient schools in common. Villages should be grouped so as to make the economic provision of primary schools possible.

At the secondary stage, the establishment of small and uneconomic institutions should be avoided, and existing uneconomic schools should be consolidated.

Vocational schools should be located near the industry concerned.

School Curriculum

In recent years, the explosion of knowledge and the reformulation of many concepts in science have highlighted the inadequacy of existing school programmes and brought about a mounting pressure for a radical reform of school curriculum. A unified approach should be taken to the framing of the entire school curriculum, a new definition of the content of general education and a new approach to the place of specialisation.

Essentials of Curricular Improvement : School Curricula should be upgraded through research in curriculum development undertaken by University Departments of Education, training colleges. State Institutes of Education and Boards of School Education; (b) periodical revision based on such research; (c) the preparation of textbooks and teaching-learning materials; and (d) the orientation of teachers to the revised curricula through in-service education.

Schools should be given the freedom to devise and experiment with new curricula suited to their needs. A lead should be given in the matter by training colleges and universities through their experimental schools.

Ordinary and advanced curricula should be prepared by State Boards of School Education in all subjects and introduced in a phased manner in schools which fulfil certain conditions of staff and facilities.

The formation of Subject Teachers' Associations in the different school subjects will help to stimulate experimentation and in the upgrading of curricula. The State Education Departments, State Institutes of Education and NCERT should help these associations in their educational activities and coordinate their work.

Organization of the Curriculum : In non-vocational schools, a common curriculum of general education should be provided for the first ten years of school education, and diversification of studies and specialisation should begin only at the higher secondary stage.

Standards of attainment should be clearly defined at the end of each sub-stage.

At the lower primary stage, the curriculum should be simple with reduced load of formal subjects and emphasis on language, elementary mathematics and environmental studies. A study of problems relating to beginning reading accompanied by a vigorous programme of improving reading instruction at the lower primary stage should receive great emphasis.

At the higher primary stage, the curriculum will broaden and deepen, teaching methods will become more systematic, and standards of attainment will be more specific.

At the lower secondary stage, study of subjects will gain in rigour and depth.

At the higher secondary stage, courses will be diversified in such a manner as to enable pupils to study a group of any three subjects in depth with considerable freedom and elasticity in the grouping of subjects. In order to ensure the balanced development of the adolescent's total personality, the curriculum at this stage should provide half the time to the electives, one-fourth of the time to the languages, and one-fourth to physical education, arts and crafts, and moral and spiritual education.

At the higher primary stage, enrichment programmes should be provided for the talented children. It may take the form of additional subject or greater depth in the same subject.

At the secondary stage, courses should be provided at two levels—ordinary and advanced—beginning with Class VIII. The programme may be done within or outside school hours or on a self-study basis. A beginning may be made with advanced courses in mathematics, science and languages at the lower secondary stage and in all the specialised subjects at the higher secondary stage.

Study of Languages : The language study at the school stage needs review and a new policy regarding language study at the school stage requires to be formulated.

The modification of the language formula should be guided by the following guiding principles :

(a) Hindi as the official language of the Union enjoys an importance next only to that of the mother-tongue ;

(b) A working knowledge of English will continue to be an asset to students ;

(c) The proficiency gained in a language desends as much upon the types of teachers and facilities as upon the length of time in which it is learnt.

(d) The most suitable stage for learning three languages is the lower secondary (Classes VIII—X) ;

(e) The introduction of two additional languages should be staggered ;

(f) Hindi or English should be introduced at a point when there is greatest motivation and need ;

(g) At no stage should the learning of four languages be made compulsory.

The three language formula modified on these principles should include: (a) the mother-tongue or the regional language ; (b) the official language of the Union or the associate official language of the Union so long as it exists ; and (c) a modern Indian or European language not covered under (a) and (b) and other than that used as the medium of education.

At the lower primary stage the pupil will ordinarily study only one language—the mother-tongue (or the regional language) and the official language of the Union (or the associate language). At the lower secondary stage, he will study three languages, the mother-tongue (or the regional language); the official or associate official language; and a modern Indian language, it being obligatory to study the official or the associate official language which he had not studied at the higher primary stage. At the higher secondary stage, only two languages will be compulsory.

The study of important modern library languages other than English should be made possible in selected schools in each State with option to study them in lieu of English or Hindi. Similarly, in non-Hindi areas, the study of modern Indian languages should be made possible in selected schools with a similar option to study them in lieu of English or Hindi.

The Study of English and Hindi will be indicated in terms of hours of study and level of attainment. Two levels of attainment should be prescribed in the official and associate official languages—one for a three-year and one for a six-year study.

The study of a language should not be compulsory in higher education.

A nation-wide programme should be organized for the promotion of the study of Hindi on a voluntary basis but the study of the language should not be forced on unwilling sections of the people.

The burden of studying languages is made heavier by the great differences in script. Some literature in every modern Indian language should be produced in Devanagari and Roman scripts. All modern Indian languages should also adopt the international numerals.

The teaching of English should ordinarily not begin earlier than Class V after adequate command has been acquired over the mother-tongue. The introduction of the study of English earlier than Class V is educationally unsound.

The study of classical Indian languages such as Sanskrit or Arabic should be encouraged on an optional basis from Class VIII and should be positively emphasized in all universities. Advanced Centres of Study may be set up in selected universities in these languages. No new Sanskrit University should be established.

Science and Mathematics Education : Science and mathematics should be taught on a compulsory basis to all pupils as a part of general education during the first ten years of schooling.

The Study of Science : In the lower primary classes science teaching should be related to the child's environment. The Roman alphabet should be taught in Class IV to facilitate understanding of internationally accepted symbols of scientific measurement and the use of maps, charts and statistical tables.

At the higher primary stage emphasis should be made on the acquisition of knowledge and the ability to think logically, to draw conclusions and to make decisions at a higher level. A disciplinary approach to the teaching of science will be more effective than the general science approach.

A Science corner in lower primary schools and a laboratory-cum-lecture room in higher primary schools are minimum essential commodities.

At the lower secondary stage, science should be developed as a discipline of the mind. The newer concepts of Physics, Chemistry and Biology and the experimental approach to the learning of science should be stressed.

Science courses at an advanced level may be provided for talented students in selected lower secondary schools with necessary facilities of staff and laboratory.

Science teaching should be linked to agriculture in rural areas and to technology in urban areas. But the levels of attainment and avenues to higher education should be the same in both types of schools.

The Study of Mathematics : Special attention should be given to the study of mathematics in view of the importance of qualification and the advent of automation and cybernetics.

The mathematics curriculum needs to be modernized and brought up-to-date at all stages with emphasis on laws and principles of mathematics and logical thinking.

Methods of Teaching Science and Mathematics : Methods of teaching mathematics and science should be modernized, stressing the investigatory approach and the under standing of basic principles. Guide materials should be made available to help teachers adopt this approach. Laboratory work will need considerable improvement. There should be flexibility in the curriculum in order to cater to the special needs of the gifted.

Social Studies and Social Science : An effective programme of social studies is essential for the development of good citizenship and emotional integration.

The syllabus should stress the idea of national unity and the unity of man.

The scientific spirit and method of the social sciences should permeate the teaching of social studies at all stages.

Work-Experience : Work-experience should be forward-looking in keeping with the character of the new social order. It will take the form of simple handwork in the lower-primary classes, and of craft in the upper primary classes. At the lower secondary stage, it will be in the form of workshop training, and at the higher secondary stage, work-experience will be provided in the school workshop, farm or commercial and industrial establishments.

Where school workshops cannot be provided, suitable kits of tools and materials should be made available at low cost.

The training of teachers, provision of workshops, mobilisation of local resources, preparation of literature and the phased introduction of the programme are essential to the success of the scheme.

Social Service : Programmes of social service and participation in community development should be organized at all levels as suited to the different age-groups, in a phased manner.

Labour and social service camps should be run throughout the year ; and for this purpose, a special organization may be set up in each district. These camps will facilitate the organization of social service programmes in schools. Such programmes may be started as a pilot project in 5 per cent of the districts and extended gradually to the others.

Physical Education : Physical education is important for the physical fitness and efficiency, mental alertness and the development of certain qualities of character. The programme of physical education, as it is in force today, needs to be re-examined and redesigned in the light of certain basic principles of child growth and development.

Education in Moral and Spiritual Values : Organized attempts should be made for imparting moral education and inculcating spiritual values in schools through direct and indirect methods with the help of the ethnical teachings of great religions.

One or two periods a week should be set aside in the school time-table for instruction in moral and spiritual values. The treatment of the subject should be comprehensive and not divorced from the rest of the curriculum.

Creative Activities : The Government of India should appoint a Committee of Experts to survey the present situation of art education and explore all possibilities for its extension and systematic development.

Bal Bhawans should be set up in all parts of the country with substantial support from the local community.

Art departments should be set up in selected university centres to carry out research in art education.

A variety of co-curricular activities should be organized to provide pupils opportunity for creative self-expression.

Differentiation of Curricula for Boys and Girls : The recommendations of the Hansa Mehta Committee that there should be no differentiation of curricula on the basis of sex is endorsed. Home science should be provided as an optional subject but not made compulsory for girls. Larger provision should be made for music and fine arts ; and the study of mathematics and science should be encouraged.

The New Curriculum and Basic Education : The essential principles of basic education, namely, productive activity, correlation of curriculum with productive activity and the environment, and contact with local community, are so important that they should guide and shape the educational system at all levels, and this is the essence of the proposals made in this Report. No single stage of education need be designated as basic education.

Teaching Methods, Guidance And Evaluation

Teaching Methods—Discovery and Diffusion : The continual deepening of the curricula should be accompanied by an equally vigorous improvement in the method of teaching and evaluation. The main factors responsible for the dull and uninspiring school teaching today are the rigidity of the educational system and the failure of the administrative machinery to diffuse new educational practices to schools. These weaknesses should be overcome.

Elasticity and Dynamism : A good educational system should be dynamic, flexible and discriminating enough to help institutions and teachers to proceed along different leve's of development—the good schools be free to go ahead on creative and experimental lines while the weaker ones should be supported to gain a sense of security.

Such elasticity and dynamism are possible if the experimenting teacher is supported by the administrative authority, a general atmosphere of reform, the encouragement of the head of the institution, a mastery of subject matter, leadership provided by training institutions, and the availability of teaching materials.

Elasticity in a school system will have lasting value if new practices developed are not diffused to schools and teachers given skilled help in trying out innovations. The educational administration can encourage and hasten the diffusion of new teaching methods by :

Combining permissiveness with persuasion ;

Approaching the new methods in stages according to the ability of schools ;

Giving necessary in-service training to teachers ;

Providing adequate guide materials which should be constantly revised and improved.

At the same time the administrator has to guard himself against letting any 'progressive' measure settling down into another orthodoxy.

Textbooks, Teacher's Guides And Materials

Provision of quality textbooks and other teaching-learning materials is a key programme for raising standards at comparatively low cost.

A comprehensive programme of text-book production at the national level should be implemented by mobilizing the best talent in the country on the lines already being attempted by NCERT. Such books will facilitate the definition and practical indication of expected standards. They will also help in national integration.

The Ministry of Education should take steps to establish in the public sector, an autonomous organization, functioning on commercial lines for the production of textbooks at the national level, especially scientific and technical books. A small Committee may be set up to workout the details of the project.

The effort at the national level should be supported and augmented by each State setting up an expert section for the production of textbooks.

The preparation, try-out and evaluation of textbooks should be the responsibility of the State Education Departments. The production aspect of the textbooks may preferably be done by the State Education Departments, wherever possible, through their own textbook presses. The sale and distribution of textbooks are better left to the student cooperatives and not be assumed directly by the Departments.

The production of textbooks and teaching aids at the State level should preferably be entrusted to an autonomous agency functioning in close liaison with the Education Department.

The machinery set up should be such that the textbooks are subjected to continuous revision and improvement.

Atleast 3 or 4 books should be provided in each subject to provide a multiple choice of books for the schools.

Liberal policies should be adopted for remunerating authors.

The entire organisation of State production of textbooks should be run on a no-profit-no-loss basis.

Manuscripts should be invited from a variety of sources including teachers, and a High Level Committee of professional persons should select and approve manuscripts.

Teacher's guides and other instructional material should supplement texsbooks.

Lists of minimum teaching aids and equipment needed by each category of schools should be prepared and steps by taken to provide the equipment to every school on a high priority basis.

Education Departments should work with the All-India Radio for the use of radio lessons, supplemented by printed guide materials for teachers and pupils. Broadcasting of special radio talks specially designed for teachers in the mornings and evenings will help teachers in lesson preparation. Sophisticated forms of newer techniques would not be suitable at present in the general run of schools but may be tried out experimentally in teacher training institutions.

Teachers should be helped and trained to rely on inexpensive and locally available or improvised teaching aids. Costly equipment should be shared by schools in a neighbourhood.

Class Size : Classes of somewhat larger size than what is strictly considered as desirable cannot be avoided in our country for a long time. However, it is necessary to restrict the number of pupils admitted to each class to a maximum of 50 in the lower primary, 45 in the higher primary, and lower secondary, and 40 in higher secondary classes.

Multiple Class Teaching : Research should be undertaken in the problems and techniques of multiple-class teaching. Training institutions should orient teachers to these techniques.

School Buildings : In view of the present unsatisfactory position regarding school buildings, it is necessary to take steps to clear the backlog of unconstructed school buildings as well as to provide additional buildings for new enrolment.

Allocations for construction of school buildings should be increased in the Central and State budgets, and community resources mobilised on the basis of equalization. Loans and grants-in-aid should be given on a liberal basis to private schools for the construction of buildings.

Reduction of Costs : The norms and guidance already available for spacing and planning of school buildings should be put into practice.

In view of the shortage of traditional building material and the cost involved, well-designed and constructed kacha structures should be accepted as part of the school system.

Buildings in Rural Areas : In rural areas, efforts should be made to encourage local initiative and contribution in putting up school buildings. The 'nucleus' approach suggested by the Ministry of Education is recommended for general adoption.

Buildings In Urban Areas : Economy in these buildings should be effected by using locally available materials, omission of certain finishes, and acceptance of a lower standard of construction. Temporary structures may be used wherever possible, and improved techniques of construction may be adopted in putting up pucca buildings.

Expeditious Construction : In order to accelerate provision of school buildings, construction in rural areas may be entrusted to local communities or village panchayats, and in urban areas, municipalities and corporations may be utilized for the purpose.

In order to supervise and guide the programme of construction of school buildings and to introduce improved techniques, an Educational Building Development

Group should be set up in each State within the Public Works Department and should work in close association with the Education Department. These groups will standardise details of construction in the region so as to make possible the mass production of the comments on a factory scale. A similar Building Development Group should be set up at the Centre to coordinate the work of the State groups.

To avoid delays in the construction of Government buildings, a separate unit of the PWD should be set up for the execution of education building programmes. At a later stage an Education Building Consortia may be set up to exploit the advantages of industrialized buildings.

The economy measures worked-out by the Educational Building Development Group should be made known to private institutions and grants-in-aid given on the basis of upper cost limits.

Guidance and Counselling: Guidance and councelling should be regarded as an integral part of education, meant for all students and aimed at assisting the individual to make decisions and adjustments from time to time.

Guidance at the Primary Stage: Guidance should begin from the lowest class in the primary school and in view of the large numbers of schools involved, the programme may be introduced through simple measures such as: (1) familiarising teachers under training with diagnostic testing and the problem of individual differences; (2) organizing in-service courses for primary teachers; (3) producing occupational literature; and (4) helping pupils and parents in choice of further education.

Guidance at the Secondary Stage: Guidance at the secondary stage should, among other things, help in the identification and development of the abilities and interests of adolescent pupils. The ultimate objective should be to introduce adequate guidance services in all secondary schools with a trained councellor in charge of the programme. But in view of the limited financial and personal resources, a short-range programme should be adopted for the next 20 years consisting of:

(1) A minimum guidance programme for all secondary schools through a visiting school counsellor for a group of ten schools, assisted by the school teachers in the simpler guidance functions;

(2) Comprehensive guidance programme in selected schools, one in each district, to serve as models; and

(3) Provision of necessary supervisory staff in the State Bureaus of Guidance.

All secondary school teachers should be introduced to guidance concepts through pre-or in-service training. The training colleges should be suitably staffed for the purpose.

General: Arrangements should be made for the professional training of guidance workers by the State Bureaus of Guidance and Training Colleges. Advanced training should be organized at the national level.

Ancillary programmes should include the production of guidance literature and materials and research into problems of guidance in the Indian situation.

Search for and Development of Talent: The search for talent must be a continuous process, pursued at all stages, but the secondary stage is the most crucial.

In addition to programmes of enrichment and advanced curricula, a variety of extra-moral programmes should be organized for the talented such as summer schools, visits to places of educational interests and provision of hostels and day-centres for those whose home environment is not conducive to study.

Teachers should be oriented to the special techniques of dealing with the talented children, especially to the need for providing an atmosphere for free expression and creative work.

The Backward Child: Neglect of backward children leads to wastage of educational facilities and human resources and it is necessary for a developing country to reduce this wastage to the minimum. In particular, attention has to be given to the under-achievers who represent a loss of potential manpower often of high ability. Steps should, therefore, be taken to diagnose the causes of under-achievement and to formulate and implement remedial programmes within the school system, with the help of interested teachers and child guidance clinics, where available, and parent-teacher associations.

Evaluation: Evaluation in a continuous process, forms an integral part of the total system of education and is intimately related to educational objectives. It exercises a great influence on the pupil's study habits and the teacher's methods of instruction and thus helps not only to measure educational achievement but also to improve it.

The new approach to evaluation will attempt to improve the written examination so that it becomes a valid and reliable measure of educational achievement and to devise techniques for measuring those important aspects of the student's growth that cannot be measured by written examinations.

Evaluation at the Lower Primary Stage: Evaluation at this stage should help pupils to improve their achievement in the basic skills and development of right habits and attitudes.

It would be desirable to treat Classes I to IV as an ungraded unit to enable children to advance at their own pace. Where this is not feasible, Classes I and II may be treated as one block divided into two groups—

one for slow and the other for fast learners. Teachers should be appropriately trained for the ungraded system.

Evaluation at the Higher Primary Stage : In addition to written examinations, weightage should be given at this stage to oral tests as a part of internal assessment. Diagnostic testing should be through simple teacher-made tests. Cumulative record cards are important in indicating pupil's growth and development but should be very simple and should be introduced in a phased manner.

External Examination at the end of the Primary Stage : Although the first national standard of attainment is to be set at the end of the primary stage, it is not considered necessary or desirable to prescribe a rigid and uniform level of attainment through a compulsory external examination. However, for the proper maintenance of standards, periodic surveys of the level of achievement of primary schools should be conducted by district school authorities through refined tests prepared by State Evaluation Organisations.

A Common External Examination or Inter-School Comparability : The district educational authority may arrange for a common examination at the end of the primary stage for schools in the district, using standardised and refined tests. This examination will have greater validity and reliability than the school examination and will provide inter-school comparability of levels of performance.

The certificate at the end of the primary course should be given by the school and should be accompanied by the cumulative record card and the statement of results of the common examination, if any.

In addition to the common examinations, special tests may be held at the end of the primary course for the award of scholarships or certificates of merit and for the purpose of identifying talent.

Improvement in External Examinations : External examinations should be improved by raising the technical competance of paper-setters, orienting question papers to objectives other than to acquisition of knowledge, improving the nature of questions, adopting scientific scoring procedures and mechanising the scoring of scripts and the processing of results.

Certificate given by the Board and School : The certificate issued by the State Board of School Education on the basis of the results of the external examination should give the candidate's performance in different subjects for which he has appeared and there should be not remark to the effect that he has passed or failed in the whole examination. The candidate should be permitted to appear again, if he so desires for the entire examination or for separate subjects in order to improve his performance.

The student should receive a certificate also from the school, giving the record of his internal assessment as contained in his cumulative record card and this should be attached to that given by the Board.

Establishment of Experimental Schools : A few selected schools should be given the right of assessing their students themselves and holding their own final examination at the end of Class X, which will be regarded as equivalent to the external examination of the State Board of School Education. The State Board of School Education will issue the certificates to the successful candidates of these schools on the recommendation of the schools. A Committee set up by the State Board of School Education should develop carefully the workedout criteria for the selection of such schools. The schools should be permitted to frame their own curricula, prescribe their own textbooks, and conduct their educational activities without external restrictions.

Methods of Internal Assessment : Internal assessment by schools should be comprehensive and evaluate all aspects of student growth including those not measured by the external examination. It should be descriptive as well as quantified. Written examinations conducted by schools should be improved and teachers may be trained appropriately. The internal assessment should be shown separately from the external examination marks.

Higher Secondary Examination : During the transition period, higher secondary students will have to appear for two successive external examinations—at the end of Classes X and XI, within one year. Where however the courses in Classes IX to XI are integrated, the examination at the end of Class X need not be insisted upon.

School Education : Administration And Supervision

A sympathetic and imaginative system of supervision and administration is essential for initiating and accelerating educational reform.

The Common School System of Public Education : The Common school System of Public Education would include all Government schools, all local authority schools and all aided private schools. Only two types of schools will remain outside it—indepandent schools and unrecognized schools.

The objective of educational policy should be to evolve, over the next 20 years, a common school system of public education which would cover all parts of the country, provide equality of access to all children and will maintain such a standard that an average parent will not feel the need to send his child to an independent or unrecognized school.

The following steps will have to be taken to create the common school system of public education :

(a) The existing discrimination between teachers

working under different managements should be done away with ;

(b) Tuition fees should be abolished in a phased programme—at the primary stage by the end of the Fourth Plan and at the lower secondary stage by the end of the Fifth Plan ;

(c) The existing discrimination between schools under different managements should be reduced to the minimum and all schools should be provided with the minimum essential conditions necessary for good education;

(d) The neighbourhood school plan should be adopted at the lower primary stage so as to eliminate the segregation between schools for the privileged and schools for the under-privileged.

Government and Local Authority Schools : Government and local authority schools do not generally maintain requisite standards because teachers in these schools develop little institutional loyality and the contact with the local community is either neglible or absent. These weaknesses should be overcome by the following measures :

(a) A School Committee with local representation should look after the management of every Government and local authority school or a group of schools in an area. Each Committee will operate its own school fund for the provision of services in schools ;

(b) Rational policies of transfers should be formulated so that teachers are not changed too often ;

(c) Greater freedom should be given to these schools.

Private Schools : It is the responsibility of Government to see that private aided institutions are satisfactorily managed through adequate support. Those, that are not so managed, should be taken over or eliminated.

A discriminating policy needs to be adopted in respect of assistance to and control of private aided institutions. The better schools should be given more freedom and assistance so as to enable them to develop into the nucleus of the common school system.

With the abolition of tuition fees, most private schools will come within the common school system and should be assisted to strengthen their management in the following ways :

(a) Each private school should have a Managing Committee consisting of representatives of the management, the Education Department and teachers ;

(b) The staffing of these schools should be broadly on the pattern of Government or local authority schools;

(c) Grants-in-aid should be improved on the basis indicated in the Report.

It should be an invariable rule that educational institutions must be conducted by non-profit-making bodies in order to be eligible for assistance.

Grant-in-aid codes should be amended to authorize the State Education Departments to take over the management of private schools which do not satisfy requirements and which have persistently failed to come upto prescribed standards.

Good Quality Private Schools : Good private schools which abolish tuition fees under the common school system should be helped to maintain existing standards and grant-in-aid should be adjusted on the basis of the quality schools as recommended in the Report and not on the basis of the level of the ordinary schools.

The Neighbourhood School : The present social sergregation in schools should be eliminated by the adoption of the neighbourhood school concept at the lower primary stage under which all children in the neighbourhood will be required to attend the school in the locality. This plan should be implemented in a period of 20 years as follows :

(a) During the first ten years, all primary schools should be improved to the minimum level and about 10 per cent of schools should be raised to a higher standard;

(b) Simultaneously the neighbourhood school system should be introduced at the lower primary stage as a pilot project in areas where public opinion is in favour of it.

To encourage children to study in the common school system, scholarships at the school stage be given by Government and local authorities should be tenable only in a school functioning within the common school system of public education. Similarly, ninety per cent of the scholarships awarded from public funds at the university stage should be open only to those students who have received their secondary education in schools functioning within the common school system.

A Nation-wide Programme of School Improvement : In view of the great need to improve standards of education at the school stage, a nation-wide progrmme of school improvement should be developed in which conditions will be created for each school to strive continually to achieve the best results of which it is capable. From this point of view, the following steps should be taken :

Each institution should be treated as a unit by itself and helped to grow at its own individual pace. For this purpose, it should prepare its own developmental programme of optimum utilization and growth.

The emphasis on these plans should be on motivating human agencies to make their best effort for the improvement of education rather than on increasing physical resources. Physical facilities should be improved through the cooperation of the local community.

The success of the programme will depend upon the degree to which the effort is sustained over a period of time.

Evaluate criteria for schools should be worked out by each State and may be used by schools for self-evaluation and by Inspecting Officers for their annual and triennial inspections. On the basis of these criteria, the schools should be classified on a three-point scale, norms being defined at optimum and minimum levels.

During the next ten years, atleast 10 per cent of the schools at the primary stage and one secondary school in each block should be raised to the optimum level. At the lower primary stage, access to these schools will be for the children in the neighbourhood. At the higher primary and secondary stages admission will be on the basis of merit.

Supervision : Reorganization of the State Department : The State Education Department will be the principal agency to deal with educational matters and will, therefore, be responsible for :

The development and implementation of a programme of school improvement ;

The prescription and enforcement of standards;

The training and supply of teachers ;

Inspection and supervision ;

The establishment and maintenance of a State Evaluation Organization ;

The maintenance of quality institutions and provision of extension services ;

The establishment and maintenance of a State Institute of Education ; and

The coordination and eventual assumption of responsibility for vocational and technical education at the school stage.

In view of the importance of strengthening the departmental organization at the district level :

(a) The District Education Officer should be given adequate status by including the post in the proposed Indian Educational Service;

(b) Adequate authority should be delegated to the district level ;

(c) Scales of pay and qualifications of inspectoral staff at the district level should be upgraded ;

(d) The strength of the district staff should be increased with the addition of 'specialists' and a statistical cell ; and

(e) A fair proportion of the district staff should consist of women officers in order to encourage girls' education.

Headmasters should be selected carefully and are specially trained. They should be vested with necessary authority and freedom.

Role of the School Complex in the New Supervision : The District Education Officer will be in touch with each school complex and as far as possible, deal with it as a unit. The complex itself will perform certain delegated tasks and deal with the individual schools within it. Adequate powers and responsibilities should be delegated to the complex so that better mathods of teaching and evaluation are made possible, facilities are shared, in-service training programmes are facilitated and new programmes are tried out.

The scheme should be first introduced in a few selected districts in each State as a pilot project before being implemented on a large scale.

The school complex should not only encourage experimentation en bloc but also foster individual experimentation within the unit.

The New Supervision : Supervision being in a sense, the backbone of educational improvement, it is imperative that the system of supervision should be revitalized.

Administration should be separated from supervision, the District School Board should deal with the former and the District Education Officer with the latter. But the two should function in close collaboration.

Recognition should not be a matter of course but should continuously be earned by every school, irrespective of its management.

Every school should have two types of inspections : An annual one by the officers of the District School Board for primary schools and by officers of the State Education Departments for the secoudary schools ; and a triennial or quinquennial inspection organized by the District Education Officer for the primary schools and by the State Boards of School Education for the secondary schools.

The provision of guidance and extension services to schools is one of the major responsibilities of the new supervision.

In-service training should be provided for all supervisory and administrative officers by State Institutes of Education and the National Staff College for Educational Administrators.

State Institutes of Education : An academic wing will have to be developed in the State Institutes of Education to look after the in-service training of departmental officers, improvement of teacher education, curricula and textbooks, guidance and evaluation, and research and evaluation of programmes.

State and National Boards of Education : In order to secure continuous improvement in standards, an adequate machinery should be set up at the State and national levels.

Standards should be defined at the end of the higher primary and lower secondary stages and later on, at the end of the higher secondary stage also when it covers a period of two years.

All these standards should be prescribed by the State Government in the light of local conditions ; the State Evaluation Organization and the State Boards of School Education will assist in defining, measuring and periodically revising these standards.

The National Board of School Education will coordinate standards at the national level and help States to raise them continuously.

The National Standard will only indicate the minimum below which no State should fall. These minima should be kept rising from time to time.

State Evaluation Organization : To assist the State Education Department in this programme of prescribing, maintaining and revising standards, a State Evaluation Organization should be set up in each State, as an independent institution, preferably autonomous, and its services should be avaiblable to all concerned.

The State Evaluation Organization will assist the District Education Officers in improving evaluation practices in schools, will advise the State Education Departments on curricula geared to expected standards, preparation of textbooks and other materials and meausure accomplished standards from time to time.

An Advisory Committee presided over by the Chairman of State Board of School Education will assist the State Evaluation Organization.

State Boards of School Education : In each State, a State Board of School Education should be established and it should take over the functioning and the responsibilities of the existing Boards of Secondary Education and allied agencies. The Board should be established by law and should have large powers and freedom to enable it to function and discharge its responsibilities satisfactorily. This would be greatly facilitated if its finances are pooled together in a separate fund managed and maintained by the Board. The Board should function as an integral part of the Department.

The Board will be in charge of the entire school stages in respect of curricula. Recognition of primary schools will be given by the District Education Officer and of secondary schools by both—the Department and the State Board of School Education.

In addition to conducting the external examination at the end of the lower secondary stage, the Board will also conduct examinations in general education at the end of the higher secondary stage.

In the long run, it would be desirable to bring all school education-general and vocation—within the scope of a single organization like the State Board of School Education. But this step may not be immediately practicable. Therefore, separate organizations may be set up, for the time being, for different vocational courses at the State level. There should, however, be a close coordination between these bodies and the State Board of School Education and there should be overlapping membership to some extent.

A Special Commitee of the Board should be established to look after the higher secondary stage. Half of its members should represent the schools and other half, the universities.

The time taken for the declaration of examination results should be minimised by : (1) mechanising the procedures, and (2) setting up sub-Boards to cover one or more districts in order to handle smaller numbers of candidates.

Role of the Centre : A National Board of School Education should be established in the Ministry of Education to advise the Government of India on all matters relating to school education. It will define expected standards at different stages of education, revise these standards from time to time, evaluate the standards attained in different parts of the country, and advise and assist State Education Departments in curricular reform and in improving standards. It will maintain close collaboration with the UGC and the universities.

A large programme should be developed in the Centrally-sponsored sector for the development of school education, particularly in respect of the establishment of vocational institutions, developing quality institutions and provision of scholarships.

The Central Board of Secondary Education should conduct some high standard examinations in individual school subjects at two levels—Classes X and XII—in consultation with the National Board of School Education. Curricula for these examinations should be prescribed in relation to the national standards. A beginning may be made with mathematics and science subjects. It should be open to the student of any recognized secondary school in the country to appear at these examinations and he should be awarded a certificate about his performance therein, separately for each subject. Such examinations would help in raising standards.

Unrecognized Schools : It may be desirable to introduce legislation for the compulsory registration of all educational institutions and it should be made an offence to conduct an unregistered institution. Power should also be vested in the State Government to remove any educational institution from the register if stipulated conditions are not fulfilled.

Higher Education Objectives And Improvement

Objectives of Universities : In broad terms, the functions of the universities in the modern world may be said to be the following :

To seek and cultivate new knowledge, to engage vigorously and fearlessly in the pursuit of truth, and to interpret old knowledge and beliefs in the light of new needs and discoveries;

To provide the right kind of leadership in all walks of life, to identify gifted youth and help them develop their potential to the full by cultivating physical fitness, developing the powers of the mind and cultivating right interests, attitudes and moral and intellectual values;

To provide society with competent men and women trained in agriculture, arts, medicine, science and technology and various other professions, who will also be cultivating individuals, imbued with a sense of social purpose;

To strive to promote equality and social justice and to reduce social and cultural differences through diffusion of education; and

To foster in the teachers and students, and through them in society generally, the attitudes and values needed for developing the good life in individuals and society.

In addition to these broad functions which they share in common with all universities, Indian universities will have to shoulder some special responsibilities in the present state of our social and educational development. For instance:

They must learn to serve as the conscience of the nation; and from this point of view, they should encourage individuality, variety and dissent, within a climate of tolerance;

They should develop programmes of adult education in a big way and to that end, evolve a wide-spread net-work of part-time and correspondence courses;

They should assist the schools in their attempts at qualitative self-improvement;

They should shake off the heavy load of their early tradition which gives a prominent place to examinations and strive to improve standards all-round by a symbiotic development of teaching and research; and

They should create atleast a few centres which would be comparable to those of their type in any other part of the world and thus help to bring back the centre of gravity of Indian academic life within the country itself.

If these objectives are to be realised, we need a well-conceived and comprehensive plan for the development of higher education, spread over the next twenty years, which will include, among other things, the following three programmes of high priority :

A radical improvement in the quality and standards of higher education and research;

Expansion of higher education to meet the manpower needs of national development and, to some extent, the rising social ambitions and expectations of the people; and

Improvement of university organization and administration.

Major Univerities : The most important reform in higher education is the development of some 'major universities' where first-class post-graduate work and research would be possible and whose standards would be comparable to the best institutions of their type in any part of the world. The UGC should select, as soon as possible, from amongst the existing universities, almost six universities (including one of the IITs and one Agricultural University) for development as major uiversities. The programme should begin in 1966-67.

A major university should have a 'critical mass' of students and teachers of outstanding capacity and promise. From this point of view:

(1) Each major university should be assigned with a number of scholarships for the under-graduate stage which will provide it with enough talented students for its post-graduate classes. Of these scholarships, about half should be from outside the area of the university.

(2) Each department or faculty of a major university should have a specially appointed Personal Advisory Committee, which should work in close collaboration wlth the appointing authorities of the university. The search for staff, instead of being limited to the State or the region, shou ld be made nation-wide and, in a sense, world-wide. Where necessary, the selected candidates should be offered advance increments. What is even more important, they should be assured of research opportunities, opportunities for study leave and the possibility to achieve professional excellence. There should be room for flexibility in the appointments and promotions. The UGC should place at the disposal of each university a contingency fund which may be used to provide more attractive salaries to persons of exceptional promise and performance.

It is necessary to establish 'clusters' of advanced centres in the major universities. They will add strength to, and enrich one another and be specially helpful in promoting inter-disciplinary research. About fifty such centres should be established, including some in modern Indian languages over the next five to ten years. Atleast one of them should concentrate on developing an inter-disciplinary approach to education. Other important areas to be covered are agriculture, engineering and medicine.

The administration of a centre, subject to the overall supervision of the universtty's Executive Council should be the responsibility of its Director assisted by a small but representative committee of his colleagues.

The original selection of a university department as a centre should be made on the basis of the quality and extent of work already done by it, its reputation for good teaching, its contribution to research and its potentiality for further development. The process of selection should be so devised that it will win the confidence of the universities and the academic community generally.

The privilege of being a centre of Advanced Study

should be continually earned and deserved. Each centre of advanced study should have, say, once in three to five years, a visiting committee, consisting of outstanding Indian and, where possible and necessary, foreign experts who will conduct a review and appraisal of the accomplishments of the centre.

The centres within a university should function in close collaboration with other centres and departments which are not centres of advanced study and measures should be adopted to involve the entire staff of the university in functioning as an intellectually effective community.

The major universities should constantly strive to enlarge the area of their excellence. For this purpose, they might be given a grant in proportion to the number of centres they already possess, to be used for the purpose of raising other departments within the university to their level.

Centres for advanced study should seek to bring the relevant teachers of their affiliated colleges into close contact with their work.

The recurring and capital costs of the major universities should be met by the UGC.

Improvement of other Universities. The major universities should be utilized to provide teachers of quality to the other universities and to the affiliated colleges. From this point of view:

(1) Every effort should be made to induce talented students from the major universities to join the teaching profession and to place a majority of them in universities and colleges, other than their own, so that they can help to raise standards.

(2) The UGC should sponsor a scheme for instituting a number of fellowships at three levels—lecturers, readers and professors. Outstanding persons, who may otherwise be lost to the profession, should be granted these fellowships and seconded to work in suitable departments of universities, care being taken to see that they are appointed against permanent posts as early as possible.

(3) The universities and affiliated colleges should be encouraged, so far as possible, to pre-select their new teachers and attach them to the major universities for a specified period.

(4) Strong inter-university links should be formed among members of centres of advanced study, members of aspirant centres, leading university departments and outstanding affiliated colleges, in particular fields of research.

(5) Invitations may be given to promising scholars and scientists from other universities or affiliated colleges to do research work and to conduct seminars (say for a term or a session) at one of the centres of Advanced Study.

(6) The other universities should be helped, through concentration of resources, to develop exicellence in selected departments and ultimately to raise them to the level of Centre of Advanced Studies.

Development of Affiliated Studies There are several colleges of long-standing which have done and are doing as good work as any good university and it should be an objective of educational policy to encourage them. The following steps may be taken to assist in this process ;

Affiliated colleges should be classified in terms of the level of their performance and assistance should be related to such classification.

Where there is an outstanding college (or a small cluster of very good college) within a large university which has shown the capacity to improve itself markedly, consideration should be given to granting it an 'autonomous' status. This would involve the power to frame its own rules of admissions, to prescribe its courses of study, to conduct examinations and so on. The parent university's role will be one of general supervision and the actual conferment of the degree. The provision for the recognition of such autonomous colleges should be made in the constitution of the universities. It should be possible, by the end of the Fourth Five Year Plan, to bring atleast fifty of the best colleges under this category.

Improvement and Teaching of Evaluation : The number of formal class-rooms and laboratory hours should be somewhat reduced. The time thus saved should be devoted, under the guidance of instructors, to independent study, assigned reading, writing of essays, solving of problems and small research projects in which the student seeks art and learns to use independently the books and documents he needs.

Every effort should be made to build-up good libraries in universities and colleges

It is most important to emphasize original thinking in the study of all subjects and to discourage memorizing.

There should be a possibility of under-graduates coming into occasional contact with senior and outstanding teachers, particularly when a new subject has to be introduced for the first time.

The content and quality of lectures in general needs to be considerably improved. One way of characterizing the level of class-work is that every one hour of instruction should receive about 3-4 hours of study-time to digest the lectures.

It may be laid down as a rule that no teacher should be away from his institution during 'term time' for more than seven days in a year.

All new appointments should be made during vacation time so that teachers join their new posts at the beginning of the academic year. Further, unless there be compelling reasons, no teacher should be permitted to leave an institution to take up another appointment during 'term time'.

There is great need for experimentation, especially in two important areas. One such area concerns the manner of handling larger number of students without a proportionate increase in educational expenditure or the number of faculty members. Another desirable experiment would be to have a certain amount of teaching done by research students and by selected post-graduate students after their first year.

The problem of teaching methods in higher education has been relatively neglected. It should be examined by the UGC through a special committee appointed for the purpose. The schools of education should make a special study of the teaching methods, not only at the school stage, but also in universities and affiliated colleges.

In all teaching universities, external examinations should be replaced by a system of internal and continuous evaluation by the teachers themselves.

In universities with affiliated colleges, a system of internal assessment should supplement the external examination.

The University Grants Commission should set up an Central Examination Reform Unit to work in collaboration with the universities. Special units for examination reform should also be set up in some universities who can be pursuaded to organize examination reform in a big way.

University teachers should be reoriented to adopt the new and improved techniques of evaluation through a large programme of seminars, discussions or workshops.

Early measures should be taken to abolish payment of remuneration to examiners. As a first step, the total number of scripts to be examined by any teacher during a year should not exceed 500.

Medium of Education : The regional languages should be adopted as media of education at the university stage in a phased programme spread over the years.

At the earlier stage of the under-graduate course, the bulk of the instruction may be given through the regional language while at the post-graduate stage, it may be in English.

In due course, all teachers in higher education should, as far as possible, be bilingual and post-graduate students should be able to follow lectures and use reading materials in the regional language as well as in English.

The maintenance of colleges, teaching through the medium of Hindi in the non-Hindi areas or of Urdu in any part of the country where there is a reasonable number of Urdu-speaking students, should be permitted and encouraged.

Centres of Advanced Study should be established for the development of all modern Indian languages including Urdu.

The classical and modern Indian languages should be provided as elective subjects, no language being made a compulsory subject of study at the university stage.

Adequate facilities should be provided in universities and colleges for the study of English. Special units for teaching English should be established in universities to give a good working knowledge of it to new entrants by the adoption of modern teaching techniques. It would also be an advantage to teach same English as part of the elective subject course in the first year of the degree course.

The teaching of important library languages other than English should be stressed, in particular the study of Russian, on a larger scale.

Student Services : Student services are not merely a welfare activity but constitute an integral part of education. These should include orientation for new students, health services, residential facilities, guidance and conselling including vocational placement, student activities and financial aid.

All institutions of higher education should organize orientation programmes for new students in the beginning of the academic year to facilitate adjustment. Each student should be assigned to an academic adviser who would assist him in planning and organizing his programme and studies. Every member of the teaching faculty should be expected to serve as an academic adviser to a group of students.

Steps should be taken to organize, on a high priority basis, adequate health services in universities and colleges. Adequate provisions should also be made for health education of students. The UGC may explore the possibility of organizing health services for university teachers and students on the lines of the Contributory Health Services of the Government of India.

Hostel accommodation should be provided, as soon as possible, for about 25 per cent and 50 per cent of the enrolment at the undergraduate and postgraduate stages respectively.

Day-study Centres, with subsidized or low-cost cafetarias, should be provided for about 25 per cent of the non-resident students.

There should be atleast one counsellor for every thousand students. A project for training the counsellor should also be organized in some university. A combined information and employment centre should function directly under the supervision of the dean of students in each university.

It is necessary to develop a rich and varied programme of co-curricular activities for students not only during 'term-time' but also during vacations.

There should be a full-time dean of students welfare for the administration of welfare services.

Student Unions : Each university should decide how its student union will function, an experimentation in this matter is welcome.

Membership of the student union should be automatic but every student should be expected to choose atleast one activity oıganized in the union,

The office-bearers should be elected indirectly by the different student societies in the university, those who spend two or more years in the same class being disqualified for the purpose.

Joint Committee of teachers and students should be established and fully utilized to ascertain and redress the genuine difficulties of students.

The UGC should take initiative in convening and financially supporting an annual conference of representatives of the student unions in universities and colleges.

Student Discipline : Education should enable young men and women to learn and practise civilized forms of behaviour and to commit themselves to special values of significance.

The responsibility for indiscipline taking place is multi-lateral and no effective solution is possible unless each agency—students, parents, teachers, State Governments and political parties—does its own duty.

Earnest efforts should be made to remove the educational defficiencies that contribute to students unrest and set up an adequate consultative and administrative machinery to prevent the occurrence of acts of indiscipline.

The incentives to positive discipline have to come from opportunities that the institution presents to the intellectual and social demands it makes on the students. A better standard of student services is also necessary.

The whole university life should be treated as one and polarization between teachers, students and administration should be avoided.

Higher Education : Enrolment And Programmes

Expansion of Facilities : The expansion of facilities in higher education should be planned broadly in relation to manpower needs and employment opportunities. On the basis of the present trends, it appears that the enrolments in undergraduate and postgraduate courses will have to be increased from about 1 million in 1965-66 to 4 million in 1985-86. Facilities in professional courses such as agriculture, engineering or medicine and those at the postgraduate stage will have to be specially expanded.

Selective Admission : Since the demand for higher education will be much larger than the provision that can be made for it or is needed on the basis of manpower needs, a system of selective admissions will have to be adopted. Three measures would have to be adopted from this point of view :

The determination of the number of places available in an institution in relation to teachers and facilities available to ensure that standards are maintained at an adequate levels.

Prescription of eligibility by the universities ; and

Selection by the institution concerned of the best students from amongst those who are eligible and seek admission.

While the use of examination marks as a major basis for admissions may continue until better se'ection methods are devised, their arbitrariners or lack of reliability should be compensated, to the extent possible, by making due allowance for the socio-economic handicaps of students so as to relate selection more directly to inmate talent. The final selectors should also take into consideration such factors as the school record and the proficiency of the student in fields not tested in the examination. This is especially important in border-line cases. In exceptional cases, the universities should have the right and courage to suspend the rules and give admissions to students whose talent has been identified but who may not have been able to fulfil the entrance requirements. The procedure proposed for selecting students on the basis of 'school clusters' for the award of scholarships may also be adopted for making admissions to quality institutions.

Each university should constitute a Board of University Admissions to advise the university about all matters of admissions.

The University Grants Commission should set up a Central Testing Organisation for the development of appropriate selection procedures for different courses of higher education.

Part-time Education ; Opportunities for part-time education (correspondence courses, evening colleges) should be extended widely and should include courses in science and technology. By 1986, about a third of the total enrolment in higher education could be provided through a system of correspondence courses and evening colleges.

College Size : The general policy should be to encourage the establishment of bigger institutions which tend to be more efficient and economic. A college should normally have a minimum enrolment of 500 and it would be preferable to raise it to 1,000 or more in as many colleges as possible. From this point of view :

(1) The UGC should undertake a study of the planning of the location of colleges with special reference to small colleges.

(2) In granting affiliation to colleges, the universities should emphasize the expansion of existing colleges, rather than establishing new ones.

(3) In granting affiliation to a new college, care should be taken to see that its location is so planned that it does not interfere with a proper growth of an existing institution of its own.

Post-graduate Education and Research : Post-graduate education and research work should ordinarily be organized in the universities or in university 'centres' where a good programme can be developed cooperatively by a group of local colleges. The increase in enrolments at the post-graduate stage should always be contingent on adequate increase in material and staff resources. A rigorous test of admission should be introduced and adequate scholarships should be available (to cover 50 per cent of the students) and these should be supplemented by loan scholarships. The Government of India should be made almost exclusively responsible for post-graduate education and research.

Education of Women : At present, the proportion of women students to men students in higher education is 1 : 4. This should be increased to about 1 : 3 to meet the requirements for educated women in different fields. For this purpose, a programme of scholarships and provision of suitable but economical hostel accomodation should be developed.

At the undergraduate stage, separate colleges for women may be established if there is a local demand. At the post-graduate level, however, there is no justification for separate institutions.

Women students shouild have free access to courses in arts, humanities, sciences and technology. Courses in home science, nursing, education and social work need to be developed as these have attraction for a large proportion of girls. Facilities for advanced training in business administration and management should also be provided.

Research units should be set up in one or two universities to deal specifically with women's education.

New Universities : The establishment of new universities is inescapable. The metropolitan cities of Bombay, Calcutta, Delhi and Madras should have, by the end of the Fourth Plan, two universities each which would supplement to some extent, the work of each other. The demand from the States of Kerala and Orissa for additional universities is justifiable. The proposals for the establishment of a university for the hill areas of North-Eastern Region should be supported as a major measure for spear-heading economic and social development in the area.

In establishing new universities, the following principles should be kept in view :

The establishment of a new university can be justified only if it leads to a substantial improvement in standards and in the output and level of research.

No new university should be started unless the agreement of the UGC is obtained and adequate provision of funds is made.

Cooperative effort by postgraduate centres to provide facilities for postgraduate education should be developed as a first step towards the establishment of a university. A new university should not ordinarily be established in a place where a university centre has not been in operation for some time.

Good university organization would be one in which a university has a strong core of teaching departments combined with about 30 affiliated colleges in close proximity.

The UGC may explore the possibility of bringing together all universities in a State in a 'consortium' to operate all the affiliated colleges in the State.

A time of two to three years should be allowed to elapse between the appointment of the first Vice-chancellor and the direct commencement of the university's work, the Vice-chancellor being assisted by a Planning Board during the period.

Larger resources should be placed at the disposal of the UGC so as to increase the amount of Central assistance to all State universities on the basis of their performance and merit.

Calcutta University : The State Government in consultation with the UGC and the Government of India may have the affairs of the University of Calcutta examined with a view to finding a way out of the difficulties created by a rapidly increasing undergraduate population.

Inter-University Collaboration : Universities should join together, at the regional and national levels, in cooperative programmes and supplement mutually their available facilities, especially in research. It should be the special responsibility of the UGC to promote collaborative and cooperative programmes which cut across State, regional or linguistic frontiers.

Reorganization of Courses : The combination of subjects permissible for the first degree should also be more elastic than at present, both in the arts and in the sciences. It should not be linked too rigidly to the subjects studied at school.

There should be general, special and honours courses at the undergraduate stage. Universities which have better facilities should only provide for special courses or for general (Honours) courses. Affiliated colleges should have an option to provide either the general eourses—both at the pass and honours levels—or the special courses, minimum enrolment being prescribed for the general (honours) and special courses to economize on costs.

It is an urgent need to introduce flexibility and innovation in the organization of the courses for the Master's degree. The curricula should be framed as to provide a general broad-based course or intensive training in one or two special fields.

A student should be expected to work from two to three years for a Ph.D. degree which should be regarded as the beginning and not the climax of the research career of the student. During the first year of the Ph.D. courses, students should attend lectures and tutorials of advance nature to overcome inadequacy of preparation at the Master's degree stage.

Students for the Ph.D. courses should be carefully selected, a time-limit being set within which a student is expected to submit his thesis. There should also be a limit on the number of students to be guided by a teacher at any given time.

The procedure for evaluation of the Ph.D. degree should be improved, a deference of the thesis being considered on essential requirement for the degree.

A study of a second world language should be obligatory for all Ph.D. students and compulsory for the Master's degree in certain subjects.

It would be desirable to institute the degree of Doctor of Science as the highest award given on the basis of recognized research work.

Special efforts should be made to promote inter-disciplinary studies in universities which have adequately staffed departments in related subjects. To further this objective, a broad-based staffing pattern is also needed.

The Social Sciences : The social sciences should be given a significant position in Indian universities and research institutions. From this point of view :

There should be adequate provision of scholarships in the social science courses;

The choice of subjects at the first degree stage should be elastic and it should be possible for students to combine study of a social science with any other group of subjects;

The financial assistance available to universities for the development of social sciences should considerably be increased; and

High level schools or Centres of Advanced Study for allied groups of social sciences should be developed in a number of universities.

Area Studies : It should be our endeavour to develop a significant and effective programme of area studies in a few selected universities and institutions. Such a programme would require intensive courses in the languages of the areas concerned and the introduction of optional groups of papers in certain social science subjects having reference to the different areas selected for intensive study. Close inter-disciplinary collaboration would also be necessary.

Study of Humanities : The need for strengthening the humanities cannot be overstressed. In science education, we shall have to depend inevitably on developments in advanced countries with which we will not be able to catch up in the foreseable future. To redress the balance, our scholars should strive to make significant contributions to the sum total of human knowledge and experience in the fields of the social and pedagogical sciences and humanistic studies, where our old traditions and the present challenges posed by social development present unique opportunities for creative work.

Educational Research : Urgent steps have to be taken to develop educational research and relate it effectively to the formation of educational policies and improvement of education. From this point of view, the following programmes need to be developed:

A documentation centre and a national clearing house in educational research should be developed at the NCERT.

Educational research has to be developed in teams and in inter-disciplinary fields. While all training colleges should do some research, the restriction of educational research to training colleges has hampered its growth. It will be the special responsibility of Schools of Education to develop educational research in a big way in collaboration with other developments.

It is desirable to set up a National Academy of Education consisting of eminent educationists, broadly on the lines of the National Institute of Science to promote educational thought and research. This should essentially be a non-official, professional body. But it should receive adequate financial support from the Government of India.

An Education Research Council should be set up in the Ministry of Education for the promotion of research.

There is urgent need to provide good specialized training for research work and services for data-processing, statistical analyses and consultation.

It would be the responsibility of the NCERT at the national level and the State Institutes of Education at the State level to bridge the serious gap between the educational research and current school practices. A similar role will have to be played by the UGC in the field of higher education.

The total expenditure on educational research has to be increased considerably, the goal being to devote about one per cent of the State expenditure on education to it.

The Governance of Universities

Universities should evolve dynamic techniques of

management and organization suited to their special functions and purposes. The UGC should encourage the formation of groups in universities to study the problem of educational administration and management of university affairs.

University Autonomy : The proper sphere of university autonomy lies in the selection of students, the apointment and promotion of teachers and the determination of courses of study, methods of teaching and the selection of areas and problems of research.

Autonomy within a Univeisity : The representation of the non-academic element on university bodies should be mainly for the purpose of presenting the wider interests of society as a whole to the university but not to impose on them.

The universities should give onsiderable autonomy to their dependents. The principle that good ideas often originate at the lower levels must be recognized and respected in the governance of a university. Wider administrative and financial powers should be delegated to a Committee of Management to be set up in each Department under the chairmanship of the head of the department.

The freedom and antonomy of colleges must be recognized and respected in the same spirit as the university wants it for itself.

There should be Joint Committees of teachers and students in each department and in every college, and a Central Committee under the chairmanship of the head of the institution for the discussion of common problems and difficulties. Student representatives should also be associated with the Academic Councils and the Courts of Universities.

In India, the tradition of university antonomy is fairly strong and will have to be consolidated in time. This imposes special responsibilities on Government, UGC, IUB, the public and the universities themselves. In particular, the following need emphasis :

A suitable machinery for consultations between universities, the UGC, IUB and the Government should be developed for reaching decisions regarding number of students to be trained, courses of study and problems of applied research.

The UGC, the IUB and the intelligentsia have an important role to play in creating a strong public opinion in favour of university autonomy.

The universities have to continually earn and deserve their autonomy by discharging their intellectual and public opinion in favour of university autonomy.

The universities have to continually earn and deserve their autonomy by discharging their intellectual and public obligations effectively.

University Finances : The State Governments should place adequate financial resources at the disposal of universities and simplify rules and procedures for operating them.

The UGC should be enabled to give both development and maintenance grants to State Universities.

There should be some reasonable sharing of developmental expenditure on universities between the UGC and State Governments.

UGC should take steps to resolve problems faced by some universities on account of the non-payment of grants on committed expenditure by State Governments.

The system of grant-in-aid from the State Governments to the universities should be reorganized on the basis of a suitable system of block grants.

The finance of universities should be placed on a sound footing on the basis of advice given by the UGC to the State Governments and the universities after periodical review.

Universities should be immune from direct governmental intervention and also from direct public accountability.

Role and Appointment of the Vice-Chancellors : While the choice of the Vice-chancellor should eventually be left to the university concerned, for the time being, the present 'Delhi' pattern, or some variation of it may be adopted. The members of the Selection Committee for the Vice-chancellor should be known for their eminence and integrity and there should be no objection to one of them being connected with the university but he should not be a paid employee of the university.

The authority to appoint the Vice-chancellor during the first years of a university's life should vest in the Visitor/Chancellor.

The Vice-chancillor should, as a rule, be a distinguished educationist or eminent scholar with adequate administrative experience.

The term of office of the Vice-chancellor should be five years and he should not be appointed for more than twe terms in the same university.

All posts of Vice-chancellors should be whole-time and carry a salary.

The retirement age for the Vice chancellor should be 65 years, an exception being made in the case of exceptionally qualified persons of all-India eminence.

It wouid be an advantage if the successor to a Vice-chancllor could be designated, so far as, possible, in advance by a year or so.

Adequate powers should be vested in the Vice-chancellor for the efficient working of the university.

Legislation for Universities : The Court should be the policy-making body of the university with a membership of not more than 100, of which about half should be external.

The Executive Council with the Vice-chancellor as Chairman should consist of 15-20 members, about half being internal and half external.

The Academic Council should be the sole authority for determining the courses of study and standards.

A Standing Committee of the Academic Council should deal with urgent matters, if the Academic Council cannot meet frequently enough for the purpose.

Each university should have an Academic Planning Board for permanent planning and evaluation, detached from day-to-day administration.

The IUB should appoint a Committee to go into the question of reform of ritual and procedure of convocation functions.

The Governors of the States should be the Visitors of all universities in the State and should have power to direct inspection or inquiry into the affairs of a university.

The Ministry of Education and the UGC should take the initiative to revise existing university legislation in India and to amend it in the light of the recommendations made.

The constitution of a university should be formulated in sufficiently general terms so as to leave room for, and promote, innovation and experimentation.

A suitable machinery for tripartite consultations between the UGC, the Ministry of Education and the State Governments should be evolved before legislation relating to universities is enacted.

Universities and the Law Courts: The Government of India may request the Supreme Court to frame a suitable policy to help the maintenance of university autonomy and the proper development of higher education.

Affiliated Colleges: Affiliation of colleges should be granted by the universities after consultations with the State Government.

A Committee of Vice-chancellors in the State should be set up to advise the Education Department regarding the grant-in-aid to affiliated colleges.

There should be a Council of Affiliated colleges in every affiliating universty to advise the university on all matters relating to affiliation of colleges.

The existing machinery for the grant of affiliation to colleges and for their periodical inspection should be strengthened.

Affiliation should be regarded as a privilege which is to be continually earned and deserved.

The UGC may examine the question of a small nucleous staff being sanctioned to each affiliating university for the proper organisation of an inspection programme.

The most important reform which alone will make it possible to improve affiliated colleges is to relate emoluments to the facilities available.

Government Colleges: Different approaches to suit local conditions and traditions may be devised for the management of Government colleges, e.g., the establishment of a separate Directorate of Collegiate Education, or an autonomous organization for all Government colleges in a State, or placing each college under an autonomous Board of Governors.

Private Colleges: A discriminating policy should be adopted so that greater freedom and assistance to the really good private institutions could be given.

The procedure for calculation and payment of grants-in-aid should be simplified on the lines recommended.

The Inter-University Board: All statutory or deemed universities should become members of the IUB automatically.

The degree or diplomas granted by a statutory or deemed university in India should receive automatic recognition from all the other statutory and deemed universities.

The IUB should be strengthened financially to enable it to develop advisory, research and service functions for and on behalf of the universities.

The University Grants Commission: All higher education should be regarded as an integrated whole and the UGC should eventually represent the entire spectrum of higher education. For the time being, however, it would be more feasible to set up separate UGC-type organizations for agricultural, engineering and medical education and to create a machinery that would effectively coordinate them.

The UGC should consist of 12-15 member: Not more than one-third should be officials of Government and at least one-third of the universities. There should be no objection to a serving Vice-chancellor being appointed as a member of the UGC.

The UGC should adopt a practice of working through Standing Committees set up to deal with important responsibilities entrusted to it.

The visiting committee appointed by the UGC should visit each university every three years and work in greater detail and depth.

Considerably larger funds should be available to the UGC to enable it to deal effectively with the magnitude and importance of the problems and responsibilities as envisaged.

The responsibility of coordinating standards should continue to vest in one body, viz., the UGC. State UGCs should not, therefore, be created.

Education For Agriculture

A programme of eductaion for agriculture will have to be based on an effective organic link between the three main elements of teaching research and extension.

Agricultural Universities: Atleast one agricultural

university should be established in each State.

Beginning with traditional agricultural specialities, these universities should gradually extend their scope of studies to cover a wide range of specialized courses to suit the need of the day.

A clear delineation of responsibilities between Agricultural Universities and the State Departments of Agriculture is necessary. The former should take over all research, education and extension programmes.

Postgraduate work should become a distintic feature of the Agricultural Universities which should be staffed with adequately trained personnel. The intake at the postgraduate level, particularly in the hitherto neglected areas, will have to be considerably increased. To ensure maintenance of standards, however, this expansion should be related to available personnel and facilities and no institution should be allowed to undertake postgraduate instruction unless it has adequate integrated facilities for education and research.

Central Research Institutes like the Indian Agricultural Research Institute (IARI) and the Indian Veterinary Research Institute (IVRI) and the National Dairy Research Institute (NDRI) and the Agricultural Universities would constitute suitable centres for strong postgraduate schools in agriculture. Close coordination among these institutions on the one hand and with ICAR on the other should be established.

Admission to postgraduate courses should not be restricted to agricultural graduates only. Talent from as many fields as possible should be harnessed to the betterment of agricultural research and education.

To enable the students to undertake independent study and to ensure their introduction to research as early as possible, each university should have a well-equipped library with adequate staff.

Coordinated, problem and production-oriented research projects recently evolved by the ICAR should be developed futher.

Duration of first degree course should ordinarily be five years, after ten years' schooling.

Teachers : For as many of the staff members as possible, there should be integerated assignments between classroom teaching and laboratory research, experimental research and work in the field with rural people.

The UGC scales of pay should be extended to Agricultural Universities also. Other conditions of service should be made attractive.

The strength of any faculty should be determined by needs and quality of staff and not by any rigid hierarchy. Merit should be the main consideration for promotion within a faculty.

The faculties should have reasonalble academic freedom.

External examinations should be reduced in importance and abolished as early as possible.

A large scale programme of teacher training should be undertaken immediately in 5 or 6 existing high quality centres, offering attractive scholarships to graduates in science and agriculture.

Students : Scholarships awarded should cover not less than 25 per cent of the students in Agricultural Universities.

To attract talented students the present scales of pay offered to agricultural graduates should be improved.

Farm : Well-managed farms, about 1,000 acres in size and with not less than 500 acres of cultivated area, should be attached to every agricultural university.

Internship: Possibilities of providing one year internship on a well-managed State university demonstration farm before awarding the degree to the students should be explored.

Number, Size and Organization : In the process of establishing one agricultural university in each State, the possibilities of converting existing universities into agricultural universities should also be studied.

While some experimentation should be allowed, it is essential that all agricultural universities should conform to some important principles such as, being single campus universities without any affiliated colleges. If for any exceptional reasons, the university should take over the responsibility for colleges outside its campus, they should be made constituent colleges under a unified administration.

Contribution of other Universities for the Development of Agriculture : Other universities wishing to introduce agricultural studies should be given all assistance.

An academic relationship between some of the agricultural universities and the IITs should be developed. This can take the form, among other things, of an exchange of students and staff, and arranging common programmes of study and research.

The possibility of organizing agricutural faculties in one or two of the IITs and in some leading universities should be explored.

Agricultural Colleges : New agricultural colleges should not be established and the training of undergraduates and post-graduates in agriculture should be done in agricultural universities.

Where agricultural colleges are constituent colleges of a university, it should be assisted to develop strong agricultural faculties.

Every agricultural college should have well-managed farm of atleast 200 acres.

Quinquennial inspections of agricutural colleges jointly by ICAR and UGC should be undertaken, and such colleges, as do not come up to the requiste standards should be disaffiliated. Some of the colleges may be converted to offer courses at a higher technician level instead of degree.

Agricultural Polytechnics : Agricultural polytechnics at post-matriculation level should be organized on a priority basis. These should be attached to agricultural universities and be large institutions with enrolments around 1,000 students. To meet immediate needs, courses may also be added to existing polytechnics located in predominantly rural surroundings.

The polytechnics should be multipurpose institutions providing training for imparting the wide range of skills needed in agriculture and allied fields. While reasonable flexibility should be allowed in their organization, these courses should be distinctly practical in nature. Courses offered should be predominantly terminal in character leading to specific employment, with adequate provision for the exceptionally brilliant students to take up courses in higher education through further study. In course of time, the polytechnics should offer short condensed courses, particularly for the young farmers and also of special interest to girls and women in rural areas.

Attractive scales of pay and adequate qualifications should be prescribed for the staff of these polytechnics.

Agricultural Education in Schools : Attempts to train for vocational competence in farming through formal schooling in agriculture at primary and lower secondary levels have failed and further efforts should be held in abeyance.

Instead of any narrow vocational training, the school should impart a sound general education with particular emphasis on mathematics and science, as the best preparation for coping with the inevitable rapid changes characterizing our future agriculture.

The proposal for setting up a large number of junior agricultual schools is beset with several difficulties and may fail to serve its objectives. It should be abandoned.

Agricultural Education as part of General Education : In all primary schools including those in urban areas, some orientation to agriculture should form an integral part of general education.

Agriculture should also be made an important part of the work-experience at the school stage.

Undergraduate and postgraduate courses in the colleges and universities should give prominence to orientation to rural and agricultural problems. UGC and other authorities should take suitable steps in this regard.

Similar orientation in agriculture and rural problems should be introduced in all teacher training progammes.

Extension Programmes : In raising the professional and technical competence of the VLWs and of the specialists who support them, the agricultural university and polytechnics should render all necessary assistance by making available the specialist staff and by organizing special courses.

When the proposed separation of supply services from the extension work takes place, the extension part of it should be transferred to the agricultural university maintaining, at the same time, closest liaison between the extension work, supply and other programme services of the department of agriculture.

The target should be to set up atleast one primary extension centre in every Community Development Block for purposes of extension work, within cycling distance of the area served. It is essential that these centres are manned by staff with a practical knowledge superior to that of the farmers whom they are educating and also that they receive the strongest support and guidance from the extension services of the agricultural university.

Greater use should be made of successful farmers in the carrying out of extension work in education about agriculture generally.

The individual village farmers attending courses at primary extension centres should be encouraged to start Farmers' Study Circles in their villages.

Fullest use should also be made of radio, films and other audio-visual aids in educating farmers and the rural community.

Mainpower Needs : Steps should be taken for preparing more accurate estimates of the requirements of manpower in the agricultural development. In the meantime, vigorous efforts should be made atleast to double the output of graduates and to produce an equal number of diploma holders, in the next ten years.

The Role of the ICAR and UGC : Responsibility for ensuring that agricultural education is launched on the basis of an integrated approach to teaching, research and extension can best be carried out by ICAR.

To enable the ICAR to fulfil its responsibility in this regard, a special Standing Committee of the Council should be set up with a scholar or scientist of national repute at its head.

There should be some overlap in the membership of the UGC and the above Standing Committee and they should evolve common programmes for the development of higher education in agriculture.

Vocational, Technical and Engineering Education

A concerted and sustained programme is needed to ensure that by 1986, some 20 per cent of all enrolments at the lower secondary level and some 50 per cent beyond Class X are in part-time or full-time vocational and professional courses.

Vocational education courses at school stage should be predominantly terminal in character, with adequate oportunities, for the exceptionally gifted child, to rejoin the main stream and more higher, through further study.

Training Semi-skilled and Skilled Workers: There should be a further expansion of facilities in ITIs, beginning by atleast a doubling of available places in the Fourth Plan. The minimum admission age should be gradually lowered to 14, with suitable adjustments in courses.

Junior Technical Schools should be renamed Technical High Schools and along with the existing Technical High Schools should offer courses clearly terminal in character. There should be greater use of available time to meet the requirements of the Apprenticeship Act. Enough flexiblity and experimentation should be permitted in the organization of the various courses.

Training in ITIs and technical schools must be production-oriented.

Skilled workers' training courses with entry requirements below Class X should also be attached to polytechnics to make better use of existing facilities.

Facilities for vocational and technical training for school leavers entering employment should be greatly expanded on a part-time, day release, correspondence, sandwich or short intensive course bases. Rigidity of approach in the organization of these courses, should be avoided.

Technician Training: The overall ratio of engineers to technicians should be raised from the present figure of 1:1.4 to 1:2.5 by 1975 and to 1:3 or 4 by 1986.

Courses for the training of technicians should be revised in the light of periodic investigations to be carried out in cooperation with industry, aimed at job analysis and specifications in terms of levels and clusters of skills and responsibilities for technicians.

Diploma training should be more practical, by including industrial experience. This practical training should be of a project or problem-oriented type.

Polytechnics should be located only in industrial areas, while those already functioning in rural areas should develop courses allied to agriculture and agro-industries.

Teachers for polytechnics should be increasingly recruited from industry, by relaxing, if necessary, academic admission requirements. Salaries should not be linked to academic qualifications only.

To give training in as near realistic conditions as possible, vacations should be used by the students and staff to do production work on simple tools either for equipping secondary schools or for sale.

Teaching of science and mathematics in polytechnics should be strengthened, particularly in the first two years. Technician courses should include introduction to industrial psychology and management, costing and estimation.

Polytechnics should increasingly adopt sandwich type of courses in cooperation with industry.

In view of low mobility of diploma holders in the country, the courses offered in polytechnics during the Fourth and Fifth Plans should be designed largely with local requirements in view, keeping at the same time, a watchful eye on total national needs.

Courses of special interest to girls should be offered in all polytechnics at both the certificate and diploma levels and girls completing the lower secondary course should be encouraged to take them up.

Every effort must be made to reduce the present high wastage rates in polytechnics to a minimum and to expand existing polytechnics to their optimum size.

Selected polytechnics should provide post-diploma courses for technicians with some years of experience in industry to qualify as higher level technicians.

Other Vocational Education: At the higher secondary level (Classes XI & XII), alongside the polytechnics, there is considerable scope for starting a range of interesting courses in commercial, clerical, scientific and industrial trades and in areas of special interest to girls. This should be fully exploited.

Products of Technical High Schools and polytechnics should be encouraged to set up small enterprises of their own or to join together with others in creating small-scale workshops, industries and services needed in the community.

Education of Engineers: All institutions not conforming to the standards should be improved, converted to institutions training technicians or should be closed.

For selected branches of engineering such as electronics and instrumentation, recruitment of well-qualified B. Sc. students should be encouraged, with courses suitably adjusted.

Anomalies in the scales of pay between staff members in science and technology faculties in engineering institutions should be removed. An appropriate number of posts in each of these faculties should be reserved for well-qualified persons of the other faculty.

Practical training for full-time degree students should commence from the third year of the course, and should be properly prepared and supervised in cooperation with the industry. Wherever possible, sandwich type of courses should be adopted.

Workshop practice should be more production-oriented.

Courses at both degree and diploma levels should be diversified to meet the changing needs.

For colleges and institutes of technology to become more concerned with the needs of industry, research design projects sponsored either by industry or Government should be made a part of the curriculum.

Syllabus should be continually revised in consultation with Expert Committees carefully avoiding any rigid conformity.

Development of courses and manpower estimates in new fields such as electronics, instrument technology including automation, chemical technology, aeronautics and astronautics, and nuclear power generation should be carefully planned in advance.

Teachers : Teachers should be allowed to undertake consultancy for industry. Widespread summer institutes should be organized.

Suitable salary scales should be offered to make the profession attractive and to ensure that well-qualified engineers may work in teaching and research for significant periods in their careers.

Institutes of technology should undertake large scale teacher training programmes for graduate and postgraduate students. All such courses should include a study of a second modern 'world language' such as Russian or German The scheme for centres of advanced study should be extended to cover technological field also.

Frequent transfers of teachers and principals in Government colleges for other than professional reasons must be stopped.

Equipment : Special consideration should be paid for the timely release of foreign exchange and the stock-piling of essential equipment.

Polytechnics should be discouraged from acquiring sophisticated equipment which is used for only a few days in the year.

Institutions should be encouraged to manufacture proto-type substitutes for imported items of equipment.

Postgraduate Courses : Admission requirements to these courses should include atleast one year's experience within industry. Rigid uniformity in the organization of these courses is not desirable.

Research at this level should be diverted towards problems of industry. Larger numbers of those taking up post-graduate courses should be sponsored by industry.

A regular Doctorate degree for professional development work within industry in addition to a Ph. D. research degree should be created.

Indiscriminate proliferation of courses should be avoided and location of highly specialised courses should be determined at the national level.

The practice of levying capitation fee for awarding seats in engineering colleges should be stopped.

Manpower Requirements : There is need for rigorous and more refined studies for estimating technical manpower requirements at all levels. Opening of new training facilities and admissions to courses should be linked to such forecasts.

In the immediate future, attention should be given to the elimination of present high wastage rates at all levels and to improvement in quality of instruction offered. Existing facilities should be expanded to their optimum size and part-time courses developed for those already in employment.

Existing marked variations in the socio-economic background of students in technical institutions can be reduced by a greater equalization of educational attainments in secondary schools between urban and rural areas and by adoption of better admission tests.

Medium of Education : At the secondary and polytechnic stages, the regional language should be the medium of instruction. Its use at higher levels should be related to the position in science faculties. Vigorous action is required for the preparation of good technical text books in regional languages.

Practical Training : Industrial concerns or Departments selected under the Central Government Practical Training Scheme as also the trainees, should be carefully chosen. The number of training places needs to be increased. If for any reason, the apprenticeship schools started by some public sector undertakings are to be closed down, Central Government should take them over.

Cooperation with Industry : A Central scheme of subsidy to industrial concerns providing training facilities should be started. Suitably qualified training officers should be posted to such industry or groups of industries.

Professional Societies : Adequate safeguards have to be devised to ensure that requisite standards are maintained by the professional bodies in all the examinations by them. These professional societies should also be associated with the recommended programme of organizing a wide range of part-time technical courses at higher secondary level (Classes XI and XII).

Correspondence Courses : An immediate begining should be made to develop a wide range of vocational and technical courses through correspondence. However, before this medium could be adopted extensively, very careful preparation and testing would be required.

Administration : A UGC-type organization for technical education with a full-time Chairman should be set up with adequate representation for UGC, professional bodies, industry and concerned Ministries.

The Institutes of Technology and comparable institutions should be given full university status, while retaining their individual names and characteristics.

As part of Boards of School Education, Directorates of Technical Education should be set up at the State level, with adequate powers, among other things, for recruitment of staff thus removing a number of procedural delays.

Chairmen of Boards of Governors of Regional Engineering Colleges should be drawn from a panel of distinguished educationists.

Principals of colleges should have, among other powers, full discretion in matters relating to the building up of educational facilities in their institutions within financial ceilings and policy guide-lines.

Science Education And Research

General Principles : The progress, welfare and security of the nation depend critically on a rapid, planned and sustained growth in the quality and extent of education and research in science and technology. It is unfortunate that India today is almost at the bottom end of the ladder of GNP per capita, as also of the ladder of per capita expenditure on education and research. In view of the limited resources available, the following measures are needed to make rapid progress :

1. A rigorously selective approach has to be adopted.

2. In postgraduate studies and research, the standards of attainment must bear international comparison. The only way this can be done is through a most careful selection of subjects for advanced study and research, selection of the most able students for such courses, and by building a small number of centres of excellence and assigning to each of these, resources exceeding a certain critical size.

3. In the utilization of our scientific manpower we must strive our utmost to achieve high efficiency—higher even than in the industrially-developed countries. We should determine our priorities and programmes in education and research on the basis of hard 'indigenous' thinking and needs, and not follow the fashion set by other countries whether highly 'advanced' or not so advanced.

4. The development of science must derive its 'nourishment' from our cultural and spiritual heritage and not bypass it.

5. The need from the earliest stage of science education for a proper understanding of the basic principles and the process of scientific abstraction and creative thinking must be emphasized.

Science Education : Apart from improving the standard of the postgraduate courses, the postgraduate enrolments in science and mathematics need to be expanded several-fold in the coming decades to meet the demands of rapidly expanding secondary and higher education and of research and industry.

It is necessary to develop a number of Centres of Advanced Study in science and mathematics. Their academic staff should be of the highest quality and should include, wherever possible, some persons of international standing. There should also be a number of visiting professorships on contract appointments for a period of two to three years. The UGC should constitute an All-India Committee to make offers of such visiting professorships. Some of the internationally famous Indian scientists at present working abroad as well as distinguished foreign scientists could be invited under this scheme.

The regional imbalances in the development of science education should be reduced to the minimum. The development of science and technology in a State should be related closely to its potential for economic growth.

There is an urgent need to revise drastically the undergraduate and postgraduate curriculum in science.

In our science departments a proper balance between experimental and theoretical aspects should be maintained. Special and urgent attention should be paid to the development of experimental physics and chemistry. In the field of biology, the study of micro-organisms and their role in medicine and agriculture deserves much more attention than is generally the case. Astronomy and astro-physics also need emphasis.

There should be well-equipped workshops in every college and university department of science. Students should be encouraged to learn the use of workshops tools and get acquainted with some of the essential laboratory techniques and practices. The workshops should work far more intensively than is usually the case. It would be desirable to permit their use by industrial workers enrolled for evening and correspondence courses.

Students in science subjects should have some knowledge of the theory of errors, basic statistical concepts and statistical design of experiments.

Apart from the evaluation of class records and the experiments performed by students, there need be no practical examinations as part of the final examination.

There is urgent need to introduce an elegent of flexibility and innovation in the organization of courses for the Master's degree. Combination courses consisting, of, say, one major subject and one subsidiary subject should be provided.

It will be a great advantage if major depertments in life sciences have on their academic staff a small number of physical scientists (including mathematicians) specially selected for their interest in the study of biological phenomena.

The need of the day is to bring science and technology closes together in our educational system.

Apart from the regular two-year M. Sc. courses there is need to provide one-year courses, or of even shorter period, for specialised training in subjects relevant to present scientific, industrial and other needs. These courses could be provided by selected science and technology deparments in universities, engineering and agricultural institutions or the National Laboratories.

It would be desirable for universities and engineering institutions to enrol qualified industrial workers for evening and correspondence courses. Apart from the usual diploma and pass degree courses, special courses to train precision machanics, laboratory technicians and other skilled operators should be organized.

There is need for the introduction of a new degree beyond the M. Sc. stage. The course should include with advantage, on an optional basis, elements of pedagogy.

The programme of the summer science institutes brings together, in active participation, school and college teachers and leading university professors. It is a major instrument in the country's effort towards the improvement of science education. It should be expanded and followed up.

The IUB and the UGC should take a lead to ensure that, by the end of the Fourth Plan, most of the books required at the undergraduate level and a considerable number at the postgraduate level are produced in the country.

We welcome the steps taken for the evolution of a scientific terminology in the Indian languages. It has to be pursued further. It would be an advantage if science students are taught the few Latin roots from which a large number of international terms are derived.

Investment in Research : In an age characterised by science and technology, research is almost a necessary pre-condition for all kinds of human endeavour. In the industrially advanced countries the growth of investment in research and development and of manpower engaged in these activities, has surpassed all expectations. The Indian expenditure on R and D is 0.3 per cent of the GNP ; and the total strength of scientists and engineers is only a few hundredths of one per cent of the labour force. The number of qualified scientists and engineers is of the order of a hundred thousand. Our effort in R and D will have to be stepped up.

University Research in Science : A major weakness of Indian education and research is the relatively very small part played by the universities in the sum total of Indian reseach which itself is far smaller than what it should be in relation to our capabilitles and needs. A stage has now been reached when deliberate support and encouragement of advanced study and research in the universities should become a fundamental goal of our national policy.

The creative scientists and engineers of a country the one of its most precious and scarce assets and should find place in the universities where their 'multiplier effect' is generally maximum : they contribute not only to scientific research but also to the building up of new talent.

It is important that more and more university people—that is teachers and students—should perform more and more research work and of a better and still better quality. As an ultimate goal, every university researcher should become a teacher and every teacher, a researcher.

Publication of qualitative research apart from good teaching ability, should be come one of the basic criteria for advancement of teachers in their university career. Gifted students even at the undergraduate stage should be encouraged to participate in some form of research activity.

Wherever practicable, active scientists in the CSIR, AEC and other research institutions outside the university system should be invited and inducted to participate in teaching and research work, full-time or part-time, for short or long periods.

It should be made possible for selected postgraduate students to spend, during their course work, a term or two in another university or institution specializing in the subject of their interest.

The UGC scheme of assisting teachers, research workers, and laboratory technicians to visit universities and research institutions for short periods (a few weeks to a few months) should be considerably expanded.

The development of team-work is an essential condition for the improvment of the of university. But it should be real. It should be a part of university research policy to eliminate ruthlessly spurious and parasitic 'team-work'.

The number of research studies under the supervision of the head of the department or any other teacher should be limited. Research students should also be assigned to younger members of the staff.

The qualifications for Ph. D. enrolment need to be upgraded. We should encourage research-minded engineering graduates to go in directly for Ph. D. in mathematics, physics and other science subjects.

Mathematics : It is important that a deliberate effort is made to place India on the 'word map of mathematics' within the next two decades or so. Advanced centres of study in mathematics should be established at three or four universities in the next five to ten years.

At least one of the major departments of mathematics in the universities should be encouraged to take an active interest in exploring the possibilities of programmed learning in mathematics for upgrading the knowledge and understanding of school and college teachers.

One or two special secondary schools for pupils with unusual mathematical ability should be set up in the near future.

A special effort should be made by the UGC to provide computation installations and training in programming on a selective basis in the universities. By the end of the Fourth Plan a good proportion of the universities should have basic computer facilities to serve the requirements of study and research in science, mathematics and social sciences.

It would be desirable to support energetically and develop one or two active centres for the study of brain and psychosomatic phenomena, using modern techniques and also drawing upon past Indian experience in this field which even today in some ways is of great significance.

Equipment : Measures will have to be found for efficient use of exisiting equipment and only such equipment as cannot be produced within the country and whose import is inescapable should be imported.

The UGC and the CSIR should actively encourage and support some of the universities and national laboratories to organize instrument calibration and rapair service for the general use of the universities. Traning of laboratory technicians should receive high priority.

A special unit should be set up to study and do research in laboratory design.

Administration of Science Departments : The administration of science departments needs to be radically reorganized, and without delay. If it is to make the fullest use of its resources, it is necessary to associate its staff with administration and decision-making in the department.

Pure and Applied Research : It is wrong to assume that universities should perform almost exclusively pure (basic) research, leaving applied research and development in all branches of science to other institutions. The universities, in the industrialized countries, as shown by the distribution of the national research potential and programme, make a substantial contribution to applied research, and some of them to a small degree even in development research.

Today, with the advance of science and technology, the distinction between pure and applied research—between a research scientist and a research engineer—has become artificial, and in service fields (e.g., electronics) it has almost disappeared. Applied work such as developing important new techniques (new for the country) or designing and fabricating special instruments or apparatus should receive proper recognition, and it should be made possible for such work to earn Ph. D. awards.

Left to itself, there is nearly always a tendency for research (even in project oriented laboratories) to become 'purer and purer'. This needs to be kept in view in the organization of research in technological institutions. These should place special emphasis on applied and industrial researches.

A survey has not yet been made showing how in India the university research potential is distributed along basic, mission-oriented basic, applied and development research. It is essential that this survey be made as soon as possible.

Expenditure on University Research : University research receives far too small an allocation and if this is not radically corrected, the future of the entire research effort in the country will be in jeopardy. By the end of the decade, something like a quarter of the total university expenditure should be devoted to research.

It would be desirable that in the early stages the UGC makes separate allocations to the universities for support of research.

A related matter of great importance is the provision of adequate foreign exchange.

Basic Research outside the Universities : At present there are a number of institutions in the country which devote almost their entire effort on university type of research but function outside the university system. A serious effort should be made to bring them within the universities, or at any rate, to link them intimately with universities.

Brain Drain : A considerable proportion—we have no precise estimates—of those who go abroad tend to stay indefinitely and a sizeable number accept foreign nationality. The migration is largely to the USA. Not all who go out of India are necessarily first-rate scientists, nor are they of critical importance to the country's requirements. But the problem is of sufficient importance to merit a close and systematic study.

Fellowships for Overseas Training : Apart from fellowships awarded by foreign agencies, there is a real need for institution by the government of a limited number of research fellowships, say about 100, to be awarded every year for study and research abroad. These fellowships should be awarded to persons of outstanding ability and there should be some form of 'bonding' for them to return to their country.

National Science Policy : It is most important for the governmental authorities at the highest level to ensure that on major scientific issues they can get advice which is as impartial and objective as it possibly can be. For this it is essential to have an advisory body which should have on it, besides heads of major agencies concerned with scientific research, persons who have a high standing and regard to their professions and who inspire general confidence—a proportion of these numbers should be distinguished young scientists in their thirties. The number of such persons should not be less than the agency heads. They could be from the universities, research institutions (Government or Non-government), industry and public life. The advisory body should also have on it not only scientists and technologists but also economists and social scientists and persons with experience of industry and management. The Scientific Advisory Committee to the Cabinet should be reorganized on the above lines and provided with an effective secretariat and with a professional component adequate to its tasks. The Committee should be in a position to assess the broad scientific needs of the country including the universities and advise Government on scientific policy and allocation of total resources between different sectors of scientific activities. It should also review continuously the national research policy situation.

Bodies concerned with science policy and implementation and which have executive and managerial functions requiring detailed and expert examination of diverse issues should ordinarily have professional scientists, engineers or science administrators of high standing as their chairmen,

It should be a major task of the national research policy, and policies of the universities to provide a 'climate' conducive to research, and to prevent and eliminate, through energetic and public measures, all dangers and infringements of autonomy and freedom of action in research.

In determining our priorities for research, we should be guided by our own national needs and not be unduly influenced by what may happen to be the current fashion in science.

Science Academy : In India the role of a National Academy is performed partly by the National Institute of Sciences. However, it may need some drastic reorganization, if the institute is to exercise a vigorous leadership in science and play a more significant role in the scientific activities of the nation.

India is almost the solitary case of a country which is not represented on the ICSU by a professional Academy but by the Government. This function should be a responsibility of the Academy.

Adult Education

Liquidation of Illiteracy : Every possible effort should be made to eradicate illiteracy from the country as early as possible and in no part of the country, however backward, should it take more than 20 years. The national percentage of literacy should be raised to 60 by 1971 and to 80 by 1976.

As a first step to arrest the growth of illiteracy, the following measures should be taken :

(a) Expansion of universal schooling of five years' duration to the age-group 6-11 ;

(b) Provision of part-time education to those children of age-group 11-14 who either miss schooling or drop prematurely out of the school ;

(c) Provision of part-time general and vocational education to the younger adults of the age-group 15-30 ;

For the liquidation of illiteracy a two-fold strategy comprising the selective approach and the mass approach should be adopted.

Under selective approach, programmes should be adopted for specified groups of adults which could be easily identified, controlled and motivated for intensive literacy work. All employers in large farms and commercial, industrial, contracting and other concerns should be made responsible, if necessary by law, for making their employees functionally literate within a period of three years of their employment. Big industrial plants in the public sector should take the lead immediately and set the pace in this important direction. Every devlopment project should include, as an integral part, a plan for the education of its employees, more especially of those who are illiterate. Literacy programme should constitute an essential ingredient of all schemes launched by Government for economic and social developments.

Under mass approach, all available educated men and women in the country should be mobilized for raising a fore to combat illiteracy and utilize it in a well-planned literacy campaign. In the organization of mass campaign, the teachers and students and all educational institutions should be actively involved. The students in the higher primary, secondary, higher secondary, vocational schools and those in the undergraduate classes of the universities and colleges should be required to teach the adults as a part of compulsory national service programme. Teachers in schools of all types should be required to teach and participate in the campaign. Every educational institution should be given responsibility for liquidating illiteracy in a specified area. The school in particular should be transformed into a centre of community life.

No literacy campaign should be launched without careful planning and preparation. The various measures to be taken for this purpose have been discussed in the Report.

In order to promote literacy among women, condensed courses for women sponsored by the Central Social Welfare Board should be adopted ; appointment of 'village sisters' should be encouraged for teaching village women and organizing adult education among local communities.

The mass media of communication should be effectively used as a powerful instrument for creating the climate and imparting knowledge and skills necessary for improving quality of work and standard of life.

In order to retain the literacy achieved, literacy campaigns must have adequate follow-up including further education, the use of library. and the production of reading material.

Continuing Education : Educational institutions of all types and grades should be encouraged and helped to throw open their doors outside the regular working hours to provide such courses of instruction as they can to those who are desirous of receiving education. A parallel part-time system of education should be created to provide adults with opportunities for taking the same diplomas and degrees as students in schools and colleges.

Educational institutions should give the lead in organizing ad hoc courses which will help people to understand and solve their problems and to acquire wider knowledge and experience.

Further education should be provided for workers for improving their knowledge and skills, widening their horizon in life, inculcating in them a sense of responsibility towards their profession and improving their careers. Special part-time and sandwich courses should be offered for them which would lead them step by step to higher courses.

Special institutions such as those run by the Central Social Welfare Board for Adult Women and the Vidyapeeths in Mysore State should be established. The existing institutions should be frequently reviewed in order to enable them to be of service to the rural community.

Correspondence Courses : In order to bring education to those who are unable even to attend part-time courses, widespread organization of correspondence courses should be organized.

Students taking correspondence courses should be provided opportunities to meet the teachers occasionally; they should be given the status of recognized students, and where possible be attached to some colleges in order to enable them to make use of the library and other facilities.

Correspondence courses should be supported by well-coordinated radio and television programmes.

Correspondence courses should not be confined to preparing students for the university degrees but should also provide agricultural, industrial and other workers such special courses of instruction as would help them to improve production.

Correspondence courses should be made available for those who desire to enrich their lives by studying subjects of cultural and aesthetic value.

Correspondence courses should be developed for the teachers in schools to keep them abreast with new knowledge as well as with new methods and techniques of teaching.

The Ministry of Education in collaboration with other Ministries should establish a National Council of Home Studies, for the purpose of accreditation and evaluation of agencies which provide correspondence courses, identification of the areas in which different types of correspondence courses would be of benefit, promote creation of such courses through proper agencies, and conducting evaluation and research.

Opportunity to talce examinations conducted by the Secondary Education Boards and Universities in the country should be made available to those who wish to work on their own without any assistance.

The Libraries : The recommendations of the Advisory Committee on Libraries relating to the establishment of a net-work of libraries throughout the country should be implemented.

School libraries should be integrated in the system of public libraries and be stocked with reading materials of appeal both to children and neo-literates.

The libraries should be dynamic and set out to educate and attract the adults to use them.

Role of Universities : The Universities in India should assume a much larger responsibility for educating the adults. Some of the important programmes which the University could undertake are described in paragraphs 17.62 and 17.63.

In order to have an efficient machinery for launching carefully planned adult education programmes, each university should establish a Board of Adult Education with representatives from all departments involved in adult education programmes. Universities should also set up Departments of Adult Education.

Universities should be financed and equipped for carrying out the adult education work.

Organization and Administration : A National Board of Education on which all relevant Ministries and agencies would be represented should be established. The functions of the Board are stated in paragraph 17.67. Similar bodies should be set up at the State and district levels.

Voluntary agencies working in the field of adult education should be given every encouragement, financial and technical.

Educational Administration

Planning : There has been an over-emphasis on achievement of targets in enrolments and expenditure and there is, therefore, a need to take a more comprehensive view and evolve a broader pattern of goals, especially those relating to qualitative improvement.

The general policy so far has been to do something in every sector of every programme with the result that the meagre resources available have been spread thinly over a very large area leading to considerable wastage. It has now become important to concentrate on a few crucial programmes.

In the existing situation where finances are limited, programmes which call for a determined effort, organization, talent and hard work rather than large financial investment, need greater emphasis.

There should be deep involvement of universities, professional organizations, training colleges, etc., in a periodical evaluation of all major programmes included in the plans and in the development of large-scale research programme.

The Ministry of Education, in collaboration with the Asian Institute of Educational Planning, should undertake studies of educational planning in the different States and conduct intensive courses for training the personnel involved in the planning process at different levels.

The University Grants Commission should also consider the possibility of setting up an Advanced Centre for Studies in Educational Planning Administration and Finance.

The process of educational planning in a Federal democracy has to be the right blend of centralization in the appropriate sectors and especially in administration. One useful suggestion which can be made in this context is to adopt a system of priorities at different levels—national, State and local.

School education is predominantly a local-State partnership and higher education is a Centre-State partnership. It is this basic principle that should guide the evolution of the delicate balance between centralization and decentralization which our planning needs.

The Role of Private Enterprise : The future role of private enterprise in education should be broadly based on the following principles:

(a) As most private enterprise has played an important role in the development of education in modern India the State should make all possible use of the assistance that can come from the private sector for the development of education;

(b) The State has now rightly assumed full responsibility to provide all the needed educational facilities and private enterprise can, therefore, have only a limited and minor role.

The Role of Local Authorities : The normal practice should be that a local authority gets the right to administer education as a privilege subject to two conditions—good administration and promoting the cause of education—and that this privilege would be withdrawn if any of these conditions is violated. The future role of local bodies in education may be defined as follows :

1. As an ultimate objective, it is essential that schools and their local communities should be intimately associated in the educational process.

2. It would, however, not be proper to press for the universal and immediate adoption of this principle without reference to local conditions;

3. The immediate goal in this respect—and this should be adopted immediately as a national policy in all the States—is to associate the local communities, namely, village panchayats in rural areas and the municipalities in urban areas, with their local schools and to make them responsible for the provision of all non-teacher costs with the help, where necessary, of a suitable grant-in-aid from the States.

4. The ultimate goal to be reached is the establishment, at the district level, of a competent local education authority which may be designated as the District School Board and which would be in charge of all education in the district below the university level. This should also be accepted as national policy.

5. In all association of the local authorities with education, adequate safeguards should be provided to ensure that the teachers are not harassed and that they do not get involved in local factions and politics.

District and Municipal Boards : The jurisdiction of the District School Board should cover the entire area of the district with one exception, namely, the big municipalities in the district. The Zila Parishad, municipalities, educationists and concerned Departments should be represented on it. A senior officer of the State Government should be the whole-time Secretary of this Board, which should be provided with the necessary administrative and supervisory staff.

The functions of this Board should cover all school education in the district—general as well as vocational. It will directly administer all Government and local authority schools within the district, and it will also remain in charge of giving grants-in-aid to all private institutions in the district in accordance with the rules framed by the State Government for the purpose.

It should be a responsibility of the Board to prepare plans for the development of school education within the District and it should also be the principal agency within the district to develop school education, the finances and guidance required for the purpose being provided by the State Government and the State Education Department.

In big towns with a population of one lakh or more, it would be desirable to establish Municipal School Boards on the above lines since these would be viable administrative units. The composition, powers and responsibilities of these Boards should be similar to those of the district school boards.

Each School Board will maintain an education fund. The Zila Parishads (or Municipalities) will approve the budget of the school boards. They will also raise the resources expected of them and credit them to the School Board. In all day-to-day administration, the School Board would be autonomous. The same relation would hold good between a Municipal Board and its Municipality.

Recruitments and transfers will be done by a special committee consisting of the Chairman of the Board, its Secretary and the District Education Officer, subject to rules framed by the State Government, the general policy being to reduce transfers to the minimum and to allow teachers to develop loyalties to Individual institutions.

It may be better in some cases not to burden the School Boards with full administrative responsibility all at once. Powers may be conferred on a board as it becomes experienced and shows its capacity to exercise them.

The Role of the Central Government: Besides institutions in the scientific and technical sector, it is also necessary for the Centre to establish institutions specializing in social sciences including pedagogical sciences and the humanities. These should be established in close association with the universities and be an integral part of the university system.

The Centre can also develop education in the Union Territories, particularly in Delhi, to serve as a pace-setter for the other areas.

The Centre should scout for talent in different fields and make the services of the best people in the country available to the State Governments for advice and assistance in all matters.

Funds for specific special programmes in the educational sector within the State Plans may not be earmarked. The total allocations for education, however, should not be altered without the approval of the Planning Commission. But within it, the State Governments should be free to use funds at their discretion.

Considerable Importance should be attached to the expansion of the Central and the Centrally-sponsored sector. It is through this mechanism that the Centre will be able to stimulate and guide educational developments in the national interest in crucial sectors.

Education should not be fragmented keeping one part in the concurrent and the other in the State list. In a vast country like ours the position given to education in the Constitution, is probably the best because it provides for a Central leadership of a stimulating but non-coercive character. The greatest need is for elasticity and freedom to experiment.

An intensive effort should be made to exploit fully the existing provisions of the Constitution for the development of education and evaluation of a national educational policy. The problem may then be reviewed again after ten years.

Ministry of Education: The present practice of giving the post of Secretary to the Government of India to an eminent educationist, who is designated as Educational Adviser to the Government of India and Secretary to the Ministry of Education should continue. This should be a selection post and the selection should be made from amongst all persons available, official, non-official, IES, university men, etc. It should also be a tenure post given only for six years in the first instance with an extension in exceptional cases for three or four years but not renewable further.

About half the posts of Additional or Joint Secretaries should be filled by promotion from officers seconded from the State Education Departments and the remaining half should be filled from eminent educationists and outstanding teachers in universities and schools. The term of eaeh tenure should be five years to be renewable at the most for a second term.

The clearing-house function of the Ministry of Education needs considerable strengthening and expansion. A well-staffed Division should be created to perform this function on an adequate scale.

The Ministry of Education may set up a Committee to examine the various types of studies required and to prepare a programme for action.

It is a major responsibility of the Ministry of Education to maintain a good statistical service for educational planning, policy making and evaluation. In order that this function may be discharged properly, the Statistical Section of the Ministry should be reorganised and strengthened along the lines recommended. The statistical units of the State Departments of Education will have to be reorganized and strengthened likewise.

The Central Advisory Board of Education with its Standing Committees should be functionally strengthened.

National Council of Educational Research and Training: The NCERT should be developed as the principal technical agency functioning at the national level for the improvement of school education and operating through and in collaboration with the National Board of School Education, State Departments of Education and their technical agencies like the State Institutes of Education.

The governing body of the NCERT should have an All-India character with a majority of non-officials. It is desirable to have atleast one outstanding teacher from secondary schools and a person specializing in primary education, preferably a primary teacher.

The Council should have its own full-time Director and Joint Director. The Director should be an eminent educationist in the field and his status should be that of a Vice-Chancellor. His term of office should be five years, renewable for not more than one term. The Joint Director would be needed mainly for the purpose of assisting the Director and relieving him of routine administrative matters.

The Central Institution of Education, under the NCERT, should be transferred to the Delhi University.

It is desirable that there should be considerable interchange and flow of officers from the NCERT to the State Education Departments and vice-versa.

The campus of the NCERT should be developed speedily and the building programme be given the highest priority.

Educational Administration at the State Level : It is desirable to create at the State level, some machinery to coordinate educational programmes which are spread over a number of departments and take a unified view for purposes of planning and development.

A Statutory Council of Education should be created at the State level with the State Minister for Education as the Chairman. Its membership should include representatives of universities in the State, all Directors in charge of different sectors of education and some eminent educationists. Its principal functions would be to advice the State Government on all matters relating to school education, to review educational developments in the State and to conduct evaluation of programmes from time to time through suitable agencies. Its annual report along with its recommendations should be presented to the State Legislature.

A Standing Committee at the officers' level which would include all State level officers in charge of different sectors of education should meet periodically under the chairmanship of the Education Secretary.

The Education Secretary also, like the Educational Adviser to the Government of India, should be an educationist rather than an administrative officer. It will be desirable to make this appointment a tenure post.

Broadly speaking, the role of the Education Secretariat should be to examine educational problems from the administrative and financial point of view and in the wider context of governmental policies for development. It should give due weightage to the views of the Directorate in technical matters and assist the Director to function as the effective head of the Department.

Indian Educational Service : The Indian Educational Service should be a service agency to teaching and research and should consist of persons who have teaching experience with the possibility of the educational administrator returning to teaching and the teacher going over to administration at least on a tenure assignment. Its method of recruitment should be as follows :

(a) Only one-third of the posts should be filled by direct recruitment at the level of the junior scale. Even these selected persons should not be placed in administration direct. Their first assignments for a minimum period of 2-3 years should be in teaching and it is only after this initiation that they should be assigned to administration ;

(b) The remaining two-thirds of the posts should be filled partly by direct recruitment and partly by promotion at the level of the senior and higher scales ;

(c) Some posts of the IES should be available for being filled by tenure appointments of teachers for specified periods. In the same way, some posts in teaching and research should also be available for tenure appointments of persons from the IES.

As there are insuperable difficulties, the idea of creating a teaching wing in the IES should be abandoned. The service should encadre only the posts of Directors and officers of the Directorate, District Educational Officers and headmasters of higher secondary schools in the State, and at the Centre, educational officers of the Ministry of Education and other Ministries and Education Departments of Union Territories.

An adequate number of posts comparable to the higher scales of pay in the IES should be created in the universities and colleges to prevent a drain of talent from teaching and research to administration.

It should be a convention that only about 50 per cent of the IES officers are assigned to their own States and there should also be a possibility of inter-State transfers (in addition to deputation to the Centre). To facilitate this, each member of the IES should be required to study and pass, within a given time after recruitment, tests in two other languages (Hindi and one more Indian language which is not his mother-tongue) to certain prescribed depth.

State Educational Service : There should be an adequate number of posts at higher levels, namely, in Class I and Class II. The Secretaries of the District School Boards should be in Class I. The District Educational Inspectors (who will be in the IES) should have adequate assistance from officers of Class I and Class II status. In order to attract talented persons, recruitment is needed at three levels : Assistant Teachers' level, Class II level (50 per cent for freshers and 50 per cent for promotion) and Class I level (75 per cent for freshers and 25 per cent for promotion).

A major reform now needed is to reorganize the State Education Departments where necessary on the basis of specialized functionaries and what is even more urgent and important is to make adequate arrangements for their specialized training with the help of the universities.

To reduce anomalies in the salaries of the departmental staff and enable transferability, it is proposed that : (a) the scales of pay in the teaching and the administrative wings should be identical, and (b) the scales of pay of the departmental staff should be correlarted with the UGC scales of pay for univeasity teachers.

Training of Educational Administrators : The State Institutes of Education, in collaboration with universities where necessary, should organize the in-service educational programmes of all the non-gazetted staff on the administrative and inspectional sides. In addition, they should also organize conferences, seminars and workshops for the gazetted staff.

The old practice of giving furlongh leave to administrators for undertaking special studies in educational problems should be revised.

Some incentives should be provided for the officers who improve their qualifications materially through programmes of in-service education.

National Staff College for Educational Administrators : The Ministry of Education should establish a National Staff College for Educational Administrators. It should provide in-service education for all the senior officers in the Educational Services—IES and State Educational Services. It should conduct two types of courses—a longish induction course for new recruits and shorter courses of three to six weeks for officers in service. It should have a research wing for conducting studies in problems of educational administration and function as a clearing house of administrative procedures and practices in the States and Union Territories. It should also conduct periodical conferences, seminars and workshops on matters relating to educational administration.

Education Departments : The present position in most States is that the Education Departments are understaffed because the growth of the departmental staff does not precede but follows the growth in the number of educational institutions; the norms fixing the number of officers required are not, even if fixed, observed in practice; the expenditure for increasing the departmental staff always has a low priority. The reversal of these policies is necessary subject to one reservation, viz., it is better to have a fewer officers at a higher level and on adequate scales of pay than a large number of officers at the lover level.

Procedures : There should be a change in the attitudes of administrators who should cultivate an openness of mind at a spirit of enquiry rather than a rule-of-the thumb approach which tries to stick to established practices even when they cease to be meaningful.

The practice of holding periodical reviews, say, every three or five years, of important administrative practies with a view to chopping off dead wood and puttiag in fresh grafts where necessary should be established.

Inter-State contacts should be built up and comparative studies in different State practices in all administrative matters should be encouraged. Periodical comparative studies in educational administration which would involve the State Education Departments closely should be made.

The evolution of the technique of detailed programming of the plan projects and the training of officers in them is the responsibility of the State Institutes of Education and the National Staff College for Educational Administrators.

The modern 'officer-oriented' system where most of the work will be done by the officers at their own level with the help of a small secretariat staff should be adopted.

Education Acts : Education should be given a statutory basis everywhere and in all sectors and Education Acts should be passed in all the States and Union Territories. These should be comprehensive and consolidated measures which will replace all the miscellaneous laws which now exist and which will also provide a statutory basis for certain important aspects of administration (e.g., grant-in-aid code) which now exists merely in the form of executive orders.

The Government of India should issue a statement on the national policy in education which should provide guidance to the State Governments and the local authorities in preparing and implementing educational plans in their areas.

The possibility of passing a National Education Act may also be examined.

Educational Finance

Total Expenditure on Education : If education is to develop adequately, educational expenditure in the next 20 years should rise from Rs. 12 per capita in 1965-66 to Rs. 54 in 1985-86 (at constant prices). This implies that the educational expenditure, which increased from Rs. 1,144 millions in 1950-51 to Rs. 6,000 millions in 1965-66, will further rise to Rs. 40,364 millions in 1985-86 and that the proportion of GNP allocated to education will rise from 2.9 per cent in 1965-66 to 6.0 per cent in 1985-86.

Allocation of Funds : While the broad pattern of educational expenditure in the different sectors of education during the next two or three decades will be to devote two-thirds of the available resources to school education and one-third to higher education, the relative emphasis on programmes should change from decade to decade as follows :

1. From 1965 to 1975, the relative emphasis should be on a larger expenditure at the school stage. This will be necessary in order : (i) to upgrade the salaries of school teachers; (ii) to transfer the PUC and the Intermediate classes from the university to the school stage; (iii) to provide at least five years of effective education to all children; and (iv) to vocationalize secondary education.

The programmes to be emphasized during the decade

1975 to 1985 will include the provision of seven years of effective primary education, the addition of one year to the school stage and vocationalization of secondary education. During this decade, emphasis should begin to shift in favour of higher education.

After 1985, there will be increased emphasis on the development of higher education and research.

Sources of Educational Finance: Although most of the responsibility for the support of education will be placed on governmental funds, a total centralization of all financial responsibility for education in the Government will not be desirable. Attempt should, therefore, be made to raise contributions from local communities, voluntary organizations and the local authorities for this purpose.

The assistance of the local communities should be mobilized through the organization of school improvement conferences for improving the physical facilities in schools and the creation of school funds.

In order to provide financial support to District School Boards, the Zila Parishads should raise funds for education by levying cess on land revenue. The State should prescribe the minimum rate of the levy and authorize the Zila Parishads to raise it to a eertain prescribed to maximum. In order to stimulate the collection of funds, the Government should give grant-in-aid proportionate to the additional revenues thus collected by the Zila Parishad.

Grant-in-aid to Zila Parishads: The system of grant-in-aid from the State Government to Zila Parishads should be reformed on the following lines:

(a) 100 per cent grant for salaries and allowances of teachers and other administrative and supervisory staff sanctioned by the Government. Definite norms regarding the number of teachers required and the administrative and supervisory staff needed should be fixed;

(b) For non-teacher costs, of block grant per child in attendance should be given. The amount of this grant should be fixed separately for each category of schools and should be revised after every 3 to 5 years;

(c) The resources raised locally by a Zila Parishad as well as the State grant thereon should be left with the Zila Parishad for such developmental programmes as it deems necessary; and

(d) Grant-in-aid for non-recurring expenditure should be given separately, preferably at about two-thirds of the expenditure.

The amount of grant-in-aid given by the State Government to Zila Parishads should be allowed to be funded and not made to lapse at the end of the financial year.

Grant-in-Aid to Municipalities: It should be made obligatory for the Municipalities to bear a certain proportion of the cost of education. For this purpose, they should levy a cess on lands and buildings.

For the purpose of Government grants, the Municipalities should be classified into groups on the basis of their wealth and the poorer Municipalities should be given grant-in aid at a higher rate than others.

All Corporations should be made responsible for supporting at least primary education within their jurisdiction. The Government grant to them should be on a proportional basis so that the Corporations may contribute a certain percentage of the expenditure from their own funds,

The Role of the Centre: The Central Government should assume a larger financial responsibility for education by expanding the Central and Centrally-sponsored sectors. It should have the following characteristics:

1. It should include programmes of crucial importance and national in character.

2. In the Centrally-sponsored sector, it should be possible for some programmes to vary from State to State according to their needs.

Central assistance for programmes in the Centrally sponsored sector should be given for five years which may in certain cases be continued upto ten years and not for plan periods only as at present.

Economies and Utilization: Even with the mobilization of maximum resources for education, the funds will still be inadequate to meet even the minimum needs of educational reconstruction, if conventional techniques involving large wastage and stagnation continue. It would, therefore, be necessary to adopt measures for economy, for eradiction of wastage and for most efficient utilization of funds. Some of these measures have been indicated in paragraph 20.44. These and all other measures, which promote economy consistent with efficiency, should be adopted.

Research: Studies conducted in some other countries indicate the importance of education for economic growth, but no such studies have been conducted in India so far. In view of the importance of the subject, the UGC should encourage studies on the subject to be conducted in a few universities.

AIR PORT SECURITY COMMITTEE, 1964—REPORT

New Delhi, Ministry of Home Affairs, 1964. 50p.

Chairman : Shri G. Mukharji (retired and replaced by Shri Asoke Sen).

Members : Shri M. Panchappa ; Shri V. Subrahmanyam ; Shri G.C. Arya; Dr. D. Chaudhury.

Secretary : Shri R.N. Manickam.

APPOINTMENT

Great Public concern was felt, when on September 26, 1963, Danial Walcott was able to escape in his own plane from the Safdarjang Airport in violation of procedural formalities. This was followed on June 9, 1964 by the neat get-away from the Santa Cruz Airport (Bombay) of Walcott and his associates—Peter John Philby, Brian McAllister, and J.C. Novak,—who had been to India on a smuggling mission. Their plane suffered an accident while trying to land on the beach at Murud about 200 miles south of Bombay, but its occupants nevertheless managed to bluff their way through Health, Immigration and Customs at Santa Çruz Airport and flew off in a Pakistan International Airways Plane. It was natural that these two events, one coming close on the heels of the other, should lead to the voicing of anxiety and misgivings in Parliament and outside and raise doubts about the effectiveness of security arrangements and procedure at Airports. The Government of India have had under consideration the question of reviewing the existing arrangements at the various Airports in the country with the object of strengthening the security and examining other connected matters. The Government have accordingly decided to constitute a Committee. The Airport Security Committee was constituted by the Ministry of Home Affairs Vide their Resolution No. F. 18/18/64-Poll., dated July 24, 1964.

TERMS OF REFERENCE

(i) To examine the existing arrangements and procedure at the Airports in relation to Customs, Immigration, Health Checks, Passenger facilities and Security ;

(ii) To make recommendations on the measures to improve and strengthen the system, wherever necessary.

CONTENTS

Introduction ; The Nature of the Problem ; Existing Arrangements (Security Measures in Airports ; Immigration/Emigration checks at Airports ; Customs checks at Airports ; Functions of the Department of Civil Aviation at the Airports ; Health Formalities at Airports ; Passenger Handling and Facilities at Airports ; and Summary of defects and drawbacks in the existing system) ; Airports under Defence Control ; Abandoned Airfields In India : Recommendations ; Summary of Recommendations ; Appendices ; Questionnaire ; List of witnesses—Official and Non-official examined by the Airport Security Committee at various Airports.

RECOMMENDATIONS

A well-disciplined unit called "Airport Protection Force" should be raised.

Perimeter security fencing should be of a uniform standard and strength in all the airports.

Perimeter roads should be improved to enable patrolling by jeeps or cycles in all the airports.

Adequate number of vehicles either jeeps and/or cycles should be supplied for carrying out mobile patrol duties.

The authority issuing passes for entry into the airports should be one and not many. All passes should be standardised into : (i) Permanent, and (ii) Temporary.

Immigaration and Customs Departments should have a small cell of staff to carryout "vigilance watch" on people on whom such watch should be exercised in the airport.

Uniform methods should be adopted for selection of suitable officers from the State Police to function as Immigration/Emigration Officers in the airports. They should be given special training which should be organised by Government of India.

Officers constituting the "Air Customs Pool" for manning checkposts at the main airports should join duty without delay.

Foreigners, when rules require, should be got registered at hotels instead of at the police stations or offices of the Foreigners Registration.

Passports should not be withdrawn and detained by authorities as a measure of control except in rare cases of suspects or undesirable.

The three unnecessary questions, namely: (1) Purpose of visit, (2) Expected duration of stay, and (3) Visa number, place and date of issue, may be scrapped from the Embarkation/Disembarkation card as a measure of saving time. Strict instructions should be issued that no corrections will be made on the passenger mainifest without due care and caution by way of cross-checks with relevant records.

The index card system of maintaining 'look-out cards' should be modernised. A compact index book should be prepared by the Immigration and the Customs Departments for ready reference.

Immigration and Customs Officers should go in for a rubber stamp with date and identification mark of each checking officer thereby avoiding writing work.

Foreigners Regional Registration Officers in India may be authorised to grant return visas to foreigners who qualify for the "No objection to return to India Endorsements".

Departure customs check should be minimised and done right at the airline counter itself in the interest of speed and convenience to passengers.

Standardisation of procedures adopted by public authorities in air ports should be done without delay. Local modifications of procedures according to the whims and fancies of local official should not be accepted.

Communication facilities between airport authorities and the local police in all airports should be strengthened wherever possible.

The Department of Civil Aviation in every airport should go into the question of allround improvement in providing adequate facilities for wash and rest for officials working in airports.

Physical arrangements of passport, customs and health control should be in the "comb" form and should be infiltration proof. This should be ensured in the existing as well as the proposal terminal buildings.

A distinct red line of demarcation between the domestic and international apron and bay should now be made and this line should be kept under constant watch by security staff to prevent mix-up and escape of undesirables from airports.

Sufficient number of channels of clearance should be provided in every airport to cope with peak hour traffic. Necessary instructions should now be issued from the respective Ministries.

Sanitary standards in airports call for all-round improvement. Toilets and baths seem to require particular attention.

Enclosure comprising the Immigration. Customs and Health Checks should invariably be air-conditioned in all the international as well as important airports in India.

Fresh efforts should be made by all public authorities working in the airports to put an end to the irregular procedure of admission of people etc., when VIPs depart or arrive.

The Indian Aircraft Act of 1934 needs revision. Special provision should be made in this Act to disable an aircraft likely to fly away without air Traffic Control Clearance.

Relevant rules applicable to foreign aircraft making forced landing/take-off should be taught in the various police training schools and colleges. Attention of the magistracy in India should also be drawn pointedly to such provisions.

Departments of Civil Aviation, Immigration, Customs and Health should now draw their "standing orders" for the guidance of staff members, if they have not done so already.

SUGAR ENQUIRY COMMISSION 1964—REPORT

New Delhi, Ministry of Food & Agriculture, 278p.

Chairman : Drs. S.R. Sen.
Members : Shri S.C. Chaudhri ; Shri N. Krishnan ; Shri S.C. Gupta ; Dr. Dharm Narain.
Secretary : Dr. P.K. Mukherjee.

APPOINTMENT

Whereas the Central Government is of opinion that it is necessary to appoint a Commission of Inquiry for the purpose of making an enquiry into certain matters connected with sugar, sugar industry. In exercise of the powers conferred by Section 3 of the Commissions of Inquiry Act, 1952 (60, of 1952), the Government of India appointed the Sugar Enquiry Commission by Notification No. S.O. 2670, dated August 3, 1964 (Appendix I).

TERMS OF REFERENCE

The Commission was asked to enquire into :

(a) The determination of the price, and the system

of distribution of sugar ;

(b) The policy regarding liecnsing of new sugar factories and the expansion of existing sugar factories.

The Commission was asked to submit an interim report regarding the determination of the price of sugar by September 10, 1964.

Subsequently, the Government of India also referred the question of exports of sugar to the Commission and asked for its recommendations on the following issues :

(i) Desirability of sugar industry bearing a portion of the loss on exports, what this portion should be and how the same should be recovered from sugar factories. Would the Commission suggest enactment of a new legislation for the purpose and, if so, on what lines ?

(ii) Desirability of recouping a portion of the loss from the consumer, what this portion should be and the manner in which it should be collected, e.g., special levy or through a system of marketing in which the portion of loss to be recouped is added on the consumer price ;

(iii) In case the export loss is to be recovered from the consumer through a marketing system, whether the work of internal distribution and exports should be entrusted to the Food Corporation or a separate Corporation should be set up for this purpose ;

(iv) Economy in the manufacture of raw sugar with reference to the actual cost of production ;

(v) Remission of purchase tax by State Governments on sugarcane used for manufacture of sugar exported and the method of securing the same.

The Commission was further asked to examine the question of production of A and B grades of sugar and whether it costs more to produce sugar of A and B grain sizes and, if so, to what extent ?

The Government of India also referred the Report of the Committee on Rehabilitation and Modernisation of Sugar Factories in India, 1965 (under the chairmanship of S.N. Gundu Rao) to the Commission on August 27, 1965 for its comments.

The Commission started its work on August 4, 1964 and submitted the interim report to the Government of India on September 9, 1964.

CONTENTS

Introduction ; Historical Background ; Problems of Development ; Price and Distribution Policy ; Licensing Policy ; Conclusions and Recommendations ; Appendices from I to XII ; Statistical Tables from I to IV.

RECOMMENDATIONS

Economics Of Growing Sugarcane

1. From an analysis of available data, the broad conclusions that emerge are as follows :

(i) Maharashtra seems to possess a comparative advantage in the cultivation of sugarcane over other usgarcane producing States ;

(ii) Amongst the States considered Punjab, Rajasthan and Madhya Pradesh, on the one hand, and West Bengal, Assam and Orissa, on the other, do not, at present, appear to be wellplaced for a large-scale extension of sugarcane cultivation. In this group ; Punjab suffers from several handicaps, like low per acre yield of sugarcane, low sugar recovery, water-logging and frost ;

(iii) Madras, Andhra Pradesh and Mysore have the advantage of higher per acre gross value of sugarcane than Uttar Pradesh and Bihar. On the other hand, the latter States possess a comparative advantage over the former when one considers farm business income or net returns from sugarcane and its competing crops. On balance of considerations, it appears that all these five States—two in the sub-tropical belt and three in the tropical belt—are more or less similarly placed so far as scope for the development of sugarcane cultivation is concerned ;

(iv) Even within the regions where there is greater scope for the development of sugarcane cultivation, there are some districts which need to be given special attention for sugarcane development.

2. These broad inferences may be viewed in the light of two other considerations. These are : (i) Development potential of the areas through larger application of water and fertilizer ; and (ii) Economic and social development of backward areas. In the sub-tropical belt, the current rate of application of water and fertiliser is grossly inadequate. The number of irrigations given and the amount of fertilizer put in per acre of land are appreciably less than those in Maharashtra and Madras. Further, it has been found by research stations located in the sub-tropical that per acre yield can almost be doubled in this belt. It is also possible by propagating suitable varieties to increase to some extent the level of sugar programmes for sugarcane cultivation in Utter Pradesh and Bihar. Further, the eastern region of Uttar Pradesh and the northern region of Bihar are economically backward. Sugarcane happens to be the main cash crop in these areas and being a hardy crop provides security of income to the agriculturists in the event of failure of other crops due to frequent natural hazards. Further, these areas do not enjoy the advantage of having mineral resources or other raw materials for setting up large scale industries.

Gur And Khandsari

(1) While favouring appropriate measures for minimising the diversion of cane supplies away from sugar factories in the factory areas, it is emphasised that steps for the improvement and stabilisation of the

gur and khandsari industry should be taken.

2. The following measures should be taken to deal with the problem of diversion of cane in the factory areas :

(i) Re-delimitation of reserved areas so as to :

(a) Make them compact ;

(b) Either exclude existing khandsari units and power crushers completely from reserved areas or provide adequate cane both for the sugar factory concerned and such khandsari units or power-crushers as already exist in the reserved areas ;

(ii) Licensing of all the existing khandsari and power-crusher units and banning of new units in reserved areas of sugar factory : or within the radius of 15 to 20 kilometres of a sugar factory ;

(iii) Shifting of all the existing khandsari and power-crusher units from the Intensive Development Blocks ;

(iv) Imposing excise duty or some other suitable levy (if necessary on a compounded basis) on khandsari units and power-crushers (and, if possible, 'kolhus' above a certain size) upto such a level that their ability to pay a price for sugarcane higher than that fixed by Government for sugar factories is restricted

(v) Enforcing the existing procedure for regulating the supply of sugarcane grown in reserved areas to sugar factories through Cooperative Cane Unions, where they exist, also in the case of cane supplies to khandsari units and power-crushers. Once the cane supplies to the khandsari units and power-crushers are regulated, it would be possible to get a fair idea of the volume of their production and, if necessary, also to control their production and prices.

3. If the measures suggested above regarding certain types of control on the production of gur and khandsari are strictly adhered to, it may not be necessary to resort to the fixation of maximum prices for gur and khandsari.

4. Sugar, gur and khandsari are eminently suitable for being dealt with from the approach of "common production programme" which has been accepted by Government for certain other industries. Since gur and khandsari will continue to be produced freely in three-fourths of the area under sugarcane and most of the restrictions mentioned above will apply primarily in the areas reserved for sugar factories, they should not be treated as detrimental to the interests of village and small-scale industries, but as instruments for balanced growth of both small-scale and large-scale industries as essential parts of a common programme.

5. Apart from a number of undesirable effects of a ban on inter-State movement of gur and khandsari, gur being an item of consumption for the low income group, it is not generally desirable to ban its movement from surplus areas.

6. The question of allowing forward trading in gur has been considered. The production and prices of gur are generally subject to wide fluctuations giving rise to hardships both—for producers and consumers. Since gur has a poor keeping quality, it may be difficult to control these fluctuations through a buffer stock policy for gur. However, if the buffer stock policy for sugar which has been recommended elsewhere in the report is operated keeping in view not only sugar prices but also gur prices, it should help indirectly stabilise gur prices also. If such buffer stock operations are supplemented by the development of a well-organised and properly regulated future market in gur under the supervision of the Forward Markets Commission, it may help to prevent undue fluctuations in gur prices.

7. Government should take measures to provide adequate and satisfactory warehousing facilities for the storage of gur, especially in those areas where gur is traded on a large scale.

8. It has been represented that the sugar factories located in the Meerut and Muzaffar Nagar districts of Uttar Pradesh should be allowed to manufacture gur in their factory establishments. Such a permission will not be in accordance with the common production programme approach. The solution for the problem faced in these areas would be to undertake intensive programme of sugarcane development so as to ensure adequate supply of sugarcane for both gur and sugar. In this context, the provisions for tubewells and proper drainage facilities in these districts deserves special attention.

Utilisation Of by-Products

1. Greater attention should be paid to adequate and proper utilisation of by-products of the sugar industry. This is necessary to prevent national waste of scarce raw meterials and also to improve the economy of sugar factories.

2. The following steps should be taken by Government to provide incentive to sugar factories and distilleries for proper storage and utilisation of molasses:

(i) Sugar factories and distilleries should be required, if necessary as a stautory obligation, to build steel tanks of adequate capacity for proper storage of molasses and this should be rigidly enforced. Factories producing both raw and white sugar should store separately edible and inedible molasses ;

(ii) The controlled price for molasses fixed by the Government is very low and does not provide enough incentive to sugar factories to undertake adequate investment on steel tanks for proper storage of molasses. The prices of molasses, therfore, should be raised by at least 50 per cent. The price of edible molasses should be fixed at somewhat-higher level than that of inedible molasses;

(iii) Government should assign on a long-term basis a few sugar factories to each distillery for supply of molasses, keeping in view the convenience of transport. Since it would not be economical to set up a distillery in a small sugar factory and the cost of transporting molasses would be substantially higher than that for alcohol, it would be desirable for the distilleries and sugar factories to be in close proximity to one another; the distilleries and the linked sugar factories should work out an agreed programme of storage and supply of molasses;

(iv) Sugar factories, which are not located near any distillery or paper factory and are not large enough to set up distilleries or pulp plants of their own, should explore the possibility of manufacturing cattle feed based on edible molasses, bagasse and other ingredients, both for export and domestic market;

(v) Government should provide facilities for developing the production of and export market for potable alcohol and cattle feed based on molasses;

(vi) The export policy, both for molasses and alcohol, should be determined on a long-term basis and export procedures simplified.

Research And Development

1. Every effort should be made to ensure proper supply of the required amount of input factors and, at the same time, develop a proper extension agency for the purpose of ensuring healthy and clean cultivation. This would necessitate proper testing of soil for which soil testing laboratories should be set up and the testing be done without any charge from the growers.

2. Sugarcane Liaison Farms, similar to the ones existing in Andhra Pradesh, should be set up in other sugarcane growing States also.

3. The sugar factory areas in Punjab and Western Uttar Pradesh suffer from lack of adequate irrigation facilities and also water-logging. High priority should be given by these States to installation of a sufficient number of tubewells in the factory areas which would ensure adequate supply of irrigation water and also minimise the adverse effects of water-logging.

4. The evolution of early, mid and late varieties suitable for different regions and their propagation with the help of appropriate incentives or disincentives should be expedited.

5. In consultation with the Sugarcane Breeding Institute, Coimbatore, and the State Government, the Government of India should draw up a list of approved varieties for different States. This list should be reviewed from time to time. The cultivation of unapproved varieties should be discouraged by adopting control measures similar to those for cotton and also prescribing that the minimum price fixed for sugarcane would either not apply to these varieties or be subject to a sufficiently large discount of say; 20 per cent.

6. The reduction of the present size of the factory area, making it more compact, for the purpose of execution of development programme is urgently called for.

7. Pending the delimitation of the factory area, the development work should be intensified in the I. D. Blocks, and the propagation of unapproved varieties within such blocks, should be statutorily banned. In the remaining part of the reserved area, the factory management should be given an opportunity to take up development work with financial assistance on a pro-rata basis out of the funds earmarked for that area. This would provide a healthy competition between the existing development agency and the factory management regarding development work.

8. Construction of roads and provision of adequate transport facilities should be given very high priority in the developmont programme of both the States and the factories.

9. Courses for specialised training should be started at the two national institutes at Lucknow and Coimbatore. These courses should be open to employees of State Government and sugar factories and also to growers.

10. A significant proportion of the revenue realised from purchase tax on sugarcane should be earmarked for its development work.

11. Certain factories in the private sector in the tropical belt have undertaken active development programme and thereby have reaped significant advantage in terms of efficiency, both of sugarcane cultivation and sugar manufacture. This has also helped in bringing the factory closer to the growers. Such examples should be multiplied especially by the industry in the sub-tropical belt.

12. A small Standing Committee including the Directors of the three national Institutes and one representative each from Government, industry and the growers, should be constituted by the Government of India.

Prospective For 1975-76

1. The target for annual export of sugar should be set at 7.5 lakh tonnes by 1970-71 and 10.1 lakh tonnes by the end of 1975-76. In case, the actual exports turn out to be higher or lower, the buffer stock recommended later in the report should provide some cushion and if, in the light of experience, that is not considered adequate, there could be adjustment in the licensing policy at the time of the mid-term appraisal of the Fourth and Fifth Plans.

2. The aggregate demand for sugar, gur and khandsari in 1970-71 and 1975-76 is likely to be as follows :

(lakh tonnes)

Item	1970-71	1975-76
Sugar for domestic consumption	37.6	53.4
Sugar for exports	7.5	10.0
	45.1	63.4
Gur	69.6	80.4
Khandsari	4.5	5.6
	119.2	149.0

After making an allowance for chewing, seed etc., at the usual rate (12 per cent), the targets for production of sugarcane in 1970-71 and 1975-76 will be roughly about 134 and 169 million tonnes, respectively.

Price Policy For Sugar And Sugarcane

1. The portion of the excise rebate, which has accured to the factories on the basis of production in 1964-65 and which has not been passed on to the growers in the form of a higher cane price, should be constituted into a development fund.

2. The agency entrusted with the task of formulation of policy should be separated from that responsible for its implementation.

3. Stability is a vital need of the sugar economy. Two alternative approaches have been considered. The first one consists of the replacement of the present system of direct controls, with all their defects, by instruments of indirect stabilisation. The other consists of the continuance of the present system of controls but with improvements in those aspects where it is found most wanting. Each alternative has its own logic and requirements in terms of specific measures and for its successful operation, each set of inter-related measures needs to be treated as a package. as it were, to be implemented not piecemeal, but as a whole.

Decontrol Of Sugar With A Buffer Stock Policy

4. In view of the perishability of the cane crop and the weaker bargaining power of the sugarcane growers vis-a-vis the sugar manufacturers the regulation of sugarcane price is both desirable and necessary. However, what needs to be ensured is only a minimum and not a fixed price. Decontrol of sugar price, by enabling the cane price to vary above the prescribed minimum level, will help maintain the above parity and thus reduce fluctuations in sugar output.

5. The flexibility of sugar price, though necessary to enable the sugar industry to complete with gur and khandsari for the available supply of cane, needs to be confined within certain limits. To enable the industry to pay the minimum price the growers, it is necessary to prevent sugar prices from falling below a certain level, is just as to protect the interests of the consumers, they must be prevented from fixing a ceiling. And both the above objectives can be realised through a buffer stock policy in sugar. Such a policy will allow sugar prices to fluctuate within a limited range, given by the minimum and maximum prices fixed for sugar. Sugar will be acquired and stocks accumulated when sugar prices threaten to fall below the minimum and it will be sold, depleting stocks, when prices threaten to rise above the maximum.

6. Although the trends of supply of and demand for sugar have been largely in balance, there are short-period fluctuations and since these imbalances partake of a cyclical character baffer stock policy seems an eminently suitable remedy.

7. Since the demand for cane is drived from the demand for sugar, the minimum price for cane will need to be derived from the minimum price fixed for sugar.

8. The minimum price for sugar will depend upon : (a) what may be called the 'Pivot' price for sugar; and (b) the range within which it will be allowed to fluctuate around the 'Pivot' price. It is best to equate the 'Pivot' price with either a five-year or at least three-year moving average of sugar price, depending upon the extent of variability that is considered tolerable in sugar price.

9. For the next five years, the range of fluctuations to be allowed in the sugar price may be fixed at 8 per cent of the 'Pivot' price.

10. Initially the stocks of sugar required for a change-over to this (buffer-stock) policy from the present policy of control should be of the order of 12 lakh tonnes.

11. In the past, sugar consumption has almost invariably recorded a sharp increase in the year in which sugar has been decontrolled. Since, for the suceessful execution of this policy it is vital that stocks should not prove to be inadequate, it is important to emphasise that, in the matter of the initial size of the buffer stocks, it is desirable to err on the side of safety rather than otherwise.

12. The magnitude of the annual stock required to be held on an average (over the period of a cycle) is likely to be significantly lower than 12 lakh tonnes and may be assumed to be of the order of 8 lakh tonnes.

13. The buffer stock should consist of two parts : one which the industry should be obliged to hold and the other which should be held by the buffer stock agency. The control over the releases of both, however, should be exercised by the buffer stock agency.

14. The industry should be subjected to the statutory obligation of carrying stocks which shall at no time

be less than 20 per cent of its total production in the preceding season.

15. The buffer stock agency will undertake to buy sugar, from ans factory which wishes to sell, at the floor price and sell-sugar, to any whole-sale dealer who wishes to purchase it, at the ceiling priee,

16. When the agency is actually called upon to buy, it may, if it so desires, pay to the factory for the quantity purchased without physically lifting this quantity; it will then merely keep a record of the amount it holds with the different factories. In view of their experience in carrying stocks and the storage facilities already available with the factories, the Commission feels that the entire buffer stock may with advantage be left in the physical custody of the factories, the agency confining itself to exercising control over its releases and meeting financial obligations pertaining to stocks held on its account.

17. The agency will have to maintain a revolving fund for making payments out of it to the factories from whom it purchases and for receiving payments into it from the dealers to whom it sells. Since the agency will be buying when prices are low and selling when they are high, it will be making a profit out of which it will pay to the factories the storage cost of the stocks they hold on its account. This storage cost mainly consisting of the cost of godown facilities can be easily estimated and prescribed per ton of sugar per month held by the factories for the agency.

18. On the basis of a sugar output of 35 lakh tonnes, the industry's obligation to carry minimum stocks would amount to 7 lakh tonnes. Assuming an average buffer stock of 8 lakh tonnes referred as before the part to be held on Government account would come to 1 lakh tonnes and on the basis of the initial buffer stock of 12 lakh tonnes, it would work out to 5 lakh tonnes. The adoption of this policy would involve for Government an interest liability of the order of 5 paise per kilogram per annum for the stocks held on its account.

19. The exercise of control on releases should be strictly confined to the buffer stocks in sugar and should be free to market whenever and wherever they like. This is because the decontrol of sugar price when accompanied with a control on the release of the entire output of sugar tends to run counter to the interests of the consumers and in favour of the producers. It prevents the most important advantages of the competitive mechanism in promoting efficiency and reducing thereby the cost of production and, therefore, the price of sugar, from being reaped by the society. Finally, it retains all the defects emanating from ad-hoc-ism and suspicions of discrimination, connected with the administration of control. In applying any selective credit control suitable relaxation should be made for the sugar industry keeping in view the seasonal character of its operations and the need for maintaining large buffer stocks.

20. In addition to the above measures, the system of rebate on excise duty on sugar should be continued, even in a period when the price and distribution of sugar are relieved of direct controls and subjected only to indirect regulation through a buffer stock policy in sugar. The present system of excise rebate for sugar, however, needs to be modified along the lines suggested in section III.

21. Government should operate the buffer stock policy through the instrumentality of the Food Corporation of India and with the advice of the Agricultural Prices Commission. Similarly, the quantities required for exports, defence personnel and distribution through fair price shops should be purchased from the sugar factories at a negotiated price by the Food Corporation of India.

Alternative II : Control On Sugar

22. Price control on gur and khandsari is difficult to enforce and control on the movement of these commodities is undesirable. Measures for dealing with the problem of diversion of cane supplies to gur and khandsari in the factory areas are listed as before.

23. In addition to the above measures, through a rebate on excise on sugar a certain margin for manoeuvrability should be provided to the sugar factories in their competition with the gur producers.

24, The rebate to be effective for meeting the gur competition and for ensuring the crushing of surplus cane has to be large enough. This would be possible only when there is a sufficiently high excise duty. The fact that the present excise duty on sugar is high enough for the purpose is thus a very helpful factor in the situation.

25. The excise rebate should be allowed every year on the sugar production of each factory in excess of 90 per cent of what may be called "effective production capacity".

26. Until the early and late varieties of sugarcane are propagated, it would not be in the social interests deliberately to encourage sugar production outside the normal crushing season in view of the loss of sugar it entails. Since, however, early cane varieties happen to be generally low yielders, excise rebate on early crushing would be required to enable the factories to pay a higher price for this cane to encourage early varieties. It would be in the social interest to extend the crushing period and thus economise on overhead costs by encouraging these varieties, so long as the economy exceeds the additional can cost of these varieties. When

employed for this purpose, excise rebate will have to be a continuing feature and will need to be announced in advance, for, say, each five-year period.

27. If early cane varieties are to be promoted, the farmer and the factory have to be enabled to plan ahead, the former on the assurance that he will be compensated for the lower yield of these varieties and the latter on the assurance that it will be allowed a cushion through excise rebate to enable it to pay a higher price to the grower for these varieties. Since the promotion and popularisation of these varieties itself would take time, such an assurance of a continuing incentive becomes all the more necessary. The present differentiation between the rebate for early and late crushing encourage uneconomical crushing beeause of the loss of sugar it entails. If such a system is repiaced by a single uniform rebate for the entire season, the factories would not only be free, but would be under an inducement, to concentrate as far as possible their crushings in the optimum crushing period. Instead of the present basis of having separate rebates for the early, late and normal crushing seasons, there should be a uniform basis for rebate on a slab system.

28. The rebate on excise duty, applicable to the entire year's production should be calculated on the basis of the fol.owing rate of production in excess of 90 per cent of the 'effective production capacity' as defined before :

(i) On the first 10 per cent over 90 per cent of the 'effective production capacity,	20 per cent
(ii) Next 10 per cent	40 per cent
(iii) Balance	50 per cent

Such portion of the rebate as may not be passed on to the grower through price or transport charges for cane should not be included in profit but should be constituted into a development fund for the factory concern.d to be earmarked Inter-alia for sugarcane development work.

29. The system of sugar price fixation should not be allowed to degenerate into a 'cost plus' basis. In the existing situation, the tystem of fixing sugar prices on a zonal basis is favoured, but zones are to be few and so democrated as to be broadly homogeneous from an agro-economic point of view.

30. In the interest of stabilizing the sugar availability for the consumer, providing stability to the industry and the grower, and rendering the working of controls smooth and effective, a stock policy in sugar becomes a necessary accompaniment of a sugar control policy.

31. In years of short cane crop, the Commission would emphasise the desireability of considerably stepping up the releases of the sugar at the time of Dussehra or Diwali, whichever happens in the year concerned, to be nearer the time when Kolhus are set up for gur manufacture, so as to discourage the setting up of Kolhus in the factory areas. Alternatively, the farmers who supply cane to the factory, especially in areas where gur competition is acute, should be entitled to the same quantity of sugar as is allowed to people in urban areas. To be effective in their purpose, it is important that these measures be accompanied with adequate publicity.

32. In order to minimise the cost of transport of sugar, the time taken by its movement and the load on the railway system, it is necessary to reduce the cross-haulage of sugar to the minimum.

33. The machinery for the distribution of sugar in a period of control should be, as far as practicable, the same as exists for the handling and distribution of foodgrains. During the period of control on sugar, the system of retail distribution of sugar should be on the basis of identity cards and the distribution of a certain quantity of sugar through fair price shops should continue when control is lifted from sugar.

34. There is no need for the establishment of a Sugar Marketing Organisation.

35. The releases and movement of sugar should be managed by the Food Corporation of India. The export policy should continue to be decided by Government as at present but the implementation of export policy should be handed over to the State Trading Corporation of India. The Agricultural Prices Commission should be entrusted with the task of :

(i) Fixing the sugar price and minimum sugarcane price ;

(ii) Reviewing the composition of zones for fixation of each prices, and

(iii) Advising on Stock Policy.

Regulation Of Sugarcane Price

36. The present system of regulation of cane price, under conditions of a free market in sugar, is inequitous for the sugar industry in different regions. If a free market in sugar is to be achieved and long-term efficiency in sugarcane cultivation is to be promoted, the present system of regulation of cane price needs to be reformed.

37. If premia could be cast on the Principle of proportionality and supplemented with like discounts or in the alternative, the specified level of recovery could be lowered sufficiently so as to approximate the lowest regional level of recovery observed in the country, the regional differences in the cane cost of sugar could be so largely narrowed down as to make the minimum cane price regulation consistent with an ex-faetory price of sugar uniform throughout the country. With the exception of the incidence of short duration, the differences in the cost of manufacturing

sugar would then reflect not so much the regional differences caused by natural factors as the relative efficiency of the sugar factories. As far the very short duration of crushing season in certain parts of the country, the remedy lies in the shifting of these factories to more favourable areas within the State concerned or alternatively in a vigorous drive for the development of sugarcane cultivation in these areas.

38. The reason which prompts the pitching of the specified level of recovery high is the same which keeps the premia at a less than proportionate level and indeed allows for no discounts at all ; it is to enable the sugar factories to pay a higher cane price in regions where gur competition is acute without allowing a corresponding increase in case price in other regions, so as to moderate the overall increase in sugar price. The reason flows from the desire to use minimum cane price regulation for purposes other than those for which it is intended, namely to afford protection to the growers and to induce efficiency. The measures which will enable the factories to withstand gur competition and receive an adequate flow of cane supplies have been suggested elsewhere. Therefore, premia should be cast on a proportionate basis. In view of the difficulties involved in introducing a system of discount as also in drastic lowering of the specified level of recovery in the immediate future, the latter should be brought down to 9.4 per cent in 1965-66, if possible, and 9.0 per cent in 1966-67, in any case. The detachment of minimum cane price regulation from extraneous ends will go a long way in removing that ad-hoc-ism which so much characterises the present policy and gives rise to suspicion and inter-regional tension.

39. The principles that ought to guide the determination of the level of minimum price of sugarcane would be different according to whether the cane price is to be determined in the context of a free market in sugar subject to regulation through a buffer stock policy or in the context of a control on sugar prices.

40. In the former case, the minimum price for cane would be derived from the minimum price fixed for sugar. The minimum price for cane per quintal should be a certain (appropriate) percentage (as in several other sugar producing countries) of the net realisation from sugar (valued at its minimum price) obtained from one quintal of sugar cane. Once this percentage is determined, the minimum price for sugarcane will vary accordingly as the minimum price for sugar varies over time.

41. The principal implication of such an arrangement is that it involves deferred payment. Despite the fact that in India a sugar factory is fed by a very large number of small growers, the existence of cane co-operative unions, make the above arrangement a feasible proposition. Arrangements should be made to ensure that the deferred payment is made not later than 3 months from the close of the season, the minimum price being paid at the time of the delivery of the cane by the growers. In this connection, it would be also underline the desirability of paying to the cane grower on the basis of the sucrose content of the cane delivered by him rather than the recovery of sugar therefrom, for the latter depends not only upon the former but also of the efficiency of the sugar monufacturer. Besides a system of payment based not on the sucrose content of a grower's cane but on the average recovery of sugar from cane supplied by all the growers to a factory seriously undermines the incentive it is intended to provide to the cane grower for taking to the cultivation of high sucrose content varieties of cane. A system of incentive to be effective ought to be based not on an average but on the quality of cane supplied by each individual grower. The National Sugar Institute has evolved a method in this regard which can be introduced without any difficulty. This method of payment should be implemented from the 1966-67. season and necessary measures, including enactment of a Statute, should be initiated immediately.

Under a system of control on sugar prices, the minimum price for cane has already to be known before the controlled price for sugar can be determined. Unlike a system of free market in sugar, it cannot be derived from the sugar price. In this case, in principle, the minimum price of cane should be so fixed as to cover the bulk-line opportunity cost of cane cultivation, the bulk-line referring to that around which the opportunity cost of largest number of cane growing regions lies. Once so determined the minimum price of cane should be adjusted from year to year on the basis of an index of the prices of competing crops so as to preserve the parity between the price of sugarcane, on one hand, and the prices of competing crops, on the other. The objective underlying this principle of prices fixation for sugarcane is to prevent a net diversion of area, especially from foodgrain crops, to sugarcane. Since with improvements in cane cultivation and the consequent reduction in its cost of production (per tonne), such an adjustability will not preserve the parity between the net profitability of sugarcane and that of competing crops, it will be necessary to conduct a cost enquiry for determining this parity and thence the base price (minimum) of sugarcane, periodically, say, on a five year basis.

The alternative of fixing the minimum cane price with referrence to the opportunity, cost of regions, where this cost is the highest, is not desirable, for it contains a built-in stimulus for the overall expansion of cane acreage in the country. The task of fixing the minimum price of cane from time to time is best entrusted to the

Agricultural Prices Commission.

If the level of recovery for which the basic minimum price of cane is fixed, is too high, as it presently is at 10.4 per cent, it destroys the incentive on the part of the growers to take to sugarcane varieties with a higher sucrose content, in regions whose recovery falls short of this level by a wide margin.

Irrespective of the diffiulties involved in a drastic lowering of the specified level of recovery (or in the alternative, of introducing a system of discounts) in the immediate future, the specified level of recovery should be brought down to 9.4 per cent in 1965-66, if possible and 9.0 per cent in 1966-67 in any case.

Having regard to the prospects for the sugarcane crop in the coming year, i.e., 1965-66, the minimum price of sugarcane which was initially announced for the year 1964-65, is adequate for 1965-66 considering the returns for competing foodgrain crops. There is a strong case for fixing the minimum price of sugarcane for 1965-66 at Rs. 4.96 per quintal (Rs. 1.85 per md.) for 9.4 per cent recovery, subject to an increase of 4.4 paise per quintal (1.5 paise per md.) for every 0.1 point increase in recovery above this level, especially for preventing diversion of land and other inputs from foodgrains to sugarcane in the present emergency. If that is found difficult, the principle of proportionality in fixing the premium should be followed in any case from 1966-67 when the minimum price of sugarcane should be fixed at Rs. 4.82 per quintal (Rs. 1.80 per md.) for 9.0 per cent recovery subject to an increase of 5.36 paise per quintal (2 paise per md.) for every 0.1 point increase in recovery above this level. The announcement of the minimum price for 1966-67 should be made by December 1965. i.e., well in advance of the commencement of sowings.

The price of Rs. 4.96 per quintal (Rs. 1.85 per md.) for 9.4 per cent recovery for 1965-66 is for cane delivered at the factory gate and is, therefore, subject to a deduction for cost incurred by the factory in transporting such cane as is not delivered at the factory gate. The minimum price of sugarcane should not be fixed on an ex-field basis because it implies the inclusion of the entire cost of transporting cane from the field to the factory in the sugar price. In order to avoid loss through driage, it is important to discourage long haulage of cane and this requires that the minimum cane price be fixed not on an ex-field but on an ex-gate basis, subject to a certain, but not excessive, deduction from the cane price for the cost incurred for transporting cane by the factory. At present, a deduction upto 32 Paise per quintal is allowed from the minimum price for sugarcane delivered at the cane purchasing centre connected by rail, and a deduction of 2.5 paise per quintal per kilometre, subject to a miximum of 32 paise, in the case of sugarcane delivered at cane purchasing centers connected by road, if such cane is transported by the sugar factory at its own cost. No distinction need be drawn between the cost incurred by a factory in transporting cane from an outside purchasing centre and that incurred in transporting it from the farmer's field.

In view of the urgent need for discouraging the cultivation of disease-ridden or othewise unsuitable varieties of sugarcane, the minimum price fixed for cane should be applicable to only the approved varities (announced for each region from time to time), or, in the alternative, it should be subject to a discount of 20 per cent for non-approved varieties.

In view of the present emergency and the fact that the requisite stock of sugar has yet to be built up, the control on the lines of Alternative II should be continued during 1965-66. Every effort, however, needs to be made to augment the present stock so as to reach a size of 12 lakh tonnes by October, 1966. This target is well within reach if care is taken to maximise sugar production and necessary caution is exercised in respect of its releases. If stock of about 12 lakh tonnes (including the carry-over from 1964-65) is built up by October, 1966, Alternative I may be adopted from the beginning of the 1966-77, promises to be good in regard to the prospects for sugar production, even a shortfall launching the policy of decontrol of sugar.

During a period of control on sugar, a rebate on excise duty is designed to serve, as a solution of the problem not only of surplus cane in a bumper year but also of that of diversion of cane in the years of short crop, without recourse to ad hoc increases in the prices of sugarcane and sugar which make for a drift in the direction of 'cost-plus' basis of price fixation. It is designed also to promote the cultivation of early varieties of sugarcane which are low yielders and the popularisation of which would take time and, therefore, require the assurance of a continuing incentive. During a period of free market in sugar, the excise rebate is required not only for the promotion of early cane varieties but also for reducing the inequitous effect of the present system of cane price regulation on the sugar industry in different regions. The sugar industry in regions where recovery is low has to be provided relief, so long as the system of cane price regulation is not reformed. Even when it is reformed, some relief would be needed for the indust y in regions where it may not get adequate cane supplies without offering a higher price. Since, in the interest especially of the growers, the existing factories in most of the unfavourable areas may have to continue, they would require some relief in the short run. The excise rebate serves both the purposes. In a period of decontrol, excise rebate has thus three objectives :

(i) To remove inequity inherent in the present system of cane price regulation ;

(ii) To promote cane development, whether through the propagation of early and late varieties by compansating for lower yield and recovery or in other ways, so as to increase the economic viability of the existing industry in 'problem areas' as well as promote efficiency generally ; and

(iii) To create an inducement for a full, or even on overful, utilisation of capacity in the industry thus making for a progressive increase in sugar production.

The rebate as contemplated should not involve any burden on the exchequer, as it would be more than covered by the excise collected on the additional output which would not be produced but for the rebate.

The desirability of encouraging the production and consumption of off-colour (raw) sugar in preference to that of white sugar should be emphasised. The production of off-colour sugar by helping economise on the consumption of sulphur will save foreign exchange. It can help augment the production of sugar in the country without additional resources in the sense that a given installed capacity of the industry can produce more off-colour than white sugar. Unlike in the case of white sugar, the molasses produced as a by-product of off-colour sugar are edible and constitute a valuable cattle feed. The fact, that the present market for molasses for the manufacture of industrial alcohol faces the prospect of being captured by naptha-based alcohol in the future, makes it important to plan ahead for an alternative utilisation for molasses, e.g., as cattle feed. And this requires that the production of off-colour sugar should be encouraged so that the produced are edible. The double-cured raw sugar of 99.4 Pol (i.e., off-colour sugar) has a fairly good keeping quality and does not, in respect of taste, compare unfavourably with white sugar. In view, however, of consumer's preference for white sugar, the consumption of off-colour sugar will have to be encouraged through necessary publicity and an adequate price differential between the two types of sugar. This can be achieved by having different rates of excise duty on white and off-colour (or raw) sugars and keeping the rate on the former sufficiently higher (say, by 25 paise per kilogram) than that on the latter.

The sulphitation factories should be required to produce a certain appropriate proportion of their sugar output in the form of raw sugar.

Cost Schedules

The following five zones are recommended for the purpose of fixation of ex-factory prices of sugar:

Zone I : Gujarat, Maharashtra, North Mysore, and North Andhra Pradesh ;

Zone II : Orissa, rest of Andhra Pradesh, South Mysore, Madras, Pondicherry and Kerala ;

Zone III : Meerut, Muzaffarnagar and Bulandshahr districts of West Uttar Pradesh, Punjab Rajasthan and Madhya Pradesh.

Zone IV : Central and rest of West Uttar Pradesh ; and

Zone V : East Uttar Pradesh, Bihar and West Bengal.

Assam may be treated as a Zone by itself on account of its location.

When the potentialities of sugarcane development from agroclimatic point of view are appropriately exploited in future through research and development works like irrigation, drainage, it should be possible to reclassify the sugar producing areas in the country into five regions as suggested by the Sugarcane Breeding Institute, Coimbatore. Till then, the zones recommended as before.

Although an increase of 50 per cent in the price of molasses has been recommended, credit has been taken only at current rates in the fixation of ex-factory price ; the margin left should be utlised for providing proper storage facilities for molasses.

The purchase tax in Mysore is out of line with that in the neighbouring States. It is desirable that the purchase tax in different States should be more or less uniform.

Even where there are no out-station purchase-centres, no distinction should be made between purchases of cane from out-station-centres and those from the fields of the farmers for the purpose of income-tax.

As the actual incidence of emergency risk insurance is not known, no provision has been made for this in the schedules. Suitable adjustment has to be made for this before notifying the prices.

In addition to what has been provided in the schedules, a contingency allowance of 50 paise per quintal of sugar may be added to the ex-factory prices uniformly for both white and raw sugar in all the Zones.

The cost schedules prepared by the Commission should be in force for a period of five years ending October. 1970 subject to adjustments, whenever called for, for variations consequent upon governmental action.

No separate schedule has been prepared for Assam as there is only one factory in that State. The ex-factory price for Assam should be fixed on the basis of the price fixed for Zone V plus the average cost of transport from a suitable railway point in north Bihar to the factory site in Assam.

The schedules of manufacturing cost (including cost on cane), packing, etc., per quintal of sugar for the five zones, based on 10 per cent recovery, for different durations are given in Tables X. 4A—E.

There is no need for separate prices for factories working on carbonation process.

No premium is recommended for A & B grades of sugar.

The rate of return of 12 per cent is not unreasonable and should encourage expansion of the industry.

There is no justification for providing the full difference between the replacement cost and the historical value of the assets without taking into account the return earned from the use of the depreciation fund, the development rebate earned by the industry and also the improvement in design, etc., resulting from technological development reflected in the assets at the time of replacement.

Any provision for rehabilitation added to a uniform price applicable to all units in the industry may not give adequate relief to those units which are in need of rehabilitation while those not in need of it would get undue benefit.

The provision of depreciation on the basis of the standard block or the cost of a new plant would result in unwarranted discrimination and unjustifiable concession, in varying degrees, as between different units in the industry.

The industry's contention that under the present system of determining prices on the principle of average for a Zone, there is no incentive for heavy investment in block, does not seem to be well-founded.

What the industry ought to be concerned with is the ultimate ex-factory price. To take out of context one element of cost that goes into the total cost and then to plead that because the incidence in respect of that element of cost is low in the case of old plants some allowance should be given to the industry as a whole, is not justified.

An appropriate way of giving assistance to old units for rehabilitation and modernisation would be to arrange for them loans, where necessary, at market rate of interest and extend to them the development rebate on the investment on the authorised programme for rehabilitation, modernisation and expansion on the same basis as for new units.

Government may consider providing finance for rehabilitation through the existing financial institutions like the Industrial Development Bank and the Industrial Finance Corporation etc. There is no need for creating a special financial institution for the sugar industry. Additional funds to the extent necessary may be provided through the existing financial institutions. Advances through these institutions to the industry should be given at the normal rates of interest. Financial institutions may also extent concessions like deferred payment of interest and principal.

Loans should not be given to all the units as a matter of course. The application of each unit should be carefully examined from the technical as well as the economic point of views. Periority should be given to the expansion of such units as are below the economic capacity of 1250 tonnes. Where the cost of rehabilition and modernisation is very high relative to the cost of a new plant, the desirability of replacing the old plant by a new plant should be examined.

If for any reason a particular factory which ought to be rehabilitated in order to survive as an economic unit in the industry, fails to take advantage of these facilities within a reasonable time, the Govenment should consider taking it over or running it as a joint venture in the social interest, especially of the growers, and rehabilitate, modernise and, if necessary, expand it.

Export Policy

Exports of sugar should not only be continued but also augmented and efforts should be made to obtain as large a quota as possible under all the three agreements.

The need for reducing the cost of production of sugar in India, in order to improve her competitive position in the world market, is urgent. In the first place, cane price being the largest constituent of the cost of manufacture of sugar, it will be necessary to reduce gradually the current minimum price of sugarcane. This will be possible if adequate steps are taken to increase appreciably the per acre yield of sugarcane so that the grower does not suffer any reduction in the total returns from sugarcane cultivation. Second, any reduction in the cost of manufacture of sugar would necessitate an all-round improvement in the efficiency of the sugar factories. In this context, it has been suggested that big factories should be set up in order to reduce the cost of manufacture. An increase in the size of a factory brings about only a small reduction in the cost of manufacture. Further, this reduction in the manufacturing cost is offset to a large extent under existing conditions in India by various disadvantages, such as higher transport cost and greater driage of cane. Since it involves a number of considerations including the question of proper utilisation of by-products, such as, bagasse and molasses, this matter should be examined carefully before Government takes any decision to set up large-size factories.

Currently, the entire export loss is being met by the Government of India out of the revenue proceeds of the excise duty on sugar. While during the period of control, the incidence of this burden is passed on to the consumer in the form of higher domestic price, during control the incidence will be shared by the producer and the consumer in a proportion depending upon the relative elasticities of supply of and demand for sugar.

There seems to be no justification for a special levy on the sugar manufacturer so long as this levy can be passed on to the consumer. In a period of control, since the rate of return, which is considered fair, is allowed by the Government for the purpose of price fixation, it will not be appropriate to make the industry pay for the export losses out of this return. The Government of India and the State Governments should bear the entire loss on export of sugar. The current rate of excise duty may be raised for the purpose if it is considered necessary. If, however, it is felt that on account of social or international considerations, the manufacturers should be made to share a part of the export loss, an appropriate way of distributing it among the sugar factories would be on a basis. pro-rata to the effective 'production capacity' as defined elsewhere in the Report. There will be relatively less scope for the manufacturers to shift the burden on to the consumers if the levy is based on capacity rather than actual output.

The State Government levy cane cess/purchase tax on sugarcane crushed by sugar factories. The State Governments can share the burden of export loss by forgoing a certain proportion of this revenue. A formula for an equitable sharing of export loss by the sugar producing States has been output.

It would be desirable to assign the task of handling exports to an independent agency. It is, however, not necessary to set up a new sugar marketing organisation for this purpose alone. The State Trading Corporation (STC), which is already acting as an export agency of the Government for various other commodities, should be considered an appropriate agency for the export of sugar also.

The question of economy in the cost of manufacture of raw sugar has been examined by the Commission and it appears that the cost of manufacture of raw sugar is significantly lower than that of white sugar. Separate cost schedules for raw sugar, constructed by the Commission may be followed for the determination of of ex-factory prices for raw sugar for different zones.

Till such time as sufficient distillery capacity is created in order to utilise the entire production of non-edible molasses, Government should liberalise the export policy for molasses. Unless a sustained and regular market is created for Indian molasses, it may be difficult to increase the export of this commodity in future when the production of molasses would be more than what could be utilised by the indigenous distilleries. Some procedure should be devised whereby such sugar factory delivering one tonne of molasses to a distillery may be given an export permit of, say, half a tonne without delay. Some of the alcohol-based industries, such as, polythene, synthetics. etc., may use in future alcohol made from naptha instead of molasses as their basic raw material. It would, therefore, be necessary to plan ahead for a proper utilisation of alcohol manufactured from molasses. It appears that there is a good demand for the potable alcohol in the foreign markets. It should not be difficult for the distilleries to change over from the production of industrial alcohol to potable alcohol.

In order that an export market for potable alcohol is properly developed, Government should liberalise the export policy for alcohol. It should also fix a minimum quota for exports, so that the foreign buyer can plan ahead on the basis of an assured supply from India. The liberalisation of export policy for both molasses and alcohol would earn for the country a substantial amount of foreign exchange without calling for subsidisation of the export of these commodities on any significant scale.

Licensing Policy

At the end of 1970-71 and 1975-76, the requirements of sugar for internal consumption work out to 37.6 and 53.4 lakh tonnes respectively. If the export demands of 7.5 lakh tonnes and 10 lakh tonnes during the Fourth and the Fifth Plan Periods are added to the above estimates, the total demand for sugar works-out to 45.1 and 63.4 lakh tonnes at the end of 1970-71 and 1975-76 respectively.

The additional capacities that may have to be installed during the Fourth and Fifth Plan Periods work to about 12.5 lakh tonnes (1,04,000 tonnes of cane crushing capacity per day) and 18 lakh tonnes) (1,50,000 tonnes of cane crushing capacity per day) respectively. In view of the usual lag between licensing and establishment of capacity, licensing may have to be suitably higher than this figure.

For the present, the minimum economic size of a factory should be fixed at 1250 tonnes per day, with provision for expansion upto 2000 tonnes. The question of determination of economic size of a sugar factory may be reviewed at intervals of, say, 5 years in the light of further developments in sugar technology.

The various merits and disadvantages of having a large size factory have been considered. The economies of scales, which result from having large units and captive by-product plants, are well-known. These will, however, have to be weighed against certain disadvantages peculiar to an industry which depends on a raw material that is perishable and is produced by a large number of small farmers. A large-size factory of 2000 tonnes or more would require an area of nearly 20 thousand acres to feed it in the sub-tropical belt. Unless such an area consists of big plantations or is distributed over a small number of large-size farms, the above economics may be off-set to some extent, by increase in cost of transport of cane from long distances and greater driage of cane leadings to loss in recovery. In addition, sugarcane cultivation in small holdings scattered widely would render intensive development work by the factories difficult.

As regards big factories of 4000-5000 tonnes capacity for purpose of export, these will prove economic only if they are based on large plantations.

The modernisation of agriculture and development of rural areas call for the promotion of agro-industries of which sugar is one of the most important. If a large number of factories of the minimum economic size is set up, it should help the dispersal of the industry and provide a larger number of "growth points" over a wider area. This would also help promote a more rational location pattern for the sugar industry reducing in particular, the cost of transport of sugar. However, the need for the expansion of some of the existing units also cannot be overlooked.

Against the target of additional capacity of 30.5 lakh tonnes (or 254 thousand tonnes of cane crushing capacity per day) to be installed during the next ten years period (1965-66—1975-76), about 25.6 lakh tonnes (or 214 thousand tonnes of cane crushing capacity per day) would be required, half for the creation of new units and half for the sxpansion of existing units. The decision about the balance of 4.9 lakh tonnes (or 40 thousand tonnes of cane crushing capacity per day) may be taken only towards the end of the Fourth Plan Period in the light of export prospects and the recommendations of the Committee which has been appointed by Government to look into the question of establishment of large-size factories for export.

Out of the capacity to be set aside for the expansion of existing units, first priority should be given to the expansion of uneconomic units having installed capacity of less than 1250 tonnes per day.

The uneconomic units, located in unfavourable areas, may be asked either to merge so as to operate more efficiently or to shift to areas better suited to sugarcane cultivation preferably within the same State. In case neither of the above is feasible, the State Government should take up urgently special measures for the improvements of cane cultivation in the reserved areas of these factories. In the light of improvements made, suitable expansion in the capacity of these units may be considered some time later.

Regarding the need for expansion of those units whose capacity is above 1250 tonnes each, the Commission recommends that: (a) factories, which can establish that, with small expansion, not exceeding 300/400 tonnes, they would become significantly more balanced and economic than now, should be allowed such expansion; (b) factories asking for further substantial expansion upto 2000 tonnes should be permitted such expansion if it is established that they have taken requisite steps to improve the yield per acre of sugarcane from their existing reserved area; (c) Factories above 2000 tonnes should not normally be permitted to expand unless these units fulfil the condition mentioned in (b) above and also satisfy the authority concerned that : (i) they would set up by-product industries like alcohol and pulp, and (ii) a substantial part of their sugar production would be supplied for export.

The additional capacity of 3.5 lakh tonnes to be created during the Fourth Plan Period should be distributed over : (i) new units, and (ii) the expansion of existing uneconomic units, to enable them to expand to a capacity upto 1250 tonnes; it is expected this would absorb practically the whole of it. However, if any balance is left, it may be issued against the genuine demands for small expansion, of, say, 300/400 tonnes for those factories which, with such an expansion, would become more balanced and viable. The question of issue of licences for substantial expansion of factories above 1250 tonnes may be considered against the additional capacity to be created during the Fifth Plan Period.

Proper technical examination of each application for expansion of existing capacity should be undertaken before expansion is granted by the Government. For this purpose, the feasibility of setting up a well-equipped cell for consultancy service in the National Sugar Institute should be explored.

In view of the fact that there is a large scope for increasing the yield per acre of sugarcane from its present level by suitable provision of irrigation, drainage and fertilizer and also the fact that the current minimum price fixed for sugarcane is highly attractive to the cultivator, and gives him higher returns than those from cultivation of foodgrains, it would be necessary to restrict, as far as feasible, any expansion of area under sugarcane cultivation. This has become particularly important in view of the present emergency which requires that there should be no net diversion of area from foodgrains. The Commission, therefore, recommends that the Government should fix a compact area for each factory based on the present licenced capacity and should not allow any expansion of this area in futnre, especially in regions where there is a substantial scope for improvement in per acre yield. If measures are taken to improve the supply of sugarcane is assured, the factory may, in due course, be allowed suitable expansion in its capacity.

Well defined criteria should be laid down and adhered to rigidly by the Government when deciding upon the location of new sugar factories. These criteria should be ; (a) agro-climatic considerations, (b) comparative economic advantage of growing sugarcane vis-a-vis competing crops, and (c) consideration of freight advantage from a surplus sugar producing area to the area in which it is proposed to set up a new factory.

On the basis of the criteria (a) and (b) Punjab, Jammu and Kashmir, Rajasthan, North Madhya Pradesh, Coastal Orissa, West Bengal, and Assam do not appear to be favourab'y placed, under present conditions for the expansion of the sugar industry. Location of a new factory in these areas may, however, be considered if the higher cost of manufacture of sugar in these areas is counter-balanced by the cost of transporting sugar from a neighbouring surplus sugar producing area.

So far as the scrutiny of applications for setting up new factories that should be set up during a particular period, of, say, five years and invite applications from all the States. The decision should be based on a comprehensive examination of all these applications in the light of the criteria mentioned as before.

Regions, A, B and C should be generally preferred for the location of new units during the next five years or so. Within these regions again certain districts enjoy greater advantages over others and in deciding about the location of new units, these differences may be kept in view. Further, the eastern districts of Uttar Pradesh & the northern districts of Bihar are economically backward and have no mineral resources or other important raw materials on the basis of which the major industries could be set up. From consideration of balanced regional development, these areas may be given a somewhat higher priority than they would otherwise deserve. The Commission recommends that, for the next five years, no new units should be allowed in those areas where competition from gur and khandsari mauufacture is currently acute and where agricultural conditions, at present, are not favourable for substantial increase of sugarcane production. In such of these areas as are considered suitable for sugar industry, necessary corrective action (e.g., irrigation, drainage, varietal improvements, etc.,) may be undertaken during the next five years and the question of setting up of new factories in these areas be reviewed on the basis of changed agricultural as well as economic conditions after that period.

The Commission found that the setting up of a sugar factory had helped significantly in the economic and social betterment of the area around it. The setting up of a co-operative sugar factory has, thus, acted as a nucleus for social and economic development of the area around it and has helped to develop a new class of rural entrepreneurs. However, cooperative sugar factories in States other than Maharashtra have not shown similar satisfactory results. The Commission would like to impress upon co-operative sugar factories located in other parts of the country to study closely and emulate developments in Maharashtra.

While the Commission generally agrees with the Government's policy that new units should be confined to the co-operative sector, it feels that where it is difficult to set up a co-operative factory, the State Government concerned may set up factories either under its own aegis or in collaboration with the joint stock sector. In the latter case, the State Government may usefully hold the majority share capital so as to have a predominant voice in the management of such a joint venture. The Commission would further recommend that such a joint venture should be given sufficient autonomy in day-to-day management and operations. It also recommends that those sugar factories, joint-stock as well as co-operative, which are found to be badly managed for more than three years, should be taken over and run by Government for a certain number of years and then handed back to the owners subject to certain conditions regarding sound management practices being followed. The Industries Development and Regulation Act, 1951, should be suitably amended with a view to facilitating this. Government should also maintain a nucleus technical organisation for this purpose. Since sugarcane is a perishable crop and the fate of a large number of farmers is depend upon it, the Government cannot afford to permit any sugar factory to be mismanaged.

The Commission has noted that some joint-stock units have recently sought to bring into their fold farmers as shareholders in order to achieve a better identification of interest between the factory and the farmer. It feels that this is a commendab'e step worthy of emulation by others, but, in order to be really useful, it should be done on substantial rather than on a token scale.

A standing Export Committee including the Director of the Sugarcane Breeding Institute Coimbatore, the Director of the National Sugarcane Institute, Lucknow, the Director of the National Sugarcane Institute, Kanpur, a representative each of the Department of Food, Ministry of Industry, Planning Commission, Agricultural Prices Commission and two independent experts—one an economist and another a technologist—should be set up to examine the applications for licences for expansion of existing factories and setting up of new factories and advising on their location and site in the light of the technical examinations envisaged in as before and the criteria for licensing mentioned in as before.

Conclusion

The real remedy of the problem facing the sugar

industry should, therefore, tackle the basic causes, natural as well as man-made. The natural causes may take a somewhat longer time to be remedied. The man-made causes can be corrected more quickly, but, since these causes have fairly deep roots, it may be difficult to correct them unless a comprehensive policy based on well-defined principals, is formulated and implemented firmly, and short-term or sectional considerations and concomitant 'ad-hoc-ism' in policy are definitely eschewed.

The long-term recommendations of the Commission have been presented as a self-contained package, as it were. The various components of this package have no doubt their own individual merits and demerits looked at from sectional points of view. But, taken together, they make a balanced whole, individual components supplementing one another. The package should, therefore, be considered in its entirely and not piece-meal.

COMMITTEE ON SOME PROBLEMS OF UNIVERSITY ADMINISTRATION, 1964—REPORT

New Delhi, University Grants Commission, 1967, 22p. (This Committee was appointed by the U.G.C. following the report of the Santhanam Committee on "Prevention of Corruption"

Chairman : Shri D. C. Pavate.
Members : Shri B. Shiva Rao; Dr. A. C. Joshi ; Shri K. Santhanam ; Shri S. Ratnam (could not attend any meeting of the Committee) Shri P. K. Rau.
Secretary : Shri R. K. Chhabra.

APPOINTMENT

The University Grants Commission at its meeting held on August 5, 1964 considered the following observations made by the Committee on Prevention of Corruption set up by the Government of India:

"Universities are the main source of supply of officers for our public services, especially at the higher level. It is, therefore, of supreme importance that they should set standards of integrity which will become an integral element of the intellectual and psychological outfit of every graduate. It is a matter of great regret that in some universities, conditions are far from satisfactory for the admission of students, recruitment of lecturers and professors and the general management of university funds. We suggest that the University Grants Commission and the Inter-University Board should take immediate steps to institute an inquiry into the malpractices that may be prevailing in the universities and evolve measures to fight them."

The Commission after consideration of the above observation appointed the following Committee on August 5, 1964.

TERMS OF REFERENCE

The terms of reference of the Committee are as follows:

To examine the extent of malpractices prevalent, if any, in the universities.

CONTENTS

Introduction; Appointment of the Committee; Nature of Complaints; Observations and Recommendations; Appendices I and II.

RECOMMENDATIONS

We have studied the procedures obtaining in various universities relating to appointment, examinations, admissions and elections to university bodies. A note on the procedures in the universities relating to appointments, examinations, admissions and elections to university bodies is given in appendix I.

The Committee visited Delhi University on 5th August, 1966 and had detailed discussion with the Vice-Chancellor, the representatives of teachers and students. We were informed that the University registered all applicants and admissions were made strictly on merit and their system of central registration for admission of various colleges for undergraduate courses was working very well. The students have to register at various centres fixed by the University for admission to undergraduate courses in arts and science. The selection for arts course is left to the colleges which generally select students according to the marks obtained in higher secondary or equivalent examinations, except in a few cases where some concession is given for proficiency in sports etc. For science courses allotment to the colleges is done by the University. The colleges are quite alive to their responsibility and there has practically been no complaint against the present system of admission through central registration. The University very firmly resists attempts to influence admissions. We were also informed that in regard to the appointments of professors, readers and lecturers the University is satified with the normal procedure. The University ensures that all experts are present at the time of the meeting of the Selection Committee and the University does not accept any decision of the selection Committee that is not unanimous.

We have considered the problem referred to us at some length and feel that corruption and malpractices do exist in our universities to some extent. Where they occur, the reason frequently is weak and inefficient administration by unexperienced officers, who are unable to resist undesirable interference. It may also happen that some of the university personnel are unscrupulous. We are of the opinion that malpractices in administrative matters may be dealt with in the same way as in those in Government and public organisations i.e, their should be strict accountability, close watchfulness, proper procedure in relation to contracts and prompt enquiry, when there are complaints or reasonable suspicion of malafides.

Universities in India have a crucial part to play in the life, welfare and development of the nation. Their function is not only to preserve, disseminate and advance knowledge but also to impart an intellectual and moral tone to society. They have to provide traiced personnel to man the various services and stimulate the country's prosperity. The report of the Education Commission has very lucidly brought out to the following functions of the universities in the modern world:

"(a) To seek and cultivate new knowledge, to engage vigorously and fearlessly in the persuit of truth and to interpret old knowledge and belief in the light of new needs and discoveries ;

(b) To provide the right kind of leadership to all walks of life, to identify gifted youth and help them develop their potential to the full by cultivating physical fitness, developing right interests, attitudes and moral and intellectual values;

(c) To provide society with competent men and women trained in agriculture, arts, medicine, science and technology and various other professions who will also be cultivated individuals imbued with a sense of social purpose;

(d) To strive to promote equality and social justice and to reduce social and cultural differences through diffusion of education;

(e) To foster in the teachers and students and through them in society in general the attitudes and values for developing the 'good life' in individual and society."

We feel that the universities cannot perform these functions efficiently unless they have freedom from external control alongwith a healthy administrative system and participation of the academic community in the formulation and implementation of university policies and programmes. An atmosphere of complete independence, non-interference and integrity is essential for the proper working of a university so as to ensure purity of public administration, public life and in fact of every aspect of social activity where the influence of a university-trained person is bound to prove decisive. This would be possible only if the universities are free from nepotism, misconduct, submission of undue influence and discrimination on grounds of caste, religion, creed and other factors which are not in harmony with the ideals of university education. The various corporate bodies should be vigilant and jealously guard the reputation of their university.

The key person in the administration of any university is the Vice-Chancellor who is its academic and executive head. The tone of a university depends on the responsibility of its Vice-Chancellor. Apart from being a distinguished scholar with administrative capacity, the Vice-Chancellor should be a person of the highest integrity who can withstand undue pressure from persons of influence, wealth or power. He should inspire confidence in students and teachers. In order to ensure this we consider it necessary that the method of appointment and conditions of service of the Vice-Chancellors should be such as to attract persons of highest ability and character. We also suggest that the universities should have proper procedural and institutional arrangements which would enable the Vice-Chancellor to deal with lapses on the part of students or teachers promptly and effectively.

There has been a rapid growth of university enrolment after the country attained independence. Various factors make it increasingly difficult for universities and colleges to apply adequately high standards to the selection of students. In a country which is passing through a period of national awakening, the right to higher education is widely looked upon as almost a fundamental right. It is also to be noted that in many quarters in India higher education appears to be a means of social uplift. Any attempt to deny access to university education is bound to meet with serious opposition. Again in India, the expansion of higher education is supported not only on the basis of popular aspirations but also by the bearing it has on the economic and social development of the country. The chapter on education in the Third Five Year Plan pointed out that it was one of the major aims of the

Third Plan to expand and intensify educational effort so that in all branches of national life education becomes the focal point of planned development. The accentuation of such effort may have repercussions on the quality of students in universities of an unwholesome nature ; but their complete avoidance may prove to be a counsel of perfection in view of the over-riding policy of the Government.

We have considered in some detail the practice of certain institutions charging capitation of high admission fees for admission. We were informed that the University Grants Commission had already expressed itself strongly against institutions charging capitation or a high fee for admission to different courses. There are complaints that a number of malpractices have developed round such institutions. We recommend that the authorities concerned should look into these allegations.

The Committee considered the question of admission to engineering and medical colleges about which complaints of favouritism and nepotism are frequently heard. The admission of less qualified students in preference to better qualified ones constitutes a long-term danger to society. We were informed that in some States, the State Governments constitute committees for such admission. We recommend that the universities should be represented on such committees so that proper academic standards are maintained.

We have referred already to the malpractices in our examination system—in the mode of appointment of examiners and invigilators, in the proportion of external and internal examiners, disclosure of question papers, improper influences in marking papers etc. Examinations which have the following three functions should be conducted with impartiality. Firstly, the assessment made by universities of the performance of students indicates to the outside world, including employing agencies, the competence and attainments of students on completing their various courses of study. Secondly, it is a measure of the development of the student himself as a result of the educational process which he has undergone in the university. Thirdly, it indicates to the other universities and professional institutions the suitability or otherwise of the students for entrance to an institution of different areas of study and training. All these require on the part of the universities an appreciation of the crucial importance of the role of examinations and of the need to conduct them with the utmost sense of responsibility, care and competence.

Further, an examination is an aspect of the educational process which is intimately linked with its other important aspects—teaching and learning. In fact, teaching, learning and examination actually constitute a unity of functions. Teaching as well as learning are bound to be adversely affected to a serious extent by malpractices in the examination system.

In view of the importance of the examination system in our present day educational process, it is of paramount importance that there should be a proper selection of the examiners ; and this obviously implies resistance to any attempt at influencing the examiners. One defect of the examination system brought to our notice is the substantial income earned by teachers from examination work. Examinerships are sometimes awarded to the teachers on a reciprocal basis. As this is an additional income to the teachers, there is a unwholesome tendency in the universities to secure the maximum of examination work. We were further told that some teachers receive a large number of answer papers from different institutions, with the result that they spend too much time over marking the papers and neglect their normal duties ; or they devote too little time to them with careless and hasty marking of the answer books. We Note that the Education Commission has recommended* the abolition of the payment of remuneration to teachers for the evaluation of answer books as evaluation is a part of teaching. We are also of the view that there should be no payment for evaluation of answer books. However, if it is not possible to eliminate this practice, the universities should lay down some limit for the income of teachers from examination work relating to their own university and other universities.

We are also informed that in some universities examiners are appointed not on their merit but on the basis of certain other considerations. In order to avoid this possibility, we recommend that every university should prepare a detailed list of teachers, their qualifications, research work to their credit etc., and these factors should be made use of at the time of appointment of examiners. Another step which we suggest for removing malpractices in the examination system in the universities is that the UGC should undertake a systematic study of the examination results in relation to the performance of the students in various universities. Even within the university or college itself the teachers should be asked to submit a statement of the performance of these appearing for examinations in a common form prepared by the UGC. We also recommend that the UGC should prepare a model code of conduct for examiners to be sent to the universities for incorporation in the service conditions of teachers ; and salient features of this code may be brought to the notice of the teachers at the time of their appointment as examiners.

*Report of the Education Commission (1964-66), para 11-57.

The most important factor in the field of higher education is the type of person entrusted with teaching. Teaching cannot be improved without competent teachers. For improving the quality of education we have to find teachers who have not only a thorough knowledge of the subject but also have genuine interest in their work. The most critical problem facing the universities is the dwindling supply of good teachers. It is not an easy thing to produce competent and devoted teachers in sufficient numbers. This difficulty is bound to be accentuated as further expansion of education takes place. The selection of the right type of teachers assumes, therefore, a vital role in the educational advancement of the country. We, therefore, recommend that teachers should be selected purely on the basis of their merit through regularly constituted selection committees on which there should be outside experts. The recommendations of the selection committee in the order in which the names are recommended should ordinarily be binding on the authorities of the universities.

We have considered the suggestion that the Vice-chancellor who is normally the chairman of the selection committee should not be associated with the selection committee. It has been pointed out that if the Vice-chancellor is not associated with the selection committee, he can take a dispassionate view of the recommendations of the selection committee and would therefore be in a better position to select the best from among the available candidates. Normally, the choice of selection committee would be binding on the university ; but in case of difference of opinion, the Vice-chancellor, if he is not associated with the committee, would be in a better position to exercise his judgement independently. The committee does not suggest any rigidity in regard to this matter. There are other considerations which cannot be ignored in approaching the problem. Many of our universities are yet in a formative stage and their standards can be raised only by dedicated Vice-chancellors. At times, the Vice-chancellor may have to persuade outstanding people to join the university. Moreover, even the experts in the selection committees have often their own people in mind and try to advance their claims, although they may not have the requisite merit. In fact, the presence of the Vice-chancellor in a selection committee may, on occasions, prove to be a moderating factor and facilitate proper selection. The most important thing is to appoint competent Vice-chancellors of proved integrity.

Our attention had also been drawn to the following recommendations made by the report of the Committee on the 'Model Act' for Universities set up by the Government of India :

"The selection committee should consist, besides the Vice-chancellor, the head of the department concerned and a certain number of experts. This number may vary in accordance with the category of teachers to be appointed. For professors it should be necessary to have two or three outside experts. In the case of lecturers a smaller number may be adequate. Great care should be taken in choosing the experts. It may be an advantage to have one nominee of the Chancellor/Visitor on the selection committee. The court or academic council should not elect a representative to the selection committee. It should be a clear rule that the executive council should accept the selection unanimously recommended by the selection committee. In rare cases, if for good reasons the executive council is unable to accept the recommendations of the selection committee, efforts for a better selection may be renewed in the following years".

We are in general agreement with the views expressed above by the Committee on the 'Model Act' for Universities and recommend that for the appointment of professors in the universities the selection committee should have outside members in a majority. It may comprise as follows :

1. Vice-Chancellor
2. Head of the department concerned
3. Three outside experts
4. One nominee of the Visitor/Chancellor.

The report of the selection committee should be finalised before the meeting is adjourned and signed by the members. If any member has to give a dissenting note, this may be done at the time of signing the minutes.

Apart from the selection of the right type of teaching personnel, it is of paramount importance that the teachers should be given proper service conditions so that talented people might be attracted to and retained in this profession. We were informed that the University Grants Commission has already appointed a committee which is looking into the question of framing model service rules for university and college teachers for guidance of universities and colleges. In this connection we have also considered a suggestion with regard to departmental promotions to teaching posts. It was suggested that if suitable departmental candidates were available, the posts should not be advertised. We are not inclined to agree with this suggestion and feel that this would amount to limiting the field of choice.

Every university should jealously guard its reputation for integrity and immediately look into complaints such as leakage of papers and other abuses in examinations, discrimination in admission, allegations of misconduct or any other complaint either appearing in newspapers or sent to the university in writing or even brought to the notice of the Vice-chancellor orally. For the prestige of any university the unqualified support of public opinion is essential. We, therefore, recommend that in every university the Vice-chancellor should appoint a high level committee comprising teachers and others of high eminence and integrity. The Committee should take prompt steps to enquire into any allegation which appears to violate ethical principles or evades well-established standards and procedures. This committee should report its findings to the Vice-chancellor.

We also feel that the UGC which is charged with the co-ordination and maintenance of standards of higher education, should play a more effective role in the eradication of malpractices in universities and colleges. The commission, we recommend, should evolve a system of studying the reports of committees set up by the Vice-chancellors so as to keep the universities informed of the steps that may be required to improve administration and eradicate corruption.

The Committee was also apprised of the complaints regarding the abuse of postal voting in elections to the senate. It was pointed out that the agents of the candidates sometimes collected the votes from the university graduates which, the Committee felt, was not in the interest of fair elections. The Committee gave a good deal of thought to the malpractices reported in elections to various university bodies and felt that whenever elections are to be held to university bodies, the university administration should ensure the secrecy of the ballot. We would, therefore, suggest that for all elections to the university bodies there should be secret ballot.

APPENDIX I

A Note on the Procedures in the Universities Relating to Appointments Examinations, Admissions, and Elections to University Bodies

1. Appointments

(a) Authority empowered to create new posts both academic and non-academic and the mode of recruitment to various posts whether by promotion or through advertisements.

The authorities empowered to create posts in the universities are the syndicate and senate. In some of the universities the authority empowered to create academic posts is senate and for the non-academic posts syndicate. In others, the executive council or the syndicate is the authority empowered to create all posts. Generally, the recruitment to the posts is made through advertisements, while some of the universities have intimated that in some cases, the recruitment is done through promotion also.

(b) Ratio between appointments through promotion and direct recruitments.

The information supplied by almost all universities indicates that there is no specific ratio prescribed by the university authorities between appointments by promotion and direct recruitments specially for teaching posts. However, in one or two cases, for the administrative staff certain quota is fixed for recruitment through promotions.

(c) The constitution of selection committees for various posts.

The constitution of the selection committee is invariably headed by the Vice-chancellor of the university and includes besides the head of the departments a few specialists in the subjects also. In some areas, the nominees of the university bodies like academic council, syndicate etc.; are also included in the selection committee. In the case of Bihar University the selections are made by the State Public Service Commission ; while in the case of Jabalpur University (M.P.) the Chairman of the State Public Service Commission is a member of the selection committee.

(d) Whether qualifications are relaxed in the case of departmental candidates. If so, to what extent ?

In a majority of the cases it is found that there is no relaxation of qualification in the case of departmental candidates. One university has intimated that there are no definite rules of relaxation and every case is judged on its merits. While in another, it is provided that relaxation in qualification in favour of departmental candidates may be made if a definite recommendation to that effect is made by the selection committee.

(e) Are the recommendations of the selection committees binding ?

If not what is the authority to over-rule recommendations of the selection committee ?

Of the 16 universities taken up for analysis, in 10 universities the position is that the recommendations of the selection committee are not binding and syndicate is the authority to over-rule the recommendations of the selection committee. In two cases, the recommendations to the selection committee are stated to be binding and there is no question of over-ruling by university authorities. In some cases, if the syndicate does not accept the recommendations of the selection committee, reference is made to the Chancellor or the Visitor or the matter may be referred back to the selection committee for reconsideration.

(f) Whether selection committee is competent to recommend advance increments ? If so, to what extent ?

In almost all the cases it is observed that the selection committee is competent to recommend increments which may even be up to the maximum of the grade. In a few cases, it is stated that the selection committee is not competent to recommend advance increments which may only be done by the syndicate.

2. Examinations

(a) Mode of appointment of examiners and invigilators.

The position about the mode of appointment of examiners and invigilators varies in the universities. But generally the examiners are appointed by the syndicate on the recommendation of the board of studies or the examiner's committee. In some cases, the academic council is also involved in the appointment of examiners. With regard to invigilators, in some cases, senior most teachers are appointed for invigilation by the Vice-chancellor and certain percentage is met from outside the university or college. In others, the invigilators are appointed by the centre-superintendent. In the case of Karnataka University, a list of suitable persons for appointments as examiners/invigilators is received from the neighbouring universities. Selection is made by the boards of studies from out of the names received and the panel forwarded to the examiner's committee which makes recommendation to the syndicate for appointment. In Kurukshetra University the invigilators are appointed by the Registrar.

(b) The proportion of internal and external examiners.

The internal and external examiners are appointed generally on 50 : 50 basis. In some universities there is no fixed ratio. In Bombay University for the pre-degree examinations the ratio between the internal and external examiners is 75 : 25 while for the degree examinations the ratio is 50 : 50.

(c) Maximum number of answer books which can be allotted to the examiner.

In some universities there is no limit for the number of answer books to be examined by an examiner. But in others a definite ceiling has been laid down which varies from 100 to 600.

(d) The period for which an examiner can continue.

In some universities there is no limit to the period for which an examiner can continue ; while in others, the period has been prescribed down which generally varies from 3 to 4 years. However, even in such cases also a relaxation is made for professional examinations and for postgraduate courses.

(e) Steps taken to maintain uniformity of standards in making the papers.

The position about each university has been explained in the annexure to this note dealing with examinations. In some cases, the board of examiners decides the mode of marking of papers and necessary instructions are issued by the Chief examiner to all the examiners. In others, model answer books are sent to the examiners, while in still others the moderator draws a scheme for the guidance of the examiners which include model answer books and indicate marks to the awardee.

In some universities the question papers are moderated by boards of moderators. In some cases, the head examiner convens the meeting of the examiners and discusses the mode of alloting marks for various questions and he also scrutinizes 5% of the answer books of examiners to see how instructions have been carried out.

(f) Checks exercised by the head examiner.

Generally, the head examiner checks a certain number of answer books to find out whether marking has been done in the proper manner. In others, the head examiner can appoint additional examiners to evaluate the answer books already marked.

(g) Steps taken to ensure safety and secrecy in the conduct of examinations i.e., whether fictitious roll numbers are allotted and whether the centre-superintendent knows the examiner to whom the answer books are sent.

The practice varies in different universities. In about 50% of the universities taken up for analysis the system of alloting fictitious roll numbers is not in vogue. In some universities, the fictitious roll numbers are allotted only for honours and post-graduate answer books. In majority of the cases, the centre-superintendent does not know the examiner to whom the answer books are sent as the answer books are first sent to the university office from where they are sent to the examiners.

3. Admissions

(a) Criteria adopted for admissions.

The admissions are generally made on merit on the basis of the percentage of marks obtained by the students in the examination which is the minimum qualification laid down for admission to the course. In some universities there are qualifying tests and the students are admitted in order of merit. In some cases, selection committees are constituted to interview the candidates which make recommendations about the admission of students to the courses. The University of Magadh has intimated that for post-graduate courses, a portion of the seats is reserved for the Magadh University graduates in order of their attainment. In Delhi University the admission committee recommends principles to be adopted for admissions and these are reviewed and approved by the standing committee of the academic council;

(b) Is there any system of reservation of seats for scheduled castes, scheduled tribes and backward classes and different areas and regions ?

In some universities there is reservation of a portion of seats available for admission to scheduled castes, scheduled tribes and other backward classes. While in others, there is actually no reservation but students belonging to these communities are given certain weightage while determining their marks which qualify them for admission to the courses. For example, in Udaipur University 5% concession in marks is given to students belonging to these communities, for admission. In Allahabad University such candidates are given weightage of 10% marks secured in qualifying examinations. In Banaras Hindu University, 10% weightage in marks is given to such students in all colleges and 15% in marks in the faculty of technology. In Calcutta and Poona Universities there is no reservation of seats for scheduled castes, scheduled tribes and other backward classes, Calcutta University has, however, reported that certain seats are reserved in some departments for the nominees of the Central Government. In Jadavpur University there is reservation of seats on merit on all-India basis and certain seats are also reserved for other States where such facilities are either not sufficient or are limited;

(c) Are any domiciliary restrictions imposed on the admission of students ?

Generally there are no domiciliary restrictions in universities for admission of students to courses. However, in Udaipur University a limited preference is given to students of Udaipur District. In the case of Delhi, women students registering with the Advisory Board of (Non-collegiate) Women's Education, their presence in Delhi is required. In Jadavpur, although there are no domiciliary restrictions but there is reservation of seats for various States.

(d) Is there any system of capitation fee or donation fixed for admission to professional colleges ? If so, the amount of donation fixed for the purpose ?

In almost all the universities there is no system of capitation fee or any donation fixed for admission to professional colleges. However, Karnatak University has reported that in some private colleges (engineering and medical) donation system is prevailing and the donation ranges from Rs. 2,000 to Rs. 5000.

4. Election To University Bodies

(a) The procedure for election to various bodies of the universities—Executive Council, Academic Council etc., etc.

(b) Method of nominations if any to these bodies. Generally the universities have intimated the constitution of various university bodies instead of giving the information asked for.

(c) Procedure for election to students' bodies in the universities.

(d) Whether the elections are conducted by students themselves or under the supervision of the university ?

Magadh, Poona, Karnatak and Sri Venkateswara Universities have intimated that there is no provision for students bodies in the universities. Kurukshetra University has reported that no procedure has been prescribed by the university for election to the students' bodies. In most of the universities, the elections to the students' bodies are conducted under the supervision of the university or the teacher appointed by the university. In Kerala University the elections are not conducted under the supervision of the university.

COMMITTEE ON COOPERATIVE MARKETING, 1964—REPORT

New Delhi, Ministry of Food, Agriculture, Community Development and Cooperation (Development of Cooperation), 1968. 383p.

Chairman : Prof. M. L. Dantwala;

Members : Dr. Punjabrao S. Deshmukh (expired and in his place Shri B. Mazumdar was appointed); Shri P. S. Rajagopal Naidu; Shri G. D. Goswami; Shri R. T. Mirchandani; Shri K. C. Cheriyan; Shri M. L. Batra (replaced by Shri J. S. Varsheny.

Secretary : Shri Veda P. Sethi.

APPOINTMENT

Cooperative Marketing has a key role to play in the economy of the country in ensuring a fair return to the cultivation for his produce and in promoting the expansion of production credit on a sound basis. The slow progress of Cooperative marketing particularly with regard to agricultural produce has inhibited to a large extent the flow and growth of production finance to the rural areas. Cooperative marketing has therefore, to be strengthened, as an integral part of the structure of credit, to subserve the need of increased agricultural production. It is also essential for marketing societies to ensure timely distribution of all production requisities to farmers and undertake proceedings of agricultural produce as well as direct sales to consumers cooperavites.

The question was discussed at length in the conference of State Ministers of Cooperation, held at Hyderabad on the 19th and 20th of June 1964. In view of the complex nature of the problem and its far reaching implications the conference recommended that an expert committee should be appointed to review the present pattern of organisation of cooperative marketing of agricultural produce, distribution of production requisite and supply of consumer articles of different levels, consider the difficulties that now stand in the way and recommend measures as can enable cooperative marketing societies to play their due role in integrated structure of credit, supplies and processing.

The Government of India in the Ministry of Community Development and Cooperation (Department of Cooperation) have considered the recommendation and have decided to set up the expert Committee on Cooperative Marketing Vide their Notification No. F. 13.5/64-C.M. dated August 6, 1964.

TERMS OF REFERENCE

(i) To review the present pattern of Cooperative marketing of agricultural produce, distribution of production requisites and supply of consumer articles at different levels (village, regional, State and National) and indicate the future pattern of development with particular reference to interse relationship between the Organisations at different levels;

(ii) To indicate the role of cooperative marketing in an integrated structure of credit, supplies and processing and how best this role can be discharged.

CONTENTS

Introductory; Existing Pattern of Agricultural Marketing in India and its Deficiencies; Need for Cooperative Marketing of Agricultural Produce; History of the Growth; Present Role and Progress of Cooperative Marketing in India; Recommendations; Annexures from I to XX.

RECOMMENDATIONS

Pattern of Organisation of Cooperative Marketing and Processing Societies at Various Levels

The future pattern of organisation of marketing cooperative should be a two-tier structure, with the apex society at the State level, primary marketing societies at mandi level and branches of the apex marketing society at district or regional level.

In States where a three-tier structure already exists, the existing district federations need not be disturbed. Such district federations should, however, gradually divest themselves of those functions which legitimately fall within the purview of the primary marketing societies in favour of the letter.

For various practical reasons it is advantageous for marketing cooperatives to undertake both agricultural marketing as well as distribution and supply functions. There is no need now to form separate societies for distribution and supply functions alone.

No rigid approach is desirable relating to organisation of single commodity marketing societies. In non-specialised (general) crop areas, the general purpose marketing society can itself deal with all crops. In areas where cooperative marketing is not developed, general purpose societies should be organised to begin with, as specialisation is not possible at that stage. In areas of concentrated development of a particular crop, which requires specialisation, e.g. sugar cane, cotton, jute, plantation crops, fruits and vegetable, separate commodity societies may be organised, provided they can be viable.

While the single commodity marketing societies may deal exclusively with the marketing and processing of the specified crops, the general purpose marketing societies may deal with all other crops in the area. Distribution of Agricultural inputs should be undertaken only by the general purpose marketing society through the agricultural credit societies. Commodity societies, including cooperative processing societies, should not undertake such functions.

To obviate the likelihood of excess recovery of production loans simultaneously by two or more marketing societies located in the same area, the marketing societies, in such cases, should make effective arrangements for coordination, or in the alternative they may remit the entire sale proceeds to the village society concerned, which, after recovering its dues, may pay the balance to the farmer.

The recommendations of the Saraiya Committee on Cooperative Processing (1961) that ordinarily processing units not involving substantial outlay of block investment, should be established by marketing societies as an adjunct to their normal marketing operations are endorsed. In cases, however, where specialised crops like fruits and vegetables, etc., which requires special skill and attention, are grown in considerable quantities, in addition to the main crop of the area, a separate processing-cum-marketing societies can be formed for the purpose, subject to its being viable. Similarly even if initially an existing marketing society sets up a processing unit for a commodity, and at a later stage the need for a separate society is felt in view of the expansion of production to setting up of a separate society for the commodity by transferring the processing unit along with the share capital of the members producing that particular crop, provided such a society can be viable and does not affect the viability of the parent society.

When a marketing society dealing with more than one crop or activity sets up a processing unit, such unit should be treated as an independent subsidiary unit of the main society, with separate accounts, Balance-sheet, trading and profit and loss accounts. etc., and independent legal status. The membership of the subsidiary unit and its share capital should likewise be kept separately from the main society, so that the profits as well as the risks involved in processing can be borne by the members concerned without involving other members. Suitable steps may be t ken to amend the existing cooperative law in the various States, wherever needed, to facilitate the formation of such subsidiary units.

Wherever primary marketing societies are not located at the mandi centres, immediate steps should be taken to shift the headquarters of such societies to the mandi centres. It is also necessary to realign the areas of operation of the primary marketing societies, wherever necessary, so as to ensure that they are co-terminus with the hinterlands of the markets concerned.

In the prevailing conditions, the suggestion to confine the membership of the primary marketing societies to village societies alone may not be workable for a long time to come. This can be the ultimate goal to be achieved, when the village service societies become strong units covering the entire agricultural community and capable of undertaking assembling, grading and pooling of the produce.

For the present, for various practical reasons, a mixed membership consisting of both village service/credit societies and individual growers is essential at the level of primary marketing societies.

Concerted efforts are needed for not only physical affiliation of all agricu'tural credit/service societies to the respective primary marketing societies, but also to forge an effective business link between them. Special attention in this regard is particularly necessary in West Bengal, Assam, Kerala, J & K. Orissa, Punjab and Union Territories, where a large number of credit societies are yet to be even formally affiliated.

State Governments and cooperators should launch an intensive membership derive through a programme of education, propaganda and persuasion to control individual growers as members of primary marketing societies. Intensive efforts are needed particularly in Bihar, Assam, Madhya Pradesh, Punjab, Rajasthan, Orissa and Jammu and Kashmir where the average membership is very low.

It is desirable to confine the membership of district marketing societies to primary marketing and processing societies alone, so that they could function effectively for the benefit of their affiliated marketing societies and also to avoid conflict of interest, which is inevitable in the present heterogeneous membership. Efforts should be made to gradually disaffiliated credit and other types of societies, not directly concerned with marketing and processing, from these district societies. The primary marketing societies should have a predominant voice for individuals at the district level society and every effort should be made to eliminate the existing individual members in these societies.

Membership of the apex marketing societies should be open to all the district/regional and primary marketing societies as well as processing societies in the State so that the apex societies can effectively represent them and coordinate their activities. It is not desirable to have agricultural credit and other types of societies as members of apex marketing societies and individuals should have no place whatsoever at this level. It will be necessary to reorganise the present membership of the apex marketing societies by dis-affiliating gradually the societies not directly concerned with marketing and processing of agricultural produce as well as individuals.

Immediate steps are also necessary to affiliate all marketing and processing societies in each State with the apex marketing societies.

Management and Personnel

Management: As recommended by the Study Team on Cooperative Marketing of Specified Plantation Crops, both individual producer-members and member societies should have a certain minimum representation on the managing committee of primary marketing societies, provided that a certain minimum number of individual producers and agricultural societies was enrolled as members of such societies. Such minimum may be determined in the light of local conditions, but it should be ensured that the share of agricultural credit societies is not less than one-third of the strength of the board of management, if more than fifty per cent of such societies in the area have been affiliated.

In addition to the above minimum representation, individual producer members and member-societies may share the remaining seats on the managing committee generally in proportion to the extent to which these categories of members were having dealings with the marketing society.

With a view to ensuring that only bonafide producers are elected to the managing committee of primary marketing societies, it is desirable to prescribed in the by-laws of the societies that to be eligible for selection, a representative of an affiliated society or an individual member should heve sold a sizeable share of the marketing surplus of his produce through the marketing society in the preceding two years. He should also undertake to sell his produce through the marketing society during his term of office, failing which he should be disqualified from continuing as director.

It is also desirable to lay down in due course similar qualifications for voting rights of individual members so that only such members who consistently sell their produce through the society will have a voice in its management.

For filling up the seats reserved for member-societies and individual members, there should be separate electoral colleges for each of the two categories of members. In course of time it may be desirable to restrict the voting rights to the representatives of only such societies which have arranged for collection of produce of their members and its sale through the marketing society.

There are a few primary marketing societies which, besides dealing in the main crop of the area, also deal in other crops, such as fruits and vegetables, etc. In such cases, if the corp concerned is exclusively grown by a sizeable number of farmers, it is necessary to provide a separate and equitable representation for them on the board of management to look after their interests.

Government nominees on the boards of management of marketing societies should be restricted to the absolute minimum, which may be determined by the State Governments with reference to local conditions such as the extent of development of the society concerned, backwardness of the area, availability of enlightened cooperative leadership etc.

The recommendations of Ramniwas Mirdha Committee on Cooperation (1965) regarding nomination by Government to the board of management of cooperative societies and the duties and responsibilities of government nominated directors are endorsed.

The recommendation of the Ramnivas Mirdha Committee on Cooperation (1965) that producer-cum-traders should not be allowed to become full members of marketing societies and that they may become associate and nominal members, without right to vote or participation in management, is endorsed.

Apart from a provision in the by-laws of marketing cooperatives to prevent infiltration of traders in their management, it is necessary that the supervisory staff of the cooperative department, central financing agencies, and supervising unions, who inspect the societies, should be made responsible to ensure that such elements are kept away from the marketing societies. As recommended earlier, compulsory sale of agricultural produce through the society for eligibility to become a director should be insisted upon. As a further safeguard, a record of the extent of land cultivated by each member should be maintained by each marketing society and no pledge or other loans in excess of his genuine requirements based on his normal production from the land should be given to any member nor should overtight purchases to made from such members in excess of such limits.

As the district marketing societies are mainly federations of primary marketing societies, it is necessary that the representation to primary marketing societies should be raised suitably so that they may have an effective and predominant voice in their management. Special provision should also be made for representation to independent processing and special commodity societies, if they are in sufficient number and function through the district society concerned.

It is desirable to reserve a percentage of seats on the managing committees of apex marketing societies separately for district, primary and independant processing societies, as well as special commodity societies. The exact proportion may, however, be left to be decided by each society concerned taking into consideration various local factors.

Apart from the apex marketing societies, the membership of the National Agricultural Cooperative Marketing Federation should also be open to bigger cooperative processing societies of growers as well as special commodity federations. There is no need for special representation to the Bharat Krishak Samaj in a purely cooperative organisation as the National Federation.

Central and State Cooperative Banks may make suitable provision in their by-laws for special representation exclusively to primary/district marketing societies and processing societies at the district level and to the apex marketing society at the State level, wherever such a provision does not exist already.

It is desirable that the local marketing societies or the district marketing society, as the case may be, are represented on the management of the cooperative wholesale stores. The wholesale stores may like-wise be represented on the district marketing societies. Similarly, mutual representation on the management of apex/national marketing societies and State/national consumers cooperative federations is desirable.

Personnel : In order to attract competent managerial personnel, common managerial cadres should be created for the cooperative marketing societies in each State. Pending creation of a common cadre, a beginning should be made by creating a pool of managerial personnel with the apex marketing societies, which could form the nucleus for a common cadre. Thus, the apex marketing societies may recruit a limited number of personnel with the requisite qualifications and experience on suitable scales of pay and give them intensive training for manning the posts of managers/secretaries, etc. of marketing societies at the district and primary levels. The personnel from this pool can be deputed to marketing societies to replace government officers now on deputation or when vacancies arise. Similar arrangements should be made for accountants and other senior posts. Graded scales of pay may be fixed to suit the needs of marketing cooperatives with different stages of development and business turnover.

The apex societies should be given a suitable subsidy in the initial stages, when the candidates recruited will have to be given training and to provide for periods of unemployment, leave, etc. The scheme formulated by the National Cooperative Development Corporation in this regard, may be implemented expeditiously in all States so that the cadres could be established as early as possible.

With a view to ensuring that unqualified managers are replaced as early as possible, a condition that the marketing society concerned should employ a trained manager from the common pool available with the apex society or otherwise where no pool is available, may be stipulated by the State Governments before contributing the additional share capital or giving managerial subsidy to marketing societies.

It is necessary that rules governing the recruitment to the various categories of staff should be laid down for all marketing societies, either as part of the cooperative rules or in the by-laws, so as to prevent appointment of unqualified staff.

It is desirable to set up, for recruitment to the posts of managers and to other senior posts in primary marketing societies, a selection board-consisting of representatives of the Board of directors of the society and the State Cooperative Department, so that local influence, which it will be otherwise difficult to avoid in such appointments, could be reduced to the minimum and really efficient personnel could be recruited.

The managerial subsidy should be made available to existing societies also to replace the unqualified staff with trained personnel and it should be spread over a period of 3 to 5 years on a sliding scale.

In a few States, a large number of government officers of the State Cooperative Departments have been deputed to work as managers/secretaries of cooperative marketing societies. In such cases, it seems that the suitability of a particular officer for the job is not always borne in mind and the postings are made mostly to suit the administrative convenience irrespective of the aptitude, training and competence of the officer concerned for the job. This procedure is not sound in principle, as every officer of the Cooperative Department will not necessarily have the requisite aptitude and business acumen, particularly to run a marketing society.

If a government officer has to be deputed to a marketing society, he should be deputed on the usual foreign service terms and the board of management of the society concerned should have full control over him in all matters relating to his selection, disciplinary control, sanction of leave, writing of annual confidential reports on his work and conduct, etc. If financial assistance needs to be granted to a society, it should be in the form of cash subsidies to meet the cost of such officers deputed, either in full or in part according to the patterns of assistance. The recommendations of the Mehta Committee on Cooperative Administration (1963) in this regard are endorsed.

Directors of marketing societies, while laying down in the broad policy and principles and ensuring their proper observance by the manager, should not interfere with the day to day working of the societies which should be the responsibility of the manager. The demarcation of functions between the board of directors and manager should be clearly laid down in the bye-laws and strictly observed.

There is a large number of untrained managers working in cooperative marketing societies. It is essential that the existing untrained managers are either deputed for training or if this is not possible, they should be replaced as early as possible. Exceptions should, however, be made in respect of those who have acquired the required knowledge and experience through their long service and who may not, therefore, need any further training and are otherwise considered suitable.

In suitable cases, where the marketing societies are weak and unable to meet the cost without affecting their financial position, it is desirable that the government should meet the expenditure on the training of the existing personnel including their salary during the period of training, to enable the marketing societies to increasingly depute their managerial staff for training. Suitable agreements should be obtained from the personnel sent for training at the cost of the societies or government, requiring them to serve the society concerned for a minimum period after completion of training and to refund the cost of training in case of failure to do so, in order to prevent desertion of the candidates after training.

The special course in cooperative marketing now conducted by the Committee for Cooperative Training has to be more job oriented. The trainees should, as a part of their practical training, be attached to the marketing societies for a few weeks during the peak season so that they can observe and learn the marketing practices, business techniques, etc. through first hand observation. This apart, the need for employing well qualified teaching staff with the requisite background of marketing business requires no emphasis. It is hoped that the special committee constituted by the

Committee for Cooperative Training for revising the syllabus, etc. for the course will suitably revise the syllabus and content of the course to suit the present needs and for different categories of managerial personnel and also prescribe suitable qualifications for the teaching staff to make the course more useful and effective.

It may also be desirable to admit a limited number of well-qualified private candidates (e.g. graduates in commerce or Business Management, or Cooperation or those who had undergone the basic course in cooperation in a cooperative training institute or the diploma course in cooperation conducted by a University) with necessary aptitude, to the special courses in cooperative marketing. This would help in building up a cadre of qualified personnel for recruitment to the managerial posts of marketing societies straightway without further training. The content of the course can be suitably amplified to suit the needs of such private candidates. The Committee for Cooperative Training and the Union Department of Cooperation may consider this suggestion.

Special emphasis may be given to 'cooperative marketing' in the syllabi for the special courses in 'Marketing' conducted by the Agricultural Marketing Adviser to Government of India so as to make instruction in cooperative marketing more comprehensive. Close coordination between the Agricultural Marketing Adviser and the Committee for Cooperative training is also desirable in conducting the special courses in 'Marketing'.

Finance For Cooperative Marketing Internal Resources

An average primary marketing society will need a capital base of about Rs. 2 lakhs to enable it to have a reasonable business turnover. Systematic efforts will, therefore, be necessary to augment the share capital of primary marketing societies to enable them to have a minimum capital base of Rs. 2 lakhs.

The establishment of a link between cooperative credit and marketing should form an integral feature of the programme of agricultural credit. It is, therefore, necessary that all primary agricultural societies/service cooperative in the area of operations of a primary marketing society should, as a rule, get themselves affiliated to that society. The central cooperative banks, officers of the State Cooperative Departments and the cooperators should take effective steps to achieve this end through a phased programme.

Each primary agricultural credit/service/multi-purpose cooperative society should be required to contribute to the share-capital of the marketing society to which it is affiliated at the rate of two per cent of its annual loan turnover in the preceding cooperative year, rounded off to the nearest multiple of a share unit. Central cooperative banks should, as part of their promotional activities, render, through their supervisory staff or otherwise assistance in computing the share-capital to be subscribed and in its collection and remittance to the marketing society concerned.

Efforts should be made, through pursuation and education, to enrol as large a percentage of the individual growers (including those who are already members of agricultural credit societies) as possible in the next five years. Each such member should be required to take one share as the minimum. A phased programme should be drawn up for each marketing society and the active assistance of the supervisory staff of the bank, officers of the State Cooperative Departments and others should be availed of for this purpose.

It is desirable that each grower member of a primary marketing society should be required to subscribe to the share-capital of the primary marketing society in relation to the services received by him from the society. To begin with, every member obtaining a loan on the pledge of his produce, should be required to invest a sum equivalent to 2 and half per cent of the loan taken by him, as share capital in the marketing society over and above the minimum share capital already subscribed by him at the time of his admission. In other words, the member should have as his share capital not less than one fourtieth of the amount of pledge loan outstanding against him at any time.

Every primary marketing society should also endeavour to collect annually about one per cent of the value of sale by each member, towards share capital, irrespective of the fact whether the produce was brought by him direct or through the village society. Such collection may stop when the member has accumulated share capital equivalent to approximately 10 per cent of his average annual scales of Rs, 1,000, whichever is lower or when the society has collected adequate share capital and is not in need of further capital. To begin with, such compulsory collection may be made by well established primary marketing societies and extended to other societies gradually through a phased programme.

Members should be pursuaded to reinvest the dividend on the share capital and bonus on sales in the marketing society as additional share capital.

Government contribution to the share capital of primary marketing societies should be raised substantially so as to reach a minimum of Rs. 1 lakh per society, so that, with its own matching contribution, each primary marketing society may have a minimum share capital of Rs. 2 lakhs. This limit of Rs. 1 lakh may be suitably enhanced by the State governments, wherever necessary on merits of each case with reference to local conditions and special needs either in respect of a specified category or class of societies or in respect of an individual society, e.g. societies dealing in plantation crops, etc. requiring large capital or those in under-developed areas where members may not be able to raise matching contribution (In the ratio of 1 : 1).

The enhanced government contribution of Rs. 1 lakh should be paid in four equal instalments of Rs. 25,000 each or in such larger number of instalments as the State governments may deem fit in merits of each case. Each successive instalments may be paid to the society concerned without prior matching contribution from its members, if the State government concerned is satisfied that the society will be able to raise the member's part of share capital within a reasonable time. Such matching contribution should, however, be raised within a period of two years from the date of government contribution and further instalments should be paid only after the earlier contributions are matched.

In the case of new primary marketing societies, the first instalment of government share capital should be contributed only after the society concerned has raised a certain minimum amount of share-capital from its members. Such minimum may be fixed by the State governments for each such society with reference to local conditions.

Primary marketing societies whose share capital from their members is below Rs. 25,000 should be asked to bring it up to at least a minimum level of Rs. 25,000 within a stipulated time. If a society falls to do so, it would be preferable to cancel its registration. The State governments should review the position in this regard and give an ultimatum to such societies to take effective measures to raise their members' share capital within a stipulated time.

The apex marketings/societies should take steps to affiliate the marketing/processing societies which have not been affiliated so far. Each primary or district marketing society may be required to invest in the share capital of the apex society an amount equal to 5 per cent of its own share capital. In turn, each apex marketing society may be required to invest 5 per cent of its total share capital in the share capital of the National Federation.

The ratio of government contribution to members' contributions to the share capital of primary marketing societies already prescribed by the National Cooperative Development Corporation are generally adequate and require no modification. For the purpose of computing the matching contribution of members of subscribing government share capital in respect of primary marketing societies, the total owned funds of the society concerned may be taken into account instead of members' share capital alone.

The State governments should, as already indicated by the National Cooperative Development Corporation, have discretion to further relax the ratios between the members and government contributions to the share capital of primary marketing societies in suitable cases within the State with reference to local conditions and needs, either in respect of a specified area because of its backwardness, etc., or for a specified category or class of societies or in respect of an individual society based on its special needs and circumstances. Similarly, the State Governments should be free to prescribe a higher ratio for members' contribution in respect of well developed societies, even though for the State as a whole a lower ratio has been prescribed.

Central and State governments should not insist on any ratio between members' share capital and government contribution in respect of marketing societies at the National, State and district/regional levels. Similarly on the analogy of State/district level credit institutions, there should be no upper ceiling for these institutions and the quantum of government share capital should be decided with reference to needs and merits in each individual case.

The procedure adopted by some of the State governments in requiring marketing cooperatives to retire the government share capital in annual instalments soon after the receipt of State contribution defeats the very object of such State participation. The retirement of government share capital may be commenced after the society concerned has collected share capital from its members to the extent of Rs. 2 lakhs or 10 years after the date of last instalment of government contribution or 15 years from the date of first instalment of government contribution whichever is earlier. The retirement, after it has commenced, may be spread over a period of ten to fifteen years, depending on the stage of development of the society concerned.

As regards the national, apex and district/regional marketing societies, as in the case of similar organisations in the field of cooperative credit, government share capital should be for an indefinite period, unless the society concerned desires to retire it earlier.

The pattern of graduated scale of interest followed by the Reserve Bank of India in respect of interest on its loans to State Governments from the National Agricultural credit (Long term operations) Fund for share capital contributions to credit institutions may be adopted by the National Cooperative Development Corporation also in respect of its loans to the State governments for share capital contribution to marketing societies. The loans for the purpose from the Central Government to the National Cooperative Development Corporation may also be on similar terms.

Retirement of government share capital should be

made only from out of the additional contributions from members to the share capital after the optimum level is reached, so that members' share capital can take the place of government share capital to the extent the retirement of the latter is effected. It is not considered necessary to create a separate 'capital redemption fund' from out of profits for such retirement, as such a procedure will only weaken the capacity of the institution to declare dividends, without any corresponding benefits either to the institution concerned or to the government. There should however, be no objection in strengthening the normal reserve funds of the societies and for redemption of government share capital from out of such funds.

It is necessary to increase the members' deposits in the marketing societies, because they will not only provide sufficient funds to the cooperatives, but also inculcate the habit of thrift among the members. In many foreign countries the system of 'revolving fund' is adopted by marketing societies, wherein each members allows the society to retain a part of his sale proceeds and other amounts due to him as a deposit repayable with interest after a fixed period. In India, the arecanut marketing societies in Mysore and cotton sale societies in Gujarat have built up sizeable deposits from their members. The practice adopted by some of these societies is to have a current account for each member to which all amounts due to him by the society are credited. Although most of the amounts so deposited are withdrawn, yet a sizeable amount still remains with the society. The above practices may be adopted by the other marketing cooperatives for collecting deposits.

Fifty per cent of the statutory reserve fund of primary marketing societies may be invested in the higher tier of the cooperative marketing structure, while the remaining fifty per cent may be utilized in their own business. The apex marketing society may, however, be permitted to utilize its reserve fund for its business operations.

Marketing societies, which have invested bulk of their reserve funds in government securities, debentures, etc. and also in fixed deposits of cooperative central banks, should take suitable measures to encash such securities and/or to withdraw the deposits with banks so that the funds would become available for marketing activities.

As suggested by the Reserve Bank of India, marketing societies, which have invested large funds in the shares of other cooperative institutions with which they have no direct business dealings, should take suitable steps to dispose of or reduce such investments as early as possible. Similar economies in regard to investments in furniture, fittings, buildings, transport vehicles etc. should also be made so that the available owned resources with the societies could be conserved for their marketing operations.

Finances for Cooperative Marketing External Resources

State Bank of India should give high priority to the requirements of cooperative marketing structure. The Bank should take immediate steps to provide adequate funds to meet the requirements of marketing cooperatives in consultation with the State Governments concerned.

The Reserve Bank of India may consider permitting the State Bank of India to borrow from it additional funds at bank rate to enable the State Bank to meet the requirements of marketing societies in regard to their marketing activity in all areas and distribution functions in areas selected for intensive agricultural development. Such advances to the State Bank may be to the extent of the advances made by the bank for financing marketing cooperatives either directly or indirectly over and above the credit limits sanctioned to such societies as on March 31, 1966.

The Government of India may also explore the possibilities of obtaining advances from PL 480 account with a view to augmenting the resources of the State Bank of India for meeting the short-term financial requirements of marketing cooperatives.

Considering the overall benefits and in the interests of maintaining an integrated cooperative structure, it will be advantageous for marketing societies to obtain marketing finance from the State Bank of India through the normal cooperative banking structure. It is desirable, therefore, to route the State Bank of India finance through the normal cooperative banking structure as far as possible.

It is not, however, desirable to follow a rigid pattern in this regard. A flexible approach is necessary depending on the needs, circumstances and merits of each case. Thus while, as a general rule, the marketing-societies should obtain their finance from the cooperative banking structure as far as possible exceptions may have to be made in case of individual societies according to local needs and other factors. In areas where cooperative financing agencies are week or unwilling to finance marketing/processing societies, the State Bank of India may finance such societies directly with the concurrence of the Registrar of Cooperative Societies or the State Cooperative Bank concerned. Such consent may be a general one or special one for the occasion as the case may be, according to needs.

The cooperative central banks are now required to give their consent to enable marketing societies obtain marketing finance directly from the State Bank of India. Some of these banks are reported to have been reluctant to give such consent, even though they were unable to finance or the State Cooperative Bank will be fully aware of the financial condition etc. of the Cooperative Central Bank concerned, it should be sufficient for either of them to give the concurrence to enable the marketing society to obtain finance directly from the State Bank of India.

It should be ensured that the margin of interest between the State Bank of India lending rate to the State Cooperative Banks and the lending rate of marketing societies does not exceed three-fourth per cent in all, in respect of marketing finance obtained from the State Bank of India.

Considering the security involved and the saving in time, labour and establishment charges, etc. that would result to the State Bank of India in case of bulk lending through the cooperative banking structure, as against dealing with numerous individual societies, the State Bank of India may consider reducing the rate of interest to cooperative banks in respect of marketing finance so that the difference between the direct and indirect. pending could be eliminated altogether or reduced to the minimum.

While there is need for initial government contribution to the share capital of marketing societies to make them viable for carrying on their normal functions, such contributions on a large scale merely to enable them to raise additional finances required for special schemes such as procurement work price support schemes are not desirable and should be avoided.

The present limits stipulated by the Reserve Bank of India for borrowings by marketing societies may by and large, be sufficient to enable the developed marketing societies to undertake their normal operations. But these standards will require relaxation when the societies undertake special schemes such as price-support and procurement schemes, etc., involving large outlay of finance, with little trade risks. Where the need for additional finance is justified with reference to the activity proposed to be undertaken and the operational efficiency of the society concerned and if the State government concerned guarantees the repayment of such loans, there should be no specific limit for such borrowings in relation to the owned funds of the societies concerned. The cooperative banks should thus have discretion. In such cases, to grant clean limits beyond twice the owned funds of marketing societies on merits of each case, taking into account the nature and extent of government guarantee and the requirement of funds in relation to the activity proposed to be financed. The government guarantee in such cases should be against default and not only against losses.

The following relaxations in respect of the Reserve Bank's directives are recommended till the end of the Fourth Plan period to enable the marketing societies to strengthen their capital base in the intervening period. Such relaxations should not, however, be made in respect of all marketing societies, as a matter of course but only on merits of each case after proper scrutiny taking into account the needs, its operational efficiency and other relevant factors ;

(i) The relaxation (a) to grant clean credit to marketing societies along side of a pledge and or hypothecation limit, and (b) to permit reduced margins in respect of pledge/hypothecation loans in cases where the business is wholly on government account or if the margin is guaranteed by the government, now allowed by the Reserve Bank of India upto 30th June, 1967, may be extended up to the end of Fourth Plan period, wherever necessary.

(ii) Central cooperative banks may be allowed discretion to grant, on the recommendation of the State Registrar of Cooperative Societies, clean credit upto twice the owned funds of marketing societies on merits of each case with reference to actual needs for both marketing and supply/distribution activities and the soundness of the society concerned without insisting on government guarantee.

(iii) The total owned funds of a marketing-cum-processing society, including investments in fixed assets but excluding losses incurred and/or the unrealiable assests, may be taken into account for the purpose of determining the extent of clean accommodation to be allowed by a cooperative bank to such society. The clean credit limits in such cases need not, however, be granted always to the full extent of the owned funds, but limited to the actual needs on merits of each case.

(iv) Marketing societies should, as a general rule, arrange to recover the dues of village credit societies from the sale proceeds of the produce brought by their members and/or from pledge loans granted to them. But since such compulsory recovery may not be practicable immediately in all cases for various reasons, it may be introduced in select areas in each State where cooperative marketing is well developed and extended to other areas gradually in a phased manner.

Where relaxation from compulsory recovery of dues to credit societies is given as indicated above, clean and pledge/hypothecation loans should not be withheld by the cooperative banks for non-recovery of such dues.

So long as the system of 'trade credit' exists and is not legally prohibited and the marketing societies are required to follow the practice, measures will have to be found to provide the marketing societies with adequate funds for the purpose. 'Trade credit' should, therefore, be brought within the purview of 'marketing of crops' for purposes of utilising Reserves Bank's credit, so that cooperative banks could advance credit to marketing societies for the purpose and be eligible for refinance facilities from the Reserve Bank of India.

Marketing societies should take suitable precautions against misuse of 'trade credit' by the traders and also against losses. They should maintain a confidential record of the credit worthiness and solvency of buyers, who may be selected with great care. Appropriate credit limits as well as the duration of such credit should be fixed and revised from time to time and the buyer should be allowed 'trade credit' only within the limits so fixed. It is also necessary to ensure that the overall trade credit outstanding at any time does not exceed the owned funds of the marketing society concerned. The supervisory staff of the State Cooperative Departments as well as the cooperative financing agencies should also scrutinise carefully the 'trade credit' accounts during their inspections with a view to preventing malpractices such as repayments by book-adjustments, etc. Where such credit remains unpaid for an unreasonably long period, interest should be charged. Buyers who are allowed 'trade credit' should be admitted as 'nominal' members of the marketing society to facilitate settlement of disputes through 'Arbitration' under the Cooperative Societies Act instead of going to civil courts.

The possibilities of evolving a suitable system of credit insurance by the Insurance Companies may also be explored so as to cover the risks involved in this regard.

It is understood that the commercial banks, in certain cases, allow the removal of goods by the buyer of the goods without repaying the pledge loan granted by the banks, provided (i) the credit rating of the owner of the goods is good and the bank will be able to realise the amount even if the buyer does not ultimately make payment for the goods or pay a smaller amount than what was originally agreed upon, and (ii) a hypothecation agreement and a trust deed are executed by the original owner and the buyer of the goods hypothecating the goods to the bank and agreeing to clear the loan to the bank within a specific period. The Reserve Bank of India may examine if a similar procedure could be adopted by the cooperative banks.

Besides the laons granted on pledge of agricultural produce to marketing societies, the cooperative banks, particularly those whose own resources may not be adequate for the purpose, may be permitted to utilise Reserve Bank's finance for 'marketing of crops' for the drawals under clean limits granted to marketing societies for (i) grant of loans on pledge of agricultural produce of their members pending its repledge to the bank, (ii) for making outright purchases of agricultural produce from their members, and (iii) for providing 'trade credit' to buyers of agricultural produce where such system is in vogue.

The agricultaral credit societies should accept full responsibility for the purchase of the agricultural inputs from marketing societies and for their sale to their members on their own account, the marketing societies undertaking only the procurement of the inputs, their stocking and supply to the village societies. The State goverment should take suitable measures to strengthen the resources of the agricultural credit societies.

It was recommended that the agricultural inputs should be supplied by the State governments to marketing societies on 'consignment' basis. But it may take some time for implementing this procedure. The Reserve Bank has recently allowed credit for financing distridution of fertilizers. The marketing societies will need funds for procuring other inputs and consumer goods. To the extent marketing societies are required to pay cash for these goods, they should be allowed by the cooperative banks, pledge/hypothecation credit and also, where necessary, clean limits, subject to over all limits recommended earlier, for the above functions.

As cooperative banks will not be able to utilise Reserve Bank's funds for the purpose and since many of these banks may not be in a position to meet such requirements from their own funds, the State Governments should make suitable arrangements with the Reserve Bank of India and/or the State Bank of India to provide the necessary funds to the cooperative banking structure for the purpose.

(i) It was suggested that in order to induce the cooperative banks to enlarge their financing operations for agricultural marketing, a 'special marketing finance risk fund' might be created at the level of each cooperative central bank on the lines of the 'special bad debt reserve fund' might be created at the level of each cooperative central bank on the lines of the 'special bad debt reserve fund' created in credit institutions for financing weaker sections and also industrial cooperative. The apex and central banks may contribute to the fund annually at a certain percentage of the margin of interest earned by them on the total amount of marketing finance, including clean, pledge/hypothecation loans, provided by them during the year, while the State governments may contribute at a percentage of the additional marketing finance advanced by the cooperative banks during the year over and above the loans advanced by them in the preceding year. The borrowing marketing societies may also be required to contribute at a percentage of the amount borrowed. Any losses incurred by cooperative banks in financing marketing societies are to be met from this fund subject to the prior approval of the registrar.

(ii) Another suggestion made was that, on the analogy of the scheme for financing industrial cooperatives by the Central Cooperative banks, the Government of India and State Governments may bear a proportion of the losses arising out of non-recovery of marketing finance granted to marketing societi es.

The Committee could not examine these suggestions in greater detail for want of adequate data. However, as the arrangement's suggestions may satisfy the cooperative banks and will be in the interests of both the banks and the marketing cooperatives as well as the State governments, who are often required to stand guarantee in each individual case, the Goverment of India may consider the suggestions further.

The criteria recommended by the Mehta Committee on Cooperative Credit for reckoning the 'owned funds' of cooperative societies may be adopted for reckoning the 'owned funds' of marketing societies at various levels for purposes of fixing their credit limits.

The existing ratio between the share capital investment and borrowing limits in respect of clean loans obtained by marketing societies from cooperative banks is high in many areas and requires reduction. The ratio may be reduced suitably with reference to local conditions so that the burden on marketing societies may be reduced.

The present ratio between the share capital investment by marketing societies in cooperative banks and their borrowing limits in respect of pledge or hypothecation loans may be reduced to 1:100 wherever the ratio is now higher, i.e., for every share of Rs. 100, the society should be eligible for a pledge/hypothecation loan of Rs. 10,000. To enable the cooperative banks to borrow adequately from the Reserve Bank of India, the State government may contribute additional share-capital to the central cooperative banks, wherever necessary.

The present maximum borrowing limits of marketing cooperative prescribed in their by-laws may be re-examined and wherever they are found to be inadequate, they may be suitably enhanced to meet their needs in respect of pledge/hypothecation credit or separate limits may be fixed for such credit.

In some of the States, it was reported that under the existing law or under various agreements, the State Governments have a statutory first charge over all the assets including stocks, etc. of the cooperative societies in respect of the amounts due to the Government. This stands in the way of marketing societies obtaining adequate finance from the banks. This is a very undesirable practice which would strangulate the societies as no bank will be willing to risk its funds in the face of Government's first charge. The State Governments should immediately re-examine this aspect and remove the impediment, so as to enable the marketing cooperatives to function efficiently.

In view of the need for large amounts of finance by marketing societies during the Fourth Plan period, the State governments may assist the deserving societies by standing guarantee for their borrowings wherever necessary, in pursuance of an accepted economic policy. The guarantee should be against default and not only losses.

The scheme of guarantee to cooperative banks, State Bank of India and its subsidiaries and select commercial banks for the finance provided to consumer wholesale stores and State and National Federations of consumers' stores recently introduced by the Government of India may be made applicable to the apex and district/regional marketing cooperative societies, as well as primary marketing societies having a sizeable turnover of consumer business, in respect of finance required by them for undertaking distribution of consumer goods in rural areas.

Whenever cooperatives are utilized for procurement or price-support operations under Government schemes, the State Governments, Food Corporation of India, State Trading Corporation or other Government agencies, as the case may be, should assume full responsibility for providing the cooperatives with sufficient advances to enable them to undertake the operations. Such advances, which should be interest free, should be provided to the apex marketing societies, which should in turn distribute them to the primary/district marketing societies according to needs.

Wherever, however, the State Governments, etc. are unable to provide the funds for the purpose from their own resources, they should themselves make arrangements to obtain such finances directly from the State Bank of India or other agencies and advance them to the apex cooperative marketing society concerned, as the owned resources of cooperative marketing societies cannot permit such large scale borrowings.

Marketing cooperatives should not be required to bear the burden involved in holding buffer stocks on behalf of the Government. Payment for stocks delivered to government, etc. should be made without undue delay. In case marketing societies are required to hold the stocks for some time, the government or other agencies concerned should pay the marketing societies for the stocks and allow the societies to keep them in storage as agents of government, etc. through suitable arrangements regarding storage costs, insurance etc.

With the expansion of cooperative credit as well as cooperative marketing envisaged in the coming years, it is necessary that all cooperative central banks should open branches of the headquarters of all primary marketing societies, which are located in the 'mandis'. It will be preferable if both the branches and the marketing societies are located in one and the same building or in adjoining buildings.

Note: Shri K. C. Cheriyan, representative of the

Reserve Bank of India on the Committee, is not in agreement with the recommendations, 73 (ii), 74 and 77 of Chapter VIII, given in the summary of Conclusions and Recommendations. These have reference to paragraphs 8.38, 8.45 and 8.49 respectively.

Business Techniques

The goal of every marketing cooperative should be to endeavour to undertake the sale of its members' produce after grading, pooling and bulking, processing where necessary, in the most favourable consumers/terminal markets through the aid of higher level organisations so that the grower could get the best price for his produce without involving any risk to the society. For this purpose, the marketing societies, the cooperators and the State Governments should undertake a systematic campaign for acceptance of the practice by the grower.

It will be advantageous if only one or two varieties of the same crop are grown in a village or group of villages under similar conditions, as it would help in pooling of the produce, grading, as also their transport and bulk storage. The State Governments and also the cooperatives may make concerted efforts in this direction through distribution of uniform variety of seeds best suited to the area and through education and propaganda.

Even while selling the produce of their members as commission agents, the marketing societies should undertake grading and processing, where necessary, before sale so that the consequential benefits in price could be passed on to the producer.

It may be difficult to do so in respect of the produce of the smaller growers in view of the small lots involved. But it should be the endeavour of these societies to pursuade such smaller growers to agree to pooling of their produce, after sorting each lot into separate grades.

While sale after pooling and grading as agents of members, is an ideal arrangement for cooperative marketing societies, for a variety of reasons pooling of produce may not always be practicable under the prevailing market practices. If the marketing cooperatives are to serve the small producers, they should be prepared to make outright purchases, subject to certain limitations, so as to conform to the present normal practice adopted by the trade. Such outright purchases should, however, be considered as an un-aviodable necessity under certain circumstances and they should, therefore, be viewed as a transitional stage in the development of cooperative marketing.

The scheme of outright purchases by marketing cooperatives formulated by the Government of India may be continued duriug the Fourth Plan period and it may be extended to all good working marketing societies satisfying the prescribed conditions during the course of next two years. It is also necessary that the progress in implementing the scheme should be reviewed periodically, both at the State and National levels, in order to pool experience and also to remove any difficulties or deficiencies found in its working.

Looses arising out of the outright purchases made under the scheme should be met from the contributions to the price fluctuation fund by the Government and the society in the ratio of 2:1. In other words, two-thirds of the loss may be met from the price fluctuation fund of the society concerned contributed by the government, while the remaining one-third may be met from the price fluctuation fund created by the society and where it is not enough to meet it, from out of its other genera funds.

As far as practicable, outright purchases may be undertaken jointly by higher level organisations such as the district or apex marketing societies and the primary marketing societies. The funds, risk and profits may be shared jointly by these institutions on an agreed basis.

The apex marketing societies and the National Federation should endeavour to find avenues for the sale of the produce of their member societies at the most favourable terminal markets and arrange to sell the produce at such markets directly, undertaking intra or inter-State trade or export where necessary for the purpose.

It would be advantageous both to the consumer and the producer if an effective link is established between marketing and consumers organisations at various levels. If the measures already suggested by the National Coop. Dev. Corporation and the National Marketing Federation for forging an effective link between marketing and consumers cooperatives are implemented, considerable progress can be made in this regard. The Central and State Governments, which have invested considerable funds in the consumers cooperatives may, in the larger interests of both the consumers and the producers, pursuade these cooperatives to obtain their requirements, as far as possible, from the marketing cooperatives.

Every primary marketing society should arrange for grading of the produce before its marketing. To begin with, the marketing societies selected under the scheme of outright purchases, as also those selected for procurement of foodgrains, etc. under State procurement schemes may undertake such grading, as these societies will be in a position to pool the produce.

As grading is a necessary adjunct for the orderly marketing of agricultural produce, the State governments should provide adequate facilities for grading of farm-produce at all assembling points. This service may be made available to the cooperative marketing societies at a normal cost. Where a cooperative marketing society handles a sizable share of the arrivals of the produce in the market concerned, the special grading Staff may be provided to it by the Government.

The Directorate of Marketing and Inspection may arrange to fix broad regional grade specifications for all important agricultural commodities wherever they have not already been fixed.

In the absence of compulsory grading for internal consumption, the Central/State Governments should take suitable measures to popularise grading through government publicity media.

All marketing societies dealing in agricultural produce, which require to be processed, should take suitable measures to establish processing units as adjuncts to their marketing activity. Such units may be set up by the district or State marketing societies, where they are intended for the benefit of a group of marketing societies.

The primary marketing societies should take suitable measures to provide creature comforts like provision of accommondation to stay, facilities for drinking water, parking of carts etc. at the mandi centre, to their members coming to the mandi, in the same way as private traders do.

The primary marketing society situated at the mandi can play a key role in undertaking certain service functions for the benefit of the farmers in its area of operations. Thus, besides undertaking marketing of their agricultural produce, distribution of agricultural inputs and supply of consumer goods, a marketing cooperative can establish a small workshop for undertaking repairs and servicing of agricultural implements like pump sets, oil engines etc. It can employ a few mechanics who can go round the villages periodically for undertaking servicing and minor repairs on the spot. It can also own small tractors, oil engines or other modern agricultural implements for hiring to the farmers. It can, in collaboration with the Government departments concerned, set up an information centre, wherein latest methods of farming together with results of demonstrations with new fertilisers, seeds, implements can be exhibited. The State Governments can provide suitable grants to the marketing cooperatives for the purpose.

These functions should, however, be taken up only as a supplement to their normal economic functions which should not be neglected.

All good working marketing societies having a sizeable turnover may be enabled to purchase lorries of their own during the Fourth Plan period.

Public carrier permits may be given liberally to the marketing societies owning lorries, so that the lorries could be utilised during the idle periods and thus reduce the overhead costs. In order to enable the marketing societies to transport their produce to the consuming markets, inter-district and inter-State route permits may be given to such societies liberally wherever necessary.

As a general rule, marketing cooperatives, subject to availability of wagons, may be given higher priority in allotment of wagons for the movement of agricultural produce by railway for intra, inter-State and export trade.

Government departments and Government controlled or aided institutions may give positive preference to marketing cooperatives in obtaing their requirements of agricultural produce. Wherever the State marketing society or the national federation is in a position to undertake supplies on terms comparable to those prevailing in the markets, they should, as a general rule, be given contracts by the Government departments etc. The rates may be fixed through negotiations with refrence to prevailing wholesale market rates and previous contract rates.

The Agricultural Marketing Adviser to the Government of India may, in consultation with the Departments of Cooperation at the Centre and the States, undertake a detailed study of the provisions of the Agricultural Produce Markets Acts in various States vis-a-vis ihe working of the marketing cooperatives and suggest suitable measures to remove the impediments, if any, for the proper functioning of cooperatives in the Regulated Markets.

Marketing societies should be enabled to make outright purchases of agricultural produce from the producers either directly or through the village societies, both at the village level and in the market area, without being required to bring the produce to the market yard or to purchase it through open auctions, through the regulated markets, In such cases, the Regulated Market Committees should, however, be furnished with details of all such transactions by the marketing societies for purposes of their record. The marketing societies may also remit the necessary market fees to the Committee. Marketing societies should also be permitted to recover. from the sale proceeds of the produce of their members (including those of their affiliated agricultural credit societies), the production loans and other charges due to the societies from such members.

The measures suggested by the Conference of Apex Marketing Societies and Joint Registrars (Marketing) held at New Delhi in August, 1964 for promoting inter-State trade by cooperatives are endorsed for early implementation. The marketing societies, which undertake outright purchaser should, as far as possible, arrange to dispose of the produce so purchased directly in the terminal markets after pooling, grading, wherever necessary, with the help of the apex and national federations. In regards to foodgrains and some other commodities which are subject to certain restrictions on their movement, the State Governments should encourage and give positive preference to cooperatives for inter-State trade, wherever movement of such restricted commodities from State to State is allowed.

The National Federation should explore the foreign markets and undertake export of agricultural produce increasingly in conjunction with the apex marketing societies.

The National Federation may set up Export Cells in its office for various commodities for the purpose of collecting market intelligence regarding foreign markets, information regarding export policy and procedures, establishing contacts with the buyers in foreign markets, etc. and to draw out specific programmes for promotion of export. They should also render advise to the apex and other marketing societies on various problemsing relation to export of agricultural produce.

The National Federation may, wherever justified by the nature and quantum of its business, participate in Trade Fairs and Exhibitions held in foreign countries and also send trade delegations. Suitable financial assistance may be provided by the Government of India for the purpose, either from the Marketing Development Fund maintained by the Ministry of Commerce or otherwise.

Suitable facilities may be afforded to the cooperatives in obtaining shipping space at reasonable cost.

It will be of great help to the cooperatives if the Commercial Attaches and Trade Representatives attached to the Indian Embassies in foreign countries could provide to the National Federation periodically information about the requirements of agricultural commodities in those countries, the form in which they are required, the price trends and other market intelligence. They can also assist in arranging contacts between the cooperatives of this country and their counterparts and other trade interests in the foreign countries.

The State Trading Corporation may give preference to cooperatives in the matter of export. Agricultural commodities which are scarce and export of which is restricted, may be entrusted to cooperatives, wherever they have the requisite competence.

In the initial stages, cooperatives may be given suitable assistance by the Government to meet any unforeseen losses incurred by them on account of undertaking exports, particularly in respect of new commodities or perishable items like fruits.

Cooperatives should make attempts to sell their produce adopting modern packing methods according to consumer preferences. The National Federation should undertake necessary market research, if necessary, in collaboration with the consumer stores, for study of consumer preferences, so that the producers could be guided through their cooperatives to produce the qualities needed by the consumers. The National and Apex Federations may also open model show-cum-sales shops of their own in the terminal markets and in the larger cities for popularising their branded goods and also to continuously study the consumers changing preferences.

Study tours may be arranged by the State Governments to enable the office bearers of marketing societies to visit successful marketing societies in other areas and study at first hand the methods and practices which have led to such success.

Each State Government should draw up a phased programme to revitalise the inactive and marginal societies within a period of 3 to 5 years. The aim should be that such societies should, within the above period, be able to handle a reasonable minimum marketing and other business, which may be fixed by the State Governments individually for each society with reference to local conditions. If any society fails to achieve a reasonable minimum business within the above period, it should be liquidated.

Inefficiently run societies, which fail to improve within a reasonable time, should not be given any Government assistance in the form of share capital, loans, subsidies, nor should they be entrusted with other functions such as distribution of fertilisers, etc. In such areas, the apex marketing societies or the district society, where one exists, should make suitable alternative arrangements for the above purpose.

Periodical seminars may be held at district, State and National Levels by the apex and the National Federations.

Marketing cooperatives may be exempted from sales/purchase taxes in respect of their business as agents of their members in cases where primary growers of the produce concerned are exempted from such tax. Where the marketing societies dispose of their produce through the district or apex or other marketing societies, such transactions should be taxed only at a single point.

At present marketing cooperatives at all levels are exempted from Income-tax in respect of the income derived by them through: (i) sale of agricultural produce of their members, and (ii) distribution of agricultural implements, seeds, live-stock, or other articles intended for agriculture. They are, however, liable to the tax in respect of their other activities, if the profits attributable to such activities exceed Rs. 15,000. It was represented that the exemption may also be extended to the profits derived through purchase and supply of essential consumer goods to the farmers. As this is a general issue concerning both marketing and consumers cooperatives, which under the present policy undertake supply to both members and non-members, this suggestion may be examined by the Government of India.

Linking Of Cooperative Credit With Cooperative Marketing

The first pre-requisite for an effective link of cooperative credit with cooperative marketing is that adequate and timely credit should be provided to the farmer for agricultural production and partly for his consumption, so as to wean him away from the trader. It is, therefore, necessary to streamline the entire cooperative credit structure so as to ensure that the full needs of the agriculturists based on realistic estimates of their credit requirements (including their needs for harvesting operations and also for their consumption requirements during the loan periods when they usually resort to the money-lenders) are met in time.

Agreements should invariably be obtained by the agricultural credit societies from their members who are given credit, requiring them to sell their surplus produce through the marketing society and also authorising the latter to recover the dues to the credit society from the sale proceeds. Wherever this is not being done away now, it should be introduced immediately.

There should also be an agreement between the credit society and the marketing society defining their mutual responsibilities regarding collection of produce and its transport, recovery of loans, mode of remittance, etc.

Instead of obtaining lengthy agreements every time a loan is issued, it would be advantageous if a provision is made in the by-laws of the credit societies in this regard. A suitable provision in the Cooperative Societies Act can also be made for enforcement of such marketing contracts incorporated in the bye-laws.

The credit societies should be enabled to have a statutory charge on the crop for the crop loans issued through a suitable provision in the Cooperative Societies Act is recommended by the Committee on Cooperative Law (1957) wherever it is not existing now.

Besides creating a perpetual first charge on the crops of the borrower members in favour of the agricultural credit societies, it is desirable to make a suitable provision to compel the buyers of such crops to recover the dues to the cooperative society from the sale proceeds or other sums due to the farmer from such buyers and for a simplified procedure for enforcing such recoveries. Though enforcement of this provision may be difficult and often it may not be possible to establish the identity of ownership of crops and also to prove that the purchase was not made bonafide, nevertheless is considered that even a few cases of effective detection would have a salutary effect on both the farmer and the trader and would thus prevent any attempt to commit breach of the agreement with the society.

The views of the Bombay Crop Loan Evaluation Committee regarding the need for suitable arrangements for following the movement of produce and ensuring recovery of crop loans are endorsed. Each cooperative central bank should have, on its staff, a senior officer of the rank of an Assistant Secretary or Assistant Executive Officer to exclusively attend to the implementation of the scheme through the bank's supervisory staff, which should be strengthened, wherever necessary, for the purpose.

The suggestions communicated by the National Cooperative Development Corporation in its Circular No. 5-1/64.M, dated 28-2-1966 regarding responsibilities of central banks, grant of awards to managers of agricultural credit societies who are able to achieve maximum linkage of credit with marketing in their societies and reckoning of the extent of linkage for determing the audit classification of credit societies may be implemented early.

The primary marketing society should appoint the village cooperative societies as its agents for collection or purchase, as the case may be, of agricultural produce of the farmer members at the village level. The marketing society, in turn, should arrange for supply of scales, gunny bags, etc. and also for transport of the produce to its godowns. In case of outright purchases, it should also provide advances to the village society for making immediate payments to the growers. Suitable commission may be allowed by the marketing society to the village societies for undertaking the collection etc. of the produce.

It is desirable to have, among others, a suitable provision in the bye-laws of agricultural credit societies to disqualify the Directors and also their delegates to cooperative central banks, who do not sell their produce through the marketing society, and also to prescribe sale of agricultural produce through the marketing society for a minimum period as a qualification for future election of such Directors/delegates.

The coercive measures suggested above should be implemented gradually over a period according to a phased programme, preceded by intensive propaganda and education At the same time, the marketing cooperatives should streamline their methods of business so as to increase their efficiency which alone can ensure members loyalty.

The arrangements suggested in the Manual of Short-term and Medium-term loans for Agricultural Purposes (1966) issued by the Reserve Bank of India regarding recovery of the marketing societies of the dues of credit societies are endorsed. The exact percentage of the sale proceeds to be set aside for repayment of such dues may, however, be fixed separately for each society with reference to its stage of development and other local factors.

Linking should not be considered primarily as a tool for the recovery of loans of credit societies. Although this is important, it is equally important to place emphasis on the development of efficient marketing, processing and distribution system for the benefit of both the producer and the consumer. The development of cooperative credit and cooperative marketing are so interlinked with each other that neither of them can develop in isolation without the active support of the other. All efforts should, therefore, be made to ensure an effective co-ordination between the two.

Attempts to hasten the pace of progress of linking through forcible methods have, in a few areas, led to adoption of certain malpractices by a few marketing societies. The cooperative departments and the co-operators concerned would take all precautions against such malpractices. It is also necessary that the targets for effecting such linkage in relation to individual societies and supervisory officers should be fixed in a realistic manner so as to ensure that no undesirable practices are adopted merely to fulfil them.

The proposed Agricultural Credit Corporations, when established, should co-ordinate their working with the marketing societies in their areas of operations in the same way as agricultural credit societies would have done. They should make full use of the existing marketing societies both for grant of production loans and for their recovery through sale of produce.

Relationship Among Marketing Cooperatives At Various Levels And With Village Cooperatives

Primary marketing societies should, to the maximum extent possible, operate through the village cooperatives in the matter of collection, transport and outright purchase of agricultural produce and also for distribution of agricultural inputs and consumer articles at the village level.

As a general rule, marketing societies should not be permitted to grant production credit in areas where agricultural credit societies are working. But in areas : (i) where there are no agricultural credit societies or (ii) where they are not in a position to advance credit or (iii) where they are no chances of organising a viable credit society, e.g., in tribal areas or in plantation crop areas, marketing societies may be permitted to grant such credit.

But any such arrangement in respect of the areas referred to in items (i) and (ii) above should only be as an interim measure till such time as credit societies are formed in the area or they are in a position to take over the function.

The village credit societies should enhance the individual maximum credit limits fixed in their bye-laws so as to enable them to meet the production credit needs of larger farmers also.

Where the marketing societies are already advancing production credit, the change-over should be made gradually in a phased manner so as not to adversely affect the business of the society concerned. Such changes should be made only after making adequate arrangements to meet the credit needs of the members of these marketing societies through the local village cooperatives.

These and other marketing societies, which are required to grant production credit should be treated at par with primary agricultural credit societies for loan facilities from cooperative central banks for providing such credit.

Where, in a given area, a general purpose and a special commodity society functions with overlapping areas of operation, it should be clearly defined in their by-laws as to the commodities each will deal with, the type of other functions each will undertake, etc. so that there can be no duplication of functions nor competition between the two types of societies.

In areas where commodity marketing societies exist in addition to a general purpose marketing society, the latter should be entrusted with the distribution and supply functions in respect of all farmers in the area.

The district marketing societies, where they exist, should co-ordinate the activities of their affiliated primaries so as to avoid duplication of activity and unhealty competition among them. The district societies should not compete with the functions of their affiliated primary marketing societies, but only supplement them,

The district marketing societies should not directly undertake marketing distribution and supply activities at the village level in areas where primary marketing societies exist.

Cooperative wholesale stores are being organised almost in all important towns in every district and it may be cheaper to obtain consumer goods from such stores locally rather than through apex/district marketing societies. It may, however, therefore, be desirable and advantageous for the primary marketing societies to obtain their requirements through such consumer stores wherever they exist.

In the federal structure visualised for agricultural cooperative marketing, the apex marketing society at the State level has a crucial role to play. For effectively discharging its functions, it is necssary that all primary and district marketing societies in the State are affiliated to the apex marketing society.

The apex marketing societies should increasingly undertake marketing operations on behalf of their affiliated societies, particularly in the fields of inter-State trade and export of agricultural produce. The apex societies may also undertake, where necessary, other allied activities such as establishment of : (i) large scale processing units for the benefit of a number of primary marketing societies, (ii) manufacturing units for production of straight fertiliser mixtures, improved agricultural implements, etc., and (iii) provision of technical guidance for construction of godowns, etc. They can also arrange for agricultural extension functions.

The apex societies should function through their affiliated societies and a share of their profits should be passed on to the primaries on an agreed formula. They should set up expert cells for dissemination of market intelligence and rendering other services to the affiliated marketing societies and the village societies.

It should be ensured that the apex marketing society plays a promotional role and supplements the efforts of its affiliated societies. Under no circumstances should it compete with its affiliated societies in the field of marketing of agricultural produce or in the field of distribution and supply functions. In undertaking Inter-State trade, an apex marketing society should, as a rule, deal with its counterpart in other States or through the National Federation. The areas of business where there is the possibility of the interests of two or more apex societies coming into conflict should be left to the National Federation.

The National Federation should coordinate the activities of apex societies and render expert advice and guidance to them on problems relating to cooperative marketing in general and inter-State and export trade in particular. It should provide technical know-how to marketing and processing societies on international and Inter-State trade, market and price trends, commercial intelligence, business techniques, etc. It should have a separate cell with expert staff for each of the different functions. The National Federation should function through the State marketing societies only and it should not normally deal directly with the Central and primary marketing societies except in areas where the apex marketing society is not effectively functioning or with its consent for other practical reasons. It should keep away from the fields where the State societies may themselves can function effectively without competing with each other.

It would be desirable and advantageous if all exports/imports are undertaken by the National Federation instead of individually by each apex society, so as to effect economy in costs and also to ensure close co-ordination.

Where, however, any apex society is already undertaking export of certain commodities and has acquired specialisation in it, there is no need to disturb the existing arrangements so long as they are working satisfactorily and there is no competition in the same trade among more than one apex society, But where two or more apex societies desire to undertake export of the same commodity, it would be desirable to associate the National Federation to facilitate economy in costs and avoid unhealthy competition.

It is not desirable for marketing cooperatives to be entrusted with the management of regulated markets. There is, however, need to give adequate representation to marketing societies on the Regulated Market Committee.

Role Of Marketing Cooperatives In State Procurement Schemes And Their Relationship With The Food Corporation Of India

Wherever the State Government concerned is satisfied that the apex and other level marketing societies can make satisfactory arrangements to procure the requisite quantities of foodgrains or other agricultural produce, the Food Corporation of India and another State trading agencies should, as a general rule, give positive preference to them in regard to appointment as agents/sub-agents under their procurement/purchase programmes.

The apex marketing societies should act as the main agency for dealing with the Food Corporation of India or other State trading authorities. There should not ordinarily be any direct relationship between a primary marketing society and the State agency.

In the case of specialised crops like jute, cotton, etc. where more than one State may be involved and procurement may be on an All-India basis, the National Federation may be associated.

While the apex marketing society should be the agent of the Government or rather State agencies for procurement, the apex society, in turn, must invariably utilise the local marketing society concerned as its sub-agent. Only in cases where the primary marketing society is defunct or does not exist or is not in a position to undertake the work, should the apex or district society set up a branch of its own.

Marketing societies should obtain the produce, directly from the producers and they should on no account obtain it through traders. In areas where the primary producers are accustomed to dispose of their produce at the village level, marketing societies should make suitable arrangements at the village level for collection of the produce.

Marketing cooperatives should not associate themselves with enforcement functions under State procurement schemes. Within limits of Government policy, cooperatives should functions always in the best interests of their own members and it should be ensured that the growers do not have a feeling that their society is working against their interests. The Government should accept direct responsibility for every step where decisions enforceable by authority are involved. In such cases, the services of cooperatives should be utilised for collection, storage, processing, etc. as agents of Government.

As a general practice, the Food Corporation of India or other Government agency concerned should undertake the task of post-procurement storage, which is essentially in the nature of storage of buffer stocks. Where, however, cooperatives have storage accommodation to spare, they may undertake post-procurement storage on behalf of the Government agencies. In such cases, the Food Corporation of India or other State agencies should fo mally take over the stocks on payment of the costs to marketing societies and also allow suitable remuneration of the societies which act only as storage agents.

Wherever the system of maximum prices or compulsory levy on traders, etc. is enforced, the State Governments should see to it that all traders observe them strictly and cooperatives are not put to any disadvantage on that account. If for any reason, the State is not in a position to enforce these measures. the proper course would be to reimburse the cooperatives the loss suffered by them due to the State policy.

Food Corporation or other State agencies concerned should fix suitable margins for the cooperatives in consultation with the apex marketing society concerned and the State Registrar, after examining, on a realistic basis, the elements of various costs, including cost of storage, transport handling, etc. at various levels. If the cooperatives are required to pay interest on the advances for procurement operations, that element should also be taken into account. At the same time, cooperatives should observe the utmost economy and efficiency in their operations and reduce their over-head costs. In the case of paddy, marketing societies should undertake its processing either in their own rice mills or in private mills which may be hired for the purpose, as this would provide a higher margin to them and reduce transport and storage costs, while it would at the same time facilitate the work of the Food Corporation.

The "hundi system" suggested by the Reserve Bank of India to marketing societies in order to conserve and utilise the available funds to the maximum possible extent may be adopted by marketing societies. It should, however, be ensured that only nominal margins are charged by the State and Central cooperative banks for discounting the 'hundis' under this system.

Cooperative Storage

The measures suggested by the National Cooperative Development Corporation in regard to selection of societies for construction of godowns with a view to facilitating the optimum utilisation of godowns and avoiding overlapping, are endorsed.

The apex marketing societies can coordinate the work of construction of godowns by undertaking bulk purchase of construction material, arranging fabrication and manufacture of standard items and employing full-time engineering staff for supervising the construction.

With a view to encouraging the cooperative to complete the construction of godowns expeditiously and according to prescribed standards, the entire amount of Government assistance (including the subsidy portion) may be given as a loan in the first instance, with the condition that 25 per cent of the loan would be converted into a subsidy if the society completes the construction within the stipulated period and according to prescribed standards. Where, however, the construction is delayed for genuine reasons beyond the control of the society concerned, extension of time can be granted by the State Governments on merits of each case. In the alternative provision can be made for converting the subsidy already given into a loan subsequently, in cases where the godown is not completed in time and/or according to specifications.

It is desirable that smaller rural godowns with provision for future expansion may be constructed to begin with so as to reduce the costs and ensure fuller utilisation.

There is a large number of village societies, particularly in the backward and under-developed areas which for considerable time to come, will not be able to maintain a godown from their own resources. Yet these societies need godowns for their service functions. In such cases, instead of burdening the societies with loans, which they will not be able to repay, the State Governments themselves should construct rural godowns as part of their rural development programmes and hire them to the cooperatives on rent at subsidised rates. In due course, the ownership of these godowns may be transferred to the cooperatives on payment of their depreciated value.

With a view to ensuring that the godowns are properly utilised and also to take prompt remedial steps in cases of mis-utilisation or under-utilisation, it is necessary that a periodical assessment of utilisation of all godowns should be made in each State. The study should, among others, cover the extent of utilisation during the marketing season, the utilisation by members and others, the methods of storage, etc. As the present methods of conducting such surveys vary from

State to State and are not satisfactory, a study might be undertaken by the National Cooperative Development Corporation in consultation with the Directorate of Storage and Inspection and the Central Warehousing Corporation, if necessary, to devise suitable methods to assess the effective capacity of godowns of different sizes under different conditions for the guidance of the State Governments.

It is desirable that some working arrangements are made with the Central and State Warehousing Corporations, as the case may be, for periodical inspection of the cooperative godowns by the technical staff of the nearest warehouse and also for technical guidance such as proper methods of storage, fumigation, etc. It is also necessary that marketing cooperatives should depute their godown-personnel to the training course conducted by the Warehousing Corporations.

Each State Government should undertake a detailed study of the requirements of godowns of cooperative at the village level, marketing cooperatives at the mandi, district and State levels. Such studies should take into account the actual requirements of each cooperative for the next ten years with reference to its marketing programme, requirements for storage of agricultural inputs, consumer goods, etc. and should suggest suitable phased programmes for the purpose. The National Programme should be revised with reference to such studies, so that the construction of godowns could be planned and regulated according to needs on a realistic basis.

The following suggestions with regard to coordination between the marketing cooperatives and Warehousing Corporations in construction of godowns/warehouses are endorsed :

(i) It will be necessary to equip each marketing society with at least one godown of a reasonable capacity with reference to local needs. However, for any further expansion, the State Registrar of Cooperative Societies may take note of the availability of warehousing facilities at the place before sanctioning the additional godowns to a marketing society. In this connection, besides mere availability of warehousing, the Registrar should also take into account the reasonable costs of warehousing and other facilities vis-a-vis cooperative godowns ;

(ii) Before constructing a State/Central Warehouse, the Corporation may take note of the availability of cooperative storage facility ;

(iii) The State Registrar should suitably coordinate the programmes of cooperative godowns and warehouses.

Godowns of good working marketing societies, which have trained godown staff and employ scientific methods of storage, may be recognised as 'warehouse' under the Warehousing Act.

Role Of Cooperatives In The Distribution Of Agricultural Production Requisites

(a) **Fertilisers :** Wherever a cooperative has been rendering efficient service, no attempt should be made to establish a duplicate agency at the same place for distribution of chemical fertilisers. Before entrusting the distribution to a private agency, the State Government concerned should examine the necessity for the second agency with reference to the performance of the cooperatives in that area, including their potential with reference to the additional facilities of credit, higher margins, etc. now proposed and only in cases where it is felt that cooperatives cannot cope up with the work, should alternative arrangements be allowed. For this purpose, an evaluation of the existing arrangements for distribution of fertilisers through cooperatives may be undertaken in each district to determine the reasons for slow progress, etc. and take remedial steps to remove differences, if any.

The system of supply of fertilisers on consignment to marketing societies upto the level of the primary marketing society may be continued in all States particularly in under-developed States during the Fourth Plan period, by which time the use of various types of fertilisers, it is expected, may become popular in all areas.

Where, however, the State Governments are not in a position to supply fertilisers on 'consignment' basis, they should make suitable arrangements to enable marketing societies to obtain stocks of fertilisers on credit for 6 to 8 months as recommended by the Committee on Fertilisers.

Where a marketing society is required to obtain credit from the cooperative banks under the Reserve Bank scheme and it is not in a position to find the necessary funds for providing the 10 per cent margin, the State Government concerned may assist such societies by providing the margin themselves.

Marketing societies which receive stocks of fertilisers on consignment basis or on credit from governments should supply them to village societies on credit, which should be interest-free. Such supplies should be on outright sale basis and not on consignment basis. The cooperative central banks should undertake the responsibility, through their supervisory staff for the prompt repayment of such credit to the marketing societies from out of the production credit granted to the village society concerned or from the sale proceeds in respect of cash sales. It is expected that in normal conditions such credit should not exceed 3 to 4 months.

The Officers of the State Agriculture/Extension Departments and the supervisory staff of the State Cooperative Departments and central banks should assist the village cooperatives in assessing their requirements of fertilisers on a realistic basis with reference to anticipated demands, so as to avoid overstocking or shortages. At the same time every care should be taken to ensure that marketing societies do not attempt to dump their stocks on the village societies without reference to their demands in order to reduce their own stocks. Suitable provision should be made to return to the marketing society, unsold stock up to a certain percentage of the total supplies, particularly in areas where fertilisers are not popular and also in respect of new varieties, so that the village societies may not be put to hardship in carrying over the stocks for the next season with the attendant risks and losses.

The recommendations of the Fertiliser Distribution Enquiry Committee (1960) and the Committee on Fertilisers (1965) regarding the need to keep the costs of distribution as low as possible and to allow adequate remunerative commission to the agencies at the retail level are reiterated. The margins of cooperatives at various levels should be fixed with reference to the actual services rendered at each level.

It would be necessary for cooperatives to build up, within their set up, an organisation for aggressive salesmanship with a two-fold purpose of doing more business and retaining their present position as State preferred instruments for distribution of fertilisers. Such an organisation could also look after, besides fertilisers, promotion and distribution of other agricultural inputs such as improved seeds, insecticides, agricultural implements, maintaining close liaison with the Agriculture/Extension staff at various levels, to plan and promote sales and also for training the sales personnel of the cooperatives at various levels including the village societies. The main responsibility for propagation of the use of fertilisers, etc. should however, continue to vest with the State Agriculture/Extension departments and the cooperatives should only supplement their efforts in this regard.

As the propagation of increased use of fertilisers, improved seeds, etc. is mainly the resonsibility of the government and the cooperatives would be sharing that responsibility with the government, it would be proper for the government to subsidise the cost of technical staff that may be employed by the cooperatives for the purpose.

The Fertiliser Promotion Corporation proposed by the Committee on Fertilisers (1965), when it is formed, may utilise the services of the cooperatives in implementing its promotional programmes so as to avoid overlapping of functions.

(b) Improved Seeds

Since cooperatives have covered most of the villages, the village cooperatives may be increasingly utilised by the State Governments for the distribution of improved varieties of seeds to the farmers.

The measures suggested by the Conference of State Cooperation Ministers held in Bombay in November, 1965 on larger involvement of cooperatives in the distribution of improved seeds are endorsed.

The State Agriculture departments should continue to be primarily responsible for ensuring purity of seeds at all levels. Cooperatives should undertake distribution of only such seeds as are certified by the Agriculture department as pure stock and they should not undertake the responsibility for certification of seeds themselves. Even in cases where, for sake of convenience, cooperatives undertake seed testing and certification, the officers of the State Agriculture department should be closely associated.

As marketing and village cooperatives, in their present stage of development, connot undertake multiplication of seeds, particularly as they do not have the requisite men and material for the work, it is desirable and necessary that they should, for the present, confine themselves to distribution work only.

Primary marketing societies may undertake the distribution of seeds certified by the Agriculture department through the village societies.

It is not necessary to involve the apex or district marketing societies for distribution of seeds, as seeds are mostly multiplied locally. The primary marketing societies may obtain their requirements directly from the Agriculture department and be accountable to them, so that duplication of functions and overhead costs could be minimised. Although the primary marketing society may be accountable for all drawals of seeds in its area, it should arrange for lifting the stocks by village societies direct from the seed depots, etc. to avoid unnecessary transport and storage costs.

In respect of seeds imported from outside the State, e.g. from National Seeds Corporatlon or from state level seed farms etc., the apex society may be associated in procuring the seeds through the agency of the National Federation where necessary and for their distribution.

The State Agriculture departments should render all help and guidance to the marketing and village societies through their technical staff and village level workers in storage and distribution of the seeds.

The State Governments should supply the seeds to marketing societies on 'consignment basis' with suitable safeguards. They should also allow suitable margins to the cooperatives to cover their distribution costs.

The issue of seeds to village societies by the marketing societies may be made on outright sale basis, but on interest-free credit for a period of 3 months, with a provision for return of unsold stocks upto a percentage of the total quantity of seeds supplied, to provide for new or unsaleable varieties, etc. The central cooperative bank concerned should, through its supervisory staff, undertake the responsibility for prompt repayment of the credit to marketing societies.

(c) Pesticides/Insecticides

It will be advantageous to the farmers if the distribution of less poisonous varieties of pesticides/insecticides and also spraying/dusting equipment, which are commonly used, is entrusted to the village societies as part of their service functions. In regard to highly poisonous varieties, these may be handled by primary marketing societies having adequate facilities.

The working arrangements suggested by the late Ministry of Community Development and Cooperation in 1961 regarding distribution of pesticides/insecticides by cooperatives are adequate and may be adopted with suitable modifications to meet local needs.

Since insecticides, etc. have to be largely imported from outside the State or obtained from manufacturers in bulk, the apex marketing societies in each State should make the necessary arrangements and undertake the distribution through the primary marketing societies and village cooperatives. The services of the State Agriculture/Extension Staff should be made available to the marketing and village cooperative for preparing indents, arranging distribution and for other services needed by these societies for the work.

The State Governments may procure the pesticides, etc. and supply them to the apex marketing societies on 'consignment basis'. The apex societies in turn may supply them to primary marketing societies on 'consignment basis'. The issues to village societies may, however, be made on outright sale basis, but on interest-free credit for 3 months. The central cooperative bank concerned should accept the responsibility for the prompt recovery of such credit and payment to the marketing societies.

To the extent cooperatives perform the above functions, there will be considerable savings for the State governments both in men and money, as otherwise the State would have been required to meintain a large number of retail depots with heavy expenditure. Since cooperatives cannot be expected to incur any loss on this account, they may be allowed adequate margins for distribution of pesticides etc. so as to cover distribution costs. Village societies may be supplied with spraying/dusting equipment at subsidised rates for being hired to the smaller farmers at concessional rates. Subsidies, if any, available to growers from government should be routed through cooperatives instead of being given directly.

While cooperatives may not procure independently the same type/brand of pesticides, etc. supplied by the Agriculture department, they should, however, be free to procure other types of pesticides, etc. from the manufacturers directly with reference to local needs, wherever necessary.

(d) Agricultural Implements

The distribution of agricultural quota of iron and steel, G.I. Sheets, cement, etc. required for rural areas, should, as far as possible, be entrusted to the apex marketing societies, which should arrange to distribute them to the farmers through the primary marketing and village societies.

As the use of improved agricultural implements is not yet popular among the small farmers and the marketing cooperatives cannot afford to lock up their funds in stocking such implements the State governments may arrange to procure such implements from the public and private manufacturers and supply them to the apex socities should, in turn, supply the implements to primary marketing societies on 'consignment basis', while the supplies to village societies may be through outright sales on credit, with suitable provision for return of unsold stocks. The cooperative bank concerned should be responsible for the prompt recovery of such credit. The State Governments should allow suitable margins to the cooperatives to cover their distribution costs. The marketing societies should, in turn, allow a larger margin to the village cooperatives.

Distribution Of Essential Consumer Articles In Rural Areas Through Cooperatives

For various practical reasons, the village credit societies themselves should undertake supply of essential consumer goods to the farmers as part of their service functions.

The measures recommended by the Conference of State Cooperation Ministers (1956) for developing the supply of consumer articles in rural areas through cooperatives are endorsed.

In areas where wholesale cooperatives stores exist nearly, the village cooperatives may obtain their requirements of consumer goods direct from such consumer stores relieving the marketing society of the work.

Till such time as consumer stores are organised in the 'mandi' or nearby towns, the primary marketing societies may continue to undertake supply of essential consumer goods to the village cooperatives as envisaged in the present scheme under implementation. Where necessary, these marketing societies may also undertake supply of consumer goods to the population of the 'mandi' towns. As and when wholesale consumer stores are organised in the area and are in a position to supply the requirements of rural areas, the marketing society concerned should relinquish the function in favour of the former.

In areas where there are no chances of organisation of wholesale stores, the primary marketing societies may continue to undertake the function. After they achieve a sizeable turnover, such societies may be organised as wholesale stores for purposes of supply of essential consumer goods as well as for sanction of government assistance, etc., admissible to consumer stores.

In regards to method of procurement of consumer goods by primary marketing societies undertaking this activity, it will be desirable and advantageous for such societies to obtain their requirements of such goods directly from the wholesale stores if one exists in the area so that economies of bulk purchases could be realised. Further, under the recent scheme of government guarantee to consumer stores for their borrowings, the marketing societies will be eligible for a line of credit from wholesale stores as in the case of primary consumer stores.

For this purpose, the primary marketing societies may get themselves affiliated to the nearest wholesale consumer stores and provision should be made in the by-laws of the wholesale stores to provide for adequate representation to marketing societies on the board of their management.

Care should be taken to see that the consumers goods are not overstocked either by the primary marketing societies or by the village cooperatives. The village societies should assess their demand carefully with reference to local requirements and should not normally stock such articles in excess of 2 or 3 months' requirements.

Village cooperatives have to strengthen their capital base through revision of the existing ratio between the borrowings of their members and their share capital investment and also by collection of additional share capital at the rate of one share from each member. Till such time as the village societies are in a position to augment their resources, the State Governments may take suitable measures to strengthen the resources of village societies by contribution to their share capital and/or by assisting them to get liberal loans from financing banks.

To the extent primary marketing societies need additional finances for undertaking supply of consumer goods, they may be allowed clean and/or pledge/hypothecation credit by the financing banks within the overall limits recommended earlier.

Unless the village cooperative, which is the base for all cooperative activities, and on the efficiency of which the development of cooperative credit, marketing, processing and allied programmes mostly depends, is sufficiently strengthened and enabled to play its role fully, it will not be possible to develop cooperative marketing. Many of the village societies, as they exist now, will need considerable time to attain vaibility of their own and till then they will not be in a position. Alternative arrangements have, therefore, to be made to assist such societies to employ full-time Managers immediately to enable them to undertake the credit and other service functions efficiently.

General

The National Cooperative Development Corporation should be counterpart of the Agricultural Credit Department of the Reserve Bank of India in so far as development of cooperative marketing, processing, storage and supplies is concerned. For this purpose it is necessary that the National Cooperative Development Fund of the Corporation is sufficiently strengthened to enable it to play its role fully.

On the analogy of the procedure adopted in the case of the erstwhile National Cooperative Development and Warehousing Board, and the Agricultural Credit (Long Term Operations) Fund maintained by the Reserve Bank of India, the entire assistance to the Corporation for financing the schemes included in the Plan may be given by the Central Government by way of grants each year for the next five years. The position may be reviewed after a period of five years and further grants may be regulated with reference to needs. This procedure would enable the Corporation to build up a sizeable corpus of its own over a course of next 10 to 15 years, so that it would be in a position to promote schemes of its own without government aid by adopting a flexible policy to suit regional and individual needs.

If, however, for any administrative reason, it is not possible to adopt this procedure immediately, in the alternative, the Central Government may make adequate recurring grants each year to the National Cooperative Development Fund for the next ten years. These grants may be in addition to the loans and grants required to meet current needs, so that the Corporation, together with the repayments in respect of earlier loans from its own funds, can build up a sizeable corpus for financing cooperative marketing/processing and allied schemes.

A specific provision may be made in the National Cooperative Development Corporation Act to enable the Corporation to provide assistance directly to national and inter-State Cooperative Federation.

Suitable measures may be taken to include tobacco, lac, kuth and such other commodities not covered now, within the purview of the National Cooperative Development Corporation.

All large-scale cooperative processing units including

spinning and textile mills, fertiliser factories etc., may be included under the Central sector for purposes of grant of financial assistance to them.

There is need to avoid any encroachment of the public sector in fields reserved for cooperative sectors as far as possible. No dogmatic approach is, however, desirable and each case will have to be decided on merits. But before establishing a public sector unit in the field of agricultural marketing/processing and other allied activities, the possibilities of establishing such activity in the cooperative sector should first be explored by the Central and State Governments. Only when it is not possible to do so, or where inordinate delay is envisaged, should such units be set up in the public sector. Even when initially such units are set up in the public sector, it should be the endeavour of the Central/State Governments to turn opportunity. Such public sector units, where they exist, should maintain close coordination with the cooperatives credit and marketing institutions in matters relating to linking of credit with marketing, procurement of raw material, distribution of agricultural inputs, promotional measures, etc.

It would be more appropriate if the Registrar of Cooperative Societies, who deals with cooperative marketing, which is expected to cover the entire country, is placed incharge of both the Cooperation and Marketing Departments as already done in a few States, so as to ensure a close and effective coordination at all levels.

As the functions of Marketing and Cooperative Officers at the district level are quite different, the Marketing Department should, however, be kept as a separate and distinct wing under a senior officer with separate field staff at district and other lower levels, subject to the over-all control of the Registrar.

If, however, for any administrative reasons this is not immediately possible, the marketing functions should be separated from the Agriculture Department and constituted into a separate department, wherever the marketing functions are now with the Agricultural Department.

An effective co-ordination among the various departments concerned with agricultural marketing, viz., Marketing, Cooperative and Agricultural department is necessary for the orderly development of agricultural marketing in general and cooperative marketing in particular. Such coordination may be brought about either at the level of Agricultural Production Commissioners in the State or through forming a co-ordination committee consisting of the Heads of the above departments.

The State Marketing Officers, in cases where the Marketing Department is not under the Registrar or in other cases the Senior Officer Incharge of marketing wing may be nominated to the Board of Directors of the apex marketing society so as to guide the society. Similarly, the Marketing Officers at the district or taluk levels may be associated with the district/primary marketing societies.

In each State, an Officer of the status to Joint Registrar of Cooperative Societies should be employed exclusively for the work relating to cooperative marketing and processing with adequate supporting staff. As recommended by the Municipal Committee on Cooperative Administration, at the district level, each Assistant Registrar should be given an officer of the rank next below the Assistant Registrar to attend to the above work. There should also be sufficient field staff at taluk or other levels as per the norms suggested by the above Committee till such time as the space societies are in a position to provide effective supervision and guidance to the primary societies.

In States, where considerable progress has taken place in regard to large-scale cooperative processing, such as cooperative sugar factories, spinning mills, etc., a separate senior officer should be employed for such societies in addition to the Joint Registrar (Marketing).

The State Governments may review the existing arrangements in this regard and take early measures to strengthen the staff.

State Governments should ensure that the audit of all marketing societies is completed and audit reports issued within six months from the close of the cooperative year.

Institutions like masketing societies, which undertake a variety of business activities involving risks, concurrent audit is essential in the interests of the members and the office bearers themselves, so as to enable them to rectify mistakes, if any, promptly. The system of employing concurrent auditors for a group of societies situated nearby adopted in Madras and Andhra Pradesh States may be usefully adopted by other States in respect of primary marketing societies which do not have full work for an auditor exclusively. Other primary marketing societies with larger turn over and district/apex marketing societies may employ one or more full-time concurrent auditors ot the Cooperative (Audit) Department exclusively. Similarly the National Federation should arrange for such concurrent audit.

Forms used for preparation of audit reports in respect of marketing societies are in most cases obsolete, and requires revision to suit the present needs. The Union Department of Cooperation/National Cooperative Development Corporation may suggest model forms for audit of marketing/processing cooperatives at various levels or adoption by State Governments with such modifications as may be needed to suit local needs.

Apart from the need for timely audit, there should be other built-in-methods by which the working of the marketing societies could be constantly supervised and guided by higher level organizations. The apex marketing societies should take suitable measures to ensure proper supervision and guidance over the primary marketing societies.

The National Cooperative Development Corporation, which is now incharge of the work relating to cooperative marketing and processing at the national level, should set up a separate Research and Development Cell in its office for undertaking: (i) continuous research in the methods and trends of cooperative marketing/processing and other agricultural marketing practices, as well as on specific problems relating to them arising from time to time, (ii) evaluation of the working of marketing and processing cooperatives at various levels by obtaining periodical statements and thorough visits by the officers of the Corporation to select societies, and (iii) to plan and promote programmes for the development of cooperative marketing/processing by undertaking area-wise surveys, etc. This apart, the Corporation should undertake through its officers, a systematic inspection of the marketing/processing societies assisted by it at various levels in the same way as the Reserve Bank of India undertakes in respect of cooperative banks and other institutions. Such inspections should be so designed as to be both constructive and in broad details complementary to and not in duplication of the inspections conducted by the State Cooperative Departments.

The Marketing Research Cell of the Directorate of Marketing and Inspection may be suitably strengthened to undertake: (i) maintenance of up-to-date information on important key indicators such as marketable surplus, price levels and trends, etc., and their analysis, (ii) study of marketing costs, margins, grades, etc. on a continuing basis, and (iii) study of the impact of various improvement programmes on the development of agricultural marketing. It is desirable to establish similar research cells in the State Marketing Departments for collection and analysis of the above data on a continuing basis at the State level.

The National Cooperative Development Corporation may undertake periodical publication of the working of successful marketing/processing societies indicating, in particular, the methods adopted leading to their success and circulate them to all marketing/processing societies.

Suitable measures may be taken by the State Governments to furnish the Annual Statistical Statements, complete in all respects, to the Reserve Bank of India or other compiling agencies within three months after the close of the cooperative year, so that the present delays in the publication of the Statements could be minimised. For this purpose, it is necessary to streamline and strengthen the administrative arrangements for collection, tabulation, etc. of the data, both at this district and State levels. The State Governments should review the Present arrangements in this regard and take suitable measures.

Details of working of all individual apex district and primary marketing societies as well as processing societies may be compiled and published by the National Cooperative Development Corporation annually as in the case of credit institutions now included in the statistical statements of the Reserve Bank of India, so that the working of individual societies could be analysed.

The data now furnished in the Statistical Statements in respect of marketing/processing cooperatives is not adequate in many respects. The National Cooperative Development Corporation and the Union Department of Cooperation may, in consultation with the Reserve Bank of India, take suitable steps to review the existing tables relating to cooperative marketing and processing societies so as to make them more informative and useful.

There is a possibility of inaccuracies and also duplication in furnishing the statistics at the primary levels. The State Governments may ensure that proper checks are instituted through adequate supervisory staff at the district and State levels to avoid any errors. Test cheking of the data furnished in the annual statements at the primary level with the final audit report of the year concerned may also be undertaken by the cooperative auditors during their audit, and suitable instructions be issued to avoid mistakes detected during such checking atleast in subsequent years. It would be useful if small pamphlets giving instructions in simple language for filling each columns, is distributed to all reporting societies and also to the bank and departmental supervisory staff at all levels for guidance in filling up the statements.

STUDY TEAM ON IMPORT AND EXPORT TRADE CONTROL ORGANISATION, 1964—REPORT

New Delhi, Ministry of Commerce, 1965. 112p. (Part I)

Chairman : Harish Chandra Mathur.

Members : Shri P. Sabanayagam; Shri N. K. Mukharji; Shri N. J. Kamath; Shri R. K. Raisinghani; Shri S. S. Kumar; Shri C. S. Khrishna Moorthi; Shri A. T. Bambawale; Shri S. P. Mukherji.

Secretary : Shri Sushil Kumar.

APPOINTMENT

The Study Team on Import aud Export Trade Control Organisation was appointed by the Government of India in the Ministry of Commerce to review the Working of the Import and Export Trade Control Organisation and to recommend measures for improvement, vide their letter No. O. & M. 12(9) 64-dated August 7, 1964 as a follow-up action on the recommendations made by the Santhanam Committee.

TERMS OF REFERENCE

The Team will examine the organisation, structure, methods of work and procedures of the office of the Chief Controller of Imports and Exports, particularly with a view to locating the points at which delays occur, where bottlenecks exist and where administrative failures are possible and would suggest measures for improvements so that opportunities for corruption are eliminated.

CONTENTS

Introductory; General Procedure and Policy in Licensing; Actual Users—Small Scale Industries, Scheduled Industries borne on the books of the Director-General of Technical Development, Scheduled Industries not borne on the books of the Director-General of Technical Development and Non-scheduled industries other than Small Scale ; Other Procedural matters regarding Actual Users Licences Issued late; Established importers; Summary of Conclusions and Recommendations in Part I; Appendices from I to VII; Ministry of Commerce Resolution, dated 31st March, 1965 containing decisions of Government on the recommendations of the Study Team.

RECOMMENDATIONS

Introductory

The question whether the existing method by which the objectives of import control are achieved is the best available method, and other questions like nationalisation of import business, creation of an autonomous organisation for the issue of licences, auctioning of licences, participation of the trade in the distribution of licences, etc., need a comprehensive examination; and perhaps a survey of the experience of other countries with similar problems may be necessary. An Expert Committee should, therefore, be appointed to go into these questions at the time of extension of the present term of the Imports and Exports Control Act which expires in 1966.

General Procedure and Policy in Licensing: Several provisions in the confidential General Licensing Instructions (GLIs) are such as should be known to the trade. As a guiding principle, nothing of interest or relevance to the trade should be kept back for publication in the Red Book or Hand Book and that G.L.I.s should communicate foreign exchange ceilings and the formulae, if any, in calculating the entitlement of various categories of importers as also such departmental instructions for the guidance of the licencing authorities with which the trade and applicants are not normally concerned.

Actual Users—Section I

Small Scale Industries : In numbers and in spatial dispersal, small scale industry presents practical problems and as such the task of applying control mechanism in this sector is inherently difficult and calls for more than ordinary administrative skills and courage. The tackling of a vast number of applicants through various levels in the State and at the Centre, the concomitant work-load, duplication of effort, multiple scrutiny, etc., involved are time consuming and a fertile ground for malpractices. As such, the present complicated procedure requires drastic simplification even if that involves unusual degrees of administrative and financial decentralisation.

While it is necessary to obtain the recommendation of the sponsoring authority on the licence application, this should be secured in a single line processing of the import application itself. The applications for licences should, therefore, be made to the licensing authority through the sponsoring authority concerned in a simplified form of application as suggested vide Annexure to Appendix III. This would eliminate the stage of applying for essentiality certificate altogether.

The Directors of Industries and other sponsoring authorities in the case of small-scale industries should be placed at par with the sponsoring authorities in the large-scale sector (e.g., D.G.T.D.); and they should not only certify essentiality but also recommend actual allocation on a unitwise basis. For this purpose, they should be informed of the ceiling within which they can then fit-in their unit wise allocation. This would make the recommendations of the sponsoring authorities more effective and would incidentally make them more responsible and participative in the import control so far as it affects the small-scale sector.

The right authority to evolve a basis and to make actual State-wise allocations each year is the Development Commissioner, Small-Scale Industries. Without wishing to fetter his discretion unduly, it is considered that, for an equitable basis the distribution of ceiling to the States will ultimately have to be based on the installed capacity to be assessed on a uniform basis on an All-India norm by the D.C.(SSI) and the Directors of Industries jointly. So long as this is not done, an ad hoc formula is neceseary which should take into account the need to maintain the tempo of industrial production already attained in different States and also the special development needs of backward.

In the first year, the allocation of available foreign exchange should be made in proportion to the average of licences issued to each State for the last three-yearly licensing periods by taking say Rs. 12 crores as the 'crore' allocation, i.e., if the allocation in 1965-66 is Rs. 12 crores or less, the State-wise allocation may be made on the basis of the ratio arrived at by taking 3 years average. If the allocation is more than Rs. 12 crores, the first Rs. 12 crores should be allocated in the ratio mentioned above. Out of the balance, 50 per cent should be allocated to different States in the same ratio to meet the requirements of normal growth. The remaining 50 per cent should be allocated keeping in view the special development needs of the various States. The allocation for the subsequent years, i.e., for 1966-67 onwards should be according to the same formula except that instead of Rs. 12 crores, the allocation of the preceeding year should be taken as the 'core' figure. The inter-State ratio will be based on the preceding year's State-wise allocation.

Before the commencement of each licensing period, the D.C.(SSI) may issue general instructions for the guidance of Directors of Industries about restrictions on new units in crowded sectors, priority attention to the needs of selected industries of national importance and so on. This extent of centralisation would be justifiable from an All-India angle.

The ceiling for imports from rupee area may also be distributed to the States along with the free foreign exchange ceiling. Inter-State ratio for rupee ceiling may be based on the actual licensing done in 1964-65.

All the Units in the small-scale sector should be allowed the benefit of annual licensing. This will mean making an annual allocation to the SSI sector, thus making an advance allocation for the second-half year. The allocation made to SSI sector being small in comparison to the total commercial quota, the reduction in the share of the small-scale units in the second half-year, if any is not likely to create such a burden for the large-scale sector as to cause any serious distortion in the economy as a whole. On the other hand, if there is half-yearly endorsement on annual licences, it will result in a fair amount of work continuing to be done in the second half-year both for the D.I.'s and for the CCI&E. However, in order to safeguard against remittances exceeding the availability, it may be laid down that even though a party can enter into commitment for the full amount of the licence even during the first half-year, remittances will have to be spaced in such a way as to have 50 per cent falling in the first half and remaining in the second half of the period. This will, of course, be subject to the existing concession to the licences valued upto Rs. 5,000 remaining intact.

The ceiling for Small-Scale Industries may be allocated in advance in the beginning of April on the basis of the best available data at that time.

So far as the small scale sector is concerned, the import policy may provide only two categories of items namely, 'banned' and 'open' and the restricted list may be altogether done away with. The need for a restricted list will, of course, continue for the scheduled sector and adjustments will have to be made in that sector where import is required to supplement indigenous production.

The new procedure for processing and disposal of applications for licences should be clearly spelt out and the role of the D.C., S.S.I., D.I.'s and Port Licensing Authorities defined in specific terms. The outline of the new procedure which will be found in Appendix III should be adopted subject to such amplification and spelling out as is deemed necessary at the stage of drafting fresh instructions.

A time table should be prescribed for various individual stages of processing of applications for lieences so as to finish the licensing work in S.S.I. sector latest by the 30th September. Such a time-table is feasible and should be accepted and a continuous watch should be kept to see that there is punctual adherence to it by all concerned.

The D.C., S.S.I. and the Directors of Industries should be called upon to make an immediate review of their arrangements for handling the work falling to their share in the new scheme of things so as to be prepared fully and in time.

The same procedure should also apply in the case of small-scale units sponsored by the State Drugs Controllers, the Textile Commissioner, the Directors of Handloom and the State Directors of Fisheries.

In order to give necessary training to the Staff of the Directorates of Industries in the States in the new procedure for processing of Import applications, short-term "familiarisation" courses should be held where the officers of the level of Assistant, Deputy and Joint Directors of Industries and various licensing authorities from the port offices should be brought together and the whole scheme and its implications explained. Also, selected Assistant Controllers from the regional port offices may be sent on one year's deputation to the State Directorates to guide the sponsoring work. There should also be frequent meetings between the sponsoring authorities and the licensing authorities during the first year of implementation of the new procedure CCI&E should initiate an urgent action programme for all these points in consultation with the D.C.(SSI) where necessary.

The D.C. (SSI) should be closely associated at the stage of processing this report as he has to play a crucial role in the new procedure for licensing.

CCI & E should take urgent steps to give publicity to the new procedure by explaining it in simple language to the trade.

The "pack value" system may be extended to embrace more and more industries during each licensing period. However, a regular review of both the pack value and the items to be imported should be undertaken at the commencement of each period in the light of the indigenous angle and other relevant factors.

The work relating to the grant of licences to SSI units for import from rupee payment area should be decentralised.

The State Directors of Industries should be authorised to pool together the small requirements of raw materials/components of actual users (say Rs. 250 in each case) for import and distribution through the State sponsored Corporations.

Section II

Scheduled Industries Borne on the Books of the DGTD: In future all import applications may be invited in duplicate only, of which a copy may be retained in the D.G.T.D. and the original forwarded to CCI & E with the recommendation.

The form of application to be adopted for scheduled industries should be as in Appendix VI.

The applicant may be asked to send an extra copy of the list of goods applied for, which, with such amendments as the D.G.T.D. may make, will be returned to the applicant.

An industrial undertaking should, for each industry handled by it, apply only once covering its requirements of raw materials, components as also spare parts but excluding non-ferrous and ferrous metals for which separate applications have to be kept. There should not be a separate application for spare parts.

The CCI & E's organisation may make suitable adjustment in the filing number and indexing system to mesh with the processing of import applications on the code numbers allotted by the D.G.T.D. to scheduled units.

A delayed application received from the D.G.T.D. with his recommendation import items will be handled by the CCI & E's office on the presumption that the delay has been condoned by the D.G.T.D. unless the contrary is indicated.

By 1st of August, the unit-wise allocation should be finalised and by 31st August all recommendations forwarded to CCI & E's office by the D.G.T.D. The D.G.T.D. should endeavour to maintain an even flow of recommendations. The CCI & E should then be able to issue licences by 30th of September.

The necessity of requiring the party to get a non-availability certificate can be entirely done away with by allowing a certain percentage of the assessed requirement of an item out-right and considering further import only when the D.G.T.D. is satisfied that the demand cannot be met from indigenous sources. There shouid be only 3 lists, namely, (a) banned items: (b) open items and (c) restricted items which are to be allowed to a certain percentage of balanced requirement] without reference to other Directorates of D.G.T.D. The lists once finalised in the beginning of the licensing period should be adhered to for that period. The list of indigenous manufacturers should be published by the D.G.T.D. in consultation with the D.C. (SSI) simultaneously with Red Book.

While the applicants should be required to indicate itemised quantities, the D.G.T.D. should make recommendations for licences without indicating itemised quantities except in case of speculative and indegenously available items. The list of goods should invariably be appended with recommendations sent to the CCI & E. The flexibility upto 25 per cent should be allowed for importing those items for which quantitative limits have been indicated, subject to the overall value of the licence. The licensee should also be allowed to utilise upto 25 per cent of the value of the licence for 'permissible' spare parts and small tools not indicated in the licence. Within this 25 per cent, upto 5 per cent, or Rs. 2,500 whichever is less, may be allowed to be utilised for the import of even the spares which are not otherwise permissible but which are not banned and are required for servicing, maintenance or replacement of the plant installed in the licence-holder's factory.

The recommendation of the Technical Directorate need not be signed by two technical officers. Only one signature will do. A copy of the recommendations containing the reasons for rejecting or reducing the amount of any item, should be sent to the applicant. The form of 'check list' should be finalised between the D.G.T.D. and CCI & E's organisation to avoid back references.

Attested lists of goods should be sent by D.G.T.D. in all cases along with the recommendation. Clean copies of the list should be attested by the CCI & E without requiring the party to come through the D.G.T.D. for attestation.

The CCI & E should be able to issue licences within a period of one month of the receipt of recommendation. A copy of the licence may be sent to the D.G.T.D. only where the advise has not been observed in its entirety.

A time-table should be observed in such a manner that all the applications are received by the D.G.T.D. by 15th May, and all licensing is completed by 30th September. If the foreign exchange allocations can be made earlier than 15th June, the time-table will be advanced accordingly.

As a logical corollary to the decision of the Government on the recommendation of Swaminathan Committee, the licensees may be allowed to place orders and commit against 75 per cent of the face value of the licence even in the first half of the year in advance of the second half year's allocation subject to the condition that, out of the 75 per cent committed, not more than 50 per cent of the total licence value shall be paid in the first half.

The existing facility of utilisation in one lot of licences valued upto Rs. 5,000 may continue.

In order to avoid the irksome procedure forgetting licences endorsed for the second half-year and considering the small percentage of foreign exchange involved in possible variation, the holders of licences valued upto Rs. 15,000 may be allowed the concession of committing the entire amount at any time during the validity period subject to the condition that not more than 50 per cent of the value is paid during the first half of that period. The load of additional foreign exchange cut, if any, borne by the licensees above Rs. 15,000 can be taken into account by augmenting their allocation in a suitable manner during next licensing period.

Section III

Scheduled Industries not Borne on the Books of the D.G.T.D. and Non-scheduled Industries other than Small Scale : The import applications should be routed through the sponsoring authority concerned. The procedure for sponsoring and processing of the applications should be the same as in the case of D.G.T.D.'s units.

The licences may be issued only once a year on annual basis by doubling the amount of half-yearly ceiling subject to the same restrictions and relaxation about utilisation, commitment or payment as suggested in the case of D.G.T.D.'s units.

The Textile Commissioner should place a certain foreign exchange ceiling at the disposal of Director of Industries, Punjab to be utilised for import of spares by woollen hosiery manufacturers at Ludhiana. Such an arrangement should also be made for similar cases in other areas.

Section IV

Other Procedural Matters Regarding Actual Users : Necessary changes should be made in the accounting procedure so that the parties to whom licences are issued after the close of the ceiling for no fault on their part, should not be made to suffer in their entitlement. Also in such cases, where the delay in sending the recommendation to the licensing authority is on the part of the sponsoring authority, the value of licence issued should be treated as a first charge on the monetary ceiling to be allocated to the sponsoring authority concerned for the next period.

The period of 30 days which is allowed to the applicants to make up deficiencies in their applications should count from the date on which the applicant is informed of the deficiencies and not from the last date for submission of applications.

The first day of the licensing period, i.e., 1st April should be taken as the date on which stocks and expected arrivals should be taken into account by the sponsoring authorities for calculation of entitlements of actual users, instead of taking, for such purposes, the date of submission of the application itself.

The work relating to the issue of licences for machine tools which is at present being done by the Development Officer (Tools) should be transferred to the CCI & E.

The details of items the import of which is canalised through a recognised agency and the procedure for allotment/distribution of the imported goods should be published in the Red Book.

Special arrangements should be made like earmarking separate staff for quick disposal of applications for amendment or revalidation of licences and it should not take more than two days to dispose of an application for amendment and 7 days to finalise a request for revalidation. Also 'counter system' should be introduced in all licensing offices for entertaining requests for minor amendment or revalidation, etc., which do not require detailed examination. The applications should be received at the counter against a proper receipt and the applicant should be given fixed date for collecting back the licence on production of receipt.

Mangalore District of Mysore State and Coimbatore District of Madras State should be brought under the territorial jurisdiction of the Controller of Imports and Exports, Bangalore, and Joint Chief Controller of Imports and Exports, Madras, respectively.

Established Importers: An application for quota certificate should not take more than 21 days in disposal.

Except in doubtful cases, the documents of imports should be verified after the issue of Quota Certificate and such verification should not take more than a month.

The application for licence should include a column requiring the applicant to furnish a declaration regarding the selection of common basic year by different branches of the applicant firm.

Licences valued upto Rs. 5,000 should be issued on annual basis and allowed for utilisation in one lot without any endorsement or cut in the second half-year.

Licences valued over Rs. 5,000 should also be issued on annual basis without the necessity of any endorsement or cut during the second half-year but such licences should be subject to the condition that remmittances of foreign exchange in respect of second half of the value of the licence will be permitted by the Reserve Bank only after the commencement of the second half of the licensing period.

Appendix II

Outline of the New Procedure for Disposal of Applications for Import of Raw Materials/Components received from S.S.I. Units: The form of application for the import of raw materials, components and spares, to be used by the small scale units will be as annexed thereto. This is an application-cum-recommendation form. There will be no separate form of application for submission to the sponsoring authority for obtaining his recommendation for licence. The form of application which has been suggested has three parts. Part I of the form is for use in the licensing office, Part II is for use by the sponsoring authority and Part III which is to filled in by the sponsoring authority will contain his recommendation for licence. Part III of the application form will be in duplicate having perforated arrangement. If any sponsoring authority finds any column in Part II of the application form unnecessary and wishes to delete it or if the sponsoring authority wishes to add any additional column to Part II of the form, he may do so.

The actual user will submit to the sponsoring authority concerned the application for licence in duplicate along with Treasury Challan showing the payment of application fee. The sponsoring authority will issue an acknowledgement-cum-deficiency letter to the applicant within a period of 7 days from the receipt of the application, acknowledging the application and pointing out any deficiencies therein. For the purpose of pointing out deficiencies, the sponsoring authority will scrutinise the information given in Part II of the application and also the I.V.C. Number and the Treasury Challan furnished by the applicant. In regard to the I.V.C./number, the sponsoring authority will only see whether the number quoted by the applicant in his application is valid for the licensing period concerned or not. As regards the Treasury Challan, the sponsoring authority will check up whether the applicant has paid the correct amount which he is required to pay on the value applied for. The applicant will be given a specified time to make up the deficiencies.

The recommendations for licences will be made by the sponsoring authority in terms of the import policy in force and the general directions given by the Development Commissioner Small-Scale Industries (DC, SSI), as may be required from time to time and within the foreign exchange ceiling allocated to each State. The sponsoring authority will prepare four copies of his recommendations for licence in each case in Part III of the application. Of these four copies, one copy will be sent by him to the applicant, one will be retained in his own office and two copies will be sent to the licensing authority along with one copy of the application and the Treasury Challan furnished by the party.

On receipt of the application the sponsoring authority will check up entries in Part I of the application form including I.V.C. Number and the Treasury Challan. If any deficiency is found therein, it will be communicated by the licensing authority to the applicant within a period of 7 days from the date of the application giving the applicant a specified time to make up the deficiencies. In case of applications having no deficiencies the import licence or the rejection letter, as the case may be, will be issued to the applicants within a period of 15 days from the date of receipt of the application forms by the sponsoring authority. In case of incomplete applications, the period of 15 days will count from the date the deficiencies are made good by the applicant. After examining the application on the check points, the licensing authority, while sending to the applicant a licence or a rejection letter, as the case may be, will simultaneously send back to the sponsoring authority one copy of his recommendation indicating therein the item deleted and the consequential reduction in value, if any. This will enable the sponsoring authority to correct the account of progressive utilisation of ceiling maintained by him and will also enable him to note the items which have been deleted by the licensing authority.

The sponsoring authority will also send a weekly statement to the licensing authority showing the progressive utilisation of the ceiling placed at the disposal of the sponsoring authority. This will serve as a double check for the licensing authority to ensure that licences are not issued in excess of the ceiling allocated to a particular State. If any licence is recommended by the sponsoring authority in excess of the ceiling at his disposal, the licensing authority will reject the application under intimation to the sponsoring authority concerned.

The sponsoring authorities will also introduce security seals to be affixed on their recommendations while sending the same to the licensing authorities in order to avoid any forged or fabricated recommendations being made.

New Units : In order to ensure rational growth and expansion of capacity in the small scale sector in the country the DC (SSI) will, at the commencement of each licensing period, that is, on 1st, April, prepare for issue in the Red Book a list of industries for which new capacity is not to be encouraged. This list which may be known as "Restricted Industries List", hereinafter referred to as 'R.I.L.' will be circulated to the Directors of Industries in the States and to the licensing authortties. This list will remain in operation for one licensing year. If a Director of Industries receives an application from a new unit for the import of materials required in the manufacture of an end-product included in the 'R.I.L.' he will normally reject the application. But, if he is convinced of its necessity, he will forward the application to the DC (SSI) with his comments and such application will be recommended for the grant of a licence only after clearance to this effect has been granted by the DC (SSI). A suitable column for indicating whethsr the industry falls in the 'R.I.L.' and, if so, whether the Director of Industries has obtained the necessary clearance from the DC (SSI) before recommending the licence, has been provided in the proposed form of application-cum-recommendation. Wherever the DC (SSI) gives clearance for the grant of a licence, he will send his communication in this regard to the Director of Industries, in duplicate. The Director of Industries will enclose one such copy of the DC (SSI's) communication with the application while forwarding his recommendation to the licensing authority. The licensing authority will issue a licence to such new units only after the DC (SSI) has given the necessary clearance; otherwise the recommendation of the Directors of Industries will not be accepted. The DC (SSI) will also intimate to all other Directors of Industries the fact of clearance of a unit falling in the 'R.I.L.'. indicating the reasons for which such clearance has been given.

In the case of new units other than those referred above and in the case of all existing units, it will be open to the Director of Industries to recommend a licence for any value for permissible items within the ceiling allocated to him, subject to such general directions as may be given by the DC (SSI), and the policy laid down in the Red Book. The DC (SSI). while distributing the ceiling may make due provision for the development and growth of industries of a priority nature like defence-oriented industries, ancillaries, etc., which may have to be supported under any policy of national importance. The licensing authority will issue a licence on the basis of the recommendations of the Director of Industries. Although it will be within the discretion of the Director of Industries to recommend a licence to such units for permissible items for any value within his ceilings, the Directors of Industries will be well advised to adhere, as far as possible, to the principle whereby the existing industries may not be recommended licences for permissible items for values less than those permitted to them in the immediately preceding licensing period, provided the foreign exchange allocation remains unchanged and the production of the unit has not fallen or the indigenous content of the finished product has not gone up or phased programme of indigenous content admits of less foreign exchange or there is any other reason to the contrary.

In case of the small scale industries, the import policy will provide only two catagories of items, one of banned items and the other permissible. For the latter, no non-availability certificate or indigenous clearance will be necessary. In the case of items which are banned but the Director of Industries desires to recommend, he will refer such cases for advice to the DC (SSI) before recommending the licence. In the office of the DC (SSI), such reference from the Director of Industries will be placed before a Committee consisting of the representatives of the D.G.T.D. and the DC (SSI). The minutes of the meetings of the Committee will be circulated to the Directors of Industries and the licensing authorities. The Directors of Industries will recommend the licences on the basis of recommendations made by the said Committee which may be known as the SSI Committee. The SSI Committee functioning at present in the office the CCI&E will cease to function. Though with the abolition of the restricted items of import, reference to D.G.T.D. and other technical authorities will be minimised, to clear even those few cases of banned items. where the Directors make a recommendation, it may be necessary for the Committee to meet more frequently from 15th May to 31st July. The meetings may be arranged in such a manner as to enable the Directors of Industries by turn to get all their cases disposed of in one or two meetings. The Directors of Industries themselves may in such a case be able to attend the meetings also. If any item is licensable in consultation with any other technical authority, the Director of Industries will consult such authority before recommending the licence and an endorsement to this effect will be made in the recommendations of the Director of Industries. If, for any reason, the Director of Industries recommends the licence for any of such items without obtaining the necessary clearance from the SSI Committee or the technical authority concerned, the licensing authority will not issue the licence for such items under intimation to the Director of Industries.

In the cass of items which are permissible for a specified end-product only, Director of Industries will ensure that the licences recommended are for items permissible for the specified end-products; otherwise the licensing authority will disallow the item under intimation to the Director of Industries.

In the case of items for which the requirements are to be met by the actual users through an approved agency such as the S.T.C., the Director of Industries will recommend a licence only after the said agency is not in a position to supply the goods in a reasonable period. A certificnte to this effect will also be given by tye Director of Industries in the proposed form of recommendation.

In cases where the Director of Industries recommends any new item to actual users it will be his responsibility to see that the c.i.f., price quoted by the applicant in his application is correct. For this purpose, the Director of Industries will either ask the applicant to produce the pro forma invoices or he will compare the c.i.f. price quoted by the applicant with the price for the same item quoted by other parties.

After the issue of licence, it will be the responsibility of the Director of Industries to check up whether the imported materials have been properly utilised by the licensee. In case of contravention of the conditions of the licence, the report will be sent by the Director of Industries to the CCI&E to enable the latter to initiate action against the parties concerned under Imports and Exports (Control) Act, 1947. In the case of new units, the Director of Industries should inspect the unit before recommending the licence whereas in the case of existing units inspection may be done at least once in four years.

Since the DC (SSI) has to play a crucial role in the distribution of foreign exchange ceilings to the DIs as also in respect of planned growth in the crowded secto and has to ensure promotion of priority industries in the small scale sector in the fields of ancillaries, defence production, backward areas etc., he will have to establish a deeper functional rapport with the State Directors. Besides informal discussions, etc., a mechanism of feedback of information from the Directors to the DC (SSI) will have to be built in. This can be effected by requesting the Directors to send abstracts of their recommendations periodically to the DC(SSI) in a form which will be most informative but least cumbersome for the DIs to send and DC (SSI) to examine. Limiting feedback of information to the strategic sectors of small scale units may be useful to start with.

The specific role of the organisations of the DC (SSI)-the Directors of Industries and the Licensing Authorities in the grant of licences to SSI units in terms of the revised procedure is summarised below :—

(a) Role of the DC (SSI)

(i) To distribute ceiling to the States on the basis laid down.

(ii) To prepare and circulate 'R.I.L.', consider cases of relaxations and to inform all the Directors of Industries where relaxations are allowed indicating reasons for the same.

(iii) To give general directions to the Directors of Industries as may be required from time to time.

(iv) To convene meetings of the SSI Committee and circulate its decisions promptly.

(v) To undertake post-facto check of the recommendations made by the D.I.'s with a view to seeing whether the Directors of Industries have followed the overall import policy and the general directions given to them.

(vi) To coordinate the work of licensing to SSI units between the licensing authorities and the sponsoring authories.

Note: In the case of pharmaceutical industries sponsored by the State Drugs Controllers, the function of the DC (SSI) will be performed by the Drugs Controllers of India.

(b) Role of Sponsoring Authorities

(i) To recommend applications for grant of licences within the ceiling allocated to them and forward the same to the licensing authority concerned in accordance with the prescribed procedure.

(ii) To ensure compliance with the general directions issued by the DC (SSI) and the policy laid down in the Red Book in the matter of assessment of requirements.

(iii) To obtain clearance from the DC (SSI) in respect of Industries appearing in the "R.I.L.".

(iv) To devise a policy to govern recommendations in cases other than those covered by (ii) and (iii) above.

(v) To obtain clearance from the SSI Committee and the technical authorities, wherever necessary, before recommending licences.

(vi) To ensure that in respect of items available from the STC or indigenous manufacturers, the licences are recommended only after obtaining the necessary clearance from the STC, or the indigenous manufacturers, as the case may be.

(vii) To ensure that recommendations do not exceed the ceiling allotted to that State and also to see that a small cushion is kept in reserve for implementing decisions in appeals.

(viii) To send an abstract of the recommendations made to the DC (SSI).

(ix) To undertake post-check of the industrial units to see whether the imported material has been properly utilised and to report cases involving misuse of such material or breach of conditions of licences to the licensing authority.

(c) Role Of Licensing Authorities

(i) To issue licences on the basis of the recommendations of the Director of Industries where such recommendations are in consonance with the policy/procedure indicated above.

(ii) In the case of rejections, to communicate reasons therefor to the applicants.

(iii) To take penal action against the licenses or importers for violations of import and export control regulations.

(iv) To watch utilisation of ceilings State-wise.

Annexure To Appendix III

Form of application for import of goods (other than those falling under CG Licensing procedure) by Actual Users who are not borne on the Books of Directorate General of Technical Development.

Part I

(To be filled in by the applicant for use in the Licensing Office).

A. Particulars Of Applicant

1. Name of the Applicant
2. Full Postal Address
   (i) House/Shop No.
   (ii) Name of Street/Road
   (iii) Name of Locality
   (iv) Name of State
3. Telegraphic Address
4. Address of Location of Factory

B. Particulars of Application

1. Registration No. allotted to Income Tax Verification Certificate or Exemption, therefrom.
2. Treasury Receipt No. and date (Treasury Receipt to be attached in original).
3. Licensing period in respect of which application is made.
4. Where shipment is to be effected from a country different from a country in which the goods originated, full statement of reasons for the same should be given.
5. Is a letter of authority desired? If so, name of the firm in whose favour it is desired.

(Note : Documentary evidence as required should be furnished.)

C. General Information To Be Furnished

1. Date of Establishment of business in India.
2. Nature of the concern, whether Public Company or Private Company, Partnership or Hindu Undivided family concern.
3. Names of Directors, Partners, Proprietor or Karta as the case may be.
4. Details of branches or associated companies (Name and Locations) :—
   (i) In India
   (ii) Abroad
5. Has any application been already made by the applicant for goods falling under the same S. No. or sub-item of serial No. for the same period from any country in any category? If so, give details.
6. Have any branches or associate companies mentioned in (4) or any of the gentlemen named in (3) applied for an import licence for import goods falling under the same serial number or sub-item of serial number for the same period?
7. Is any branch/associate concern of applicant holding an Established Importer quota for particular item/items covered by this application? If so, details of quota Certificates/Established Importers licences may be given.
8. The Customs House where the import licence, if granted, will be registered.
9. Full details of the enclosures attached with the application (Every copy of the document should be marked as a true copy and signed beneath by the applicant).

Part II

(To be filled in by the applicant for use by the sponsoring authority).

1. Name of the Industry and the purpose for which the raw materials/components are required.
2. Description of goods manufactured.

3. Production capacity.

4. Actual production in the preceding two years.

5. Estimated production in ensuing year.

6. Capital investment :

(i) Machinery and equipment (Details of machinery to be attached).

(ii) Land and buildings or rent of premises.

7. Registration No. allotted by the State Director of Industries.

8. Particulars of raw materials/components to be imported :—

Item with I.T.C. Serial No.	Quantity Number	Value (c i.f.)

9. Particulars of licences issued and imports effected during the last three periods.

10. Actual sales of the manufactured products during the preceding year.

11. Value of exports, if any, of the manufactured products during the preceding year.

12. Stocks or raw material/components applied for, on the date of the commencement of the period, i.e., on 1st April :

(i) Imported.

(ii) Alternate Sources.

13. Expected arrivals of the goods applied for on the date of the commencement of the period against licences in hand.

14. Period for which stock and expected arrivals of raw materials to last.

15. Consumption of the imported material applied for during the 12 months.

Items with I.T.C. Serial No.	Quantity Number	Value

(1) I/We hereby declare that if this licence is granted, the goods will be utilised only for consumption as raw materials/components or accessories in our factory and that no portion thereof will be sold to or permitted to be used by any other party.

(2) I/We hereby declare that the above statements are true and correct to the best of my/our knowledge and belief. I/We fully understand that any licence granted to me/us on the basis of the statements furnished is liable to cancellation, in addition to any other penalty that the Government may impose having regard to the circumstances of the case, if it is found that any of the statements or facts therein are incorrect or false.

Date.........

Signature...........
Name in Block Letters..............
Designation.........
Residential.........
Address..............

Part III

(To be filled in by the Sponsoring Authority in duplicate)

1. Particulars of goods recommended :

Item & I.T.C. Serial No.	Requirements quantity Numbers as per installed capacity	Requirements in Value (cif) as per installed capacity	Quantity Number recommended for Import	Value (cif) recommended for Import	End-use
1	2	3	4	5	6

2. (a) Whether the applicant is a new or existing unit.

(b) If new unit, whether the industry is included in the List of Restricted Industries circulated by DC (SSI).

(c) If the industry is included in the List of Restricted Industries, whether clearance from DC(SSI) has been obtained and if so, a duplicate of the DC (SSI)s' letter may be enclosed.

3. (a) Whether the items recommended are licensable in consultation with DGTD/DC (SSI) or any other technical authority.

(b) If so, whether the clearance from the concerned technical authority has been obtained (The No. and date of the reference of the technical authority may be given).

4* In the case of items available indigenously whether the applicant has produced evidence to show that indigenous manufacturer(s) are unable to supply.

5 In the case of items which are being imported by STC, whether the STC have expressed their inability to supply the material (The No. and date of their letter may be quoted).

Signature of Sponsoring Authority

* To be filled in respect of items where the import policy provides clearance from indigenous manufacturers.

Appendix VI

Form 'C'—Special Form of Application for the Imports of Raw Materials/Spare Parts for Certain Specified Industries as well as other Industrial Units borne on the List of the Directorate-General of Technical Development.

The following amendments in the existing form are recommended:

(1) At present, there is no separate form for the import of spare parts and this very form is used for that purpose also. It is, therefore, recommended that the heading of the form should be changed as follows:

"Form 'C'—Special form of application for import of raw-materials, components and spare parts for certain specified industries as well as other industrial units borne on the list of the Directorate-General of Technical Development."

(2) At present, three copies of this application form are received, of which one is retained in the Directorate-General of Technical Development and two copies are passed on the Chief Controller of Imports and Exports. The Chief Controller of Imports and Exports, however, requires only one copy of the application. In order to make the position very clear, the entry on the top of the form should be amended as follows:

"This application should be submitted to the Chief Controller of Imports and Exports through the Directorate-General of Technical Development. Only two copies should be submitted, of which one would be retained by the Directorate-General of Technical Development and the other passed on to the Chief Controller of Imports and Exports."

(3) The following entries should appear on the top of this form:

"Licensing Period............
Code No............

(4) Section B

(a) In Serial No. 4, omit sub-item (ii).

(b) In Serial No. 5, omit sub-item (ii).

(c) Serial No. 6 may be omitted after the system of code numbers has been introduced.

(5) Section C

In Serial No. 5 for the words "the first twelve months" substitute the words "the last twelve months".

(6) Section D

Serial No. 8 should be omitted after the system of code numbers has been introduced.

(7) Section D should be renumbered as Section E and the following should be introduced as a new Section D.

"D. Spare parts: c.i.f. value of the spares to be imported (list of spare-parts indicating the quantities required to be attached".

(8) In the tabular form attached to the application, the heading of Column 8 should be rewarded as follows:

"Quantity consumed during the last three calendar years, (information to be furnished for each year separately)''.

STUDY TEAM ON DIRECTORATE GENERAL OF TECHNICAL DEVELOPMENT, 1964—REPORT

New Delhi, Ministry of Industry and Supply, Department of Supply and Technical Development, 1965, 130p. (Part 1).

Chairman : Shri Harish Chandra Mathur.
Members : Shri N.J. Kamath; Shri N.K. Mukharji; Shri P. Sabanayagam; Shri R.K. Raisinghani; Shri S. S. Kumar; Shri P. C. Kapoor; Shri S.P. Mukherji.
Secretary : Shri S.S. Puri.

APPOINTMENT

In pursuance of the recommendations made by the Santhanam Committee to look into the functioning of the organisation of the Directorate General of Technical Development the Government of India in the Ministry of Industry and Suppy, Department of Suppy and Technical Development appointed the Study Team on Directorate General of Technical Development Vide their Letter No. 21(8) '64'V, dated August 12, 1964.

TERMS OF REFERENCE

The Team will examine the organisation, structure, methods of work and procedure of the Directorate General of Technical Development, particularly with a view to locating the points at which delay occur, where bottlenecks exist and where administrative failures are possible and, would suggest measures for improvement so that opportunities of corruption are eliminated.

CONTENTS

Introductory ; Role, Functions and Organisational pattern of the Directorate General of Technical Development ; Guiding Principles followed by the Study Team ; Scope of Import Work; Allocation of Foreign Exchange; Import of Raw Materials, Components and Spares by Undertakings borne on the books of the Directorate General of Technical Development ; Import of Capital Goods ; Indigenous Clearance for Imports Effected by Public Sector and Departmental Undertakings ; Import Applications from Universities, Educational, Scientific and Medical Institutions and Municipalities ; Summary of Conclusions and Recommendations; Appendices from I to XII.

RECOMMENDATIONS

Allocation Of Foreign Exchange

Allocation made to the Directorate General of Technical Development as a whole :

The function at present performed by the Department of Iron and Steel in respect of steel allocation to private sector industry, from the stage of obtaining demands to the stage of allocations should be transferred to the Economic Adviser.

The foreign exchange allocation now separately indicated for imported steel should be added to the consolidated bulk allocation which the Department of Economic Affairs makes to the Ministry of Commerce for commercial imports. The requirements of the D.G. T.D. borne untis should be created for out of the bulk allocation earmarked for the Directorate General of Technical Development by the Economic Adviser under a single head.

The functions at present being performed in regard to sub-allocation of the non-ferrous allotment by the Department of Mines and Metals should be transferred to the Economic Adviser.

As in the case of steel allocation, the allocation to Directorate General of Technical Development borne units for their requirements of non-ferrous metals should be amalgamated with the bulk allocation made to Directorate General of Technical Development under a single head.

Wherever possible commodity-wise allocation may be done away at least so far as the D.G.T.D. borne units are concerned and that the Directorate General of Technical Developments' share in the allocation for such commodities should be amalgamated with their bulk allocation under a single head even though some of the items are canalised. Similar treatment may be given as far as possible to other sponsoring authorities for their total needs which are looked after by the Economic Adviser.

Special care may be taken to see that the amalgamation of ceilings proposed does not in any way lead to a reduction in what the Directorate General of Technical Development may have received by way of a total allocation under the existing system.

Import licensing for the steel requirements of the D.G.T.D. borne units should be transferred from the Iron and Steel Controller to the Chief Controller of Imports and Exports and should preferably by done at the Head quarters. There should be a single consolidate licence issued from the Headquarters of the Chief Controller of Imports and Exports for the total needs of a particular unit for raw materials, components and spares excluding the canalised items which should be imported against sub-allocations carried out of the bulk allocations of individual sponsoring authority. This sub-allocation is to be determined by the sponsoring authorities concerned.

Once allocation of foreign exchange has been made to the Director General, Technical Development, its inter se apportionment between the industries should rest solely with him. The inter se priority which the concerned Ministries wish to be adopted for their group of industries may be intimated to him will in advance for his consideration but such an advice should not have mandatory force.

The Director General of Technical Development's hands should not be tied by indicating his allocation in two groups, viz.,Chemicals and Engineering and that his allocation should be given as one figure only.

The Directorate General of Technical Development's industry-wise apportionment of foreign exchange should be completed within 15 days of his receiving foreign exchange allocation.

The present varying patterns of unit-wise allocation in the different Directorates should be replaced by the basis set out in the main report.

If any change is made in the basis mentioned above in future, it should be made known to the industry.

Import Of Raw Materials, Components And Spares By Undertakings Borne On The Books Of The Directorate General Of Tecenical Development

The application should be submitted in duplicate instead of in triplicate. The form of application has been recommended for simplification. The applicant may be asked to send an extra copy of the list of goods applied for, (i.e. in triplicate) which would be sent back to him by Directorate General of Technical Development with suitable amendments, conforming to recommendations made.

The unit may be asked to submit only one application for a particular end-product. A consolidate application both for raw materials, components and also for spare parts may be submitted.

It should be impressed on all industrial undertakings that applications for import should be made after very careful consideration and requests for changes or additions avoided.

The Chief Controller of Import and Exports' organisation should not question an application if duly recommended by the Directorate General of Technical Development merely because the application is time-barred. The recommendation of the Directorate General of Technical Development about condonation should be presumed unless the contrary is stated. The last date prescribed in the Red Book should be 'the date by which the application should be received by Directorate General of Technical Development's organisation.

For easy identification of sponsoring Directorate each industrial undertaking should be allowed a code number related to the end-product. The referencing within the Directorate General of Technical Development and Chief Controller of Imports and Exports' organisation should be on the basis of these code numbers.

At present an application is registered twice, once in the Receipt and Issue Section and again in the Coordination Section before it goes to the sponsoring Directorate. To save time, it is recommended that registration in the R & I should be reduced to the barest minimum.

For checking applications received without treasury challans or with under valued treasury challans, the Chief Controller of Imports and Exports will assist the Directorate General of Technical Development by locating in the Dirsctorate General of Technical Development a unit which will screen them and return such as are deficient in fee.

The Import Cell of the Co-ordination Directorate through which all import applications will pass, will prepare periodical list of cases which are not disposed of in time and bring them to the notice of the Industrial Adviser concerned so that the latter may arrange their disposal at Industrial Advisers' meeting.

Technical scrutiny of import applications should be conducted in advance of the foreign exchange and acknowledgement-cum-deficiency card should be sent to the applicant within 7 days of the receipt of the application. Formal references to other Directorates, if absolutely necessary, should be completed before the unit-wise allocation is made. Based on working norms the entitlement of each unit should be assessed and a master chart of unit-wise entitlement should be prepared in advance of foreign exchange allocation. The recommendatory letter should also be completed in advance of the foreign exchange allocation. All the scrutiny and action should be completed within a period of three weeks from the issue of acknowledgement letter.

Clarifications from the applicants should be sought in one lot avoiding piece-meal references and the party should be given 10 days to furnish all necessary clarifications.

To facilitate the technical scrutiny a list of check points should be standardised on a Directorate-wise basis.

All industrial undertakings may be impressed to furnish complete monthly production returns regularly failing which the import applications are liable to remain unsponsored.

All import applications received in each Directorate should be registered industry-wise in a chronological order and taken up for action on the same chronological order.

On the basis of a master chart, unit-wise allocation should be finalised within 15 days of industry-wise allocation after due clearance from the indigenous availability angle.

In the case of spare parts, the Development Officer will continue to make allocations on the basis of his judgement of the requirements of an undertaking and his past experience. It will be necessary for the Directorate General of Technical Development to indicate a separate allocation for raw materials and components and separate allocation for spares. The Chief Controller of Imports and Exports may issue only one licence showing the two allocations separately. It should not be open to an undertaking to divert any portion for spares for the import of raw materials and components.

The Directorate General of Teehnical Development's publication "Hand-book of Indigenous Manufacturers" should be brought out at the same time as Chief Controller of Imports and Export's Red Book and kept up-to-date by issuing quarterly supplements.

The policy formulated in the Red Book regarding indigenous clearance in respect of raw materials and components should not normally be changed during the licensing period.

The necessity of requiring the party to get non-availability certificate should be entirely done aways with. There should be only 3 lists namely : (a) banned items, (b) open items ; and (c) restricted items in respect of which quantitative restrictions may be imposed by the Directorate General of Technical Development on the basis of indigenous availability.

So far as small scale sector is concerned, the import

policy may provide only two categories of items namely, "banned" and "open". The restricted category may be done away with. The need for restricted list will of course continue for the scheduled sector.

While the applicant should be required to indicate itemised quantities, the Directorate General of Technical Development should make recommendation for licences without indicating itemised quatities except in cases of speculative and indigenously available items. Quantitative restrictions should be applied uniformly to all undertakings in the same industry. The list of goods should invariably be appended with the recommendation sent to the Chief Controller of Imports and Exports. The flexibility upto 25 per cent should be allowed for importing those items for which quantitative limits have been indicated, subject to the overall value of the licence. The licencee should also be allowed to utilise upto 25 per cent of the value of the licence for "permissible" spare parts and small tools not indicated in the licence. Within this 25 per cent, upto 5 per cent or Rs. 2,500 whichever is less may be allowed to be utilised for the import of even the spares which are not otherwise permissible but which are not banned and are required for servicing, maintenance or replacement of the plant installed in the licence-holder's factory.

A revised form of the covering letter (Appendix IX) with which the recommendation should be sent to the Chief Controller of Imports and Exports is recommended. To facilitate legitimate representation and follow-up by the trade, a copy of the Directorate General of Technical Development's covering letter should be sent simultaneously to the applicant for his advance information (without any commitment). A copy of the list of items recommended should also be sent to him. If the Chief Controller of Imports and Exports wants a fair copy of the list he should ask the applicant to prepare a clean copy from his own list. The applicant should not, in any circumstances, be required to get clean copies of the list attested by the Directorate General of Technical Development's organisation.

For speeding up matters in the sponsoring Directorate for the despatch of recommendation to the Chief Controller of Imports and Exports' office, it is recommended that : (a) the draft letter and the list need not normally be put up to officers above Development Officer's level, (b) the fair copies should ordinarily be prepared within 2 days of the approval of a draft, and (c) the fair recommendatory letter and the list need not be attested by two Technical Officers as at present.

The Co-ordination Directorate should not take more than 24 hours in the transmission of applications received from the sponsoring Directorate to the Chief Controller of Import and Exports' organisation. However, where an officer oriented pattern has been introduced the sponsoring Directorate should send its recommendation to the Chief Controller of Imports and Exports' organisation direct.

The time-table as proposed should be observed so that all applications are received by the Directorate General of Technical Development by 15th May and all licencing is completed by 30th September. If the foreign exchange allocation can be made earlier than 15th June, the time-table will be advanced accordingly.

The Chief Controller of Imports and Exports should be able to issue licences within a period of one month of the receipt of recommendation. A copy of the licence may be sent to the Directorate General of Technical Development only when the recommendation has not been observed in its entirety by the Chief Controller of Imports & Exports.

As a logical corollary to the decision of the Government on the recommendations of Swaminathan Committee, the licences may be allowed to place orders and commit against 75 per cent of the face value of the licence even in the first half of the year in advance of second half-year's allocation subject to the condition that, out of the 75 per cent committed, not more than 50 per cent of the total licence value shall be paid in the first half-year.

The licences upto Rs. 5,000 should continue to get the concession of total commitment in one lot at any time during the validity period.

The holders of licences between Rs. 5,001 and Rs. 15,000 may also be allowed the benefit of annual licensing without any endorsement during the second half and also the concession of being able to commit the full value of the licence at any time subject, however, to 50 per cent limit on payment during the first half of the licensing period.

In order to provide for marginal adjustment where the value of the licences is in excess of Rs. 15,000 but does not exceed Rs. 30,000 the licences should be authorised to place orders upto the value of Rs. 15,000 in one lot subject to the condition that remittance of foreign exchange in the first half year will not exceed 50 per cent of the value of the licence. Also, any cut which might have to be imposed on such licences in the second half year should not result in the total value of the licence being reduced below Rs. 15,000.

The allocation made to small valued licence holders should be considered as the first charge on the total amount of foreign exchange allocated to the Directorate General of Technical Development during the second half year, leaving the balance to be distributed among the holders of larger licences in all industries.

Miscellaneous Recommendations

Licences in advance of foreign exchange allocation:

Issue of licences in advance of foreign exchange allocation to the extent of 75 per cent of allocation in the proceeding year will not be of any particular advantage to the trade. On the contrary this will throw up additional work load on the trade as also on the Directorate General of Technical Development and on Licensing Offices.

Intimation of unit-wise allocation to the applicant in advance of the application itself: The present practice of intimation of unit-wise allocation to the applicants in advance of the receipt of application itself in certain Directorates should be discontinued.

Revalidation of Licences : Where the industrial undertaking has already made the necessary commitment or opened a letter of credit but due to some reason the delivery period falls outside the validity period of the licences, revalidation in such cases should be left to the Chief Controller of Imports and Exports alone and on consultation with the Directorate General of Technical Development should be necessary. However, where industrial undertaking has neither made any commitment nor opened a letter of credit or has entered into commitment only for a part of the licence, then revalidation of the whole licence in the former case and of the un-utilised postion of the licence in the latter case, should be decided by the Chief Controller of Imports and Exports in consultation with the Directorate General of Technical Development.

Licensing of machine tools : In order to relieve the Directorate General of Technical Development from non-technical work, the work of issue of licences of machine tools may be taken over by the Chief Controller of Imports and Exports organisation. Directorate General of Technical Development however should continue to give technical advice as before.

Requirements of workshop office buildings etc. : Where a workshop holds an industrial licence for the manufacture of various articles under different headings or sub-headings of the first schedule to the Industries (D&R) Act, 1951, its requirements such as cement, pig iron, coke etc., common to more than one end-products, should be decided by the Directorate to be determined by the Deputy Director General or Directorate General of Technical Development quickly in cases of doubt.

Handing over the documents to the trade representatives : There need be no objection to handing over to the bonafide trade representatives copies of communications sent to his firm asking for information etc.

Policy cards for import policy : Policy cards which are sent to the Chief Controller of Imports and Exports should be prepared only in respect of those items for which a change in the import policy is considered necessary by the Directorate General of Technical Development.

Release of materials through the State Trading Corporation : Where materials are released by the State Trading Corporation etc. on the recommendation of the Directorate General of Technical Development, a copy of the Directorate General of Technical Development's recommendation should be sent to the applicant also.

Ex-post-facto Scrutiny of Import Cases : A separate Cell in the orgynisation should be created under a suitable technical officer who will work directly under the control and guidance of the Director General,

Reasons of Excercise of Discretion to be Recorded on file : In order to facilitate the ex-post-facto scrutiny recommended in the above para, reasons for exercise of scrutiny should be recorded in brief on the file itself.

Import of Capital Goods

DGTD borne units : All DGTD borne units should submit their applications to the Chief Controller of Imports and Exports through Directorate General of Technical Development. The revised form of application (Appendix XI) should be adopted for use by the DGTD borne units. The same form can be used for all other categories of Capital Goods applications without difficulties.

An application may be invited in duplicate only and the party should send in all 7 copies of the list of Capital Goods applied for by it.

While there need not be any restrictions on the timings or the number of applications in respect of a new scheme, reasonable restrictions should be imposed in regard to the frequency of applications from existing firms for replacement/balancing, modernisation needs. However, applications made in emergent situation like break down can always be permitted as special cases and so would applications linked to specific credits.

All applications should be received in the Import Cell located in the Co-ordination Directorate and this Cell should not take more than 24 hours for registering an application and sending it to the sponsoring Directorate concerned without any forwarding memo. No paper should be retained in the Import Cell except the maintenance of register on the lines recommended for applications dealing with the import of raw materials.

In order to facilitate referencing and processing of applications, DGTD borne units submitting applications for the import of Capital Goods should indicate code numbers allotted to them on these applications.

The sponsoring Directorate concerned should scrutinise the application with the help of check list recommended for the purpose.

After carrying out the necessary scrutiny, an acknowledgement-cum-deficiency card should be sent to the applicant within a period of 7 days. The party should furnish information/clarification within 10 days.

The question of indigenous clearance should be examined by the Directorate General of Technical Development in respect of only those cases/items where essentiality is certified. Where essentiality cannot be certified the application form may be forwarded to the Chief Controller of Imports and Exports with the recommendation for rejection.

The existing instructions that all inter-Directorate references should be made direct and not through Co-ordination should be strictly enforced.

Where a Development Officer finds any difficulty in disposing of a reference within the prescribed time limit, he should obtain the order of the industrial Adviser.

It should be made mandatory for sponsoring Directorate to place all applications which are not cleared from indigenous angle within the prescribed time limit, before the industrial Adviser's Committee which should take a final decision. The Sponsoring Directorate should withdraw the application from whichever Directorate on that particular date and submit it to the Committee. Only the Industrial Adviser's Committee should handle these cases.

The fact that the Industrial Adviser's Committee is required to clear outstanding items should not act as a bar to disposal of items through formal or informal consultations wherever practicable.

With a view to be more realistic the Director General, Technical Development may amend the existing orders regarding delegation of decision-making powers to bring them in conformity with facts and the requirements of proper scrutiny.

The fair recommendations should be signed by only one technical officer.

Wherever Officer Oriented System is working, the sponsoring Directorate itself should forward the recommendations to the Chief Controller of Imports and Exports' office/administrative Ministry concerned with a copy to the Import Cell for their information and record.

In such cases where essentiality is not in doubt, but all items are indigenously available the Directorate General of Technical Development should, while sending their recommendation to the Chief Controller of Imports and Exports, mention names of indigenous manufacturers in the case of items not already covered by the Hand-book of Indigenous Manufacturers.

When both essentiality and the indigenous angle are cleared, the Directorate General of Technical Development's recommendation to the Chief Controller of Imports and Exports should invariably be accompanied by an attested copy of the list of items to be allowed for import, and by mention of the names of indigenous manufacturers as indicated above. Simultaneously the Directorate General of Technical Development should inform the applicant that his application has been forwarded to the Chief Controller of Imports and Exports and give a gist of recommendations made, covering items not considered essential and items not cleared from the indigenous angle. The standard form of communication to be sent to the applicant at the stage, should be devised.

A time-table for handling applications within a range of 15 to 31 days within the organisation has been recommended.

The Import Cell should keep a watch on the disposal of these applications within the prescribed time limits.

Applications from sources other than DGTD borne units : Instead of making application-wise references to the Directorate General of Technical Development, it should be possible for the Development Commissioner, Small Scale Industries, in cases of Small Scale Sector, to obtain package clearance from the Directorate General of Technical Development at the commencement of a licencing period in regard to items of Capital Goods commonly applied for by small units and on the basis of such a package clearance, the Development Commissioner, Small Scale Industries, could himself proceed to give indigenous clearance in individual cases. Necessity to consult the Directorate General of Technical Development may arise only where the package clearance list does not cover a particular item without sending the whole application.

For cases from all non-DGTD borne units, the Import Cell will play a positive sponsoring role analogous to that of sponsoring Directorates for the DGTD borne units.

The Development Commissioner, Small Scale Industries should inform the applicant that his application has been forwarded to the Chief Controller of Imports and Exports and give him the gist of recommendations made.

In respect of other sponsoring authorities, the Directorate General of Technical Development's recommendations accompanied by an attested list of cleared items should be sent direct to the Chief Controller of Imports and Exports. A copy of this should be responsible for informing the applicant about the gist of recommendations.

Miscellaneous Matters

Validity of indigenous clearance should be renewed at the end of one year.

The Directorate General of Technical Development officers should equip themselves with up-to-date information regarding international prices of capital goods and check prices indicated in the invoices while scrutinising the items.

Where the party has placed an order or entered into commitment within the period of validity of the licence, revalidation may be allowed by the Chief Controller of Imports and Exports without consulting the Directorate General of Technical Development but in other cases the Directorate General of Technical Development should be consulted.

Applications for minor amendments should also be sent by the licencees direct to the Chief Controller of Imports and Exports. However, where an amendment in value or description of goods is sought to be made, the application should be made through the relevant sponsoring authorities. The Directorate General of Technical Development's role in regard to indigenous clearance on such applications from those other than DGTD borne units should be the same as for original applications.

Indigenous Clearance For Import Effected By Public Sector And Departmental Undertakings

Maintenance And Operation Items Of Spares And Stores : The present position of a separate allocation for maintenance and operational spares and stores which exists for some projects should be extended to all departmental/public sector undertakings and State Electricity Boards/Projects so that no reference to the Headquarters either on indigenous clearance or on release of foreign exchange is required.

There should be a separate application in a separate form for import of items of maintenance and operational stores and spares, distinct from the application for import of raw materials.

The application should be sent direct to the licensing authority concerned with necessary certificates about non-availability etc. indigenously and clearance from Directorate General of Technical Development on banned items.

References for indigenous clearance to the Directorate General of Technical Development should be made only for banned items and such reference received in Directorate General of Technical Development should be sent direct from the Receipt and Issue Section to the nominated officer, who should dispose of the reference in the same manner as prescribed for references on raw materials. To help the Directorate General of Technical Development in giving a decision expeditiously the project authorities may indicate the quantity or value of banned items required to be imported by them. It should be open to the discretion of the Directorate General of Technical Development to indicate a quantitative limit on any particular item. Unless a quantitative limit is specifically indicated by the Directorate General of Technical Development the clearance would be presumed to be without any quantitative restriction.

The project authorities may adopt the practice of a general inquiry for eliciting response from indigenous manufacturers and indicating the result of such an inquiry in the reference made to the Directorate General of Technical Development should not call upon the project authorities to approach individual indigenous manufacturers.

The 'Hand book of indigenous Manufacturers' should be kept up-to-date by issuing quarterly supplements. The book should be attempted to indicate the description of goods in the same pattern and sequence as the Red Book indicates.

The project authorities need not send their applications to the Headquarters for licencing but should deal direct with Port Licencing Offices.

The list of maintenance and operation items of stores and spares need not be sent for ex-post-facto scrutiny to the Directorate General of Technical Development.

(II) Raw Materials, Components And Major

Assemblies

On the basis of the presumption of project-wise foreign exchahge allocation and full dele ation to the project authorities, for operation within the allocation eliminating the Department of Economic Affairs as also the administrative Ministry, a new procedure has been visualised as follows :

(i) Indigenous clearance should be obtained usually not more than once a year;

(ii) The project authorities should get packet clearance during October-November of the preceding year and before demand for foreign exchange allocation is made;

(iii) The items to be imported may be divided into two lists viz. list A and list B. In list A should be included items which are already open. This list need not be cleared by Directorate General of Technical Development ;

(iv) The items which are banned or not open should be listed in list B. General open enquiry be floated for these items and those indigenously available should be deleted. Thereafter a certificate should be appended about non-availability;

(v) List B with itemised requirement certificate should be sent to Directorate General of Technical Development by the end of October.

(vi) Directorate General of Technical Development should clear the list by the end of November in accordance with the procedure indicated subsiquently;

(vii) The demand for foreign exchange should be sent to administrative Ministry on the basis of list A and cleared items of list B;

(viii) After import policy is announced, the project authorities may get further clearance from Directorate General of Technical Development in case some items of list A or list B come in the banned category or new items not included in these lists are required to be imported;

(ix) The project authorities should apply to Chief Controller of Imports and Exports direct on the basis of list A and packet clearance of list B items within the foreign exchange ceiling;

(x) The Licensing offices after checking up list A and list B items with reference to Red Book and Directorate General of Technical Development's packet clearance issue licences without further reference to Directorate General of Technical Development administrative Ministry or Department of Economic Affairs.

Processing Of Indigenous Clearance References Under The Revised Procedure With In The Directorate General Of Technical Development

All applications may be sent direct from R & I Section to the nominated officer concerned.

The nominated officer should be responsible for the disposal of each case.

Inter-directorate references should not be routed through Co-ordination Directorate.

Where more than one Directorate is involved, the project authorities may be advised to furnish extra copies for simultaneous reference to other Directorates.

The nominated officer should collect in advance as much information regarding indigenous manufacture of items as possible.

The nominated officers should not advise indigenous clearance on list 'A' item or items for non-banned items of operational and maintenance stores and spares.

An indigenous clearance obtained from the Directorate General of Technical Development should be valid for the entire licencing year under reference subject to certain conditions.

The nominated officer should dispose of a reference on indigenous clearance within a period of 30 days.

In no case should a project authority be required to approach indigenous manufacturers individually.

Adequate clerical support should be given to the nominated officer for maintenance of files and issue of fair copies within 3 days of the decision taken.

Directorate General of Technical Development need indicate itemised limits only in the cases where import may be allowed of an item for a nominal quantity or where there is indigenous manufacture but the manufacturers are not able to supply the total requirements.

(III) Capital Goods

Like raw materials applications, capital goods applications also should be received direct by the nominated officer and should not be sent to the Coordination Directorate at all, except at the stage of despatch of recommendation to the Chief Controller of Imports and Exports' organization. A nominated officer will be personally responsible to obtain the clearance within a period of 21 days and ensure its final disposal within a period of 30 days.

In order to conform to actual position the Development Officer should be formally authorised to dispose of cases of capital goods. We would leave it to the Directorate General to amend the existing order suitably.

The public sector undertaking should submit a consolidating application for items of balancing equipment preferably not more than twice for a particular licencing period.

The indigenous clearance on capital goods items should be valid for one year : The Directorate General of Technical Development would impose quantitative restriction on indigenous clearance only in respect of those items which are either banned or partially available in the country. Where the accessories are indigenously available, indigenous clearance may have to be restricted.

The project authorities may apply direct to the Chief Controller of Imports and Exports for emergency replacement and break down items of capital goods and no reference to the Directorate General of Technical Development for indigenous clearance on individual cases should be necessary. The foreign exchange should be met out of a bulk allocation made to the Chief Controller of Imports and Exports for this purpose.

Miscellaneous Recommendations: A Development Officer by designation should be nominated for specific related public sector projects by name.

Public sector undertakings should be fully informed of the procedure regarding imports. Diversity of procedures from undertakings to undertakings should as far as possible be avoided but where there is such diversity the same should be clearly indicated. It may be desirable to have a separate chapter on public sector undertakings in the Hand-book of Rules and Procedures on Import Trade Control.

Import Applications From Universities, Educational Scientific And Medical Institutions And Municipalities

Since the requirement of these organisations for operational and maintenance stores are not likely to be large, it is recommended that there should be only two lists ; (i) list of open items without any restrictions ; and

(ii) list of banned items, so that references from those organisations to the Directorate General of Techn'cal Development in regard to store which otherwise might have been included in the restricted list would be avoided.

As regards the import of scientific equipment and apparatus and other capital goods, it should be the responsibility of the Co-ordination Directorate to keep a watch and to ensure that these applications are disposed of within a time limit of 15 days.

COMMITTEE ON COOPERATION, 1964—REPORT

Delhi, Manager of Publications, 1966. 71p.

Chairman : Shri Ram Nivas Mirdha

Members : Shri Rama Krishna Hegde ; Ch. Brahm Parkash; Shri Digambar Singh Chaudhuri; Shri Nand Kishore Narain ; Shri L. N. Bongirwar ; Shri M.L. Batra.

Secretary : Shri A.C. Bandyopadhyay.

APPOINTMENT

Government of India in the Ministry of Community Development and Cooperation Constituted the Committee on Cooperation Vide their Notification No. F. 11-64/64 Coord. dated August 17, 196'.

TERMS OF REFERENCE

(i) To lay down standards and criteria by which the genuineness of Cooperative Societies of various types may be judged and to suggest measures for weeding out non-genuine societies and preventing their registration.

(ii) To review the existing cooperative laws, rules and practices with a view to locating the loopholes which enable vested interests to entrench themselves in cooperative institutions and recommend measures—legislative as well as administrative—for the elimination and prevention of such vested interests.

(iii) To examine the factors inhibiting self-reliance and self-regulation in the cooperative movement and to suggest appropriate remedies.

CONTENTS

Introductory ; Historical Background ; Cooperative Principles ; Criteria of Genuineness ; Vested Interests ; Audit and Supervision ; Resources for Cooperatives ; Education in Cooperation ; Summary of Conclusions and Recommendations ; Appendices from I to IV.

RECOMMENDATIONS

Historical Background

1. The cooperative movement in India started as an agricultural credit movement and it continued to concern itself primarily with agricultural credit activities for many years till the dawn of independence. Though some beginning was made during this period to extend the movement to other activities like urban banking, consumer service, transport undertakings, and purchase and sale of agricultural commodities, it was only after independence and particularly after the rural credit survey that systematic efforts were made to extend the movement to diverse economic activities.

2. During the last decade or so, the cooperative movement has shown unmistakable signs of growth. There has been substantial progress in co-operative agricultural credit, cooperative agricultural marketing and processing, cooperative consumer movement, and there has been a diversification of the movement to embrace activities like village industries, transport, labour, housing and forming.

3. The movement no doubt suffers from various short-comings and defects. Many of them are more an outcome of deliberately accelerated pace of expansion rather than inherent and inevitable weaknesses. These could be remedied successfully with vigilant administration and supervision at official as well as non-official levels.

4. The movement as a whole, in our opinion is proceeding on right lines, has thrown up good leadership in various sectors and has made itself serviceable to an over increasing membership. It has to its credit a vast network of societies with millions of sincere members which can be energised into a tremendously vibrant force, once the necessary financial, administrative and supervisory inputs are assured.

Cooperative Principles

5. The following cooperative principles are essential

for the sound growth of the movement :—

(i) Open Membership ;
(ii) Democratic Control ;
(iii) Distribution of surplus to members in proportion to their transactions ;
(iv) Limited interest on capital ;
(v) Mutual Aid ;
(vi) Thrift and self-help ;
(vii) Promotion of Education ;

6. The above-mentioned principles find expression in the cooperative laws prevailing in India today in some form or the other. Those State laws which do not have suitable provisions on any of these principles may make suitable provisions on the lines suggested in our report.

7. The cooperative movement offers an organisation most suitable to protect the small man from exploitation by the powerful and the rich. It is an instrument for promoting social justice. This should be clearly recognised in State policy and reflected in cooperative legislation.

8. Within the frame-work of these objectives and principles of the co-operative movement, certain conditions are laid down by cooperative law to be fulfilled before a society is registered. The pattern of conditions suggested in clause of the Model Cooperatives Societies Bill is sound. We suggest that it may be supplemented by a further requirement that the aims of the proposed society facilitate the establishment of a socialistic pattern of society.

9. In addition to these general conditions to be fulfilled before a society is registered, detailed conditions intended to ensure a minimum performance may be prescribed by the Registrars for fulfilment before a society is registered. These may be mostly in terms of a minimum membership and a minimum share capital to be achieved before registration. We also suggest that promoter members should all be persons from different families. We recommend that in each State detailed conditions may be prescribed by the Registrar in consulation with the apex institutions concerned. Even within each State different sets of conditions may be prescribed, if necessary, for different regions considering the general level of socio-economic development and other factors.

10. Scrutiny at the time of registration is essential. Careful watch after registration is even more so. The Registrar should be empowered to cancel the registration of a society which remains dormant or has ceased to function or has departed from cooperative principles. This power should be exercised in consultation with the apex institutions concerned.

Criteria Of Genuineness

11. In organising new societies either in the credit or in any other sector, planning must ensure that targets have some relation to financial resources and administrative preparedness.

12. Agricultural credit service society should admit all the rural population within its area who are willing to participate in its services, the only exception being that moneylenders should not be admitted as members. Where moneylending as a business by private persons is not controlled or regulated by law, suitable legislation should be enacted.

13. The problem of dormancy of a large number of agricultural credit service societies is very disturbing and quick action is needed to eliminate societies which have no chances of revival. A programme of revitalisation based on a survey of the potential for growth should be carried out quickly.

14. Admission to agricultural marketing societies should be restricted only to agriculturists. Traders in agricultural commodities should be negligible for admission.

15. Many of the drawbacks from which cooperative farming societies suffer are the results of inadequate pattern of financial and other assistance and inadequate preparedness. Any expansion in this programme should be preceded by careful planning.

16. A labour cooperative should not admit a contractor as a member. Admission of non-labourers other than contractors to the membership may be allowed up to 5 per cent of the total membership subject to a maximum of 5 in a society. A well-developed labour cooperative movement would make for economical and efficient execution of government works. It would tend to bring down construction costs and break up the vicious hold of the contractor system. It is, however, found that labour cooperatives have not generally been able to elicit support and sympathy of the government departments. A re-orientation of policy and outlook is very much called for in this respect.

17. Admission to transport cooperatives should be restricted to workers, traders and machanics. Persons who have their own transport business should not be allowed membership. Others may be allowed up to 5 per cent of the total membership subject to a maximum of 5 in a society provided they are prepared to work for the society and promote its growth. Lack of finances has often impeded the growth of genuine transport societies and special attention of the Government is necessary to the aspects.

18. There have been many malpractices in the cooperative housing programme. This is a sector of the movement which has done much to tarnish the emage of cooperative. People of small means should be the primary beneficiaries of cooperative housing programme. The safeguards, we have suggested in our report, should

be vigorously implemented.

19. Traders in consumer commodities should not be admitted into the membership of consumer societies. A consumer society should try to build up a mutual loyalty between the consumer movement and the marketing movement so that an integrated attempt is made at satisfying the needs of the consumers as well as the producers.

20. Membership of industrial societies should be confined to workers, artisans and such other persons who may wish to serve an industrial society faithfully. The number of the latter type of members in an industrial society should not exceed 5 per cent of the total membership subject to a maximum of 5. Persons who run industries of their own should not be allowed to join a society undertaking similar industrial activities.

Vested Interests

21. Enforcement of the principle of open membership is a vital check against the growth of vested interets. There must be a provision for appeal against refusal to admit a member; such appeal should be heard and decided by a committee at the district or State-level as the case may be, consisting of representatives of the cooperative federal bodies concerned and of the Registrar.

22. Sanction of loans in favour of the members of the managing committee of a credit society and their relatives should be reported to the general body in its next meeting for information. Cases of default in repayment of such loans should also be similarly reported.

23. We do not favour imposing statutory restriction regarding the number of terms that a person may hold office in the committee of management or the number of societies in which office may be held simultaneously by a person. The general body of each society must be the final authority to decide such things. It would, however, be a welcome step if some convention is gradually evolved in this direction from within the movement.

24. The practice of holding annual elections for electing the full committee or replacing a few members who retire by rotation is, in our opinion, inconvenient. We would prefer a gap of at least two years between one election and another in the same society, whether it be for electing the full committee or a few members. We suggest this because the holding of election in a society every year keeps up a sort of election atmosphere throughout the year and does not enable the committee members to settle down to their work.

25. Conscious efforts should be made by the Committee members to associate the general members in the management of the affairs of a society. Formation of sub-committees to which general members can be co-opted will be a helpful step in this direction. A sense of participation among the general members should be fostered.

26. Delays in holding elections to the committee of management usually arise due to non-receipt of audit reports, non-preparation of accounts and wilful default made by the committee in arranging elections.

27. Arrangement for audit must be tightened up. Concurrent audit provided in all big institutions with heavy transactions Dates must be prescribed for keeping the accounts ready for audit and members of the committee of management must be answerable for non compliance. Penal provisions such as apply to Directors of Companies should be made in the cooperatives law and applied to bigger cooperatives who can afford to maintain qualified people to write accounts.

28. Holding of elections to the committee of management is the function of the general body meeting. Meetings of the general body must, therefore, be held regularly both for considering the accounts of the society and also for holding elections. This will be a check against growth or continuance of vested interests. The committee members must be answerable for not holding the general meeting in due time and penalty for non-compliance should be provided in the cooperative law.

29. We do not consider it necessary to set up a separate election machinery for conducting elections to cooperative institutions nor do we think this function should be taken over by the cooperative department. Cooperative institutions should continue to conduct their own elections as they have been doing in the past. The federal bodies, however, should keep watchful eyes over their constituents and should depute observers to watch election proceedings in the constituent societies. Any irregularities coming to the notice of the observer should be promptly reported to the federal body and to the Registrar. If an election dispute comes to the Registrar, due not should be taken of the contents of the observer's report before the Registrar comes to a decision.

30. Societies should follow a clear structural pattern i.e., a primary society should consist of individuals, a central society should consist of primaries, an apex society should consist of central societies and a national society should consist of apex societies. Individual members should not normally, be allowed in central or apex or national societies.

31. In the committee of a management of a federal society, all important interests reflected by member-societies should be represented. For this purpose constituencies should be delimited and seats allocated on territorial or functional basis.

32. Nomination by government to the committee of a society should be kept to the minimum, and in any

case the nomination should not exceed one-third of the committee members or three which ever is less. Only government servants should be nominated and not any non-official.

3. A code of conduct should be evolved for the nominated directors in order to ensure that they realise their responsibilities and discharge them in the best manner possible. In evolving such a code of conduct the important points to be kept in mind are; (i) regular attendance in committee meetings; (ii) recording a minute of dissent when the nominated director considers the decision of the majority to be wrong or harmful for the society; (iii) bringing nominated directors within the same discipline regarding surcharge and other penalties as is applicable to elected directors.

Audit And Supervision

34. Audit should embrace a scrutiny as to how far the activities of a society conform to cooperative principles and to what extent the benefits of a society have accrued to the weaker or smaller among its members. More emphasis on financial soundness is not enough, whether the society takes active promotional interest in cooperative education is also one of the points to be looked into.

35. Audit machinery should be strengthened in all States on the basis of the yardsticks suggested by the Committee on Cooperative Administration as a matter of high priority.

36. In order that audit may be more objective and may provide a faithful indicator of the trends in the cooperative movement, it should be entrusted to an agency under the government but independent of the Registrar. This agency may function under the Finance Department or on the lines of the Organisations of Local Fund Audit. This will be a step in the direction of audit being finally taken over by the cooperatives themselves who may form audit unions or entrust this to the State Cooperative Unions and the National Cooperative Union. While, therefore, audit may be generally entrusted to an independent agency in each State under the State government, a pilot project in a carefully selected area may be undertaken for having audit done by cooperatives themselves through a suitable machinery devised for the purpose.

37. Federal cooperative bodies should increasingly take more responsibilities for supervision of the activities of their primary constituents. Assistance should be given to them by the Government to maintain adequate supervisory staff for this purpose. Efficient supervision by federal societies will pave the way for the eventual transfer of some of the statutory functions of the Registrar to them.

38. Central and State Government should follow the policy of promoting and strengthening central and apex societies in those cooperative sectors where they do not exist at present or exist as weak bodies. They should help the central and apex societies to build up cadres of qualified and trained personnel for effective discharge of the supervisory and other responsibilities.

Resources For Cooperatives

39. Central and State Government should come to the assistance of the cooperatives in a big way. The existing policy of State partnership in cooperative societies should continue. The Long-term Operations Fund of the Reserve Bank should be augmented, if necessary, to enable State governments to borrow larger amounts for share capital participation.

40. Adoption of the crop loan system by agricultural credit societies over the entire country is essential for meeting the credit needs of cultivators. This will, however, lead to an increase in the credit requirement. We suggest that an overall assessment of credit requirement, short, medium and long-term, should be made. Generally, there is a shortage of medium and long-term resources and these require to be augmented during the Fourth Plan.

41. Cooperative Institutions should be enabled to collect more deposits by removal of legal and administrative obstacles which at present prevent local bodies, statutory corporations etc. from using Cooperative Banks as their bankers. A suitable system of insuring or guaranteeing the deposits should be evolved so that public confidence in these institutions may be assured.

42. As a logical culmination of a process that has been going on for years, steps may be initiated for setting up a national cooperative bank which would form the apex of the cooperative financial structure in the couutry. All finance to be provided by the Central Government as well as by the Reserve Bank of India may flow to the cooperative movement through this national institution. This will be a step in the direction of promoting self-reliance within the cooperative movement. We recommend that details of the proposal may be worked out and a blue-print prepared by cooperators themselves as well as the Government.

Education In Cooperation

43. For the cooperative movement to be self-reliant and to develop on sound and healthy lines, utmost emphasis should be laid on the programme of Cooperative Education.

44. The National Cooperative Union and the State Cooperative Unions should take complete responsibility for running the training institutions. The training centres in several States which are still administered by State governments should be transferred to the concerned

State cooperative unions as early as possible.

45. It is essential that societies should contribute to Cooperative Education Fund out of their net profits. Those States which have not yet made legal provision for this purpose should do so quickly. The pattern followed in Maharashtra is commended to other States in this regard.

46. It will, however, take time before cooperatives develop their own resources and become self-supporting so far as training arrangements are concerned. They must, therefore, be assisted in a generous measure by the government for several years to come.

47. The Member Education Programme is of basic importance in the promotion of the cooperative movement. The revised programme which has been chalked out should be implemented vigorously. For this purpose formation and strengthening of district unions and formation of committee at the block level are essential steps to be taken.

48. In order to give a practical bias to Member Education Programme, it is necessary to actively involve cooperative business federations in it. It should not be difficult to work out mechanisms of collaboration between State Cooperative Unions and Business Federations in this programme.

49. It will act as a check against the formation of non-genuine societies if the programme of member education precedes the programme of organisation of societies. There should also be a programme of education of new members. There must be a tie-up between the member education programme and the drive for increase of membership in village societies.

50. Strengthening of cooperation unions is important from the point of view of de-officialisation of the movement. Cooperative training should seek to develop the quality of leadership among members. This underlines the importance of the role envisaged for Cooperative Unions which have to be the nurseries of cooperative leadership.

51. The member education programme should be linked up with the national drive for promotion of literacy. A concerned and massive programme of adult education in the country can be launched through the cooperative movement. It would be a tremendous national achievement if the target of imparting literacy to the total cooperative membership is achieved. It will usher in a revolution of light and learning in rural India.

52. We suggest that the Cooperative Department in each State should prepare a detailed annual report not only containing the relevant facts and figures regarding the cooperative movement in the State but also bringing out the weaknesses in the movement that have come to light in the course of the year. This report should be placed before the Legislature which may provide adequate time and opportunity to discuss it.

STUDY TEAM ON THE CENTRAL PUBLIC WORKS DEPARTMENT, 1964—REPORT

New Delhi, Ministry of Works and Housing, 1965. 147p.

Chairman : Shri M. Govinda Reddy.

Members : Shri N.G. Dewan (replaced by Shri B.K. Guha) ; Shri G.P. Shahani ; Shri S.G. Gokhale.

Convener : Shri R.F. Isar.

APPOINTMENT

The Committee on Prevention of Corruption (Santhanam Committee) found that administrative delays were one of the major causes of corruption and therefore recommended inter alia that each Ministry/Department/Undertaking should immediately undertake review of all existing procedures and practices to find out why and where delays occur and to devise suitable steps for their avoidance. It also recommended that a thorough study should be made of the extent, scope and modes of corruption, the preventive and remedial measures prescribed, if any, and their effectiveness.

The Government of India have had under consideration the question of examining the organisation, structure, methods of work and procedures of the offices of the Central Public Works Department with particular reference to the points at which delays occur, where bottlenecks exist and where administrative failures are possible, in the context of combating corruption. The Government of India in the Ministry of Works and Housing constituted the Study Team on the Central Public Works Department Vide their Resolution No.

14 (30)/64-EWI dated August 17, 1964.

TERMS OF REFERENCE

To examine the existing rules, manuals, codes and procedures of the Central Public Works Department.

CONTENTS

Introduction ; Organisation and Functions of the Central Public Works Department ; Planning of Works ; Structure and Staffing of the Central Public Works Department ; Contractors ; Tenders ; Conditions of Contract ; Earnest Money ; Award of Works ; Security Deposit ; Materials and Stores ; Supervision of Works ; Technical Examination ; Payment to Contractors ; Arbitration ; Reduction of Works in Divisional Offices ; Eradication of Corruption ; Summary of Recommendations ; Appendices from I to XII.

RECOMMENDATIONS

Recommendation	Action to be taken
1	2
The C.P.W.D should be allowed the time that is necessary and irreducible for the proper planning and designing of each particular work with a view to obtaining the best results. A minimum period of 12 to 21 months depending on the nature and the size of the work is reasonably required by the Department for proper planning and desiging of a work.	Circular to be issued by the Ministry of Works and Housing to all Ministries/Departments and para 86 (A) of the C.P.W.D. Code to be amended.
Availability of the site is a prerequisite for planning and designing of work and no Ministry should call upon the Department to initiate planning until the site is physically in their possession.	Circular to be issued by the Ministry of Works and Housing to all Ministries/Departments and suitable provision to be made in Section IV of the C.P.W.D. Code.
Ministries should work out their requirements accurately and comprehensively at the earliest possible stage so that once the planning is begun changes are kept to the minimum and no substantial or radical change is asked for. While there are no objections to clarifications, modifications or improvements to a plan that has already been well thought out and the main scope of which is understood major or large scale changes in the conception or size of the work that disrupt the smooth and even flow of architectural drawings should be discouraged.	Circular to be issued by the Ministry of Works and Housing to all Ministry/Departments and suitable provision to be made in Section IV of the C.P.W.D. Code.
No budget provision should be made for any work that has not previously received administrative approval.	Instructions to be issued by the Ministry of Works and Housing that the provisions of Note 4 under para 53 of the General Financial Rules, 1963 and Rule 6 of Appendix 5 of the C.P.W.A. Code, 1965 should be strictly followed.
Token budget provision, if at all necessary, should only be made for procurement of land.	Suitable provision to be made in Note 6 under para 53 of G.F.R., 1963 and Rule 6 of appendix 5 of C.P.W.A. Code, 1965.
Expenditure section should be issued along with administrative approval by the administrative Ministry. Queries or objections raised by the Ministry of Finance should be answered by the Additional Chief Engineer directly provided that where departures from the specifications of the administrative Ministry are proposed these should have the concurrence of the administrative Ministry.	Para 131 of G.F R., 1963, Para 2.1.1. (2) and note under para 4.4.1 of C.P.W.A. Code, 1965, Paras 61, 62, 63, 66, 68, 72 and 73 of C.P.W.D. Code, 1959 and Section I of C.P.W.D. Manual Vol. II, 1958 to be amended. Circular to be issued by the Ministry of Works and Housing in supersession of their O.M. No. B. II-20(17)/57 dated November 30, 1957.
Complete architectural and structural drawings and specifications should be made available to the tenderers along with the Notice Inviting Tenders.	Chief Engineer, C.P.W.D. to issue instruction for strict compliance with para 6.303 of C.P.W.D. Manual Vol. II, 1958.

1	2
Government should take a decision about the work-load that a Senior Architect Unit can reasonably be expected to handle in a year. On the basis of the yardstick that may be decided, the Architect Wing should be properly staffed to enable it to take up the work-load expected of C.P.W.D.	To be examined by the Ministry of Works and Housing in consultation with the Ministry of Finance.
Central and State Governments should take steps to start a 3 years diploma/certificate course in architecture in Polytechnics and other institutions.	The matter to be pursued by the Ministry of Works and Housing with the Ministry of Education.
In order to attract graduates in architecture, Government should consider the creation of a grade of Architectural Assistant in the scale of Rs. 325-15-475-EB-20-575.	Posts to be sanctioned in relaxation of the ban. On creation of new posts recruitment rules to be framed by the Ministry of Works and Housing.
Units the Architect Wing of the Department is adequately strengthened and staffed. The designing of some selected works should be entrusted to private architects.	Necessary authority to the C.P.W.D. with terms of appointment of Private architects to be issued by the Ministry to Works and Housing.
The Surveyor of Works Organisation should be bifurcated in a suitable manner at Zonal and Circle levels so as to provide separate units for structural planning and contract work. An Assistant Surveyor of works with one Section Officer and Grade I Draftsman should be provided in each Divison. There should be at least two Assistant Surveyors of works under each Surveyor of works in a Circle. The Electrical Circles in the Calcutta and Nagpur Zones should each be given a Surveyor of works for planning works up to the value of Rs. 2 lakhs. A post of Additional Chief Engineer (Electrical) should be created. A Central Designs Office should be set up in the office of the Chief Engineer. Divisional Accountants should be replaced by S.A.S. Accountants.	Additional posts to be created in relaxation of ban on creation of new posts and approval of the Expenditure Finance Committee to be obtained.
Government should take steps to ensure that the workload of the Divisions is such that the Department can carry out its tasks efficiently.	To be examined by the Ministry of Works and Housing in consultation with the Ministry of Finance.
The eligibility period of 5 years of service as Assistant Executive Engineer and 8 years as Assistant Engineer for promotion as Executive Engineer should be restored at the earliest stage.	Position to be reviewed by the Ministry of Works and Housing in consultation with the U.P.S.C.
For conversion of temporary posts into permanent ones the workload of the preceding three years should be taken into account for determining work of a permanent nature.	To be examined by the Ministry of Works and Housing in consultation with the Ministry of Finance.
Permanent strength of Engineers in the C.P.W.D. should be in creased by 20% to provide a deputation reserve.	To be examined by the Ministry of Works and Housing in consultation with the Ministry of Finance.
The period of training of direct recruits to Engineering Service should be increased to 52 weeks.	Instructions to be issued by the Ministry of Works and Housing to the Chief Engineer, C.P.W.D.
Section Officers should be given training in Public Works Accounts and Engineering Practice.	Necessary arrangements to be made by the Chief Engineer, C.P.W.D.
Clerks with special aptitude in accounts should be given	Necessary arrangements to be made by the

1	2
training in Public Works Accounts and should remain in Accounts Branches of the Divisional Officers.	Chief Engineer, C.P.W.D.
Clerks in Accounts Branches of the Divisional Offices should be rotated between the Divisions and Sub-Divisions periodically.	Necessary instructions to be issued by the Chief Engineer, C.P.W D.
Action should be taken to weed out or revert unsuitable officers to lower posts in accordance with the various alternatives open to Government.	To be noted for guidance by the Ministry of Works and Housing and the appointing authorities in the C.P.W.D.
Fundamental Rule 56(c)(iv) should be suitably amended so that the Engineers who do not attain the rank of Superintending Engineer may be retired on reaching the age of 50 years.	Amendment to F.R. 56(c)(iv) to be issued by the Ministry of Finance.
Section Officers should be made eligible for allotment of scooters from the Government quota irrespective of their pay.	Instructions to be issued by the Ministry of Industry and Supply.
Government should review the rates of conveyance allowance admissible to officers.	Matter to be examined by the Ministry of Finance.
Transfer rules should not be rigidly applied.	Instructions to be issued by the Ministry of Works and Housing.
Officers who are transferred from one station to another should be given priority in the allotment of Government residential accommodation.	Rules regarding allotment of Government residences to be amended by the Ministry of Works and Housing.
Government should construct parmanent residential accommodation for Engineers and Section Officers of permanent maintenance Divisions.	Chief Engineer, C.P.W.D. to furnish estimates for sanction to the Ministry of Works and Housing.
Where large construction projects are undertaken in out of the way places Government Should construct temporary or semi-permanent accommodation for field staff.	Chief Engineer, C.P.W.D. to make provision in the works estimates.
Early steps should be taken to start Central Schools at stations where there is a need for them.	Matter to be taken up with the Ministry of Education.
A review of the list of approved contractors to cover the period 1958 to 1964 should be carried out. Thereafter the review should be carried out every three years.	Chief Engineer, C.P.W.D. to take necessary action.
Foreign exchange and other facilities should be afforded to the contractors to import brick-making plants and other essential machinery.	Ministry of Finance and Ministry of Commerce and Industry to note the recommendation.
Time limit between the date of call of tenders and opening of tenders should be 7 days in the case of works costing up to Rs. 1 lakh, 2 weeks in the case of works costing between Rs. 1 to Rs. 10 lakhs and 3 weeks in the case of works costing more than Rs. 10 lakhs.	Para 6.320 of C.P.W.D. Manual, Vol II, 1958 to be amended.
Executive Engineers should personally satisfy themselves that the instructions regarding issue of tender notices are meticulously followed.	Provision to be made in Section III of C.P.W.D. Manual, Vol. II, 1958.
Tender notices should be issued only when all tender documents are ready. Tender forms should not be sold on the date on which the tenders are the due to be opened. In case of tenders costing less than Rs. 2 lakhs, the sale of tender forms should be stopped 24 hours befor the time fixed for opening of the tenders.	Para 6.331 of the C.P.W.D. Manual, Vol. II, 1958 to be amended.
Conditions of contract should not be issued with indivi-	Conditions of contract to be printed in a

1	2
dual tenders but should be consolidated in the form of a saleable pamphlet.	saleable pamphlet and necessary provision to be made in Section III of the C.P.W.D. Manual, Vol. II, 1958.
Divisional Accountants should be made responsible for the safe custody of tender documents during the stage these remain in the Accounts Branch until submission to the Executive Engineer.	Provision to be made in Para 4.2.4. of C.P.W.D. Code, 1965 and Para 6.343 of C.P.W.D. Manual, Vol. II, 1958.
The provision regarding acceptance of tenders within 90 days in case of Delhi works may be extended to other stations after assessing its success in Delhi.	Chief Engineer, C.P.W.D. to review the position in April, 1966.
The work of comparative study of contract forms in other countries with a view to considering improvement in the conditions of C.P.W.D. contracts should be completed as expeditiously as possible.	A Committee to be appointed for considering the revision of conditions of contract.
Amount of earnest money to be deposited should be fixed at 1% ad valorem of the estimated cost of the work, subject to a minimum of Rs. 100 and a maximum of Rs. 20,000.	Instructions to be issed by the Ministry of Works and Housing and para 6.401 of the C.P.W.D. Manual, Vol. II, 1958 and relevant rules for enlistment of contractors to be amended.
Exective Engineers should be authorised at their discretion to dispense with the condition of calling for earnest money in case of works costing Rs. 5,000 or less.	
Executive Engineers should periodically review the tender registers with a view to ensuring that the earnest money is refunded in time. If the tenderers do not come forward to get their challans endorsed for refund, the challans should be sent to them by registered post within a week after expiry of the prescribed period.	Necessary instructions to be issued by Chief Engineer, C.P.W.D. and provision to be made in Section IV of C.P.W.D. Manual, Vol. II, 1958.
The power of the Superintending Engineers and Additional Chief Engineers to accept single tenders should be raised to Rs. 5 lakhs and Rs 25 lakhs respectively. The powers of the Chief Engineer/Additional Chief Engineers to award a work by acceptance of a tender other than the lowest should be raised to Rs. 25 lakhs. The powers of the Chief Engineer to award a work by negotiation with a tenderer other than the lowest should be raised to Rs. 25 lakhs. The powers of the Chief Engineer/Additional Chief Engineers to award a work by noegtiation without call of tenders, after an infructuous call of tenders or with a firm which has not quoted should be raised to Rs. 50,000.	A consolidated schedule of the financial powers of officers of the C.P.W.D. to be issued by the Ministry of Works & Housing and to be incorporated in the C.P.W.D Code and C.P.W.D. Manual, Vol. II, 1958. Isolated Paras relating to the powers to be deleted from the C.P.W.D. Code.
No negotiations should be resorted to when the lowest rates obtained through call of tenders are within marginal limits.	Ministry of Works & Housing letter No. 5/53/61 Cont. dated April 2, 1962 to be amended.
Provision for deposit of security in any of the forms mentioned in the General Financial Rules should be in corporated in the general conditions of contract.	Clause I of the conditions of contract to be amended.
Executive Engineers should personally keep a close watch on delays in the refund of security deposits.	Provision to be made in Section V of C.P.W.D. Manual, Vol. II, 1958.
A Liaison Office should be set up in the Directorate General of Supplies and Disposals to expedite procurement of stores required by the C.P.W.D.	Necessary posts to be sanctioned in relaxation of the ban on creation of new posts.

1	2
There should be a larger allocation of cement on a higher priority basis for C.P.W.D. works.	Instructions to be issued by the Ministry of Industry & Supply.
No tenders should be invited unless the stipulated materials are likely to be available.	Instructions to be issued by the Chief Engineer, C.P.W.D. and incorporated in the C.P.W.D. Manual, Vol. II 1958.
Billets should be supplied to rerollers on the understanding that the bars produced to that extent would be made available to meet the requirements of Governments indentors.	Instructions to be issued by the Ministry of Steel & Mines in consultation with the Ministry of Industry and Supply.
The C.P.W.D. should not undertake the responsibility for supply of decontrolled categories of steel except to the extent stocks permit.	Instructions to be issued by the Chief Engineer, C.P.W.D. and incorporated in the C.P.W.D. Manual, Vol. II, 1958.
The C.P.W.D.'s requirements of steel should be accorded second priority.	Instructions to be issued by the Ministry of Steel and Mines.
In respect of mathematical and survey instruments not manufactured by National Instrument Factory normal powers of purchase upto the value of Rs. 5,000 should be utilised. Where the supply of instruments manufactured by the factory is likely to be delayed enhanced powers should be given to C.P.W.D. officers for local purchase.	Instructions to be issued by the Ministry of Works and Housing and para 155 of C.P.W.D. Code, 1959 to be amended.
The C.P.W.D. should purchase construction/machinery upto a limit of about Rs. 2 crores.	Chief Engineer, C.P.W.D. to send an estimate for sanction to the Ministry of Works & Housing. Ministry of Finance to release the required foreign exchange.
The D.G.S. & D., should be asked to conclude Rate Contracts for more items frequently required in substantial quantities by the C.P.W.D.	Chief Engineer, C.P.W.D. to send a list of items with approximate quantities required to the D.G.S. & D.
For local purchase of stores, quotations should also be invited directly from manufacturers or recognised dealers.	Instructions to be issued by the Chief Engineer, C.P.W.D. and Para 7.211 of the C.P.W.D. Manual, Vol. II 1958 to be amended.
A scientific study of the procedure followed in the Stores Divisions should be undertaken.	A Committee to be appointed.
The minimum qualification for the post of Work Assistant should be Matriculation or equivalent. Condidates should have a working knowledge of elementary engineering.	Recruitment rules to be framed and issued by the Ministry of Works and Housing.
Defective work should be pointed out during execution and got rectified immediately.	Executive instructions to be issued by the Chief Engineer, C.P.W.D. and para 6.1205 of C.P.W.D. Manual, Vol. II. 1958 to be amended.
If the experiment of reduction of supervisory staff in the case of works entrusted to the N.B.C.C. proves successful it should be extended to other public sector undertakings and to contractors of proved integrity and technical competence.	Chief Engineer, C.P.W.D., to review the position in 1967.
The Chief Technical Examiners' Organisation should continue under the Central Vigilance Commission.	Planning Commission (Committee on Plan Projects) to be apprised of the decision.
All items of work should be measured by the Section Officer except those specifically entrusted to the Assistant Engineers. Instructions regarding recording and checking of measurements by the Departmental Officers should be revised.	Para 5.605 of the C.P.W.D. Manual, Vol. II, 1958 to be revised.
The prescribed time schedules for payment of bills and issue of completion certificates should be rigidly enforced.	Chief Engineer, C.P.W.D., to issue executive instructions.
In case of contracts up to the value of Rs. 1 lakh the power	Para 10.2.18 of the C.P.W.D. Code, 1965

1	2
to sanction advance payment of running bills should be delegated to the Executive Engineer.	to be amended.
Detailed instructions should be issued regarding advance payment (without measurements) at pre-determined levels.	Ministry of Works & Housing issue detailed instructions in consultation with the Accountant General, Commerce, Works & Miscellaneous in persuance of the note under para 10.2.25 of C.P.W.D. Code, 1965.
Superintending Engineers should be given power to authorise payment of alternate running bills when monthly payments cannot be made on the basis of recorded measurements.	Para 6.1209 of C.P.W.D. Manual, Vol. II, 1958 to be amended.
Detailed measurements of 5% of the total number of units need only be recorded in cases where not less than 50 units of a repetitive type of building are constructed.	Provision to be made in para 10.2.7. of the C.P.W.A. Code, 1965.
The lump sum form of contract should be increasingly used.	Chief Engineer, C.P.W.D. to issue necessary instructions.
The proposal for payment of interest at 1% per annum for delay in payment should be implemented.	Clause 7 of the conditions of contract to be amended.
Where a tenderer offers a rebate for timely payment this should be accepted.	Chief Engineer, C.P.W.D. to issue necessary instructions and provision to be made in Section III of the C.P.W.D. Manual, Vol. II, 1958.
Steps should be taken to reduce disputes with contractors.	Chief Engineer, C.P.W.D. to issue executive instructions.
To reduce arrears of arbitration cases, the number of arbitrators and counsel should be increased.	Required number of posts to be sanctioned in relaxation of the ban on the creation of new posts.
If a contractor fails to claim reference to arbitration within 30 days of the intimation that his final bill is ready for payment his claim should be deemed to be finally extinguished and time barred.	Clause 25 of the conditions of contract to be amended.
Generally all issues should be referred to arbitration and the decision whether any issue is or is not within the purview of the arbitration clause should be left to the arbitrators.	Instructions to be issued by the Ministry of Works and Housing in consultation with the Ministry of Law.
The numbers of periodical returns should be reduced.	Ministry of Works and Housing and Chief Engineer, C.P.W.D. to issue necessary instructions.
The limits of minor works should be raised to Rs. 1 lakh.	Para 2.1.1 (36) of C.P.W.D. Code, 1965 to be amended.
Central Public Works Department should be absolved of the responsibility of evaluating the houses of officers suspected of possessing disproportionate assets.	Ministry of Works and Housing to inform the Ministry of Home Affairs.
Payment of the rent for private buildings should be made by the Directorate of Estates in all places where it operates and not by the Central Public Works Department.	Ministry of Works and Housing to issue necessary instructions.
Allotment and recovery of rent of Government residences where there is no organisation of the Directorate of Estates should be done by the administrative Ministries concerned and not by the Central Public Works Department.	Do.
The Central Public Works Department should not be called upon to furnish certificates of non-availability of Government accommodation or to certify the reasonableness	Item 18 of Schedule V of the Delegation of Financial Powers Rules, 1958 to be amended.

1	2
of the rent of private buildings or to hire private accommodation for other Ministries.	
Preparation of capital and revenue accounts for residential buildings should be dispensed with.	Para 22.4.31 of C.P.W.A. Code, 1965 to be deleted.

ONE-MAN INDEPENDENT BODY TO ENQUIRE INTO THE QUESTION OF DEARNESS ALLOWANCE PAYABLE TO CENTRAL GOVERNMENT EMPLOYEES, 1964—REPORT

Delhi, Manager of Publications, 1965. 61p.

Member : Shri S. K. Das.

APPOINTMENT

The One-man Independent Body was constituted under the Government of India, Ministry of Finance (Department of Expenditure), vide their Resolution No. F. 1(5)-E. II (B)/64, dated August 27, 1964.

TERMS OF REFERENCE

To examine and report whether in the matter of dearness allowance payable to Central Government employees, compensation already sanctioned by them from time to time in the various pay ranges is adequate and to recommend what changes, if any, are necessary therein.

CONTENTS

Part I—Priliminary—Terms of Reference; General Principles; Cost of Living Index and the Rise in Prices; The State of the Economy—Impact of Increased Pays on Prices and Other Relevant Factors; The Nature and Number of Pay Ranges, the Upper Pay Limit up to which Dearness Allowance should be granted; Neutralisation; Financial Implications of the Recommendations.

Part II—Dearness Allowance Formula.

Part III—Appendices I to VI.

RECOMMENDATIONS

It would be unwise on principle and inexpedient in practice to grant dearness allowance to Central Government employees on a local or regional basis. As to controlled commodities, I see no objection to the adoption of controlled rates. Any other method would be tantamount to accepting as legal, something which is clearly illegal.

It would be unfair and unjust to deny to Government employees adjustment of dearness allowance to compensate for the fall in their real income.

The upper pay limit should now be raised to Rs. 1,200 with marginal adjustments in the pay range of Rs. 1,201 to Rs. 1,289; it is at that range that the safety cushion drops almost to nil. It is to be remembered that I am not recommending full compensation to persons in the upper pay limit. Far from it, the neutralisation in their case, as I shall presently show, will be the lowest. The point is that they deserve some compensation to be provided against the phenomenal rise in prices.

The suggestion that all those who come within the taxation limit under the Indian Income-tax Act should not get dearness allowance does not conform to the general scheme of dearness allowance formulated by the Second Pay Commission, nor do I think that tax concessions under the existing scheme of Income-tax Law can give them sufficient relief for the fall in their real income. Prices fluctuate frequently and the rise may be steep or gradual. It is obvious that taxation law cannot be changed as frequently as prices fluctuate, and tax relief can seldom keep pace with price fluctuations. As to the standard of living of employees in the higher pay ranges, I do not think that it is an undesirable thing in itself that middle class families maintain a better standard of living. It is well-known that what distinguishes the middle class from the working class is that the latter spends a major part of its income on primary necessaries, whereas the former spends somewhat less on primary necessaries and more on education and other amenities of life. It is indeed true that when there is a rise in prices, particularly of essential commodities like foodgrain, middle class families can cut down their expenditure on non-essential articles and thereby mitigate the effect of the rise. This they can do to a much greater extent than poorer people who have to spend almost the whole of their income on primary necessaries of life. That is the reason why neutralisation must descend rather steeply when the first category of middle class families (say Rs. 400 and upward) is reached. But there is a danger of pushing this argument too far, because there are certain other considerations which must also be taken note of. I do not think that it is a sound policy, either of economics or administration, to "depress" the middle class to the position of the working class. The administration must always require persons of skill, special knowledge of administrative ability, and they are usually recruited from the middle classes. Depressing the standard of living of these classes may ultimately affect the recruitment of suitable persons in the higher pay ranges; it may, in the end, be a very doubtful gain to deny them some compensation for a fall in their real income. A contented service is generally an asset; and a discontented service a liability. It is also to be recommended that the temptation to make currupt or illegal gains is always stronger in an insufficiently paid service, which has to look to other means for supplementing the normal income. The problem is not one of pound, shillings and pence only; that is a relevant factor, but it is also an administrative and human problem.

My recommendations as to the pay ranges and the upper limit are:

Pay Ranges

1. 70—109
2. 110—149
3. 150—209
4. 210—399
5. 400—599
6. 600—799
7. 800—999
8. 1000—1200

Some Associations, particularly of lower paid groups asked for a percentage calculation on the basis of full neutralisation or slightly less than full neutralisation for each employee in the lower paid groups. In my opinion, such a scheme would mean a departure from the basic formulation of the Second Pay Commission, and would involve administrative difficulties in calculating dearness allowance, and also very heavy outlay of expenditure which the national economy would not be able to bear.

It is my considered opinion that the dearness allowance granted by Government from time to time is not adequate and requires modification. It is based on neutralisation which falls far short of a fair and reasonable compensation for the fall in real income of Central Government employees as a result of the abnormal rise in prices, a rise which has reduced the income to less than half its former value within a very short period. I am aware that Government is not committed to a cent per cent neutralisation even in respect of the lowest man in the lowest pay range.

I have come to the very definite conclusion that a just and adequate neutralisation must start at 90 per cent in the lowest category and descend progressively in the higher pay ranges. Any thing less will be inadequate and unreal as a compensation for the fall in income due to the abnormal rise in prices. If the price line is not held in future, even a 90 per cent neutralisation may prove illusory.

Giving my best consideration to all the factors involved, I recommend the following graduated scale of neutralisation:

	Pay Ranges		Neutralisation of each pay range on the basis of the lowest paid employee of the range
1.	70—109	...	90 per cent
2.	110—149	...	85 per cent
3.	150—209	...	80 per cent
4.	210—399	...	70 per cent
5.	400—599	...	40 per cent
6.	600—799	...	30 per cent
7.	800—999	...	24 per cent
8.	1000—1200	...	20 per cent

The scale of neutralisation follows the pattern of the scheme of the Second Pay Commission and starting from 90 per cent in the lowest category, goes down to 20 per cent in the highest. It follows the well-established principle—"higher the salary, lower is the neutralisation". At the end of the marginal adjustments in the pay range of Rs. 1201 to Rs. 1289, neutralisation drops down to nil in all compensation cases.

There is, however, one point which requires some elucidations here. It may well be asked why neutralisation descends so steeply (i.e., from 70 per cent to 40 per cent) when the pay-range of Rs. 400-599 is reached. One reason is that the earlier pay range (Rs. 210—399) is a combination of two pay-ranges to give effect to observations of the Second Pay Commission. The second reason, which in my view, is the real reason, is that neutralisation must descend steeply when middle class families are reached. I have said that the cushion which they had earlier has either disappeared or shrunk to a negligible limit by reason of the abnormal rise in prices; therefore, they are now entitled to some compensation and should come within the upper limit of the grant of dearness allowance. But employees in this group are also in a position to meet the rise in prices of essential commodities by cutting down their expenditure on non-essential goods. This they are able to do much better than the poorer sections of the community. I had referred to this aspect of the problem earlier in my report. The sum and substance of the matter is that middle class families should get some compensation, because they are also hit by the rise in prices ; but in their case neutralisation, that is, the extent of compensation must be much less. This is the ratio of the steep descent from 70 per cent to 40 per cent when the pay range of Rs. 400-500 is reached. Therefore, there is again a gradual descent.

Recommendations Regarding Neutralisation and Dearness Allowance

*Pay ranges	Neutralisation for the lowest paid employees of each pay range	D.A. at 135 points+			D.A. at 145 points+		Estimated** No. employees (in lakhs)	Average* of neutralisation for the entire pay range
		Method (a)	Method (b)	What Govt. has already given	Method (a)	Method (b)		
1. 70—109	90%	22	23	20.50	28	29	13.20	79%
2. 110—149	85%	33	29	25.50	42	38	4.40	73%
3. 150—209	80%	42	44	52	54	56	2.42	71%
4. 210—399	70%	51	49	50				
				35	66	64	1.51	56%
				20				
				20				
5. 400—599	40%	55		—	70		0.29	34%
6. 600—799	30%	65		—	80		0.07	27%
7. 800—999	24%	65			85		0.05	22%
8. 1000—1200	20%	70			90		0.02	18%

*Pay ranges adopted by the Government for the purpose of granting D.A. have been kept in fact in the lower pay ranges except that the pay range of Rs. 300—400 has been combined with the immediately preceding pay range i.e., 210—300. This has been done to give effect to the recommendations of the Second Pay Commission in this regard in paragraph 9 of Chapter IX of their report.

+The actual D.A. for each pay range has been adjusted to the nearest rupee in the case of the first four pay ranges and thereafter to the nearest multiple of five rupees.

Method (a) *:* The method followed in this case is to neutralise to the specified extent the increase of 35 points/45 points in the All-India working class consumer price index (base 1949-100).

The method followed in this case is to neutralise to the specified extent the increase of 20 points/30 points in the consumer price Index, for each of the first four pay ranges and then to add to this the D.A. already granted on the basis of the Second Pay Commission's recommendations (when the index stood at 115). For the next four pay ranges the entire increase of 35 points/45 points has been neutralised to the specified extent, since the Second Pay Commission's recommendations did not give any relief to these categories.

**The figures for the different pay ranges have been estimated on the basis of the data contained in "Census of Central Government employees—1962". The total No. of Central Government employees in 1964 has been assumed at 22 lakhs.

* The averge neutralisation for each pay range has been computed as a weighted average of the neutralisation percentages for smaller pay groups (of five rupees in the first pay range, of ten rupees in the second and third pay ranges, of twenty rupees in the fourth pay range and of fifty rupees in the remaining pay ranges) within the pay range. The weights are the estimated numbers of employees in each of these smaller pay groups.

At the annual average of 145 points which was reached in September, 1964, I would recommend the payment of dearness allowance from October 1, 1964 as follows :

	Pay Range	Dearness Allowance as recommended from October 1, 1964
1.	70—109	Rs. 28
2.	110—149	Rs. 42
3.	150—209	Rs. 54
4.	210—399	Rs. 66
5.	400—599	Rs. 70
6.	600—799	Rs. 80
7.	800—999	Rs. 85
8.	1000—1200	Rs. 90

There should be marginal adjustments for employees drawing pay of Rs. 1201 and above but below Rs. 1290 in order to avoid anomalies.

The real basis of compensation is neutralisation which must bear a just proportion to the fall in income and the principle followed is, "higher the salary, lower is the neutralisation". I do not think there is any principle that the amount of dearness allowance must also progressively decrease (irrespective of neutralisation) beyond the pay range of Rs. 300. Such a principle, if it can be called a principle, is likely to be artificial and even arbitrary. It seems to me that the limit of Rs. 300 is itself some what arbitrary, and the second Pay Commission clearly envisaged that Government employees in the pay range of Rs. 300—399 should be grouped with those below Rs. 300 in future upward adjustments of dearness allowance. I have found it somewhat difficult to appreciate on what principle Government gave a sum of Rs. 20 only as dearness allowance to employees in the pay range of Rs. 400-599, when an employee on a lower pay range got Rs. 50 as dearness allowance. The grant was no doubt an ad hoc grant ; but I can discover no recognised principle behind it.

I would recommend, though not without some hesitation, against retrospective operation of the recommendations to a period beyond October 1, 1964.

NARMADA WATER RESOURCES DEVELOPMENT COMMITTEE, 1964—REPORT

New Delhi, Ministry of Irrigation and Power, 1965. 224p.

Chairman : Dr. A.N. Khosla.
Members : Shri Moti Ram ; Shri G.N. Pande ; Shri H.R. Bhatia ; Shri V. Ananda Rao.
Secretary : Shri K.S.S. Murthy.

APPOINTMENT

The Narmada Water Resources Development Committee was constituted under the Ministry of Irrigation and Power, vide their Resolution No. DWII-32(4)/64, dated September 5, 1964.

TERMS OF REFERENCE

(i) To collect, with the assistance of the Central Water and Power Commission and the State Governments of Madhya Pradesh, Maharashtra and Gujarat, the relevant reports, correspondence and data and draw up a Master Plan for the optimum and integrated development of the Narmada water resources ;

(ii) In consultation with the three State Governments recommended the projects to be taken up in the first instance, and the order in which they should be started so that after execution of the first group the further development of the valley becomes self-financing, if possible, and provide maximum benefits to the State concerned ;

(iii) To examine in particular Navagam project together with alternative projects, if any, and suggest appropriate full reservoir level and consequential adjustments ;

(iv) To suggest the distribution of benefits and costs among the States ; and

(v) To make recommendations on any other ancillary matters.

CONTENTS

Introduction ; Appointment of Committee and Terms of Reference : Meetings, Tours, Discussions ; Narmada River System; Historical Review ; Hydrology; Proposals of State Governments and General Review; Crop Pattern and Water Requirements; Water Resources of Mahi and other rivers crossed by the Navagam Canal in Gujarat ; Navigation ; Flood Control ; Committee's Approach to the Plan of Narmada Development ; Terminal Storage Dam, Optimum Height and Power Studies ; Distribution of Costs and Benefits ; Committee's Master Plan for Optimum and Integrated Development of Narmada Water Resources; Organisational set-up for implementation of the Plan ; Summary ; Committee's recommendations ; Tables ; Annexures ; Plates.

RECOMMENDATIONS

Approach To The Master Plan

Regarding the Master Plan for the optimum and integrated development of the Narmada water resources. the Committee recommend that it should aim at :—

(i) Giving highest priority to National interest, while safeguarding, at the same time, the legitimate rights and needs of the States concerned ;

(ii) Providing for maximum benefits in irrigation, power generation, flood control, navigation, fish culture, tourism, recreation, etc. ;

(iii) Extending irrigation to maximum area within physical limits of command, irrespective of State boundaries ;

(iv) Extending irrigation to the arid areas of Great Rann of Kutch in Gujarat, and Barmer and Jalore in Rajasthan, both having a long common border with Pakistan, to enable peasants to settle permanently in such border lands and produce more food ; and

(v) Reducing to the unavoidable minimum the waters going waste to the sea.

Assessment Of Areas To Be Irrigated And Water Requirements

The Narmada river at Navagam—where it debouches into the Gujarat plains—has a mean annual run-off of 36 Million Acre Feet against 32.8 MAF of the three Punjab rivers—the Sutlej, Beas and Ravi combined for irrigation of over 124 lakh acres. According to the Committee's assessment this run-off of 36 MAF will fully provide for irrigation of 65 lakh acres in Madhya Pradesh, 45.81 lakh acres in Gujarat, 10,000 acres in Maharashtra and 1,00,000 acres in border areas of Rajasthan or a total of 111.91 lakh acres and after generation of all possible power, still leave 7.15 to 5.60 MAF going to the sea.

Water Account For Various Plan Periods

Navagam FRL+500

	1975	1980	1985	1990	1995
	MAF	MAF	MAF	MAF	MAF
Consumptive use for irrigation	4.1	9.3	15.75	20.50	23.80
Utilisation for power	22.25	17.89	11.53	6.85	3.90
Evaporation losses	2.50	2.70	2.70	2.70	2.70
Water going to sea utilised for irrigation or power	7.15	6.11	6.02	5.95	5,60

After careful assessment, the Committee recommend the following areas for irrigation and water requirements in the various States, assuming a uniform delta of 2.4 ft. at canal head inclusive of reservoir losses which figure has been derived from a study of realistic crop pattern, natural rainfall, drainage facilities and regeneration, use of subsoil waterable in areas in plains as a result of irrigation which will make available large volumes of water in subsoil reservoirs for use in lift irrigation by pumps or otherwise and thereby preventing water logging (see table on next page).

Equivalent water-supply of Mahi thus released shall be transferred for use in Rajasthan.

The above is subject to the provision that Madhya Pradesh will have unrestricted use of water for their projects except in years of poor rainfall when sharing of stored supplies will have to be done.

Sharing Of Water For Irrigation In Years Of Low Run-off

The Committee recommend that sharing of water for irrigation between Madhya Pradesh and Gujarat should start when the total storage in all the Madhya Pradesh reservoirs including medium and minor and Navagam reservoir is less than 16.00 MAF on the Ist October. Madhya Pradesh will be entitled to three-fifths and Gujarat two-fifths.

If minor irrigation reservoirs and areas irrigated by them are excluded, then sharing will become necessary when the combined storage in all the medium and on the 1st october. This storage will be shared by Madhya Pradesh and Gujarat in the ratio of 4:3, respectively.

If the total storage is more than 14.5 MAF, but Navagam has less than 6.2 MAF of storage, then Madhya Pradesh reservoirs will have to make adequate releases to make up the deficit in Navagam reservoir.

Navagam Canal

For irrigation of areas in Gujarat and Rajasthan, the Committee recommend FSL +300 for the Navagam Canal.

Location Of Terminal Storage Reservoir, Optimum Level And Installed Capacity

The Committee recommends the Navagam site, at the downstream and of the 10 mile Hiranphat-Navagam gorge, as the best location for a terminal dam and reservoir.

The Committee further recommends FRL of +500 as the optimum for a reservoir at the Navagam Site.

The Committee also recommends that the installed capacity at the river bed power station and the canal power station should be 1,000 MW and 240 MW, respectively with one standby unit in each.

These recommendations are based on considerations of economics, power development flood control and reducing to the minimum wastage of water to the sea.

Implementation Of Projects In Madhya Pradesh

The Committee recommends that all dams and other works located in Madhya Pradesh should be the exclusive concern of and be executed by that State.

Areas to be Irrigated and Water Requirements

Project	Madhya Pradesh		Maharashtra		Gujarat		Rajasthan		Total	
	Irri. lakh acreas	Water allowance MAF	Irri. lakh acreas	Water allowance MAF	Irri. lakh acreas	Water allowance MAF	Irri. lakh acreas	Water allowance MAF	Irri. lakh acreas	Water allowance MAF
Major Projects ...	25.00	6.00	...	...	34.74	8.33	1.00	0.25	60.74	14.58
Medium Projects ...	32.00	7.68	0.10	0.10	...	...	...	...	32.10	7.78
Major Projects ...	8.00	1.92	...	...	...	...	...	...	8.00	1.92
Great Rann of Kutch ...	...	...	...	...	4.50	1.08	...	...	4.50	1.08
Mahi Command transferred to Nevagam Canal. ...	...	...	...	...	6.57	1.58	...	...	6.57	1.58
Total ...	65.00	15.60	0.10	0.10	45.81	10.99	1.00	0.25	111.91	26.94
Deduct contribution of Heran and ...	...	...	...	...	...	0.34	...	...	...	0.34
Orsang	...	...	...	...	...	10.65	...	...	...	26.60

Implementation Of Navagam Pradesh

In respect of Navagam dam, power plant and appurtenant works, the Committee recommends that these should be treated as a joint project. These should be executed by the Government of Gujarat under the overall financial and technical control of a Control Board which should have representatives of the three State Governments, constituted generally on the Bhakra model. The Control Board should be assisted by a Board of Consultants as for the Bhakra Project.

The construction of Navagam Canal and any power development on this canal or river system in Gujarat, will be the responsibility of the Gujarat Government. The latter may set up a suitable Control Board for the purpose and may have a representative of Rajasthan for only the canal portion of the project.

Sharing of Benefits

The Committee further recommends that the costs and benefits of the project be shared by the participating Governments in the proportions set forth below—the cost of irrigation part being wholly borne by the Gujarat State.

The Committee have proceeded on the assumption that Madhya Pradesh should get as much power from Navagam as it would have got if a dam with FRL+465 had been constructed at Hiranphal, and that the other two States should share the balance equally.

Calculated On This Basis, The Shares For Navagam FRL+465 For The mean Year 1985 would be—

Madhya Pradesh		Gujarat		Maharashtra
1.64	:	1	:	1

Almost the entire submersion of culturable areas will be in Madhya Pradesh. Although compensation under the Land Acquisition Act would be paid by the project both for culturable and other areas, the resettlement and rehabilitation of the persons displaced will pose a major human problem for the State.

The Committee, therefore, recommends that the ratio of sharing for the mean year, as well as for all other years, should be Madhya Pradesh (2), Maharashtra (1) and Gujarat (1) for Navagam FRL+465.

The Committee further recommends sharing for this and higher levels of Navagam reservoir as given in the Table on next page :—

Proportionate Shares of Power for Different FRLs of Navagam Reservoir

FRL of Navagam reservoir	Culturable area submerged			Proportionate share of		
	Madhya Pradesh	Maharashtra	Gujarat	Madhya Pradesh	Maharashtra	Gujarat
	Acres	Acres	Acres			
+465	25,600	1,900	2,500	2.00	1	1
+480	52,500	1,950	2,500	2.15	1	1
+490	73,500	2,000	2,600	2.30	1	1
+500	94,500	2,050	2,630	2.50	1	1

The consequent share of power of each State for different reservoir levels and different years is given in Table :

Shares of Power for Different FRLs of Navagam and Different Stages of Development

FRL of Navagam	Share of Madhya Pradesh					Share of Maharashtra					Share of Gujarat				
	1975	1980	1985	1990	1995	1975	1980	1985	1990	1995	1975	1980	1985	1990	1995
+500	585	632	527	386	283	234	254	212	155	114	234	254	212	155	114
+490	...	...	473	...	...	...	...	205	...	...	...	...	205	...	...
+480	...	...	434	...	...	...	...	201	...	...	...	...	201	...	...
+465	521	531	388	269	185	261	266	194	135	92	261	266	194	135	92

NOTE :— When full utilisation for irrigation, the quantity of power generated goes down, the Hydro-Power Station can be used as a peaking station with load factor of 30 per cent or lower, thus making full use of the installed capacity.

The Committee also recommend that power surplus to the requirement of any of the State be sold to other participating State in proportion to their shares specified in Table.

Gujarat will be free to generate power on the canal and river system in the State at their own expense. The development of power at the head regulator of the canal will be in the common pool.

Allocation Of Cost Between Irrigation and Power

The allocation of costs between irrigation and power has been based on the mean year 1985. The allocation to power will, therefore, remain the same all years for the same FRL of Navagam reservoir. For other FRLs of Navagam reservoir, this allocation will very on the basis mentioned above.

Sharing Of Cost

Shares of cost will, accordingly, be as given in Table.

Sharing of Power Portion of Cost of Navagam Dam, Power Plant and Appurtenant Works for Different FRLs

FRL of Navagam	Total cost of production	Shares of		
		Madhya Pradesh	Maharashtra	Gujarat
			Rupees Crores	
+465	119	59.5	29.75	29.75
+480	132.3	68.5	31.90	31.90
+490	140.5	75.3	32.60	32.60
+500	147	81.6	32.70	32.70

The above costs are inclusive of the amounts mentioned in the Paras.

400 KV Transmission Link between Navagam and Barwaha : The Committee recommend the construction of 400 KV transmission link between Navagam and Barwaha Power Stations. Cost of the link up to Hiranphal only, with sub-station at Hiranphal, is estimated at Rs. 8 crores, which will be charged to the power part of the Navagam Project.

Allowance for Regulated Releases from Punasa Reservoir: Navagam Project will be utilising regulated releases from the Punasa Project unstrained. The Committee do not accept the principle that part of the cost of upper riparian project be allocated to the projects down below. However, under the special circumstances of Navagam Project, the Committe recommend charging a fixed sum of Rs. 13 crores, irrespective of the actual cost of the Punasa dam, to Navagam Project on account of this.

Out of this, Rs. 8 crores will be chargeable to the power part of Navagam Project and Rs. 5 crores to the irrigation part.

Cost of Power Generation : Cost of power generation at Navagam for FRLs+465 as well as+500 for the different years is given in Table :—

Cost of Power Generation at Navagam

	1975		1980		1985		1990		1995	
	Rs. Per Kw	Paise Per Kwh	Rs. Per Kw	Paise Per Kwh	Rs. Per Kw	Paise Per Kwh	Rs. Per Kw	Paise Per Kwh	Rs. Per Kw	Paise Per Kwh
Navagam +500 capital cost Rs. 147 crores	1,393	1.73	1,290	1.98	1,545	2.65	2,110	3.61	2,880	4.93
Corresponding to sum at charge	1,380	1.43	800	1.28	438	1.14	51	0.97	Nil	1.19
Navagam +465 capital cost Rs. 119 crores	1,140	1.73	1,120	1.91	1,533	2.63	2,210	3.75	3,230	5.52
Corresponding to sum at charge	1,090	1.43	621	1.16	308	1.01	Nil	0.86	Nil	1.26

Navigation : The cost of providing navigation facilities in the form of list Weirs, locks, connecting channels, raising of bridge, etc. upto Bargi reservoir has been very roughly estimated between Rs. 50 and 60 crores.

The Committee recommend that the designs of navigation works should be taken up simultaneously with the design of canals, regulators, dams, etc., so that both works can be taken up for construction at the same time.

It would be desirable to provide navigation facilities as soon as the inland waterways become available for navigation.

The Committee further recommend that the Central Government should assume full responsibility for the capital cost involved in the construction of structures necessary to provide facilities and share the revenues therefrom with the concerned States on an agreed basis.

Phasing Of The Master Plan

The Committee recommend for implementation in full, the Master Plan for the optimum and integrated development of Narmada water resources, consisting broadly of 13 major irrigation and Power Projects, 12 of which are in Madhya Pradesh and one in Gujarat. In addition Madhya Pradesh would be free to take up medium and minor irrigation Projects to the extent resources in staff, funds and material permit.

In the phasing given for the implementation of this Plan, the Committee have presumed that preliminary works on phase I of the Plan will be authorised in 1965-66.

The first Phase : The Committee further recommend that besides expanding the projects already sanctioned, viz., Tawa and Barna, the Madhya Pradesh Government should take up Punasa and Bargi Projects ; and Gujarat should take up Navagam Project in the first phase of development.

The canal system under Navagam Project should also be started at an early date to enable Gujarat to take full advantage of the large supplies which would be available in the Narmada in earlier years of irrigation development and to carry waters to the Great Rann of Kutch and Rajasthan areas bordering on Pakistan.

The Second and Subsequent Phases: In the second and subsequent phases, the rest of the dams in Madhya Pradesh, viz., Barwaha, Burhner and Kolar and any other project which Madhya Pradesh Government may like to take up for irrigation or power or both, may be built, subject to availability of resources, etc.

The Committee recommend that preference should be given to the construction of the Barwaha dam to utilise the regulated supplies from Punasa.

Programme of Irrigation and Power Development : In drawing up the phased programme of basinwise development, the Committee have kept in view the acute shortage of food, the all-round power shortage, the necessity for raising additional financial resources and the reported decision of the Planning Committee to make massive allocation for irrigation and power in the Fifth, Sixth and subsequent Plans.

Irrigation is essential for producing more food but, in the present context of low water rates, irrigation projects are unproductive and an increasing burden on the State exchequer.

Power projects, on the other hand, raise substantial additional financial resources apart from stimulating industrial development.

The Committee Recommend : (a) That question of raising water rates and imposition of betterment levy be given serious consideration to enable irrigation projects to become self-supporting.

(b) That power units be installed to ultimate maximum capacity as soon as each dam gets completed, so that maximum power can be generated and maximum resources raised from the very start of operation of the project, as there will be large quantities of water otherwise going waste to the sea in the early stages of irrigation development.

The load forecasts of the three States confirm that power will be used up to any extent as soon as generated.

Waterlogging And Drainage

With the introduction of large-scale irrigation in Madhya Pradesh and Gujarat, substantial quantities of water will be stored up in sub-soil reservoirs, which will raise sub-soil water level to varying depths below the surface, resulting in waterlogging of low lying areas. It would be necessary to keep this water level in the areas in plains within safe limits for crop production.

The Committee recommend that the natural drainages of the commanded area should be taken care of simultaneously with the introduction of large-scale irrigation and that supplemental irrigation by pumping should also be undertaken simultaneously, which besides, controlling the rise of sub-soil water level, will also help to conserve supplies in surface reservoirs for use in extending irrigation and generating power.

Necessity For Investigation

The Committee would like to stress the necessity for immediate start on large-scale investigations under a economics of any project well in advance of authorisation for its implementation. These will also provide a wide choice for selection of projects.

The number of discharge sites on the Narmada and rain gauges of Indian Meteorological Department standard in the free catchment below Punasa are few. The Committee recommend that their numbers should be adequately increased.

The Committee recommend that training of personnel for the implementation of the various phases of the Master Plan should be given immediate consideration. This training can well be arranged on major projects already under construction in the country, such as the Beas, Yamuna, Ramganga, Sabarigiri, Rana Pratap Sagar, Sharavathy and several projects in Madras and other States.

Resettlement And Rehabilitation

The resettlement and rehabilitation of persons displaced as a result of the construction of projects, particularly those included in the first phase, will present a major human problem. It would be necessary to find alternative lands for their resettlement.

The Committee recommend that the best solution would be to reclaim waste lands on the fringes of the reservoirs and provide them with perennial irrigation from medium and minor works constructed on the major streams or from the reservoirs themselves. The Committee also recommend that the lands on which the bustees are to be resettled should be selected, made ready and allotted well before their original lands are submerged. Work on resettlement programme should, therefore, start simultaneously with that on the dams and with equal ergency. Efforts should also be made to resettle the inhabitants of a group of villages in contiguous areas to preserve communal life.

Cost Of The Plan

The total cost of all the projects contemplated under the Master Plan has been estimated at Rs. 1,050 crores to be spent in the course of thirty years from start of construction for full development.

Financing Of The Plan

The probable expenditure on development has been estimated roughly at Rs. 643 crores for Madhya Pradesh and Rs. 300 crores for Gujarat.

The Committee recommend that this should either be treated as a loan to the State concerned, outside the State plan or, alternatively, the Government of India may assume financial and technical responsibility for the key major components of the plan to began with.

The Committee stress the desirability of speedy implementation of a project once it is sanctioned, so that construction costs can be kept at the minimum and substantial resources can be raised from the very start of operation of the project, particularly, the power part.

Fish Culture

The Committee recommend the development of fish culture on a large scale in the reservoirs with a view to earning revenues and providing valuable nutritious foods which are in short supply.

The per acre yield of fish from reservoirs is miserably low at present and the Committee recommend that concentrated research be undertaken to raise this yield manifold. As an illustration, the Chilka Lake in Orissa yields 75 lbs. of fish to the acre, and the Hirakund reservoir only 0.5 lb. to the acre, whereas in a number of highly development fish ponds abroad, the yields are as high as 2,000 lbs. and more per acre.

Tourism

The Committee recommend that large reservoirs, such as Punasa and Navagam, should be specially developed to provide attractions and facilities for tourists who would visit the sites in large numbers.

Integrated Development Of The Mahi And Sabarmati Waters

The Committee recommend that the optimum development of the Mahi and Sabarmati rivers for irrigation and power should be undertaken in integration with the Narmada development. For the optimum of utilisation of the water resources of the Mahi, it would be necessary to construct four dams, viz. ; Banswara, Baneshwar and Kadana on the Mahi, and Anas, on the tributary by that name. Of these, Banswara and Kadana Projects are likely to be sanctioned shortly by the Planning Commission. The Committee recommend that investigations for the remaining two projects, namely, Baneshwara and Anas, should be completed as early as possible and projects finalised.

As indicated in the Table above, it is proposed to transfer for the area under Mahi command in Gujarat to Navagam canal and to transfer the corresponding Mahi waters to irrigate higher areas in Rajasthan which cannot be commanded by Navagam canal.

The Committee recommend that the cost of the dams and works chargeable to power and irrigation, respectively, on the Mahi system and the benefits therefrom should be shared in the ratio of 2 for Rajasthan and one for Gujarat subject to such marginal adjustments as may be mutually agreed upon.

The Committee further recommend that the State Governments of Gujarat and Rajasthan should consider the question of setting up a Control Board for the execution of Projects under the Mahi-Sabarmati complex.

COMMITTEE ON SCARCE RAW MATERIALS, 1964—REPORT

Delhi, Manager of Publications, 1966. 64p.

Chairman : Dr. P.S. Lokanathan.

Members : Shri A.R. Bhat ; Shri G.L. Bansal ; Shri S.S. Kumar and later on Shri P.C. Kapoor ; Dr. D.K. Malhotra ; Dr. S.T. Merani.

Secretary : Shri S.V.S. Sharma.

APPOINTMENT

The International Perspective Planning Team which was invited early in 1962, to review the progress made by small scale industries since the programme was initiated in 1955, found even to the outset of their study that the supply of raw materials was the major problem facing the small industries. Members of the Team devoted full attention to this problem in their interviews of businessmen and officials in the States. At the instance of the Team, a working group of foreign and Indian economists undertook an extensive study of the raw materials and the import allocations and their price control system in the Centre and in eight States. Special studies were made of selected firms in various States to determine how the present allocations and price control system affected business operations. A second group of studies was undertaken of State Government allocation records to determine how the system was being run by the State officials. On the basis of these studies the Team concluded, "Of all the present difficulties, raw material supplies available at competitive prices appear to be the greatest. The evidence points out that the inequities in the distribution of raw materials and imports are so severe that they tend to override all other types of assistance offered to small firms by the Government. These difficulties are apparent from the studies of the firms conducted by the Working Group in both industrially developed and underdeveloped States".

According to Team nearly 60 per cent of the firms analyzed provided evidence that critical shortages of materials and components that could only be purchased at higher black market prices made it unprofitable for them to expand their production to fuller utilisation of capacity. Another 18 per cent of the firms stated they could not get additional supplies at any price. Nearly half of the firms which found it unprofitable to increase production because of the black market prices of raw materials, were facing competition with larger firms making similar products, and the larger firms getting allocated inputs at fixed prices.

A number of large firms producing similar products were checked by the Team as to the allocations ; they received at fixed prices through the department of Technical Development and it was found that on the average, they were allocated 85 per cent of their one shift requirements. In contrast, similar competitors received allotments to cover only 33 per cent to 40 per cent of one shift requirements. There was also an extreme range of the ratios of allotments to small firm ; for one shift operation. Some small firms bought all their raw materials and components in the black market. The largest group was seen to cover about one third of one shift capacity; few got above 75 per cent.

The Team found that the percentage of capacity covered by allocation seemed to depend primarily on the size of the firm. It had little, if anything, to do with the priority of the product being manufactured. It was all too evident to the Team that the allocations system worked to the advantage of the larger firms, at the expense of the smaller ones.

The Team also noted that the relative cost disadvantage was significant for the small firm in competition with the large. Even if costs were higher, but equal for both, the small firms would not be confronted with such a difficult situation.

The Team concluded, "Solutions for the raw materials and imported components allocation and price problems must be sought within the shortage conditions existing today. Shortages of various inputs will persist as long as Indian planners press their growth plans to thefullest. We are not concerned with just a small part of the industrial economy because it happens to be small industry. As has been pointed out previously that these modern small factories constitute one third of all registered factory production. They also furnish 38 per cent of all registered factory employment. Their role is not significant in either case, and whatever discriminates against them certainly requires study and correction in the national interest. Continuation of the present inequities clearly weakens their ability to mature and multiply and strengthen the economy."

The International Perspective Planning Team is quoted in extent to have only to bring out that in spite of these findings of the Team, the allocations to small scale sectors were not increased or the system modified to any significance. The Team's report has led to further criticism and the feeling has gained ground that the small scale sector is not receiving just treatment. At the 21st and 22nd meetings of the Small Scale Industries Board this matter received a good deal of attention and criticism were levelled from all sides about 'discrimination' meted out to the small scale sector in the matter. Some members even said that it was not a "crisis of foreign exchange" but a "crisis of faith" of the Government in the programme of development of small scale industries that was responsible for the State of affairs. It was in this background that at 22nd meeting of the Small Scale Industries Board, held in New Delhi on 13th and 14th August, 1964, the Appointment of the Committee on Scarce Raw Materials was formally announced by the Late Shri H.C. Dasappa, Minister of Industry and Supply announced the appointment of the Committee in their Resolution No. SSI(A)—20 (68)/64 dated September 10, 1964.

TERMS OF REFERENCE

(a) How best to secure the equitable distribution of available scarce raw materials among the three sectors, viz. :

(i) Scheduled sector units with capital over Rs. 25 lakhs ;

(ii) Units with capital above Rs. 5 lakhs and not more than Rs. 25 lakhs ; and

(iii) Small scale units with capital not exceeding Rs. 5 lakhs ;

(b) How best to ensure that the materials so allotted are utilised to the fullest advantage for the purpose for which they are allotted.

Scarce raw materials shall include :

(i) Raw materials/components licenced by the Chief Controller of Imports and Exports ;

(ii) Steel, both indigenous and imported ;—

(iii) Non-ferrous metals ;

(iv) Basic organic chemicals and intermediates ; basic inorganic chemicals like caustic soda, soda ash, titanium dioxide, etc. ; pharmaceuticals and drugs ; plastics, synthetic and natural rubber etc.

CONTENTS

Introduction ; Availability of Scarce Raw Materials ; The Procedure ; Disabilities of Small Industries ; Recommendations ; Appendices from I to IV.

RECOMMENDATION

It became evident early during the course of our work that the present system of allocation of scarce raw materials was operating to the disadvantage of the small scale sector. As we were unlikely to complete our work and finalize our recommendations before the allocations for the second half of the year 1964-65 were finalized, we decided to make an interim recommendation that the then existing allocations of foreign exchange to this sector amounting to about Rs. 20 crores per half year should at least be maintained till our report was submitted. A copy of the letter addressed by the Chairman to the Secretary, Ministry of Industry, in this connection, is given in the Appendix. We are constrained to record that the Government did not find it possible to implement the recommendation which we considered modest and absolutely essential. This has further strengthened our conviction that the present ad hoc system of allocation can only work to the detriment of the small scale sector.

The items of scarce raw materials under our examination are likely to continue to be relatively scarce for quite some time to come. The increased indigenous production of steel, basic inorganic chemicals, PVC, etc., may, perhaps, make the position regarding these items somewhat easy but even these items will continue to be in short supply relative to their total countrywide demand. We are convinced that a rational, equitable and enduring system of allocation can only be based on an accurate, dependable and uniform assessment of production capacities and actual production in three sectors. A system of determination of priorities of end-products is essential in the context of the present raw material shortages. We are emphatic that there should be no disparity in availability of scarce raw materials between different units producing similar end-products. We are also convinced that the small scale sector, which opened up vistas of opportunities for our enterprising middle class youngmen, has an expanding role to play in stimulating the new entrepreneurial class, harnessing latent capital resources and decentralizing the economic structure of the country.

At the same time, in view of the present and anticipated shortages of scarce raw materials, we feel that the entry of new units requiring scarce raw materials, should be clearly known to the Government and be subject to advice and guidance by the Directors of Industries of the State Governments. But the decision to set them up or nor will rest entirely upon the new entrants. It is not our intention that the new entrants should obtain licences as in the case of the large scale sector. The prospective entrepreneurs will do well in their own interest to consult the State Directors of Industries in advance and apprise them of their production programme so that the Directors may be able to assess the priority of the end-products, the availability and requirements of the scarce raw materials etc. and guide the entrepreneurs accordingly. The role of the State Director of Industries that we envisage in this context is not that of a censor but that of a guide and counsellor. By this method, we envisage some advance assurance of scarce raw material for the new entrants. This system of guidance need not be insisted upon where the unit is depending entirely on indigenous or freely available raw materials or where the import content is a negligible percentage of the total raw material requirements of the units. We feel that in this way while the entrepreneures will be still free to choose the line of industrial activity they want, they can expect proper guidance in cases where their raw materials are scarce, even before they invest time and money in the enterprise. A suitable and simple procedure for guidance, such as that contemplated above, may be drawn up on a uniform basis for all States by the Central Small Industries Organisation in consultation with the State Directors. The CSIO will also have to guide the States regarding the industries in which there is scope for new units requiring scarce raw materials.

Recommendations—Short Term

During the course of our working, we became painfully aware of the fact that dependable, uniform data regarding different small scale industries is not available for over a period of time. We recommend that this basic deficiency should be set right as quickly as possible. We hope that adequate data to form a basis for the implementation of our recommendations will be available in the States in about 18 months' time if immediate steps are taken to organise their collection and analysis on a uniform basis in all the States.

From the analysis of the availability of scarce raw materials, it is borne out that, generally speaking, the units in the small sactor were able to secure scarce raw materials to the extent of about a third of their requirements, whereas units in the large sector were able to utilize nearly two-third of their production capacities with the scarce raw materials allotted to them although in recent years the position has deteriorated.

The Non-Ferrous Metals Survey conducted by the CSIO in 1964, the various studies conducted by the International Perspective Planning Team during 1962, the studies conducted by the Directorate of Industries, Maharashtra and U.P., at our instance, all confirm the position so far as the small scale sector is concerned. The Central Statistical Organisation's paper on 'Utilisation of Installed Capacity in Selected Industries of India—1957—61' throws light on the position regarding the large scale sector.

In order to ensure an equitable distribution to the two sectors, we feel that immediate relief should be given to the small sector. We, therefore, recommend that the total availability of foreign exchange for import of components, spare parts, non-ferrous metals, steel, etc., to the small scale sector should be increased to at least Rs. 25 crores per half year (as against the range of Rs. 17 to Rs. 20 crores per half year in recent years), for the next three half years as a short term measures.

The implementation of this recommendation involves the immediate provision of an extra Rs. 8 crores for the small scale sector over the allocation made for the half year ending March 31, 1965. We feel that this extra amount should be found, in the national interest, without cutting the allocation of the large sector. If this is not possible, we recommend that suitable adjustments may be made in the allocations to the other sectors of the economy. An adjustment of about Rs. 8 crores from the total foreign exchange available will not cause hardship to any sector in particular. We strongly recommend that this should be implemented with effect from the allotment period starting from 1st April, 1965.

Our recommendation for the interim period is intended only to mitigate the immediate hardship of the small scale sector. However, as we have already mentioned, a long-term, enduring solution is allotment on the basis of dependable facts about all the sectors.

Comparability Between The Two Sectors

Sponsoring authorities like the Textile Commissioner, Jute Commissioner, etc., are responsible for allocations to all units engaged in industrial activity falling under their respective spheres. The sector-wise differences arise more in the case of industries looked after by the DGTD and the CSIO. Therefore, we attempted to reclassify the industries looked after by these two authorities so as to put them on a comparable basis.

A whole field of industrial activity is undertaken by private firms of varying sizes. Some units produce a number of products while others concentrate on particular products. The products of some units have a higher national priority but that does not mean that those of other units are not essential. All these units are contributing to industrial production of the country and their production has adequate demand which, but for their production, would have remained unsatisfied. At the one end, there are small one-man or two-man units located in a single room working with one or two machines undertaking mainly job orders. At the other end, there are huge industrial establishments employing thousands of workers with investment running into crores of rupees. These have been divided into three sectors as large, medium and small scale for convenience in administering various programmes of regulation and assistance. They all have a legitimate claim on the scarce raw materials. We, therefore, recommend that the scarce raw materials should be equitably distributed without reference to the sector to which the units belong subject only to the overall national priorities of their end-products. For determining the equitability we have broadly divided these units into the following categories, on the basis of the present definition of the large (including medium) and small scale sectors.

(i) Units producing such goods/services which could only be undertaken in the large (including medium) scale sector.

(ii) Units producing goods/services which could be manufactured depending upon economies of scale, either in the large (including medium) sector or in the small sector.

(iii) Units which fall in the small scale sector but produce goods/services/components/sub-assembilies or other items, which are of a primary nature, in the national interest, though they may not have comparable units in the large (including medium) scale sector.

(iv) Other units in the small scale sector.

Each of the above categories of units has its respective role to play in our national economy.

All units on the registers of the DGTD and the State Directors of the Industries may be reclassified as above and scarce raw material allotted within each group on a uniform basis.

We have attempted as an illustration a reclassification of industries now handled by the DGTD so as to group them into categories (i) and (ii) above and this is given in Appendix I.

To implement this recommendation, the DGTD will have to somewhat modify the present system of preparing estimates of requirements of scarce raw materials Directorate-wise. Estimates will not have to be prepared for each directorate for each of the categories mentioned above, but this should not involve much additional work.

In the small scale sector, however, the whole work has to be organised for the first time. For all category (i) and category (iii) industries, estimates of production capacities, past production and requirements of different items of scarce raw materials will have to be prepared in each State by the State Directorate of Industries and coordinated and consolidated at the Centre by the CSIO. The lists, thus prepared, would be comparable to the directorate-wise category-wise estimates prepared by the DGTD. These two sets of lists can then be considered by the allocating authority, like the Ministry of Industry, Ministry of Steel, etc., for directorate-wise category-wise allotment in the two sectors as is now being done for the large sector alone.

We have considered the additional work load involved in implementing this recommendation by the small scale sector. As the data in chapter two disclosed, the Chief Controller of Imports and Exports alone is now receiving about 45,000 applications and is issuing about 18,000 licences per annum to this sector. The number of licences issued to the large scale sector was about 8,000 in 1963-64. A systematic and purposive scrutiny at the State level will eliminate a number of applications and facilitate further work. Even when this entire work is distributed over all the State Directorates of Industries, it will be seen that the work load involved is heavy but is absolutely justified in view of the systematization and orderliness achieved. It will also help to expose and eliminate bogus firms, inflated and untenable claims and give scope for the further growth of genuine units. We recommend appropriate strengthening of the Directorates of Industries and of the State Governments at the technical statistical and administrative levels to enable them to cope up with the size and quality of work.

Category IV

It is conceived that a large number of units in this group will not qualify for inclusion in the three groups listed before ; it cannot, however, be denied that they are rendering valuable service to the community. Their employment potential is considerable. In fact, this category serves as the starting point for skilled workers, technicians and entrepreneurs to try out their new ideas and slowly graduate into category (iii) or category (ii) industries in the small scale sector. It will be a serious disadvantage to the national economy to restrict the entry of such new entrepreneurs, who, through ingenuity and innovation, provide goods and services and employment quite out of proportion to their meagre requirements of scarce raw materials.

As we have already mentioned, it is necessary to guide the entry of new firms requiring scarce raw materials so that there may be no further strain on our meagre foreign exchange resources. But even so we feel that provision should be made as a long-term programme for new entrants into the sector. We suggest that, depending upon availability and as a residual measure, an ad hoc allocation of a small amount per half year for all imported scarce raw materials, components of spare parts, non-ferrous metals and steel might be allowed for this category. The CSIO will guide the State Directors of Industries as to the type of Industries which could be fostered under this category. The State Directors of Industries will be the sponsoring authorities, as usual, for these allocations. It might, however, be made clear to such entrants that allocations to them would depend on availability and the priority of their end-products. When these units prove their technical feasibility and viability, they may be transferred either to category (ii) or category (iii) above, giving scope for new entrants again.

Priorities of Industries: The foreign exchange resources of the country are limited and have to be conserved to the utmost extent and utilized with utmost care. Therefore, even at the risk of leaving a part of investment under-utilised, it will be necessary of feed industries which have a higher national priority. Thus, even amongst the comparable industries in the two sectors, priorities may have to be drawn up so that those industries with higher priority get higher allocations and provide the much more needed goods/services. We recommend the following categories and the industries must fall under one or the other of these categories.

(i) Defence requirements :

(ii) Industries directly concerned with the development of agriculture and the food production.

(iii) Export-oriented industries.

(iv) Import substitution industries.

(v) Transport and power.

(vi) Units producing components, etc., required in certain vital sectors like railways and others ; those producing accessories, components, etc. which are imported and essentially required for keeping plant and machinery in the above industries running.

(vii) Producer goods and essential consumer goods industries.

It is expected that units which are working as ancillaries to a particular large scale unit would get, to that extent, the priority of the principal unit.

We recommend that in these industries the existing capacities sh uld be more fully utilized and that additional raw material should be secured, to the extent possible, to utilize existing production capacities.

Under the heading 'Producer Goods and Essential Consumer Goods', we recommend the inclusion of industries given in Appendix II.

The Role Of CSIO And State Directorates

In the case of medium and large scale units, the DGTD or the other authorities like Textile Commissioner, Jute Commissioner, etc. have all particulars about the concerned units on their registers and are able to estimate their requirements and allocate accordingly. In the small scale sector, however, the work will have to be jointly undertaken by the CSIO and the State Directors of Industries.

The State Directors of Industries, as sponsoring authorities, will be responsible for estimating the requirements, allocation and inspection of utilization. They will also have to play an important role in the distribution of scarce raw materials through the State Small Industries Corporations. The CSIO on the other hand, will have to work as the central coordinating and controlling organisation for this work and be in liaison with other Central authorities concerned with the allocations of scarce raw materials. Details of the role that we envisage for these two agencies are given in Appendix IV.

In most of the State Directorates, a senior officer is now looking after the entire work regarding small industry programmes. The administrative, technical and statistical sections in the Directorates need reorganisation and considerable expansion to fulfil the role envisaged for the Directorates. We recommend that the pattern of reorganisation and the actual strength required should be worked out immediately by all State Governments. The DC(SSI) should help the State Directorates in this regard. In some States, a full-time Joint Director may be needed for the work relating to raw materials. He may be assisted by a Deputy Director (Statistics) and other adequate supporting staff both at the headquarters and in the districts.

The CSIO has been concentrating, during the last ten years, on industrial extension service. Matters regarding supply of raw materials were, perhaps, considered as regulatory work and did not receive adequate attention till recently. It is surprising that even now there is no separate directorate to tackle this important but difficult problem. In view of the role envisaged for the CSIO in our recommendations, it is necessary to post immediately a senior officer exclusively for this work. He will have to be supported by adequate statistical and other assistance.

Allocation : At the national level, joint committees, including representatives of the concerned administrative Ministry, DGTD and CSIO should allocate raw material on the basis of overall requirements and availability to the different industry groups. Once the availability to the particular industry group in the small scale sector is decided, the CSIO will redistribute it to the States in accordance with their estimated requirements and will also inform the States about the entitlement of the industry groups so that there may be equitable distribution between the different units in the same industry group in the different States.

Distribution : The large scale units which receive bulk allotment are able to import directly in view of the large quantities involved. As far as possible, scarce raw materials to small scale units should be channelized through raw material depots opened by the State Small Industries Corporations. In States where such Corporations are not existing we recommend that they should be constituted immediately. The raw material depots might be established at convenient places so that a small industrialist may not have to travel more than a hundred miles to secure his raw materials. These raw material depots should be recognised as controlled/registered stockists by the Iron and Steel Controller and as agents for distribution of imported material by the Minerals and Metals Trading Corporation/State Trading Corporation and such other organisations. State's quotas of other source materials, like caustic soda, PVC, etc., might also be allotted to the Small Industries Corporations.

When industrial scrap available with defence establishments, railways, public undertakings, etc. is disposed of, an appropriate portion may be made available to the small scale units at a price which has some relation to the auctioned price, wherever the latter procedure is in force. The State Small Industries Corporations can play a useful part in this.

It has been represented that these raw material depots might become yet another link in the chain of distribution and add to the total cost of the raw material. We feel that the recognition of the Corporations on the lines suggested above will actually eliminate many middlemen and, in view of the assured supplies at controlled/fair price, justify the small charges levied.

Inspection : We note that already the State Directors of Industries are doing inspection work on behalf of the DGTD at the latter's request. We recommend that this practice be extended to the extent desirable. We feel that there should be such inspection of all the units at least once in a year.

It would also be a definite advantage to have central teams of inspection consisting of representatives of DGTD and CSIO to visit a few large and small scale units at random.

Assessment Of Capacities

The CSIO recently completed an assessment of the production capacities of the non-ferrous metal using small scale units, with the cooperation of the State Directorates. Similar assessment will have to be conducted, on an industrywise basis, for all industries under category (ii) and category (iii) above. We recommend that this work should be taken up immediately and completed in the time indicated.

In order to realise our objective of equitable distribution of the scarce raw materials between the two sectors it is necessary to have a proper assessment of the capacities of the different units in the two sectors. It is also to be ensured that such assessment is on a uniform basis. We, therefore, recommend that suitable norms, in respect of raw materials, for the purpose be evolved by mutual consultation between the DGTD, the CSIO and the State Directors of Industries. We further recommend that in the actual assessment work, the State Directors be associated wherever necessary.

The assessment of capacities suggested above will yield valuable information regarding the capacities in the small scale sector. It should be analysed and passed on to the DGTD and the Chief Controller of Imports and Exports and the Licensing Committee for their use.

There could be better co-ordination between the CSIO, DGTD and the CCI &E with a view to plugging the loopholes in the import of spare parts etc. Some parts/components which could be made in the country are still imported. This, from the National point of view, is serious drain.

We recommend that joint panels of representatives of DGTD, CSIO and CCI&E should scrutinize the lists of parts components now imported with a view to examine whether these could be produced within the country.

We recommed that these joint panels should scrutinise the Directorate General of Supplies and Disposals imports also with a view to encouraging industrial units in the country to take up their production.

In regard to indigenous scarce raw materials such as steel, aluminium, basic organic chemicals and intermediates, including dyes, basic inorganic chemicals like caustic soda, soda ash, titanium dioxide, etc.; pharmaceuticals and drugs; plastics, synthetic and natural rubber, etc., we recommend that an equitable proportion should be set apart for the small scale units at reasonable prices. In the pooling and retail distribution of such indigenous materials the Small Industries Corporation can play a useful role.

COMMISSION OF RAILWAY SAFETY, RAILWAY ACCIDENT INVESTSGATION ON ACCIDENT TO 12NB BANDEL-NAIHATI LOCAL AT NAIHATI JUNCTION STATION OF EASTERN RAILWAY ON 14TH SEPTEMBER, 1964—REPORT

Delhi, Manager of Publications, 1971. 17p.

One Man Commission : Shri H. S. Hart

APPOINTMENT

The Commission was constituted under the Ministry of Tourism and Civil Aviation vide Rule 9 of the Railway Board's Notification No. 1926-T dated March 19, 1930.

TERMS OF REFERENCE

To inquire into the accident to 12NB "Bandel-Naihati Local" that occurred while it was entering Naihati Junction on the Northern Suburban Section on the Sealdah Division of Eastern Railway on the morning of the September 14, 1964.

CONTENTS

Preamble ; Relief Measures ; Local Conditions ; Summary of Evidence ; Observations and Tests; Discussion ; Conclusions ; Annexure.

RECOMMENDATIONS

Cause Of The Accident

From the evidence available I have come to the conclusion that the ladder of the Branch UP Advanced Starter Colour Light Signal at Naihati was strack and distorted inwards towards the Down line by the protruding latch of the tower bolt of an open door of a covered wagon of the load of Diesel 280 Down.

I have also come to the conclusion that the first two coaches of 12NB Local, which followed Diesel 280 Down 12 minutes later, struck against the infringing signal ladder of this Branch UP advanced. Starter Colour Light Signal, resulting in slight damage to the coaches in question and injuries to some passengers.

Responsibility For The Accident

(a) The Guard of Diesel 280 Down, Shri N. C. Das was directly responsible for the damage sustained by the ladder of the Branch UP advanced Starter signal in that he failed to ensure that all the doors of the wagons of his train were secured in the closed position. He thereby violated the Asansole Divisional Circular No. TGB/41/60 Pt. I. dated the September 3, 1964. His responsibility should be viewed in the light of the possibility of the wagon doors having been opened by miscreants shortly before the train approached Naihati.

Shri N. C. Das who is nearing 29 years of age, was originally appointed as a Probationary Guard (Grade 'C') in the Traffic Training School, Sealdah, underwent practical training for 7 weeks on the Asansol Division before taking over independent charge as a Guard (Grade 'C'). He was last medically examined in March 1964 and declared fit for service in Class A2. He has had no punishments since his appointment.

The Permanent Way Inspector, Naihati Shri S. K.

Bakshi also was responsible in that he slewed the Down line without receipt of an authorisedsslew chart and without first ensuring that the Branch Up Advanced Started Colour Light Signal was shifted. As a result, after the slewing, this signal infringed the Downline. He thereby violated General Rule 197 and Para 612 of the Indian Railways Way and Works Manual. However, it cannot be said with any degree of certainty that the ladder of this infringing Branch Up Advanced Starter Signal would not have been struck and distorted by the latch of the tower bolt of the open door of a covered wagon if he had ensured that the clearance of the signal from the centre of the Downline was kept at the distance prescribed by the Schedule of Dimensions for the curvature and super elevation obtaining at the spot.

Shri S. K. Bakshi, was originally appointed as an Apprentice Permanent Way Inspector in April 1945. He has been working as a Permanent Way Inspector continuously from July 1955, and has been Permanent Way Inspector, Naihati since July 1961. He has been twice censured since January 1953.

Relief Measures

These were prompt and satisfactory.

REVIEWING COMMITTEE OF THE TELECOMMUNICATION RESEARCH CENTRE OF THE POSTS AND TELEGRAPHS DEPARTMENT, 1964—REPORT

New Delhi, Department of Communications, 1965. 43p.

Chairman : Dr. S. Bhagavantam.
Members : Dr. S. Husain Zaheer : Shri Jagdeesh Prasad; Shri S. K. Karanjilal.
Secretary : Shri C. P. Vasudevan.

APPOINTMENT

The Committee was constituted under the Government of India, Department of Communications by the Ministry of Communications vide Order No . TRC. 17-47/61 dated the September 26, 1964, to review the work and progress of the Telecommunication Research Centre, attached to the Telegraph Board.

TERMS OF REFERENCE

(i) To review the work and progress of the Telecommunication Research Centre; and

(ii) To recommend the lines on which the activities of the Telecommunication Research Centre should be developed and directed so as to secure the maximum benefit for the development of telecommunications in India.

CONTENTS

Part I —(A.—Terms of Reference and General; B—History and Background of the Telecommunication Research Centre); **Part II**—Work and the Progress Achieved so far (Section 1—Designs and Telecommunication and Related Equipments; Section 2—Techniques Developed in the Telecommunication Research Centre; Section 3— Consultation, Assessment, Training and other Activities of the Telecommunication Research Centre); **Part III**—Review of the Work done so far and the Committee's Comments Thereon; **Part IV**—Programme of Work of the Telecommunication Research Centre for the Period upto the end of March 1971; **Part V**—Proposals Regarding the Activities and the Set-up of the Telecommunication Research Centre for the Future (Section 1—Main Divisions of the Work in the Telecommunication Research Centre; Section 2—Staff Requirements ; Section 3—Set-up of the Telecommunication Research Centre vis-a-vis the Posts and Telegraphs Department; Section 4—Financial Requirements; Section 5—Other Recommendations and Conclusions); Appendix.

RECOMMENDATIONS

Review Of The Work Done So Far And The Committee's Comments Thereon

The Telecommunication Research Centre was set up in 1956. In the ten-year period, the organisation has been built-up by able direction into an efficient and powerful research organisation. In spite of the usual difficulties in recruiting personnel and training them and the time taken to obtain the equipments and materials under Indian conditions, the progress achieved in this period is remarkable.

There has been a well directed effort in several

directions, viz., in the drawing up of the programme, in the direction of the research work, in the translation of these designs to manufacture (generally in conjunction with the Indian Telephone Industries Limited) and in getting this into practical application (in conjunction with the Planning Branch).

The programmes have been drawn up not on the basis of the past practices but have, in all cases, taken into account the trends in development and techniques. This has resulted in the designs, when they become ready, in being modern and useful. The programme has been drawn up to meet the requirements in a given time and, for this, the studies and outline of the systems, the design of the different units of the system and the development of the necessary scientific and engineering disciplines as well as the economic aspects have been set out and tackled in a well directed manner and reviewed to keep these in proper perspective. In addition, the economic aspects have been continuously kept in view, so that the range of application is as wide-spread as possible. The time element is always an important factor in applied research. In order to meet the targets in the minimum time, considerable amount of advance planning and coordination between the Telecomunication Research Centre, the Planning and other branches of the P &T and the manufacturers (usually the Indian Telephone Industries Limited) has been maintained. This aspect has been given great importance at all stages.

The results achieved have been set out in Part II of this Report. The number of items designed and in manufacture are considerable and meet almost all the big needs of the P & T Department.

The equipments designed in the Telecommunication Research Centre are modern and sophisticated and call for a wide and detailed knowledge over many aspects of electronics and communication engineering of methods of fabrication and production as well as of the communication needs of the country to provide modern and economical service on a scale which could not have been envisaged a decade ago.

The achievements of the Telecommunication Research Centre together with the activities of the Planning Branch and of the Indian Telephone Industries Limited have resulted in providing the country many new and modern services such as Telex and Subscriber Trunk Dialling. It has also provided for massive expansion of the long distance networks with modern carrier systems of different types. As a result, the number of carrier channels added in any one year from out of the production in this country is much larger than the total number of such circuits in 1961. There has been a considerable advancement in the knowledge now available to the Department and the Telecommunication Research Centre has played an important and vital role in spearheading modern forms of communication such as micro-wave, new switching systems, etc.

There has been a considerable amount of savings of foreign exchange and this has in turn permitted the expansion of the P & T which would otherwise have not been possible. The equipments have been available to the P & T steadily from indigenous sources reducing the effort in having to go through the considerable effort in getting international tenders and of placing orders. The ability to design special equipments needed and the capacity to alter the designs to meet the special requirements has resulted in being able to provide communication under difficult conditions and to complete some of the big projects.

The work of the Telecommunication Research Centre has also shown that it is possible, with proper direction, to design and manufacture complex equipments with indigenous know-how rapidily and on a competitive basis. There are a number of examples in the work of the Telecommunication Research Centre where this has been done and the requirements have been met satisfactorily from indigenous sources and in a shorter time. The setting up of production is quicker and the hold-up can be reduced by a quick reference to the designer. It is also possible to make alterations, to make improvements or to include indigenous components or materials on a continuous basis.

The Telecommunication Research Centre has in addition to meeting the requirements of the P&T, also designed equipments for other uses such as Railways where all the items for communication and signalling for the Railway Electrification Project are made indigenously to the Telecommunication Research Centre designs. The Telecommunication Research Centre has also played a notable and significant role in acting as consultants as well as for technical advice and in training up persons in advanced fields.

The Telecommunication Research Centre is now taking up a very ambitions programme for meeting all the communication needs of the P & T and keeping apreast of the world development. The capabilities that have been builtu-p in the Telecommunication Research Centre are such that, with adequate expansion, it can do this with the same success.

The Committee is very appreciative of the achievements of the Telecommunication Research Centre and the contribution it has made in several directions. The Committee wishes to record their appreciation of the co-operation and work done in the Indian Telephone Industries Limited and the Planning and other Branches of the P & T. This working together to achieve a desired objective has been a considerable factor in the progress made and the setting up of a large complex industry in the country or indigenous know-how—a unique performance. The Committee wishes to record its appreciation of the work done by the personnel of the Telecommunication Research Centre under the able direction of its Director. The Telecommunication Research Centre has added considerable resources to the development of communication and of electronics in the country.

Programme Of Work Of The Telecommunication Research Centre For The Period Up To The End Of March, 1971

A programme of work on broad lines for the period up to the end of the Fourth Plan is outlined in this Part. The principal areas of activity so far have been in the fields of carrier systems, electro-mechanical switching, electronic measuring instruments and power plant. A beginning has been made in the field of the microwaves, V.H.F. and in the pulse and digital techniques.

The work will have to be continue in all these areas and the scope expanded to meet the likely requirements of equipments and services in new areas also.

In addition, since developments are considerable, every effort should be made to improve our systems and services continuously. Further indigenous materials and components are becoming available and design efforts are required to make use of these of the maximum extent possible.

The scope of activities and the amount of work involved to meet the needs of the P & T is very considerable. In addition, the requirements of some of the other users such as Railways and Defence Services can in many cases be met by modifications or additions to the range of P & T designs. The amount of professional electronic equipments required in the next decade has been estimated by the Bhabha Committee at a figure of several hundred crores of rupees. The P & T Telecommunication Research Centre must play its part in fulfilling these needs, where necessary, in close collaboration with others working in these fields.

A brief outline of the areas of development with regard to the minimum programme to meet the requirements of the Fourth Plan of the P & T is given below.

Carrier Telephone System

This must continue to be a major area of activity. The most important items of work in the field are :

(a) Design of transistorised coaxial cable systems for 4 or 6 Mc/s;

(b) Design of 4 Mc/s coaxial systems for small tubes ;

(c) Value type and later transistorised type 2,700 channel systems for large tube coaxial cables ;

(d) Re-design of the existing systems and circuits extensively to accommodate indigenous components as well as for making improvements ;

Carrier Telegraph Systems : The existing carrier telegraph systems should be re-designed to incorporate the new improvements to provide for indigenous materials and to eliminate electro mechanical relays. In addition, higher speed telegraph systems—3 or 4 types—occupying greater bandwidth of 360, 480, 960 cycles and the whole VF bandwidth will require to be designed. These high speed systems are required for various applications such as in data and picture transmission, for telemetry, etc.

Electro Mechanical Switching System : Two major developments are taking place. The first is the scheme to introduce subscriber trunk dialling over the entire country and the second, the application of the crossbar switching systems using different principles of switching. These two programmes necessitate a large amount of work to lay down the pattern of development in clear terms. In addition, a large number of relay sets and other circuits are required to inter-work with the new systems or to provide new facilities in the existing systems consequent on the changes.

In addition, the following items of work have to be tackled :

(a) The equipment designs—quasi-electronic—to achieve automatic billing and accounting of trunk calls. This requires design of systems for calling line identification and of using computer techniques ;

(b) The design of indirect type teleprinter exchanges with additional facilities for routing and for introduction of regenerative repeaters ;

(c) The design of a fully automatic tape relay system for telegraph message switching ;

(d) Design of new systems and improvement of existing systems through new circuit and equipment designs to provide new services and facilities for improving the flexibility and working of strowger exchanges.

Subscribers' Apparatus : With the introduction of subscriber trunk dialling and the need to dial long numbers, new facilities at the subscribers' premises have to be provided. Amongst the more important ones are the design of systems for repertory dialling, push botton dialling, for new Private Automatic Branch Exchanges with inward dialling and extension metering, introduction of load speaking telephones, the design of answering services, means for intercepting calls and giving of recorded announcements. There is also need to continuously improve the telephone subscriber set and to introduce new schemes for improving the intercommunication at the subscriber's premises. The design of a centrex system has also to be taken up.

Electronic Instruments : A wide variety of electronic

measuring instruments will have to be developed in keeping with the new equipments and services. In addition, the existing instruments have also to be modernised continuously and improved in performance. Amongst the new instruments to be designed are :

(a) Production instruments to be used in factories bases on 'go' and 'no go' indications and set up for use by workman to check complex equipments ;

(b) Instruments for testing microwave and VHF equipments and for making transmission and other tests at these frequencies ;

(c) Testing Equipments to automatically check the large numbers of circuits now becoming available ;

(d) Traffic measuring and monitoring equipments ;

(e) Special and general purpose instruments for making different types of measurements.

Power Plant : The range and capacities of the power plants will have to be extended to meet the new requirements. With the expansion of the telecommunications, very large units become necessary.

In addition work will have to be undertaken to harness new sources of power supplies such as thermoelectric generators fuel cells, etc., for scattered or remote installations.

Special efforts will have to be directed to design improved standby power supplies.

The power equipments designed already will be continously improved by the use of new materials, components and techniques that are becoming available.

Microwave Systems : The development of the P & T network as well as those of other communication users will be extensively based on the use of microwave equipments. A number of types are required differing in capacities, frequency requirements, economics, etc.

Of these, the most important are the line-of-sight microwave systems in the 2, 4, 6, 7 and 11 Gc/s. bands with different capacities from 60 to 1800 channels per radio bearer. These systems must provide for all the usual variations such as for different types of order wire and supplementary control, use of diversity and combining and, where necessary, for an all solid state design. The design of economical systems for each application is an essential part of the progamme. The systems should be complete including antennas, etc.

Microwave systems for over-the-horizon, for scatter, and for satellite communication are also required. These call for several special techniques.

The design of the full range of microwave systems is a matter of great importance and must be tackled on a priority basis with vigour. The amount of work involved is considerable.

VHF Systems : VHF systems have an important role in the development of new and vital services. In many areas, these are the only practical systems.

The main use of VHF in the P & T is for mobile services of different types which are now-a-days provided by all telephone administrations. These include interlinking with the city network, of the ships and other vessels at sea or in the harbour, or providing communication to vehicles used for ambulance, fire brigade, taxis, etc., and by members of the public such as doctors, etc. These are also necessary to provide communication to vehicles on highways and on trains, etc.

VHF is also advantageous to open up telecommunications in large areas of the country that are backward. In these cases, special designs can provide trunk circuits to remote areas economically, including those for geological and oil exploration sites, oil companies, etc. Other designs can replace long rural subscriber loops effectively and economically.

Other needs to be served by VHF equipments include 'paging' services over wide areas.

These and other services are already being provided in other countries and there is considerable demand for these in this country. Other users such as the Defence Services also use VHF extensively. VHF equipments to meet these different needs have to be developed.

Digital Communication Systems : With the advent of solid state technology, digital communication systems have an important role in the future. Amongst the systems that show considerable promise are the pulse code modulation systems of small capacity say, 24 channels, to provide short distance circuits such as for junctions and subscriber lines. The use of these systems in combination with concentrators will considerably reduce the requirements for cable conductors which at present account for a large part of the total network cost as well as for expenditure of foreign exchange on copper. Other important systems are PCM systems to be used in conjunction with VHF equipment. There is also need to develop large capacity multiplexing systems using digital techniques for telephone, telegraph, and data transmission to be used in conjunction with the different transmission media including wave guides.

Data Transmission Equipments : A new area of communication which is emerging rapidly is for transmission of large volumes of data between one location to another. The demand for data transmission circuits is growing very rapidly in America and Europe and the same pattern is expected in our country. Even now, there are enquiries from important units for these services. The design of the data transmission equipment calls for special coding and de-coding equipments to ensure adequate security of transmission as well as mechanical and electronic devices to transmit and receive data. General types of data equipments have to be designed, for example, those that work on telegraph or built-up telex circuits, those for telephone circuits and higher speed data circuits operating on wider bands.

Picture, Facsimile and Television Transmission Equipments : There is a considerable demand for facsimile and picture transmission, and India is amongst the few countries which have not provided these services With the coming of television in a few years, equipments for television transmission have also to be specially designed. These require a wide range of equipment designs including a fair amount of precision mechanical items.

Use of Computer Programming for Telecommunication Applications : Electronic computers are now being extensively used by all the telecommunication administrations. A computer is under installation and priority should be given to establishing a powerful group in order to bring the benefits of computer economy to various activities in the Department, some of which are given below :

(a) Evolving computer programmes for designs of circuits, networks and equipments, preparation and prediction of propagation conditions, other scientific and technical applications ;

(b) Preparation of traffic tables and the study of traffic pattern in the different parts of the network ;

(c) Analysis of the particulars of the telegraph messages as well as of telephone calls for the accurate planning of telephone and telegraph networks ;

(d) Design of telecommunication networks for meeting various design objectives such as flexibility, lower costs, etc. ;

(e) Automatic message billing accounting with regard to the telephone and telegraph revenues ;

(f) Programming for normal commercial applications, viz., inventory control, maintenance of accounts, programme evaluation, etc.

Electronic Switching : This is another field of considerable importance. In the U.S.A. electronic systems have already been standardised for commercial use. Many European countries are finalising the design of electronic exchanges and these are expected to be standard systems in a few years. The electronic exchanges have a number of advantages over electro-mechanical exchanges and it is known that when economical and reliable systems can be designed, these will take over from the electro-mechanical exchanges. In India, it is extremely important that we should be in a position to instal commercial electronic exchanges in the early seventies. This calls for massive amounts of development work in the next few years and the target should be to instal one (or more) large scale electronic exchanges at least in the year 1969-1970. The design of the electronic switching systems is complex and difficult and requires the development of new circuits and techniques and fabrication processes. Since our investments in switching systems are large, high priority should be given to meeting the above targets.

Proposals Regarding Activities And Set Up Of The Telecommunication Research Centre For The Future

Main Divisions of the Work in the Telecommunication Research Centre : The Telecommunication Research Centre, in order to meet the minimum requirements in the next few years, has to tackle problems covering a much wider range of subjects. The amount of work involved has to increase several fold. This calls for the organising of the work in the Telecommunication Research Centre in a systematic way.

The actual work to be done in the next few years has been set out in part IV of this Report. These items of work have to be grouped together based on similarities, systems and techniques. The principal areas of activity and their grouping taking into account the similarity as well as the amount of work to be done given below :

(a) Carrier telephone systems, carrier telegraph systems, special error protection systems ;

(b) Microwave line-of-sight systems, over-the-horizon systems, microwave circuits including low noise amplifiers, solid state circuitry and high power amplifiers ;

(c) VHF fixed systems for single and multi-channel operation, VHF mobile systems paging systems, solid state and high power VHF circuits ;

(d) Electronic instruments, active electrical circuits, materials, devices and electronic components ;

(e) Electrical networks, filters including microwave filters, microwave passive devices, magnetic materials ;

(f) Digital communication systems, telemetering, telecommand and remote supervision systems ;

(g) Data transmissission facsimile, picture transmission and television transmission systems;

(h) Electronic switching systems ;

(i) Digital, logic and memory circuits for electronic exchanges and for digital systems, micro miniaturisation using solid state and thin film techniques ;

(j) Electro-mechanical Switching Systems including quasi-electronic systems—networks designs—subscribers' Apparatus – traffic tables and measurements ;

(k) Prototype construction, fabrication methods, external plant, gas pressure systems, microwave and VHF Antennas, design of microwave towers and structures ;

(l) Field work, propagation measurements, collection of data, performance checks, follow up on the Telecommunication Research Centre designed equipments, maintenance of equipments and standards ;

(m) Computer engineering and programming, analyis of data ;

(n) Power Supplies and Associated Equipment ;

Servo Systems for antenna control for recording data and for remote operation.

A few of the above groups are in existence now, but even here, the amount and the pattern of work in quantity and in complexity will increase as compared with the existing position The organisation into groups specified on the above lines will be the only way in which the degree of specialisation now required can be developed and sustained. The degree of sophistication now required in the developments is increasing from year to year.

Taking up of the work in any new field requires considerable amount of preparatory work at all levels involving as it does complete system trends and a survey of the techniques available and the drawing up of all programmes of research and devising the ways for realisation. This work involves the breaking down of the system requirements into unit requirements, drawing up of the specifications and examining of alternative techniques and methods (if necessary after some exploratory work) before an actual laboratory programme can be undertaken. At this stage the necessary materials and equipments are procured and this is the starting point of the detailed development and research work.

The technical and scientific work connected in each of these areas will normally be done by a Deputy Director supported by the required number of Assistant Directors and Scientific and Technical officers with the necessary supporting staff at lower levels. This set up is essential for ensuring that the work in each area is tackled on an adequate and efficient basis.

Staff Requirements

The work to be taken up immediately in the context of the requirements of the Fourth Plan is itself very considerable. For meeting these needs, the Telecommunication Research Centre must be strengthened quickly and effectively. The expansion is to be limited only by the capacity of the Centre to organise work Programmes, recruit personnel and utilise them effectively.

The rate of expansion that is generally feasible is an increase of 25% annually as compared with the position existing at the beginning of the year. This is only a rough guide and should not be adhered to rigidly. The actual number required at any level will depend on the state of activity in the division. Usually, the proportion of staff at higher levels is more in the preliminary stages of development in order to organise the work properly and to take up the task of training and reorientation of the group to tackle the problems and meet the objectives. Further when special programmes or requirements have to be met, greater expansion at an earlier stage may be desirable even though the overall average rate over a period of years should be kept in order to consolidate the position effectively.

Taking into account the work actually to be tackled and the aspects set out in the above paragraphs, the Telecommunication Research Centre will increase by about four times in the next six years ending in March, 1971. At this stage, it will have about 140 Scientific and Technical officers, Grade I, 65 Asst. Directors and 14 Deputy Directors.

The Telecommunication Research Centre also requires considerable strengthening at the top to make for an effective and smooth working research organisation. There is need to tackle not only the expanded activities of research, both in depths as well as in range, but there is also need to make the implementation of the programmes effectively in the shortest period of time. This requires additional activities in the formulation of programmes, drawing up the details of research work and assignments and in the total technical activities.

The amount of work required in the effective coordination of the activities in the Telecommunication Research Centre with the planning and other branches of the P & T as well as with the manufacturing organisations is very large. The entire success of these activities of the Telecommunication Research Centre depends on the proper formulation of the total programme, the supervision of the activities and of coordination at all stages leading to effective implementation. The quantum of work involved is such that the present set up in which the Director, Telecommunication Research Centre exercises all these functions is inadequate. It is necessary that the post of the Director, Telecommunication Research Centre, should be made equal to a Member of the P & T Board. He should be assisted by two officers in the Senior Administrative Grade who will be responsible along with the Director for the formulation of research programmes, supervision of research, technical advice, coordination with the Department and with the manufacturing units, consolidation of the activities of the research organisation, dissemination of the information, training progrommes, implementation and review of the research work.

This increase in the officer strength at the highest level is essential for formulating the programmes and guiding the research activities as well as running the research organisation effectively and for enabling these policies to be dealt with at the highest levels in the Department for speedy utilisation of the fruits of research and technology in all matters. The changed set up will, in addition, be in line with other recommendations on recruitment, scientific direction, etc., which are dealt with in latter parts of this Report.

It is important that the persons employed in the Telecommunication Research Centre should have the aptitude for research and the necessary competence. Only in this way can effective research be conducted. In a research organisation, the problems to be faced in any subsequent year are newer and more difficult than the problems solved earlier unlike in the maintenance organisation. This also calls for greater knowledge, experience, abilities and mature judgment. Recruitment to the organisation should be done on the basis of suitability and aptitude for research work. Persons found suitable in the Telecommunication Research Centre should continue in the organisation. The total amount of research work is, at this stage, limited only by the number of suitable men available in the particular activity and should be subject only to these limitations. The benefits of research are considerable and hence it is necessary that special considerations should be given to the needs of research and arrangements made to ensure that continuity is maintained irrespective of whether a person is due for promotion or the ordinary rules require tenure considerations for assignments in the Department.

There should be full flexibility in the Telecommunication Research Centre in regard to the number of posts in any cadre. The set up with regard to creation of the posts should be such that the interests of research are the foremost and that the personnel are retained in the research organisation and not disturbed merely for lack of incentives or avenues of promotion. Within the total number in the four grades (Scientific and Technical Officers, Grade II, Grade I, Assistant Directors and Deputy Directors) there should be flexibility to adjust the posts marginally between one grade and the next. This flexibility is extremely important.

The recruitment of personnel the Telecommunication Research Centre must be free from normal governmental methods in order to secure the services of those most qualified for research. The sources from which the requirement is made should be as wide as possible. There is need for departmental engineers in the organisation since the research work is user-oriented. The selection of these persons should be governed only by their suitability and aptitude. Considerations of seniority or age should not play any role in the selection which may be done by the appropriate departmental committee. The selection of outside candidates must be done by a special committee consisting of departmental and outside high level scientific and technical personnel. This committee should be empowered to adopt procedures for ensuring that the best persons are recruited to the Telecommunication Research Centre. Direct recruitment should be possible at all levels including that of Asst. Directors and, if necessary, for Deputy Directors. This will enable the organisation to tape all the available sources of qualified personnel including those who are occupying positions in other organisations especially overseas :

Set Up Of The Telecommunication Research Centre Vis-a-Vis The Posts And Telegraphs Department

The Telecommunication Research Centre may continue as at present as part of the Posts and Telegraphs Department. However, as far as the working of the Centre itself is concerned, it should be invested with considerably more powers so as to be in practice autonomous in all its activities.

The continuation in the Posts and Telegraphs Department gives the Centre benefits by way of ready availability of funds within the large budget of the P&T, of being able to retain close and continuous touch with the requirements of the Department not only at the top level but at different levels also, and of being able to coordinate the different activities in order to bring the benefits of technology to rapid application for the betterment of telecommunication services. This structure also enables the Centre to act directly and quickly in an advisory capacity in all technical matters.

While this is so, it is very essential, specially with the massive programme which has to be undertaken, that the organisation be fully autonomous within the frame work. The Director should have full powers in relation to all the activities in the Centre subject to only such limitations as may be inescapable. With regard to the programme of work, he will be guided by an advisory committee consisting of high level scientific and technical personnel drawn from the department and outside.

The Director of the Telecommunication Research Centre should have complete powers within the budget provision to undertake all the activities of the Centre and for the creation and filling up of the posts. However, with regard to the creation of senior posts, he may be required to get the approval of the Advisory Committee. The procedure to be followed for filling the posts has been outlined elsewhere in this Report.

Financial Requirements

The expenditure incurred at present by the Telecommunication Research Centre is very small compared with the rest of the activities of the Department. The current rate of revenue expenditure of the Telecommunication Research Centre is about Rs. 16 lakhs. In addition, there has been a Third Plan provision for capital works of Rs. 40 lakhs. In view of the need to strengthen the research organisation to meet the requirements in the Fourth Plan, the revenue expenditure will increase steadily from year to year and at the end of the Fourth

Plan will require an expenditure of about Rs. 65 lakhs (based on present scales of pay and prices) in about six years' time. In addition, the capital expenditure during the Fourth Plan will need about Rs. 100 lakhs of equipments additionally in the Telecommunication Research Centre together with additionally amounts for experimental installations, especially of electronic exchanges and of high power micro wave systems.

Other Recommendations

There is need to build-up a workshop to manufacture prototypes in the Telecommunication Research Centre as well as to take some of the designs one step further to speed up implementation. The setting up of a model workshop has been hampered by lack of accommodation. However, for proceeding smoothly and rapidly to the stage at which the designs are ready for industrial development, it is essential to have an efficient and effective model workshop on an adequate scale.

As research progresses, there is need to train new recruits as well as to retrain research personnel already in the Telecommunication Research Centre in new systems, techniques, methods, etc. A training class must form part of the Telecommunication Research Centre in order to meet these requirements systematically and effectively. This organisation is important and vital for manning the posts in the research branch adequately and effectively.

The persons working in the Telecommunication Research Centre should keep in coutinuous touch with the progress in other countries. Without this, the organisation will become backward. It is, therefore, essential that research personnel should be given facilities for further training as well as for participation in conferences, seminars, discussions, etc. In view of the rapid growth of technology in this field, this point is of importance.

It is essential for speedy implementation that the officers in the Department are aware of the trends and thinking in the research organisation as well as the products that are likely to emerge in the near and in the distant future. It is also essential that there should be close contact between the executive persons in the field and the research organisations. This is best done by having regular groups of these officers posted to the Telecommunication Research Centre for short periods of between 2 and 4 weeks so as to bring themselves up-to-date and to have mutual discussions in the Telecommunication Research Centre. This will greatly increase the understanding all-round and speed up the application of the latest knowledge and technology. It will also given the Telecommunication Research Centre a very useful basis to formulate the future programmes.

There is need to consolidate the fruits of research and to make them available to all the persons working in the field. It is, therefore, essential to prepare thoroughly and adequately technical memoranda, scientific papers, books, etc., so that all information is freely and readily available to the persons working in the research organisation and others who are working in the field in this country. The techniques available in the Telecommunication Research Centre and the techniques likely to be available are useful to all the persons in the field of electronics and communication and every effort should be made to disseminate this information freely. Special attention should be given to this aspect and, if necessary, a separate section should be set up and adequately staffed to deal with this item.

Conclusion

In the context of the needs of the country, the Telecommunication Research Centre has an extremely important and vital role to play in the development of telecommunication and of electronics. To keep such an organisation effective is not an easy task and can be done only, if its importance is kept in view at all times and every effort directed to sustain, expand and stimulate its activities. The Telecommunication Research Centre should be given facilities, personnel, organisation etc., to meet as effectively as possible the needs in every way. The work of the Telecommunication Research Centre should be treated as one of the national importance and should not be subordinated to departmental procedures or considerations.

COMMITTEE TO STUDY THE QUESTION OF LEGALISATION OF ABORTION, 1964—REPORT

New Delhi, Ministry of Health and Family Planning, 1967, 143p.

Chairman : Shri Shantilal H. Shah.
Members : Smt. Achama Mathai; Smt. Avabai P. Wadis; Dr. (Mrs.) S. Bhatia; Smt. Masuma Begum; Shri Narendra Pragji Nathwani; Dr. B.N. Purandare; Dr. H.N. Shivapuri; Smt. Shyam Kumari Khan; Dr. V. N. Shirodkar.
Secretary : Lt. Col. B.L. Raina.

APPOINTMENT

In pursuance to the recommendations of 16th meeting of the Central Family Planning Board held in Bombay on August 24, 1964, it has been decided to constitute a Committee to study the question of Legalisation of Abortion in the country. So the Ministry of Health and Family Planning (Deptt. of Family Planning) constituted a Committee vide their letter No. F. 4-30/64-F.P.II dated September 29, 1964.

TERMS OF REFERENCE

To examine the question of legalisation of abortion in all its aspects—medical, social, legal and moral and to make recommendations.

CONTENTS

Letter of Transmission to the Ministry of Health and Family Planning, Government of India from the Chairman of the Committee; Members of the Committee; Introduction (Appointment of the Committee; Terms of Reference; Programme of Work; Acknowledgement); The Problem (The Incidence of Abortion; Mortality; Mortality and Complications; Abortion and Birth rates; Abortion as related to age and parity; Marital status and Abortions; Repeated Abortions; Motives for seeking Abortion [(a) Summary—statement of laws regarding abortion in different countries; (b) Abortion Laws in India]; Views expressed by persons interviewed); General Appraisal; Recommendations; Supplementary Note by Dr. H.N. Shivapuri; Appendices.

RECOMMENDATIONS

The abortion law in India at present is as follows :—

Section 312: Indian Penal Code. "Whoever Voluntarily causes a women with child to miscarry shall, if such miscarriage be not caused in good faith for the purpose of saving the life of the woman, be punished with imprisonment of either description for a a term which may extend to 3 years or with fine or with both; and if the woman be quick with child, shall be punished with imprisonment of either description for a term which may extend to seven years and shall also be liable to fine.

Explanation: A woman who causes herself to miscarry is within the meaning of this section.

The word miscarriage is used in the section includes not only abortions but also expulsion of viable foetus before the normal birth. The only exception is in case of miscarriage caused in good faith for the purpose of saving the life of the mother.

(i) The Committee considers the above provision too restrictive; and therefore recommends that it should be liberalised to allow termination of pregnancy by a qualified medical practitioner acting in good faith not only for saving the pregnant woman's life but also :—

(a) When the continuance of pregnancy would involve serious risks to the life, or gave injury to the health, whether physical or mental, of the pregnant woman, whether before, at, or after the birth, or

(b) When there is a substantial risk that if the child were born it would suffer from such physical or mental abnormalities as to be seriously handicapped in life; or

(c) When the pregnancy results from rape, intercourse with an unmarried girl under the age of 16 or intercourse with a mentally defective woman.

(ii) The Committee further recommends that the following conditions be complied with in connection with any treatment for the termination of a pregnancy, that is to say—

(a) Abortions authorised under the above recommendation can be performed only by a person who holds a qualification granted by an authority specified or notified in any of the schedules to the Indian Medical Council Act, 1956 (202 of 1956), as modified up to 1st December, 1964;

(b) The treatment must be carried out in a place for the time being approved for the purpose, by the Government of India or State Government;

(c) The opinion must be certified in writing by the practitioner who carry out the termination of pregnancy before the treatment is begun;

(d) There should be before treatment a consent in writing by the pregnant woman, of, if under eighteen years of age, the pregnant girl and one of her parents or of the pregnant girl and her guardian for the termination of the pregnancy.

Provided that where the practitioner is of the opinion formed in good faith, that the termination is immediately necessary in order to save the life of the pregnant woman (and certifies his opinion in writing either before or after carrying out the treatment) conditions (b) and (d) need out be compiled with.

(iii) The Government should prescribe rules requiring the qualified medical practitioner who terminates a pregnancy to give notice of the termination, and such other information relating to the termination as may be prescribed by the regulations within such period as may be prescribed; and with respect to the disposal of certificates.

The information so furnished shall not be made public or divulged to any person other than a police officer especially authorised to obtain such information or under order of a Court of Law.

The Committee had the opportunity to see a Draft Medical Termination of Pregnancy Bill recently discussed in the British Parliament and has utilised its provisions in making the above recommendations.

The Committee is aware that it may be difficult to distinguish genuine from non-genuine cases. The Committee, however, feels, that the likelihood of a few non-genuine cases should not prevent protection to a large number of genuine cases.

The Committee while making the above recommendations also strongly recommends that :

(a) In order to prevent the danger of repeated abortions in the case of woman who are not fit to bear the strain of further pregnancies the medical practitioner should advise the woman and/or her husband to undergo voluntary sterilization.

(b) The idea of small family norm achieved through control of conception should be vigorously promoted.

(c) Readily accessible services for family planning should be extended.

(d) Family Life Education to develop healthy and responsible attitudes towards sex ; marriage and parenthood should be promoted.

There is very little statistical and other material available in India on this highly controversial subject of induced abortion. If has attracted public attention only recently. The Committee is aware that its recommendations are likely to be criticised either as falling too short or as going too far according to the critics attitude. Nevertheless it is of the view that they should be placed before the Government for their consideration as it feels that the recommendations are practicable and necessary under present conditions.

MATHEMATICS REFORMS COMMITTEE, 1964—REPORT

New Delhi, University Grants Commission, 1966. 24p.

Chairman : Dr. D.C. Pavate.

Members : Prof. R.S. Verma; Prof. V.S. Huzurbazar; Prof. N.S. Nagendranath.

Secretary : Dr. V.S. Patankar.

APPOINTMENT

To meet the challenge of the continuous growth of scientific knowledge, the universities have to maintain some balance between the old and the new in their programme of studies. The University Grants Commission realised the great hiatus between the course of studies in various subjects in our country and those of the advanced countries in the other parts of the world. The U.G.C., therefore, appointed a few years back "Review Committees" in a number of important subjects in Physical and Biological Sciences, Humanities and Social Sciences, to survey and assess the standards of teaching and research and the facilities available for the purpose. Accordingly in 1959, a 'Mathematics Review Committee, consisting of some of our distinguished mathematicians was appointed for the purpose. This Committee reviewed the position as it existed towards the end of the Second Plan period, about the standards of teaching and research in mathematics in this country. One significant suggestion made by this Committee was the desirability of reviewing and revising the syllabus once in five years in view of the rapid pace at which knowledge is growing in these days. In pursuance of this suggestion of periodical revision of the mathematical education in this country, the U.G.C. appointed the second Review Committee in October 1964.

TERMS OF REFERENCE

The desirability of reviewing and revising the syllabus once in five years in view of the rapid pace at which knowledge is growing in these days.

RECOMMENDATIONS

Existing Facilities For Teaching Mathemaitcs In Our Universities

Though the previous Review Committee made several useful suggestions, they made little impression on the undergraduate teaching of mathematics, although we are aware of some notable exceptions. The reasens for this state of affairs are :

(i) The large and steady increase in the number of students in colleges and the lack of corresponding increase in the number of well qualified teachers.

(ii) The teachers are, by and large, not inclined to keep themselves abrest of modern developments. Well-qualified teachers are inclined to join the post-graduate departments rather than do unde rgraduate teaching. The status of a postgraduate teacher is much higher than that of an undergraduate teacher although the work of the latter is in no way less important than that of the former.

(iii) The questions asked in the competitive examinations of U.P.S.C., continue to be old fashioned and are not based on modern subjects like Abstract Algebra and Topology.

(iv) The engineering colleges attract a large number of potentiality good mathematics students and at least in our country waste eventually their talents. The process creates a drain of mathematical talent at the present moment. Suitable in essentivc such as special scholarships for good mathematics students even at the undergraduate stage and opportunities of employment need to be provided.

(v) In some universities the language load is inclined to be heavy at the B.A., or B.Sc. classes. This partly effects the standard of mathematics. While we have no objection to the retention of English or any other European language such as French, German and Russian, the retention of regional language does not serve any useful purpose at the stage.

Somehow a beginning has to be made to modernise the courses of studies in mathematics, but it will not be possible unless we are able to organise seminars every year during the summer vacations, for the education of the teachers. There should be discussion groups and we must indicate to the teachers the lines on which broad advances have been made in mathematics during the last fifty years. Simultaneously, good text-books in mathematics should be got written. Without seminars and without good text-books, no improvement in the mathematical education of undergraduates is possible. It is gratifying to note that some universities and higher secondary school boards are making efforts in this direction and their experiments are well worth encouraging. All the same, great efforts are necessary to modernise the mathematics course as early as possible.

Actually much reform is needed in the secondary school mathematics. The introduction to logic could, with advantage, begin from Standard VI and be continued through the higher secondary stage. The emphasis should be laid on the discovery and understanding of general principles, but this is a matter which should be seriously considered by the colleges of education and the departments of public instruction. Universities have no say regarding the content of education in the secondary schools except through the colleges of education. The lead in the reform of teaching mathematics in the schools should, therefore, be taken through the Colleges of education. The works produced by the American School Mathematics Group will be of great use in this connection.

Many universities in India control the examinations of standard XI of the higher secondary schools directly or indirectly by at least laying down the requ'rements of admission to colleges. Some universities have pre-university classes corresponding to stan lard XI of the higher secondary schools. It is, therefore, possible to begin the reform in the teaching of mathematics from standard XI or the pre-university class onwards. Hence we suggested in the interim report a few changes in the courses in these classes. Much depends also on the enthusiasm and knowledge of the teachers themselves. Given the will and drive, it is possible to make radical changes in the teaching of mathematics in the colleges and raise the general standard by holding regular annual seminars, etc. and being our syllabus considerably closer to that followed in advanced countries.

Many educationists hold the view now-a-days that the pre-university course should of two years' duration and that this could be followed by a three years degree course. If this is possible, it will make for considerable improvement in the mathematical education in our country. In that case, the first years, B.A. and B.Sc. course will automaticaliy be transferred to the higher secondary schools (or pre-university classes) and the undergraduate course can be extended by one year. This will enable us to have a standard comparable to that obtaining in Europe or America to some extent at least. In the present financial stringency, however, it is doubtful whether government will be in a position to find the additional funds required throughout the country. Hence we have made our recommendations in this report on the assumption that the present educational structure, viz. 10-year school education, 1-year pre-university (or 11-year higher secondary school) education, three-year degree course and two-year Master's course will continue at least for the next five years at the end of which there will be another

Committee to review the situation.

At present there are three patterns of undergraduate courses of three years for B.A. and B. Sc. Some universities believe in a three-year general education so that in addition to English they provide for three different courses of the same level. This means that mathematics will have only one-third of the teaching time available. We may put such universities in category I. The standard of mathematical education is bound to be low in such universities at the undergraduate level. The students in such universities will have to depend only on two-year M. A. and M. Sc. course for their real mathematical education and it seems to us that this period is too short for students of mathematics. The difficulties of these students in tackling research problems or to be effective mathematics teachers in schools and colleges will be also very great indeed.

The second category of universities provide a three-year honours course in mathematics immediately after the pre-university or XIth standard of the higher secondary schools. The only possible criticism against this arrangement is that the students general education tends to be poor as a result of specialisation at an early stage.

Finally, there are a number of universities which have been taking a sort of middle path between the first and the second categories we may put such universities in category III under this scheme, the students are required to have general education up to the intermediate (or the first year of the B. A., and B.Sc.) stage, followed by a special course in mathematics for two years. The latter course of two years in mathematics closely resembles the honours course in universities in category II. The general standard of mathematical education is more or less the same in universities of categories II and III, although the scheme under the universities of category II has been obviously more advantageous than in those of category III. For instance, the universities under category III provide general education as well as specialisation. This system would be still more advantageous if it were possible to have a three-year honours or specialised course based on a two-year pre-university course. In the present circumstances, however, we have to see how best we can improve the standard of undergraduate education in mathematics in all the three categories of universities.

Mathematical education at least according to the British pattern usually consists of training in Pure Mathematics and Applied Mathematics. Pure Mathematics provides the basic tools and Applied Mathematics usually consists of Mechanics, Hydrostatics, Hydrodynamics, Electricity and Magnatism, Elasticity and Thermodynamics. These are applications of mathematics to physics. There are also vast applications of mathematics to engineering with which we are not ordinarily concerned in arts and science colleges. Similarly statistics which has developed into an independent branch of mathematics has many applications to problems both in social and physical sciences. Mathematical treatment of economics has been developing on a large scale during the last thirty years. We have to make provision for the teaching of econometrics at least at the post-graduate level. However, it is not possible to make provision for the teaching of several subjects in pure and applied mathematics in all universities. Some universities, however, should provide for mathematical economics. We can, however, select a few core subjects which could be taught compulsorily at a high level in all the three categories of universities. Now what are these core subjects ? They are : Modern Algebra and Analysis. Not long ago, a mathematician was one who could solve all sorts of difficult examples in Algebra, Trignometry, Calculus, Pure and Analytical Geometry, and Machanics etc., by learning the trick of the trade. There was hardly any attention paid to fundamental ideas and logical thinking. Even now, several universities in our country suffer from these inhibitions in so far as the teaching of mathematics is concerned. The reason for this is the use of out-of-date text-books and the tendency on the part of teachers to stick to what they had learnt in their days. Supreme efforts are, therefore, necessary to remove this inertia and hence fresh thinking is necessary on the content of mathematical syllabus.

Statistics is studied as an independent subject both at the undergraduate and postgraduate levels in several universities. In view of its great importance, it should, in our view, be made a compulsory subject for students taking mathematics as an honours or a major subject at the first degree level. We have given in this report a sort of model syllabus for all the three categories of universities at the undergraduate and postgraduate levels.

Examinations

(i) Nobody be a paper-setter for any examination for more than two consecutive year.

(ii) The examples be fresh, i.e., should not have been taken bodily from the previous years' papers or standard text-books, as far as possible, and the number of questions to be set should not exceed the number of questions to be solved by 25% in the first two years and 50% at the B.A. and B.Sc. and postgraduate examinations;

(iii) The paper-setters be given at least six months in which to set the papers and supply the answers;

(iv) The book-work or the theory portion should not

carry more than 40% marks in an examination up to the first degree examination;

(v) Universities encourage all colleges under them to have periodical tests which may carry up to 25% of the total marks to start with, the exact percentage depending on the sincerity and honesty of the colleges and correlation between these marks and the marks obtained at the annual examinations by the candidates; and

(vi) The practice of supplying to the candidates the actual marks obtained by them at any examinations be done away with, the results being declared only in four classes, keeping the actual marks obtained by them strictly confidential.

Proposed Syllabus In Mathematics

We have studied the syllabic of several universities in India. Having regard to the comments we have made and the general principles laid down in the body of this report, we suggest the following syllabus for the guidance of the mathematics boards of our universities with a view to modernising their courses. The universities are, of course, free to modify them to suit their special requirements. The syllabus should be reviewed periodically and revised once in every five years, as suggested by the previous Committee. We would like, however, to emphasize the need to change the pre-university and the undergraduate courses, as they provide the basic foundations.

Pre-University (Or Standard XI) Courses

Algebra one paper and Geometry and Trigonometry one paper. The time required for teaching the course is one hour a day roughly and not less than 160 hours during the year for covering the ground for both the papers.

Paper I—Algebra

Elementary theory of sets : Union, Intersection, Complimentation of a set. Vehn Diagrams.

The number systems : The sets of Natural numbers, Zero as a number, Integers, Rational numbers, Real and Complex numbers. The fundamental operations with them and basic Laws of the rational and real numbers viz. Closure, Commutative, Associative, Distributive, Indentity elements, inverse cancellation.

Indics, surds and logarithms, theory of quadratic equations. Relations, functions and their graphs, simple treatment of A.P., G.P., H.P., and also of A.M., G.M., and H.M., and the relations between them. Sum. to nifinity of geometric series. Mathematical Induction. The values of Σn and Σn^2. Permutation and combination. Elementary course in Theory of Probability.

Binomial theorem for a positive integral index. Partial fractions, simple properties of determinants of second and third order. Solution of simultaneous linear equations by determinants.

Paper II—Geometry And Trigonometry

(i) **Pure Geometry** : (**Plane and Solid** : Basic concepts, important definitions and postulates in Geometry. Line, Plane, Angle between two skew lines. Angle between a line and a plane and angle between two planes. Dihedral Angle.

Tetrahedron, Pyramind, Cone Cylinder (general discussion only).

(ii) Similar triangles, mean proportionals. To find a third and a fourth mean Proportional. Important theorems on similar triangles.

Triangular Prism (No formal proofs for the areas and volumes are required).

The proofs of the following theorems only may be required in Solid Geometry :

1. If a straight line is perpendicular to each of two intersecting straight lines at the point of intersection, it is also perpendicular to the plane in which they lie.

2. All straight lines drawn perpendicular to a given straight line at a point on it are coplanar.

3. If two intersecting straight lines are respectively parallel to two other intersecting straight lines not in the same plane with them, the first pair and the second pair contain angles.

4. If two straight lines neither of which intersect nor are parallel, then (i) there is one straight line perpendicular to both of them, and (ii) this common perpendicular is the shortest distance between the given lines.

5. The lines joining the middle points of opposite sides of a tetrahedron are concurrent and bisect one another.

6. The lines joining the vertices of a tetrahedron to the centroids of opposite faces are concurrent at a point which divides each of these lines in the ratio 3:1.

7. Any plane section of a sphere is a circle.

(iii) **Analytical Geometry** : Rectangular, Co-ordinates, Section formulae.

Straight line : Standard forms of its equation.

Conditions for parallel and perpendicular lines, Angle between two lines, bisectors of Angles, distance of a point from a straight line. Simple Locus Problems.

Circle : Equation of the circle, tangent, condition that a straight line be tangent to a circle, orthogonal circles, conditions for orthogonality, radical axis.

(iv) **Trigonometry** : Angle as being generated by the rotation of a ray. Radiant measure. Trigonometrical ratios and their signs. Trigonometrical ratios of

$$\frac{\pi}{6}, \frac{\pi}{4}, \frac{\pi}{3}, \frac{\pi}{2}$$

and of and angle between 0 and 2π. Simple identities. Trigonometrical functions of

$$\left(\frac{\pi}{2}-0\right),\left(\frac{\pi}{2}+0\right),\ \pi-0 \text{ etc.}$$

Solution of right angled triangles and simple problems on heights and distance. Sine and Cosine Laws and geometric interpretation of the Cosine Law. Solution of triangles. Addition and multiple angle formulae. Simple identities. Simple equations involving trigonometric functions. Periodicity and graphs of sin θ, cosθ and tan θ.

Note : It may be possible for some universities to delete some portions of Geometry and Trigonometry and include in their place an elementary course in Calculus.

B A. And B Sc. Part I (or Intermediate Or The First Year Mathematics Course In Engineering)

The time required is roughly one hour a day or a minimum of 150 hours during the year.

Paper I—Calculus And Geometry

Differential Calculus : Functions, the Concepts of Limit and Continuity, Derivatives of Algebraic, Trigonometric, Exponential and Logarithmic Functions, Differentiation of Composite, Inverse and Implicitly defined functions and Functions defined parametrically. Successive Differentiation, Leibnitz's Rule, Tangents and Normals. Maxima and Minima of functions of a single variable.

Integral Calculus : Integration of standard forms, Integration by Partial Fractions, by substitution and by parts, Reduction Formulae, Evaluation of simple Definite Integrals, Definite Integral as an area and as the limit of a sum. Applications to area, Lengths of curves, volume and surface of a solid revolution.

Analytic Geometry of Two Dimensions : Standard Equations of Parabola, Ellipse and Hyperbola and their simple properties.

Rigid Motion : The general idea of rigid motion, congruence of geometrical figures under rigid motion, Geometrical transformations of plane figures : (i) translations, (ii) reflections, and (iii) rotations under rigid motion.

Paper II—Algebra And Trigonometry

Sets, Real numbers—Postulates and consequences. The ordering of the real numbers, the ordered field, the Basic Inequality Postulates—the trichotomy, the transitive, the addition and multiplication of inequalities, Simple Inequalities, Absolute values. Relations, functions and mappings. Complex numbers, Inequality.

Division or Eulclid's Algorithm ; Polynomials : Synthetic Division, Rational Roots and the Fundamental Theorem of Algebra. Relations between co-efficients and roots of a Polynomial Equation. Graphing of Polynomial functions, quadratic, cubic and quartic curves.

Simple treatment of Matrices and determinants. Addition and Multiplication of Matrices. Rank of a Matrix. Solution of a system of linear equations involving not more than 4 variables.

Infinite Series : Limit of an infinite sequence, convergence of an infinite series—the comparison tests, the ratio tests, Cauchy's root test, alternating series. A monotonic sequence. Power series—convergence of Binomial and exponential logarithmic series.

Trigonometric functions, Inverse functions, Principal values, Complex numbers—geometrical representation of a complex number, De Moivre's theorem. The nth roots of unity. Series for Sine and Cosine, Hyperbolic functions, Logrithms of a complex number, Summation of trigonometric series (simple cases only).

Syllabi For B.A. And B.Sc. Parts II And III

We have studied the syllabi adopted by some of our universities for the second and third years of the three-year degree course in mathematics. Some universities have an honours (major or principal) course and provide eight or six papers in Pure and Applied Mathematics. We are submitting below an eight-paper scheme for the honours course of which four papers are to be taken at the end of the second year and four others at the end of the third year. Some provide for the study of mathematics as one of the three different subjects taught in arts or science, while some provide for it as a Pass course or as a minor subject. In these cases, there are usually three or four papers to be taken at the end of the two years. In the scheme given below a four-paper scheme is given of which two are to be taken at the end of second year and the two others at the end of the third year. In view of the vast importance of Calculus (or Analysis) and Modern Algebra for all students no matter whether their interests lie in physics, engineering or economics, we consider that papers on these subjects should be common to all. The students who offer mathematics even as a minor or pass course could with advantage take Papers I and II at the end of the second year and papers IV or V, and VII of the honours course at the end of the third year.

The students of honours or major mathematics should take all the four papers I to IV at the end of the second year and the papers V to VIII at the end of the third year of the three-year degree course. In some universities, honours students have to take other subjects as well and may have time for only three papers each year in mathematics. In such cases, they may choose any subject they like from the remaining two paper (i.e. Papers III and IV and Papers V and VIII). Since we have recommended that there should be an examination of the university at the e d of every academic year (if not at the end of every semester or term), we have divided the course into two p rts-one for each year.

We have not suggested any textbook as there are many available. The teacher should choose them caref ully. Most of these books are, however, expensive foreign books. We suggest that the UGC should get cheap books written by competent scholars, perhaps, with a subsidy for production.

B.A./B.Sc. (Part II)

Paper I—Algebra And Geometry

(a) **Mathematical Logic** : Notion of logical inference. Rules of inference and proof. Truth and validity—truth values and truth functional connectives.

Tautology—Predicates and universal quantifier.

(b) **Modern Algebra** : Elementary properties of Integres, starting with Peano's axious. The Modulo system. Euler's function. Fermat's, Wilson's and Lagrage's theorems. Integral domains, Nothions of groups, rings, fields and vector spaces.

(c) **Geometry** : General equation of a conic section and its reduction to standard forms. Polar coordinates. Equation of a conic section and its tangent in polar coordinates. Equation of a plane and a straight line. Standard equation of a sphere, cyliner, ellipsiod, paraboloid and hyperboloid and general properties of central conicoids.

(d) Elementary treatment of finite differences and interpolation formulae.

Paper II—Calculus (Analysis)

(a) The principle of the point of accumulation. Limits of sequences, Cauchy's convergence test. Monotonic sequences. Upper and lower bounds of a set. Upper and lower limits. Functions of a real variable. Continuity of functions. Properties of continuous functions.

(b) Derivatives of algebraic, trigonometric, exponential and logarithmic functions and inverse functions: Higher derivatives and Leibnitz's theorem. Properties of derivatives. Rolle's theorem and Mean value theorem. Taylor's and Maclaurin's series, Maxima and minima. Indeterminate forms.

(c) The definite integral as the limiting value of upper and lower sums (Riemann Integral). Fundamental rules of operation. Indefinite integral, the derivatives of the indefinite integral. The fundamental theorem of the integral calculus. The mean value theorem of the integral calculus.

Reduction formulae. Integration of rational functions involving trigonometric and hyperbotic functions. Evaluation of definite integrals.

(d) **Differential Equations** : Differential equations of the first order. Exact differential equations. Simple equations of the second order.

(e) **Applications** : Length of an arc of a plane curve. Concavity and convexity. Points of inflexion. Asymptotes. Surface area. Volumes of solids or revolution. Particle falling freely under gravity including air resistance. Simple harmonic motion.

Paper III—Probability And Elementary Statistics

(a) Frequency, definition of probability. Axiomatic approach to probability. Fundamental concepts of experiment, outcome sample, space (discrete case only), events and probability of events. Conditional probability, Bayes' Theorem, Independent events.

(b) Discrete random variable defined as functions on discrete sample spaces. Intuitive treatment of continuous random variable, Distribution function and probability density function. Expectation, moments, characteristic funtions of measures of location, dispersion, skewness and kurtosis. Standard distributions—Binomial, Possion, Hypergeometric, Negative Binomial, Uniform, Normal, Beta, Gemma and Cauchy distribution.

(c) Distributions of more than once variable. Conditional and marginal distributions. Dependent and independent random variables. Conditional expectation, correlation and regression. Bivariate normal distribution.

(d) Tchebysheff's ϕ Lemma. Convergence probability. Weak law of larger numbers. Statement and applications of central limit theorem. Poisson and normal limits of the Binomial distribution.

(e) Chi-square, t and f distributions. Sampling distribution of mean and variance in samples from a normal population. Standard errors of statistics. Large-sample standard errors.

(f) Elements of statistical inference-Unbi-assedness, efficiency and consistency of estimaters, Method of maximum likelihood. Testing of simple hypotheses. Confidence intervals.

Paper IV—Vector Analysis And Mechanics

(a) **Vector Analysis** : Vectors and scalars. Rules of vector algebra. Vectors as an ordered triad of three real numbers. Scalar and vector Products. Vector equations. Independent and dependent vector.

(b) **Dynamics** : Newton's laws of motion. Equations of motion of a particle. Motion in a straight line, work, energy and power. Motion of a system of particles. Laws of conservation of energy, linear momentum and angular momentum.

Impulsive forces. Tangential and normal components of acceleration. Radial and transverse components of acceleration.

(c) Equilibrium of a particle and a rigid body under coplanar forces. Principle of virtual work. Centre of mass. Friction. Equilibrium of freely hanging strings and strings on rough plane curves.

(d) **Hydrostatics** : Fluid pressure, centre of pressure. Floating bodies and meta centre. Gas laws and atmospheric pressure.

B.A./B. Sc. Part III—(Final Year)

Paper V—Set Theory, Topology And Infinite Series

(a) **Set Theory** : Basic notion of set theory. The concepts of a set and its subsets and set algebra. The cartesian product of two sets and definition of a general function. One of one mappings and their inverses. Composite functions. Sequences. The number of elements in a set. Countable sets. The set of all real numbers is uncountable. The notion of a cordinal number.

(b) **Topology** : Notion of a topological space. Open sets, closed sets, derived sets. Elosure, neighbourhood, limiting point. Metric spaces. The real number system and its topological properties. Bolzano Weierstrass theorem. Continuous mappings, homeomorphism, compact and connected spaces. Application of compact and connected spaces in real analysis. Heine Borel Theorem.

(c) **Infinite Series** : Tests of convergence including comparison d' Alembert's Cauchy's integral tests. Dirichlet's theorem on rearrangement of terms of an absolutely convergent series. Multiplication of series. Uniform convergence. Power series.

Paper VI—Calculus (Analysis)

(a) Derivatives in polar coordinates. Vector functions and their derivatives.

(b) Functions of two or more variables. Limits continuity and differentiability of functions of more than one variable. Partial derivatives of a function of more than one variable. Total differential. Jacobians. Implicit functions and there differentation. Maxima and minima of functions of two or more variables, Lagrange multiplies.

(c) Improper integrate. Infinite integrals.

(d) Differentiation and integration under the integral sign. Term by term differentiation and integration of series.

(e) Multiple integrals. Evaluation of simple, double and tripple integrals. Beta and Gamma functions.

(f) Osculating circle and the circle of curvature. Involutes and Evolutes, Envelopes and singular points.

(g) Elements of Numerical integration.

Paper VII—Differential Equations, Linear Algebra And Complex Variables

(a) **Differential Equations** : Singular solution. Standard linear differential equantial with variable coefficients. Simultaneous differential equations. The equation $Pdx+Qdy+Rdz=0$. Partial differential equations of the first order.

(b) **Linear Algebra** : Matrices and determinants and their application to solutions of linear equations. Quadratic forms and their reduction to normal forms.

(c) **Complex Variables** : Analytical functions. Cauchy-Riemann equations. Cauchy's theorem. Taylor and laurent series. Residue theorem and contour integration.

Paper VIII—Electricity And Magnetism Or Spherical Astronomy

Electricity and Magnetism : Inverse square law. Potential. Gauss's theorem. Electrostatic field. Lines and tubes of force. Equipotential surfaces. Conductors and insulators. Mechanical force on a conductor. Solution of simple electrostatic problems, method of images, boundary conditions, Condensers dielectric constant, condensers in series and in parallel, capacity of a parallel plate condenser and of a sphere. Energy of charged bodies.

Steady currents, Ohm's law. Distribution of steady currents in closed circuits, Wheatstones' bridge.

Field of a magnetic double. Magnetic induction. Bar magnets, magnetic susceptibility and permeability. Magnetic field due to a steady electric current. Uniform magnetic shell. Forces between currents and magnets. Induced magnetism, Electromagnetic induction.

OR

Spherical Astronomy : Fundamental formulae of spherical trigonometry and solution of spherical triangles (only as much of spherical trigonometry will be required as has a direct bearing on problems in spherical astronomy).

The celestial sphere and different systems of celestial co-ordinates. Twilight atmospheric refraction. Planetary motions and phenomena. Sidereal time, mean time, conversion of time. Equation of time. Aberration. Parallaxes of the moon and the Sun and annual parallax of stars. Precession and Nutation. Elementary theory of eclipses.

M. A./M.Sc. Part—I

Paper I—Real Analysis

(a) Dedekind and Cantor theories of irrational numbers. Continous functions of one and more than one variable. Functions of bounded variation and their properties. Partial derivatives, and partial differentials. Total differential Partial differential derivatives of the second order. Young's and Schwarz's theorems. Implicit functions. Young's existence theorems.

(b) Fundamentals of set theory. Concept of cardinal numbers. General concept of function. Measure of plane sets. Measure an semirings. Extension of Jordan measure. Complete additivity. General problem of extension of measures. Lebesgue's extension of a measure defined on a semi-ring with unity. Extension of Lebesgue measure in the general case. Measurable functions and their fundamental properties. Sequences of measurable functions and their convergence under different concepts of convergence. Lebesgue integral of simple functions. The general definitions and fundamental properties of the Lebesgue integral. Passage to the limit under the Lebesgue integral. Comparison of Lebesgue and Riemann integrals. Products of sets and measures. Fubini's theorem. The integral as a set function. Riemann-Stieltje's and Lebesgue-Stieltje's integrals and their properties.

Square integrable functions. Mean convergence. Two spaces with countable bases. Orthogonal sets of functions. Orthogonalisation Fourier series over orthogonal sets. The Riesz-Fischer theorem.

Paper II—Modern Algebra

Semi-groups and groups. Cyclic groups. Coset decomposition of a group. Homeomorphism and Isomorphisms of groups.

Rings, sub-rings, ideals, Homeomorphism and Isomorphisms of rings. Anti-isomorphism. Characteristic of ring. Algebra of subgroups to the additive groups of a ring.

Extensions of rings and fields. Polynomial rings. Structure of any field. The number of roots of a polynomial in a field. Symmetric polynomials. Rings of functions. Elementary factorisation theory. Gaussian and Education domains.

Groups with operators, M-Groups, Schreier's refinement theorem. The Jordan-Holder theorem. Fields : separable and inseparable. Algebraic extensions. Transcendental extensions. Perfect fields. Galois fields.

Paper III—Mathematical Methods

Advanced Vector analysis. Gradient divergence, Curl and Laplacian. Theorems of Gauss, Green and stokes. Serrent-Frenet formulae. Curvature aad torsion of curves. Cartesian Tensors. Covariant and contravariant tensors. Equation of a geodesic in a Riemannian space. Ordinary differential equation. Self adjoint operators, eigen-value problem for the Sturm-Liouville equation. Orthogonality. Eigen-function expansion Partial differential equations. Laplace's equation, transformation of Laplace's equation from rectangular coordinates to curvilinear coordinates. Tbe maximum, minimum property and the fundamental properties of harmonic functions. Euler's problem in the Calculus of variations. Fourier and Laplace transforms.

Paper IV—Functions Of A Complex Variable

Analytic functions. Liouville's theorem. Morera's theorem. Singularities of analytic functions. Behaviour of an analytic function in the neighbourhood of a singularity. Rouche's Theorem. Argument principle. Mittag-Leffler's theorem. Maximum modulus theorem. Hadamard's three circle theorem. Schwarz's Lemma. Analytic continuation Monodromy theorem. General analytic function. Power series and the formula for its radius of convergence. General tests for singular points. Convergence of the series and regularity of the functions. Abel's theorem and its converse. Tauber's theorem and Littlewood's theorem. Functions with natural boundaries. Conformal mapping, linear transformations, normal families. Riemann mapping theorem. Schwarz-Christoffel formula.

Paper V—Topology And Functional Analysis

Sets : Set operations, Product sets, denumerable and non-denumerable sets, Equivalence of sets. Cardinal number. Equivalence relation. Mappings. Partially ordered sets, Zorn's lemma (without proof)

Metric Spaces: Definition and examples. Neighbourhoods. Convergence, limit points and closure. Open and closed sets. Separable metric spaces, Continuous mappings. Homeomorphism Isometry, Complete metric spaces. Sets of the first and second category. Baire's theorem. Diameter of a set. Bounded and totally bounded sets. Sequential compactness. Compact and locally compact sets. Connected sets. Principle of contraction mapping in a metric space.

Existence theorems for Differential Equations. Existence theorems for Integral Equations. Arzela's theorem and its applications Generalised Arzela's theorem. Real function in a metric space. Extension of continuous functions from closed sets. Continuous curves in a metric space.

Normed Linear Spaces: Definition. Examples. Convex sets. (Linear funtionals. Confugerate space. Benach spaces. Hahn Banach's theorem. Closed graph theorem. Weak and strong convergence. Linear operators. Bounded operators. Inverse and Adjoint operators. Hilbert spaces. Schwarz's inequality. Orthogonal complements. Riesz-representation theorem. Separable Hilbert spaces. Orthnormal systems. Fourier coefficients. Bessel's inequality. Parseval's equality. Riesz-Fisher-theorem.

Definition and examples of generalised functions (distribution) on the real line. Dirac's function. Derivative and convergence of generalised functions.

M.A./M.Sc.—Part II

Here we do not want to restrict the teacher's freedom of choice of topics. Hence we mainly indicate the subjects to enable the teachers to carry out as much advanced work as possible in these subjects.

Pure Mathematics

Paper VI—Special Functions and Integral Transforms.

Paper VII—Advanced Real Analysis.

Paper VIII—Algebraic Geometry or Differential Geometry including Riemannian Geometry.

Two papers IX and X may be chosen from Schedule A and/or from Schedule B.

Applied Mathematics

Paper VI—Analytical Dynamics and Gravitation.

Paper VII—Mechanics of Continuous Media.

PaperVIII—Electromagentic Theory and Relativity.

Two papers IX and X may be chosen from ScheduleB.

Schedule A—Pure Mathematics

Set Theory, Foundations of Mathematics, Mathematical Logic, Algebraic Theories, Theory of Groups, Hilbert spaces, Combinatorial Topology, Probability. Theory (Advanced), Stochastic processes, Infinite Matrices and Summability. Linear Operators, Information Theory, Integral Equations, Theory of distributions, Econometrics, Sequences and function spaces, Theory of numbers, Harmonic Analysis.

Schedule B—Applied Mathematics

Hydrodynamics, Aerodynamics, Elasticity and Plasticity, Quantum Machanics, Theory, Theory of waves and vibrations, Partial differential equations of mathematical physics Non-Linear analysis, Stellar structure, Relativity, Classical Mechanics, Ballistics, Information Theory, Cybernetics, Special Functions, Celestial mechanics and satellite motion, Statistical mechanics and Thermodynamics, Turbulence, Magnetohydrodynamics.

Note : Subjects like probability, statistical Inference, Numerical Analysis, Stochastic processes can be classified as either Pure Mathematics special subjects or Applied Mathematics special subjects.

Finally, we thank the University Grants Commission for appointing this Committee to review the position of mathematics in our universities and we must say that we have enjoyed this work and done our best to give a workable solution to the problem of modernising the teaching of mathematics at the undergraduate as well as at the postgraduate classes. Whether this report will serve any useful purpose or not will depend on the seriousness with which the teachers of mathematics view the urgency of the problem. We may venture to suggest that the University Grants Commission can also effectively bring to the notice of the universities the desirability of improving the courses in mathematics. Whether any university does real valuable work in mathematics can to a great extent be judged by the modernisation of their courses and development of progressive schools of research. The U.G.C. is the custodian of university interests and it is open to the Commission to see whether the funds advanced by them have been actually put to good use or not. Even the sanction of further development schemes should depend on the earnestness of the universities to improve the quality of mathematical education. Some people may complain that the number of papers has been increased to ten from eight for M. A. or M. Sc. examination. In this connection, we would like to remind them that in Mathematics Tripos they set six papers each year.

As pointed out by Academician Alexandrov, in a programme for improvement of mathematics teaching, computational mathematics is very much to be emphasised. It is, therefore, necessary that at least some selected universities should be encouraged to have computors to enable them to teach computational mathematics. We suggest that at least 10 universities be provided with computors during the Fourth Five Year Plan.

AD HOC COMMITTEE ON EXPORT OF MINOR FOREST PRODUCTS, 1964—REPORT

New Delhi, Ministry of Food, Agriculture, Community Development and Cooperation (Department of Agriculture), n.d. 64p. (memeographed)

Chairman : Shri Hari Singh.

Members : Shri R. T. Mirchandani; Director of Agriculture, Himachal Pradesh; Chief Conservator of Forests, Jammu and Kashmir; Director of Agriculture, Jammu and Kashmir; Shri F. C. Gera. (replaced by Shri J. S. Sarma); Shri K. Srinivasan (replaced by Smt. S. L. Singla); Shri J. S. Matharu.

Secretary : Shri S. L. Katyal (replaced by Shri A. Oswald).

APPOINTMENT

On the recommendations made by the Estimates Committee in their 48th report, the Government of India have decided to set up an Ad hoc Committee on the Export of Minor Forest Products to go into the problems connected with the export of forest products with special reference to Myrobalans, Walnuts and Mushrooms so that concerted measures may be taken to increase their exports vide their Resolution No. 14-15/64 E.P. dated November, 28, 1694.

TERMS OF REFERENCE

(i) To establish on the basis of available material the availability of forest products with special reference to myrobalans, walnuts and mushrooms;

(ii) To consider and suggest long-term policies for the export of forest products, especially, myrobalans walnuts and mushrooms;

(iii) To recommend steps to be taken for increasing the availability of forest products with special reference to myrobalans, walnuts and mushrooms for export purposes; and

(iv) To suggest specific schemes, with estimates of expenditure involved for developing various forests products with an export potential.

CONTENTS

Preface; Introduction; Development of Minor Forest Products; Myrobalans; Walnuts; Mushrooms; Gum Karaya; Kuth; Katha or Cutch; Agarwood; Rosin and Turpentine.

RECOMMENDATIONS

Myrobalans

The State Forest Departments should be requested to protect trees of 'Terminalia Chebula' in particular, in addition to the other species of Terminalia which yied myrobalans, where this has not been done. These species should not be felled in the coupes. Where possible, plantations of Termination Chebula, should be raised.

It is necessary that a high tan bearing myrobalans planting stock should be selected by practical trials and this alone should be used for further propagation of the plant in suitable regions of the country. The fruits should be harvested at the proper time of its development while grading and marking should be made compulsory.

Scientific methods of collection, grading etc. have only recently been introduced in this trade. Consequently the Indian myrobalan has been receiving increasingly less support from the various buyers both in Indian and overseas markets.

Cooperatives should be established for collection and grading of myrobalans in the raw form and for export to foreign countries. Adulteration or 'chebulic myrobalans' with other kinds should not be allowed.

States concerned may be asked to take steps to reduce the sales tax on this commodity.

The old railway freight concession may be restored.

The myrobalan trade should be given a higher priority in the allotment and movement of wagons.

Export incentive should be given to exporters of myrobalans as has been given to some other export commodities.

The indigenous manufacture of myrobalans extract and its export should be encouraged. The extract should be in a form acceptable to the importers in foreign markets.

Walnuts

The economic importance of the Walnut trees lies mainly in their three important issues, namely :

(a) Supply of timber which is greatly prized for decorative wood work and for furniture;

(b) Supply of kernels for edible purposes ; and

(c) Extraction of a high grade dyeing oil from the waste kernel for artist's paints and colours.

At present walnut plantations are located mainly in inaccessible forest areas and there is no organised efforts for the production of quality walnut fruits, their collection, grading, handling, storage and utilisation. In order to step up the production of walnuts in the country, the existing plantations should be improved through adoption of better horticulture techniques. Improved strains of walnut should be developed for obtaining better quality fruits.

New plantations in compact blocks should be raised in the States of Jammu and Kashmir, Himachal Pradesh and Uttar Pradesh. Suitable personnel should also be trained in horticulture to look after these plantations more effectively. Private growers should also be encouraged to grow quality walnuts in sizeable areas. For this purpose suitable planting material and subsidy should be given to them, together with the necessary guidance in its cultivation, in the use of fertilizers and plant protection measures.

Good varieties of walnuts form from USA, France and other advanced countries should be introduced for trial in the Himalayan regions of India.

The practice of debarking the trunk of trees for use as a dentrifice should be discontinued.

At present, chiefly the medium varieties of walnuts are being exported. These have medium-sized kernels and in the European market there is a tendency to prefer small wholes particularly in the confectionary industry. Supply of small wholes should, therefore, be progressively encouraged.

The methods adopted for bleaching, sorting, drying, shelling, grading, storage and packaging are crude and cumbersome and call for improvements. This can be effected by :

(i) Harvesting the nuts at the optimum stage of maturity;

(ii) Drying them adequately;

(iii) Standardising bleaching methods;

(iv) Better packaging; and

(v) Effective fumigation.

In advanced countries, subsidiary industries have been successfully built up for the profitable utilisation of green husk, dried shells and inedible kernels and for the production of oil for artist's paints and colours. It is, therefore, desirable that the feasibility of setting up similar industries for the profitable utilisation of these materials, which are commonly wasted in India, may be examined. This would also reduce costs.

Agmark standards provide for sorting out of the produce according to size, colour, good cracking quality and also guard against invisible or internal defects, visible or superficial defects, insect infestation and extraneous matter. It is hoped that with the proper and strict observance of the compulsory quality control scheme; there would be a significant improvement in the quality of our exports. This is essential if Indian walnuts are to compete successfully with the produce of other countries, notably U.S.A., France, Italy and China

Harvesting of the fruits should be undertaken under expert guidance so that their collection, storage and handling do not result in any wastage. The fruits should be properly graded and marked before marketing.

The walnut producing states should conduct a survey to assess the areas under walnuts and the annual production thereof. This will help in scientific planning and augmenting production for the future.

The research and development departments of the State Governments need to be geared upto extend technical help and supply grafted plants of high quality walnuts at subsidized rates to the prospective growers.

Mushrooms

All practical data gathered as a result of researches being done under different organisations like Indian Council of Agricultural Research and Council of Scientific and Industrial Research for Cultivation of Mushrooms should be disseminated to encourage the private sector to undertake the organisation of mushroom cultivation in suitable areas of the country, on a commercial scale.

Enterprising private sector organisations should be encouraged to set up industrial units for the mass production of edible mushrooms and they should be provided necessary facilities such as planting material, machinery and financial assistance.

A delegation consisting of two or three technical officers connected with the development and research of mush room cultivation in India, should be deputed to Japan to study the cultivation practices of mushrooms on a commercial scale and to acquaint themselves with the latest techniques employed for the advancement of this industry.

The technique of the artificial cultivation of some important edible mushrooms should be standardised and pure culture spawns should be prepared for supplying to different growers. A centre for the supply of spawn should be set up under the aegis of the I.C.A.R.

Prospective growers should be trained in various aspects of mushroom cultivation and given technical guidance.

Mushrooms should be classified separately as an independent item in the "Monthly Statistics of the Foreign Trade of India". This would facilitate the assessment of progress in the export of mushrooms and also in planning for increased production for export purposes.

Quality control should be introduced in mushrooms before export.

Gum Karaya

The Forest Departments of the States where the species 'Sterculia urens occurs' naturally may be requested to protect the trees and to raise this spec es in plantations where possible. Young plants that come up naturally in the forest should be encouraged.

Existing methods of tapping must be improved to ensure that the trees are not unnecessarily damaged and killed by excessive tapping, The Forest Research Institute, Dehradun may be asked to evolve improved tapping techniques for this purpose and to ensure the maximum sustained production of the gum. The highest priority should be given to this work.

Collection of the gum has to be improved to ensure the exclusion of chips of bark, dust etc. For this purpose, the collection of the gum would have to be organised to allow for frequent collections. Tribal Co-operative Societies could undertake the collection and marketing cf the gum. Under the supervision of field officers, better quality can be ensured. In the collection, packing and storage of the gum, the Forest Research Institute, Dehradun, in collaboration with the Central Food Technological Research Institute, Mysore, could advise on improvement of methods of collection, packing and storage.

The storage of the gum at the exporting centres has also to be improved to protect the gum from extraneous matter. Since Gum Karaya is an edible product, sanitary conditions in storage must be ensured. For this purpose, it may be necessary to prescribe inspection of export consignments.

The Indian Standards Institution may be requested to undertake the preparation of standards for Gum Karaya particularly for the foreign market.

Kuth

Efforts should be made by the State Trading Corporation to develop the recently found foreign markets of Hong Kong, Ceylon, France and Afghanistan for the export of Kuth, as exports to China, the earstwhile major buyer, have been stopped since 1962.

Small quantities of Kuth roots have been used indigenously in the manufacture of Indian attars. The roots have also been exported to France for the distillation of its essential oil and for the extraction of resinoids. This export of Kuth roots to overseas manufacturers of essential oils, resinoids etc. should be encouraged.

On account of the fall in the demand for Kuth roots and also because of careless handling by the contractors who obtain the right of extracting the roots in the forest areas, the market for the roots is rapidly dwindling. This has resulted not only in loss of an important trade item to the country but also in unemployment among the people engaged in the cultivation and collection of the root in the States of Jammu and Kashmir, Himachal Pradesh and Uttar Pradesh. Consequently, every effort has to be made and high priority given to revive the trade on sound and scientific basis.

The research and development work carried out at Forest Research Institute, Dehradun, on the economic utilisation of Kuth roots has shown, encouraging results. Its further extension by the scientists at National Chemical Laboratory, Poona has now given a new opening for expanding the scope of utilisation of Kuth roots. An effective method for extraction of the oil of Kuth roots in the form in which it is found to be present in the roots has been developed by National Chemical Laboratory and is also being exploited on a pilot plant basis for the production of oil and its export. The reports received from the overseas users have been extremely encouraging. It is, therefore, suggested that the method for the extraction of oil from Kuth roots, as developed by the National Chemical Laboratory, should be encouraged as widely as possible in view of the large potential for the export trade for this new produce from India. At the same time, costus resinoid which has a large demand in the perfumery trade should also be manufactured and exported.

In order to have a high quality perfumery product which should receive increasing attention on the part of overseas perfumers; it is necessary that sound and scientific methods for collection of the roots and its drying, storage etc. should be introduced under expert advice. The age-old method of smoking the roots over any fuel (leaves, bark and other such wastes) is responsible for the poor quality of the roots and introduces therein a 'burnt' odour which is difficult to remove from the end product. This has been responsible for a large scale refusal of the Indian costus roots, the oil and other related materials produced therefrom, in the international market. Proper drying methods require to be introduced to ensure a good quality.

The creation of a suitable machinery to undertake proper grading, quality control and marketing of the material is an urgent necessity.

Distillation plants for the extraction of the oil, using improved techniques, should be encouraged in the private sector.

Katha Or Cutch

A complete suryev of Khair bearing areas and an assessment of the existing potential should be carried out. It would entail the enumeration State-wise of Khair trees, both on forest and non-forest lands.

On the bas's of the above survey, a regular working scheme for the management of these Khair bearing forests should be prepared. This should include prescriptions for the scientific exploitation, regeneration and extension of Khair trees. The exploitation of Khair on non-forest lands should be controlled and restricted and exploitation of Khair in these areas should also vest with the State Forest Departments. The cooperation of the State Revenue Department and action at Government level will be required for this purpose. Planting stocks should be supplied to Gram Panchayats and individuals at subsidized rates under the Farm Forestry Scheme.

A major inhibitory factor in the manufacture of Katha and Cutch by the factory method is the lack of assurance of sustained and adequate supplies of Khair wood be cause of the policy of the State Governments to auction Khair trees on short leases. Unless there is an assurance of supplies of raw material on a long-term basis there is an understandable hesitation on the part of private entrepreneurs to invest in Katha factories. Leases of 5—10 years are, therefore, recommended to encourage the establishment of new factories so that the production of Katha and particularly Cutch is increased.

It was reported that some Katha traders are unable to take up large scale production of Katha by the factory method because of inadequate financial backing, It is, therefore, recommended that long-term loans on east conditions at low interest could be floated to encourage such private entrepreneurs.

The country method of extracting Katha should be discouraged and the proper scientific method of extraction in factories encouraged because of the wastage of Cutch in the former. Cutch is very important by-product of the factory method and has considerable export potential. The State Forest Departments should, therefore, take immediate action to encourage the setting up of Katha factories and gradually prohibit the manufacture of Katha by the country method.

Research conducted at the Forest Research Institute, Dehradun, into various improvements which could be made in the country method should be brought to the notice of the contractors employing the country method. The improved methods recommended by the Forest Research Institute, Dehradun, would also ensure a higher quality of Katha together with a recovery of some Cutch as by-product.

The Indian Standards Institution may be requested to complete the prepartion of Standard specifications for Katha and Cutch on a priority basis.

Agarwood

For increasing the production of Agarwood, artificial insulation technique to accelerate the rate of obolary formation needs to be evolved. University of Gauhati has already started work in this direction and this work should also be taken up by the Forest Research Institute, Dehradun. The mode of infection, the casual agent and other relevant information in this field is also necessary to be collected.

Steps are necessary to be taken to evolve suitable methods for distillation to increase the yield. Intensive research work in this aspect needs to be taken up by the Forest Research Institute, Dehradun.

A Pilot Plant to extract oil which will have a ready market is necessary to be set up to explore market possibilities of ready-made oil.

Strict measures for quality control in order to promote export trade are necessary.

Instead of the wood, the exporters should be encouraged to export oil extracts which will have a wider market.

Protection of plantations and natural forests containing this species is necessary to preserve this important tree which constitutes substantially in earning foreign exchange for India.

Rosin And Turpentine

Concerted efforts should be made to increase the production of resin from the forest areas in the Himalayas.

Arrangements should be made for the proper handling of resin from the source to the delivery point. Contamination from storage tins and adulteration from extraneous matters during transit should be minimized. In order to purify it from iron contamination, oxalic acid is used but this changes the composition of resin. It would, therefore, be desirable to prevent the contamination itself by using good quality containers.

The export of Turpentine should be restricted so as to encourage its utilization in indigenous industries. This will result in saving the foreign exchange now being utilised on imports.

The overseas markets require various grades of Resin It is not enough to supply them with only WW or WS grades. There is a demand for N grade and it might even be possible to find some demand for B & D grades. Efforts should be made to meet all these demands. 70% of the total production of WG and 40% of N grades produced should be reserved for export.

Uniformity in quality should be maintained for all grades and the Indian Standards Institution should standardised these grades.

Pine oil can be extracted from the needles of the pine trees and the exhausted material c n be turned into pure wool which is very good shock absorber and is used as a packing material. The utilisation of the high boiling sesquiterpene fractions of longifolene and carenes from the oil of turpentine is important and costly perfumery chemicals such as jasmine, jasminal etc. can be produced from this. Some work on this aspect has been done in the National Chemical Laboratories but it is yet to be started on a commercial scale. Research and development of this industry has to be intensified at National Chemical Laboratory and in the Private Sector.

To encourage exports :

(i) Rosin and Turpentine should be brought under the schedule of items eligible for subsidies for export by Commerce Ministry;

(ii) Railway Ministry should be approached to allow 50 per cent concession in railway frieght on the quantities that are moved for export; and

(iii) That a special quota of bright tin plates should be made available to the Industry to reduce the cost of production of Rosin.

INQUIRY INTO THE WASH-AWAY OF NO. 653 DOWN PAMBAN—DHANUSHKODI PASSENGER TRAIN BETWEEN KMS. 681 AND 682 NEAR DHANUSHKODI STATION (SOUTHERN RAILWAY) ON 23RD DECEMBER, 1964—REPORT

Delhi, Manager of Publications, 1967. 10p.

Member : Shri Arya Bhushan.

APPOINTMENT

The Commission was constituted under the Ministry of Transport and Aviation (Commission of Railway Safety) in accordance with Rule 9 of the Railway Board's Notification No. 1926-T dated 19th March, 1930 on December 23, 1964.

TERMS OF REFERENCE

To inquire on the Wash-away of No. 653 Down Pamban-Dhanushkodi Passenger between Rameswaram Road and Dhanushkodi Stations of the Madurai Division of Southern Railway on the night of 22/23-12-1964.

CONTENTS

Summary ; The Inquiry ; The Accident ; Casualties and the Number of Passengers ; The Train ; Damage ; The Relief ; Restoration of Traffic ; Local Conditions (The Locality ; Weather and Visibility) ; Inspection of Site and Observations ; Summary of Evidence ; Discussion (An Abnormal Accident) ; Time of the Accident ; Speed of the Train ; Cource of Events ; The Conduct of the Engineering Officials ; Position of Signals at Dhanushkodi ; Whether Constable Narayanan Nair on the ill-fated Train ; Newspaper Reports ; Conclusions ; Recommendations made by the Commission of Railway Safety in connection with Wash-away of No. 653 Down Pamban-Dhanushkodi Passenger Train between Kms. 681 and 682 near Dhanushkodi station of Southern Railway on 23rd December, 1964.

CONCLUSIONS

From the evidence available, I have come to the conclusion that the accident to No. 653 Down Pamban-Dhanushkodi Passenger on the night of 22/23 December, 1964 occurred as a result of unprecedented tidal wave from the Palk Straight on the northern side which swept away the whole train resulting in all the train crew as well as passengers being carried away by the current. I do not hold anybody responsible for this accident and classify it as an Act of God. I am also satisfied that there has been no negligence on the part of the railway staff which would have reduced the effects of this catastrophe.

1965

GROUP OF EXPERTS ON LAND ACQUISITION, 1965—REPORT

New Delhi, Ministry of Food, Agriculture, Community Development and Cooperation (Department of Agriculture), 1967. 24p.

Chairman : Shri B. Sivaraman.

Members : Shri K. Sen; Shri V. M. Joshi; Shri M. Lal; Maj. Genl. Harkirat Singh; Shri K. S. Sivasubrahmanyan; Shri B. S. D. Baliga; Shri K. A. Ramasubramaniam; Shri Gajendra Singh; Shri A. N. Seth; Shri D. B. Kulkarni; Shri K. G. George; Shri A. Das; Shri K. N. V. Nambisan; Shri Nau Nihan Singh; Shri Jagmohan.

Convenor : Shri Saran Singh.

APPOINTMENT

The Group of Experts on Land Acquisition was Constituted of under the Ministry of Food, Agriculture community Development and Cooperation (Department of Agriculture), in 1965.

TERMS OF REFERENCE

The Group was required to go into all questions relating to land acquisition with particular reference to the procedure for acquisition and the principles for determining compensation, to examine the difficulties experienced and to suggest remedies, in particular, for the delays occasioned in completion of the proceedings. In doing so, the group was also expected to examine the various recommendations made by the Law Commission in its Tenth Report.

CONTENTS

Introduction ; Terms of Reference and Meetings; Constitutional Limitations; Definition of Public Purpose; Need for Uniformity in the Laws on Land Acquisition; Procedural Delays—Remedies examined ; Some Important Provisions discussed; Compensation and Solatium; Rehabilitation of displaced Persons as a Result of Acquisition of Land; Conclusion:

RECOMMENDATIONS

The legislation regarding acquisition has to be in conformity with the constitutional provisions.

By the subsequent amendment of article 31(2), the question of adequacy of compensation has been made non-justiciable. If a law lays down principles which are not relevant to the value of the property acquired at about the time it is acquired, it must be said that they are not principles contemplated by article 31(2), and do not pertain to the domain of adequacy and in such circumstances their validity would be open to scrutiny by courts. Further, when the compensation as prescribed in law is in fact illusory, the Court would have jurisdiction to deal with the matter. Thus the Court would have jurisdiction if the Legislature, though ex-facie purporting to provide for compensation, or indicating the principles for its ascertainment, in fact and substance, takes away property without providing compensation, or provides for illusory compensation, or for its ascertainment on arbitrary principles, for in that case, the Legislature would be enacting a law in a fraud of its power under article 31(2).

Consequently, the exercise of the legislative powers by the State is subject to the limitations laid down by the Court and the interpretation of the constitutional provision. This limitation has to be borne in mind while considering any amendment of the principal Act.

In a matter concerning acquisition of private property, the laws relating to the rights and liabilities of the citizens and the powers of the State should as far as possible be uniform.

There is a great danger in replacing the Land Acquisition Act, 1894, as may new legislation will not enjoy the protection afforded by Article 31(5) of the Constitution.

Procedural delays can be eliminated by taking administrative action to streamline the working of land acquisition office, by providing efficient staff and by enforcing the greatest measure of supervision.

Acquisition of good agricultural land for non-agricultural purposes should be avoided as far as possible. The requisitioning department should take care to consider this aspect in detail and wherever good agricultural land can be saved, alternative acquisition proposal should be submitted.

The requisitioning department should also certify that the project for which land is required has the administrative approval of the Government and the necessary budget provision has been made to meet the cost of acquisition.

The entire proceedings for acquisition, from the preliminary notification upto the taking of possession after the award is made, should be completed within a specified period, which may not exceed, say, five years from the date of issue of notification under Section 4(1), it was of the opinion that it would not be expedient to lay down specific time-limits for completion of each stage of the proceedings. As a matter of fact, it was felt that any rigid time-limits set within the framework of the law may cut both ways. Thus, if the specified action is not taken within the mandatory period, the whole proceedings would become vitiated, necessitating the entire process to be gone through all over again. This might defeat the very purpose of fixation of such time limits. Instead of making a rigid time-table as a part of the law, there may be an over-all time-limit in the Act, leaving the detailes to be included in the rules and administrative instructions. At any rate, the group felt that some restrictive provision should be made that in case the awards are not completed within a given period, say, of five years from the date of notification under Section 4(1), the valuation for determining the compensation should be as on a date five years prior to the date of the award.

Considering the constitutional limitation and keeping in mind the Supreme Court rulings, the following conditions may be stipulated :

(i) If the draft declaration under Section 6 was not published within three years of the date of notification under Section 4(1), the preliminary notification should become invalid;

(ii) If the award is not made within 5 years of the publication of Section 4(1) notification, compensation should be antedated on the basis of the market value as on a date 5 years prior to the award. Alternatively, it was suggested that interest may be payable on the compensation money in case the 5 years limit is exceeded; the latter course may be more practical considering that the former would introduce an element of uncertainty and also the antedating of the market value would compel a revision of the estimates of the project concerned; and

(iii) In computing the period, the time spent in litigation should be excluded unless the Court rules otherwise.

Section 4 : Limited powers could be delegated to the Collector. Power should be conferred on the Collector to initiate proceedings and issue notification under Section 4(1) in all ordinary cases. Consequential draft declaration under Section 6 should, however, be sent upto Government for approval and publication. In cases involving Section 17 i.e. where urgency clause is applicable, notification under Section 4(1) read with Section 17 should be invariably published by government as at present.

Section 5 : Simultaneous action should be taken with regard to survey, demarcation and measurement of land and the hearing of objections, but that fixing of a time limit was unworkable.

One of the contributory causes of delay is the service of notice. The group considered the question of valid service of notice inviting objections under Section 5A and suggested that a notice sent under "registered acknowledgement due" post should be deemed to be a valid service of the notice inviting objections.

Section 6 : In cases of big project, the practice has been to notify the entire area proposed to be acquired under Section 4 and thereafter to issue piece meal declarations under Section 6 in respect of parts of the area as the project proceeds. The group took note of the fact that in a recent judgement pronounced in February, 1966. The Supreme Court has held that declarations under Section 6 cannot be issued piece-meal and once a single declaration under Section 6 is issued, the force of the notification under Section 4 is extinguished. The judgement is based on the principle that the action under Section 4(1), 5 and 6 is an integrated action and one notification under Section 4(1) cannot be followed by several declarations under Section 6 issued on different dates and separated by considerable intervals of time.

This means that the Act will have to be amended so as to provide for more than one declaration under Section 6. But the advice of the Ministry of law has been that any such amendment must steer clear of the provisions of Articles 14 and 31(2) of the Constitution and mere amendment of the Act would not solve the problem. To achieve the purpose, it would be necessary to amend Article 31(2) of the Constitution so as to include therein, inter-alia a special definition of the expression "compensation" which may be less than the "just equivalent" of what is being acquired. Further, the Act would also require to be so amended as to avoid discrimination when more than one declaration under Section 6 is allowed to be issued in respect of land covered by a single omnibus notification under Section 4(1) of the act, bearing in mind the principle of reasonable classification applicable in relation to Article 14.

The alternative would be to have an amending and validating legislation enacted by Parliament, amending the Act with restrospective effect and to include the same in the Ninth Schedule to the Constitution. This would automatically attract Article 31B which is a constitutional device to place the statutes specified in the Ninth Schedule beyond any attack on the ground that they infringe Part III of the Constitution. The latter course appears to be safer and more feasible.

The limitation imposed by Section 17 on the type of land which can be acquired under the "emergency clause" has been the biggest factor contributing to delay in the execution of projects. The restriction under Section 17, confining the power to take immediate possession of "waste and arable" lands should be removed. The words "waste and arable' should be deleted from Section 17(1).

The emergency provisions of this Section should be extended to all projects of national importance including Defence. The special provisions with regard to railways in Section 17(2) need not, however be altered.

Section 31(1) : At present, payment by cheque is not covered under this provision according to some judicial interpretations. It is suggested that all orders of payment on treasury or bank should be covered by the word "payment" referred to in Section 31(1) of the Act.

The requisitioning department should take active part in assisting the Land Acquisition Collector in arriving at a fair value and should not remain a mere spectator. It should be competent for the requisitioning department to produce evidence in regard to the market value of the land.

When the Land Acquisition Collector is considering the evidence pertaining to market value with a view to making the award, the requisitioning department should take active part in producing evidence on valuation. The collector has to follow the procedure of a civil court. Documentary evidence regarding valuation is, therefore, admissible. The requisitioning department should present the case before the collector.

The proviso to Section 50 (2) may also need amendment.

No damages need, however be paid under Section 48 (2) in case government department withdraws from acquisition prior to the publication of the draft declaration under Section 6. This may be stipulated by means of a suitable amendment.

The group was in favour of retaining the payment of solatium of 15 per cent for the compulsory nature of the acquisition. In this connection, the group endorsed the view of the Law Commission that it is not enough for a person to get the market value of the land as compensation in order to place himself in a position similar to that which he would have occupied had there been no acquisition. The person concerned would have to spend a future amount for settling himself more or less in the same position as before.

ARCHAEOLOGICAL REVIEW COMMITTEE, 1965—REPORT

Delhi, Ministry of Education, 1965. 114p. (Memographed)

Chairman : Sir Mortimer Wheeler.
Members : Shri Nihar Ranjan Ray; Shri H.D. Sankalia; Shri S. Nurul Hasan.
Secretary : Mrs. S. Rao.

APPOINTMENT

The Committee was appointed by the Ministry of Education in March 1965.

TERMS OF REFERENCE

(i) To assess the work of the Archaeological Survey of India;

(ii) To make recommendations about the lines on which it should work during the next five years, and

(iii) To make suggestions for closer cooperation with the States and the Universities.

CONTENTS

Introduction; Conservation; Exploration and Excavation; The Pre-history Branch; Printing and Publication; Science and the Survey; Training; Indian School of Archaeology Abroad; The Survey and the Universities; The States and Archaeology; The Survey Libraries; The Survey's Museums; The Survey's Gardens; Epigraphy; The Archaeological Atlas, and Documentation; The Temple Survey Project; Location and Accommodation; Staff Salaries; Technical Grades; Administration and Recruitments; Summary of Principal Recommendations; Appendix A : Proposed Circles; Appendix B : Staffs—proposed changes.

RECOMMENDATIONS

Conservation

To equalize more nearly the responsibilities of the Circles and generally to facilitate their administration, a re-shaping of some of them and the addition of a new Circle are necessary, making 11 in all. Also, the Delhi Circle should be reconstituted, in view of its metropolitan importance.

To enable Circle Superintendents to concentrate more effectively upon the primary functions of the survey—the preservation of India's archaeological heritage—extraneous activities, notably exploration and excavation, must be removed from their function, and special steps must be taken to attract qualified Engineers and suitable Conservation Assistants. Further, it is essential that every Circle shall have an Administrative Officer Grade II.

Exploration

The D.D.G.A. (Exploration and Excavation) shall in future be responsible for the important village to village survey, previously under the over-worked Circle Superintendents.

Excavation

The tendency of the Survey to operate an excessive number of excavations at the expense of other activities, including the preparation of reports, must be controlled. The plea for the constitution of a second Excavations Branch, in view of the fact that in the whole of India the Survey is, and will probably remain, the only body equipped for sustained large scale excavation, is accepted; but only when the existing Excavations Branch has cleared up its arrears, i.e. in something more than a year's time. For this purpose, and for general efficiency in its complex task, the Branch requires an Assistant Superintendent in addition to its Superintendent. It should also have an Administrative Officer Grade II.

Meanwhile, as a special project requiring less elaborate provision than a normal Excavations Branch operation, it is recommended that sufficient work be done at Fatehpur Sikri at least to recover the street-plan of Akbar's city. This would be a complete innovation in Indian archaeology and would encourage a whole range of medieval and later studies which have in the past been neglected by Indian archaeologists.

Printing And Publication

The Printing and Publication of the Survey's reports and other works are gravely in arrears and the printing has been of inadequate or even deplorable quality. It is absolutely essential that, within its budget allocations, the Survey, as a technical department, be given of, and dealings with, its printers.

The Constitution of a Printing and Publications Branch under a Deputy Director General is an essential and urgent provision.

Archaeological Science Laboratory

The immense international developments in the application of science to archaeological problems during the past fifteen years are not reflected in the present organisation of the Survey's Chemistry Branch. An immediate, if modest, widening of the scope of this

Branch, under the more comprehensive name here suggested, is essential for the credit of India's reputation both in the scientific and in the hermanistic field.

Training

The scope of the excellent Survey's school of Archaeology should be widened to take more cognizance of the cultural environment of India. Also, regular (annual) training-courses in archaeological conservation must be organised, to ensure adequate and uniform standards throughout the survey.

Indian Schools Of Archaeology Abroad

Permanent schools or institutes in appropriate countries, where Indian scholars can work under conditions similar to those of their American, British, French, German and other conferers, are a necessary development as soon as economic conditions permit.

The Universities

The awakening of several of the Indian universities to the value of archaeology is reflected in an appreciable total of grants from the Survey towards the cost of university excavations. This promising trend is at present in its early stages, but can usefully be developed by close cooperation between the Survey and the Universities in the choice of problems and the insurance of sound standards in the field and in prompt reporting. Certain difficulties are discussed.

The States And Archaeology

With exceptions, the States have not yet taken up archaeology in a suitably scientific spirit, and the position will have to be watched, particularly in respect of conservation. The Centre, which has only some 3,500 monuments under its control—an astonishingly small number having regard to the number and high importance of ancient buildings and sites in India—should hesitate before deprotecting monuments and sites and surrendering them to State control. Very few States are at present equipped to assume this responsibility.

The Survey's Libraries

Whilst the Central Archaeological Library is of first class value, some of the Branch and Circle libraries are considerably below standard. A greater measure of centralized control within a reorganized library service is recommended. A Documentation Centre should be included in the Central Archaeological Library.

The Survey's Museums

A similar procedure is recommended for the Survey's 14 (proposed 22) museums.

The Gardens Branch

This is thoroughly efficient, but requires certain minor adjustments, which are particularized.

Epigraphy

This is in the main satisfactory, though its remoteness at Ootacamund is inconvenient, and the isolation of its Superintendent for Arabic and Persian inscriptions at Nagpur should be remedied. He should have an Assistant Superintendent.

Archaeological Atlas

This scheme will be discontinued, save for certain features of it which will be of value as the nucleus of a Documentation Centre, to be set up at the Central Archaeological Library.

Temple Survey Project

This project, already in an advanced stage, should continued but should be shared with, or supplement by, an urgent architectural survey of selected Indian domestic buildings, which are rapidly disappearing without record.

Accommodation

The present temporary headquarters of the survey should be replaced by a suitable building designed for the purpose. It is essential that this headquarters should be at Delhi, preferably in the vicinity of the new University site. Moreover a uniform building should be designed for the various Circle headquarters, which are often in adequately and shabbily housed.

Salaries Of Technical Grades

Great difficulty is experienced in recruiting and retaining several of the technical grades, for which there are increasing openings in commerce and industry. The salary-scales of all these grades have been carefully reviewed by the Committee with a view to providing a sufficiently attractive career in a service which is otherwise to be regarded as a "dead end".

Finally, the Committee has carefully reviewed the salaries, duties and status of the senior staff. It most urgently asks that the Director General, whose salary equates with that of a Joint Secretary of the Government of India, should now be ex-officio a Joint Secretary, with direct access to the Secretary and, if necessary, the Minister.

COMMITTEE OF OFFICERS ON THE REORGANIZATION OF THE STRUCTURE AND WORK PROCEDURES OF THE MINISTRY OF WORKS AND HOUSING, 1965—REPORT

New Delhi, Ministry of Works and Housing, 1965. 178p.

Chairman : Shri C.P. Gupta.

Members : Shri T.N. Bahel; Shri N.K. Mukarji; Shri K.C. Joshi; Shri G.P. Shahani; Shri P.K. Sen; Shri S. Chaudhuri; Shri R.M. Agarwal; Shri K.N. Zutshi.

APPOINTMENT

The Committee of Officers on the Reorganization of the Structure and Work Procedures of the Ministry of Works and Housing was constituted under Government of India, Ministry of Works and Housing dated January 15, 1965.

TERMS OF REFERENCE

To undertake a study of the method of handling work in the Ministry with the object particularly of reorganising the procedure of work as also the structure of organisation of the Works and Establishments Works wing of the Ministry.

CONTENTS

Introduction; Functions and Organisation of the Ministry of Works and Housing; Guiding Principles; Works Division (Delegations from the Ministry to the Attached Office; Delegation of Financial Powers from the Ministry of Finance to the Ministry of Works and Housing; Procedural Simplifications; Single File System; Filing System; Structural Reorganisation; Implementation); Summary of Recommendations; Appendices I to XVI also Ministry of Works and Housing Office Memorandum No. 3/13/65-WSU, dated 22nd September, 1965, containing the decision of Government on the recommendations of the Committee of Officers.

RECOMMENDATIONS

Having identified powers and functions in respect of which delegations were possible from the Ministry of Works and Housing to the CPWD, proposals were evolved and divided into two categories viz, administrative and financial. The delegations recommended are set out and explained in the form of 45 broad sheets at appendix VII.

Based on a study of cases referred to the Ministry of Finance by the Works Division of the Ministry of Works and Housing over a period, and taking account of the history of delegation of financial powers, a set of proposals for delegating financial powers from the Ministry of Finance to the Ministry of Works and Housing has been evolved. The delegation's recommendations are stated and explained in the form of broad sheets at appendix VIII.

In the procedure prescribed for sanctioning of the building schemes of the various Ministries, the two separate stages of consideration, viz., administrative approval and expenditure sanction, should be combined into one in which the administrative Ministry will, in consultation with Finance, accord its approval after due scrutiny from administrative and financial angles. Thereafter, a scheme will only need processing for allotting priority at the stage of inclusion in the budget. Internal arrangements may be made in the Ministry of Finance under which schemes costing not more than Rs. 5 lakhs are advised on by the associated Finance of the Ministry concerned, schemes costing more than that only being referred to Works Division of the Ministry of Finance. The cost limit for referring schemes to the Expenditure Finance Committee may be raised to Rs. 25 lakhs. The various steps of the new procedure are outlined in appendix IX(B).

The time taken in scrutinising preliminary estimates could be significantly reduced if comprehensive information is given by the CPWD alongwith the estimates. A checklist of information points should be drawn up by the Works Division in consultation with the Works Division of the Ministry of Finance and the CPWD taking account of the comprehensive range of queries usually raised in the absence of full details.

Although the scrutiny of proposals relating to additions and alternations is of a routine character and the work is largely repetitive, a separate file is opened for each proposal. Each proposal for addition or alteration should be made on a form, giving all the information regarding various considerations involved and providing a standardised drill for its processing as in Appendix X.

Duplicate files in the recipient office should be eliminated and so should duplicate consideration at office level as far as possible by introducing the single file system. The existing items of works handled in the Works Divisions should be divided into three lists :

List I—Items of work to be covered by the delegations recommended, and thus to be excluded from the Ministry's purview.

List II—Items of work which would continue to be handled in the Ministry, but on the files of the CPWD under the single file system.

List III—Items of work which would continue to be held in the Ministry on its own files.

The compilation of List I will follow what is decided about delegations. Specific proposals for items to be included in List III are set out in appendices XI(a) and XI(b). With the Lists I and III settled, the remaining items should form List II and be handled on the single file system. A drill for operating the single file system is in appendix XII.

To ensure successful functioning of an officer oriented pattern, the filing system should be so simple that files both current and recorded can be picked out without difficulty even when the dealing officer or his personal staff is not available. For this a scientific filing system is necessary, which eliminates the disadvantages of the present system. Equally important is the storage of records. The filing and storage system recommended is in appendix XIV. A standard file index recommended for the files to be maintained by the Works Division is given in appendix XIII.

The steno-typist attached to the dealing officer should be incharge of all current files. These and recorded files which are not more than 3 years old should be stored in filing cabinets or filing almirahs kept as near the basic dealing officers as possible. Files over three years old should be maintained in the record-room.

With non-essential work cleared out through delegations, and with various procedural simplifications including the single file system introduced, the Works Division should be reorganised according to an officer oriented basis.

The posts of O.S.D. (Work Charged Establishment) will continue until his work has been studied.

An organisation charge of the Works Division based on the recommended staffing pattern is given at appendix XVI.

As indicated in appendix XVI, the revised staffing pattern at the bottom level will be manned by new functionaries styled principals and assistant principals. In this arrangement, it would not be the case that an assistant principal channelises his work to a principal or that an under secretary channelises his work to a Deputy Secretary. While there may be two scales of pay in the bottom level and also two in the middle level, the flow of work will not be governed by the number of scales of pay but would go from one level of consideration as such to another.

For the present, ad hoc arrangements for securing the right type of staff as principal and assistant principals will be necessary :

(i) The basic pay scales of principals and assistant principals may be identical with those of Section Officer and assistant but in recognition of their additional responsibilities, they may draw special pay of Rs. 125 and Rs. 75 p.m. respectively.

(ii) Personnel to be posted as principals and assistant principals should be hand-picked through a process in which merit and suitability play the major role.

The duties of steno typist attached to officers should be enlarged beyond merely shorthand and typing and should additionally include :

(a) Opening of files with the help of file index and under the guidance of dealing officers ;

(b) Maintenance of current files and internal movement diary and collection of relevant papers ;

(c) Routine liaison work.

A "registry" with an assistant in charge should be set up to handle work relating to receipt and despatch, typing preservation of non-current files, watching external movement of files outside the Ministry and maintenance of some necessary registers.

To ensure that the change over from the present to the new system is as smooth as possible and not unnecessarily long drawn out, careful planning will be necessary. An implementation organisation on the following lines may be set up :

(i) The responsibility for procuring the report for acceptance or otherwise of its recommendations as well as for over-seeing the implementation of the recommendations that are accepted should rest with the O & M Unit of the Ministry neaded by a whole-time under secretary who can not only work out all the details involved but will also be continuously available to help in solving difficulties in the course of the implementation.

It will be useful for the O & M Unit to keep in close touch with the Department of Administrative Reforms during the stage of implementation.

It would be useful if internal arrangements are made in the Ministry to ensure that the O & M Unit works directly under the joint secretary who has functioned as Chairman of the Committee of officers which has produced this report.

In case the processing of the recommendations is handled by an empowered committee presided over by the Secretary of the Ministry of Works and Housing it would be useful if that committee were to continue functioning even after it has taken decisions on the recommendations as such so as to keep an eye on the prompt and correct implementation of what is accepted.

Some of the consequential tasks that will arise out of acceptance of the recommendations are listed in Para 4.51.

COMMISSION ON THE HILL AREAS OF ASSAM, 1965-66—REPORT

New Delhi, Ministry of Home Affairs, 1966 ; 198p.

Chairman : Shri H. V. Pataskar.
Members : Shri Shankar Prasad; Shri G. S. Rau.
Secretary : Shri B. N. Tandon.

APPOINTMENT

The hill areas of Assam comprising the Garo Hills, the United Khasi and Jaintia Hills, the Mizo Hills, the United Mikir and North Cachar Hills districts are administered subject to the special provisions of the Sixth Schedule to the Constitution which confer a certain measures of autonomy on these areas. It has been represented to the Government of India from time to time that for accelerating the pace of and ensuring fuller participation of the people in the development of these areas, and for safeguarding more effectively the interests of the tribal people, it is necessary to widen the autonomy enjoyed at present by these areas. The Government of India after giving careful consideration to the needs of these areas and the necessity in the interest of the people of hill areas themselves of enabling them to participate in the larger political and economic life of the State, have come to the conclusion that it would be desirable for the hill areas to have a full measure of autonomy subject to the preservation of the Unity of Assam, the continuance of a common legislature for the whole State of Assam and the maintenance of the Cabinet Government of the accepted form functioning on the basis of collective and joint responsibility of the State Assembly.

The general pattern of the administrative set up which might be evolved for the hill areas of Assam was discussed by the late Prime Minister Sh. Jawaharlal Nehru, with some of the hill leaders and certain broad conclusions were reached. The Government of India consider it necessary that a detailed scheme for the reorganisation of the administrative set-up of these areas on the basis of those discussions and conclusions should be drawn up by a Commission to be appointed for the purpose, after careful study of the various aspects of the problem involved. The Government of India, Ministry of Home Affairs have accordingly, in consultation with the Government of Assam decided to appoint a Commission on the Hill areas of Assam vide their Resolution No. 4/2/64S-R(R)-A dated March 16, 1965.

TERMS OF REFERENCE

(i) To recommend a detailed scheme for reorganizing the administrative set up of the hill areas having regard to the main objectives of conferring a full measure of autonomy on the hill areas, subject to the preservation of the unity of the State of Assam, the continuance of a common legislature for the whole State and the maintenance of the cabinet form of government functioning on the basis of collective and joint responsibility to the State Assembly;

(ii) To recommend "the administrative, financial and legal measures necessary for giving effect to" the proposed reorganization;

(iii) To recommend, after examining the working of these councils, changes in their powers and functions as also in the Sixth Schedule in the light of the scheme to be recommended.

CONTENTS

Resolution; Procedure of the Commission; General description of the hill districts; Summary of earlier discussions and evidence; Some Economic and Financial Aspects; Basic Considerations; Autonomy of the Hill Areas; Legislation for the Hill Areas; Machinery of Government; Financial Administration of the Hill Areas; Hill Areas Development Council; District Councils—Generals Legislative Functions of the District Councils; Financial Administration of the District Councils; The District Fund and its Audit; Administration of Justice; Small Tribes and Regional Councils; The Non-tribal Residents of the Hill Districts; Composition and Functioning of the District Councils; Administration of Forests; Language; Summary of Conclusions and Recommendations; Appendices from I to XII B.

RECOMMENDATIONS

Our enquiry has ranged over a wide field and the following is a summary of the conclusions we have reached and the main recommendations we have made in accordance with the terms of reference given to us :

Economic And Financial Aspects

Dissatisfaction with the economic progress of the hill districts is at the root of the unsatisfactory general relationship between the two regions—the hills and the plains—of Assam.

A comparison of the revenue and expenditure of the two regions shows that :

(a) The relative contribution of the hill districts of the State revenues is much less in proportion to their population; and further it has gone down over a period of 12 years since 1951-52.

(b) The per capita contribution of the hill districts to the State revenues is much less than that of the plains. While the per capita contribution of the plains has more than doubled during the past 12 years that of the hills has remained more or less the same.

(c) The share of the hill areas in revenue expenditure has always been more than their share of population. It is also much in excess of their relative contribution to the State revenues.

(d) The per capita expenditure in the hill districts, which is 5 to 6 times as large as it was in 1951-52, is much more that in the plains.

(e) The capital expenditure in the hills has been relatively small but since 1956-57 it has been stepped up.

(f) While the allocations of the Plan outlay for the hill districts have not been unfair vis-a-vis their population, as a percentage of the total outlay these have gone down slightly during the third Plan period.

(g) The hill districts have recorded a higher rate of increase than the plains in respect of the State and per capita incomes.

There is no evidence of any deliberate neglect of the hill areas in the matter of development; nor has there been any diversion of funds allocated to the hill areas for the benefit of the plains.

In respect of certain pressing needs of hill areas, such as means of communications, the progress has been unsatisfactory.

The financial assistance by the Central Government has generally been on a more generous scale to Nagaland, NEFA, Manipur and Tripura than to the hill areas of Assam. This has contributed to the dissatisfaction in the latter areas.

While there has been no failure on the part of the State Government to take cognizance of the difficulties of the hill districts, the need of these districts are greater than those of the plain areas. The exceptional difficulties of these districts justify exceptional treatment.

Basic Considerations

The basic problem of the hill areas is that of economic development, for which the two regions of Assam—the hill areas and the plains—are interdependent. The links of the hills with the plains constitute a factor of importance to both of them; and there is great need of preserving these links.

There should be active participation of the hill people, through their district councils, in the development programmes. The necessary guidance and councelling to these councils should also come from their own representatives functioning at higher levels.

Social and personal matters of the tribal communities should be left entirely in their own hands.

Autonomy Of The Hill Areas

The scheme of autonomy that emerged from the discussions between the Prime Minister and the hill leaders did not envisage a completely separate administration for the hill areas with only a national superstructure remaining common with the rest of Assam.

The scheme assured the hill people that the State Assembly would pass laws applying to them with the approval of their representatives, and that they would have full opportunity to control their social, cultural and personal matters and the development of their areas within the framework of the larger political and economic life of Assam.

Legislation For The Hill Areas

The broad principle enunciated by the Prime Minister on the legislation applicable to the hill people is already embodied in the Sixth Schedule in respect of certain matters. No basic changes is proposed in that position.

The MLA's of hill districts should constitute a Hill Areas Committee of the State Assembly. The latter should refer to this Committee all "proposals relating to legislation concerning the hill areas". If a question arises whether a Bill concerns the hill areas or not a certificate issued by the Governor should be final.

Normally the State Assembly should accept the recommendations of the Hill Areas Committee. But in case of difference of opinion the speaker will submit the matter with relevant records to the Governor for decision in his discretion. The Governor should convey his decision in a message to the Assembly, which, on being reported to the House by the speaker, should be deemed to be the decision of the Assembly itself.

Autonomy of the hill areas in the legislative field should be provided by making a provision similar to article 371(1) of the Constitution in the Sixth Schedule. A Presidential order under that provision should then lay down the Constitution, functions and the procedure of the Hill Areas Committee.

Ministers For Hill Areas

In the new set up the Cabinet Minister in charge of hill districts should be called the Minister for hill areas. He should be assisted by as many junior ministers as may be necessary.

In making appointments of the hill ministers the Chief Minister should consult the hill MLA and obtain their views in an appropriate manner.

The number of hill ministers and the allocation of ministerial business etc., to them are matters which should be decided by the Chief Minister as the head of the Cabinet.

Departments Of Hill Areas

There should be a separate department of hill areas in the Assam Secretariat.

The department should be entrusted with the administration of the following subjects in the hill districts :

"Agriculture including minor irrigation; horticulture; cooperation; animal husbandry and veterinary; forests and soil conservation; community development, national extension service and tribal development blocks; education including higher and technical education; public health; local government; social welfare; revenue; public works (roads and buildings); small scale and rural industry; sericulture and weaving; publicity and information; market and fairs; burial and burial grounds; cremation and cremation grounds; and prevention of cattle trespass".

The department should also be responsible for the following :

(i) Matters relating to district councils ;

(ii) Supervision over the development programmes of these councils;

(iii) Special development programmes for the hill districts out of grants under article 275 of the Constitution; and

(iv) Even in respect of subjects not transferred for administration to the department of hill areas the hill ministers should be consulted on all important matters.

Commissioner For Hill Areas

There is great need for strengthening the administrative machinery at the field level. It should be presided over by a Commissioner, who should not have any additional responsibilities not connected with the hill districts. His main duty should be to guide, direct and supervise administration and development work in the field in the hill district.

Senior officers of the rank of additional joint deputy heads of departments should be put in charge of the administration of their respective subjects in the hill areas. Administratively these officers should work directly under the Commissioner, but for technical purposes they should seek necessary guidance from their respective heads of departments.

There is no need for separate cadres or sub-cadres exclusively for the hill areas; the present practice of common cadres for the whole State should continue. But the manpower requirements of the hill areas should be fully taken into account in the management of cadres In the development of personnel also the views of the hill ministers should be given full consideration.

Financial Administration

As far as practicable the general economic condition of the hill areas should be raised to the level of the plains within a reasonable period of time. The Central Government should accept special responsibility for the development of these areas. As a general principle the total development expenditure in the hill areas of Assam should at least be of the same order as in the neighbouring territories of Nagaland, NEFA, Manipur and Tripura.

Merging of Article 275 grants in the State Plan outlay and in the Central assistance given for the purpose tends to make these grants subject to the same kind of downward adjustments which occur in the case of State Plan provisions. It would therefore to desirable to treat Article 275 grants as special allocations earmarked for the tribal areas.

Hill Areas Budget

The form of the State budget should suitably be modified to include a new "area budget" to show allocations for the hill districts in respect of subjects transferred to the department of hill areas. In respect of other i.e. "non-transferred" subjects also, the budget allocations for the hill districts should be shown separately. For the convenience of the Assembly, a supplementary statement giving at one place the total receipts from and expenditure on the hill districts in respect of both transferred and non-transferred subjects should be prepared and presented to the Assembly along with other budget documents.

The Hill Areas Committee should be given an opportunity to express its views on the budget for the hill areas before it is presented to the State Assembly. The discussion of the State budget in respect of an autonomous district by the district council concerned should be dispensed with.

The control of the area budget should vest in the department of hill areas. The savings in the funds allotted for the hill districts in respect of non-transferred subjects should also not be diverted for other purposes without consulting the minister for hill areas. The department of hill areas should have its own financial adviser, who should have the widest possible measure of delegated authority to enable him to carry out his duties satisfactorily.

Hill Areas Development Council

At the head quarters of the State Government there should be Hill Areas Development Council with the Chief Minister of Assam as its Chairman. The main duty of the Council should be to advise the State Government on the administration and development of the hill areas.

The Sixth Schedule should contain a provision for the setting up of such a council. Similarly the new administrative arrangements should be based on appropriate provisions in the Sixth Schedule and the Assam Rules of Executive Business framed in pursuance of Article 166(2) and (3) of the Constitution.

District Councils

There is wide spread dissatisfaction with the district councils. The criticism and suggestions made on their working raise two fundamental questions, namely, whether the present organization and functions, of the district councils are adequate in relation to the needs of the hill areas; and whether the financial relationship between them and the State Government is satisfactory.

In view of the setting up of the Hill Areas Committee there is not much need to widen legislative authority of a district council. Only amplification of the existing powers in respect of certain subjects is recommended.

Executive Functions of the District Councils : A wide extension of the sphere of the activities of a district council is desirable and necessary. The administrative and executive functions of a district council is desirable and necessary. The administrative and executive functions of a district-council should include the following :

"Land and revenue administration, establishment, construction, management and administration of primary schools and educational institutions upto the higher secondary stage and in particular the prescription of the language and the manner in which education in the primary, middle english and middle language schools is to be imparted; the establishment, construction, management and administration of roads and waterways within the district, community projects, national extension service and tribal development blocks; agriculture and minor irrigation; animal husbandry, veterinary services and dairy farming, cooperative ; fisheries; small scale and rural industries, and sericulture and weaving; rural water supply; public health; works programmes for rural manpower utilization; social welfare; village planning and rural housing; publicity and information".

A district council may undertake any commercial business or other enterprises, including means of transport, and industry authorised by the Governor.

The policy of democratic decentralization should be extended to the working of a district council; and subordinate and village councils should be set up at the block and village levels respectively for the successful implementation of rural development programmes.

The services of the gazetted and inspection staff should be made available to a District Council by the State Government on deputation. A district council should recruit its own clerical and subordinate staff but this should be done through properly constituted recruitment board or boards.

The post of the secretary to district council should be filled by deputation of an officer of the rank of additional district magistrate belonging to the Assam Civil Service Class I.

District Development Board : Each hill district should have a District Development Board under the chairmanship of the deputy commissioner to help the district council in the execution of welfare and development schemes.

The question of creating separate civil districts for the North Cachar Hills and Jowai should be favourably considered by the State Government.

Financial Administration of the District Council : A detailed examination of the financial administration of the district council show that :

(i) The Council have not fully exploited the financial resources available to them.

(ii) There is reluctance to impose taxes, and laxity in realising them with the result that sizeable arrears have accumulated in all the councils.

(iii) The Councils have very often not been able to balance their receipts and expenditure.

(iv) The expenditure on staff and establishment is unduly heavy and there is clearly an urgent need for economy.

(v) The Councils have been able to devote only meagre funds, if at all, to the development programmes which have been mostly financed out of government grants.

Investing a district council with additional powers of taxation will not improve its finance materially. The most satisfactory arrangement would be to help a district council by way of increased grants-in-aid from the State government.

Having regard to the need for both accelerating development and economy in administration of a council the State government should evolve a system which would encourage financial discipline and thrift on the part of a district council.

At the beginning of each financial year a district council should be informed of its shares of taxes on motor vehicles and royalties on minerals on the basis of averages for the preceding three years. Actual payment should then be made quarterly, the necessary adjustments being made in the last quarter of the year or the first quarter of the following year.

District Fund and its Audit : There should be uniform District Fund Rules framed by the Governor for all the district councils. The Rules should provide for the laying of the audited annual accounts before a district council. A district council office should have a separate, well organized, finance and accounts branch. The service of an SAS accountant should be obtained on deputation from the Accountant General, Assam to supervise the working of this branch. An examiner of accounts should be attached to the staff of commissioner for hill areas for conducting a review and internal audit of the council's accounts.

The Accountant General should present an audit report on the accounts of the grants received by the district councils as a separate section of his audit report of the State as a whole. This report would be examined by the Public Accounts Committee of the State Assembly, which should co-opt three representatives of the Hill Areas Committee for the purpose. The secretary of the hill areas department should assist the Public Accounts Committee in examining the report.

Administration Of Justice

No change in the existing system is recommended. It may however be got examined after a few years if any modification is required in the law and procedure followed by the tribal communities.

Regional Councils

The Sixth Schedule provides for setting up of Regional Councils for different tribes in an autonomous district. So far only one council—the Pawi Lakher Regional Council has been very unsatisfactory. In the nature of things such a council can hardly make only substantial contribution to the well-being of the tribal people. The institutionalization of autonomy of each and every tribe inhabiting an autonomous district is not desirable. The setting up of Regional Councils is therefore not recommended. The existing Regional Council should also be abolished. The existing provision empowering the Governor to set up Regional Councils should accordingly be deleted from the Sixth Schedule.

Non-Tribal Residents In The Hill Districts

There is no evidence to show that the district councils have administered the restrictions on non-tribals in acquiring and disposing of land in an arbitrary or unreasonable manner. No change in the present position is recommended.

While a district council should continue to frame regulations to control money lending and trading activities within its jurisdiction these regulations should uniformally apply to both tribals and non-tribals.

The Governor's assent should be necessary for giving effect to the taxation laws passed by the district council.

The State Government should have the right to extend their Town Planning Act to Shillong and the adjoining areas within a growing radius of ten miles or more according to the progress of urbanization; and the town of Shillong should be completely excluded from the jurisdiction of the district council.

Composition Of The District Councils

There should be a provision in the Sixth Schedule itself laying down the term of a council as five years subject to the condition that the governor may extend it by not more than six months at a time and in no case by more than two years in all.

The delimitation of the constituencies of a council should be done by a "District Council Delimitation Committee" appointed by the governor under the chairmanship of an officer of the rank of district judge.

While in view of the peculiar conditions of the hill areas it may be necessary to prescribe residential qualifications for the non-tribal population for voting at a council's elections, the present requirement of 12 years' residence is in the nature of an excessive and unreasonable restrictions. The legitimate interest of the tribal people would remain fully protected, and the harshness of the restriction on non-tribals would be mitigated if this period is reduced to two years.

The Governor should be responsible for the conduct of elections and related matters.

Not more than four seats in a district council should be reserved to be filled by nomination of persons to provide representation to special interest such as minorities etc. In making these nominations it should not be necessary for the Governor to be bound by the advice of the council concerned.

The Governor's authority with regard to annulment or suspension of an act or resolution of a district council should not be confined to cases where safety of the country is endangered but all acts or resolution prejudicial to public orders should be brought within its ambit.

As regards dissolution of a council and the assumption of its administration by the Governor the existing provisions seem to be satisfactory.

When the Governor is satisfied that a situation has arisen in which the administration of a district council cannot be carried on in accordance with the provisions of the Sixth Schedule and the rules made there under he may assume to himself all or any of the functions of the district council concerned. The Governor's order in this regard should be laid before the state legislature.

The administration of forests in the hill districts should vest in the minister for hill areas, assisted by an Advisory Committee of all the chief executive members of the district councils.

A district council should be empowered by frame regulations within the general framework of the forest policy and any consequential legislation to control "jhum" cultivation.

Before we conclude we wish to place on record our deep appreciation of the manner in which our Secretary Shri B. N. Tandon has carried out his duties. His responsibilities were heavy. He has had to deal with a large mass of factual information, memoranda, evidence etc. received from the Central and State Governments, a number of associations and individuals. He has had to collate and formulate tentative proposals for our consideration. He has discharged these heavy responsibilities cheerfully with energy and great devotion. His knowledge of economic and administrative matters was particularly valuable to us.

Our thanks are also due to the entire staff of our secretariate from whom we received the best service we could expect. In particular we would like to mention Shri R. K. Goel and Shri A. N. Sharma. Shri Goel's experience and knowledge of financial accounting matters has been of use in our investigations.

Finally, we must mention the help rendered to us by Shri N. C. Sharma and Shri S. S. Washist, who have had to work often under great pressure, in typing in time the final Report.

CANCER COMMITTEE, 1965—REPORT

New Delhi, Director General of Health Services, 1966. 192p.

Chairman : Dr. K. N. Rao.
Members : Dr. J. C. Paymaster ; Dr. Amiya Sen ; Prof. P. N. Wahi ; Dr. T. B. Patel ; Dr. S. Krishnamurthi ; Dr. B. Mukherji ; Dr. H. Syed Ali; Dr. S. Mukherji.
Secretary : Dr. M. J. H. Writer.

APPOINTMENT

The Government of India in the Ministry of Health Family Planning, set up a Committee on Cancer under their letter No. F.42-4/65-RISM, dated April 26, 1965, to examine the question how and on what pattern the Cancer Hospitals at Ahmedabad, Bombay, Calcutta and Madras can be developed as Regional Cancer Hospitals and Research Centres.

TERMS OF REFERENCE

(i) "To examine the present development of the Cancer Hospital, Ahemdabad ;

(ii) To recommend its phased development; and

(iii) To report the immediate requirements, recurring and non-recurring expenditure, for the Third Five Year Plan and the later development during the Fourth Five Year Plan".

The Committee should also examine the working of the Cancer Hospitals at Bombay, Calcutta and Madras and recommend how the already functioning Cancer Hospitals could be developed into Regional Cancer Hospitals.

CONTENTS

Appointment of the Committee; Extent of the Problem; Survey of existing Centres; Recommendations; Finance; Acknowledgements; Appendices from 1 to 19.

RECOMMENDATIONS

Sh. M. P. Shah Cancer Hospital, Ahmedabad, Gujarat.

The Committee in consultations with the Health Ministry agreed to an ad hoc interim grant of Rs. 2 lakhs to the Gujarat Cancer Society and another Rs. 3 lakhs by the end of the Third Plan, and future grants would be made on recommendation of the Cancer Committee.

The Gujarat Cancer Society may complete the present project in hand in the shortest possible time, without, however, undergoing expenses on any new constructions, additional staff and equipment.

The Gujarat Cancer Society should hand over the buildings, equipment etc.. to the State Government of Gujarat on completion The Government of Gujarat should take them over as soon as possible. This will facilitate the integration of the B. J. Medical College and Hospital and this specialised hospital along with other specialised hospitals as Eye, E.N.T., Dental etc., situated in the same campus. The Cancer Hospital to take patient—care responsibility only when the basic services as nursing, kitchen, sterilisation etc., are available.

The establishment of the Cancer Researeh Centre should be fully financed by the Government of India, Ministry of Health on the analogy of the Chittaranjan National Cancer Research Centre, Calcutta. The integration of the Cancer Hospital and the Centre should be taken up at the appropriate time by the State Government and the Government of India. The type of management to be evolved may be left open till the Research Centre is established and a common pattern developed for Calcutta, Madras and Hyderabad.

No additional staff should be appointed by the Gujarat Cancer Society till the future of the Hospital is finalised. It should be noted that there would be an overall review of the staff needed and it is the responsibility of the B. J. Medical College, Ahmedabad to give specialist services to the patients in the Cancer Hospi al. The Committee, however, recommends that, in the interest of economy, efficiency and good inter-relationship, the staff of the B. J. Hospital should be utilised to the fullest extent.

Cancer patients should not be levied any fee either in the out patient or in-door for general ward patients.

The development should be phased progressively according to the resources available. As the society is in a position to collect funds from philanthophists, it should be encouraged to function as an independent organisation with its own Governing Council even after the Cancer Hospital is taken over by the State Government or by a separate Board of Management.

The Committee enunciated the following recommendations for immediate acceptance by the Government of India in respect of the Cancer Hospitals and Research Centres for Calcutta, Madras, Hyderabad, Ahmedabad, etc., with special reference to the patient load, trained personnel, equipment, available facilities and potentialities for future development on an uniform all-India pattern.

Urgency of the Cancer Problem: Cancer in India constitutes a health problem and should be tackled early and comprehensively through a multi-pronged collaborative attack by different groups of medical and non-medical scientists and health service personnel during the Fourth Plan, as a joint venture between the State and Central Governments and the Voluntary Organisations, their efforts channellised through one Central agency so that the development programme follows a uniform and co-ordinated pattern.

Method of Approach: A comprehensive coverage of the Cancer problem is possible through a five-fold programme of Prevention, Diagnosis, Treatment, Rehabilitation and Research. Cancer consciousness through mass Health Education, should be awakened. Service to cancer patients, both in door and outdoor should be without charge except in paying wards.

Control Programme: Establishment of Caneer Detection Clinics below district levels where clinical, simple endoscopic, histopathological and cytological examinations could be carried out. These clinics will collaborate with the better equipped and more advanced centres at District and Central levels.

Cancer Prevention Service:

These will include recognition of "pre-cancerous lesions". Doubt cases will be referred to district hospitals or the Regional Cancer Centres.

Control And Elimination Of Occupational And Industrial Hazards

Steps to eliminate and protect industrial workers for carcinogenic pollution of industrial environment will be the responsibility of Regional Cancer Centres when constituted.

Therapeutic Programmes

The programmes will be conducted by the :

1. Regional Cancer Centres (Hospitals) with facilities for surgery, radiotherapy, Hormone therapy;
2. Cancer Research Centres;
3. Cancer Wings in General Hospitals;
4. Mobile Cancer Therapentic Teams etc; and
5. Cancer Clinics.

Educational Programmes

1. Health Education of the public;
2. Orientation of the Medical practitioners;
3. Post-graduate education centre and Rehabilitation centres.

Socio Economic Programmes

1. Provision of free beds;
2. Provisions of livelihood assistance to families;
3. Postgraduate education centre and Rehabilitation centres.

Establishment Of Regional Cancer Centres (Regional Oncological Institutes)

The Committee unanimously agreed that the mos

effective way for the development of cancer work in India would be through the establishment of Regional Cancer Centres, on the pattern, recommended by the W.H.O. The functions of a Regional Centre should be :

1. To act as a Centre for diagnosis, treatment and follow-up of cancer patients.

2. To act as the Centre for teaching and training in cancer for the different professional levels needed.

3. To carry out research work in cancer in the region.

4. To act as the Cancer Registry Centre for the region where all cancer records are collected for statistical elaboration and analysis for the purpose of determining the cancer morbidity and mortality, for the preventive campaign and for the further development of the network of cancer facilities in the region.

5. To coordinate and lead the fight against cancer in the region through its peripheral cancer clinics, in cancer control and educational programme.

The Regional Cancer Centres should operate under the auspices of the Government of India, Ministry of Health, in areas where facilities for diagnosis and treatment already exist. The Regional Cancer Centre will operate as the Central directing agency of all cancer activities in its region. Sueh a centre must have coverage of more than one State and should receive Plan Assistance and support from the Central Government. The development can'be phased depending on the existing facilities and the finance available.

1. North-Eastern Regional Centre :

It will cover Assam, Bihar, Orissa and West Bengal.

2. Western Regional Centre :

It will cover Maharashtra (already under the Department of Atomic Energy of the Government of India), Madhya Pradesh, Goa, etc.

3. North-Western Regional Centre :

It will cover Gujarat, Rajasthan, etc.

4. South-Eastern Regional Centre :

It will cover Madras and Kerala.

5. Central Regional Centre :

It will cover Andhra Pradesh and Mysore.

6. Northern Regional Centre :

It will cover Delhi, Punjab, Jammu and Kashmir and U.P. There may be certain centres which may not come into the category of the Regional Cancer Centres. For these, Central Government assistance may be given, however duplication of effort and consequent wastage of talent and funds should be discouraged.

(i) **Activities of Regional Centres** : Diagnosis and Treatment of Cancer Patients. A well-staffed Cancer Hospital with a bed strength of 250 with separate beds allocated to Surgery, Radio-therapy and Chemo-therapy (including hormones) and facilities for Radio-diagnosis, Radio-isotopes and Resuscitation service should be available. Ancillary units for detal surgery including Prosthetic department, E.N.T. department, etc. are desirable,

(ii) Tumous Registry and Follow-up system with a statistical department,

(iii) Laboratory facilities for, both routine investigations and research, should be available in Pathology, Experimental Biology, Biochemistry and Medical Physics,

(iv) **Research on Fundamental and Applied Aspects of Cancer Problem** : Research should include human and animal biology, cell biology including tissue culture, chemo-therapy, both experimental and clinical, enzyme chemistry, genetics, micro-biology, medical biophysics and medical physics including various aspects of radiation therapy and nucleonics, radio-isotopes, etc. This may not be possible in all the Regional Centres and cooperation will have to sought from various neighbouring established university departments, e.g., in Calcutta, Madras. Bombay. etc.,

(v) Surveys of cancer morbidity and mortality, etc.

(vi) Cancer prevention with particular emphasis upon : (a) mass examination, (b) health education and (c) industrial hygiene.

(a) **Mass Examination** : Mass examination (site specific and comprehensive) on early cancer cases or symptom—free cancer cases will have to be taken up in Cancer Detection and Diagnostic Clinics in urban hospitals. district hospitals and later, in rural centres. Equidemiology and geographic distribution of cancer incidence will be worked out from such data.

(b) **Health Education** : Preventive measures are very much linked with health education. Government of India has a Health Education Bureau and each State has also a cell or a section dealing with Health Education. These bodies will be requested to help in circulating authoritative information about cancer in urban and rural areas. Much more weightage should be given to cancer propaganda during the Fourth Plan.

(c) **Industrial Hygiene** : Industrial hygiene including cigarette smoking can also be taken up for further investigative work. Public health measures can be taken where indicated. Mass prophytatic service at industries for early detection of pre-cancerous disease and initial stages of cancer is essential,

(vii) Training programmes of doctors, nurses, technicians, social workers, etc.

(a) **Doctors** : Training of cancer specialists in Regional Cancer Centres should be planned in collaboration with Medical Colleges and Research Institutions in the region and must aim at reaching a high standard of efficiency, as is obtainable in post-graduate institutions of Universities. Courses of study could be organised, for example for diploma courses in Radio-Therapy, Surgery and M.D. or Ph.D. in Oncology, the basic qualification being M.B.B.S. These specialists will be supported by adequate stipends during the training period. Non-medical scientists with M.Se., may be encouraged to take advanced course in Biochemistry, Pathology etc.

(b) **Nurses** : Registered Nurses may be given training in Cancer Hospitals.

(c) **Technicians** : Specialised training of 6m onths in a year shouid be given to technicians for x-ray work and for handling costly Radiotherapy equipment.

(d) **Social Workers** : Special training in bio-statistics for these people may be necessary. This is very important for epidemiological study and will be in the nature of post-graduate training to already qualified Social Workers,

(viii) Any other allied functions, as so indicated from time to time by their Governing Bodies, to be set up for the purpose, e.g., this may include provision of convalescent homes and occupational-therapy, organisation of the blood-bank and patient care programmes, etc., etc.

Constitution And Management Of Regional Cancer Centres

(a) **Governing Body** : There should be one representative Governing Body consisting of about 9 to 11 members under the aegis of the Central Health Ministry.

The Chairman should be either the Union Health Minister, or the Union Health Secretary or a scientist of international calibre nominated by the Ministry of Health. The tenure of the Chairman and non-official members may be for a period of 5 years.

A Committee consisting of :

Director General of Health Services, Government of India, New Delhi. Financial Adviser, Govt. of India, Ministry of Health, New Delhi. One prominent scientist in the cancer field to be nominated by the Govt. of India.	3 Central Govt.
State Health Secretary (one). Director of Health Services of the State in which the Centre is located.	3 State Govt. (number can be adjusted depending on participating States.)
Two to be nominated or elected from the respective bodies offering assistant to the Regional Centres	2 from Voluntary Agencies.
Director of Regional Centre would be the Member-Secretary of the Government Body of Regional Centre.	1 member-Secretary
Total	9

Two members to be cootped whenever necessary.

(b) **Director** : The Director of the Regional Cancer Centre should be a Senior Medical Scientist familar with Oncology, with high professional qualifications and mature research experience and leadership. He should be a full-time paid worker of the Regional Cancer Centre.

(c) **Central Hospital of Regional Cancer Centre** : The hospital attached to the Regional Cancer Centre should have an optimum bed strength of 250 and staffing pattern should be as given on next page.

(d) **Training and Teaching of Future Cancer Workers** : The Regional Cancer Centres should serve not only as centres for treatment of cancer patients but also develop research, diagnosis and organisation, and methods of cancer control. These centres should be staffed with trained personnel who should undertake teaching and training of workers in this special area of (cancer) Oncology.

The objective can be best achieved if the Regional Cancer Centres are affiliated to the universities at post-graduate level. Degrees and Diplomas may be given in Oncology. Efforts should be made to get Oncology recognised as a special subject for M.D., M.S., Ph.D, etc., by the universities. Refresher courses for medical practitioners should be arranged. Orientation courses should be arranged for nurses and technicians.

(e) **Staff Salary—Regional Cancer Hospital** : The Committee unanimously agreed that the Central Health Services scales of pay and allowances and service conditions should apply to the staff of the Regional Centres.

(f) **Cancer Wings and Cancer Clinics** : As the programme progresses, the Committee anticipated that there will be need in future for the establishment of special cancer wings in some of the suitable General Hospitals. Cancer clinics should be established in all Districts and suitable facilities provided. The Primary

Staff of Central Hospital of Regional Cancer Centre

Medical Superintendent :	
Deptt. of Surgery	(1) Visting Surgeon—(Surgical and Gynaecological) for in-patient.
	(2) Visiting Dental & E. N. T. Surgeon.
	(3) Resident Surgeon and Duty Staff.
Deptt. of Anaesthesia	(1) Anaesthetist—Senior and Junior.
Deptt. of Radiology	(1) Radiologist
	(2) Asstt. Radiologist.
	(3) Radio-therapist.
Deptt. of Chemo-therapy	(1) Senior Chemo-therapeutist and Physician.
	(2) Junior Chemo-therapeutist.
	(3) Clinical Endocrinologist.
Deptt. of Pathology (including Blood Bank)	(1) Senior Pathologist.
	(2) Helping Staff and Technicians.
	(3) Blood Bank Officer,
Deppt. of Nursing	(1) Nursing Superintendent.
	(2) Senior and Junior Nurses.
	(3) General Duty Assistants.
Pharmacy	(1) Senior Pharmacist.
	(2) Helping Staff Pharmasists.

Deptt. of Social Service and Rehabilitation;
Department of Medical Records and Statistics:
Registrar and Hospital Administrator.

Health Centres and dispensaries should collaborate with the district clinics in all cancer control activities. Minimum standards for a Cancer Centre/Wing are given in Appendix 16.

(g) Cancer Education : Cancer is a deadly disease which thrives on a ignorance of the general population and it is the world opinion today that if early cancer cases are detected in time, there is a very good chance of elimination and cure in a large number of cases. The Committee felt that early efforts should be made, to bring knowledge of various facts and causation and incidence, to the public through pamphlets and other mass media of communications such as the radio, film television etc.

As a first step, the Committee suggested that a pamphlet or a booklet be published in various languages for the lay public outlining the important aspects of cancer by the Central Health Education Bureau with the assistant of the staff of the Tata Memorial Hospital.

Finance

The Committee noted that all the important cancer hospitals in India such as, the Tata Memorial Hospital, in Bombay, the Chittaranjan Cancer Hospital in Calcutta and the Madras Cancer Institute, were started by voluntary organisations with funds from private donations and charities.

Later, the State and Central Governments have come to their aid with grants for maintenance of hospital beds, equipment and research. Cancer is now a world challenge and all countries are supporting cancer research from their Government budgets.

In India it is absolutely essential that the Regional Cancer Centres should draw their finance from three sources:(1) Central Government,(2) States and (3) Voluntary agencies and private bodies. The States which do not have adequate cancer treatment facilities should be encouraged to participate in this programme through suitable contributions and by sending a representative to serve on the Governing Body of the Regional Cancer Centres. The funds should be operated by the Governing Body of Regional Cancer Centres. Assistance from the Centre would be geared to the expansion of activities. Aid in the shape of foreign exchange, equipment, apparatus. etc. should be sought from international agencies only, through the Health Ministry of the Government of India.

The Committee estimated Rs. 80 lakhs to be the probable cost of each Regional Centre which consists of research section and a hospital consisting of 50 Research beds and others as service. The bed-strength of a Regional Cancer Hospital should be about 200 which is considered the optimum. The Tata Memorial Hospital and Indian Cancer Research Centre which are under the Management of the Department of

Atomic Energy, Government of India, are taken as models with regard to cost etc. The cost of the Regional Cancer Centre without service beds is given in Appendix 15. It is considered that any Regional Centre that is already developed sufficiently and has certain equipment, would cost considerably less. The following centres are capable of being developed as Regional Centres :

(1) Bombay.
(2) Ahmedabad.
(3) Calcutta.
(4) Delhi.
(5) Hyderabad.
(6) Madras.

Some of these centres are developed and have a fair amount of equipment. Some others require supply of equipment and additional accommondation. On an average it would cost about Rs. 80 lakhs per centre, i.e., Rs. 4 crores, which may be spread out in two plan periods. As it is understood there is only a provision of Rs. 2 crores during the Fourth Five Year Plan, it is recommended that funds should be provided to each centre on the recommendation of the Cancer Committee.

The Committee noted with satisfaction that most of the State Governments consulted, have in realisation of the seriousness and urgency of the problem, agreed to bear the increasing cost of maintenance of cancer hospital beds and have requested the Centre for help in connection with equipment and apparatus needed for Radio-therapy, Chemo-therapy, etc. and Research and Training Centres. The Committee felt that in view of the present difficult situation in the country, aid-funds from voluntary agencies are not likely to be forthcoming as before and, therefore, the financial lead will have to be taken more and more by the Central Government. The service facilities, Education and Research in this field should be immediately developed on a planned basis by the Central Government. The Committee felt that the Indian Research worker has a great role to play in Cancer research, prevention, diognosis and treatment.

Appendix 16

Views of Dr. J. C. Paymaster

Facilities For Cancer Treatment and Diagnosis Other Than Regional Cancer Centre

Besides Regional Cancer Centres, there will be "Cancer Wings" or "Cancer Sections" in some of the larger hospitals and perhaps in the smaller ones, there will be "Cancer Clinics". The Cancer Wings or Sections and the Cancer Clinics must work in full co-ordination with the nearest Regional Cancer Centre. In this way there will be unformity in the matter of collection of data, diagnostic facilities and also in the treatment of cancer patients. Ultimately from these data will emerge the methods for prevention of cancer.

A. Cancer Clinics : The Cancer Clinics, being situated in smaller hospitals with limited facilities need not go in for elaborate treatment part but they must have diagnostic facilities.

For the purpose :

(1) They must use forms or proformas accepted by the Regional Cancer Centre and used throughout the clinics and Cancer Wings of the regions covered by the Regional Cancer Centre and collect information about cancer which can be filled by the Medical Officer in charge at the time of examination.

(2) There must be facilities for taking a biopsy from superficial lesion, such as those which occure on the skin, ear, nose, mouth, throat cervix penis etc.

(3) There must be mutual arrangements for such biopsies to be examined either by the nearest hospital that has a "Cancer Wing" or it must be sent to the nearest Regional Cancer Centre.

(4) The patient once suspected or diagnosed as a cancer patient, should be referred to the nearest hospital with a Cancer Wing or to the nearest Regional Cancer Centre without delay for treatment and advice.

(5) After completing treatment at the Cancer Wing or Regional Cancer Centre, the routine periodical check-ups may be done at the Cancer Clinics and information and findings passed on to the Cancer Wing or to the Regional Cancer Centre for record purposes.

B. Cancer Wings or Cancer Sections must have the Following Facilities :

(1) Facilities (Proformas etc.) for collection of data from cancer patients.

(2) Facilities for clinical examinations of patients.

(3) Facilities for taking biopsies from external and internal organs.

(4) Facilities for processing and examining biopsies.

(5) Radiological diagnosis and treatment facilities etc.

(6) Personnel trained for all types of treatment of cancer patients.

(7) Personnel and facilities for collecting follow-up information and to maintain medical report of patients.

A team from the Regional Cancer Centre should visit the Cancer Wings or Clinics and evaluate the working progress of each unit periodically.

COMMITTEE ON UNTOUCHABILITY, ECONOMIC AND EDUCATIONAL DEVELOPMENT OF THE SCHEDULED CASTES AND CONNECTED DOCUMENTS, 1965—REPORT

Delhi, Manager of Publications, 1969. 431p.+xxivp.

Chairman : Shri L. Elayaperumai.
Members : Shri C. Das; Shri R. A. Achuthan; Shri B. K. Gaikwad; Shri P. L. Majumdar; Shri Narain Din; Shri V. V. Vaze.
Secretary : Shri S. K. Kaul.

APPOINTMENT

The Committee on Untouchability, Economic and Educational Development of the Schduled Castes and Conncted Documents was constituted under the Department of Social Welfare vide their Resolution No. 14/5/64. SCT. II, dated April 27, 1965.

TERMS OF REFERENCE

(i) To study the various aspects of untouchability, in particular the working of the Untouchability (offences) Act. 1955, and the restrictions, if any, imposed on the entry of harijans into public places of worship, and to suggest remedial measures;

(ii) To study the problem of the economic uplift of the Scheduled Castes, evaluate the impact of the present schemes, and make recommendations as to the further measures that may be necessary; and

(iii) To study the problems of Education of Scheduled Castes, assess the progress achieved so far and suggest further measures that may be necessary.

CONTENTS

Part I : Untouchability—Some Basic Considerations and Issues; Legislative Measures to eradicate Untouchability; Forms of Untouchability; Role of Non-official Organisations in the removal of Untouchability; Role of Official Organisations in the Removal of Untouchability; Working of the Untouchability (Offences) Act, 1955; Formation of Boards for the removal of Social Distributors; Annexures I to XV(b).

Part II : Introduction; Occupational Pattern of Scheduled Castes; Land Allotment to Scheduled Castes; Incentives to Scheduled Castes in Agriculture; Agricultural Labour; Land Colonisation; House-sites and Housing for Scheduled Castes; House Sites; Housing; Industries; Cooperation; Indebtedness; Forced Bonded Labour; A Brief Review of the Backward Classes Sector in the Five Year Plan; Benefits derived by the Scheduled Castes from the General Sector Programme; Annexures I to II.

Part III : Introduction; Primary Education; Middle and Secondary Education; Post-Matric Scholarships Scheme and Post-Matric Education; Overseas Scholarships; Sainik Schools; The system of Public Schools; Ashram Schools/Residential Schools; Hostels; Girls Education; Anneures I to VI.

Part IV : Representation of Scheduled Castes in Central Government Services; Representation of Scheduled Castes in the Services under the State Governments/Union Territory Administration.

Part V : Need for Reorganisation of the present set-up of the Office of the Commissioner for Scheduled Castes/Scheduled Tribes; Appendices 1 to 4.

RECOMMENDATIONS

Part I—Untouchability : Some Basic Considerations And Issues

To abolish the Caste Systems and Untouchability merely on paper and by wishful thinking and empty advice or slogans is sheer nonsense or bypassing. The real solution of the only question of supreme importance to be considered is to devise and how to bring about the necessary reform of the Hindu Social Order. There must be a deliberate plan of action to be carried out through social engineering. Definite ways and means will have to be worked out in the shape of social planning. But to bring about the necessary social transformation would call for wise leadership with a clear appreciation of aims and objects, a national and experimental attitude of mind with the confidence in the outlook of science and willing to pay the price of much painful adjustments. There must be a clear-cut policy for social reconstruction of the Hindu Society and that has to be outlined in the form of a Social Policy Resolution incorporating the cardinal features of the reforms.

The most crucial question of social reorganisation is to break the hold of the institution of caste system. This can be done by deliberately creating new loyalties across caste lines, new States, systems and power structures that are not based or dependent on caste.

The hereditary priesthood in the Hindu Society should be abolished. It can be achieved even without legislation. The system can be replaced by an ecclesiastical organisation of men proessing the requisite educational qualifications after giving training in recognised institutions in priesthood. Such lines in priesthood should be open to all qualified candidates irrespective of caste, creed or race.

Untouchability being a social and collective offence has to be treated as such. Governmental displeasure on a collective scale would surely be impressive.

There should be a comprehensive scheme for biological assimilation of social groups through inter-caste marriages which can help a lot to cut through castes creating a society with lateral mobility.

Legislative Measures to eradicate Untouchability : We strongly recommend that the States which do not have any legislation permitting entry of all classes and sections of Hindus into places of public worship should enact necessary laws to the effect so that the Scheduled Castes may enter and worship in all Hindu temples on an equality with caste-Hindus.

Forms of Untouchability : Untouchability can only be removed when the mojority of Hindus realise that it is a crime against God and men are ashamed of it.

Role of the Non-official Organisations in the removal of Untouchability : There are essentially two basic considerations which demand the participation of non-official organisations in the social welfare programmes of the country. Firstly in a democratic form of Government, increasing participation of the people in the welfare programmes is essential for the success of any scheme. Secondly, it is felt that these organisations reflect the actual needs and desire of the society for reformation and change. Besides, it is also conceded that the coercive methods of law should always be buttressed by the persuasive methods of slow mass education or propaganda, and the non-official organisations could play effective role in this sphere and could contribute substantially in our efforts for the removal of untouchability. It is, therefore, inevitable that non-official agencies should also be more effectively associated with all the programmes for the removal of untouchability.

Role of Official Organisations in the removal of Untouchability : As the problem of the removal of untouchability emerges significant from the point of view of national solidarity and national integration of the country the role of official organisations in any determined efforts for its eradication affairs increasing proportions. To usher in the process of regeneration, integration and consolidation, special efforts and sincere approach to the problem by official organisations at all the level is inevitable.

Working Of The Untouchability (Offences) Act. 1955

Due action should be taken in appointing such committees in all the States throughout the country which try to eradicate the evil of untouchability.

Formation of Boards for removal of Social Distributors : The Government should appoint some Boards, which should be clothed with adequate powers to enforce the Act dealing with the removal of social and religious disabilities.

Part II –Occupational Pattern Of Scheduled Castes

It is suggested that the Scheduled Castes who like to give up their unclean occupations and endeavour to engage themselves in certain trades of Cottage Industries like weaving, basket works, blacksmithy, carpentry, masonery, processing of cereals and pulses, etc., should be encouraged.

Land Allotment to Scheduled Castes : The Scheduled Caste landless agriculturists would not be benefited much by the method of imposition of land ceilings, as the preference in allotment of such lands, as a matter of policy of the Government is always to :(1) tenants displaced as a result of resumption of land, for personal cultivation, (2) farmers with uneconomic land holdings, and (3) to landless workers. From the Government policy it appears that they have given first preference to those whose lands have been acquired for public purpose. The Committee will have no objection in giving them first preference provided they are not paid any compensation. If compensation is paid they have no right to demand Government land. As regards second category, Government are giving preference to those who have uneconomic holdings. The Committee notes with regret that though it is the duty of the Government to see that those who have no land at all, and for centuries together are suffering on account of poverty are provided with land, Government have ignored their claim. In the third category the Government have given preference to landless people. The Committee shows dissatisfaction towards this and gives the following illustration for information of the Government and public :

As the population of Scheduled Caste agricultural landless labourers is round about 50% of the total landless persons, the Committee recommends the 50% reservation should be made for landless Scheduled Caste agricultural labourers.

It should be ensured by the State Governments that only reclaimed lands are allotted to Scheduled Castes. The cost of such reclamation should not be recovered from them, and the whole expenditure should be borne by the Government from the General Sector and not from Backward Class Sector.

Schedule Caste cultivators having uneconomic holdings, (say less than 5 acres) should be allotted additional land to ensure economic viability. The minimum land allotment should not be less than 5 acres.

Immediately after allotment of land sufficient money should be given to the allottee for purchase of agricultural implements, bullocks, fertilizers, seeds, etc.

When land is allotted to Scheduled Castes, it should be ensured that the ownership is vested on the allottee, i.e., the Scheduled Caste person, on permanent and hereditary basis.

The Committee feels that the State Government should think of giving some immediate economic relief to the landless agricultural Scheduled Castes, at least till all of them are covered by land allotment. As the agricultural work is seasonal, most of them are under-employed, and their living conditions are pathetic. Some immediate relief, therefore, is required.

Incentive to Scheduled Castes in Agriculture : It is essential to have a general idea on the agricultural aid programme implemented in various States and for this purpose a Statewise review is required.

Care should be taken of the landless cultivators in providing agricultural aids. The existing rules in States should be suitably amended to accommodate the large number of these cultivators in the provision of agricultural aids.

The Committee feels that the Ministry of Food and Agriculture should set out a list of agricultural programmes and forward to States for implementation according to conditions prevailing in each State. The programme should invariably involve all the essential requirements of poor cultivators such as, supply of plough, bullocks, agricultural implements, improved seeds and fertilizers, sinking of irrigation wells, maintenance of demonstration centres, offering technical advice etc.

All the State Governments should make adequate provision in their budget for agricultural aids and all Scheduled Castes cultivators should be covered.

Agricultural Labour : On going through the minimum rates fixed by the various State Governments, the Committee observes that the rates are much low in some States, and in certain cases the rate is even lower than the market rates. The Committee recommends that as the cost of living has gone up considerably and the present market rate has also thoroughly changed, all the present conditions, should be taken into consideration for fixation of minimum wages of agricultural labour.

The agricultural labour is seasonal and they are unemployed for more than 8 months in the year. The only solution to this problem is to divert these people to some other fields of work when they have no work in agriculture. The surplus agricultural workers can be gainfully diverted into other fields such as construction, road repairing etc. as manual workers.

All Scheduled Caste persons above 60 of age, having no income and nobody to support, should be given old age pension.

50% labour in all Public Sector Undertakings should be reserved for landless Scheduled Caste agricultural labourers.

Land Colonisation

If Government can acquire land for public purposes including those of rehabilitating refugees such as Dandakaranya Project, there is no reason why similar facilities should not be extended to the members of Scheduled Castes. Such villages or colonies should be self-contained in all respects with sufficient cultivable land attached. There should be shopping facilities, approachable roads, drinking water wells, irrigation facilities, a Multipurpose Cooperative Society and also a School-cum-Community Centre.

If the State Governments are not willing to come forward to establish such special settlements, the Central Government should take up the matter. The Committee recommends that at least Rs. 20 crores should be earmarked for this purpose in the Fourth Five-Year Plan.

House-sites And Housing For Scheduled Castes

The State Governments and Union Territory Administrations should review the house-site scheme to incorporate the following measures to surmount difficulties :

Special Revenue Officers may be attached with the Directorate of Harijan Welfare to expedite acquisition of land for house-sites to Scheduled Castes as in vogue in Madras State.

Ownership right over the house-site should be given to the beneficiaries as soon as they construct their houses.

The cost of acquisition should be borne by the Government.

At the time of establishing housing colonies, consideration should be given to scope of employment opportunities for the settlers in and around the locality.

Wherever house-sites plots are proposed to be allotted or auctioned at a new place, the State Governments/ Union Territory Administrations should reserve a percentage of house-sites for members of Scheduled Castes. Such plots should be given free of cost.

Housing : Where the State Governments construct houses for Scheduled Castes under the scheme, proprietory rights over the houses should be given to the beneficiaries but it should be ensured that the beneficiaries are not alienating the house.

After grant of subsidy, follow-up action should be

taken by responsible officers of the State Government to ensure that the funds are spent for the specific purpose for which they were given.

The amount of grant for construction of houses should not be given to the beneficiaries in cash as far as possible. The State Governments should construct the houses and then allot to the beneficiaries.

The houses constructed and allotted under the scheme should have the minimum amenities of one room, a varandah, kitchen, bath-room and latrine.

It should be ensured that in all colonies adequate arrangements are made for lighting, sanitation, approach roads, medical facilities, water-taps etc.

The State Governments should ensure that the colonies for sweepers and scavengers are constructed in neat and hygienic localities.

Industry

Cottage industries programme for economic upliftment of the Scheduled Castes under the Backward Classes Sector should be institutionalised and comprehensive and coordinated efforts with proper supervision and follow-up should be made. All the State Governments and Union Territory Administrations should take a tangible step for the establishment of Backward Classes Finance Corporation for promotion of cottage industries as early as possible. The Committee also recommends that at least Rs. 20 crores should be provided in Fourth Plan for this purpose.

Government organisations like State Trading Corporation which is engaged in purchase and export of commodities should purchase the products of the Scheduled Caste Cooperative Societies at reasonable rates.

Cooperation

It is observed in Kerala that the Societies for Scheduled Castes are exempted from payment of registration fees. Similar concessions should be given by other State Governments and Union Territory Administrations.

Public Sector Undertakings like State Trading Corporation and Handicrafts and Handloom Corporation, who are engaged in purchase and export should be instructed to give preference to the products of Scheduled Caste Societies.

The Office bearers of Scheduled Caste Cooperatives should be adequately trained in cooperation before they take up their jobs. Atleast one training school for cooperation should be started in each State in which sufficient seats should be reserved for Scheduled Castes.

Indebtedness

On study of the problem of indebtedness among the Scheduled Castes, it has been revealed that the worst type of exploiter who has been sucking the very blood of these unfortunate people is the indigenous moneylender, who alone accounts for more than 20 per cent of their indebtedness.

Forced/Bonded Labour

The State Governments/Union Territory Administrations should conduct a survey of the problem of bonded/forced labour.

They should pass legislation by:

(a) Declaring this system unlawful and a punishable offence;

(b) Offering price to those bringing to notice of the police the cases of bonded/forced labour;

(c) Treating the bond as null and void;

(d) Releasing the individual of any obligations, whatsoever, of the past debt; and

(e) Making future offences under the Act non-bailable.

A Brief Review Of The Backward Classes Sector In The Five Year Plan

Economic uplift programmes under the Backward Classes Sector should be institutionalised and comprehensive and coordinated efforts with proper supervision and follow up should be made.

A large scale integrated programme should be launched for settling landless Scheduled Caste persons on land. Adequate funds for this purpose should be provided in the Backward Classes Sector of the Plan.

The Department of Social Welfare, Government of India and the State Governments should review the economic programmes for Scheduled Castes and take suitable steps to provide more funds in the State Plans during the Fourth Five Year Plan.

After taking into consideration all the points, the Committee feels that the amount of Rs. 66 crores proposed in the Backward Classes Sector of the Fourth Plan for the Scheduled Castes should be increased. It is recommended that it may be raised to at least Rs. 200 crores so that educational and economic uplift schemes for the welfare of the Scheduled Castes may be continued and expanded.

Benefits Derived By The Scheduled Castes From The General Sector Programme

It is necessary to establish at the State level a small cell in the Directorate of Social Welfare to keep a constant watch and review the orders issued by the Government to the development department for earmarking of funds and their proper utilisation for the benefit of Scheduled Castes. This cell should work under the supervision of the Director of Social Welfare with the

Secretary, Planning Department as the overall incharge.

The Department of Social Welfare at the Centre should bear all the expenditure for creation of this cell in the Directorate of Social Welfare in the States.

The Scheduled Castes persons already getting benefits from the Government should continue to get such benefits, even after their conversion to other religions, in the matters of Education and Economic developments.

Part III—Primary Education

To increase the enrolment of Scheduled Caste children in schools, the services of Gram Sevaks and Panchayat Presidents and officers may be utilised.

It is futile to make elementary education compulsory if simultaneous efforts are not made to induce the parents to send their children to school. First of all, a proper field should be prepared by providing such incentives as mid-day meals, free supply of books, stationery, etc. and then only education should be made compulsory by legislation.

Middle And Secondary Education

Lack of schooling facilities near to the villages is an all-India problem fund in all the States except a few. In a country like India, where majority of the population lives in villages, especially Scheduled Castes ; it is high time for the State Governments of change their policy of preferential treatment to towns and cities in the establishment of educational institutions. As it is an all-India problem facing all the States, this matter deserves immediate attention of Government authorities.

Scheduled Caste individuals coming up for establishing educational institutions should be given all facilities such as free land, building grant of at least 50% of the expenditure etc. All such institutions should be attached with hostels and such facilities as mentioned above should be given for establishing hostels also.

The Committee feels that the present rate of scholarship is quite inadequate in the present increased cost of living condition.

Scheduled Caste students should be exempted from payment of all special fees such as game fee, laboratory fee, examination fee, library fee, etc.

Necessary arrangement should be made by the Government to supply set of costly text-books to students on loan basis as is being done by the Tamil Nadu Government through Welfare Department.

Post-Matric Scholarships Scheme And Post-Matric Education

A uniform procedure should be adopted by all the State Governments for implementation of the scheme and disbursement of scholarship amounts. The Department of Social Welfare to which post-metric scholarship scheme has been transferred recently should evolve a uniform procedure for disbursement of grants, acceptable to all the State Governments.

A separate form of application should be prescribed for Scheduled Castes and other Backward Classes.

State Governments should be advised to complete the scrutiny within the prescribed period and scholarships should be granted to the students within the fixed time after the receipt of the applications.

The Department of Social Welfare should immediately call for information from other State Governments also on the rate of scholarships granted by them, and wherever the amount is found to be less than the prescribed rate immediate action should be taken to ensure that the minimum rates of scholarships are granted to the students.

Wherever necessary, medical aid should be made available to the post-matric scholars—the expenditure being met out of the provision for Backward Classes (Health Scheme).

The Director of Harijan Welfare in State should be empowered by the respective State Governments to watch the number of seats reserved by the institutions and how it was implemented by them. And if the Director finds any irregularity he should take up the matter with Secretary, Department of Education.

Periodical survey should be undertaken by all State Governments to enable them to make an assessment of the achievements, and also to bring out the drawbacks, if any, in the working of our education schemes.

Overseas Scholarships

The number of overseas scholarships for Scheduled Castes students should be increased from 4 to at least 15 and thereafter every year there should be an increase of one scholarship for them.

State Governments should introduce Overseas Scholarship Scheme in their State to benefit Scheduled Castes students who possess good academic qualifications.

Hostels

In the case of Scheduled Castes students admitted in private general hostels all their expenses should be met by the Government and stipends/scholarships should be increased for this purpose.

The rate of stipends should be fixed according to the cost of living and should be sufficient to meet all the expenditure.

Once a student is admitted in a hostel his continued admission in the coming years should be ensured so long as he does not fail more than two times.

Special coaching for students should be incorporated as a part and parcel of hostel life.

Untouchability and segregation in any form should not be allowed to continue in any of the hostels run by Government or Voluntary Organisation.

The Central Government should directly construct, at least some hostels in each State to accommodate needy Scheduled Caste students.

Girls Education

Preference should be given by the State Governments for construction of Scheduled Caste Girls' Hostels.

All stipends/scholarships including post-matric scholarships should be fixed at higher rates say at least at Rs. 10 p.m. more for girls, than for boys. This is essential in view of the higher expenditure of girl students compared to boys.

Girls travelling to distant places by buses/trains etc. should be paid their actual conveyance charges.

Overseas scholarships, passage grants, scholarships for study in Public Schools etc. should be awarded to all qualified Scheduled Caste women applying for the same.

In some of the districts in States, as an experimental measure at least one primary/middle/high school with attached hostels should be opened for education of Scheduled Caste girls.

Education of girls should be work-oriented. In middle and high school classes, special training may be imparted in weaving, tailoring, typing, shorthand, etc.

Part IV—Central Services

Representation Of Scheduled Castes In Central Government Services.

In Public Sector Undertakings where no reservation orders were in vogue at the time of its establishment, the Ministry/Department concerned, in consultation with the Ministry of Home Affairs and the Department of Social Welfare, should increase the percentage of reservation for Scheduled Castes in such categories of posts where suitable candidates fulfilling minimum qualifications are easily available.

State Governments Services

Andhra : Special efforts should be made by the Judicial Department to increase the intake of Scheduled Castes in the various categories of posts under them.

In view of the poor representation of Scheduled Castes in the police department it is suggested that as a special case educational qualifications may be lowered for Scheduled Caste persons to enable them to join in the rank of constables.

The State Government should issue necessary instructions to the statutory bodies and public undertakings and to make reservations in posts and services on the lines of the State Government in favour of Scheduled Castes.

Panchayati Raj Institutions should take special steps to increase the intake of Scheduled Castes in various categories of posts under them.

Bihar : A strict compliance of communal roster should be ensured on the lines of the Central Government.

Special efforts shouid be made by the local bodies to ensure that representation of Scheduled Castes increases in the various services and posts under them as early as possible.

The State Government should ensure that all the Panchayati Raj Institutions follow scrupulously the orders regarding the reservation of posts for Scheduled Castes.

Jammu and Kashmir : Special direct recruitment of Scheduled Castes should be made to fill in the gazetted posts in all Departments.

The reservation orders in posts and services for Scheduled Castes should be extended to local bodies, statutory bodies, public undertakings, etc., etc.

Other concessions like relaxation in age, exemption from payment of application fee, etc., etc., on the lines of the Central Government and other States should also be given to the Scheduled Castes in the State.

Kerala : Periodical returns regarding representation of Scheduled Castes should be furnished by all the offices which should be checked and consolidated at the State Headquarters.

Relaxation in age may be allowed to Scheduled Castes in recruitment to Class IV posts also.

Special direct recruitment of Scheduled Castes may be resorted to fill in the gazetted posts in all the Departments.

The State Government should direct all Government and Semi-Government employers to indicate clearly the posts reserved for Scheduled Castes when notifying vacancies to the Employment Exchanges.

Madhya Pradesh : There should be a proper scrutiny of the periodical returns that are submitted by the appointing authorities at the State level. An Employment Cell should be appointed.

It is necessary to increase suitably the percentage of reservation in Class III and IV Services if Scheduled Caste persons are to attain an adequate representation in services in the near future in Class III and IV Services..

Steps should be taken to increase the intake of Scheduled Castes in the Services under the High Court and the Subordinate Courts so as to bring them to the percentage prescribed for them.

Madras : Necessary arrangements may be made to establish a pre-examination coaching centre for Scheduled Castes to enable them to qualify for competitive examinations held for recruitment to various State services.

The percentage of reservation in services for Scheduled Castes should be in accordance with their percentage of population to the total population of the State.

The Khadi and Village Industries Board should extend the reservation orders to all posts under their control and amend the rules accordingly.

Maharashtra : A manual of instructions containing reservation orders issued from time to time should be printed and supplied to all appointed authorities.

Special efforts should be made by the Judicial Department to increase the intake of Scheduled Castes in the various categories of posts under them.

The State Government should persuade the High Court to make necessary reservation for Scheduled Castes in the posts under it.

Separate reservation should also be provided for Scheduled Castes Converts to Buddhism.

Mysore : Reservation orders of 15% in favour of Scheduled Castes at the time of direct recruitment should also be made applicable at the time of promotion.

A pre-examination training centre for giving coaching to Scheduled Castes to enable them to appear in the various competitive examinations for entry into State Services may be established in the State very early.

A brochure containing all the reservation orders regarding recruitment of Scheduled Castes should be published and supplied to every appointing authority.

Delhi : Periodical returns should be properly checked.

A cell should be created to ensure compliance of reservation orders.

Himachal Pradesh : Periodical returns should be properly scrutinised and the discrepancies pointed out to the defaulting Departments.

While getting officers from other States on deputation basis, the State Government should try to secure the services of suitable Scheduled Caste employees from other States.

Manipur : The Union Territory Administration should make it obligatory for all the Departments to send periodical returns regarding the intake of Scheduled Castes in services to the Government.

Training facilities should be provided to Scheduled Caste candidates to enable them to compete for various services and be available to man the reserved posts.

Pondicherry : Special direct recruitment of Scheduled Castes should be made to fill in the gazetted posts in all Departments.

Tripura : There should be some effective machinery to check the observance of reservation orders of various departments. An employment cell may be established.

Periodical returns should be prescribed.

Special steps should be taken to increase the intake of Scheduled Castes in the services and posts under the Local Bodies.

Gujarat : The Committee recommends that a separate percentage should be fixed for Scheduled Castes i.e. :

(a) According to their population and a survey should be made about the representation of Scheduled Castes in Classes I, II, III and IV.

(b) There should be a Y in all Semi-Government bodies and local bodies for Scheduled Castes.

Rajasthan : An employment cell should be established.

Reservation of vacancies should be made separately for the Scheduled Castes and Scheduled Tribes.

A pre-examination coaching centre for Scheduled Caste students to appear in the various competitive examination should be started.

The State Government should issue instructions to all the heads of the departments to indicate clearly the posts reserved for Scheduled Castes when notifying the vacancies to the Employment Exchanges.

Strenuous efforts should be made to increase the intake of the Scheduled Castes in the posts under the control of the High Court.

Assam : A Employment Cell or a separate machinery should be established to verify adherence to instructions and orders issued regarding reservation of posts for Scheduled Castes by Government, Semi-Government and Public Undertakings, etc. and to see that the orders are being strictly followed by the respective departments in filling up the posts and percentage of reservation is properly maintained.

The State Government should appoint one member in the P.S.C. from amongst the S. C. as there has been no Scheduled Castes member in the Commission since Independence.

Orissa : Periodical returns should be prescribed and these should be properly scrutinised. An employment cell should be established.

Steps should be taken to get the reservation orders implemented by the State Khadi and Village Industries Board.

The District Welfare Officers should maintain a list of unemployed Scheduled Caste candidates and that list should be supplied to the Employment Exchanges every month.

Punjab : The order reserving 50% of vacancies in Class IV posts for Scheduled Castes should be reviewed.

Public Sector Undertakings may be instructed to follow strictly the rule of reservation of posts and services for Scheduled Castes.

Special measures may be taken to increase the intake of Scheduled Caste in Classes I, II and III Services.

Panchayati Raj Institutions should take special steps to increase the intake of the Scheduled Castes in services under them.

Andaman and Nicobar Islands : Those refugees from East-Pakistan who were considered to be Scheduled Castes in East-Pakistan and those migrated from the mainland and who were declared to be Scheduled Castes, must be considered as Scheduled Castes in the Andaman and Nicobar Islands.

Reservation must be provided for them in the services under the Government and the local bodies and public sector undertakings, etc., in addition to other educational benefits and political rights they will be entitled to under the Consitution.

Goa, Daman and Diu : If the reservation in services is not made already, the Committee recommends that it should be done early.

Nagaland : Early steps may be taken by the State Goverenment to recruit Scheduled Castes to Class II posts as there is no representation at present.

Uttar Pradesh : An employment cell should be established at the State Headquarters.

The Department of Municipal Administration should ensure that reservation orders are followed by the various Municipalities.

The High Court should make the reservation for Scheduled Castes in ths services under its control on the lines of State Government. Special efforts should also be made to increase the intake of the Scheduled Castes in the posts under the control of the High Court.

Unfilled reserved vacancies of Scheduled Castes should be carried forward for 2 years on the analogy of the Central Government.

West Bengal : Urgent steps may be taken to extend the reservation orders to all the States Services.

Concession should be given to the Scheduled Castes in cases where some fee is prescribed for posts advertised by the State Public Service Commisslon, State Government Offices and statutory organisations etc.

The unfilled reserved vacancies of Scheduled Castes should be carried forward for two years on the analogy of the Central Government.

Part V—Need For Reorganisation Of The Present Set Up Of The Office Of The Commissioner For Scheduled Castes And Scheduled Tribes

The Commissioner's organisation must not only be given a really independent status with clearly defined and codified powers, responsibilities and jurisdiction of actions, but as a field organisation as existing before the 1967. Reorganisation must also be immediately restored, further strengthened and systematised.

STUDY TEAM ON TEXTILE COMMISSIONER'S ORGANISATION, 1965—REPORT

Delhi, Manager of Publications, 1966. Part I—184+ivp.

Chairman : Shri K.K. Shah.
Members : Shri R. Doraiswamy; Shri P. Sabanayagam; Shri N. K. Mukarji ; Shri A. N. Biswas ; Shri R.L. Bhinge.
Secretary : Shri R. Parameshwar.

APPOINTMENT

The Study Team was constituted under the Government of India in May, 1965 in pursuance of the recommendation made by the Santhanam Committee that it would be desirable for each Ministry/Department to undertake a review of its regulatory functions and also examine whether the manner of discharge of these functions and of the exercise of powers of control are capable of improvement.

TERMS OF REFERENCE

(i) To review the various controls exercised by the Textile Commissioner in the context of a minute recorded by the late Prime Minister in 23rd April, 1965;

(ii) To examine which of the controls were superfluous and, as such, could be removed and which were such where simplification of operation was possible.

CONTENTS

Introductory ; Organisation and Functions of the

Textile Commissioner ; Guiding Principles followed by the Study Team ; Cotton (Section I—Production of Cotton ; Section II—Cotton Price Policy ; Section III—Licensing of Cotton Dealers ; Section IV—Allocation of Indian Cotton ; Section V—Procedure in regard to Allocation of Imported Cotton ; Section VI—Accounting of Import of P.L. 480 Cotton) ; Installation of Additional Capacity in the Organised Sector ; Control on Installation of Powerlooms ; Control and Regulations Designed to Protect the Decentralised Sector (Section I—Pegging of Weaving Capacity in Mills ; Section II—Reservation of Fields of Production ; Section III—Dhoti Production ; Section IV—Supply of Yarn to the Decentralised Sector ; Section V—Excise Duty on Textiles ; Section VI—Restrictions on the Printing of Fabrics) ; Qualitative Controls ; Statutory Controls on Production and Prices ; Regulations regarding Markings on Cloth and Yarn ; Textile Machinery (Section I—Organisation for the Development of Textile Machinery ; Section II—Industrial Licensing ; Section III—Import of Capital Goods Required by Textile Machinery Manufacturers ; Section IV—Textile Machinery Manufacture in the Medium and Small Scale Sectors ; Section V—Control on Textile Machinery Production) ; Assistance rendered by the Textile Commissioner to the Textile Industry in Securing Scarce Items of Supply ; Review of Statistical Forms and Returns ; Summary of Conclusions and Recommendations : Annexures 1 to 8.

RECOMMENDATIONS

Guiding Principles Followed By The Study Team

The Textile Commissioner's organisation which was initially set up during the last war to harness production for war requirements and also to deal with scarcity conditions arising out of shortages of supplies in the civilian market, has undergone a series of changes, and today it performs a variety of functions, both regulatory and developmental.

The activities, which in the early days, were confined to cotton and cotton textiles, have become widespread and varied and the Textile Commissioner is now not only concerned with cotton and cotton textiles, but is also responsible for the development of handloom, wool, art silk and textile machinery manufacturing industries.

Having regard to the changing conditions in the country, the emphasis on the role of the Textile Commssioner should be more on functions related to growth and development of the industry than on those which are purely regulatory in nature.

The organisation should take greater initiative in organising surveys and in planning and development activities, as it is purposeful effort in this direction and is important for healthy growth.

To create a proper climate for the healthy development of the industry, it is important that there should not be too many fetters on its working. Further, today, in the highly competitive international market for textiles, if our efforts to increase exports are to be crowned with a measure of success, it is desirable that the industry should not be logged down these unnecessary and outdated controls.

Cotton

The system of controls on cotton and textiles stems from the fact of inadequate supply of cotton. It axiomatically follows that once the supply position of cotton is improved, it may not be necessary for controls to be exercised over trading in cotton.

It is possible to increase the per acre yield of cotton even in areas not under irrigation, by increased input of fertilisers, pesticides and insecticides and by adoption of modern agricultural practices.

Viewed in the context of our expending approximately Rs. 60 crores per annum on the import of cotton, there is need to step up assistance to the farmers on a substantial scale with a view to increasing the productivity of our own cotton. Increased assistance of various kinds should be such as to make a sizeable impact on the production of cotton.

It is not suggested that the wherewithal for the increased input should be found wholly by the Central and State Governments. The farmers should be enabled to finance a considerable part of the increased expenditure through loans and advances to them and to farmers' cooperatives. Those may by redeemed at the time of sale of the produce.

Leading mill owners' associations in the country shall in their own interest emulate the efforts of the Indian Cotton Mills' Federation and take up selected pockets in their respective regions for intensive cultivation of cotton. In view of their organisational ability, their active participation in the production of the basic raw material would undoubtedly yield results, as has been eloquently proved in the demonstration farms of the Indian Cotton Mills' Federation. The Textile Commissioner should take the initiative in putting the proposition to mill owners' associations.

More foreign exchange should be released for automatic spraying equipment which are in extremely short Supply. The Director General of Technical Development should also address himself to the problem of increasing the manufacture of indigenous automatic spraying equipment.

The Study Team recieved a representation that in the context of Government's efforts to increase the yield per acre of cotton, the move to abolish the Indian

Central Cotton Committee would be ill-advised In the context of the recommendation to intensify cotton cultivation, the above representation gains further weight.

Considering the uniquely important position which cotton and the cotton textile industry occupy in the nation's economy, there should be a suitable agency or body to look after the work that the Indian Central Cotton Committee was supposed to do. It is imperative that the winding up of the Committee should not leave a vacuum. The agency or body to replace the Committee should be charged with the responsibility of reviewing policies and achievements in the realm of cotton development and generally of assisting in the putting through of a really significant production programme.

In Government's efforts to intensify cotton cultivation to achieve the Fourth Plan target, the Textile Commissioner should have to play a more positive role. Just as the Textile Commissioner and the Ministry of Commerce have a system of consulting the Agriculture Ministry on price policy, there should be a system of reverse consultation with the Textile Commissioner by the Ministry of Food and Agriculture in regard to cotton development programmes. The active participation of the Textile Commissioner in these programmes would provide a channel and a stimulus for the industry to be yoked in a practical and purposeful manner to the business of helping the cotton growers to increase their productivity.

In a situation where trading (in cotton) takes place above the ceiling, it has to be noted that the increased prices do not benefit the agriculturists, but the middlemen.

If the Government is to assure the consumer adequate supplies of popular varieties of cloth at reasonable prices, it has necessarily to ensure that prices of cotton, which constitute approximately 55 per cent of the cost of cloth, are kept with in bounds. In the circumstances, ceilings on cotton prices need to be continued so long as controls over production and prices of mill-made cloth continue.

The present floor prices do not provide adequate incentive to the farmer to increase his output. Realistic support prices should be fixed for all varieties of cotton and they should be announced well in advance of the cotton season in order that growers may have an assurance of their not having to sell their cotton at distress prices. This would be the most effective inducement to the grower to intensify his effort for the cultivation of cotton.

The following measures may be considered by Government in the context of the representation that the participation of agriculturists in the fixation of price policy was not adequate:

(a) Increasing the number of representatives of agriculturists in the Cotton Advisory Board;

(b) Appointing Regional Advisory Boards in some of the major cotton growing States.

The Board should advise the Textile Commissioner on:

(i) price policy;

(ii) implementation of the price policy; and

(iii) measures for improving the productivity of cotton.

Considering the limited scrutiny bestowed on applications for renewal of cotton licences and considering also that all requests for renewal of licences are allowed as a matter of course, the system of renewal of both 'A' and 'B' class licences should be done away with.

The system of issuing 'C' class licences should be dispensed with altogether as hand-ginners who cater to a very limited market should not be subject to the rigors of licensing.

The revised system of issuing permanent licences may be commenced from the cotton season 1966-67, and the system be notified to the public some time in June. Suitable amendments to the Cotton Control Order may be made in this regard.

To deal with requests from mills for additional quantities of Indian cotton, a specific form of application is necessary, with a view to avoiding back references.

In order to avoid frequent issue of quota letters for import of global cotton, the following revised procedure is recommended:

(i) After a basic year for the allocation of Indian cotton has been determined, the quantity of cotton used by each mill during that year should be intimated by the Textile Commissioner to the Indian Cotton Mills' Federation in the form of an authorisation card.

(ii) As and when cotton becomes available for release, the Federation should be advised of the percentage of cotton vis-a-vis consumption in the basic year that should be released to individual mills.

The Indian Cotton Mills' Federation should issue a letter, along with the premium receipt, indicating the actual quantity of cotton that may be released to the mill, with a copy direct to the Joint Chief Controller of Imports and Exports, Bombay.

The certificates to be issued by the Indian Cotton Mills' Federation should be serially numbered and a weekly statement of such certificates issued to the mills should be sent to the Joint Chief Controller of Imports and Exports and the Textile Commissioner.

In order to provide a basic record showing the total allocations made to a mill under different categories of allocation, the Federation may be asked to make suitable entries in the allocation card of all the allocations made to the mill, i.e. :

(a) Retention quotas ;

(b) Special quotas for executing Defence orders ; and

(c) Quotas given for supply of yarn to handlooms.

The introduction of the card system will secure the following advantages :

(i) Avoidance of issue of quota letters to actual user mills as many times as there are cotton releases ;

(ii) Automatic procedure for cancellation and re-allocation of the surrendered cotton to other mills ;

(iii) Cumulative accounting of allocations of foreign cotton in the same card ; and

(iv) Elimination of clerical work in the office of the Textile Commissioner.

The work relating to allocation of cotton against retention quota presently done by the Entitlement Branch of the Textile Commissioner's Office may be transferred to the Indian Cotton Mills' Federation. As a measure of safeguard, a statement of such allocations made may be sent to the Textile Commissioner's Office.

The existing procedure under which mills have to obtain permission of the Textile Commissioner to transfer retention quotas to other mills is redundant and should be discontinued.

The resale of retention quotas to third parties should be prohibited by public notice so that there is no question of individual parties applying for permission to resele.

In order to avoid the present accounting complications attendant on import of cotton under the P.L. 480 programme, the entire authorisation granted under P.L. 480, should be imported by a Central agency, like the Indian Cotton Mills' Federation. The advantages resulting from such move would be :

(a) Import of the entire quantity by the Federation in one instalment, thereby utilising the full value of the Purchase Authorisation ;

(b) Avoidance of unnecessary speculation in the market in view of early/late arrival ;

(c) Avoidance of the maintenance of individual accounts by the Textile Commissioner who is none too sure as to when imports would take place and when payments would be made into the U.S. Disbursement Accounts ;

(d) Avoidance, as a corollary, of the clerical work connected with the custody of a large number of bank guarantees and their subsequent discharges.

If, during any particular year, mills do not utilise the full value of the purchase authorisation, central purchase should make it possible to build-up buffer stock for meeting possible shortages of Indian cotton.

It is not necessary to be unduly concerned about precluding mills from exercising their choice about quality. In the circumstances, the possibility of bulk imports of P.L. 480 cotton through a central agency, the Indian Cotton Mills' Federation or a specially created buffer stock association, should be seriously examined.

If, however, for any reason, Government do not find it possible to implement the above suggestion, it is suggested that the Indian Cotton Mills' Federation should be entrusted with the accounting of individual transactions of mills. In other words, the Federation should take over the functions presently performed by the Textile Commissioner as the authorised applicant.

Installation Of Additional Capacity In The Organised Sector.

The existing procedures of industrial licensing for the cotton textile industry far from helping the growth of the industry had only tended to retard its growth.

In the light of the continuous need to expand production of cotton cloth which is a basic and essential need of a growing population, the cotton textile industry should be allowed to develop freely and to expand in all parts of the country.

Industrial licensing should be dispensed with for installation of spinning capacity upto 25,000 spindles or composite capacity upto 25,000 spindles and 500 looms.

Licensing should also be dispensed with where mills wish to undertake expansion of spindleage or loomage of their existing units within their existing premises.

There should be no need to extend the validity of existing unimplemented licences for spindles.

There need not be any commitment on the part of the Government to allow the import of machinery as a matter of course.

The question of issuing installation permits in the above cases should not arise hereafter.

Statutory returns may be prescribed under which textile mills should be required to send periodical returns to the Textile Commissioner, more in the nature of "Information" for statistical purposes.

The Textile Commissioner should keep himself informed about the development of textile machinery produced by indigenous machinery manufacturers, and for this he should obtain sale details from the latter in a convenient form.

Installation of Powerlooms : Government have a very difficult task of reconciling the various assurances given to the handloom industry (which is next only to agriculture in the matter of employment) on the one hand and the rather helpless situation in the matter of unauthorised growth of powerlooms, on the other.

While some measures of regulation over the growth

of powerlooms would be useful with a view to protecting the handlooms, having regard to past experience, there is no point in expecting such controls to be exercised by a Central Govermental agency like the Textile Commissioner.

Any measure of regulation that may be considered necessary to ensure the orderly growth of powerlooms and the manner of implementation thereof should be left to the discretion of the State Governments.

The question of issue of texmark by the Textile Commissioner should not arise hereafter.

After the additional locms for the Fourth Plan are allocated to the various States, the State Governments should take necessary measures for the attainment of the targets, allotted to each State.

With the delegation of authority to the State Governments, the guiding hand of the Textile Commissioner in the development of powerlooms in the small scale sector should not be removed. The Textile Commissioner should set general guidelines in respect of all aspects of the development of powerlooms. The State Governments should ensure that whatever information is required by the Textile Commissioner is made available to him. The Textile Commissioner should also be empowered to call for progress reports from the State Governments in regard to their development programmes of powerlooms.

Unless the present pattern of excise levy is radically changed, no amount of controls and regulations will restrict the haphazard growth of powerlooms. Only by a judicious combination of fiscal instruments and development policies will it be possible to make clandestine growth of powerlooms a thing of the past.

Controls And Regulations Designed To Protect The Decentralised Sector

The de-limitation of the fields of production to help the handloom industry introduced under the Textile Commissioner's Notification No. 9 (9)-Tex. I/49, dated 15th April, 1950, has stood the test of time and has helped the growth of the handloom industry. In order to make the control more easily enforceable and to prevent encroachment by powerlooms on areas reserved for handlooms, it is necessary that the existing reservations should be made exclusive in favour of the handloom industry and that the exemption from this order granted to small powerloom units having less than five looms should be withdrawn.

Assistance to handlooms and other weaker sections should be viewed as a long-term expenditure policy and should not perpetually be dovetailed to regulatory schemes.

The existing system of allocation of dhoty quota which was introduced with a view to protecting the handloom industry has out-lived its utility as the production of dhoties by the mills is far below the dhoty quota. The system of allocation of dhoty quotas should, therefore, be discontinued.

Should, however, a situation develop where production of dhoties by mills exceed the present quantum of the dhoty quota, the system of allocation of unit-wise quotas could be re-introduced.

The withdrawal of regulation on the packing of yarn in hank form as from Ist January, 1966 is a step in the right direction.

Having regard to the increased supply of yarn during the last few years, the following restrictions/obligations imposed under the Cotton Textiles (Control) Order on mills should be given up :

(i) **Clause 12(1)**—Placing restrictions on mills to sell in each quarter not less than 1/8 of the total quantity of yarn sold by it during the years 1949 and 1950 taken together.

(ii) **Clause 12(A)(1)**—Prohibiting mills from purchasing yarn except with the permission in writing of the Textile Commissioner.

(iii) **Clause 20C(B)**—Prohibiting composite mills from spinning yarn from cotton or cotton waste not owned by them.

(iv) **Clause 12(6B)**—Requiring mills to take the permission of the Textile Commissioner to effect any alteration or conversion of the reed space of looms.

The effective way of curbing the unnatural growth of the small powerlooms would be to remove the very wide differential in excise tariff as between powerlooms and mills by giving up the levy of excise duty at compounded rates and replacement of the same by transferring excise levy to yarn and to processing.

While fixing the actual rate of duty, the level of handicaps encountered by the powerlooms vis-a-vis mills in marketing the cloth should be taken into account.

Increased supply of yarn in hank form along with the present concessional duty on yarn in this form and the withdrawal of excise concession, enjoyed by powerloom units in the shape of compounded levy would create proper conditions for the healthy growth of the various sectors and particularly the survival of the handlooms.

The existing restrictions on the printing of cloth by mills may be removed and substituted by delimitation of fields of printing for hand-printers. As recommended by the All-India Handicrafts Board, printing of sarees with headings (border or pallou) or any bed spreads, bed covers and table covers with headings and borders should be reserved for the hand-printers.

A representative of the All-India Handicrafts Board should be included in the Cotton Textiles Advisory

Committee for ensuring the working of the restrictions and for its periodical review.

The existing restrictions imposed on composite mills under clause 20 C(a) of the Cotton Textiles (Control) Order, 1948 on processing of cloth or yarn not produced by them should be withdrawn.

Qualitative Control : The specifications relating to constructional particulars of cloth laid down in Schedule II annexed to the Textile Commissioner's Notification No. TCS. 1/20, dated 22nd September, 1949 are unnecessary as they by themselves do not ensure minimum durability of cloth, but only add to the administrative work in the Textile Commissioner's Office. The Schedule may accordingly be withdrawn in so far as non-controlled categories of cloth are concerned.

Sufficient flexibility may be provided to the industry to produce varieties of cloth to cater to an increasingly sophisticated market.

The efforts of the Textile Commissioner should hereafter be directed to promoting the setting up of Quality Control Departments in the various units of the mill industry.

It is presumed that the Textile Committee in furtherence of the objectives of the Textiles Committee Act, 1963 would take steps to ensure standards in the quality of textiles and also evolve a code of discipline to be observed by the members of the industry.

The constructional particulars of dhoties and sarees introduced under Schedule IIA, as part of the control mechanism, has out-lived its utility as deviations from the Schedule in as many as 286 cases were allowed There is, therefore, little justification for the retention of this Schedule.

Statutory Controls On Production And Prices

Controls on production and prices on mill-made cloth should not be perpetuated for ever, but should be subjected to review periodically, having regard to the availability of cotton and the supply position of cloth with a view to determining the feasibility of its withdrawal.

In view of the present low level of cloth stocks, representing only about a month's production, and the inadequate production of cotton to meet the increasing consumption by mills, controls over production and prices of cloth should continue for the time being.

Markings On Cloth and Yarn

Since under the provisions of the Trade and Merchandise Marks Act, stampings relating to the name of the manufacturer, length, width and the type of cloth by which it is commonly known, are to be compulsorily stamped on cloth prices, there is no need for mere or less identical marketings being prescribed by the Textile Commissioner, The stamping of 'tex-mark' on all categories of cloth pieces may be dispensed with.

There is no utility an insisting on merchant's trade number being stamped on cloth pieces.

There should be no compulsion on mills to stamp the month and year of packing in so far as non-controlled varieties of cloth are concerned. These markings may, however, continue in respect of controlled varieties.

The manufacturer's name and the description of yarn which are required to be stamped on yarn under the Trade and Merchandise Marks Act are considered adequate and hence the markings prescribed under the Cotton Textiles (Control) order may be removed.

For cloth and yarn bales, the existing markings may continue except that the manufacturer's name may be substituted for 'texmark' and the stamping of month and year of packing may be discontinued.

Textile Machinery

It is of the utmost importance that the organisation which is to be placed in charge of development of textile machinery manufacture should be a well integrated one in order that there may not be any short fall in the production of textile machinery.

The procedures relating to licensing of textile machinery manufacture should really help and not retard the growth of the industry. The most effective way of reducing delays is to create as few agencies as are absolutely necessary in processing of applications for licences, issue of capital goods and approval of foreign collaboration. The existence of a number of agencies dilutes responsibility at various levels with the result that no agency can singly be held responsible for the attainment of targets.

There has to be close coordination between the engineering industry which produces the capital goods and the user industry which actually instals and works them. Where feasible, it is most desirable that a single agency be made responsible for both.

While the idea of entrusting the responsibility for the development of the plant and machinery to one Directorate is unobjectionable there should not be a doctrinaire approach to this problem and in cases where specialised knowledge, apart from general engineering background, is required for the development of a particular sector of the engineering industry, it should not be insisted that the work should be looked upon as a part of the general engineering industry merely for the sake of ensuring uniformity.

In all these cases, the approach should be how best the particular line of the industry can be developed and not whether a uniform approach in so far as the engineering industries are concerned is necessary or not.

Where an engineering industry can be isolated from the Director General of Technical Development, having regard to the special requirements of the particular branch of the industry, there should be no hesitation to keep it as a separate entity and seek other means for ensuring coordination with the Director General of Technical Development.

The transfer of work to the D.G.T.D. would result, apart from increase in administrative expenditure, in delays and duplication of work.

The work relating to the development of the textile machinery manufacturing industry should continue to be dealt with by the Textile Commissioner.

There is force in the criticism that the Textile Commissioner's office does not have sufficient experienced staff to look after the development of textile machinery manufacture. This deficiency can and should be made good by posting a qualified mechanical engineer who has specialised in textile engineering. If a candidate is available in the organisation of the D.G.T.D., he should be drawn from the cadre of that organisation.

The Director General of Technical Development can play a very useful role in the licensing and development of textile machinery manufacture. He should be associated in the consideration of applications for licensing of textile machinery manufacture and also be represented at meetings of the local Capital Goods Committee (Bombay) whenever applications for machine tools are considered.

The remedial measures suggested by the Mathur, Study Team on the Directorate General of Technical Development on industrial licensing procedures could be applied to textile machinery cases with advantage.

The modified role visualised by the Mathur Study Team for Administrative Ministries, will in the case of applications for textile machinery manufacture, be applicable to the MEI section.

Consistent with recommendation 85, the D.G.T.D. should also be included in list of those to be consulted so far as textile machinery applications are concerned.

The recommendations of the Mathur Study Team in regard to handling procedures within the technical advice agency and in the Ministry of Industry may be adopted with advantage.

Within the Textile Commissioner's Office, the Textile Machinery Branch should not take more than 21 to 45 days to forward comments to the secretariate of the Licensing Committee.

The recommendations made by the Mathur Study Team to streamline procedures regarding import of capital goods should be followed here too.

The revised form of application suggested by the Mathur Study Team which would ensure that parties gave all the relevant necessary information for use of the D.G.T.D. and the Chief Controller of Imports-Exports in the very first instance and reduce the need for back references should be prescribed for use by imports of capital goods.

A time table for handling applications for import of capital goods within a range of 23 to 28 days upto the stage a brief is prepared for the Local Capital Goods Committee is recommended.

As suggested by the Study Team on the Import-Export Trade Control Organisation, the Textile Machinery Branch should obtain package clearances from the DGTD in respect of items falling under general engineering industries. Such a package clearance should be considered valid for a period of one year and should be obtained at the beginning of each licensing year.

A package list may still have a number of situations unprovided for and for these the presence of a representatives of the DGTD in the meetings of the Local CG Committee (recommendation 85) should prove useful. If case is taken to send papers to the representatives well in advance, he should be able to give his advice on the indigenous angle in the meeting itself.

In instances not covered by the package list and where the value of import is less than Rs. 5 lakhs, indigenous clearance will continue to have to be obtained from the D.G.T.D. through correspondence. The Development Directorate concerned in the D.G.T.D. should give the clearance within a period of 20 days.

There is no justification for keeping under central control an industry which legitimately should be the responsibility of the States. The responsibility for the development of sub-Rs. 25 lakh units engaged in the manufacture of textile machinery should accordingly be transferred to the State Governments.

It is not intended that with the above delegation to the State Governments, the Textile Commissioner should be divested of all responsibility in the matter of development of small and medium units. The Textile Commissioner should continue to be responsible for overall planning and development of the textile machinery industry.

In respect of the non-licensed sector going over to the States, the responsibility of the Textile Commissioner should be as under :

(i) Broadly, the Textile Commissioner's role vis-a-vis the non-licensed sector proposed for transfer to the States should be analogous so that of the Development Commissioner, Small Scale Industries vis-a-vis small industries already under the charge of State Governments;

(ii) The Textile Commissioner should keep himself informed through State Directors of Industries about essential facts relating to the development of the industry. For this, he may prescribe suitable returns which bring in information about the number of units, their capacity and production, etc.

(iii) He should be competent to issue guide lines to the State Directors of Industries on various aspects. In particular, he should bring out a brochure periodically giving particulars of textile machinery items for which creation of capacity may be encouraged. There should be a positive programme of documenting the expertise available in the Textile Commissioner's Office to the maximum extent possible, and making it available to prospective entrepreneurs in the non-licensed sector through the State Directors of Industries, small industries service institutes and other suitable channels;

(iv) The bulk allocation of foreign exchange to cover the requirements of raw materials and components of the non-licensed sector should come first to the Textile Commissioner who should them make State-wise allocations having regard to all relevant factors: In the States, the allocation should be treated as an earmarked one, not to be merged with the SSI allocation. This is necessary to ensure that the gratifying progress made in the development of this important industry is maintained even in the new arrangement.

(v) Cases of new units involving foreign collaboration should have to be cleared by State Directors of Industries with the Textile Commissioner;

(vi) So should cases of import of capital goods. Capital goods applications of this sector should be processed by the Textile Commissioner and the Local Capital Goods Committee on lines similar to procedures obtaining in the DC, SSI's organisation for Capital Goods requirements of small scale industries generally.

The responsibility for approving foreign collaboration terms for the manufacture of textile machinery in the non-licensed sector should rest with the Textile Commissioner and only in cases of doubt, need cases be referred to the Ministry of Industry.

There is need for the Textile Commissioner to reduce delays in the processing of foreign collaboration cases. Not more than 15 to 20 days should be taken by the Textile Commissioner in dealing with such cases after powers have been delegated to him.

While the enabling provisions regarding direction of sale should remain, the system of registration required under the Textile Machinery (Production and Distribution) Control Order, 1962 should be done away with.

Assistance Rendered By The Textile Commissioner To The Textile Industry In Securing Scarce Items Of Supply

Considering the very limited role of the Textile Commissioner in the allocation of coal and the relatively easy position of coal supplies, it is no longer necessary for Textile Commissioner to be burdened with this work.

The millowners' Associations of Ahmedabad and Indore are playing a very useful role in "pooling" available supplies of local in their areas. The system of "pooling" may be extended to other areas.

The Indian Cotton Mills' Federation may be asked to bulk the demands of the various coal consuming units and also prepare unitwise allocation on the advice of the various mill-owners' associations. Allotments to the units may be made by the Federation.

The targets for wagon requirements can be framed by the Railway Board itself after taking into consideration previous movements, the details of which can be obtained from the different railway stations. If necessary, the Railway Board may consult the Indian Cotton Mills' Federation, the starch manufacturers' association, the machinery manufacturers' association and the East India Cotton Association and secure necessary information.

In so far as streamlining the procedure for allocation of iron and steel items to the textile industry is concerned, the recommendations of the Khadilkar Committee may be awaited.

Review Of Statistical Forms And Returns

The report of the Sub-Committee appointed to review the forms and statistical returns submitted to the Textile Commissioner is reproduced at Annexure 8. The committee has recommended elimination of four monthly returns viz. PI, CC, 'D' and the returns on cloth earmarked for cooperative stores and fair price shops. The forms, where revised are given as appendices to the report.

There is need for introducing mechanisation for tabulation of data in the Textile Commissioner's office.

It is necessary to have a standing advisory body to review continually the various statistical returns submitted by the industry.

FILM ADVISORY COMMITTEE OF MEMBERS OF PARLIAMENT, 1965—REPORT

New Delhi, Directorate of Commercial Publicity, Ministry of Commerce, 1966. 16p.

Chairman : Shri Sham Lal Saraf.
Members : Shri Ravindra Verma; Shri Krishna Chandra Pant; Shri Rameshwar Tantia; Shrimati Tarabai R. Sathe; Shri Santokh Singh; Shri P. N. Kathju; Shri D. R. Khanna.
Secretary : Shri V. R. Rao.

APPOINTMENT

An Advisory Committee of Members of Parliament was set up by an Office Memorandum issued by the Government of India, in the Ministry of Commerce vide No. 30-Pub (3)/65 of May 20, 1965. This Committee was appointed following the acceptance of a suggestion of the Informal Consultative Committee of Parliament on Commerce, for production of documentary film aimed at educating the people regarding the vital importance of exports to the economy.

TERMS OF REFERENCE

The Committee was initially constituted for giving guidance in the preparation of a documentary film intended for arousing the export-consciousness in the country. On a request of the Committee, the scope of the term of reference was later enlarged so as to cover the production of documentary film both for internal and external publicity.

CONTENTS

Preamble; Terms of Reference; Composition of the Committee; Procedure Adopted by the Committee; Need for Export; Annexures I and II.

RECOMMENDATIONS

One of the chief characteristics of a developing country like India is that she must export in order to be able to import. The massive programme of economic development framed for the country calls for an increasing volume of imports of capital goods, basic industrial raw materials, inter-mediates and components needed by the developing industries as well as technical skill and know-how to be acquired from abroad for modernisation of our factories and mills, amortisation of loans, maintenance, defence preparedness, foodgrain imports. All these items can be paid for only in foreign exchange. It is therefore, imperative that we should step up our exports to the maximum extent possible.

The Nation has set before himself the goal of attaining a self-generating economy. It is a complex task and would require a multi-pronged attack at a variety of levels. It would require increase in production and productivity so that larger surpluses can be thrown up for exports. Secondly, it would mean the curtailment of domestic consumption in the short run to the barest minimum, because production cannot be stepped up overnight. Thirdly, it would require a vigorous drive to effect sales in foreign markets where demand requires stimulation and competition from rival countries is getting ever stiffer. Government or Trading Community alone cannot solve the problem. Every individuals has to lend a shoulder. In fact, the whole nation has to mobilise itself, otherwise our economic progress would slow down which would mean a failure on our part to keep the date with India's economic destiny.

The target of attaining the exports of Rs. 5,100 crores during the Fourth Plan period, i.e. reaching the figure of 1,100 crores by 1970-71 involves an increase of nearly 30 per cent over the period of five years. But fulfilment of even this moderate target has posed numerous problems like:

Generation of an adequate export surplus of saleable commodities at competitive prices;

Building up an export minded cadre of competent exporters for transforming the export surplus into actual foreign exchange earnings;

Setting up of a dynamic institutional framework for creating and sustaining the export effort at various level; and

Mobilisation of the demand for our goods in foreign markets;

In this connection, the Committee has noted that the Government has already taken a series of measures to facilitate expansion and flow of exports to overseas markets. The Committee is glad to observe that the institutional arrangements set up is something landable.

The most important among these Institutions is the Board of Trade, a high power advisory body with the Commerce Minister as its Chairman and members drawn from various sectors of the industry and trade as also other organizations connected with them. The Committee feels that representatives of States and important growers' interests should find great representation than now.

They are also of the view that the Board should arrange its meetings at important State Headquarters so that export consciousness may permeate to a greater depth than now.

There are already eighteen export promotion councils, seven commodity boards and five corporations. The export promotion councils cover a wide range of commodities including cotton textiles, basic chemicals, cashew, chemicals and allied products, engineering goods, finished leather and leather manufacturers, marine products, mica, plastics and linoleum, processed foods, shellac, silk and rayons, spices, sports goods, tobacco and woollens. They promote exports by disseminating information on various foreign markets, guiding new-comers in the export trade, assisting in the development of products and markets, sponsoring delegations abroad, arranging publicity and participation in trade fairs, etc. The seven commodity broards which cover commodities of tea, coffee, coir, handicrafts, handlooms, silk and rubber, deal with various aspects of export promotion including production and development. In addition, there are export promotion offices set up at Bombay, Calcutta, Madras, and Ernakulam which are assisted in their work by the Honorary Export Promotion Advisors drawn from the business and trade. At State Government levels there are the export liaison officers to energies the various State organisations in the task of export promotion. Over and above, there are Government Trading Corporations, viz. the State Trading Corporation, Minerals and Metals Trading Corporation, Hondicrafts and Handlooms Export Corporation, Indian Motion Pictures Export Corporation and Metals Scraps Trading Corporation. These have provided the essential base for developing and strengthening the effort relating to specific commodities and for reaching out to various regions of the world with those commodities. Certain commodities which would otherwise have languished in the exports, or on which adequate attention may not have been paid, have been picked up by these Government Trading Corporations for intensive export efforts.

The Committee is also pleased to note that the State Trading Corporation in its export promotion activities functions like a friend and a guide in finding out markets for commodities where the sales fall and the future sometime looks dark, dim and dismal. It fills up the missing links in the chain of exporting. Its major role is in respect of coordination of India's export trade with countries having Government controlled economies. It has been successful in introducing new items in foreign markets as well as new finding markets for existing items. The State Trading Corporation is also called upon to undertake price support or buffer stock operations where the prices register a considerable fall.

The Minerals and Metats Trading Corporation handles exclusively export import trade and minerals and metals specifically allotted to it. The important commodities handled by the Corporation are iron ore, manganese ore, ferro-manganese, banxite, illemnite chrome ore, coal, non-ferrous metals such as copper, zinc, lead, nickel, tin, steel, etc. The Corporation helps also the private sector in finding new markets for traditional as well as new items. It procures at reasonable prices and holds stocks in order to maintain production at optimum level of commodities which have high export potential.

Apart from the above institutions, the Government have set up the Indian Institute of Foreign Trade for training personnel engaged in the export trade. The Institute is now running training courses in international trade and conducts seminars on export problems as also disseminates specialised export information and export techniques. There is the Export Credit and Guarantee Corporation which covers various types of risks and facilitates the availability of finance for export. The Indian Council of Arbitration which has come into existence recently is designed to facilitate arbitration of commercial disputes arising in the course of export trade. To strengthen the visual publicity abroad and to supplement the activities of the Ministry in this regard, the Indian Council of Trade Fairs and Exhibitions has been set up.

Besides the above institutional arrangements, the Committee was apprised of various incentives given to exporters. Mention may be made, in particular, of the import entitlements under various export promotion schemes under which the exporters get import licences for raw materials, components, machinery and spares, drawback of excise and customs duties in respect of materials, which are supplied to them and which go into the making of export products, manufacture in bond, enlargement of facilities in respect of medium and short term credits, etc. Very recently, besides allowing rebate @ 1/10th of the amount of Income Tax and Super Tax attributable to income arising from export, further assistance in the form of tax credit certificates has been instituted. The rate of tax credit ranges from 2 to 15 per cent. The commodities falling under these are :

Goods made wholly or mainly for jute,
Jute carpet backing cloth,
Cashew kernels in consumer packing of 2 kgs or less,
De-oiled rice bran,
Green tea,

Tea (other than green tea) in consumer packing of 1 kg or less,

Tea n.o.s.,

Calcined magnesite,

Iron ore (raw washed or pelletised),

Lumpy iron ore originating from mines, the nearest loading point of which is not less than 200 kilometers away from the Customs Station (whatever the mode of transport used),

Coal,

Fresh fruits other than nuts,

Surgical cotton and surgical dressing,

Guar gum (refined pulverised or treated),

Guar splits,

Myrobalan extract,

Crushed bones,

Refractories,

Tiles of earthen-ware,

Manganese ore containing 48 per cent or less of manganese,

Ferro-manganese,

Alcoholic beverages,

Processed mica powder,

De-oiled extractions of groundnut oil cakes,

Coir ropes, coir mats and coir mattings,

All sorts of leather and leather goods (excluding raw hides and raw skins) and

Fresh vegetables.

The Committee also noted that facilities are accorded in respect of allocation of indigenous raw materials for manufactures meant for export, freight concessions, both on rail and ocean and of trade delegations.

In this fiercely competitive world market, we can sell only if our products are of high quality and design, and meet specific requirements, tastes, etc. of consumers in markets abroad. Quality, in this age of technological development is not the monopoly of a single nation. Unless our products are of high standard, we have no chance to sell. The Committee is gratified to observe that energetic measures are bring taken to ensure the quality of various Indian products and manufacturers. In this respect the work of the I.S.I. is commendable. This Institution has evolved about 3,000 standards covering a wide range of manufactures and other products. It has evolved a certification marks scheme covering about 350 export products. Under this scheme the importer abroad is assured of products which conform to internationally recognised standards. To ensure quality, it has instituted a system of inspection and checking in respect of the goods falling under Export Quality Marking scheme. This scheme is covering more and more of export items.

The recently set up Export Inspection Council of India has, since its inception in 1964, taken vigorous action to institute quality standards and a system of preshipment inspection schemes. The Committee was glad to note that now nearly 80 per cent of our exports are covered by these schemes of the Export Inspection Council.

We are also pleased to note that export publicity has in recent years gained momentum and is done with purposiveness. Our participation in international fairs and holding of wholly Indian fairs has also been increased.

What we notice is that the creation of export consciousness or awareness has not received such attention as it deserves. On account of our developmental needs our import policy has been very restrictive and the internal market has become practically a monopoly of Indian manufacturers. The pull of the home market is too heavy to facilitate exportation. Further as the standards of living and income are rising, there is the tendency to consume the rising national gross product. It is, therefore, necessary to edecuate the public about the urgent need to maximise export, although it may involve to some extent inconvenience and a slight hardship. Export consciousness has, therefore, to be created through publicity and propaganda through various media. Services of various voluntary social organizations like All India Women's Federation, Bharat Sevak Samaj, etc., can be profitably used. Wastage, particularly at consumer level, is to be eliminated. In this respect, the housewife can play a decisive role. That is the reason why the Committee would particularly recommend that the women's organizations, both at the Centre and State levels, may be profitably used. Seminars, symposiums, exhibitions, etc., can be arranged by these organizations, if necessary with financial assistance.

Press can powerfully influence the minds of the public. The Committee would recommend greater utilization of this media. Newspapers and journals with mass circulation, both in Hindi and regional languages, may be persuaded to bring supplements on exports so as to focus public attention. Folders and pamphlets written in easily understood local languages could be profitably employed. Apart from the press publicity or propaganda, medium of documentary films can have an abiding influence.

Initially the Committee was expected only to concern itself with the production of a documentary film for arousing export consciousness in the country, but in the first meeting itself, it was felt that production of films for external publicity is closely related to the creation of export consciousness. Accordingly the terms of reference were enlarged to cover both these aspects.

There are many factors which influence public opinion and harness their cooperation. A documentary merely exhorting people to abstain from consumption and to save for export will meet resistance. As mentioned earlier our consumption standards are very low and to ask people to forego even a portion of their meagre requirements would be resented. What we have to suggest is that out of every additional production that is achieved, a part should be set apart for capital formation. To raise the consumption standards of our people we have to increase out put of food and other crops, produce more cloth and produce more and more such other items which make life worth living drugs and medicines have to be produced, hospitals have to be constructed to keep the health. Therefore, we have to set up factories to manufacture fertilizers for our fields, cloth, medicines and other necessities of life. As we don't have the necessary technical khow-how and machinery we will have to import. So the documentary films should start with the presentation of fields where better techniques of production are employed, yields are higher and factories producing host of other consumers items. Hospitals, educational institutions and others should also be presented. All these, the commentary should indicate, require the import of machinery, scarce raw materials, technical know-how, etc. This would bring in the topic of selling. We can show here the usual life of a rural family ; how he exchanges his produce with what he needs from others. The documentary should emphasis here that this is a corollary of exchange economy, be it on family level, village level or national level. From here we have to indicate what products we can export. But we cannot sell whatever we want to export unless they are required abroad. Therefore, the documentaries should cover the items that are exported or can be exported. In this connection the Committee has drawn up a list of items that are being exported or have export potential and can be covered by documentaries. The documentary will also have to indicate the various measures, institutional and otherwise, which the Government have taken to facilitate exporting. The documentary may also highlight the role of such institutions as Export Promotion Councils, Commodity Boards, State Trading Corporation, etc., and indicate how they can be helpful to exporters or would-be exporters. In respect of some items which can be exported like sugar, bananas, the documentary should highlight the need and a little hardships that their export would cause to the consumers in the country. Care has to be taken to see that all these things are hinted indirectly and it does not sound like mere Government propaganda. The documentary should also cover the following :

(i) Besides what has already been said, some shots of prominent officials, non-officials and leaders' views, speeches, etc. at various meetings and conferences.

(ii) How quality control has been introduced and standards for quality laid ("I.S.I." etc.)

(iii) Transport facilities for moving export products in bulk like ores, tea, jute, etc. by rivers, trucks, railways and sea.

(iv) Institutional arrangements such as Commodity Boards, Exports Promotion Councils, Corporations, etc.

(v) Channels of exports (both through State-owned organizations like S.T.C. and private trade).

(vi) Credit facilities to exporters.

(vii) Assistance given to exporters, and other measures taken for arousing export consciousness.

(viii) Role of India Government's Commercial Representatives abroad in promoting export trade.

(ix) Coverage of foreign families living in India, using Indian goods for their decoration, etc.

The Committee feels that a single documentary may not be adequate to cover all the aspects indicated above. There is the need, therefore, to have a number of documentaries on "Why Export", "What to Export", "How to Export", etc. And these documentaries should be of two kinds, viz., (i) Meant for appeal to the general public ; and (ii) Meant for special audience like potential exporters, chambers of commerce, trade organisations, etc.

In regard to documentary films for exhibitions abroad, the Committee had the benefit of viewing a number of documentaries produced by the Films Division at the instance of the Commerce Ministry. The Committee had also the benefit of discussions with the producer-in-chief of the Films Division, Bombay, and the Principal of the Films Institute, Poona. The Committee is of the view that documentaries for export promotion can also be usefully divided in the abovementioned two categories, viz., (i) Films for being shown to general audience ; and (ii) Films for being shown to specialised audience. After due consideration the following suggestions as guiding rules for production of export promotion films are made :

(1) Each film should be tailor-made to suit the specific requirements of the audiences for whom it is intended.

(2) Each film as far as possible, should be based on one single idea which would be properly developed. Any attempt to put too many ideas in one film reduces the usefulness of the film and dilutes its impact.

(3) Some sequences in a film could be profitably shot in foreign countries to show how Indian products are utilised in foreign homes and how they are available in foreign countries.

(4) To much of commentary should be avoided.

(5) Techniques of high pressure salesmanship should be avoided.

(6) Quality of products should not be praised in hyperbolic terms.

(7) For export promotion the films should be indirect, unobstructive and modest in claims for our products.

(8) Commentary of documentaries, as far as possible, should be got vetted and records in countries in which they are to be exhibited.

In the production of documentaries for exhibition abroad, the officers in the Commerce Ministry connected with the production of documentaries for publicity in overseas markets as well as the officials of the Films Division should have adequate knowledge of the trends and the requirements of publicity films. A first hand knowledge of some of the foreign countries abroad where this technique of publicity is developed is necessary. We recommend that two or three officials drawn from the Commerce Ministry and the Films Division may be deputed to go abroad on a study tour.

In any programme of export publicity in overseas countries we cannot be content with only one medium. All media should be utilised in a coordinated and integrated manner if publicity is to have any impact.

In regard to our Commercial Representatives abroad, the Committee is of the view that in these days of specialisation, a separate cader to man commercial posts should be drawn up. The personnel should be well conversant with the business practices in India and abroad and should have good understanding of the export problems of their country. This would enable them to play mere effective role in promotion of the country's exports.

To create necessary climate and impact, publicity including publicity through documentary films should have the necessary slant. We feel that a Standing Advisory Committee should be constituted to give general guidance in the formulation of Programmes. In the Standing Advisory Committee the Members of Parliament may also be associated.

The Committee would like to emphasize the aspect of Research which is as important in this field as elsewhere. The Committee had the benefit of visiting the Film Institute of India at Poona and observe its working. At our instance a proposal for research study on films for export promotion has been prepared by the Principal of the Institute. An analytical study of the film medium from the point of view of other methods used in sales promotion is necessary. This is so because the medium of films has its own artistic characteristics. A good film must follow the artistic logic of the medium. The film maker has to adopt and express the idea put forth by the Sponsoring Departments while making the film. Therefore, it is necessary to make an analytical study of the documentaries and public relation films of other countries. This research work should be in our view handled by the Film Institute at Poona.

ADVISORY COMMITTEE ON THE REVISION OF THE LISTS OF SCHEDULED CASTE AND SCHEDULED TRIBES, 1965—REPORT

New Delhi, Department of Social Security, 1967. 116p.

Chairman : Shri B. N Lokur.
Member : Shri A. D. Pande.
Secretary : Shri N. Sundaram.

APPOINTMENT

The Government of India have had under consideration for some time the question of revising the lists of Scheduled Castes and Scheduled Tribes. The present lists do not show a uniform pattern and several anamolies have been brought to notice. It is, therefore, very necessary that the lists of Scheduled Castes and Scheduled Tribes should be revised in a rational and scientific manner.

Proposals for revision of the lists have been received from various States and Union Territories. A preliminary examination of these proposals has been completed and it has been found that there are several controversial issues which require to be settled. The Government of India have therefore, decided to set up an Advisory Committee on the Revision of lists of Scheduled Castes and Scheduled Tribes Vide its Resolution No. F. 12/3/65-SCT. IV, dated June 1, 1965.

TERMS OF REFERENCE

(1) To advise on the proposals received by Government for revision of the existing lists of Scheduled

Castes and Scheduled Tribes.

(2) To advise whether, where caste or a tribe is listed as a Scheduled Caste or a Scheduled Tribe in relation to a particular area in a State or a Union Territory, members of that caste or tribe residing :

(i) In other areas within the same State or Union Territory; or

(ii) In other States or Union Territories, should be recognised as belonging to the Scheduled Caste or Scheduled Tribe, as the case may be.

CONTENTS

Part I : Introduction; Principle and Policy; Revision of Lists; General Recommendations; Appreciation; **Part II** : Appendices I to VII.

RECOMMENDATIONS

In revising the lists of Scheduled Castes and Scheduled Tribes, we have excluded some Castes and Tribes. These excluded Castes and Tribes are already enjoying certain educational, economic and other developmental benefits. We are of the view that they should not be deprived of these benefits abruptly; in particular, we consider that members of these castes and tribes who are participating in scholarship schemes should not be suddenly denied their scholarship benefits, thereby compelling them to give up their education. We would recommend that the benefits enjoyed by the excluded castes and tribes should be gradually withdrawn in a phased manner.

There are some communities which, though not strictly eligible to be treated as Scheduled Castes and Scheduled Tribes, deserve special assistance. It would not be sufficient to treat them merely as "Other Backward Classes" as they require larger aid than is provided to Other Backward Classes. The communities which we have in mind are the Gujjar, Gaddi and Banjara communities.

In the course of the revision of the lists, we have at times adopted local names and synonyms and altered the spelling of some castes and tribes. These nominal changes should affect continuation of privileges and benefits to those castes and tribes subject to such changes. It would be for the State Governments to ensure that the castes and tribes whose names are altered in the revised list are not denied the benefits they were previously entitled to. The State Governments should be advised to issue necessary instructions to the appropriate authorities.

We have advised that where a caste or tribe is mentioned in the lists by its generic name, it should be deemed to include all its synonyms, phonetic variations, sub-castes or sub-tribes, as the case may be. We have, no doubt, enumerated in some cases the sub-castes and sub tribes but such an enumeration is imperfect and is not exhaustive for want of complete data. The State Governments should collect the necessary information and try to prepare a comprehensive list of sub-castes and sub-tribes and give such lists a wide publicity. Such lists are necessary for the guidance of local officials and non-officials authorised to issue caste and tribe certificates; they will also prove very useful for the proper enumeration of sub-groups of the Scheduled Castes and the Scheduled Tribes at the next Census.

As has been pointed out in an earlier chapter, it is imperative that the more advanced communities in the lists are gradually descheduled. To accelerate the pace of descheduling, a dead-line may perhaps be fixed when the lists of Scheduled Castes and Tribes are totally dispensed with. In our opinion, it is only by such a process that we can bring about complete integration of the population. In order to weedout the advanced castes and tribes from the lists in time to come, it is necessary that an intensive survey be undertaken to ascertain the social, educational and economic progress made by each of the Scheduled Castes and Scheduled Tribes from time to time. The task will, no doubt, be stupendous and expensive but it is only through such periodic surveys, that the results of the various development schemes can be correctly ascertained. We would suggest, in this connection, that the possibility of the Census and National Sample Surveys authorities assisting in this task may be explored. Incidently, the Census authorities might, as we have done, endeavour to record and refer to the castes and tribes by name by which they are commonly and locally known in their respective areas. Nomenclature such as 'Bison Horn Madia' adopted by anthropologists and outsiders is now out of place, and expressions like 'Chandala' are terms of contempt which might well be dispensed with.

COMMITTEE ON THE INDIAN FOREIGN SERVICE, 1965—REPORT

New Delhi, Ministry of External Affairs, 1966. 157p.

Chairman : Shri N. R. Pillai.
Members : Shri C. S. Jha; Shri L. P. Singh; Shri D. S. Joshi; Shri Azim Husain.
Secretary : Shri N. Krishnan.

APPOINTMENT

The Government of India consider it desirable that a Committee be appointed to review the organisation and working of the Indian Foreign Service in the light of the experience gained since its inception and the changes that have taken place in India and in the world during this period. The object of such a review should be to bring about an improvement in the efficiency of the Foreign Service and in the working of Indian Missions abroad so as to make the Foreign Service better, able to meet present and future needs of India's foreign policy and diplomatic representation abroad, through a Press Note issued by the Ministry of External Affairs on June 15, 1965.

TERMS OF REFERENCE

"To review the structure and organisation of the Indian Foreign Service, with particular reference to recruitment, training and service conditions, and to consider any other matters conducive to the strengthening and efficient functioning of the service at Headquarters and abroad, and make recommendations to Government".

CONTENTS

Introduction; Evolution of the Indian Foreign Service; The Role of the Foreign Service in a Changing World; The Ministry of External Affairs; A Unified Foreign Service; Personnel Problems and Tasks; External Publicity; Recruitment; Training; I.F.S. (B), Conditions of Service; Conclusion; Annexure A to E and Tables I to XII.

RECOMMENDATIONS

The Role Of The Foreign Service In A Changing World

In the context of the changes in the international scene and the growing commitments of India abroad, the role of Foreign Service will become increasingly important, its tasks will become much more exacting, especially in the promotion of our trade. The Foreign Service should be made an effective instrument for attaining our foreign policy goals.

It will be prudent to plan for an expansion in our representation abroad and in the cadre and resources of the Foreign Service.

The Ministry Of External Affairs

The primary responsibility for the conduct of foreign relations vests in the Ministry of External Affairs. Relations of other Ministries with foreign Governments should be co-ordinated by the Ministry of External Affairs. The Ministry should develop adequate, competence within itself and effective inter-departmental liaison for discharging this responsibility.

The Ministry should be headed at the official level by an officer who can help in the pursuit of an integrated policy and speak with authority for the Ministry as a whole. A post with the designation of Secretary-General (or other appropriate designation) should be created for this purpose.

Purposive planning is today indispensable for the conduct of foreign relations. The Policy Planning and Review Committee should be made a permanent body under the chairmanship of the Secretary-General; and the Policy Planning Division strengthened with the necessary research staff.

Work should be distributed evenly among the Secretaries without burdening the Secretary-General with too much departmental work. Heads of Divisions should preferably be Joint Secretaries. Desk Officers should not be burdened with too large an area. The officer-oriented staffing pattern should be extended to cover all divisions. The Secretaries should have more time to devote to higher policy matters; there should be greater delegation of responsibility to Heads of Divisions.

Sharing, vertical and lateral, of information and views among all the divisions is essential. A new Division for Parliamentary work and co-ordination should be set up. Communication between the Ministry and Missions should be efficient. A network of two-way telex communication with Missions should be established. Personnel contacts with and among representatives abroad should be encouraged through more regional conferences.

The Ministry should discuss with the Ministry of Finance the methods by which budgeting arrangements could be improved and greater powers of reappropriation and spending within its budget grant given to it. Greater delegation of powers within the IFS Rules to the Ministry as well as to the missions is desirable; administrative procedures should be simplified. A Pay and Accounts Office should take over the accounts of the Ministry and missions abroad.

Administration should be in charge of a full-time Additional Secretary. A permanent Inspectorate in charge of a Joint Secretary should inspect all missions. An efficiency assessment of the mission's performances may also be made by Secretaries when possible.

A trained officer should be appointed to modernise filing procedures and systems and for weeding-out records. The Ministry should have proper accommodation of its own and reallocation of accommodation in South Block should be speeded up.

Research Officers should be given occasional foreign assignments; IFS Officers may also be used for research work. Pay scales and related matters of Research Officers should be examined. The Historical Division should be called the Research and Reference Division.

The Legal and Treaties Division should remain an autonomous but integral part of the Ministry; the personnel of the Division should remain distinict from the Foreign Service. Pay scales of Legal Officers may be reviewed to the extent necessary. An outstanding Research Officer or Legal Officer may occasionally be taken into IFS.

A Unified Foreign Service : Personnel Problems And Tasks

Diplomatic work forms the base for all functional tasks of the Foreign Service. The danger of over-zealousness should be guarded against; faith in the Government's policies is essential; these principles are well understood in the Foreign Service. Any tendency towards self-righteousness or timidity can be corrected by training. The representative should always be kept fully informed of all developments and current thinking in the Government.

Representational activity is not confined to one method or medium. Entertainment is of much value to the diplomatist in his work; facilities offered for this purpose should be fully adequate. Entertainment offered must be of good quality and well regulated to cover contacts over a wide range. Present system of individual representational grants for each officer should continue. A lump sum grant should be sanctioned for entertainment at restaurants.

Economic and commercial work forms an indivisible part of Foreign Service work and should be handled by officers of a single IFS cadre. Recruitment of personnel from Industry and Commerce except through the regular machinery of over-age entry is not advisable. There should be greater awareness within the IFS of the importance of this branch of its work. Preparation of officers for this work needs greater attention. A few officers may be assigned to the Central Economic Pool as associate members. A substantial increase in the officer resources devoted to commercial work abroad is necessary. Prompt transmission of economic and commercial information to missions should be coordinated by the Economic Division. Commercial Officers should concern themselves more with promotional activities.

Information work can and should be done by Foreign Service officers themselves. Expertise for this puspose should be developed within the IFS through career planning and training. Every Foreign Service officer abroad should be public relations conscious.

Consular instructions need to be reviewed. The standard of courtesy of missions in dealing with the public should be improved. Indian residents and visitors should be given all assistance permissible under the rules. Missions should take greater interest in Indian students abroad.

Ability and suitability should be the preponderant factors in Goverement promotions to selection grades; practice in this regard needs to be brought into line with policy enunciated in the Rules. Impartiality and objectivity should govern all assessments for promotion. The character rolls must be maintained up-to-date and reporting tightened up. The powers of review for premature retirement should be fully exercised.

Selection of Officers for work at headquarters and for different assignments abroad should be more carefully made. A Head of Mission should be chosen with due regard to his capacity and fitness for the post.

A frequent return to India on a home posting is necessary for renewal of contact with the country. Opportunities for this can be increased by posting IFS officers to other Ministries of the Government of India in exchange for IAS and other officers for service under the Ministry of External Affairs. Such cross postings will benefit the Administration. Bharat Darshan tours and contact with universities will be useful.

A knowledge of language is essential in the Foreign Service. Planned development and utilisation of language ability in the IFS needs improvement. The Ministry should concentrate first, on the major languages. Lump sum rewards for requalification is compulsory and optional languages will encourage language proficiency.

Specialisation in different fields should be developed within the Service without impairing the versatility of its members. Special allowance should be paid to officers who have to serve on difficult posts.

There is need for planned career development of

every officer. Planning should be flexible and take preferences of officers into account. Present classification of stations and strict rotation of officers among them should be abandoned. Normal term of duty should be four years except at difficult posts where it will be three years; term of duty should be a flexible norm and not fetter the Ministry's discretion to retain officers, especially on the commercial and information sides, for longer periods.

External Publicity

Long-term publicity is concerned with the projection abroad of a proper image of India. Current publicity seeks to explain and gain acceptance for our foreign policy objectives and actions.

Conduct of external publicity should remain with the Ministry of External Affairs. There should be close collaboration with the Ministry of Information and Broadcasting and effective day-to-day coordination.

The Joint Secretary incharge of publicity should not be burdened with other duties. Within existing limitations missions abroad are kept well informed, teleprinter link with them should, however, be further extended. Forward planning of publicity is essential. Publicity should be oriented to the needs of different areas; Information Officer should work within the territorial division while remaining under the over-all control of X.P. Division. The official spokesman should have greater authority and discretion and be brought into closer association with policy-making organs. Adequate briefing and continuous guidance of foreign as well as Indian correspondents are essential.

Success of publicity abroad will depend on the attitude and interest of the Head of Mission himself. Information Officers should concentrate on effective public relations; they should know the local language; funds for touring and entertainment should be adequate; assistance of Junior Officers should be provided in more important missions. The tenure of successful Information Officers may be extended to five years or even longer. Publicity units should be opened in another 20 missions in a phased manner.

Material for inclusion in news bulletins should be carefully chosen and sent from headquarters in a finished form. Greater selectivity and promptness in despatch of features and photographs is desirable. X. P. Division as well as publicity units should have more modern facilities for transcription and mailing. The production of pamphlets and brochures should be planned in advance; more attention should be given to quality and needs of different areas; material in foreign languages should be produced abroad; a panel of good script writers should be maintained; all these improvements will cost more money.

Documentary films and film strips exclusively designed for external publicity should be produced according to a planned programme; all films should carry commentaries in major languages. X. P. Division should bear full cost of this programme; an officer of the Division may be stationed in Bombay for achieving closer liaison with the Films Division.

The use of the External Services of All India Radio for furthering our foreign policy objectives has been neglected; weak transmitters and indifferent programme policies have greatly affected its impact. The Ministry of External Affairs should be responsible for deciding the number, duration and content of the services and allocate funds from its own budget. The appointment on deputation of an IFS Officer to take charge of External Services will encourage greater co-ordination.

Publicity agencies should be used when circumstances justify the extra cost. Libraries should be better maintained.

While information work abroad will normally be done by members of the Foreign Service, a professional expert may be appointed in exceptional cases. The indefinite continuance of a separate group of officers doing information work is not desirable; therefore, as many as are found suitable should be taken into the IFS and the rest given the option of being absorbed in the IAS.

More effective performance in publicity cannot be attained without more expenditure.

Recruitment

Recruitment through the competitive examination held by the UPSC ensures a fair and representative selection. Higher Services under the Government do not have the same degree of attractiveness today as in the past. Notwithstanding the progressive increase in recruitment, the quality of recruits to the IFS is being maintained. The present method of recruitment is the best for securing officer material for the IFS. Proposal for defferred recruitment to IFS through IAS is not desirable. Marriage is not the main reason for the wastage of women officers; an effort may be made to transfer married women officers, when necessary, to the IAS on an exchange basis.

In addition to the inclusion of "International Organisations and Relations" among the optional subjects for the examination an advanced paper on International Law may be included among the additional subjects. Languages are already included among the optional subjects and need not be made compulsory. An assessment of personality is essential for the selection of candidates for the IFS; the marks for the Personality Test should be retained at 400. There is no case for the revival of the qualifying minimum.

Taking the requirements of the future and other factors into account, an expansion of the IFS cadre to about 550 over the next ten years would appear necessary. This would necessitate recruitment through the examination of 15 per annum during the next three years and more thereafter.

Recruits drawn through the examinations will form the predominant element in the service; the service can, however, be strengthened by the induction of men with special qualifications through over-age entry; an average of two to three per annum may be taken after 1968 from candidates with high qualifications between the ages of 28—35.

Officers of the IAS and other Services may be borrowed to the extent necessary until the IFS cadre has expanded sufficiently. Officers should be drawn from other Departments for doing specialised work distinguishable from the normal work of the Foreign Service. When the work-load justifies it, they should be under the discipline of the Ministry of External Affairs.

Training

Initial training includes training and preparation of the officers for life and representational work abroad. A total period of training not exceeding two years would be the ideal. A Directorate under a Joint Secretary should be set up for giving undivided attention to training.

An IFS Officer should be attached to the directing staff of the National Academy to provide for closer liaison. A grounding in Indian history and culture should be provided during this period. Training in the districts should come soon after recruitment, District Officers should be well chosen and the programme carefully worked out. Training at the School of International Studies is important; the Directorate of Training should seek to utilise facilities available in other agencies and institutions also.

Training in the Ministry of External Affairs should have a practical orientation and be conducted under the guidance of the Directorate of Training. A good grounding in economic and commercial matters should be given. Special attention to publicity and public relations work is also necessary. Language training should preferably be given in India itself. The Ministry of External Affairs should take the initiative for the setting up of an Institute of Foreign Languages. Attachment to an Armed Forces Unit and Bharat Darshan Tour should be retained. On his first posting abroad the officer should be made a functioning member of the Mission; the Head of Mission should take personal interest in his development.

Progress during probation should be carefully watched and remedial action taken when necessary. The officer should be brought back to headquarters after two years 'service abroad. This will enable the Ministry to assess as well as guide the development of the officer during his first six years' service.

Officers going to a new area or new functions should receive some pre-post training; wives going abroad for the first time should get some orientation.

Mid-carrer training should receive much greater attention; attachments to orientation courses, seminars, etc., and sabbatical leave should be encouraged; the deputation reserve should be increased from 10 per cent to 15 per cent to facilitate the release of officers for these purposes.

A reform in the composition of the IFS(B) is necessary, an increase in the officer grades being balanced by a reduction in staff in lower grades; such re-adjustment should be achieved over a period through a reduction in fresh recruitment, so that there is no need for retrenchment of any personnel. The IFS(B) should remain one single service at present. General parity in scales with the C.S.S. may continue. The UDC's grade should remain but the strength may be adjusted to achieve a better balance with that in the LDC's grade.

No modification of the present system of recruitment of Clerks and Assistants is necessary. Fitness for Foreign Service may be assessed through a brief interview of the top few successful candidates before appointments are made. A limited competitive examination for the Assistants' grade is not recommended.

The quota for promotion from IFS(B) into the IFS should be raised from 10 per cent to 15 per cent. Selection should be made on merit from amongst officers in Grade I with three years' service. A Selection Grade above Grade I should be introduced.

Training of members of the IFS (B) should be given greater attention than hitherto. Mid-career orientation is particularly significant for promoted officers; the Directorate of Training should assume responsibility for this.

A few language officers should be trained from among staff members. Language training of direct recruits to the Attache's grade should be better organised. Lump sum rewards should be available to IFS(B) Officers in the higher grades.

Conditions Of Service

An early review of the formulae for determining foreign allowances is necessary. All missions should be inspected once every three years. Machinery for revision of allowances between inspections needs to be improved. The quantum of domestic help for representational officers should be standardised and standard wages for Indian servants reviewed.

Facilities for part-drawal of emoluments in a convertible currency should be liberalised.

Home leave should be granted regularly to officers; conditions regulating travel of servants should be reviewed. One additional special return air passage for coming urgently to home should be available during the entire service of the officer.

A special arrangement with selected schools in the country for admission of children of Foreign Service Officers should be made. Children's Education Allowance should be raised. Conditions affecting the utilisation of the concession of Children's Holday Passages should be liberalised; the upper-age limit should be raised from 18 to 20.

A special monthly allowance at a fixed rate should be paid to officers serving at "hard" stations.

The Ministry of External Affairs and the Head of Mission should have more delegated authority in applying rules relating to medical assistance abroad. Proposals for liberalisation already approved in principle should be implemented.

The rules of concessions relating to the handling of heavy baggage, transfer grant, etc. should be reviewed consequent on compulsory travel by air. Ceilings for transport of baggage allowed to senior officers should be reviewed.

The adequacy of the outfit allowance may be reviewed.

Parity in time scales and grades between the IFS and IAS should continue.

We are aware that many of these recommendations involve considerable increase in expenditure, including expenditure in terms of foreign exchange, and that their implementation may have to be spread over a period in view of the present financial position and the need for the utmost economy in Government expenditure. We have thought it our duty, nevertheless to propose measures which we consider to be necessary if the Foreign Service is to function effectively and to carry out responsibilities assigned to it.

TASAR SILK COMMITTEE, 1965—REPORT

New Delhi, Ministry of Commerce, 1966. 103p.+9 maps.
(Report on Tasar Silk Industry in India)

Chairman : Shri R.V. Ramaswamy.
Members : Shri T. S. Pattabhiraman; Smt. Jahanara Jaipal Singh; Shri Bhagwat Jha Azad; Shri Sham Lal Sarf; Shri H.C. Soy; Shri A. N. Ramachandran.
Secretary : Shri S.R. Ullal.

APPOINTMENT

Government of India, vide Ministry of Commerce Resolution No. 59(1)/65-Tex(G), dated June 16, 1965 set up a Committee to investigate into the question of developing further the production of Tasar Silk which has a great export potential and to review the working of the Tasar Industry.

TERMS OF REFERENCE

(a) To review the working of the existing schemes for the development of Tasar Industry in the States of Bihar, Madhya Pradesh and Orissa and to make a report on the working of all these schemes including : (i) the supply of tasar silkworm seeds ; (ii) running of tasar seed supply stations and sub-stations ; and (iii) other technical and administrative matters including reorganisation of existing schemes and introduction of necessary new schemes.

(b) To examine and recommend the further measures that may be needed for the speedy development of the Tasar Industry to meet the increasing export demand.

The Central Silk Board, vide its letter No. CSB/TS/65/890, dated July 19, 1965 had requested the Committee to include the following within the scope of its studies :

(c) Fixation of floor price for Tasar cocoons.

(d) Examine the proposal of the Government of Madhya Pradesh to set up urgently a Corporation under the conjoint auspices of the Central Silk Board and the Tasar States of Bihar, Madhya Pradesh and Orissa.

CONTENTS

Constitution of the Tasar Silk Committee ; Mode of Inquiry ; Global Distribution of Tasar Silk Industry and Its Position in India ; Development of Tasar Industry through Plants ; Recommendations for Future Development ; Appendices I to V.

RECOMMENDATIONS

The People's Republic of China is by far the largest producer of Tasar Silk in the world—accounting as she does for more than 90 pre cent of the global output of Tasar Silk.

Besides being used as a textile fibre, Tasar is reportedly in demand in China for ammunition bags, parachutes, acid-proof work, clothes and equipment. It is also being used extensively in the manufacture of flexible cords and tyres. In Japan the use of Tasar Silk was mainly mixed with ordinary mulberry silk for the manufacture of neckties, obis (scarves), crepe-de-chine and luxurious apparel.

Next only to Chinese Tasar, Indian Tasar occupies a position of prominence in the tasar map of the world.

Antheraea mylitta is by far the most important commercial producer of Tasar Silk in India.

The Tasar Silkworms of India are polyphagous and feed on a variety of food plants.

Tasar industry is mainly concentrated in Bihar, Madhya Pradesh and Orissa.

There are about a lakh of Tasar Silk in India in 1964 was 2.24 lakhs of kgs.

India produced 1.47 lakhs of Kgs of tasar silk waste in 1964.

The only attention bestowed on the silkworms is at the time of preparation of eggs, transference of larvae from tree to tree to ensure adequate feed and at the harvest of cocoons. It is this peculiar feature of tasar culture which exposes the tasar worms to the vagaries of weather and natural enemies and introduces an element of uncertainty in harvests. This is one of the weak spots of the industry which calls for our attention.

The departmental supplies of disease-free eggs being rather limited, seed procurement becomes an exercise which calls for considerable experience and traditional skill in selection.

It is the general experience among the tasar rearers that cocoons raised on sal trees (shorea robusta) are the best.

Controlled mating of moths does introduce the element of inbreeding depression and there appears to be a fear among the tribal rearers that the departmental seed does not give stable crops.

The most appropriate time to collect cocoons is about 7 days after spinning. The preferable time for collection of cocoons is 8-10 a.m. and after 3 p.m.

Tasar rearing is a precarious calling, the success of which depends, to a large extent, on the vagaries of weather during the progress of rearings.

The marginal returns that the industry provides are too meagre to tempt men of moderate means into this avocation. The harvests normally range from 2 to and a half Kahans of cocoons per rearer.

The 'Mahajan' with his capacity for ready credit to the ever needy tribal rearer exerts a strangle hold on the cocoons producer by advancing moneys and binding the searers to sell the produce at greatly unremunerative prices. This institution of 'Mahajans' has been menacing the orderly progress of this poor man's industry for decades.

In the opinion of the Committee, marketing is the weakest link in the tasar industry as organised at present and deserves the most immediate attention of the State and Central Governments.

Tasar culture—an unknown tribal craft has of late acquired the status of an export industry earning valuable foreign exchange for the country.

The U.S.A. has been accounting for nearly 75 percent of our total exports of tasar fabrics.

The setback in export performance (latter half of 1965) is rather disturbing and merits careful consideration of the State and Central Governments so that further deterioration could be effectively stemmed by timely adoption of palliative measures.

The fall in exports in recent months had led to the manifestation of distinctly bearish tendencies in the tasar markets.

The quantity of tasar fabrics produced in India in 1964 could be estimated at 24 lakhs of metres.

The annual average of tasar silk fabrics exported during the past three years will work out to 5.63 lakhs of metres.

The exports have accounted for less than 25 per cent of the total output of tasar fabrics in the country during the past three years when the exports were at their peak levels.

If the tasar prices are to be stabilised, tasar exports should be maintained, the exports might reach a figure of 10 lakhs of metres at the end of 1970 to earn a foreign exchange of Rs. 120 to Rs. 130 lakhs at the most.

The main bottleneck in the export supplies is limitation stemming from the handloom pattern of production.

One of the causes for the set-back in tasar exports in 1962 was the export of sub-standard fabrics which to a considerable extent shattered the confidence of importers abroad.

It anything there is a case for progressive reduction in the flexibility of this scheme (Preshipment Quality Inspection Scheme) so that exports of tasar fabrics of poor quality might be effectively curbed.

During the First Five Year Plan, the Central Silk Board has approved only 9 schemes for development of tasar silk industry and had sanctioned a Central Assistance amounting to Rs. 2.74 lakhs.

During the Second Five Year Plan, 35 schemes involving a Central Assistance of Rs. 28.65 lakhs were approved. The expenditure was Rs. 17.63 lakhs.

A perusal of the schemes under implementation during the Second Five Year Plan reveals that the accent was mainly on generating increased capacity to meet the seed requirements. But the fact remains that the host plant sector was totally neglected despite clear recommendations of the I Working Group as also the Non-mulberry Sub-Committee. This is rather disappointing.

The actual provision for development of tasar industry alone during the Third Five Year Plan was Rs. 90.53 lakhs.

Bihar has not drawn up any scheme even during the Third Plan for tackling the host-plant requirement of tasar rearings.

On the basis of the production of 1,13,000 Kahans of cocoons in 1965, the total requirement of dfls, for the State (Bihar) could be estimated at 28.25 lakhs. Against this the production is 3.67 lakhs of dfls. (13 per cent) which cannot be deemed satisfactory.

The period of training (in the Training-cum-Production Centres) could be considerably reduced from its present duration of 6 months to 3 months. These centres should also be completely peripatetic.

By and large the cooperatives in Bihar have proved a failure. The Committee is of the view that the Department should revitalise the societies and expand their scope of utility.

The impact of the State's (Bihar) scheme to tackle the problems of marketing has been negligible.

There is no cooperative organisation in the State (Madhya Pradesh) to tackle the marketing aspect. Instead six Government markets have been established.

The apex society is assuring the rearers a reasonable return disease-free layings (Orissa).

The apex society is assuring the rearers a reasonable return by giving them a stable price fixed in a meeting of the representatives of primary and apex societies.

West Bengal ranks fourth among the tasar producing States in India.

It is not quite clear why the Department is not utilising its full capacity for production of seed which is reported to be very popular with the rearers (West Bengal).

There is considerable potential for tasar production in Andhra Pradesh in districts of Adilabad, Karimnagar, Khammam, Warangal and Mahaboobnagar.

The present output of tasar cocoons in Maharashtra has been estimated at 100 lakhs or 7812 Kahans The Committee feels that this estimate is rather on the high side.

Even assuming that the actual annual production of tasar cocoons is 7812 Kahans as stated by Maharashtra, the requirements of dfls., on the basis of 25 dfls. to produce one Kahan of cocoons will come to less than 2 lakhs of dfls.

Tasar industry in Uttar Pradesh is confined to Mirzapur district which adjoins the tasar belt of Bihar and Madhya Pradesh.

Recommendations of the Sub-Committee on Non-mulberry Silk Industry set up by the Central Silk Board mainly related to host plants, have remained unimplemented by the States. This has operated as a setback to the progress of the industry.

Experiments so far conducted have shown that tasar worms fed on shorea robusta spin better cocoons with higher silk content.

The Central Tasar Research Station, Ranchi has drawn up a very comprehensive programme of research in the Fourth Plan and unless the requisite facilities, both by way of equipment, buildings and scientific personnel, are provided well in time, the efforts are likely to be hampered.

The Central Tasar Silkworm Seed Station at Lakha has no doubt shown considerable progress during the short period since it has been functioning.

'Asan' and 'Arjun' are not protected trees and have been felled for fuel purposes during the past several decades leading to a progressive reduction in the availability of food plants for tasar rearings.

What has not been sufficiently realised is that the host plants are not available in adequacy in the vicinity of human habitation to sustain large scale rearings.

In districts where tasar industry is practised, cutting down of tasar food plants should be prohibited, if need be, by legislation.

The question of utilising the facilities for afforestation under the soil conservation programmes in operation in some of the States is worth consideration.

The Committee suggests that nurseries may be set up by the Industries/Sericulture Departments in consultation with the Forest Department so that a continuous supply of tasar food plants could be assured.

The question of getting the protected and unreserved forests for tasar rearing should receive the attention of the Industries Departments.

With a little imaginative cooperation between the Industries and Highway Departments, it should be possible to utilise the road-side trees which have the advantage of being close to the rearers' habitation.

The State Departments should evince interest in the experiment relating to use of 'sat' leaves for tasar rearing and initiate field studies in collaboration with the Central Tasar Research Station, Ranchi.

The total requirement of disease-free layings for the Tasar States is 54 lakhs. The actual supply of disease-free layings including seed cocoons is hardly 40 per cent of the total requirement. This shows a serious hiatus in the organisation of the industry.

The Technical Officers of the States seem to be of the view that at present infection of Pebrine was almost negligible.

It would not be correct to lay disproportionate emphasis on preparation of disease free seed just to keep off of a possible out break of 'Pebrine'.

Supply of seed cocoons rather than examined eggs could be adopted for the present for the commercial rearings.

Exclusive seed zones should be organised.

The Committee feels that it would be worthwhile to attempt seed rearings in Reserve Forests so that the present availability of nature grown seed cocoons could be supplemented.

The study of heterosis to stabilise tasar crops should be intensified and a sense of urgency should be imparted to the experiment so that tangible findings might be able in the near future.

The Committee recommends that the Department of Industries/Sericulture should devise measures to meet the full requirement of seed cocoons free of cost

The present methods of rearing are rather crude and irrational. What is, however, recommended is a little more attention to incubation of seed to ensure uniform hatching of worms, choice of host plants in keeping with the stage of growth of the larvae, maintenance of optimum larva-forage ratio etc.

To ensure sufficiency of leaf of suitable quality, pollarding of host plants should be done on a rational basis. There is need for systematising this operation under expert direction of the departmental technicians.

There was wide divergence of opinion among the States about the effective earnings of a tasar rearer. The Committee feels that the figures furnished by Orissa and Bihar (Bhagalpur region) more or less depict the actual position, i.e., an income of Rs. 120 to Rs. 210 per rearer per annum.

Having regard to the difficulties and risks of tasar rearings this monetary return is to be deemed rather low and quite insufficient to sustain the interest of even traditional tasar rearers.

The Committee is of the view that one of the main factors which have impeded the orderly progress of tasar industry during the past several decades is the strangle hold exerted by the 'Mahajan' or 'Paikar' on the poor tribal rearers.

The cost of production of 1 Kahan of cocoons is Rs. 65 as follows :

(i) On account of seed	Re. 1.00
(ii) Dalkatli/Royalty	Rs. 3.25
(iii) Labour	Rs. 60.00
Total :	Rs. 64.25 or say
	Rs. 65.00

The Committee feels that unless the actual producer of tasar cocoons is assured of the fair price of Rs. 65 per Kahan, it will be very difficult to sustain his interest in the persuit of tasar culture.

If the tempo of exports is to be sustained the exporters should also be enabled to get raw material (cocoons) at reasonable prices. Perhaps a price of Rs. 90 per Kahan (Grade-I 1280 cocoons) would enable the exporters to enter markets abroad with confidence.

The marketing mechanism should be able to assure price of Rs. 65 per Kahan to the rearers and sell cocoons to the manufacturers at Rs. 90 per Kahan.

The Mahajans give petty loans to the rearers in their times of need and bind them to sell their cocoons at predetermined prices which are invariably unremunerative.

Bihar should send one or two of its Technical Officers to Orissa to make a complete study of the working of the cooperative societies for tasar so that the same pattern could be adopted with slight modifications to suit local requirements.

The Committee recommends that the marketing scheme of the States should get more liberal provision of funds for purchase of cocoons.

Even when the prices for tasar cocoons ruled at unprecedented levels above Rs. 160 per Kahan, the rearer was still getting hardly Rs. 50 or Rs. 60 per Kahan.

In Bihar the 'daba' cocoons were being sold at Rs.70 to Rs. 75 per Kahan while in Madhya Pradesh the State Department had to announce a floor price of Rs. 50 per 1000 cocoons (Rs. 63 per Kahan). Even in Orissa the prices were operating at Rs. 90 per Kahan of 1600 cocoons.

The Committee feels that the situation warrants the launching of price support operations on an extensive scale so that the price depression might not permanently harm the future outlook for the industry.

Regarding the price which should be offered to the rearer, the Committee feels that Rs. 65 per Kahan of 1280 cocoons as suggested by Bihar and as arrived at by the Board's survey team will be reasonable.

The Committee feels that even if the cooperatives and Government markets were to enlarge their activities manyfold it will be extremely difficult for them to effectively replace the Mahajan. The effort is likely to prove time-consuming and the result is rather doubtful.

A separate Corporation for purchase and sale of cocoons might prove to be too cumbersome to admit of efficient administration.

If the prices for tasar cocoons are to be stabilised the State Trading Corporation may have to purchase about 30,000 Kahans of cocoons during a year at the support price of Rs. 65 per Kahan.

The Committee suggests that the departments of Industries Sericulture etc. in the Tasar States should fully cooperate with the State Trading Corporation in its price support operations and if need be keep all their existing facilities like cocoons godowns, stifling equipment etc. at the disposal of the State Trading Corporation.

The reeling as also the spinning equipment at present in use in the Tasar States was of an antiquated type.

The Committee feels that there is a case for increase of the subsidy element in the scheme of popularisation of the reeling-cum-tursting machines. This should be treated as a socio-economic measure for the general amelioration of the poor tribal rearers.

The pit loom is the most inefficient device for weaving and as such the departments concerned should immediately initiate action, quick change-over, to more modern methods of weaving.

Experiments should be initiated to find out the possibilities of giving 'silicon finish' to the tasar fabrics.

The Institute at Bhagalpur should be fully equipped and staffed with adequately trained Technical Officers so that the problems of the industry which might crop up in future might be more effectively tackled.

Efforts should be made to set up Cooperative Credit Societies with a view to affording necessary financial relief to the tribal rearers at times of need.

There is urgent need to revive the proposal of the Central Silk Board to appoint a Senior Officer to effectively coordinate the development work relating to tasar industry in the Tasar States.

There should be will-knit organisation with the Central Tasar Research Station at Ranchi as the driving force and with a few field units in the States so that coordinated experiments to resolve regional problems could be laid out on systematic lines.

Immediate action should be taken to ensure coordination of work among the units at Ambikapur (Madhya Pradesh), Baripada (Orissa) and the Central Tasar Research Station, Ranchi.

Export assistance should be further liberalised by giving a total cash incentive of 25 per cent so that Indian Exporters could enter the American and European markets with confidence.

It is the exports which will impart a stability to the industry and no efforts should be spared to put our tasar exports on sound basis.

THE COMMITTEE ON COST OF PRODUCTION OF STEEL, 1965—REPORT

New Delhi, Ministry of Iron and Steel, 1966; 126p.

Chairman : Shri Harekrushna Mahatab.

Members : Shri P. Venkatasubbaiah ; Shri. S. N. Mishra ; Shri Jehangir Ghandy ; Shri S. L. Kirloskar ; Shri B. K. Sethi ; Shri Karnail Singh ; Shri B. R. Nijhawan ; Shri M. S. Rao ; Dr. Pritam Singh ; Shri N. Krishnan ; Shri D. S. Nakra.

APPOINTMENT

The Government have been concerned for some time about the rising cost of production of steel and have had under consideration the appointment of a Committee to examine this matter in detail, analyse all the factors going into the cost, assess the reasons for the increase and advise Government on the measures necessary to reduce the cost. The Government of India, Ministry of Steel and Mines, Department of Iron and Steel have now decided to constitute a Committee on cost of production of steel vide their Resolution No. coy-3 (12) 65, dated the August 28, 1965.

TERMS OF REFERENCE

"To examine the problem of the rising cost of production of steel ; analyse all the factors going into the cost, assess the reasons for the increases ; and advise them on the measures necessary to reduce the cost."

CONTENTS

The Problem and its Setting ; Analysis of Cost Trends ; Raw Materials ; Plant Operation ; Personnel Cost ; Inventory Cost ; Capital Cost ; Summary of Conclusions and Recommendations ; Role of Administration, Appendices I to II.

RECOMMENDATIONS

Introduction

We have covered the period 1948/49 to 1964/65 in our study. During this period, the selling prices of various categories of steel in our country rose faster than the corresponding ex-works prices Relatively steeper increases in Excise Duty, Equalised Freight and surcharge (during the Equalisation Fund period) contributed to this trend. The differentials between selling prices and ex-works prices are more now than in 1948-49. This steeper increase in the elements like Excise Duty, Equalised Freight and surcharge forming part of the selling prices have tended to strengthen the popular impression that our steel is excessively costly.

A comparison of our selling prices with prices of imported steel would not be a comparison of like to like. A valid comparison would be between our ex-works prices with the ex-works (Home Prices) in foreign countries. Such a comparison has been made. This discloses that even today our ex-works prices, such as they are, do not compare too unfavourably with similar internal prices (Home Prices) abroad. However, it is a matter of concern that our ex-works prices have risen faster than the corresponding prices elsewhere. We thus, seem to have lost the advantage we once had as one of the cheapest steel producing countries in the world. This conclusion is reinforced by the fact that the present level of ex-works Prices in India is related to the capital block for the three HSL plants which is about Rs. 2,500 per tonne of saleable steel, capacity at the million tonne stage and about Rs. 2,000 per tonne of saleable steel capacity at the end of current expansions.

A general study of price trends in the country discloses that the ex-works prices of steel have risen faster than the average ex-factor prices of several other commodities. Also the ex-works prices of steel has risen faster than the general level of prices.

Cost Analysis : Between 1948/49 and 1960/62, the average retention price fixed by Government for untested categories increased from Rs. 248 to Rs. 522.5 per tonne, i.e., an increase of Rs. 274.5 per tonne or 111 per cent. Of this increase, overheads constituted about 27.5 per cent, Ingot excise duty 17 per cent and the works cost 55.5 per cent. The increase in overheads was almost entirely related to the increse in the gross block. Increase in the cost of fixed assets per unit of capacity has thus contributed importantly to the increase in the ex-works prices. This is the trend in other steel producing countries as well.

To identify the important cost raising elements in Works Cost, an analysis of the Works Cost of ingot at Tatas is made for the period of 1948 49 to 1964-65, which discloses an increase of about Rs. 151 per tonne of ingot (158 per cent). Out of this total increase, the portion relating to gross materials (including fluxes) formed about 68 per cent and operating charges 45 per cent. However, there was an increase in the credit for scrap gas etc., at 13 per cent. Further, of the total increase of Rs. 15 per tonne, the portion attributable to price and expense factors represented about Rs. 146 (97 per cent) and usage factor about Rs. 5 (3 per cent). Increase in materials cost is thus the largest single item among the cost raising factors. Further, of this increase in material cost, the bulk was accounted for by coal, iron ore, limestone, and dolomite ; coal being the most important cost raising material. It should be emphasised here that an important contributory factor leading to the steep increase in the cost of coal is the deterioration in the quality of coal which has compelled the steel plants to use an increasing proportion of washed coal resulting in higher cost.

Fuel and Power, Stores and Services and labour constitute the three important cost raising factors in so for as operating cost are concerned. In regard to labour, wages per tonne or ingot have practically doubled during the period 1948/49 to 1964-65.

The methods adopted in working out costs by the different Steel Plants vray. This frustrates any attempt at a meaningful inter-plant comparison of works cost of Ingot steel in the present system of uniform selling prices and uniform ex-works prices there is a paramount need for establishing uniform accounting system in all the steel plants so that a proper comparison of costs could be made in the future. We strongly urge that steps to have this evolved should be initiated by the Government. Despite the limitations imposed by the differing cost accounting procedures, a comparison of the Works Cost of ingot at the five steel works for 1964-65 has been made and this discloses that the ingot cost ranges from Rs. 227 to Rs. 247 per tonne.

A representative analysis of the impact of Government levies on the Works Cost of ingot steel shows that the increase on account of these levies contributed as much as 24 per cent to the increase in the Works Cost of steel between 1948-49 and 1964-65. The impact of Government levies has thus been a significant cost raising factor.

Raw Materials : Although with technological innovations the unit consumption of raw materials per tonne of ingot steel is on the decline, the prices of materials have risen at such a rapid rate that their increase has more than offset the decrease in raw materials consumption. Although the prices of raw materials have increased all over the world, the rise in India is much higher than in other steel producing countries. The analysis of the coal cost in the various steel plants shows that the prices of coal, both washed and un-washed, as charged to the coke ovens, have risen progressively, and that the increase was mainly on account of the increase in the prices, of coal and freight. Another striking feature is the progressive increase in the use of washed coal by all the steel works except IISCO where it is small. The steel plants have over the years been able to maintain consistency in the ash content in the total intake only by a progressive increase in the use of washed coal. As there is no prospect of an improvement in the quality of metallurgical coal, the use of washed coal to a greater extent than now seems inescapable. The efficient operation of coal washeries, therefore, assumes considerable importance in the economy of the steel industry.

Another factor contributing to the coal cost in the steel works (as well as in the washeries) is that coals received by them have been one or two grades lower than the grades for which payments are made to the suppliers on the basis of the grading made by the Coal Controller, resulting in substantial overpayments. This situation needs immediate rectification. We have recommended that the process of regrading which now reportedly takes as much as a year should be considerably speeded up. Further, having regard to the manner in which attempt at introducing joint sampling at destination have been frustrated so long in the absence of a legal backing for this measure, it is recommended that Government should arm itself with statutory powers to make joint sampling at the destination obligatory on the coal suppliers.

The Committee attach the greatest importance to the working out of a long-term and durable solution to this vexed question of coking coal supplies to the steel industry. We have urged that no time should be cost in evolving a partical design for developing of coal production in view of the rising demand for coking coal and the rising prices. The amalgamation of coal mines and their development in public sector is one solution. It would appear that there are advantages in strengthening the association between N.C.D.C. and the steel plants in the matter of coal supplies by extending the scope of N.C.D.C.'s operations.

Coal Washeries : As indicated already, the efficient operation of coal washeries assumes considerable importance in the economy of the steel industry. Operation of the washery at full capacity is indispensable for keeping the costs down. With the anticipated increase in demand for washed coal, this should be possible utilisation of full capacity on the washery is also dependent on the regularity in the supply of raw coal and the disposal of washed coal. To achieve this, the Railways have to ensure a regulated supply of wagons to the washeries.

As the first step towards the establishment of standard cost for washeries, norms should be fixed for the operation of the washeries indicating the ash percentage at which the washed coal will have to be priduced and the yield percentage will have to be achieved.

On the raw coal supplied to the washeries, the Railways are charging the minimum distance freight of Rs. 6.50 per tonne plus siding charges. As this is a short distance movement, this rate appears to be rather high and there seems to be a case for concessional rate for this movement. It is further suggested that additional siding charges should not be levied on the washeries in view of the fact that the Central washeries have provided themselves with the necessary siding facilities.

It is suggested that the double collection of cess on raw coal and on washed coal despatched should be avoided and that the cess should be collected either on raw coal or on washed coal despatched.

The importance of regular disposal of middlings from he washeries in washery economics is underlined and the urgency of taking in hand projects for setting up thermal stations which should consume washery middlings in close proximity to the washery is stressed.

Iron Ore : Attention has been drawn to the mining cost attained in Joda East Mines of Tatas in 1964-65 which is the lowest amongst the mechanised captive mines attached to steel plants and it is suggested that although the mining conditions in Joda East may be more favourable than elsewhere, the Joda cost level could be set as the target for other captive mines.

It is shown that the increase in output from the captive mechanised mines and the substitution of purchased ore by ore from own mines which this would make possible, would help reduce the overall cost per tonne of ore to the steel works. The need for maximising the output from the Barsua mines so that the heavy investment in this mine is put to better use than at present is stressed. The urgency of installing ore bedding and blending arrangements at Rourkela is also stressed.

It is indicated that the utilisation of fines to a larger extent than now would have salutary impact on the cost of iron ore to the steel works.

A comparison of railway freight rates on mineral ores in India and USA is made and it is suggested that prima facie there appears to be a case for revising the existing freight structure for handling iron ore from mines to the steel plants. It is further recommended that by adopting close circuit movement wherever possible. These recommendations apply to limestone with equal force.

Ferro-Manganese : In the context of the recent escalation in Ferro manganese prices, the Committee has argued that Government should keep a close watch and control over the prices of the raw materials needed by the steel industry in the interest of keeping the steel costs down.

General

The Committee gather that even at the existing levels of demand, the procurement of the raw materials needed by the steel industry at the most economic cost is becoming a major problem for the steel plant managements. In view of the importance of ensuring supply of raw materials at economic rates to the steel plants, we have referred to certain difficulties in the grant of mining leases experienced by the industry and have urged on more constructive and sympathetic attitude in such matters on the part of the State Governments and other authorities concerned towards the requirements of the industry.

Plant Operation

The Committee have urged that positive steps to attain higher blast furnace productivity should be taken by all concerned without further delay as this is an area where significant results leading to cost reduction seem possible.

The need for reducing the coke rate is stressed and a target of about 750 kg/tonne of hot metal considered as attainable with Indian Coke of 23 to 24 per cent cash content. It is felt that there is scope for improvement in the level of productivity attained by our steel melting shop furnaces. The need for reducing heat consumption in these furnaces and improving their availability is also urged.

We have emphasized the need to maximise production from highly expensive rolling mills and by removing those factors which limit the optimum utilisation of such mills by making suitable balancing investments.

The importance of efficient operation of coke oven by-product plants has been stressed with a few specific suggestions in this direction. Having regard to the leeway we could make up in the matter of equipment productivity, it is suggested that arrangements should be made to enable exchange of practical experience in the technical field amongst the operatives in the various steel works.

To coordinate the research activities and programmes of all the research and control laboratories of the steel plants both in the public sector and in the private sector and of the National Metallurgical Laboratory and the Central Fuel Research Institute, the Committee advises the formation of an Iron and Steel Research Board patterned broadly on the British Iron and Steel Research Association in the United Kingdom.

Personnel Costs

The Committee noted that in most of the HSL plants, man-power has been steadily increasing even when there is no addition to capacity. This indicates the need for a tight control over manning. We recommend that norms and standards of productivity and personnel costs on a department wise or activity-wise basis should be established so that departmental performance could be assessed and pressures for increasing the work force held.

Step should be taken for standardising the classification of personnel by departmental groups and by activities so as to facilitate standardisation of accounts, classification and comparability of performance as between plants.

The incidence of overtime payments in some of the plants gives cause for concern and indicates that not only the statutory limits of overtime work are being exceeded steadily but the control over overtime authorisation is not effective. We suggest that the level to which powers for authorising overtime have been delegated may be reviewed to see if they have to be revised upwards to limit the incidence of overtime payments.

It was found that in some steel works the practice of obtaining work through job contract or through contract labour was widespread. Some of the plants and departments which have the largest incidence of costs on contract work were also the units where productivity of departmental labour was low indicating that there was considerable scope for increasing the productivity of departmental labour and reducing cost of contract work. Our studies indicate that some of the centralised services and maintenance departments are not being utilised to the extent possible and are also probably over-manned. Greater attention to the proper utilisation and manning of these departments could be a fruitful source of cost reduction.

Considerable variations exist between the five plants in regard to manning of their administrative departments. We feel that to keep the man-power in these departments in check, the possibility of revising the procedures, making the activities more officer-oriented rather than the clerk-oriented and tightening the control in regard to sanctioning additional administrative personnel might be investigated. We feel that the need exists not only for the control of man-power but for the improvement in productivity of labour by rationalisation of work force over the years even in plants which are not expanding. We consider it possible for the management and the unions together to agree to adjust the labour force and reduce heavy surpluses where they exist.

It seems to us that there are major possibilities of effecting improvements both in man-power productivity and personnel costs with each expansion of the steel plants. We consider it possible to raise the productivity in respect of works-personnel from the present level of 55 to 70 ingot tonne per man-year to a productivity index of about 125 ingot tonne per man-year and above in each of the plants. Certain specific steps in this direction are also suggested.

Inventories

The Committee noted that inventories were generally high in all the steel plants and felt that there was need to check the build-up of inventories both by budgetary control methods and by the exercise of Quality Control.

The Committee was of the view that plant managements should strive to maintain the level of wo king capital within about 25 to 30 per cent of the cost of sales. Similarly, the aggregate inventory level should be maintained between 35 and 40 per cent of the cost of sales. In terms of consumption also, they would recommend an average target of about 6-7 months, consumption against the present level which varies from 9 to 11 months between the five steel plants.

We find that the high valued items which constitute the bulk of the value of the inventory in a steel plant are confined to relatively fewer items compared to the total number of items in the inventory. Therefore, we feel that it should be possible to apply strict inventory control techniques to these selected items as a first step in the progressive application of scientific methods of inventory control.

Even in regard to consumable stores, the level of stocks seems to be on the high side but there is hope that with the establishment of indigenous capacity for the manufacture of several of these items there would be significant improvement in this respect.

In regard to spares also, the Committee noted that the steel plants carry high stocks and suggested a ceiling between 3 to 4 per cent of the original plant and equipment cost in this regard. To tackle the problem of spares, the following further steps are suggested :

(a) Pooling of spares may not be practicable at the present stage because of the different specifications and make of the equipment in the existing plants, but, for the future at least, this problem could be avoided if indigenous equipment is made to common basic designs.

(b) The dependence on imports, which is the main cause for over-stocking, has to be progressively reduced by planning educational orders in the country in a systematic manner.

(c) Production in the plant workshops should be maximised. There will be need for replacements which may not be economical for outside agencies to undertake. These will have to be manufactured in the plant workshops leaving bulk orders for execution by outside agencies. To achieve this, drawings and material specifications have to be prepared systematically over a certain period as a special programme.

The Committee would recommend a study of the problem of risks insurance spares by a specialised team consisting of operating and maintenance Engineers as well as Inventory Analysts.

The accumulation of inventories is a problem which has occurred in the steel industry in other countries too and special drives seem to have been undertaken to reduce inventories from time to time. Such a drive appears necessary in our steel-works today.

Capital Cost

Capital cost, which accounts for about 25 per cent of the total cost of steel in the HSL Plants, has a significant responsibili y in raising the cost of steel. The capital cost of the new steel plants and expansion programme in India is no doubt high as compared with other countries. But several un-avoidable circumstances account for higher cost. The more important factors have been : (i) high cost of imported plant and equipment on the basis of turnkey arrangements ; (ii) heavy customs duty on imported equipment ; (iii) provision of unutilised built-in capacity in the plants for later expansion programmes ; and (iv) the heavy cost of steel townships.

The Committee found that there is scope for the reduction of capital cost, particularly in respect of the following items : (i) plant and equipment, including its erection ; (ii) structurals ; (iii) refractories ; (iv) civil engineering ; and (v) townships.

The Committee makes the following recommendations to reduce the cost of these items :

(i) Turn-key contracts which have generally been found to be more expensive should, as far as possible, be avoided unless the need for speedy work makes such an arrangement unavoidable.

(ii) The experience of expansion programmes shows that it should now be possible to make a substantial shift to indigenous plant and equipment. Such a shift would be particularly, helpful to secure substantial savings in foreign exchange. The country is now well-equipped to design the general lay-out of a steel plant, but we have a big gap in our ability to design equipment. The Design Organisation in the country should be strengthened and encouraged to develop equipment designing.

Structurals fabrication is another item in which considerable reduction can be achieved. New designs should be developed to reduce the total tonnage of steel for the structurals. Our engineering industry is now capable of developing and implementing such improved designs.

As regards refractories, already, we are using mostly indigenous manufactures but we should make efforts to rely entirely on our own refractories. Their quality, however, needs to be substantially improved.

The Civil Engineering Works which were undertaken as a part of turn-key jobs, naturally tendered to be expensive. The foreign contractors actually got the work done from the Indian firms. As we shift from turn-key to non-turnkey arrangements, we should have direct contracts with the Indian engineering firms for all the construction work in the steel plants. The number of such firms is, however, limited and conditions should be created to enc urage the entry of new organisations in order to ensure competition, which would bring down the cost of engineering work.

The present situation with regard to steel townships needs to be reviewed. As time passes, the burden of public utility services on the steel plants will go on increasing. The State Governments should be persuaded to share the cost of essential services particularly in view of the fact that they drive considerable revenue from the location of the industry in their areas.

As regards future townships, there is a need for improving the lay-out to plan compact towns. The number of quarters per acre can be very much increased and thereby the cost of land as well as utility service is reduced.

We recommend statutory action, if necessary, to secure that the steel industry does not have to make more than such provision for depreciation as they were making before the amendment to the Indian Income Tax Rules, 1964, which introduced an additional third shift depreciation. In the case of steel industry, the third shift is an integral part of the process of seel manufacturing and the incentive for this shift is therefore not called for.

Role Of Administration

In the foregoing, we have explored several areas where there seems to be scope for the cost reduction and have advanced a number of suggestions. We are convinced that for fruitful and lasting results, the implementation of the recommendations, we have made, should be reinforced by intimate participation by everyone who has a stake in the industry, whether it be the Government, the higher managements of the steel companies or the large body of men in each steelworks from the General Manager down to the lowest unskilled worker. They must all join in an organised and sustained drive for cost reduction. This means that cost discipline cannot be conceived of as a series of spasmodic effort, but should be looked upon as a part of the very texture of perposive management. We hope that the appointment of our Committee is earnest of Government's own consciousness of their responsibilities in the matter and that this would permeate down to the last man in the industry without which positive and lasting results cannot be achieved. In particular, we believe that in these formative years of the public sector in the steel industry in which substantial public funds are invested and public aspirations are founded, cost consciousness and cost discipline would be inculcated at all levels in such a manner that it forms a permanent part of the mental outlook of all.

Impact Of Devaluation

Devaluation of the Rupee took place after the draft of this Report had been prepared, and since by that time all the detailed studies on which the Report is based had been completed, we have thought it best to finalise the Report on the basis of the old external value of the Rupee. A study of the impact of devaluation on the cost of production of steel and related matters will be not only time-taking and, therefore, a cause for further delay in the submission of this Report, but also, in the nature of things any conclusions that might be drawn in the immediate future as to the likely effect of devaluation on the steel industry will be somewhat speculative.

While immediately, because of the devaluation the steel industry will be in a better situation than before for export promotion at competitive prices, it appears that even then support with a reduced subsidy would be necessary. Conditions generated by the Indo-Pakistan conflict and subsequent events have already compelled the steel industry to plan and work for large scale import substitution by indigenous effort and these efforts must be continued with the same zeal even if foreign aid becomes more readily available and the exchange position Cases. Even so import will have to be continued on many things such as rolls, certain raw materials and maintenance spares. A rough estimate made by HSL of the probable increased costs for these imported materials because of devaluation of the Rupee, suggests that in the Public Sector Steel Plants we may have to count on an increase in expenditure of about 5 per cent per tonne of saleable steel. All of which may mean a total reduction in profitability for HSL in the year 1966-67 by Rs. 3 to 4 crores.

In the matter of capital costs also, all expansions, will entail considerable increased Outlay. In Hindustan Steel alone if the present Plants are undertaken, the increased cost is estimated at Rs. 165 crores, and that also on the assumption that during the period of this expansion which will be during the 4th Plan period and perhaps in the first year of the 5th Plan period, Indian costs will increase only about 5 per cent. But Indian costs are likely to increase by much more than 5 per cent. The hope HSL had of reducing their block capital per tonne of steel through the expansion programmes may not now be realised. However, it would not be worthwhile discussing in any further detail the effects of devaluation.

We would only say that the recommendations that we have made and the arguments that we have advanced in favour of these recommendations get reinforced emphasis in the context of the devaluation, and we confidently hope and trust that steel industry both in the Public Sector and the Private Sector will make all out efforts to further reduce the costs in order that the climate created by devaluation may help in developing vigorously both in abundance and in diversity our export market.

ROAD TRANSPORT TAXATION ENQUIRY COMMITTEE ON INTER-STATE TRANSPORT, 1965.—REPORT (INTERIM)

New Delhi, Ministry of Transport and Aviation, Department of Transport and Shipping (Transport Wing), 1966. Memiograph. 81p.

Chairman : Dr. B. V. Keskar.

Members : Shri G. Ramachandran; Shri P. N. Damry ; Shri V. M. Bhide ; Shri S. A. Iyengar ; Shri R.P. Naik ; Shri S. Mullik ; Shri G. L. Mehta ; Shri M. S. Swaminathan ; Major Gurjit Singh ; Dr. F. P. Antia ; Shri Kundan Lal ; Shri N. Balkrishna ; Shri C. R. Raja ; Shri Deokinandan Narayan ; and Dr. V.G. Bhatia.

Secretary : Shri A. S. Bhatnagar.

APPOINTMENT

The Committee was constituted under the Ministry of Transport and Aviation, Department of Transport and Shipping (Transport Wing) vide their Resolution No. 21-T (42)/61 dated September 6, 1965.

TERMS OF REFERENCE

(a) To examine the present cost of operation for haulage of passengers and goods by road transport, including the element of State and Central taxes; whether it has become disincentive to the healthy development of road transport and if so, to what extent;

(b) To examine whether there is justification for correlating the rates of motor vehicle taxes with reference to the types of fuel (petrol or diesel) used and area of operation;

(c) To survey the existing administrative machinery and the procedures connected with the levy and collection of taxes, tolls etc. on motor vehicles in the States and examine whether they hinder the smooth movement of vehicles;

(d) To recommend the principles on which Motor Vehicles Taxation should be based and also the level of taxation which will ensure adequate provision and development of efficient and economic road transport services in the country;

(e) To suggest any changes in law and procedure that may be required to give effect to any recommendations that may be made ; and

(f) To make any other recommendations germane to the subject-matter of the enquiry.

CONTENTS

Introductory ; Importance of Road Transport ; Inter-State Transport ; Regulation and Taxation of Inter-State Road Transport ; Note of Dr. V.G. Bhatia ; Note of Shri Kundan Lal ; Annexures I to IX.

RECOMMENDATIONS

Importance Of Road Transport

Increase in Motor Vehicle Population : The first motor vehicle reached India in 1898. Within the first decade of this century, the number of motor vehicles went up to 45,000. After the end of the First World War, there was a phenomenal growth of road transport. By 1929, the number of vehicles on the road had increased to 1,17,900. Because of the economic 'depression' of the thirties and the outbreak of the Second World War, there was no further appreciable growth of road transport in the next two decades. The number of vehicles in 1947 was only 1,78,000 (in British India). After Independence, there was a greater emphasis on economic development and consequently the development of road transport took place more rapidly. The number of motor vehicles rose from about 1·78 lakhs in 1.47 to over 10 lakhs in 1965-66 as will be clear from the following table :—

Year	Buses	Trucks	Scooters and Motor cycles and auto-rickshaws	Other Vehicles	Total Vehicles
1950-51	35,641	83,443	27,105	1,63,223	3,09,412
1955-56	46,461	1,19,097	40,961	2,19,041	4,25,560
1960-61	56,792	1,67,649	94,595	3,45,439	6,64,475
1965-66*	70,000	2,55,000	2,34,600	5,05,800	10,65,400

*Estimated.

Road Transport in Five Year Plans : Experience during the implementation of the projects included in our three Five-Year Plans has shown that the success of our schemes depends upon the speed with which we can carry goods. High priority has, therefore, to be given in future to the development of transport. Our increased transport requirements have thrown a great burden on the Railways which are the biggest carriers in the country. Although the capacity of the Railways has been increased considerably during the recent years, a big gap has still to be bridged on account of their inability to carry the entire traffic offerings. Next to the Railways, the most important carrier of men and materials in this country is road transport. The role played by road transport in the implementation of our development projects has been significant. Whether in our steel projects or river valley schemes, road transport has, along with railways, successfully transported the numerous materials required for their implementation. In our rural economy also, road transport has come to play an important role. It has helped to link up hitherto inaccessible areas with rail heads and business centres thereby bringing prosperity to those areas. Road Transport has become a vital link in our communications.

Advantages of Road Transport : Road transport has many inherent advantages. It is speady, flexible and easily accessible. It is more direct and offers door to door service. It has obvious advantages for particular classes of goods, i.e., costly machinery, high class manufactured goods and goods requiring delicate handling can always be carried better and in more perfect conditions by road. It does not require many transhipments. It can be supervised throughout the journey. For all these reasons, this kind of traffic is already moved in very large quantity by road and it is bound to go on increasing quickly. Even in the matter of bus traffic, passenger service on long distance routes upto 300 miles or more is already becoming common and is playing an important role in the movement of passengers in certain areas where rail communication is roundabout and leading to delay due to change of trains etc. It is also a source of substantial revenue to Government. In 1950-51, the revenue realised from road transport, both by the Centre and the States, was Rs. 47.37 crores while this figure has risen to about Rs. 350 crores at present. It has a great employment potential. Because of these advantages, road transport is becoming increasingly important in the economy of the country. It has to play a vital role in the Fourth Five Year Plan period ; both with regard to carriage of goods on long-distance inter-State routes and serving the rural areas where the Railways cannot reach. Its importance is immense, more than the Railways, in the development of the economy of the States.

Changes in the Pattern of Traffic in Foreign Countries : According to the information gathered by the Committee, the volume of traffic carried by road transport in foreign countries like Germany, Italy and United Kingdom during the last few years was much more than that carried by Railways. In the United Kingdom, two-thirds of the inland traffic was carried by road transport. In Italy, 72 per cent of the traffic was carried in motor vehicles during the year 1963. In West Germany, there has been a steady decline in the rail traffic. While the volume of rail traffic was about 50 per cent in 1955, it fell to 38 per cent in 1961. A similar trend is noticeable in the U.S.A. also. In other foreign countries too, there has been a shift from the railways to road transport during the recent past due to the advantages mentioned earlier, vide Annenure II. The same position may arise in India also in the next few years. According to the draft outline of the Fourth Five Year Plan, the volume of goods traffic carried by road is expected to increase from 33 billion tonne kilometres in 1965-66 to about 60 billion tonne kilometres in 1970-71 and to about 150 billion tonne kilometres in 1975-76. Passenger traffic is estimated to rise from 80 billion in passenger kms. in 1965-66 to 120 billion passenger kms. in 1970-71 and 195 billion passenger kms. in 1975-76. On the basis of the anticipated increase in traffic, the number of trucks would need to be increased from 2,55,000 in 1965-66 to 4,25,000 in 1970-71 and of buses from 70,000 to 1,00,000 during the same period. The Fourth Plan provides for an outlay of Rs. 65 crores in the public sector and reckons on an investment of Rs. 630 crores in the private sector to achieve expansion of the order indicated above. In keeping the general growth of road traffic, there is bound to be very great increase in the inter-State traffic also.

National Highways

Effects on Inter-State Traffic: The growth of national highways during the last three Plans has given a great impetus to inter-State transport. The national highway system has many missing links and its development has yet to reach a uniform level. However, inspite of the many drawbacks, the movement of inter-State traffic for goods is increasing very rapidly.

Differing Rules And Regulations Of Motor Vehicles Taxation

The importance of inter-State traffic growing so rapidly and becoming as important a matter for consideration as Railways for the economic development of the country bringing us to the taxation of this section of road transport. As inter-State transport by road was in a very primitive condition 20 years back, no one envisaged a future where it will be playing as important a role as Railways in the economic development of the country. Technological development was such that it was then considered to be and likely to remain a local mode of transport. In the Constitution, therefore, this was left to the States to deal with. However, the developments of the last two decades have shown that the inter-State aspect is as important as movement within the State. The question having been left to the States to decide as they considered proper, each State has developed according to its own circumstances and requirements. The result has been differing rules and regulations regarding taxation not only of vehicles for intra-State Transport but also those which are engaged in inter-State traffic. Present position in the various States regarding taxation of vehicles, both passengers and goods, is indicated in Annexures III to VII.

Constitutional Position of Road Transport Taxation : Taxes on motor vehicles or their operation on roads which are within the legislative powers of the Union are enumerated in List I in the Seventh Schedule to the Constitution and those within the legislative powers of the States are mentioned in List II. Items falling in the concurrent field of legislation are mentioned in List III. Residual powers of taxation vest in the Union.

The taxes which are, or may be, imposed on motor vehicles and the entries in the Union, State and Concurrent Lists under which they fall, are indicated below :—

Union List (List I)

Duties of customs on motor vehicles, spare parts, accessories, fuel and lubricants	—Entry 83
Duties of excise on motor vehicles, spare parts, accessories, fuel and lubricants	—Entry 84
Inter-State sales tax on motor vehicles and spares	—Entry 92-A

State List (List II)

Tax on the entry of goods into a local area for consumption, use or sale therein	—Entry 52
Sales Tax on motor vehicles, spare parts and accessories and motor fuel	—Entry 54
Taxes on goods and passengers carried by road (and inland waterways)	—Entry 56
Taxes on vehicles, whether mechanically propelled or not, suitable for use on road, subject to provisions of Entry 35 of List III	—Entry 57
Tolls	—Entry 59

Concurrent List (List III)

Principles on which taxes on motor vehicles are to be levied	—Entry 35

Motor Vehicle Tax, Passenger and Goods Tax : At present, motor vehicles tax is levied by all States. However, taxes on passengers and goods carried by motor vehicles are being levied in Assam, Bihar, Gujarat, Kerala, Madhya Pradesh, Madras, Maharashtra, Mysore, Punjab, Haryana, Rajasthan, Uttar Pradesh and Himachal Pradesh. The Governments of Nagaland and Orissa are contemplating legislation to provide for levy of these taxes.

No legislation has been undertaken so far either by the Central Government or any of the State Governments laying down the principles of taxation on motor vehicles under Entry 35 in the Concurrent List.

Freedom of Inter-State Commerce : Inter-State Commerce falls in the Union List (Entry 42). Part XIII of the Constitution deals with freedom of trade and commerce. Under Article 30D in that Part, trade, commerce and intercourse throughout the country are to be free. Under Article 302, Parliament can, by-law, impose such restrictions on the freedom of trade, commerce or intercourse between one State and another or within any part of the territory of India, as may be required in the public interest. Under Article 304, the legislature of a State can :(a) impose on goods imported from other States any tax to which similar goods manufactured or produced in the State are subject, so as not to discriminate against the goods so manufactured or produced, and (b) also impose such reasonable restrictions on the freedom of trade, commerce or intercourse with or within the State as may be required in the public interest. However, no Bill under the provision (b) can be introduced in the State Legislature without the previous assent of the President.

Previous sanction of President to Bills seeking to introduce Passenger and Goods Tax : The levy of taxes on goods and passengers carried in motor vehicles under Entry 56 in List II has been held by Courts as a restriction falling within the purview of Part XIII of the Constitution and attracting the provisions of Articles 301 and 304 thereof. All Bills seeking to impose tax on passengers and/or goods carried in motor vehicles require the previous assent of the President, before they can be introduced in the State Legislatures. The State Governments, therefore, usually refer such Bills to the Government of India for the necessary clearance before introducing them in their Legislatures.

The powers of the Centre under Entry 42 in the Union List in the Seventh Schedule to the Constitution have not been clearly defined; particularly those in relation to the taxation of inter-State transport. Apparently the expression "inter-State trade and commerce" can also be considered to inclu'e inter-State transport and the taxation thereof. This view gains support from Article 301 of the Constitution which provides for the freedom of trade, commerce and inter-course throughout the country. On the other hand, power to legislate on taxes on road transport and goods and passengers carried therein is specifically mentioned in the State List (Entries 56 and 57) in the Seventh Schedule to the Constitution. No effort seems to have been made so far for getting the position clarified. Such clarification is necessary for laying down the legal framework for the development of inter-State transport. The demarcation of powers for regulation and taxation of inter-State transport and the authority to legislate for it will have to be studied and examined thoroughly at the highest level in order to determine what legal steps might be necessary to deal with inter-State transport by any authority or Commission that might be proposed.

Inter-State Transport

Mode of Regulation of Transport Vehicles : The regulation of commercial motor vehicles is done largely through a system of permits. Section 42(1) of the Motor Vehicles Act, 1939, lays down that the owners of a transport vehicle should not use or permit the use of a vehicle in any public place except in accordance with the conditions of a permit granted or counter-signed by the proper authority. These permits specify, inter-alia, the route or the area of operation of the vehicle. Stage carriages are generally permitted to operate on specified routes and public carriers in specified regions. The area of the region so specified in the permits differs from State to State, but it has not to be less than the entire revenue district of a State or the whole area of a Presidency town as per the provisions of Section 44(1) of the Motor Vehicles Act.

Counter-signature of Permits : The Authority for the grant of a primary permit to a vehicle is generally the Regional Transport Authority. A permit granted by this Authority entitles the vehicle to operate within the region but, if it has to operate in any other region in the State, it has to obtain counter-signature on the permit by the Regional Transport Authority of the other region. The State Governments may relax this provision so that a permit granted in one region is made valid for operation in the other region within the State without counter-signature. During the past one decade, each State Government has followed its own procedures in respect of the area where the vehicles are to operate under primary permits. However, almost all State Governments have since accepted the need for the grant of primary permits valid for the entire State and this policy is being gradually implemented.

The procedure for obtaining permits for operation in inter-State regions is given in Section 63(1) of the Motor Vehicles Act, according to which, a permit issued in any one State is not valid in any other State unless counter-signed by the State Transport Authority of that other State or by the Regional Transport Authority concerned. The procedure for counter-signature of permit by the other State Transport Authority or the Regional Transport Authority is the same as that for the issue of a primary permit in the 'home' State in respect of inviting applications, hearing of objections, selection of applicants for grant of permits etc. However, this procedure may be dispensed with when counter-signature is done as a result of reciprocal agreement between the States. If a vehicle operates in two States by obtaining a counter-signature in the State other than the home State, it is considered to be possessing an inter-State permit which is just an extension of the primary permit made valid in the other State by virtue of counter-signature.

Difficulties of Inter-State Operations : The motor Vehicles Act does not contain a separate procedure for regulation of transport vehicles on long distance routes traversing more than two States; as such an operator desirous of plying his vehicle on multi-State routes has to go through all the complex procedures for obtaining the counter-signatures on his permit in all the intervening States through which he may wish to operate.

The authority in each State has the right to specify the area or route which the vehicle can traverse, the maximum laden weight which it is to carry, the freight rate to be charged, the truck terminals, repairing and warehousing facilities which are required to be maintained by the operator and supply of statistics. For example, when a vehicle registered in Delhi has to travel to Bombay, the owner of the vehicle has to obtain, in the first instance, counter-signatures on his primary permit from the authorities in Haryana, Uttar Pradesh, Rajasthan, Madhya Pradesh and Maharashtra. The operator has also to abide by the conditions which the State authorities concerned might impose under Section 63(2) of the Act at the time of granting the countersignature.

In addition to these obligations under the Motor Vehicles Act, there are several other State Acts which likewise affect the operation of motor vehicles in those particular States. The Motor Vehicle Taxation Acts require that the vehicle should pay a tax at the rates fixed by the State Governments and also obtain a token indicating therein that such a tax has been paid. The Taxation of Passengers and Goods Acts of the States also impose a similar liability on vehicle operators in regard to payment of tax, maintenance of accounts, and other details.

The Sales Tax Authorities and more recently the Civil Supply Authorities require a public carrier to carry particular types of documents in respect of the consignments carried in the vehicle with such details as may be required by them. This has resulted in the erection of numerous barriers and checkposts en-route where the vehicles are detained for verification of documents. Further, the operators are required to adhere to different laden weight restrictions in each State and also go through the vexatious procedures at every octroi checkpost falling on the route. Therefore, the liability of a public carrier is to as many authorities as may be specified in every State through which it operates.

Besides the above difficulties, inter-State operators are also subjected to multiplicity of procedures in each State. Regarding only taxes, their rates, basis of assessment, period for which they are collected, the agency for collection, the method of payment etc. differ from State to State. Four statements showing the position in respect of these matters in relation to motor vehicle tax and taxes on passengers and goods carried in motor vehicles are given in the Annexures III to VI. The Motor Vehicle Taxation Enquiry Committee has suggested in 1950 that in the interest of uniformity, the basis of motor vehicle tax should be the registered laden weight for trucks in all States. This suggestion did not involve any loss of revenue to the State Governments. Nevertheless, there are some States and Union Territories, which continue to collect vehicle tax on the basis of pay load or the unladen weight of the vehicle as the case may be.

Tax for Temporary Permit: The minimum period for which tax is payable for a temporary permit differs from State to State. In certain States this period is one week while in many others, it is one month. In Maharashtra and Gujarat, the tax period is related to the calendar month, which means that a vehicle registered outside reaching Bombay on the last day of a month and returning on the 1st day of the subsequent month has to pay two full months tax to those States. A table showing the minimum period for which the tax is payable by a vehicle for operating on temporary permit in different States is given in the Annexure VII.

Disparities also exist in the payment of taxes on passengers and goods. The minimum period for which goods and passenger tax is payable is one day in Rajasthan and three months in Punjab. While taxes on passengers and goods have been amalgamated with the vehicle tax in Andhra Pradesh and provision for compounding them exists in many other States, there are still some States which do not permit composition of either passenger tax or goods tax. Particulars are given in Annexures V and VI. All these differing rules and regulations serve as impediments to the free flow of traffic and involve delay.

Absence of Single-Point Tax: One of the impediments to the development of inter-State transport has been the obligation of the operators to pay taxes both to the 'home' State where the vehicle is registered and to the other States through which it passes. In the early years of fifties, some States had entered into mutual agreements permitting the operation of a specified number of transport vehicles on inter-State routes, but such agreements did not exist in all the States. The negotiations between the States had been generally of a prolonged nature and had often failed to produce any agreement. Instances were common of transport vehicles having had to stop at the border of a State in the absence of any mutual agreement and passengers and goods had to be transferred to other vehicles. These difficulties have, however, been mitigated to some extent at present.

The grant of inter-State permits for operation in contiguous States is at present determined by reciprocal agreements between two State Governments according to which a specified number of vehicles registered in State 'A' is allowed to operate in State 'B' without the need for the payment of vehicle tax due to State 'B' in return for an equal or agreed number of vehicles from State 'B' operating in State 'A' and enjoying similar exemp-

*Rajasthan, Uttar Pradesh, Punjab, Haryana, Assam, Himachal Pradesh, Manipur and Tripura.

tion from payment of vehicle tax. The vehicles operating under such agreements are subjected to "single-point levy". These agreements have been arrived at by the State Governments largely keeping in view the interests of their own operators and the revenues of the States. The reciprocal agreements do not generally provide for a single-point levy in respect of vehicles operating on temporary permits. In many States, the principle of single-point levy does not cover taxes on passengers and goods.

Trucks operating on long distance routes covering more than two States are required to pay vehicle tax and goods tax to all the intervening States even on regular permits.

Under Utilisation of the Trucking Industry

Although the growth indices shown in Chapter 2 suggest that there has been great progress in the field of road transport according to the number of vehicles registered in the country and the extent of traffic carried by them, yet in one section of the industry progress appears to be poor. Even after 15 years of planning, the average utilisation of a vehicle remains as low as 1,29,000 tonne-kilometres a year in 1965-66. It means that a vehicle with a pay-load of 9 tonnes with load factor at 70% operate only 60 kms. a day. This also indicates that the industry is not able to utilise even 50 per cent of its rates capacity. On the basis of the estimates in the draft outline of the 4th Plan, the utilisation of a vehicle would be increasing from 1,29,000 tonne-kilometres in 1965-66 to 1,41,000 tonne-kilometres at the end of 1970-71 as per the table given below :

Year	Tonne-kilometres carried by road transport (Millions)	Number of Trucks	Average utilisation per truck (In tonne-kilometres)
1950-51	5,500	81,888	67,000
1955-56	8,950	1,19,097	1,75,000
1960-61	17,300	1,71,045	1,00,000
1965-66*	33,000	2,55,000	1,29,000
1970-71*	60,000	4,25,000	1,41,000

* Estimated.

South Zone Agreement

The five States of Maharashtra, Madras, Mysore, Andhra Pradesh and Kerala have entered into a special reciprocal agreement for the multi-State operation of public carriers in these States. The main provisions of the scheme contained in this agreement are that each State will authorise the issue of permits to 200 vehicles to operate on all National Highways and State Highways of all the five States. In addition to the taxes payable to the home State, each vehicle will pay a surcharge comprising vehicle tax and goods tax, at the rate of Rs. 500 per annum to each of the other States ; this means that a vehicle will have to pay Rs. 2,000 per annum in all for operating in all the other States covered by the agreement. This amount is to be paid to the home State who will pass on the share due to the other States.

Study Group On Motor Vehicle Taxation

The Study Group on Motor Vehicle Taxation has made a detailed study of the problems facing inter-State road transport and suggested many remedies. Particularly in respect of taxation, the Group h s, after careful study, recommended a new scheme to eliminate the various procedural difficulties connected with taxation and also to extend the principle of single-point taxation to vehicles operating on multi-State routes. It has suggested a graded system of inter-State standard tax based on the distance covered by a vehicle outside its home State. The full scheme as envisaged by the Study Group is given is Annexure VIII.

Graded Form Of Inter-State Standard Tax

The main features of this scheme are that a vehicle operating on inter-State route will be liable to pay taxes on two counts, viz., (1) to the State Government where it is registered at whatever rates prevail therein, and (2) a uniform graded system of standard tax also payable in the home State for operating on routes outside the Home State. The maximum of this tax is proposed to be Rs. 2,500 per annum for 11 tonne RLW and Rs. 3,000 per annum for other heavy vehicles of more than 11 tonne RLW. According to the scheme, the tax liability of a truck will depend proportionately on the distance covered as per the following scales :

Distance	Tax Payable
First 50 miles outside the "Home State" (the State of registration of vehicles).	Nil
From 51 to 150 miles outside home State	25 per cent of the Standard Tax
From 151 to 350 miles outside home State	50% -do-
From 351 to 600 miles outside home State	75% -do-
Over 600 miles outside home State	100% -do-

We have carefully considered the scheme suggested by the Study Group and given our view in the concluding portion of Chapter 4.

Summing Up

The necessity to develop inter-State transport in the

present context of economic development is undisputed; such development is, however, not feasible so long as the taxation and licensing policies are not simplified and the principles of taxation and regulations governing them made uniform throughout the country. The recommendations of the various Committees, Study Groups and other bodies will, therefore, continue to be ineffective as long as there is no Central legislation to lay down uniform principles of taxation and licensing for the whole country. The Central Government will have to consider ways and means to overcome these short comings so that a Central authority can be constituted to carry out these objectives. We have discussed these matters in the next Chapter.

Regulation And Taxation Of Inter-State Road Transport

Formation of inter state Transport Commission-Background: The idea of setting up a Central agency for regulation and development of inter-State transport was mooted at the time of formulating the Second Five-Year Plan. It was felt that there was greater need to coordinate all forms of transport as adjuncts to each other in order to provide a broad base of transport supply for the realisation of Plan targets. But coordination of road transport was found difficult as each State had followed its own pattern of regulation and taxation of motor vehicles. There was not much uniformity between them. This created impediments for vehicles to operate on inter-State routes. The efforts of the Centre to bring about reciprocal agreements between the States for inter-State movement of vehicles had not borne much result. The Central Government, had, therefore, decided to take over the regulation of inter-State road transport under entry 42 of the List I—Union List—in the Seventh Schedule to the Constitution. The Joint (Select) Committee of Parliament to whom the Motor Vehicles (Amendment) Bill, 1955 had been referred, was of the unanimous opinion that a Central Body should be set up for this purpose. This was named as the 'Inter-State Transport Commission' and Sections 63A to 63C of the Act defining the set up of this body were introduced through the Motor Vehicles (Amendment) Act, 1956.

Existing Machinery: The inter-State Transport Commission was thus constituted by the Government of India on the 8th March, 1958. It consists of a Chairman and such other members, not being less than two, as the Central Government may think fit to appoint. In actual practice, the number of other members has varied between two and four. For the purpose of assisting the Commission in the performances of its functions, in relation to any area or route, common to two or more States, the Commission has to associate with itself, for such purposes as may be prescribed, representatives of each of the Governments interested, who is to be chosen by the Government concerned. A person so associated has the right to take part in the relevant discussions.

Functions as contained in the Motor Vehicles Act: Section 63(2) of the Motor Vehicles Act, 1939, describes the powers and functions of the Commissioner as under :

The Commission shall perform throughout an Inter-State Region all or such of the following functions as it may be authorised to do by the Central Government by notification in the Official Gazette, namely :

(a) To prepare schemes for the development, coordination or regulation of the operation of transport vehicles and, in particular of goods vehicles in an Inter-State Region ;

(b) To settle all disputes and decide all matters on which differences of opinion arise in connection with the development, coordination or regulation of the operation of transport vehicles in an inter-State Region ;

(c) To issue directions to the State Transport Authorities or Regional Transport Authorities interested regarding the grant, revocation and suspension of permits and of counter-signatures of permits for the operation of transport vehicles in respect of any route or area common to two or more States ;

(d) To grant, revoke or suspend any permit or counter-sign any permit for the operation of any transport vehicle in respect of such route or area common to two or more States as may be specified in this behalf by the Central Government ;

(e) To perform such other functions as may be prescribed by the Central Government under Section 63C.

Powers as contained in the Rules: The Commission has also been empowered to exercise and discharge the following functions under Rule 21 of the inter-State Transport Commission Rules 1960 :

(i) Classification of routes and areas as inter-State routes and inter-State areas for the purpose of developing road motor transport ;

(ii) Survey of the requirements of any inter-State region for road motor transport ;

(iii) Examining how best the additional requirements of such region can be met ;

(iv) Preparing detailed schemes for provision or improvement of motor transport facilities in specific inter-State regions and advising the Central Government and the State Governments regarding the manner of implementation of such schemes ;

(v) Division of traffic in inter-State regions among the States concerned ;

(vi) Specifying the conditions which may be attached to a permit in respect of an inter-State region, subject to the provision of Chapter IV of the Act ;

(vii) Fixing the maximum and minimum fares for the carriage of passengers in an inter-State region ;

(viii) Fixing the maximum and minimum freight rates for the various kinds of goods to be carried in an inter-State region, and laying down the conditions for the carriage of such goods ;

(ix) Requiring the holders of inter-State permits to furnish such periodical returns, statistics and other informations as the Commission may, from time to time, desire ;

(x) Advising the State Governments in the matter of :

(a) Taxation of motor vehicle ;

(b) Load restrictions ; and

(c) Rationalisation of goods transport services in inter-State regions ;

(xi) Assisting in the conclusion of reciprocal arrangements amongst State Governments for the smooth and efficient operation of Inter-State Motor Transport Services ;

(xii) Devising ways and means of extending road transport to inter-State regions where there is scope for its extension without creating uneconomic competition with other means of transport already available or likely to become available there ;

(xiii) Coordinating the operation of tran port vehicles with other means of transport in inter-State regions as to ensure that ;

(a) There is no uneconomic competition between the motor transport operations inter-se and between motor transport and other forms of transport ; and

(b) There is no duplication or waste of transport capacity ;

(xiv) Regulating the timings of the passenger bus services in inter-State regions so as best to serve the convenience of passengers ;

(xv) Advising the Central Government from time to time in regard to such measures as may be necessary for an integrated and coordinated development of Inland Transport Resources of the country and their optimum utilisation ;

(xvi) Visiting such places as it may consider necessary for the discharge of its functions ;

(xvii) Convening meetings of the representative of State Governments, motor transport operators, and other interested concerns ;

(xviii) Sending out its officers to inter-State regions to check whether the directions issued by the Commission are being implemented, or to carry out a census of traffic ;

(xix) Recommending to State Governments the enforcement of such traffic and safety measures in inter-State regions as the Commission may deem necessary ;

(xx) Doing all other things to facilitate the proper carrying on the functions of the Commission.

The Commission has so far been given the powers under clauses (a), (b), (c) and (e) and para 3 above. The powers under clause (d) viz., to grant, revoke or suspend an inter-State permit or counter-sign any such permit in respect of the routes or areas specified in this behalf by Central Government have not so far been vested in it.

Limitations of Powers : The powers given to the Commission are, however, restricted, regarding clause (b). Under a convention agreed to between the Ministries of Home Affairs and Transport, the Commission is to discharge its functions and statutory duties as laid down in the Motor Vehicles Act, only as long as it can secure the agreement of the States concerned. Where there is a dispute or disagreement between the Commission and the State or between one State and another which the Commission is unable to resolve, the Commission is required to refer the matter in dispute to concerned Zon al Council for bringing about a settlement. There are 5 such Zonal Councils. The Commission can issue a directive under the Act only if the said Zonal Council is unable to settle the dispute. This procedure inevitably results in delay in the settlement of disputes.

The procedure as envisaged in the convention referred to above obviously comes in the way of working of inter-State road transport. The Commission has become a mere Advisory Body whose functions are very much restricted to bring about agreement between the State Governments concerned in the matter of issuing permits.

Mysore High Court Ruling : The powers to issue directions under clause (c) have also been circumscribed by judgement of the Mysore High Court. A directive was issued by the Commission prescribing certain conditions for the selection of operators by the State and Regional Transport Authorities when a permit for a goods vehicle was to be granted in respect of an inter-State route. On appeal, the Mysore High Court held that the Commission could not issue a directive to State Transport Authorities in the matter of selection of applicants for the issue of permits as it is a judical function, which should not be influenced by an outside agency including the Inter-State Transport Commission.

It would thus appear that the Commission at present is allowed to exercise powers contained only in clause (a) in Section 63A(2) alone.

Working of Inter-State Transport Commission

Having regard to the constitutional set up and the limitations under which the Commission was required to function, the record of performance of the Commission during the last 8 years has been commendable. It has tried to bring about agreements between a number of contiguous States and it has tried to help the cause of inter-State tronsport by bringing about zonal agreements. The Commission has also tried to get greater facilities for issue of regular permits for inter-State operations and a number of such permits have been issued.

Drawbacks of Reciprocal Agreements : The various reciprocal agreements between States have helped the movement of traffic in contiguous States. However, such agreements do not lead to full development of inter-State transport as they have many drawbacks. These might be briefly mentioned here. as follows :

(a) Most of the reciprocal agreements are based on parity. This basis cannot meet the situation where the States are of in equal size, differ in traffic generation, vehicle population road condition and general economic development. For instance, there can be no parity between Goa and Maharashtra, Orissa and Andhra Pradesh. Parity between such States would not be taking into consideration the demands of traffic.

(b) There is possibility (and this was mentioned by some operators) that the principle of parity might lead to unfair competition in the States where the level of taxation is higher than in neighbouring States.

(c) As stated in para 8 of the preceding chapter, vehicles under regular counter-signature enjoy exemption from the payment of vehicle tax to the neighbouring States covered by the agreement ; but the passenger and goods tax has to be paid to both the States. Apart from the difficulty of paying it to more than one authority, it causes hardship to the operator as he has to maintain detailed accounts and submit returns to the authorities in both the States. In case of goods tax the hardship is still greater. The difficulties of multiple taxation still persist inspite of reciprocal agreements.

(d) A serious limitation of reciprocal agreements is that they provide no relief to operators plying on routes covering more than two States. There may be reciprocity between Maharashtra and Delhi but the intervening States not being the parties to such agreements, insist on the payment of vehicle tax and goods tax from the operators, even if they do not pick up or unload goods in those States.

We, therefore, feel that reciprocal agreements have not been able to remove a number of handicaps in the way of inter-State operations.

Multi-State Operation : The total number of trucks in the country is about 2 and a half lakhs ; out of those that ply under regular permits in contiguous States are estimated at 25,000. The number plying under regular permits on multi-States routes is only a few hundreds. Although the Inter-State Transport Commission has issued directions to State authorities to grant 726 multi-State permits, the number of such permits issued so far is only 163. This might be due to the difficulties to which multi-State road transport is subjected. Quite often even when an offer of permits was made, there was no operator to come forward to accept that offer. The operators are required to pay vehicle tax and also goods tax for the whole year to each and every State which the vehicles traverse. In the circumstances, the operators probably prefer taking out temporary permits only for short periods as and when they have an assured load.

Regulatory Powers of I.S.T.C. Inadequate

The facts mentioned in the preceding paras show the inadequacy of the regulatory powers vested in the Inter State Transport Commission. It is clear that the power of regulation by itself is not of much practical value as long as the Commission has no power to ensure uniform principles of taxation for inter-State movement of traffic. The taxation tariff of each State being different, the road transport operations are necessarily delayed by multiplicity of taxes and the procedures connected thereto. Smooth flow of traffic is not, therefore, possible under the prevailing conditions. Therefore, the fundamental issue to be resolved is that of taxation. Any regulation cannot become effective without the power to levy and regulate taxes. We are of the firm view that the power of taxation is necessary for enabling the Commission to carry out its work effectively. There is no denying the fact that the powers vested in the Inter-State Transport Commission, even if allowed to be exercised fully, do not enable it adequately to fulfil its intended functions of development, coordination and regulation of Inter-State Transport. We, therefore, feel that appropriate measures should be taken to vest in the Commission the authority to levy tax in Inter-State Transport within such frameworks as may be approved by Parliament.

Recommendations of C.T.P.C.

The Committee on Transport Policy and Coordination, while considering inter-State road transport proposed two sets of permits, viz., inter-State permits and Intra-State permits. While the regulation of vehicles operating within the States was to be left entirely to the control of the State Governments, the Committee suggested that inter-State transport should be taken over by the Centre. They recommended that inter-State permits both for buses and trucks should be issued under the authority of the Inter State Transport Commission, the actual permit, however, being issued by the State authorities. They also recommended that the present reciprocal agreements for determining the number of permits need not continue. In respect of taxations, the Committee desired that there should be uniform rules for all inter-State vehicles and such vehicles should be free to pass through the territory of any State lying enroute.

While we are in broad agreement with the suggestion made by the Committee on Transport Policy and Coordination, we would for practical considerations, suggest certain modifications therein. In practice, difficulties might arise in operation of vehicles of there are two sets of permits; one for purely intra-State traffic and the other for inter-State traffic. There might be complications inside a State as the State Government would have no control over an inter-State vehicle registered in the State and might not look with favour on such a vehicle. Moreover, it might not be possible to check the activities of an inter-State vehicle inside the State where it has its centre of origin. There might be complaints of contravention or rules by such vehicles indulging in intra-State traffic also.

Liability to Home State

We feel that basically a commercial vehicle should be registered in a particular State where it normally resides and the primary permit should be issued by the Home State. It will pay all the necessary taxes to the Home State, which will include vehicle tax and passenger and goods tax. Those vehicles which desire to carry on inter-State traffic also will have to obtain an additional permit which will be infact an extension of the primary permit and which will enable the vehicle to carry on operations outside the State of origin. Such additional permit for inter-State operation should be granted by the Inter-State Transport Commission, though the permit itself will be issued by the authorities in the Home State, acting on behalf of the Commission. According to the proposed arrangements, every vehicle will be resident and registered in its State of origin while the regulation of the Central authority will only be for the purpose of inter-State traffic. At the same time, the jurisdiction of the State in which the vehicle is registered in respect of levies of taxes and fees, vis-a-vis, intra-State transport will remain unfettered.

Definition of Inter-State Transport

In view of the above distinction, it becomes all the more necessary that the scope and meaning of the expression 'Inter-State Transport' should be unambiguously and authoritatively defined so as to preserve in tact the States, present jurisdiction over intra-State transport while excluding inter-State transport from their purview. Broadly all transport movement other than Intra-State Transport should, in our view, be classed as inter-State transport, intra-State being defined as transport in areas or routes falling predominantly within the boundaries of any one State of Union Territory.

Constitutional Remedy

It may well be that even under the existing provisions of the Constitution, with reference to Entry 42 of the Union List in the Seventh Schedule, Parliament is competent to legislate in the above manner in respect of inter-State transport. If so, action should be taken speedily by the Government of India to introduce legislation whereby Parliament could authorise the Inter-State Transport Commission to levy and collect taxes within the framework approved by it. Such legislation as the Parliament may pass should specifically provide for the assignment to the States of the proceeds of the levy so imposed and the principles of its distribution. We have given in the next paragraph the framework for the levy and collection of taxes for inter-State operation of goods vehicles and the basis for the distribution of tax proceeds, which might be adopted as an interim measure.

Should it be found that under the existing provisions of the Constitution taxation in respect of inter-State transport is not within the competence of Parliament, we would recommend an amendment of the Constitution for this purpose.

Inter-State Standard Tax

We have examined the proposals made by the Study Group on Motor Vehicles Taxation particularly those in respect of inter-State Standard Tax. We feel that the scheme of inter-State Standard Tax framed by the Study Group and the criterion suggested by them (vide Annexure VIII) for distribution of proceeds are generally acceptable subject to two important modifications. While the Study Group has not recommended the levy of any tax for the first 50 miles outside the home State, we are of the view that having regard to the present configuation of different States and flow of traffic, it may not be fair to deny altogether a share of the tax for States in which the route traversed by an inter-State vehicles is less than 50 miles. To obviate this anomaly, we recommend that the first two slabs proposed by the Study Group be merged with the tax payable being fixed at 25 per cent of the standard tax. While making this recommendation, we are conscious that there are short enclaves or pockets of other States through which traffic originating and terminating in the same State has sometimes to move in order to avoid traversing longer distances. With a view to eliminating hardship on such intra-State movement of traffic through short distances lying within other States, we recommend that a special provisions be made for exempting vehicles engaged in intra-State transport from payment of tax in such cases provided there is no loading or unloading in the stretch lying in the enclave or pocket of the neighbouring State. We further recommend that the quantum of inter-State standard tax which is to be eventually settled after consulting the State Governments, may as an interim measure, be fixed at Rs. 2,500 per annum on a truck with R.L.W. of II tonnes and Rs. 3,000 per annum for vehicles exceeding II tonnes R.L.W. We would, however, incidentally like to draw attention to the recent Zonal Agreement (Annexure IX) between 5 Southern States where the tax including goods tax for inter-State transport has been fixed at the maximum of Rs. 2,000 per annum for the entire zone.

The tax liability of vehicles plying on inter-State routes under the scheme recommended by us is given in the table below :

Standard tax : Rs. 2,500 upto II tonnes R.L.W.
Rs. 3,000 over II tonnes R.L.W.

Distance	Tax payable
Upto 150 miles (240 kms) outside the home State.	25 per cent of the standard tax.
From 151 to 350 miles (241 to 560 kms) outside the home State	50 per cent of the standard tax.
From 351 to 600 miles (561 to 960 kms) outside the home State	75 per cent of the standard tax.
Over 600 miles (960 kms) outside home State.	100 per cent of the standard tax.

We have not been able to consider fully the question of standard tax for passenger vehicles. We propose to consider this question at the time of recommending general principles of taxation of motor vehicles.

Set up of Inter-State Transport Commission

The Inter-State Transport Commission would be the proper agency for regulating inter-State transport and its taxation. We recommend that the Commission should be reconstituted, de novo and in addition to the powers that the present Commission has under the Motor Vehicles Act, the new Commission will have additional powers regarding taxation. The Commission will have the authority to decide the quantum of permits for each State though the actual selection and issuing of permits will be carried out by the State authorities concerned acting on its behalf. The Commission will also levy and regulate taxes on inter-State transport vehicles. The taxes levied and collected will be realised normally by State authorities acting on its behalf to be ultimately distributed to the various States according to principles laid down under Article 269 of the Constitution.

Recommendations Regarding I.S.T.C. : According to the plan that we are recommending the Commission that will come into being will be different and very much more strengthened with wider powers than the present one. Its structure and functions which we are suggesting are given below. In doing so, we are keeping in view the task that if before the Commission:

(i) All powers which at present are given under Sections 63A(1) to 63C of the Motor Vehicles Act should be given to the new Commission in the substantive Act itself by Parliament and not left to be granted by Government through notifications.

(ii) In addition, the Commission will have the power to levy and regulate taxation of inter-State transport. It will also fix the rates on the basis of the framework laid down by Parliament. It is recommended that the collection of taxes be carried out generally by the States acting on behalf of the Commission. The Commission will have the authority to recommend modifications in this regard where it thinks necessary.

(iii) The Commission should have for discharging its functions properly the power to appoint Committees of one or more persons for examinations of specific matters and enquiries. It will no doubt associate representatives of States or specialists in advisory capacity whenever necessary to enquire into or deal with specific problems in connection with inter-State transport development.

Composition of the Commission : As the existing Inter-State Transport Commission is composed of part time officers representing different interests, it will not be in a position to discharge the functions enumerated above. It will not be a workable arrangement to have a Commission representing different interests as the number of interests which should appropriately be represented is very large and decisions taken by members representing particular interests might not create an impression of impartiality which is essential for making the work of the Commission effective. Further part time members often change and it is difficult to have consistent and effective working. The Committee is strongly of opinion that having regard to the functions it is expected to perform, the Commission should be a high power independent authority. Its composition should be such as should inspire confidence not only amongst operators but also amongst the States in regard to the discharge of its functions. The Commission, in order to carry out the executive duties enjoined upon it, ought to be small with full time members. In the Committee's opinion it should be composed of three members. It should have a Chairman of a high status preferably chosen from public life who should be able to wield independent authority and taken an objective view of the demands of the various interests. The other members should have wide experience of administration or transport or finance or economics. They should also have no personal interest in any transport undertaking or automobile manufacturing concern. In order to give it requisite authority, the status of the Commission should be similar to that of the Union Public Service Commission, the Tariff Commission or the Forward Markets Commission.

We need hardly add that the Commission should be equipped with a proper Secretariat and also have a Research Wing of its own in order to discharge its duties.

The powers vested in the present Inter State Transport Commission, even if allowed to be exercised fully, do not enable it adequately to fulfil its intended functions of development, coordination and regulation of Inter-State Transport. We, therefore, feel that appropriate measures should be taken to vest in the Commission the authority to levy tax on inter-State transport with in such a frame work as may be approved by Parliament. At the same time, the jurisdiction of the State in which the vehicle is registered, in respect of levies of tax and fees, vis-a-vis intra-State Transport, will, however, remain unfettered. This makes it all the more necessary that the scope and meaning of the expression "inter-State Transport" should be unambiguously and authoritatively defined so as to preserve in tact the States, present jurisdiction over inter-State Transport, while excluding inter-State Transport from their purview. Broadly, all transport movement other than intra-State Transport should, in our view, be classified as inter-State Transport, intra-State Transport being as transport in areas or on routes falling predominantly within the boundaries of any one State or Union Territory.

It may well be that even under the existing provisions of the Constitutions, with special reference to Entry 42 of the Union List in the Seventh Schedule, Parliament is competent to legislate in the above manner in respect of inter-State Transport. If so, action should be taken speedily by the Government of India to introduce legislation whereby Parliament could authorise the Inter-State Transport Commission to levy and collect taxes within the framework approved by it. Such legislation as Parliament may pass should specifically provide for the assignment to the States of the proceeds of the levy so imposed and the principles of its distribution. We have suggested a suitable framework for the levy and distribution of taxes on inter-State Transport, which should find general acceptance amongst States as an interim measure.

Should it be found that under the existing provisions of the Constitution, taxation in respect of inter-State Transport is not within the competence of Parliament, we would have no hesitation in recommending an amendment of the Constitution itself for this purpose.

The newly constituted Inter-State Transport Commission should be a full time high power independent authority. In order to carry out the duties enjoined upon it, it ought to be a small body composed of three full time members, it should have a Chairman of a high status, preferably chosen from public life who should be able to wield independent authority and take an objective view of the demands of the various interests. The other members should have wide experience of administration or transport or finance or economics. It should have high status similar to that of the Union Public Service Commission, Tariff Commission or Forward Markets Commission.

COMMITTEE ON SOCIAL SCIENCE RESEARCH, 1965—REPORT

New Delhi, Planning Commission, 1968, 132p.

Chairman : Shri V.K.R.V. Rao.
Members : Shri D. R. Gadgil ; Shri A. Aiyappan ; Shri K. L. Joshi ; Shri J. N. Khosla ; Shri R. Mukherjee ; and Shri M. S. Gore.
Secretary : Shri Harbans Lal.

APPOINTMENT

The Government of India, Planning Commission appointed a Committee on Social Science Research vide their resolution No. F. 1-2/65-RPG dated New Delhi,

September 11, 1965. In recognition of the important contribution that social sciences can make to planning and development, suitable provision had been made in each Plan for organising, in cooperation with the Universities and other institutions, investigation and research on economic, social and administrative problems of national development. The experience of the last thirteen years in promoting social research and directing it to the requirements of planning has revealed the need for a review of the whole field by an appropriate body. Government feel that such a review would be helpful in bringing about a more coordinated growth of social research in the country as well as providing guidelines for its expansion, in the light of the emerging requirements of the developing economy. Accordingly, the Government of India have decided to constitute a Committee to review the status of social science research in the country and suggest guidelines for the future.

TERMS OF REFERENCE

"To survey the current situation in relation to research in the Social Sciences in India, and make recommendations regarding their future line of development, including the organisational steps necessary for the same."

CONTENTS

Introductory ; Output and Quality of Research ; Recommendation ; Tables ; Annexures I to VIII.

RECOMMENDATIONS

The factors impeding progress of social science research have been outlined and the tasks that will have to be attended for putting research in social science disciplines on the path of sound development are given below :

(a) Accelerating improvement in the output and the quality of research work.

(b) Promoting a coordinated and balanced distribution of research over difficult disciplines, different regions and different categories of research.

(c) Building up an expanding corps of research orkers.

To attain these objectives, a number of problems will have to be tackled and the operation of several deterrents countered. We will now turn to steps necessary for this purpose.

Need For A Policy Of Social Science Research

Government of India has recognised this in the Scientific Policy Resolution of March 1958 which declares its faith in scientific and technological research, as also the directives of action for its promotion. What is needed is an extension of this declaration to social science research with similar emphasis and expression of governmental attitude. Understanding of the social phenomena and human behaviour, knowledge about the social process and its determinants, are essential for designing policies to promote social change and to produce a dynamic society capable of absorbing and utilizing the scientific and technological developments for the welfare of human beings. The importance in this fundamental consideration.

Machinery Needed : Indian Council Of Social Science Research

Unsatisfactory stage of social science research is due to the absence of any Central or national organisation, which could, not only bring the social scientists together and provide a forum for exchange of views between them but also act as a spokesman for social science research and elicit support and recognition by government. Such a gap in the institutional set up is not unique of India.

In specific terms we recommend that an Indian Council of Social Science Research be set up by a Government of Indian Resolution in the same manner as the Council of Scientific and Industrial Research was set up (vide Department of Commerce Resolution No. 148 I and D (57)/41 dated September 26, 1942). The Council should be a registered society under the Registration of Society Act (Act 21 of 1860). This is important to give necessary autonomy to the Council and ensure objectivity in the discharge of its responsibility. The council should be under the Education Ministry for administrative and budgetary purposes, as is the Council of Scientific and Industrial Research. It should consist of a Chairman and 25 members nominated by the government. The Chairman of the Council should invariably be a leading social scientist of the country. We suggest the following composition of members.

(i) Social Scientists — 15

From universities, specialised reasearch institutions/ Associations and government representatives.

(ii) Users! Government And Private — 6

(iii) Ex-Officio Members — 5

Secretary, University Grants Commission.

Director-General, Council of Scientific and Industrial Research.

Director, National Council of Educational Research and Training.

Secretary, Indian Council of Agricultural Research.

Member-Secretary, Indian Council of Social Science Research.

The tenure of office of its members should be 5 years, after which a fresh nomination may be made by the government.

Functions Of The Council

The responsibility of the Indian Council of Social

Science Research will be as follows :

1. To indicate periodically areas and topics on which research is to be promoted.

2. To initiate and conduct research in neglected or new areas.

3. To sponsor research programmes, as well as, research projects, and administer grants to institutions and individuals for associations, standard journals and institutions or organisations engaged in the conduct or sponsoring of research.

4. To give both development and maintenance grants to research institutions in social sciences that do not constitute either affiliated or constituent institutions of statutory universities in India.

5. To provide technical assistance for the formulation of research programmes and designing of research projects by individuals or institutions, and to organize and support institutional arrangements for training in research methodology.

6. To review the progress of research and to give advice to the users of research in government or outside.

7. To coordinate research activities in the field of social sciences.

8. To encourage programmes of inter-disciplinary research through grants and technical assistance and initiate and, if necessary, conduct inter-disciplinary research when considered necessary.

9. To act as a liasion with foreign agencies sponsoring and financing research in India and undertake collaborative arrangements.

10. To develop and support Centres for documentation Service, maintenance, and supply of data, inventory of current research work and preparation of national register of social scientists.

11. To organise, sponsor and finance seminars, workshops, study circles, working groups/parties, and conferences for promoting research or utilisation of research.

12. To give grants for publication of research work and to undertake publication of research digests, periodicals and journals.

13. To institute and administer a pool of social scientists.

14. To institute and administer research scholarships, fellowships and awards for research by students, teachers and other research workers and in particular to award senior fellowships, for research in Social Sciences that will enable research workers in universities to complete their research work for publication or undertake whole time research for a defined period on topics in which they are specially interested and for doing research, on which, they are specially qualified.

15. To increase utilisation in government of social science research findings.

Operational Arrangements

The council will operate through Committees and subcommittees constituted by it from among social scientists working in different universities, institutions or government departments. It will be provided with a strong and permanent secretariat. A competent social scientist will be the Member-Secretary of the Council and head of the secretariat which will be manned by qualified social scientists representing different disciplines. The details of the secretariat set up will be as outlined in the Article of the Memorandum of the Council. The Headquarters of the Council will be at Delhi. The council will meet at least twice a year.

We have ascertained the requirements of the Council in the initial years and recommend to the Government to make a provision of Rs. one crore per year initially. This amount should, however, be progressively raised as the requirements of the Council will grow as it takes on more responsibility. The Council should, however, have powers to obtain donations or funds from other sources, such as foundations or endowments etc. and administer these funds for the purpose of promoting social science research. Provision should also be made for the Council, to supplement its resources out of such fees, sale proceeds, royalties or earnings as may accrue from its activities.

Relation With University Grants Commission

The proposed Indian Council of Social Science Research will supplement the University Grants Commission. The U.G.C. is really concerned with the development of departments in the universities and institutions etc., creation of new posts and enlargement of staff. It thus gives only structural support, to institutions of higher learning and is principally concerned with problems connected with development and functioning of universities. The proposed Council on the other hand will be concerned with provision of the facilities like documentation, data library, promotional facilities for seminars, workshops and conferences, etc. which really supplement the structure already existing in the universities and institutions. The Council will supplement the U.G.C. in another way also it will cover the growing number of research institutions, which do not qualify for the assistance from the University Grants Commission.

It is for this reason that separate Councils have been established for scientific research, medical research, agricultural research and educational research even though research and teaching in the concerned disciplines are conducted in universities or university like institutions. The composition of the University Grants

Commission provides for the representation of university administration and of all disciplines including humanities, social science, physical science and technology while the composition of Social Science Research Council will need representation of social science disciplines institutions and government departments conducting research in social sciences as also the users of social sciences research. We envisage this body to provide technical assistance for promotion of social science research and not merely be an administrative or grant making body. These later functions are incidental and its major responsibility is of building research potential and promoting its effective utilisation. Research programming, designing of research projects, technical guidance and assistance to research institutions and research workers will from the core of its activities. Sponsoring of research and financial support to research workers and research institutions or research students will only be subsequent links, in the chain of its responsibility.

Relation With Research Programmes Committee

We also recognise the useful role of the Research Programmes Committee of the Planning Commission over the past 14 years in promoting research on socio-economic problems. The Committee has been able to create a climate for socio-economic research in universities and research institutions mobilise research talents outside government for undertaking research on problems directly related to socio-economic planning and development. In the process it has succeeded in the production of some highly valuable pieces of research. In a small way, it has also created awareness of research findings among policy-makers, as well as, formulators and implementors of development programmes. As research is an integral part of planning, such an organisation has to continue within the Planning Commission, to assist the Commission in identifying areas and problems of research emerging in the process of formulating and implementing development plans and to mobilise talented research workers outside government, to bring to bear on these problems their technical expertise. The Committee is, undoubtedly, to be reconstituted and its activities more closely and directly related to the needs of the Planning Commission. The entire field of research falling outside the Scope of the R.P.C. will be the function of the Council.

Suggested Course Of Action And Steps To Be Taken By The Council

We suggest below a course of action to be taken by the Council for the coming years, which flows from our analysis in the preeding chapters.

1. Identification of Areas of Research and Designing Of Research : The Council should, soon after, its establishment, arrange to prepare a programme of research periodically identifying areas and topics to sponsor programmes and projects for research in various disciplines. It should prepare guide-lines for designing projects by research workers in universities and institutions, and provide technical assistance in designing, coding, tabulation programme etc.

2. Research Training : Adequate provision for training in research methodology is essential for improving the output and quality of research. The Council should organise or sponsor periodical seminars of summer schools for training in research methodology to research students as well as to social scientists employed in universities, colleges, research institutions or government departments. It should also arrange with foreign foundations or foreign universities for overseas training of social scientists from this country in research methodology and advance techniques of research.

3. Promotion of Research in New Areas : For encouraging research in neglected or new areas such as inter-disciplinary research, the council may, when necessary, give special grants or provide technical and such other assistance as is within the competence of the Council.

4. Data Library and Documentation Centres : There is a strong case for setting up data library and documentation centres. We recommend that the Council may in the first instance put up a strong data library and documentation centre at the headquarters and then fan out such centres to other towns in the country—at least one each in east, north-east, west, south, north-west and central region. The data library and the documentation centre should maintain catalogues, bibliographies classified by disciplines, areas and sub-areas in order to cater to the requirements of research workers.

5. Conferences, Seminars and Workshops : For promoting coordinated development in research, it may hold periodical conferences or meetings for exchange of views between research workers of different institutions as also policy-makers, administrators, representatives of industries and those who are the users of research, etc.

6. Publication Grants : Another step in right direction would be, administration of publication grants to research workers and institutions of facilitate wider dissemination of the results of their research. The Council should supplement the University Grants Commission and other agencies in financing publication of research work. Since large part of research in universities takes the form of articles or papers in standard journals, the Council should also give financial assistance to learned associations or journals connected with promotion of research in Social Sciences. It should keep itself informed of the financial position of such associations as also of research institutions conducting social science research and give such general support, as may be called for, to put them on sound financial footing. This is yet another aspect of deficiency in the existing system of financial support.

7. **Special Awards for Research** : Further, we suggest, the Council should institute special awards for research work undertaken by teachers or others on their own. The value of the award may be placed at Rs. 1000 to Rs. 5000 depending on the nature and the quality of research work. As a further incentive, the Council should extend financial assistance to teachers or non-doctoral research workers, (other than those receiving awards or assistance from other sources) through an annual grant of a value sufficient to cover the cost of conducting such work. This should be routed through the employing agency and disbursed in instalments subject to satisfactory programme of work.

8. **National Register of Social Scientists** : In addition, we suggest that the Council should also maintain a a register of all social scientists giving particulars of their qualifications, present post, salary experience, research publications and willingness or unwillingness for assignments to temporary or permanent research posts. This register will provide information on the availability of research personnel of verying qualifications and level of experience. The information will prove useful in sponsoring research projects as also in mobilising higher level research personnel with requisite qualifications and experience.

9. **National Register of Ph. D. Students** : The Indian Council of Social Research should prepare a register of all candidates working for Ph. D. degree whether financed by it or not. It should make arrangements for keeping track of the progress of their work.

10. **National Pool of Research Workers** : The Council should institute a pool of research workers carrying an emolument of Rs. 400 a month. The recruitment to the pool should be made from those obtaining Ph. D. degree in social sciences for allocating to projects sponsored by the Council or in response to the request for research personnel received from universities, institutions or government departments. The pool may also have junior sector to which non-Ph-Ds with research experience in the field surveys may be recruited. The remuneration of this class may be Rs. 300 per month. Research personnel released from a project on completion, will revert to the pool till they are absorbed in another project. During the period of their employment in projects, their salary will be charged to the project and not to the Council, funds. For selecting pool officers, the Council will set up a selection committee, consisting of the Chairman of the Council, Member-Secretary and two or three advisers.

11. **Building Research Workers** : A sustained and rapid progress of social science research requires an enlarged flow of research workers. To ensure this, it is suggested that Indian Council of Social Science Research should institute at least 200 research scholarships of the value of Rs. 300 per month in addition to the number of research scholarships granted by the U.G.C. or from university funds. We would also suggest that University Grants Commission should raise the value of its own research scholarships to Rs. 300. The research scholarships to be instituted by the Indian Council of Social Science Research should be tenable for two years from the date of admission. Provision should, however, be made for the extension beyond two years due to unforseen circumstances, and in exceptional cases for a period not exceeding one year. A lumpsum grant of Rs. 1000 per Ph. D. student should also be provided to cover expenses incidental to the preparation of his thesis such as typing, stationary, travel for collection of data, etc.

The Indian Council of Social Science Research should institute one hundred fellowships of the value of Rs. 500 per month for Post-Doctoral research by Ph. D. degree holders or others, irrespective of whether it is done for a higher degree or not. This fellowship should also carry a lump sum grant of Rs. 1000 for incidental expenditure connected with the work.

12. **Modernisation of Syllabi and re orientation of Teaching in Social Science** : We understand that the University Grants Commission is already seized with the problem of revising the syllabus prescribed for postgraduate and under-graduate teaching in Social Sciences and has setup committees for this purpose. The Indian Council of Social Science Research should be associated with this work and represented on the committee so as to lend weight to the needs of Social Science Research.

INQUIRY INTO THE COLLISION OF DOWN EMPTY RAKE WITH REAR OF NO. K-3 DOWN LOCAL TRAIN AT THANA STATION, CENTRAL RAILWAY, ON 14TH SEPTEMBER, 1965—REPORT

Delhi, Manager of Publications, 1970, 15p.

Member : Shri Arya Bhushan.

APPOINTMENT

The Commission was constituted under the Ministry of Tourism and Civil Aviation (Commission of Railway Safety) in accordance with Rule 9 of the Railway Board's Notification No. 1926-T, dated March 19, 19?0 on September 14, 1965.

TERMS OF REFERENCE

To inquire into the Collision of Down Empty Rake with the rear of No. K-3 Down Local Train at Thana Station on the Bombay-Kalyan Broad Gauge quadruple line, electrified suburban section of the Central Railway at about 05.35 hours on September 14, 1965.

CONTENTS

Corrigendum; Summary; The Accident; Casualties; Inspection and Inquiry; The Trains; Number of Passengers; Damage; The Relief; Restoration of Traffic; Local Conditions (The Locality; Than Station and the System of Train Working; Permissible speeds; Whether and Visibility); Summary of Evidence; Inspection, Observations and Tests; Discussions; Conclusions; Recommendations made by the Commission of Railway Safety in Connection with Collision of Down Empty Rake with the Rear of No. K-3 Down Local Train at Thana Station, Central Rai'way, on September 14, 1965.

CONCLUSIONS

The Cause And Responsibility For The Accident

From the available evidence and my inspection and observations at site, I have come to conclusion that the accident was caused an account of the Line Clear having been given by the Thana 'C' Cabin for reception of the Down Empty Rake while K-3 Down Local continued to occupy the section, waiting outside the Down Home Signal No. 51-C.

Responsibility : The Cabin Assistant Station Master N.H. Bhushan is responsible for the accident by having cleared the block section while train No. K-3 Down Local still occupied it. He has, therefore, violated General Rule 336.

Leverman Maruti Vishram is also considered responsible in having contributed to the accident by not taking 'OFF' signal No. 51-C for train No. K-3 Down Local when he was fully aware that the Line clear had been granted for the following train viz., Down Empty Rake and the train despatched from 'B' Cabin. He is, therefore, found guilty of being grossly negligent in his duties.

It has, however, to be mentioned here that as stated in paras 32 to 37, the work load of the Cabin Assistant Station Master was heavy and beyond the capacity of one man, facilities provided to him were inadequated, and the work was being carried out under trying conditions on account of Civil Defence measures. Similarly, the leverman was working single handled at a time when the traffic was heavy.

Service Particulars: Cabin Assistant Station Master N. H. Bhusari is 45 years old. He was originally recruited as a traffic candidate on 28-7-1943 and was promoted as Cabin Assistant Station Master on 19-12-1945. He has an accident—free record and except for being censured for failure to use lever collars he had no other punishments. His last vision test took place on 1-2-1965.

Leverman Maruti Vishram is 48 and a half years of age, and was initially recruited as Assistant Pointsman on 12-2-1939. He had his promotion as Pointsman on 30-10-1941 and as Leverman on 12-11-1954. He had no punishment in connection with train operation but was censured and fined for coming late on duty and unauthorised absence. His last vision examination took place on 9-9-1965.

Relief Arrangements

The medical attention given to the victims of the accident was prompt and satisfactory and the injured were also properly looked after later in the hospitals and I am satisfied in this respect.

PARLIAMENTARY COMMITTEE ON THE DEMAND FOR PUNJABI SUBA, 1965—REPORT

New Delhi, Lok Sabha, 1966. III, 90p.

Chairman : Sardar Hukam Singh
Members :
Lok Sabha : Dr. M.S. Aney ; Shri Mani Ram Bagri ; Chowdhury Brahm Perkash ; Shri Surendranath Dwivedy ; Sardar Dhanna Singh Gulshan ; Shri Hem Raj ; H.H. Maharaja Karni Singhji of Bikaner ; Shri Lahri Singh ; Sardar Surjit Singh Majithia; Shri K.D. Malaviya ; Shri H.N. Mukerjee; Shri Krishna Chandra Pant ; Shri Sadhu Ram ; Shri Amar Nath Vidyalankar.
Rajya Sabha : Shri Bansi Lal ; Shri Uttam Singh Dugal; Shri Jogendra Singh ; Shri Dahyabhai V. Patel ; Shri Sadiq Ali ; Kumari Shanta Vasisht and Shri Atal Behari Vajpayee.
Secretary : Shri S.L. Shakdher.
Deputy Secretary : Shri M.C. Chawla

APPOINTMENT

On the September 6, 1965, the Minister of Home affairs (Shri Gulzari Lal Nanda) made a Statement in Lok Sabha in which he referred to the several steps which had been taken in recent years to arrive at an amicable arrangement for meeting the needs of the Punjabi and Hindi-speaking regions of the Punjab State and said that "the whole question (of formation of a Punjabi-speaking State) can be examined afresh with an open mind". He had added that "Government would be prepared to have further talks on the subject. We may hope that a co-operative solution would be discovered based on goodwill and a reasoned approached". A similar statement was made in the Rajya Sabha on the same date by the Minister of State in the Ministry of Home Affairs (Shri Jai Sukhlal Hathi).

Subsequently, on the September 23, 1965, the Minister of Home Affairs (Shri Gulzarilal Nanda) recalling his earlier statement of the September 6 1965, announced in Lok Sabha Government's decision "to set up a Committee of the Cabinet to pursue this matter further" and added "I would request you (the Speaker, Lok Sabha) and the Chairman, Rajya Sabha, to set up for the same purpose a Parliamentary Committee of members of both Houses of Parliament presided over by you". Concluding his Statement, he expressed his confidence that "the efforts of this Cabinet Committee and of the Parliamentary Committee will lead to a satisfactory settlement of the question. A similar statement was made by the Minister of Home Affairs in Rajya Sabha also on the same date.

TERMS OF REFERENCE

To arrive at an amicable arrangement for meeting the needs of the Punjabi and Hindi speaking regions of the Punjab State.

CONTENTS

Composition of the Committee ; Report ; Introduction ; Evolution of the Demand for Punjabi Suba ; Working of the Regional Formula in Punjab ; Demand for Haryana State ; Merger of Hill Areas of Punjab in Himachal Pradesh ; Conclusions and Recommendations ; Notes by Members ; Appendices from I to X.

RECOMMENDATIONS

Cooperative Solution

It was the earnest desire of the Committee to find a cooperative solution of the vexed linguistic problem facing Punjab which would be universally acceptable to all. After perusing the large number of memorandas/representations received by the Committee and hearing the various view points expressed by the different witnesses representing the various shades of opinion, it soon became evident that it was not possible to arrive at any 'cooperative solution' which would be unanimously acceptable to all without reservations. Nor is unanimity possible or necessary on all matters in a democratic set up. The next best thing was for the Committee to look for a solution which would be acceptable to the largest number of people and which would also be in the best interests of not only the people and the State of Punjab but also in the best interests of the country as a whole from the point of view of affinity between the various communities and the economic and cultural well being of the people.

Various Alternative

(a) **Status Quo** : The bulk of the evidence before the Committee suggest the re-organisation of the State on linguistic basis. Even the Chief Minister of the Punjab State admitted that the present position needed a change and status quo in its entirely was not possible.

But a section of the people from the Punjab convassed before the Committee that the Status Quo might be maintained in the Punjab. In support of this argument, it was urged that the Punjab was not a unilingual State but a bilingual State with the people speaking both Hindi and Punjabi spread over throughout the State, although in varying percentages. Another argument advanced in favour of the Status Quo was that any division of the State would adversely affect the economy of the State and the resulting units would not be financially viable. A third argument advanced in favour of the Status Quo was that any reorganisation of the State would not be in the interests of the security of the country and would weaken the defences of India.

The Committee have carefully considered all the arguments advanced for and against the reorganisation of the existing State of Punjab. The witness who appeared before the Committee could not satisfactorily prove to them as to how the linguistic reorganisation of the State of Punjab would adversely affect the economy of the area or the defence of the country. The Committee has no authentic data before them to show that it would be so. The Committee requested the Ministry of Home Affairs. Government of India, to furnish a note or a paper on the viability of the proposed Punjabi-speaking State from the point of view of defence and the finance but the Government expressed their inability to comply with request as the former did not like to involve themselves either way 'in a controversy' (vide D.O. No. 38/3/66—S.R. dated the 11th March, 1966 from Shri B.S. Raghavan Deputy Secretary, Ministry of Home Affairs to Shri M.C. Chawla, Deputy Secretary, Lok Sabha Secretariat). Although this Committee are not an expert body on matters relating to the defence and finance but it should be self-evident that security or defence of the country should not be affected by a mere linguistic reorganisation of the State. Defence is a Central Subject and the State Governments have nothing to do with it. On the contrary, it should strengthen the defence of the country, if there are on the borders people whose political and economic aspirations are fully satisfied and they can devote all their energies towards the task of nation-building and development, instead of frittering away their energies in political agitations or the like. While the Committee agree that financial viability should be considered as an important factor while creating a unit, nevertheless having regard to the economic progress of the State so far (which judged from the per capita income in each region of the State, which is the highest in the whole country) it can be safely visualised that the human and material resources (both tapped and untapped) of the State are sufficient to make each unit economically viable. Looked at from another aspect, it was urged before the Committee that no State in the union is at present economically viable, as most of the State are dependent on the Union Government for grants and loans. Be that as it may, the arguments of viability has no force in denying a well-recognised and well-established principle of formation of States on linguistic basis which has been universally applied in the rest of the country.

As regards the State being bilingual, it had been already recognised in the Regional Formula that there were two distinct regions, namely, the Punjabi Region and Hindi Region. In each region were included the predominantly Punjabi speaking and the Hindi speaking districts respectively. Thus, the State was already divided into a distinct Punjabi Region and the Hindi Region. People of neither region are satisfied with the Status Quo. An overwhelming majority of the memoranda received by the Committee and of the witnesses who appeared before them were in favour of the two regions being made full-fledged States with suitable adjustment of boundaries which could be done by a Boundary Commission or any other expert body appointed for the purpose.

In the opinion of the Committee, maintenance of Status Quo in the State would cause further unrest among the people. Past experience has shown that the present bilingual State of Punjab has been the scene of internal disorder, agitations and counter-agitations. Any make-shift arrangement is not likely to provide a lasting solution to this vexed question. The Committee, therefore, feel that it is high time that some permanent and satisfactory solution of the problem is found.

An apprehension was expressed before the Committee by a section of the Punjabi-speaking Region who was opposed to the bifurcation of the existing State of Punjab that in the event of creation of a new Punjabi State, a large scale migration of population and capital, and consequent human suffering, might take place. The Committee's attention was also drawn in this connection to the "Questionnaire (Reports of the Committees of the Constituent Assembly of India (Third Series), page 222 (serial No. 19 of the Questionnaire) regarding the proposed provinces of Andhra, Karnataka, Kerala and Maharashtra" which was issued by the Linguistic Provinces Commission set up under the aegis of the Constituent Assembly of India (known as Dar Commission) where in the Commission posed this specific question and asked for public opinion as to the steps that should be taken for its prevention. The Committee note that this particular aspect was not ultimately touched upon by that Commission's report. Similar fears were expressed at the time of the formation of the Andhra State and Maharashtra and Gujarat States but experience has shown that they did not materialise. Obviously, such fears are ill-convinced and ill-founded. This is more so in the present case especially when Hindus and Sikhs have close ethenic, racial, religious and cultural relationship.

(b) Strengthening Of Regional Committees

A view was expressed before the Committee that the present State of Punjab might remain united and more powers could be given to Regional Committees, but it was not specifically stated as to how such Committees could be given more powers or what the nature of those powers was. A vague suggestion was made that the decisions of the Regional Committees could be final in respect of the subjects entrusted to them. In fact, it was also mooted that they might function something like "Sub-Legislatures", but what the powers and functions of "Sub-Legislatures" would be was never specified. As has been stated in detail in chapter third of this report, the working of the Regional Committees has been an utter failure. Suffice it to say that no body, including the Ministers of the Punjab, was satisfied with the working of these Committees and, in fact that the sooner they were scrapped the better. The Committee, therefore, feel that the idea of continuing Regional Committees in any form should be given up.

(c) Reorganisation On Linguistic Basis

It would not perhaps be out of place to refer here to the following passage from the Report of the Linguistic Provinces Commission (Dar Commission, 1948) which enunciates the cardinal principle for the formation of linguistic provinces, which rest upon two alternative grounds; "—upon the theory that these linguistic groups are sub-nations and as such contracting parties to the constitution from which the Federation and the Centre derive their existence and power ; alternatively it rests upon the administrative advantage, which may result from bringing together people speaking one language, in imparting education and in the working of courts, legislatures, governmental machinery and democratic institutions".

The only alternative which found the largest measure of support was that the present State of Punjab should be reorganised on a linguistic basis on which basis all the States in the country had been formed. This will not only satisfy the political and economic aspirations of the people of the respective areas but also end once for all the political controversy on a vexed question in this strategic boarder area and help remove the tension prevailing for the last so many years.

A suggestion was made that the question of formation of a Punjabi-speaking State might be referred to the people of Punjab for decision by a referendum and the wishes of the people ascertained. Apart from the fact that no such referendas were held for the reorganisation of the rest of the States in the country on linguistic basis, such a course is neither feasible nor desirable. The wishes of the people are easily known through their elected and representative bodies and other leaders of public opinion.

After carefully considering all the view points represented before the Committee and taking all relevant factors into consideration, the Committee have come to the conclusion that it would be in the larger interests of the people of these areas and the country as a whole that the present State of Punjab be reorganised on linguistic basis. The Punjabi Region specified in the First Schedule to the Punjab Regional Committees Order, 1957, should form a unilingual Punjabi State, the hill areas of the Punjab included in the Hindi Region of the Punjab which are contiguous to Himachal Pradesh and have linguistic and cultural affinity with that Territory should be merged with Himacbal Pradesh. The remaining areas of the Hindi-speaking region of the Punjab should be formed as a separate unit called the Haryana State. The distribution of population and density of population in the (i) Hill area, (ii) Haryana area and (iii) other areas of the existing State of Punjab are indicated in Appendix X. In case there are any boundary adjustments to be made among the three States of Punjab, Himachal Pradesh and Haryana, a Committee of experts be set up immediately to suggest the necessary adjustments.

A view was expressed before the Committee that a Vishal Haryana Prant be formed by bringing together of certain areas of Rajasthan, Uttar Pradesh, Delhi and the Haryana areas of the Punjab. The Committee have refrained from expressing opinion on these view-points or suggestions nor have they applied their mind to these proposals as the Committee consider that these matters do not fall within the scope of their competence. A suggestion was also made that the Haryana area of the Punjab might be joined with Delhi, as originally it was detached from Old Delhi Province. Here too the Committee cannot make any recommendation. The Committee leave it to the Government to consider in due course whether, after retaining New Delhi Municipal Committee area intact under the direct administration of Central Government it is feasible to join Delhi Municipal Corporation areas with the Haryana Prant which the Committee have proposed in this report.

The question of parts of Rajasthan being added to the new Punjabi State or the Haryana State was considered to be beyong the competence of the Committee and hence the Committee did not examine it.

The Committee trust that all the various political and other elements in the country in general, and Punjab in particular, will accept the solution proposed in a cooperative spirit and work for the harmony and prosperity of the heroic people inhabiting the present State of Punjab.

PANEL ON ECONOMIES IN CONSTRUCTION COSTS, 1965—REPORT

New Delhi, Planning Commission (Construction Division), 1968. 184p. (Mimeographed)

Chairman : Prof. M. S. Thacker.

Members : Maj. Gen. Harkirat Singh, Shri M. R. Chopra; Maj. Gen. K. N. Dubey; Shri N. G. Dewan (Retired, replaced by Shri B. K. Guha); Shri H. P. Sinha; Shri D. N. Chopra; Shri P. S. Bhatnagar; Shri Kulbir Singh; Shri J. K. Banerjee; Shri K. Barua; Shri K. V. Joglekar (replaced by Shri D. K. Datey); Shri P. T. Malla; Reddy; Shri I. M. Mugdum; Shri J. C. Abraham; Shri Y. G. Patel; Shri P. L. Verma; Shri H. J. Shah; Shri Uttam Singh Dugal; Shri S. Kumar; Shri S. Krishna Iyer; Shri Akshoy Bose; Shri P. C. Kapoor; Dr. Lal C. Verman; Shri C. B. Patel; Prof. Dinesh Mohan; Prof S. R. Mehra; Prof G. S. Ramaswamy; Shri G. Pandey; Prof. R. N. Dogra; Brig. S. K. Bose; Shri K. K. Nambiar; Shri J. R. Bhalla; Shri P. N. Gadi; Shri J. K. Chowdhury (replaced by Shri P. C. Khanna); Shri Hukum Singh; Shri Jamshed Burjor Aga; Shri K. M. Kantawala; Shri D. Dutt; Shri S. K. Joglekar; Maj. Gen. R. A. Loomba; Shri T. N. Subba Rao; Shri Erach A. Nadirshah; Shri M. N. Dastur.

Secretary : Shri A. N. Malhotra (replaced by Shri P. N. Gadi).

APPOINTMENT

The Panel on Economies in Construction Costs was constituted under the Planning Commission (Construction Division), vide their Resolution No. PC/Constn./Planning 6/3/65 dated October 1, 1965.

TERMS OF REFERENCE

(i) To advise on guide-lines for economy in construction costs; and

(ii) To periodically review the progress made in this field.

CONTENTS

Preface; Introduction; Preplanning; Design and other Technological Factors; Construction Materials; Business of Constructing; Administrative and Organisational Factors; Motivation, Training and Publicity; Summary of Recommendations; Appendices A to C.

RECOMMENDATIONS

Every Project should be examined and planned as completely as possible before its execution is begun to ensure that the user is not only provided with what is essential but complete phases of the project are made over to him in logical sequence.

It is necessary to associate the agency for construction of a project from the earliest possible stage with the process of project formulation so that this agency may do the necessary pre-planning and advise the sponsoring authority suitably.

Adequate surveys and data collection should be ensured with regard to construction materials, infrastructure, etc. to enable relative economies of alternative locations of projects to be worked out.

There should be continuity in data collection and pre-planning. Data should be stored in a central place for future reference.

Formation of a Central Hydrological Survey Department for collection of data in respect of water resources of the country on a continuous basis is considered necessary.

Adequate time should be allowed for the planning effort between the project formulation stage and commencement of construction.

For continuous investigation and data collection, suitably equipped permanent planning staff should be provided in every construction organisation. Large projects should be planned from the outset by the best available talent and professional expertise so that subsequent screening and criticism may not necessitate whole-sale changes in design and specifications.

Projects should be developed in suitable phases. Modern programming techniques should be adopted to determine phasing.

Optimum rate of financial input is an important factor and this should be ensured.

Detailed designs should be completed before construction is started.

There should be a periodical review of design criteria and codes of practice so that these are updated incorporating modern developments in science and technology. Handbooks illustrating standard procedures of design in fields not already covered should also be brought out by I.S.I.

Adoption of ultimate load theory in structural design should be aimed at. Necessary experimentation and testing programme should be undertaken.

Methods of structural analysis and design practices using latest advances in science and technology should be attempted wherever possible with a view to reducing overall cost of construction.

In large scale building projects, relative overall costs of multi-storeyed construction and dispersed low rise type construction should be studied in order to determine the most suitable and economical type.

For large construction projects alternate designs should be prepared and relative economies studied before making a final decision.

Temporary buildings are uneconomical and wasteful in the long run and should be resorted to only when requirement is for a very limited period and is transient in nature.

There should be wider application of modern design and construction techniques in the practice of highway and air field engineering.

Standardisation of construction materials, codes of practice, etc. is being done by the I.S.I. These standards should be adopted by all construction departments and agencies.

All construction agencies should ensure modular coordination as envisaged in IS-1233-1958 while planning and designing structures.

A suitable design organisation should be set up in every State and for every large project. In addition there should be strong Central Design Organisations with accent on specialisation. Every design organisation should have, inter alia, a work study cell attached to it.

Design talent should be developed and groomed in all construction departments without jeopardising their career prospects. Continuity of design personnel should be ensured as that will make for development of expertise and specialisation.

Design engineers should be given suitable opportunities to work in the field. They should be encouraged to visit construction sites where construction based on their designs is in progress.

Competitive designing should be encouraged, prizes being awarded for best and economical designs.

Indigenous consulting agencies could advantageously be made use of for designs in specialised fields. Consulting organisations have, therefore, to be built up, encouraged and nursed.

Foreign consultants should be engaged, with the approval of highest technical authority in the field in which work is to be executed, only when essential expertise and experience are not available in the country. If employment of foreign consultants becomes unavoidable, they should preferably be engaged through Indian Consultants and be made responsible to them.

Preparation of a National Building Code incorporating latest developments in the field of building design, construction techniques and materials has been taken up by the I S.I. The code should serve as a model for adoption by PWDs, local bodies and other construction agencies.

Existing out-dated building bye-laws of municipalities and corporations should be revised to fall in line with the Standard Code of Building Bye-laws prepared by the I.S.I.

The N.B.O. should establish Development Groups to evolve norms, space standards and lay outs and help prepare economic designs for buildings of repetitive types.

Industrialisation and mechanised methods of construction, suited to Indian conditions, should be gradually introduced in the interest of speed, quality control and reduction in cost.

Requirements of construction plant and machinery should be periodically assessed and measures taken to produce indigenously those items which are not at present being so produced.

For indigenous production, development of ancillary industries, inter-changeability of parts and speed in training of operators. the various broad categories of equipment should be assessed so that a limited number of suitable makes and sizes are standardised.

Procedures for provisioning of spare parts should be streamlined and the policy regarding their import simplified.

Proper procedures should be laid down to ensure prompt and systematic maintenance and servicing of equipment.

To ensure maximum utilisation of common categories of equipment. Equipment Pools should be set up on a zonal basis to be run on commercial lines.

For organising quality control, quality mindedness has to be inculcated in staff connected with a project.

Laboratory methods of quality control should be adopted in the lieu of present methods of visual inspection and dimensional checks.

A Building Materials Assessment and Development Cell should be set up in every State with authority to encourage development of building materials industries and to recommend setting up of new production units in public sector in case private sector is unable to meet demand. The N.B.O. should act as a coordinating agency and should lay down methodology for the purpose.

State should conduct surveys to locate and determine suitable deposits of soils for brick making and earmark sites for this purpose in Master Plans for urban localities.

Productivity in the brick making industry should be increased by adopting improved methods of manufacture, increased adoption of mechanisation and semi-mechanisation and more efficient types of kilns.

The present policy of issuing short-term licences to brick manufacturers deter them from investing capital and adopting modern techniques. Licensing and pricing policy of Government should be worked out on a long term basis to permit continuity of manufacture.

It will be advantageous to have price control on bricks and an equitable method for fixing fair prices linking these to prices of coal, labour, land rents and other inputs laid down.

Credit facilities on reasonable terms should be made available to the brick and tile industry so that new entrepreneurs are encouraged to start new units and their product are available at competitive rates.

Steps should be taken to collect regularly accurate and detailed statistics of output of construction timber and to assess trends of future production and demand.

Efficient and modern methods of felling, logging, storage, conversion and transport of timber have to be adopted on a priority basis. Every Forest Department should have a qualified Logging Officer to train personnel. Improved logging tools should be made available by indigenous production.

Methods of sale of timber trees to contractors by Forest Departments should be suitably modified to permit their sale in bigger lots and for longer periods to encourage mechanisation of operations.

The remote and hitherto unexploited or partially exploited fir and spruce forests in the Himalayas, teak and sal forests in Dandakaranya and mixed forests in Western Ghats should be opened up to permit economic harvesting of available timber.

To augment the supply of traditional species of construction timber, the large quantity of secondary species of timber available in the country should be made use of after being given suitable seasoning and preservative treatment.

Secondary species of timber should be marked in standard sizes and quality with certified markings after being properly seasoned and given preservative treatment.

Specifications for construction timber stipulated by construction deparments should be revised to permit use of secondary woods of reasonable quality. Standard cut sizes of timber specified in IS : 1331-1958 should be adopted to the greatest possible extent.

Nail jointed and laminated structures using small dimensioned and short length timbers should be adopted wherever feasible.

Governments should encourage setting up of integrated saw-mill-cum-wood/workshops with facilities for sawing, seasoning, preservation and production of prefabricated components.

Wider use of fibre boards and particle boards manufactured out of waste wood in lieu of timber boarding, should be encouraged. To bring down the selling price of particle boards, modification of the tax structure in respect of resins used in its manufacture is called for.

Railways should restrict use of timber sleepers to those locations only where their use cannot be avoided. Generally, timber sleepers should be substituted by prestressed concrete sleepers.

To encourage mechanisation of methods for quarrying stones and aggregates land leases should be given for a minimum period of, say, 10 years with possibilities of extension. Royalty and tax structures of the quarrying industry require study and rationalisation.

As the stone aggregate industry is capital intensive, it needs assistance of institutional finance.

Substitution of ordinary portland cement by cheaper cementing materials should be considered wherever possible. Increased adoption of weigh-batching and use of controlled concrete should be resorted to. Ready mixed concrete should be made available in areas of large construction activity.

It is for consideration whether ordinary portland cement should not be marketed in more grades than one with a view to achieving more intensive utilisation.

Improved methods should be evolved for packing cement so that less in transit is minimised.

Use of cement pozzolana mixes and lime reactive surkhi in lieu of ordinary portland cement should be resorted to wherever possible. Production and marketing of ready-to-use mixtures of lime pozzolana as a standard product should be encouraged.

Formation of cooperatives of small producers of

lime should be encourged. Such cooperatives should have ancillary testing facilities for controlling quality and a marketing organisation. Lime industry should be included in the list of scheduled industries so that entrepreneurs may get requisite facilities.

Measures should be taken to ensure production of light and junior series of Indian Standard Steel Sections.

Use of cold formed light gauge sections and tabular sections should be considered wherever technically and economically feasible. Incentives by way of reduction in excise duties may be offered to lower the price of these products and thus encourage their use on a wider scale.

Adoption of welded type steel structures should be encouraged. Production of weldable quality steel and electrodes should be increased. Production of high strength friction grip bolts should be increased and their use by design organisations encouraged.

Modern design methods should be increasingly adopted for steel structures as such designs require lesser quantities of steel than conventional designs.

Use of high strength deformed bars should be resorted to in lieu of plain-mild steel bars for reinforcement purposes. The integrated steel plants in the country should take up the manufacture of high strength deformed bars. National laboratories should develop the requisite indigenous know-how.

Efforts should be made to use alternative materials in lieu of scarce traditional materials wherever feasible.

Manufacture of light weight aggregates should be started in areas where stone is not readily available and has to be transported over long distances.

To reduce import of asbestos fibre and zincs asphaltic corrugated sheets and aluminised iron sheets should be produced indigenously.

In regions where price of burnt clay bricks is higher than Rs. 70 per 1,000, manufacture and use of cellular concrete, using fly ash and lime, should be considered for adoption as walling materials.

Wherever suitable clay for manufacturing bricks is not available, manufacture of sand lime bricks should be considered.

Along with production of new construction materials suitable facilities should be created for training craftsmen in the proper use of these materials.

Industrial cooperatives for producing construction materials should be encouraged by Central and State Governments by providing facilities in the form of financial assistance, marketing, laboratories for quality control, training of artisans, transport, etc.

Modern methods of materials management should be resorted to in large projects.

With a view to disseminating knowledge of improvements in designs and techniques and to displaying new materials, Building Centres should be set up at prominent locations in large cities and important towns.

Contractors carrying out construction works for Government Departments and other public bodies should be given advance payments. These payments should be made out of normal budget allotment.

(a) Against supply of acceptable non-perishable materials brought to site and not incorporated in work;

(b) In case of contracts valued at over Rs. 20 lakhs.

(i) Work advance against bank guarantee or fidelity bond of an insurance company; and

(ii) Against machinery (tools and plants) brought to site;

(c) In case of contracts valued at over Rs. 10 lakhs, on execution of essential preliminary items of work such as, hutments for labour, site offices, etc., and against guarantees.

Bank guarantees and fidelity bonds of insurance companies should be accepted towards earnest money and security deposit/retention money.

A Construction Finance Corporation with a capital of Rs. 100 million should be set up to advance funds on reasonable terms to contractors engaged on construction to construction materials industries and to consulting engineer organisations.

To develop healthy codes of conduct, improved technical competency and better general standards in the construction industry, a National Authority should prepare and maintain a National Register of Builders.

Labour cooperatives should be encouraged and offered facilities to undertake construction works.

It was considered necessary to evolve a Standard Contract Form for executing construction works so that general conditions are fair and equitable to both parties. This work has since been completed. Adoption of this form by all governmental construction agencies is recommended, with such minor modifications as may be necessitated by local requirements

Contracts should, as far as possible, be concluded on a lump sum basis.

Specialised training in Quantity Surveying should be organised.

Where the work is to be executed through the agency of contractors, selective tendering should normally be resorted to irrespective of whether the job is large or small.

The system of Technical Examination by an external agency should be abolished and steps taken to intensify internal supervision and quality control.

The existing system of settling disputes arising out of construction contracts by arbitration by an Engineer/Architect should continue.

Competent technical authorities should be empowered to settle disputes up to specified amounts without recourse to arbitration.

The system of settling disputes by a single arbitrator should continue. The arbitrator should, however, be an Engineer/Architect acceptable to both parties.

Procedure for implementation of arbitration awards should be streamlined. Chief Engineers should be authorised to decide whether or not an award should be implemented, after taking legal advice, where he considers such a course necessary. The practice of referring awards to Government or to some other department, before these are implemented, should cease.

At the beginning of each financial year, lump sum allotments should be placed at the disposal of Chief Engineers for implementing arbitration awards, recoupment being made as and when required.

An All-India Standard Schedule of Rates priced on a zonal or other suitable basis should be prepared by the National Buildings Organisation and adopted by all departments carrying out construction works out of public funds.

To enable technical heads of construction departments to discharge their responsibilities, adequate authority should be given to them by abolishing the present secretariat system of Public Works Ministries and replacing it by a system based on an executive pattern so that both responsibility and authority vest in the head of the department and his senior technical colleagues. There is also a need for streamlining administrative procedures which are at present being followed by construction departments.

The existing Ministry of Works should be suitably reorganised into a Central Ministry of Construction. Its role should be to arrange for economic and speedy execution of works financed by the Central Government to assist the construction industry as a whole in the wide range of problems which concern it, to encourage the development of new techniques and materials, to ensure proper utilisation of technical manpower and to build up expertise.

To coordinate the construction activities of different public sector undertakings, their construction should be carried out with the technical assistance of the proposed Construction Ministry without in any way interfering with the autonomy of these undertakings.

The proposed Ministry of Construction should aim at achieving economy in construction costs by proper management, satisfactory human relations, ensuring regular and coordinated supply of materials, etc., rather than by merely lowering scales of accommodation and specifications.

Construction staff of Public Sector Undertakings should be borne on a regular cadre operated by the Central Ministry of Construction so that individuals are assured continuity of service and surplus technical staff is not discharged on completion of works but is transferred from one undertaking to another or elsewhere, as necessary, and the experience gained is properly utilised.

The Central Ministry of Construction should be so organised that there is maximum centralisation of policy-making and maximum decentralisation of executive authority.

The procedure for liaison between the proposed Ministry of Construction on the one hand and the Council of Scientific and Industrial Research and the National Laboratories on the other should be laid down so that results of research in construction techniques are utilised and the problems encountered in the field are fed back to the laboratories for further research and study.

The Construction Ministry should be so constituted as to carry out all Central Government Works except those pertaining to the Ministries of Defence, Railways and Irrigation and Power.

In a State if in any branch of engineering the number of Chief Engineers is more than one, the senior most/selected Chief Engineer should function as a Principal Secretary and other Chief Engineers as Secretaries. All Chief Engineers of the branch should act as a Board for formulation of policies for the branch and for taking decisions on technical schemes above a specified limit.

To draw up integrated plan of development including judicious allotment of priorities and to review all problems of technical nature, each State should set up an Advisory Board of Engineers, Architects and other Technologists. The Chairman of the Board will be responsible for tendering advice to the State Cabinet on technical matters.

Existing rules and procedures for accounting in Public Works Departments should be modified with a view to eliminating interference, delays, etc. so that it is easier for a project authority or head of an organisation to work efficiently.

Accounting should be separated from Audit and made the responsibility of Chief Engineers. To enable a Chief Engineer to exercise the responsibility a Controller of Accounts with suitable staff should be placed under him.

All payments should be made by Executive Engineer after technical, arithmetical and primary audit checks have been exercised in his office. Prepayment audit by an external agency should be done away with. External audit parties should carry out post-payment audit.

The system of Cost Accounting should be introduced in Public Works Departments and in large projects and Cost Accounting Cells set up for the purpose.

For maintaining an optimum programme of construction on important projects, funds should be allocated over a long period and not by annual budgetary provision.

The National Buildings Organisation should be reorganised as an autonomous body to enable it to carry out not only the existing tasks but also the additional functions which have been outlined for it.

Terms and conditions of service of engineering personnel, architects and other technologists need to be reviewed. Control of technical departments from the lowest level to the highest should be in technical hands both in the States and at the Centre.

The present system which permits assessment of capabilities of technical personnel by officers of the administrative cadre should be abolished. Performance of technical personnel should be judged by their superior technical officers.

The existing disparity between salary and status of engineers, architects and other technologists in Class I service on the one hand and of officers of the Indian Administrative Service on the other should be removed and pay and status of the former should not be lower than of those in the Administrative Service for equivalent length of service. Formation of the Indian Service of Engineers should be expedited.

A technologist who during his employment acquires additional qualifications or makes an outstanding contribution should be appropriately rewarded. Whenever an engineer or a team of co-workers show higher efficiency, they should be suitably rewarded.

National awards should be instituted in the field of technology and construction economy.

Extreme degree of vigilance exercised by the Special Police Establishment, Vigilance Departments and other similar agencies, though useful to some extent, acts as a disincentive to serious and sincere workers even at senior levels resulting in loss of initiative. A review of these measures is considered essential.

Technical officers of construction services should be given training soon after recruitment, in matters of works procedure, accounts procedure, personnel administration and other administrative and departmental procedures before they are placed incharge of sub-divisions.

Technologists serving in construction departments should be put through 'in-service' training courses periodically. These courses should be in the form of refresher courses, advanced courses and specialised courses which would enable them to keep abreast of rapidly developing technology in the field of eonstruction and to acquire post-graduate qualifications.

Civil Engineers should be given special training in quantity surveying.

Subordinate supervisory staff should be put through training courses and refresher courses which should lay stress on practical aspects of construction, methods of conducting tests and precautions to obtain good workmanship

The Department of Labour and Employment should review the list of trades for which training is imparted in the ITI's. Training in building construction trades should be diversified.

Capacity for training of welders should be increased.

Forest departments should arrange training in the use of modern logging tools and in equipment for extracting and fashioning of timber.

In-service training in modern timber engineering techniques should be given to personnel employed on supervision of building construction.

Ministry of Labour and Employment should set up training centres to impart training in the operation of construction machinery and in carrying out servicing and repairs to such equipment.

To overcome the shortage of hereditary master craftsmen in the country suitable training facilities should be provided so that intelligent craftsmen with potential qualities of leadership could be selected and trained for the purpose.

Training of craftsmen should be provided for in every large project by absorbing expenditure on training in the project outlay. Public Works Departments should also devote attention to training of craftsmen.

Workers who are already skilled should be given facilities for obtaining trade certificates without having to undergo a formal course of training. The responsibility for recoganising competence of an institution to issue certificates should be vested in a Central Body such as the Labour Ministry.

The construction industry should take interest in the training of apprentices in construction trades in accordance with the Apprentices Act, 1961.

Dissemination of technical information and data having a bearing on construction economies achieved in the country in the past is necessary so that engineers, architects and others engaged on construction projects may profit from experience of others.

The NBO, IRC, CW & PC, CBI & P, ISI and other similar organisations should extend their facilities to serve as clearing houses for dissemination of technical information in their respective fields. All engineering project organisations should publish detailed reports on all matters connected with the achievement of efficiency and economy obtained through their construction operations. A specific provision therefor should be made in the project and the responsibility for writing such reports be placed squarely on the Chief Executive.

An independent journal on "Engineering Construction Economy" should be started. It should be produced attractively and made available to all concerned at a reasonable price.

COMMITTEE ON CUSTOMARY RIGHTS TO SCAVENGING, 1965—REPORT

New Delhi, Department of Social Welfare, 1969. 131p.

Chairman : Shri N.R. Malkani.
Members : Shri K.L. Balmiki ; Sadar Daljit ; Smt. Minimata Agamdas Guru ; Shri Satish Chandra Samant ; Shri Mahabir Dass.
Legal Adviser : Shri H.K. Chaudhry.
Secretary : Shri C.B. Tripathi.

APPOINTMENT

In 1949 the erstwhile Government of Bombay appointed a Scavenger's Living Conditions Enquiry Committee under the Chairmanship of Shri V.N. Barve and the report of that Committee published in 1952 touched the problem of abolition of Gharaki or Customary rights to scavenging in Gujarat. Subsequently a more detailed study of the problem was made by the Scavenging Conditions Enquiry Committee set up by the Central Advisory Board for Harijan Welfare on October 12, 1957 under the Chairmanship of Prof. N.R. Malkani. This Committee submitted its report in December, 1960 and it was published sometimes in the latter half of 1961. It briefly discussed cutomary rights of scavengers in a six-pages chapter. It observed that the nature of customary rights differed from State to State and from town to town within a State.

In order to abolish customary rights of scavengers, the Committee opined, mere municipal employment might be sufficient at some places but at others cash compensation might have to be paid and at still others, other difficulties might crop up. In order to overcome all these difficulties the Committee suggested that the State Governments and the Union Territory Adminstrations should appoint small committees to go into the whole question of abolition of customary rights. It added "they should not merely study the legal aspects of the problem but go thoroughly into other problems as well connected with it. They should draw up a phased programme for the abolition of customary rights and see that the work is completed as soon as possible but not later than a fixed target date. They should determine the basis, mode of payment and the amount".

No action was taken on the above recommendation until the meeting of the Central Advisory Board for Harijan Welfare held at New Delhi on December 7, 1963 where the late Shri Parikshitlal Majumdar explained the reasons why high priority should be given to abolition of private rights to scavenging. He opined that a small committee should be appointed to examine the legal position with particular reference to the need to pay compensation. Prof. N.R. Malkani explained that the customary rights did not prevail in all the States. These existed in some of the States like Uttar Pradesh, Rajasthan, Punjab and Madhya Pradesh. He also drew attention to the fact that the nature of the rights differed from State to State, and in this light of the matter, State level Committees might be more useful than the Central Committee. According to him what was required was the cultivation of public opinion through State-level Committees as also the preparation of scavengers for the change. Shri K. L. Balmiki described the question as intricate and reminded the Board that a Bill once introduced in Parliament was withdrawn as it was felt that the problem required deeper study. According to him the municipalities did not pay enough attention to the scavengers nor were they in a position to municipalise all scavenging. The Deputy Minister of Home Affairs, Smt. M. Chandrasekhar, pointed out that large amounts were being provided for abolition of the practice of carrying nightsoil as head loads but unless customary rights were abolished full results would not be secured for the expenditure. The Board finally recommended that the Ministry of Home Affairs might consider the constitution of a Small Committee with four or five members of whom one would from the Ministry of Law. Another year and a half elapsed before the Government of India, in the Department of Social Security, decided to constitute the Committee on Customary Rights to Scavenging vide their Resolution No.

22/5/65 SCT. III (B), dated April 23, 1965.

TERMS OF REFERENCE

"To examine the question of abolition of the customary rights to scavenging."

CONTENTS

Introduction ; What are Customary Rights ; Genesis and Growth of Brit-Jajmani (Customary Rights) ; Legal Aspect of Brit-Jajmani ; Income from Brit-Jajmani ; Evils of Brit-Jajmani ; Municipalisation of Scavenging—Attitude of Scavengers Municipalisation of Scavenging—Attitude of Public ; Municipalisation of Scavenging—Attitude of Municipalities ; Methods of Abolition of Brit-Jajmani—Alternative Employment ; Methods of Abolition of Brit-Jajmani—Cash grants and Rehabilitation ; How to start Abolition of Brit-Jujmani ; Underground Drainage and Water-Borne Latrines ; Summary of Recommendations ; Note of Dissent ; Appendices I to VI.

RECOMMENDATIONS

Legal Aspect Of Brit-Jajmani

The scavenging right is not property within the meaning of Article 19(1) (f) or Article 31 of the Constitution, and even where such right exists, no compensation would be legally payable for its abolition.

The Punjab Municipal Act, 1911, should be suitably amended so as to bring it in conformity with the provisions of other Municipal Acts and abolish the right of the scavenger to the property in nightsoil. Some reasonable compensation may be paid to the scavengers concerned.

Income From Brit-Jajmani

Pending municipalisation of scavenging the Hardwar Union Municipality should take immediate steps to rationalise the rates of house scavenging provided in the Municipal Bye-laws in 1964.

The schedule of rates of house scavenging approved by the Municipal Board, Meerut, in 1949 is defective as it does not take into account the number of members in a household. Pending municipalisation of scavenging these rates need early suitable revision.

Evils Of Brit-Jajmani

Hardly half a dozen Balmiki children were attending the Government primary school near the large sweepers' colony built by Amritsar Improvement Trust, though the total number of students in the school was 473. The authorities concerned should look into this.

Compulsory primary education should be made strictly applicable to the scavenging community and the educational authorities should make earnest and sympathetic efforts to spread education among them.

In quite a few cases a considerable portion of the income of a scavenger's family goes into the pocket of the moneylender or is wasted in drinking and gambling. This situation should be remedied.

Some representatives of Balmikis of Jasra District Ratlam, stated that Balmikis could not procure the services of music bands and palanquins in marriages, were not allowed to enter restaurants, barber shops, laundries, etc, and were not served tea in broken cups in tea stalls. The Madhya Pradesh Government are requested to look into this complaint.

In some towns in Rajasthan, Uttar Pradesh, Madhya Bharat and Saurashtra scavengers still accept left over food (Jhoothan) from the houses of their Jajmans on occasions of marriages and feasts. This practice should be stopped through publicity and education.

In some touns of Marathwada scavengers clean latrines only on alternate days. The time of cleaning the latrines is also irregular. These practices should be stopped.

In most of the towns there are no receptacles in private latrines. The authorities concerned should take necessary steps in the matter.

Often misappropriation of nightsoil and private sale of raw manure to cultivators take place in some towns in Uttar Pradesh, Madhya Bharat, Gujarat and Jammu and Kashmir. This should be stopped.

Generally private scavengers are not supplied with wheel-barrows and other implements for improving their working conditions. The municipalities are generally unwilling to supply these to private scavengers. The State Governments/Union Territory Administrations are requested to ensure that these implements are supplied to private scavengers also.

Municipalisation Of Scavenging

Attitude of Scavengers : At Bikaner the municipal sweepers complained that they were kept in the dark about their Provident Fund accounts and that the passbooks were not issued to them. The Government of Rajasthan are requested to look into this complaint.

At Bhindsar (District Bikaner) the municipal sweepers stated that the payment of their salaries was irregular. The Government of Rajasthan may kindly look into this complaint.

Attitude of Public : In certain parts of the country the people think that they can have the amenities of urban life without being required to pay municipal taxes. It is high time that our people should be educated in order to free them from this incorrect attitude.

It is astonishing that most of the municipalities in Rajasthan are not realising any property or house tax though the quantum of this tax in Rajasthan is much lower than in other States, say, in Andhra Pradesh. The Government of Rajasthan are requested to take necessary action in the matter.

In order to ensure that scavenging cess is realised regularly the Government and the public are requested to see that maximum amount of discipline and efficiency is observed by the municipalities in respect of sanitation and scavenging.

Attitude of Municipalities : A Municipal Councillor complained at Bikaner that though the Social Welfare Department of the State Government was meant to work for the amelioration of the conditions of Harijans, there were officers in the Department who themselves practised untouchability against Harijans. The Government of Rajasthan are requested to look into this.

A trade union leader, who is also a Municipal Councillor, said that the Municipal Council had not put wheel-barrows on the roads and the salaries of the conservancy staff were held up for several months. Several Municipal Boards according to him were not giving even minimum wages to their sweepers. The Government of Rajasthan may kindly look into these complaints.

Method Of Abolition Of Brit-Jajmani-Alternative Employment

It is essential that all the Municipal Acts should be suitably amended so as to declare house scavenging (scavenging of service latrine) as an essential and obligatory function of the municipalities. The function must be taken over by the municipalities as early as possible in the same manner in which it has been taken over in the remaining States.

Section 200 of the Uttar Pradesh Municipalities Act, 1916, Section, 159, 160, 161, 162 and 165 of the Punjab Municipal Act, 1911 and Sections 210, 211, 213, 214, of the Rajasthan Municipalities Act, 1959, should be appropriately amended to enable the municipalities to take over house scavenging without any hitch.

A general sanitation tax should be levied along with generat water cess or charge by all the municipalities irrespective of Brit-Jajmani. Even those who have installed water-borne latrines should not be exempted from payment of this tax.

There should be a scavenging cess for cleaning of private latrines as there is a water charge for private water connections. It should not be called or deemed a tax but payment for services rendered. Scavenging cess should be realised in advance and defaulters fined for late payment.

At present the local bodies in Jammu and Kashmir are not even levying any house tax. The Government of Jammu and Kashmir are requested to take necessary action in the matter.

Bye-laws may be provided to the effect that the income from scavenging cess cannot be spent for any other purpose than payment of salaries of scavenging staff, purchase and maintenance of tools required for house scavenging and welfare activities for scavengers and sweepers.

The age bar for employment of private scanvengers as municipal sweepers/scavengers should be relaxed and every effort made to find employment even for persons falling in the age-group 40—60. Those private scavengers who are earning only Rs. 20 to Rs. 40 p.m. may be offered part-time service if they cannot be taken up as whole-time employees.

Each municipal scavenger should be assigned cleaning of about 40 latrines in a compact area. Mostly they will be required to perform this work in the morning. Therefore, those who are engaged in scavenging in the morning must be asked to do scavenging work in the afternoon.

We strongly recommend that female employees should not be assigned scavenging work at all except on female public latrines. Female employees may be engaged as sweepers and when this is not possible, as part-time scavengers.

Unless the municipality offers better terms for employment Brit-Jajmani will not easily be ended. It is highly desirable that the Governments of the States where municipal employments are low should make serious efforts to bring up the emoluments which will enable to have a living wage.

These should be no discrimination in pay between male and female employees for performing the same duties.

Municipal sweepers/scavengers should be assured of benefits and facilities like Provident Fund, uniforms, free quarters or house rent allowance, different kinds of leave, etc., as available to class IV employees of the State Government.

The Committee records its warm appreciation of the decision of the Punjab Government (being implemented for nearly three years) to pay sweepers and scavengers Rs. 15 p.m. more than other class IV employees like peons, etc. Municipal emoluments in Punjab and Maharashtra are commendable.

The Committee expresses its disappointment at the hard lot of municipal sweepers and scavengers in Uttar Pradesh and Madhya Pradesh where even the Municipal Corporation do not pay as much as the bigger municipalities in Punjab and Maharashtra.

Every local body should have a disciplinary sub-Committee to deal with all disciplinary cases against scavengers and sweepers. This will ensure security of service for them.

After municipalisation of scavenging irregular practices as observed by the Committee at Anantapur (Andhra Pradesh) must be curbed and there should be even distribution of work among municipal scavengers and strict enforcement of discipline.

In Marathwada the problem of Brit-Jajmani is a very limited one and can easily be solved by a determined policy. At present most of the posts of scavengers in the Municipalities in Marathwada are treated as temporary. Satisfactory service conditions will hasten the process of municipalisation of scavenging in the remaining municipalities.

Some private scavengers in Marathwada may perhaps not be able to find municipal employment locally and may have to be sent to other places in Marathwada or Telangana where there is shortage of scavengers.

In Rajasthan most of the private scavengers would prefer municipal service but they require permanent employment and an assurance of amenities like provident Fund, leave, uniforms, etc. We found that in this State there was lack of uniformity in providing these amenities inspite of satisfactory rules.

In Punjab scavenging can be municipalised without much difficulty at least in those municipalities where private scavengers are not exercising right over night soil. The local bodies of new townships should also take immediate steps in this direction.

Though the municipal emoluments in Punjab are high, a large number of the local bodies have engaged only part-time sweepers/scavengers. Efforts should be made by them to have wholetime and permanent employees.

Those who cannot be taken up as whole time sweepers/scavengers should be offered on a priority basis some other municipal posts such as peons, chowkidars, etc.

Efforts should be made by the State Governments/Union Territory Administrations concerned to absorb scavengers in other jobs in Government departments and public undertakings.

The Government of India and the State Governments/Union Territory Administrations should issue appeals to private industry to provide employment to scavengers in other jobs in a big way.

We found that all over Rajasthan there was a deep prejudice among the public against employment of educated Balmikis in jobs other than scavenging. Qualified boys are rejected in a summary manner simply because they are children of Balmikis.

Methods Of Abolition Of Brit—Jajmani-Cash Grants And Rehabilitation

In recognition of the useful and essential services rendered by scavengers and their forefathers some sort of a compensation to the present private scavengers would appear necessary and reasonable. However, from the point of view of the legal position and expediency the words 'relief' or 'ex-gratia grant' would be more appropriate than compensation.

Where alternative employment secured to a scavenger falls short of his average income during the last 12 months from scavenging the loss may be compensated by payment to him in lump sum not exceeding five times the difference between the average monthly income from scavenging and the municipal emoluments.

Where the municipal emoluments are higher than the income of a private scavenger, such private scavengers need not be paid any grant if he accepts municipal employment.

Where municipal service is not available to adult scavengers certain inducement grants may be given to them by the municipality for giving up Brit-Jajmani.

Big Britdars who have ceased to scavenge but employ tenant scavengers should not be given any cash relief. However, these intermediaries should be assisted in finding gainful employment if they need it.

An old person above 60 who is at present engaged in scavenging and will not be given municipal employment should be given a pension of at least Rs. 20 p.m. for life time, irrespective of the fact whether there are other members in family to support him or not. This is desirable in appreciation of his services to the society. The expenditure on this scheme should be shared between the Government of India and the State Government/Union Territory Administrations concerned.

The amount of relief grant should be shared by the Union Government, the State Government and the local body in the proportion of 2 : 1 : 1. As some of the local bodies may find it difficult to contribute even one-fourth of the amount the Committee recommends that ;

(a) In the case of local body having a population of less than one lakh the contribution of the Central Government should be 75 per cent ; and

(b) In the case of a local body with a population exceeding one lakh the contribution of the Central Government should be 50 per cent

In either case the concerned State Government should ensure that the balance is found out either from the funds of the local body or the State Governments themselves.

The Government of India and the State Governments/Union Territory Administrations concerned are requested to take urgent steps for broadening occupational opportunities for scavengers and undertake special schemes in this regard in the Fourth Five Year Plan. Whereas all the State Governments/Union Territory Administrations concerned may be requested to undertake this programme of rehabilitation of scavengers in other trades and occupations in the general sector of their Plants, the Department of Social Welfare, Government of india, must include this scheme in the Centrally-sponsored programme of the State concerned and allocate adequate funds during the Fourth Plan purpose.

All the members of a scavenger family who offer to give up scavenging en bloc (i.e., of a family in which no members will hereafter continue scavenging work) should be provided with a stipend @ at least Rs. 45 p.m. each to ensure training in some gainful trade or occupation for a period of, say, six months or one year and after the completion of the training each of them should be provided with a grant of about Rs. 200 mainly in kind and partly in cash to settle in the particular trade or occupation for which he or she has been trained. The trades should be selected for different areas according to local conditions in consultation with the actual scavengers concerned.

No strict rules or curriculum for such a training programme will meet the district results. In this connection the example of the Plan Scheme of Economic Uplift Centres in Punjab, where similar facilities are at present being extended to members of the scheduled castes, the denotified communities and the backward classes, is recommended.

With sound organisation, sympathetic but strict supervision and suitable follow-up programme this scheme rehabilitation of scavengers in other trades and occupations can undoubtedly succeed and bring a marked change in their way of life and their status in the society.

Children of scavengers should be imparted education or technical training, if necessary, away from their parents. The Committee reiterates the desirability of setting up Ashram Schools for children of scavengers and sweepers where a certain percentage of children belonging to other communities including Sawarnas may also be admitted.

Children of these private scavengers who not only give up their Brits but scavenging itself should be given special educational facilities.

How To Start Abolition Of Brit—Jajmani

The abolition of Brit—Jagmani must begin at the State level and each State concerned should issue orders to abolish Brit-Jajmani during the Fourth Five Year Plan.

The programme must be implemented municipality-wise and not on individual basis. Each municipality should immediately conduct a survey of the number of service latrines, the number of scavengers to be employed as part-time or whole-time employees, the expenditure on their salaries, the salaries of the supervisory staff, tools, etc., and the amount of ex-gratia grant or cash inducement to be given to private scavengers. A record should also be maintained of all water-borne latrines in each municipal area.

Each municipality should start employing private scavengers not only as sweepers/scavengers but also on other pasts such as peons and chowkidars.

Each municipality should give ex-gratia grants and inducement according to local conditions and resources as outlined in Chapter X. This inducement, where necessary, must be given mainly in kind and when unavoidable in cash. It may be in the form of scaling down and repayment of debts, allotement of house sites, housing subsidies, etc. The quantum of these grants will generally be so small that it should be paid out of the municipal funds. But when the amount involved is much more the Government should give necessary financial assistance as suggested in Recommendation No. 53.

A fair beginning may be made with small and medium size municipalities letting alone big ones where there are intermediaries and trade unions.

The municipalities should prepare phased programme of municipalisation of scavenging where it is not considered feasible to straightaway municipalise scavenging in the whole town and further ensure that the programme is fully implemented within a specified period.

There should be special rates of scavenging cess when there is a big feast or a marriage, etc., in the house requiring several scavengers or harder duties for the scavenger.

Employment of minors for scavenging by the parents or any one else should be banned, if necessary by legislation, and made punishable.

In future municipal employees should be asked to give an undertaking not to do any other work on remuneration without the permission of the municipality, under penalty of fine or even suspension.

The concerned States/municipalities where scavengers are legally or illegally exercising right over nightsoil must ensure that this objectionable practice is stopped at the earliest, if necessary by legislation as in Punjab.

The municipalities which are at present neglecting their duties to prepare compost from nightsoil must take necessary steps to adopt modern and scientific methods of treatment of sewage.

The Committee expresses its distress at the utter neglect regarding utilisation of sewage in a modern and much publicised city like Chandigarh whe e underground sewage is simply diverted into a rivulet.

Mungeli Municipal Council (District Bilaspur)

Madhya Pradesh is reported to be paying some amount annually to cultivators having fields in the vicinity of the municipal boundary to allow it for disposal of night-soil in their fields. Thus a source of income there has become a liability.

The need for proper utilisation of sewage for increasing agricultural production can scarcely be overrated. Until our country becomes self-sufficient in chemical fertilizers urban organic waste including sewage must be properly utilised. The potential of sludge, a valuable manure produced by the treatment of sewage, should also be fully utilised. Plants of different sizes should be set up in the urban centres according to their size and resources. The Committee was pleased to observe the scientific and profitable methods in this regard adopted by Ahmedabad Municipal Corporation.

A big campaign for underground drainage and, failing that, for water-borne latrines will not only make big citeis more sanitary but will also weaken Brit-Jajmani. This will help in solving the problem of intermediaries.

The problem of Brit-Jajmani can be solved on a permanent footing only if a suitable machinery is set up to ensure that not a single individual seeking social transformation by giving up Brit-Jajmani and scavenging is left out of the purview of benefits under the rehabilitation plan mentioned at Recommendation No. 55.

The Government of Maharashtra deserves congratulations for appointing officers in the Directorate of Social Welfare who are exclusively incharge of sanitation and scavenging schemes. But the Committee feels that in order to have a more effective implementation of these schemes, at least the scheme for improvement of working conditions of sweepers and scavengers and the programme of municipalisation of scavenging, it wou'd be desirable that the State Governments/Union Territory Administrations shou'd appoint a Deputy Director of Health in the States where there is a combined Department of Health and Local Self-Government or a Deputy Director of Local Bodies in those where there are separate Departments of Health and Local Self-Government.

The programme of rehabilitation (Recommendation No. 55) should be looked after by the Harijan Welfare Department.

In order to coordinate and review the implementation of the various steps suggested in Chapters IX and X a State level Committee comprising the following should be appointed under the chairmanship of the Welfare Minister:

(i) Secretary/Director of Health,
(ii) Secretary/Director of Local Bodies,
(iii) Secretary/Director of Harijan Welfare,
(iv) Regional Deputy Commissioner for Scheduled Castes and Scheduled Tribes, Government of India,
(v) A few non-officials including legislators and representatives of non-official organisations working for the welfare of scavengers.

This State level body may hold quarterly meetings and report the progress to the Government of India.

Underground Drainage And Water-Borne Latrines

Earnest efforts must be made to cover most of the cities with underground drainage during the Fourth Five Year Plan. Priority may be given in this regard to the cities in the States having Brit-Jajmani, specially the cities with a population exceeding two lakhs.

Indore Municipal Corporation allocates Rs. 3 lakhs annually underground drainage from its own funds. It deserves more aid from the Government.

In areas where underground sewerage has been completed it should be made obligatory for house-owners to take connections for letrines failing which the municipality must be so departmentally and recover the expenses from the house-owners.

If Delhi Municipal Corporation implemented the statutory provisions empowering it to compel house-owners to take connections from the mains situated within 100 feet from their houses and empowering the Commissioner to execute work after giving notice to the person liable and to recover the cost of the same from him, the problem of Brit-Jajmani in the capital would have been almost solved.

Municipalities should frame bye-laws making it incumbent on every houseowner to provide a latrine in his house. If the cost of the house exceeds a certain amount, to be determined by the Municipality, the houseowner must provide a water-borne latrine.

Where new colonies are being set up or cooperatives societies are building new houses care must be taken that only water-borne latrines, preferably hand-flushed latrines, are permitted.

Wherever feasible, existing service latrines should be converted into water-borne ones and for this purpose local bodies may provide subsidies or loans to needy houseowners. The resolution adopted by Hyderabad Municipal Corporation on 2-11-1964 in this regard may be referred to.

We found that Bhavnagar Municipality was offering Rs. 300 to every householder almost indiscriminately and yet connections were not increasing in number.

Some scheme of providing financial assistance takes into consideration the distance of the latrine from the sewer as well as the income of the houseowner must be devised in respect of all new houses and made obligatory.

Either municipalities should announce a certain

period during which any houseowner can instal a flush latrine without prior permission or they should ensure prompt approval of plans from houseowners for flush latrines.

The Governments of Gujarat and Kerala have banned service latrines and made installation of water-borne latrines obligatory in new houses and buildings. The Government of Gujarat deserves congratulations for their decisions to remove service latrines from the whole State before the Gandhi Centenary, as contained in the Rural Development Department circular dated 2-2-1965. All State Governments/Union Territory Administrations are requested to follow the example of Gujarat.

In new towns, outlying areas of old towns and localities inhabited by the lower income group hand-flushed latrines should be popularised as most of the people cannot afford to have septic latrines. The Vidya Bhawan Rural Institute, Udaipur, has designed and supplies the material of such latrine at a cost of Rs. 22 only.

Marathwada has not even made a beginning in the introduction of septic tank or hand-flushed latrines in a big way.

The programme of introduction of hand-flushed latrines has been most popular in Saurashtra where the municipalities have given and are giving a subsidy of Rs. 20 to every houseowner for conversion of his service latrine into a water-borne one. The Committee recommends that wherever possible the municipalities may assist needy houseowners financially and technically in installing hand-flushed latrines in their houses.

The 'let out' latrines in Nizamabad (Andhra Pradesh) are highly injurious to public health and should be banned forthwith. If these latrines cannot be converted into water-borne ones immediately these may be converted into Khuddi type serviee latrines (cleaned by the scavenger from the front unlike sandas type latrines opening onto the road and required to be cleaned from behind by the scavenger who has to stoop too low) and municipal scavengers engaged for cleaning these. A beginning must be made for municipalisation of scavenging immediately with these 300 odd houses in Nizamabad and wherever else similar latrines exist.

The Committee generally endorses the recommendations in the paper captioned 'The Problems of Excreta. Disposal in Urban Areas and their appropriate Solutions' by Dr. Ram Das and requests the Government to implement the same.

Appendix VII

Hand-flushed latrine is a simple type of sanitary device which serves as a substitute for sewage flush latrine. It has a trap, water seal of 3/4" and a pipe. It is fixed either inside or outside the house, as the case may be, depending on the availability of space with a platform, A temporary cover wall is provided to have some privacy. The pipe is connected with a pit which is about six feet deep having a diameter of 2-3/4 feet and over which reinforced concrete pit-cover is put. It is then covered with ordinary soil from all sides to ensure that the contents of the pit are not visible and the pit does not collapse due to weight of cattle or cart, etc. The latrine is used by individuals and after use it is flushed with about one litre of water. On account of the water seal, after flushing the bad odour is not thrown back. The premises are kept quite clean. There is no maggot formation and the total cost involved in putting up such a latrine is anything between Rs. 30 to Rs. 50 including the cost of installation. This amount is within the reach of a good percentage of population in urban areas.

Experimental work in developing such latrines was done by a number of agencies in the country particularly under the Rural-cum-Action Research Project at three centres, financed by Ford Foundation, Public Health Reaserch Institute, Nagpur, and Planning Research and Action Institute, Lucknow. Some other voluntary agencies in different parts of the country also did good work on developing suitable type of hand-flushed letrines. The environmental sanitation project, run in U.P. in collaboration with WHO/UNICEF, proved to be quite successful in the introduction of hand-flushed latrines. Planning Research and Action Institute, Health, C D, and L.S.G.E.D. co-operated in the execution of the project. The results of the project were extended to other areas by conducting training classes for health and para-medical personnel and village masons. The masons were given intensive training in the construction of latrine parts and their installation. The Department of Community Development assisted this programmes and provided funds for the training of masons who were subsequently given loans to start their workshops. About 300 workshops were started by individuals, co-operative and panchayats in different parts of the State. The village communities liked the idea of hand-flushed latrines and programme became quite popular. Some private individuals in the urban areas set up their workshops and started doing good business. In the three piloted projects areas of U P., the work on the Construction Department. In the newly constructed buildings, the P.W.D. is required to put in hand-flushed latrines in U.P. Since this programme caught the imagination of a number of other agencies including some public undertakings, such latrines have become quite popular in some localities.

A number of municipalities and town areas have already permitted the installation of the hand-flushed latrines by individuals in their houses as the introduction of the Sewage Schemes in them is still a thing of the distant future. Some of the State Governments have also passed orders that Service latrines shall not be allowed to operate in the municipal areas of their States, hence have advocated the installation of hand-flushed latrines. No special techniques and precautions are necessary in the installation of such latrines. The only precaution to be followed is that the latrine pits should be constructed at a distance of about 25 feet from the wells.

In order to create suitable climate for this purpose in the country, a Committee at the Central level in the Ministry of Health is essential. Such a Committee should be incharge of the coordination work in the country for solving the present insanitary problem and may be chaired by the Minister or the Deputy Minister of Health. The concerned Ministries of Health, Education, etc. should be associated with it and representatives from the various State Governments should serve on this Committee. A few public-spirited persons like prof. Malkani should be a nember of such a Committee. It would be helpful if WHO and UNICEF are also invited to participate in the deliberations of the Committee. Perhaps, some assistance from them may be available in the Local Self-Engineering Department will the Minister of that Department as the Chairman. The Departments of Health, L.S.G.E.D. and Community Development should be associated with it. A suitable scheme for the manufacture of latrine parts and their installation should be worked out in consultation with the municipal committees. Until sewage schemes are started, municipal by-laws should permit the installation of such latrines. Part of the finances should be made available by the Local Self-Engineering Department of the Government and a part of the funds should be contributed by the municipalities for starting construction of such latrines on a sizable scale.

Some orientation training of those who will be involved in educating the public about the use of such latrines should be arranged at the local level by the trained staff of the municipalities. Hand-pump-tube wells should be installed at convenient points so that water for flushing the latrines may be readily available in the locality.

In every municipality or town area, there should be a Committee under the chairmanship of the member incharge of the health programme. This Committee should review the progress from time to time and keep the State Governments informed about it. The State Government, in turn, should keep the Central Co-ordination Committee apprised of the progress.

For the construction of latrines, special quota of materials for building the latrines, particularly cement, will be necessary for which some decision will need be taken in advance.

In order to achieve good results, the Local Self-Engineering Department of the Government, the Health and Public Health Departments of the municipalities shall have to work hand in hand. In many cases, the municipal health departments can also take up the fabrication of the latrine parts and their installation through their own contracts. Since this is a matter of local importance, details of this can be left to the local agencies concerned to fulfil that responsibility. What is needed is a proper plan and its proper execution in collaboration with the local communities and the municipalities of the States.

CHAIRMAN INDEX

ARYA BHUSHAN, 313, 384

BHAGAVANTAM, S., 291
BONGIRWAR, L.N., 23

CHATTERJEE, N.P., 140

DANTWALA, M.L., 223
DAS, S.R., 275
DAS GUPTA, K.C., 82
DIWAKAR, R.R., 112

ELAYAPERUMAL, L., 333

GOKAK, V.K., 12
GOVINDA REDDY, M., 268
GUPTA, C.P, 320

HARI SINGH, 80, 309
HART, H.S., 290
HUKAM SINGH (Sardar), 385

JOSHI, K.L., 20
JUNGALWALLA, N., 1

KESKAR, B.V., 368
KHANNA, R.K., 150
KHOSLA, A.N., 278
KOTHARI, D.S., 153

LOKANATHAN, P.S., 284
LOKUR, B.N., 352

MAHATAB, HAREKRUSHNA, 362
MALKANI, N.R., 394
MATHUR, HARISH CHANDRA, 247, 256
MEHTA, M.S., 9
MIRDHA, RAM NIVAS, 264
MUKHARJI, G., 202

NIJALINGAPPA, S., 78

PATASKAR, H.V., 322
PATEL, B.P., 128
PAVATE, D.C., 217, 300
PILLAI, N.R., 354

RAJAMANNAR, P.V., 109
RAMASWAMY, R.V.R., 358
RAO, K.N., 327
RAO, V.K.R.V., 379
REDDY, M. GOVINDA, *See* Govinda Reddy, M.

SANTHANAM, K., 48
SARAF, SHAM LAL, 348
SEN, ASOKE, 202
SEN, S.R., 203
SHAH, K.K., 340
SHAH, SHANTILAL H., 299
SHINDE, G.K., 53
SIDDIQI, M.Z., 107
SIVARAMAN, B., 315
SOHAN SINGH, 130
SUBRAMANIAN, S., 66, 75

TARLOK SINGH, 26
THACKER, M.S., 388

WHEELER, MORTIMER, 318

INDEX

Abortion, 299
—,Lagislation, 299
—,—,Abortions Authorised, 299
—,—,Miscarry, 299
—,—,Pregnancy Continuance, 299
—,—,—Results, 299
—,—,—Termination, 299
Ad-Hoc Committee on Export of Minor Forest Products, 1964, 309-313
Advisory Committee on the Revision of the Lists of Scheduled Castes and Scheduled Tribes, 1965, 352-353
Adult Education, 195
Air Port Security, 202
———,Air Customs Pool, 202
———,Airport Protection Force, 202
———,Departure Customs Check, 203
———,Foreign Aircraft, 203
———,——,Force Landing, 203
———,Index Card System, 203
———,Mobile Petrol Duties, 202
———,Perimeter Roads, 202
———,—Security, 202
———,Sanitary Standards, 203
———,Vigilance Watch, 202
———,Committee, 1964, 202-203
Arabic and Persian Studies, 107
————,Diploma Course, 109
————,Improve Teaching, 108
————,Incentives, 108
————,Manuscripts, 109
————,Post-Graduate Teaching, 109
————,Problems, 107
————,Research Methodology Course, 109
————,Seminars and Conferences, 108
————,Short-term Correspondence Course, 109
————,Syllabi, 107
————,Teaching Standard, 108
————,Value and Importance, 108
Archaeology, 318
—,Conservation, 318
—,Excavation, 318
—,Exploration, 318
—,Indian School of Archaeology Abroad, 319
—,Printing and Publication, 318
—,States and Archaeology, 319
—,Training, 319
—,Universities, 319
Archaeological Atlas, 319
—,Review Committee, 1965, 318-319
—,Science Laboratory, 318
—,Survey of India, 319
————,Accommodation, 319
————,Epigraphy, 319
————,Garden's Branch, 319
————,Libraries, 319
————,Museums, 319
————,Salaries of Technical Grades, 319
————,Temple Survey Project, 319
Assam, 322
—,Hill Areas, 322
—,——,Administration of Justice, 326
—,——,Autonomy, 323
—,——,Basic Considerations, 323
—,——,Budget, 324
—,——,Commissioner, 324
—,——,Departments, 324
—,——,Development Council, 325
—,——,District Councils, 325
—,——,——,Composition, 326
—,——,——,Executive Functions, 325
—,——,——,Financial Administration, 325
—,——,—Development Board, 325
—,——,—Fund and its Audit, 326
—,——,Economic and Financial Aspects, 323
—,——,Financial Administration, 324
—,——,Legislation, 323
—,——,Ministers, 324
—,——,Regional Councils, 326
—,—Districts, 326
—,——,Non-Tribal Residents, 326
Audit of Accounts of Panchayati Raj Bodies, 150

Backward Classes Sector, 336
Brain Drain, 194

Cancer, 327
—,Clinics, 332

—,Education, 331
—,Finance, 331
—,Control and Elimination, 328
——,Programme, 328
—,Prevention Service, 328
—,Regional Cancer Centres, 330
—,———,Central Hospital Staff, 331
—,———,Constitution and Management, 330
—,Research, 329
—,Treatment Facilities, 332
—Committee, 1965, 327-332
—Wings, 332
Central Government Employees, 275
———,Dearness Allowance, 275
———,——,Adjustment, 275
———,——,Essential Commodities, 275
———,——,Graduated Scale of Neutralisation, 276
———,——,Marginal Adjustments, 278
———,——,Neutralisation Method, 277
———,——,Pay Ranges, 276
———,——,Prices Rise, 275
———,——,Standard of Living, 275
———,——,Taxation Limit, 275
———,——,Upper Pay Limit, 275
———,——,Well-established Principle, 276
—Public Works Department, 269
————,Accounts Branches, 271
————,Architect Wing, 270
————,Bills Payment, 273
————,Budget Provision, 269
————,Capital and Revenue Accounts Preparation, 275
————,Cement Allocation, 273
————,Contract Conditions, 271
————,—Forms Comparative Study, 272
————,Contractors Disputes, 274
————,Direct Recruits, 270
————,Divisional Accounts, 272
————,Earnest Money, 272
————,Engineers, 270
————,—Permanent Strength, 270
————,Expenditure Section, 269
————,Foreign Exchange Facilities, 271
————,Interest Payment, 274
————,Liaison Office, 272
————,Minor Works, 274
————,Measurements, 273
————,—,Recording and Checking Instructions, 273
————,Planning and Designing, 269
————,Section Officers, 271
————,——,Permanent Maintenance Division, 271
————,Security Deposit, 272
————,Steel Requirements, 273
————,Stores Division, 273
————,Structural Drawings and Specifications, 269
————,Superintending Engineer's Power, 272
————,Surveyor of Works Organisation, 270
————,Tenders Acceptance, 272
————,Tender Notices, 271
————,Three Years Diploma/Certificate Course, 270
————,Work Assistant, 273
————,——,Minimum Qualifications, 273
————,Workload, 270
—Silk Board, 362
—Tasar Research Station, Ranchi, 360
——Silkworm Seed Station, Lakha, 360
—Wage Board for Non-Journalist Employees of Newspaper Industry, 1964, 53-65
Chief Technical Examiner's Organisation, 273
Commission of Railway Safety, Railway Accident Investigation on Accident to 12 NB Bandel-Naihati Local at Naihati Junction Station of Eastern Railway 14th November, 1963, 290-291
Committee of Officers on the Reorganisation of the Structure and Work Procedures of the Ministry of Works and Housing, 1965, 320-322
——Secretaries on Government Journals, 1964, 3-9
—On Cooperation, 1964, 264-268
——Cooperative Marketing, 1964, 223-246
——Cost of Production of Steel, 1965, 362-368
——Customary Rights to Scavenging, 1965, 394-401
——Hill Areas of Assam, 1965-66, 322-327
——Integration of Health Services, 1964, 1-2
——Plan Projects, 9
——Scarce Raw Materials, 1964, 284-290
——Social Science Research, 1965, 379-383
——Some Problems of University Administration, 1964, 217-223
———Indian Foreign Service, 1965, 354-358
———The Methods of Elections to Panchayati Raj Bodies, 1964, 48-53
——Transport Policy and Coordination, 1964, 26-47
——Untouchability, Economic and Educational Development of the Scheduled Castes and Connected Documents, 1965, 333-340
—To Study the Question of Legislation of Abortion, 1964, 299-300
——Suggest Ways and Means of Improving Financial Returns from Irrigation Projects, 1964, 78-80
Construction Costs, 388
——,Building Materials Assessment, 390
——,Disputes Settling, 391
——,Economics, 388
——,Industrialisation and Mechanised Methods, 389
——,Optimum Rate of Financial Input, 389
——,Standard Schedule of Rates, 392
——,Standardization of Construction Materials, 389
—Industry, 393
Cooperation, 264

—,Audit and Supervision, 267
—,Cooperative Principles, 264
—,Education, 267
—,Genuineness Criteria, 265
—,Historical Background, 264
—,Resources for Cooperatives, 267
—,Vested Interests, 266
Cooperative Marketing, 223
——,Agricultural Implements, 243
——,Business Techniques, 234
——,Cooperative Credit Linking, 237
——,Distribution of Agricultural Production Requisites, 241
——,Essential Consumer Articles Distribution, 243
——,Finance, 228
———,External Resources, 230
———,Internal Resources, 228
——,Improved Seeds, 242
——,Management and Personnel, 225
——,Pesticides, Insecticides, 243
——,Relationship at Various Levels and with Village Cooperatives, 238
——,Role, 239
—Storage, 240
Cooperatives, 140
—,Administration, 140
—,Animal Husbandry, 147
—,Consumer Service, 144
—,Farm Supplies, 144
—,Fishery Cooperatives, 147
—,Marketing, 146
—,Processing and Storage, 146
—,Rural Areas, 144
—,Training and Coordination, 149
Customary Rights to Scavenging, 395
————,Brit-Jajmani, 395
————,——Abolition Method, 396
————,—Income, 395
————,Cash Grants and Rehabilitation, 397

Directorate General of Technical Development, 257
—————,Applications from Sources, 261
—————,Capital Goods Import, 260
—————,——Indigenous Clearance, 263
—————,Foreign Exchange Allocation, 257
—————,———,Licences in Advance, 259
—————,Import Applications, 263
—————,Indigenous Clearance for Import, 262
—————,——Processing, 263
—————,Raw Materials, Components and Major Assemblies, 262
—————,——,Import, 257

Education, 153
—,Agriculture, 187
—,Backward Child, 175
—,—Classes, 168
—,Basic, 173
—,Curricula Differentiation, 173
—,Development Strategy, 164
—,Education about Religions, 155
—,Educational Opportunities, 165
—,—System, 156
—,——,Structure and Standards, 156
—,Enrolements and Manpower, 163
—,Fellowship for Overseas Training, 194
—,Governance of Universities, 185
—,Government and Local Authority Schools, 177
—,Handicapped Children, 167
—,Higher, 179
—,—,Enrolment and Programmes, 183
—,—,Objectives and Improvement, 179
—,—,Post-Graduate Education and Research, 184
—,—Secondary Stage, 156
—,———,Duration Lengthening, 156
—,Humanities Study, 185
—,Language Policy, 154
—,Loan Scholarships, 167
—,Moral and Spiritual Value, 173
—,National Awards, 161
—,—Conciousness Promotion, 155
—,—Level, 164
—,—Science Policy, 194
—,Part-time, 157
—,Physical Education, 173
—,Pre-University Course Transfer, 156
—,Primary Teachers, 162
—,Private Schools, 177
—,Regional Imbalances, 167
—,School Education, 169, 176
—,——,Administration and Supervision, 176
—,—Teachers, 159
—,——In-Service Education, 163
—,——,Scales, 159
—,Scholarships, 166, 167
—,—,National, 166
—,—,Study Abroad, 167
—,—,University, 166
—,Science Education and Research, 192
—,Secondary and Higher Education, 163
—,————,Enrolment Policies, 163
—,Social and National Service, 154
—,—,Moral and Spiritual Values, 155
—,—Service, 173
—,Standards, 157
—,—,Dynamic and Evolving, 157
—,State Boards of School Education, 179
—,——,Level, 165

—,Student Aid, 167
—,Teacher Education, 161
—,——Standards, 163
—,—Status, 157
—,Teaching Methods, Guidance and Evaluation, 173
—,—Profession, 159
—,——,Promotional Prospects, 159
—,Technical and Engineering, 189
—,Textbooks, Teacher's Guides and Materials, 173
—,Training Facilities Expansion, 162
—,—Institutions, 162
—,Tribal People, 168
—,University Stage, 159
—,——Reorganisation, 157
—,——,Scales, 159
—,Vocational, 189
—,Women, 168, 184
—,—Teachers, 160
—,Acts, 200
—And Employment, 165
——Modernization, 155
——National Objectives, 154
——Productivity, 154
—Commission, 1964, 153-202
Educational Administration, 196
—Finance, 200
——,Sources, 201
—Research, 185
English Study, 12
——,Compulsory English Course Teachers, 18
——,Higher Secondary Teachers, 18
——,Instruction Medium, 13
——,Measures to Improve, 18
——,Priorities Programme, 19
——,Second Language, 13
——,Teachers of English, 17
——,———,Training Programme, 17
——,Teaching in Colleges, 16
——,——Schools, 14
——,———,Hindi Speaking Areas, 15
——,———,Non-Hindi Speaking Areas, 15
——,———,Semi-Vocational Groups, 15
——,———,Vocational Groups, 15
Enquiry Committee on Small Newspapers, 1964, 112-128

Film, 348
—,Demand Mobilisation, 348
—,Documentary, 350
—,—,Exhibitions, 351
—,Domestic Consumption, 348
—,Export, 348
—,Quality Control, 351
—,Advisory Committee of Members of Parliament, 1965, 348-352
Films Division, 352
Finance, 110
—,Estate Duty, 110
—,Excise Duties, 111
—,Grants-in-Aid, 112
—,Income Tax, 111
—,Railway Fares Taxes, 111
—,———,Grant-in Lieu, 111
—,Union Excise, 111
—,Commissions, 1964, 109-112

General Insurance Cooperatives, 23
———,Adequate Business, 24
———,Cattle Insurance, 25
———,Crop Insurance, 25
———,Development, 24
———,Individual Policy Holders, 23
———,Loans, 24
———,National Federation, 24
———,——,Management Board, 25
———,——,Membership, 24
———,Panchayats, 24
———,Property and Business, 23
———,Rules, 24
———,State Level Societies, 24
Government Journals, 3
——,General Purpose Journals, 3
——,House Journals, 3
——,Scientific and Technical Journals, 3
Group of Experts on Land Acquisition, 1965, 315-317
Gur and Khandsari, 205
———,By-Products Utilisation, 205

Health Services, 1
——,Cadre Unification, 2
——,Common Seniority, 2
——,Comprehensive Health Work, 2
——,Equal Pay, 2
——,Inter-independence, 2
——,Medical Education, 2
——,——,Central and State Levels, 2
——,Organisational Structure, 2
——,Primary Health Centre, 2
——,Private Practice, 2
——,Re-orientation training, 2
——,Special Pay, 2

Import and Export Trade Control, Actual Users, 247-250
————,——,Other Procedural Matters, 250
————,Disposal of Applications, 251
————,Scheduled Industries Borne on the Books, 249

————,—Not Borne on the books, 250
————Organisation, 247
————,—Licensing Authorities Role, 254
————,Policy General Procedure, 247
————,Ro'e of the DC (SSI), 253
————,Sponsoring Authorities Role, 253
Indian Aircraft Act of 1934, 203
—,Council of Social Science Research, Operational Arrangements, 381
————,Relation with Research Programmes Committee, 382
————,——U.G.C., 381
————,Suggested Course of Action, 282
—Educational Service, 19)
—Foreign Service, 354
———,External Publicity, 356
———,Ministry of External Affairs, 354
———,Personnel Problems and Tasks, 355
———,Recruitment, 356
———,Role, 354
———,Service Conditions, 357
———,Training, 357
Industrial Policy Resolutions, 82
Industrial Workers, 9
——,Literacy, 9
——,—,Appropriate Agency, 11
——,—,Financial Resources, 11
——,—,Proposals, 10
——,—,Campaign, 12
——,——,Libraries, 12
——,——,Supervision, 12
——,——,Syllabus, 12
——,—Schemes, 10
Inquiry into the Collision of Down Empty Rake with Rear of No. K-3 Down Local Train at Thana Station (Central Railway) on 14th September, 1965, 384
———Wash-Away of No. 653 Down Pamban Dhanushkodi Passenger Train between K.M.S. 681 and 682 near Dhanushkodi Station (Southern Railway) on 23rd December, 1964, 313
Insurance Act and Rules, 24
Inter-State Standard Tax, 377
—Transport Commission, 376
Inter University Board, 187
Irrigation Projects, 78
——,Agriculture Department and Irrigation Department Coordination, 80
——,Capital Levy Recovery, 79
——,Financial Returns, 78
——,Irrigation Facility Charge, 79
———,Potential Created Area Programmes, 79
——,————,Optimum Utilisation, 79
——,Major and Medium Projects Priority, 79
——,New Projects, 79
——,Projects Sanctioning Criteria, 80
——,Schemes Cost Advance Contribution, 80
——,Water Rate Revision, 79

Land Acquisition, 316
——,Big Project, 317
——,Constitutional Limitation, 336
——,Cost, 316
——,Emergency Provisions, 317
——,Legislation, 316
——,Payment of Solatium, 317
——,Proceedings, 336
——,Replacing Danger, 316
——,Requisioning Department, 317
——Collector, 317
Libraries, 130, 196
—,Block Libraries, 136
—,Books Production, 135
Libraries, Central and State Levels, 131
—,————,Administrative and Advisory Organisations, 131
—,Directorate of Libraries, 134
—,Fourth Plan Schemes, 136
—,Library Personnel Training, 134
—,Public Library Development, 134
—,——Programmes, 131
—,————,Branch Libraries, 133
—,————,District Libraries, 132
—,————,Model Public Libraries, 133
—,————,State Central Libraries, 131
—,Ten-year Programme, 135
—,Union Territories and other Areas, 134
—,Village Level, 135
Library Legislation, 135
Life Insurance Corporation, 24
Liquid Cargo, 128
——,Coastal Movement, 129
——,Distribution, 129
——,Ethyl Alcohol Availability, 129
——,Handling, 128
——,Imports of Liquid Chemicals, 130
——,Molasses, 129
——,Palm Oil, 129
——,Soyabean Oil, 129
——,Tallow, 129
——,Tank Farms, 128
——,——,Bulk Storage Facilities Absence, 129
——,Weighment and Accounting Methods, 129
——,Committee, 1964, 128-130

Mathematics, 301
—,Cybernatics, 308
—,Examinations, 302

—,Pre-University Courses, 303
—,Proposed Syllabus, 303
—,Teaching Facilities, 301
—Reform Committee, 1964, 300-308
Medical Termination of Pregnancy Bill, 300
Minor Forest Products, 309
——,Export, 309
——,—,Agarwood, 312
——,—,Gum Karaya, 311
——,—,Katha Or Cutch, 312
——,—,Kuth, 311
——,—,Mushrooms, 310
——,—,Myrobalans, 309
——,—,Rosin And Turpentine, 312
——,—,Walnuts, 309
Model Public Libraries Bill, 137-140
Monopolies, 87
—,Legislative, 87
—,Monopolistic or Restrictive Trade Practice Commission, 100
—,——,Jurisdiction, Power and Procedure, 100
—Practices, 96
—,Offences and Penalities, 102
—,Proper Measures, 82
—,Restrictive Trade Practices, 97
—and Restrictive Trade Practices Act, 1965., 93
—Inquiry Commission, 1964, 82-106

Narmada Water Resources Development, 278
——,Benefits Sharing, 280
——,Cost Sharing, 281
——,Fish Culture, 283
——,Investigation Necessity, 283
——,Irrigation and Power Development Programme, 282
——,Irrigated Areas Assessment, 279
——,Mahi And Sabarmati Waters Integrated Development, 284
——,Master Plan Phasing, 282
——,Navagam Canal, 279
——,—Project Implementation, 280
——,Plan Cost, 283
——,—Financing, 283
——,Projects Implementation in Madhya Pradesh, 280
——,Punasa Reservoir, 281
——,Resettlement And Rehabilitation, 283
——,Sharing Water for Irrigation, 279
——,Terminal Storage Reservoir Location, 279
——,Tourism, 284
——,Water Requirements, 279
——,Water Logging and Drainage, 283
——Committee, 1964, 278-284
National Council of Educational Research And Training, 198
—Instrument Factory, 273
—Science Policy, 194
—Staff College for Educational Administrators, 200
Newspaper Industry, 53
——,Non-Journalist Employees, 54
——,——,Administrative Staff, 58
——,——,——,Remuneration, 58
——,——,Factory Employees, 60
Newspaper Industry, Non-Journalist Employees, Newspaper Establishments, 55
——,——,——,Classification, 55
——,——,——Reclassification, 56
——,——,Pay Scales, 60
——,——,——,Operation Date, 65

One-Man Independent Body to Enquire into the Question of Dearness Allowance Payable to Central Government Employees, 1964, 275-278

Panel on Economies in Construction Costs, 1965, 388-394
Panchayati Raj Bodies, 48
——,Accounting Procedure, 151
——,Audit, 151
——,—Manual, 152
——,—Memoes, 151
——, Consolidated Finance Account, 153
——, Elections, 48
——,—,Conduct of Elections, 51
——,—,Panchayat Samiti, 49
——,—,Political Parties Role, 52
——,—,Qualifications and Disqualifications, 51
——,—,Score for Unanimity, 52
——,—,Special Groups Representations, 51
——,—,Supervision and Control, 52
——,—,Village Panchayats, 48
——,—,Zila Parishads, 50
——, Income, 151
——, Internal Audit Machinery, 152
——, Training Institutions Capacity, 151
Parliamentary Committee on the Demand For Punjab Suba, 1965, 385-388
Posts and Telegraphs Departments, 291
Punjabi Suba, 385
——, Demand, 385
——,—, Cooperative Solution, 385
——,—, Various Alternatives, 385
——,—,——, Linguistic Basis Reorganisation, 387
——,—,——, Regional Committees Strengthening, 387
——,—,——, Status Quo, 385

Railway Accident, 290
——, Cause, 290, 384

——, Relief Arrangements, 384
——,—Measures, 291
——, Responsibility, 290, 384
——, Service Particulars, 384
——, Tidal Wave, 313
Review Committee on Arabic And Persian Studies in Indian Universities, 1964, 107-109
Reviewing Committee of the Telecommunication Research Centre of the Posts and Telegraphs Department, 1964, 291-298
Road Transport, 368
——, Advantages, 369
——, Five Year Plans, 369
——, Importance, 368
——, Motor Vehicle Taxation, Study Group, 373
——, National Highways, 370
——, Taxation, 370
——,—Inter-State Road Transport, 374
——,—,—Standard Tax, 373, 377
——,—,—Transport, 371
——,—,—Transport Commission Set up, 378
——,—,———Working, 376
——,—,Single Point Tax Absence, 372
——,—,Temporary Permit Tax, 372
—,—Taxation Enquiry Committee on Inter-State Transport, 1965, 368-379
——, Traffic Pattern Changes, 369
——,———, Foreign Countries, 369

Scarce Raw Materials, 285
———,Allocation, 289
———,CSIO and State Directorates Role, 288
———,Capacities Assessment, 289
———,Comparability between the two Sectors, 287
———,Distribution, 289
———,Inspection, 289
———,Non-Ferrous Metals Survey, 286
———,Priorities of Industries, 288
Scavenging, 395
—,Municipalisation, 395
—,Underground Drainage And Water-Borne Latrines, 399
Scheduled Castes, 333
——,Agricultural Labour, 335
——,Agriculture Incentive, 335
——,Benefits, 336
——,Central Services, 338
——,Commissioner for Scheduled Castes And Scheduled Tribes Office Reorganisation, 340
——,Forced/Bonded Labour, 336
——,Girls Education, 338
——,Hostels, 337
——,House-site and Housing, 335
——,Indebtedness, 336
——,Land Allotment, 334
——,Colonisation, 335
——,Middle and Secondary Education, 337
——,Occupational Patterns, 334
——,Overseas Scholarships, 337
——,Post-Matric Scholarships and Post-Matric Education, 337
——,——Scheme, 337
——,Primary Education, 337
——,State Government Services, 338
——,Untouchability, 333
——and Scheduled Tribes, 353
—————,Lists Revision, 353
—————,Scholarship Schemes, 353
—————,Sub-groups Enumeration, 353
Second Pay Commission, 276
Small Newspapers, 112
——,Advertisements, 124
——,Association of Newspapers, 121
——,Circulations, 113
——,Communications and Transport, 117
——,Consultancy Services, 121
——,Credit Facilities, 121
——,Feature Services, 119
——,Information Services, 118
——,Issue of Import Licences Delay, 122
——,Newsprint, 121
——,News Services, 118
——,Performance, 116
——,Photo and Feature Services, 120
——,Policy Announcement, 122
——,Price-Page Schedule, 127
——,Printing Machinery, 116
——,Staff Training Facilities, 120
Social Science Research, 380
———,Need, 380
State Educational Service, 199
Steel, 362
—,Cost Analysis, 363
—,—of Production, 363
—,———,Administration Role, 367
—,———,Capital Cost, 366
—,———,Coal Washeries, 364
—,———,Devaluation Impact, 367
—,———,Ferro-Manganese, 364
—,———,Inventories, 366
—,———,Iron Ore, 364
—,———,Personnel Costs, 365
—,———,Plant Operation, 365
—,— ——,Raw Materials, 363
Study Group on the Study of English in India, 1964, 12-20
———Wild Life and Wild Life Products, 1964, 80-82
—Team on Directorate General of Technical Develop-

ment, 1964, 256-264
———General Insurance Cooperatives, 1964, 23-25
———Import and Export Trade Control Organisation, 1964, 247-256
———Textile Commissioner's Organisation, 1965, 340-347
———the Audit of Accounts of Panchayati Raj Bodies, 1964, 150-153
————Central Public Works Department, 1964, 268-275
Sugar, 203
—,Buffer Stock Policy, 207
—,Control, 208
—,Cost Schedules, 212
—,Decontrol, 207
—,Export Policy, 213
—,Gur & Khandsari, 204
—,Licensing Policy, 214
—,Sugarcane Price Regulation, 209
—Enquiry Commission, 1964, 203-217
Sugarcane, 206
—,Research and Development, 206
—,Sugar and Sugarcane Price Policy, 207

Tariff, 66
—Commission, 78
—Revision, 66
——,Appellate Collectors, 78
——,Central Board of Excise and Customs Rulings, 78
——,Cottage and Small-Scale Industries, 78
——,————,Encouragement, 78
——,Departmental Laboratories, 78
——,Independent Appellate Tribunals, 78
——,Indian Customs Tariff, 66
——,Revised Central Excise Tariff Schedule, 77
Tariff Revision Committee (Interim), 1964, 66-75
———on the Central Excise Tariff, 1966, 75-78
Tasar Food Plants, 3(0
—Silk, 358
——,Cocoons Collection, 359
——,Exports, 359
——,Marketing Problem, 360
——,Prices, 359
——,Production, 360
——,Committee, 1965, 358-362
——,Industry, 361
———,Price Support, 361
———,Separate Corporation, 361
Teacher's Hostels, 20
——,Bath Room, 22
——,Bed Room, 21
——,Entrance Hall, 22
——,Hostels Combination, 22
——,Kichenette, 21
——,Living Room, 21
——,Material Choice, 22
——,Multi-purpose Room, 21
——,Propose, 20
——,Services, 22
——,Siting Location and Expansion, 21
——,Space Utilisation, 21
——,Steeping Terrace, 22
Telecommunication, 291
Telecommunication Research Centre, 291
———,Computer Use, 295
———,Financial Requirements, 297
———,Main Divisions, 295
———,Programme of Work, 293
———,———,Carrier Telephone System, 293
———,———,Data Transmission Equipments, 294
———,———,Digital Communication Systems, 294
———,———,Electro Mechanical Switching System, 293
———,———,Electronic Instruments, 293
———,———,Microwave Systems, 294
———,———,Picture, Facsimile and Television Transmission Equipment, 295
———,———,Power Plant, 294
———,———,Subscriber's Apparatus, 293
———,Staff Requirements, 296
———,Workshop, 298
Textile Commissioner's Organisation, 341
———,Cloth and Yarn Marketing, 345
———,Cotton and Textiles Stems Control, 341
———,Decentralised Sector, 344
———,Organised Sector, 343
———,——,Additional Capacity Installation, 343
———,Powerlooms Installation, 343
———,Qualitative Control, 345
———,Securing Scarce Items of Supply, 347
———,Statistical Forms and Returns Review, 347
———,Statutory Control on Production and Prices, 345
—Machinery, 345
Transport Policy and Coordination, 26
————,Air Transport, 42
————,Coastal Shipping and Rail Sea Coordination, 39
————,Commercial Motor Transport Taxation, 38
————,Coordination Problems, 27
————,Data Organisation and Collection, 46
————,————,Traffic Flows, 46
————,——————and Transport Costs, 46
————,—,Development Trends, 27
————,Inland Water Transport, 41
————,Machinery, 44
————,Observations, 47
————,Pipelines and Ropeways, 42
————,Ports and Harbours, 40
————,Railways, 29
————,Road Development and Road Policy, 31

———,—Transport, 33
———,Transport, 27

University Administration, 217
——, Abuse, 221
——, Admission Fees, 219
——, Admissions, 222
——, Appointments, 221
——, Corruption and Malpractices, 218
——, Education Quality, 220
——,Elections, 221
——,—,Postal Voting, 221
——,—, University Bodies, 223
——,Examination System Malpractices, 219
——, Examinations, 222
——, Freedom From External Control, 218
——, University Enrolment Growth, 218
——, Vice-Chancellor, 218
University Grants Commission, 187
——, Building Advisory Committee on Teacher's Hostels, 1964, 20-22

Wild Life and Wild Life Products, 81
————, Crocodile And Crocodile Skins, 81
————, Deer Horns, 81
————,—Musk, 81
————,Jungle Fowl Feathers and Necks, 81
————, Langurs, 83
————, Leopard Skins, 83
————, Lesser Panda, 81
————, Other Monitor Lizards and their Skins, 81
————, Panther Skins, 83
————, Peacock Feathers, 81
————, Python and Python Skins, 81
————, Slender Loris, 83
————, Slow Loris, 83
————, Water Lizards and Their Skins, 81
Working Group on Co-operatives in I.A.D.P. Districts, 1964, 140-150
———, Libraries 1964, 130-140
Works and Housing, 320
———, Reorganisation, 320
———,—,Structure and Work Procedures, 320
———,—,———,Liaison Work, 321
———,—,———,O. & M. Unit, 321
———,—,———,O.S D. Posts, 321
———,—,———,Successful Functioning, 321